*Money and its use
in medieval Europe*

MONEY
AND ITS USE
IN MEDIEVAL EUROPE

Peter Spufford

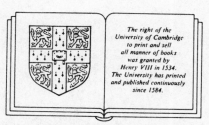

The right of the
University of Cambridge
to print and sell
all manner of books
was granted by
Henry VIII in 1534.
The University has printed
and published continuously
since 1584.

Cambridge University Press

Cambridge
New York   Port Chester
Melbourne   Sydney

Published by the Press Syndicate of the University of Cambridge
The Pitt Building, Trumpington Street, Cambridge CB2 IRP
32 East 57th Street, New York, NY 10022, USA
10 Stamford Road, Oakleigh, Melbourne 3166, Australia

First published 1988
Reprinted 1989

Printed in Great Britain at the University Press, Cambridge

British Library cataloguing in publication data

Spufford, Peter
Money and its use in medieval Europe.
1. Money – Europe – History
I. Title
332.4'94   HG923

Library of Congress cataloguing in publication data

Spufford, Peter.
Money and its use in medieval Europe.
Bibliography
Includes index.
1. Money – Europe – History.   2. Europe – Economic
conditions – To 1492.   3. Numismatics, Medieval.
I. Title.
HG923.S68 1988 – 332.4'94 86–13701

ISBN 0 521 30384 2 hard covers

Contents

v

Contents

Maps

vii

Tables

Graphs

Acknowledgements

I must first express my gratitude to the late Mr P. G. Burbidge of the Cambridge University Press, who originally suggested that I should write this book. I thought that it might take three years or even, pessimistically, five to write. I could not have imagined that it would take fifteen. Over so long a time I have incurred innumerable debts of gratitude. Most importantly I must thank the President and Fellows of Clare Hall, Cambridge, for electing me to a Visiting Fellowship in 1969–70 to enable me to undertake a complete year's uninterrupted reading, on which the whole edifice has been built. Clare Hall continued to give me open and generous hospitality for several summers to enable me to extend my reading and to write without distraction. I must equally thank the University of Keele, and in particular Paul Rolo and my former colleagues in the history department there, not only for giving me leave of absence to pursue medieval money, but for unstinting support in my pursuit. The University of Cambridge and Queens' College gave me the sabbatical that finally made the completion of the book possible. As the work progressed I was led into byways that then proved of major importance in themselves. I must thank the Social Science Research Council for their support in my work on medieval exchange rates, and the Marc Fitch Fund for its support in my work on the routes of medieval trade. The University of Louvain, by its invitation to lecture in 1972, caused me to crystallise my thoughts in the substance of chapters 15 and 16, and the University of Toruń by its invitation in 1980 my thoughts on chapter 13. The Istituto Internazionale di Storia Economica 'Francesco Datini', inspired by Fernand Braudel, through the remarkable conference that it held in Prato in 1975 on money in the European economy, provoked a number of ideas that appear in different parts of this volume. It also stimulated a general interest in the history of money amongst economic historians, so that it is now at last suddenly taking its rightful place as one of their major preoccupations.

Over the years an almost infinite number of correspondents and friends have given me assistance and encouragement. I cannot thank them all. They include Karel Castelin, Michael Dolley, Walter Hävernick, Michael Postan, Raymond De

Roover and Hans van Werveke, who are no longer alive to receive my thanks. They also include Peter Berghaus, Tom Bisson, Wim and An Blockmans, Maria Bogucka, Carolyn Busfield, Susan Cattermole, Christopher Challis, Carlo Cipolla, Pierre Cockshaw, John and Nicoletta Day, Aldo and Mariele De Maddalena, Françoise Dumas, H. Enno van Gelder, Marc Fitch, Karol Górski, Michael Hendy, Madeleine De Heusch, Jan van Houtte, Štefan Kazimír, Ryszard Kiersnowski, Frederic Lane, Robert Lopez, Antoni Maczak, Nicholas Mayhew, Michael Metcalf, Reinhold Mueller, John Munro, Graham Pollard, Robin and Catherine Porteous, Michael Prestwich, Jean Richard, Ian and Deborah Stewart, Raymond van Uytven, Terry Volk, Andrew Watson, Wendy Wilkinson, Herman van der Wee, and Philippe Wolff. I thank them for their patience and friendship and hospitality and offprints.

My two most considerable debts of gratitude are, however, to Philip Grierson and to my wife. Philip Grierson, whose myriad articles fill my footnotes on practically every page, started me on historical research. The footnotes reveal how often he has preceded me in many of my inquiries. He has not only lent me a whole range of unobtainable books, but has given me continual encouragement, and rapid, ruthless and incisive comments on anything I have dared to show him. His unrivalled collection of medieval European coins, now in the Fitzwilliam Museum, Cambridge has enabled me to handle the coins to which I refer.

My wife, by her probing historical questioning, has repeatedly made me cut out irrelevant matter, has helped me repeatedly reshape the volume, and perpetually reminded me that the proper subject-matter of the historian is past men and women and their actions, and not the artifacts that survive from them. She has also enabled me to continue writing, whenever the prospect of conclusion seemed to recede indefinitely. As it is this book has taken up all too much of our married life and of our children's childhood.

It is appropriate that I completed the draft of this book on the great pay-day of the medieval year, when, in much of northern Europe after the harvest had been sold, annual rents, annual wages and direct taxes were due for payment. On this day much of the stock of money changed hands.

Clare Hall, Cambridge   PETER SPUFFORD
University of Keele   *St Michael and All Angels, 1974*

It seems strange to publish a volume with a 1974 date in 1988. After the completion of the draft in 1974, my immediate and main concern turned to giving our daughter a kidney and to the continuous and demanding medical follow-up to a kidney transplant. I was therefore unable to deliver a revised text to the Press, as I had planned, in 1975. Unfortunately, I had by then already received my grant for work on medieval exchange rates, planned to follow *after* the completion of this book. This was published first as an *Interim Listing of the Exchange Rates of Medieval Europe* in 1977. I had also obtained the grant for the fieldwork for *The Routes of Trade in Medieval Europe*, planned to follow the exchange-rate research. In 1980 Sir Michael Postan asked me, as a matter of great urgency, to postpone the revision of this book yet further, so as to be able to rewrite entirely my chapter on medieval coinage and currency for the second edition of volume II of the *Cambridge Economic History of Europe*, which he was then trying to get to the Press. It proved impossible to delay these projects to get *Money and Its Use* revised. While I was working on these other projects a number of major works on medieval monetary history had appeared, some unthought-of when I began this work in 1969. Charles de la Roncière's and Mario Bernocchi's great multi-volume works came out on the Florentine economy and its money, John Day's on the early fifteenth-century bullion-famine, Tom Bisson's on political control of the coinage from the eleventh century to the thirteenth, and Michael Metcalf's on coinage in the Balkans. The Oxford symposia on coinage and monetary history had also meanwhile been launched. These small international gatherings, focussed on particular areas of monetary history, have resulted in most years in a volume of proceedings published by British Archaeological Reports. When I was at last able to revise my text I did so at a time of continuous publication in the field of monetary history, quite unlike the much quieter era in which I had begun writing. I felt that the Red Queen's admonition to Alice applied to me: 'It takes all the running *you* can do, to keep in the same place.' This volume was eventually revised and sent to the press at Pentecost 1983, more or less taking account of publications up to that date. The flood of new publications following the Prato conference in 1975 has in no way abated since 1983. Whilst this book was with the Cambridge University Press's excellent subeditorial department, the proceedings of the conference at Madison, Wisconsin, on the trade in precious metals has come out, as well as further volumes of proceedings of the Oxford symposia, the volume of essays on monetary history edited by John Day, and major new works on the monetary history of France, Byzantium, Greece and Venice, by Harry Miskimin, by Michael Hendy, by Alan Stahl and by Frederic Lane and Reinhold Mueller, besides my own *Handbook of Medieval Exchange*, greatly expanded since 1983 from the *Interim Listing* of 1977. I have had the chance of adding this new work to the bibliography at galley proof stage, but have had no opportunity of taking proper cognisance of it in the text. Meanwhile our daughter has needed a second kidney transplant. By some mysterious alchemy I return the page proofs of the book once more on the great pay-day of the medieval year, twelve years later.

PETER SPUFFORD

Queens' College, Cambridge   *St Michael and All Angels, 1986*

Introduction

Since historians have generally found the pursuit of happiness hard to analyse and chronicle, they have concentrated rather on the other two principal preoccupations of the human race, the pursuits of power and of wealth. In its widest sense 'money' was, in the Middle Ages, not only, with land, the major form of wealth, but also the measure of all other forms of wealth. It is therefore surprising that historians of this period have paid comparatively little attention to money. The availability and use of money have changed so much and so often over time that it must be considered one of the key variables in our understanding of medieval societies, along with population, religion and developing agricultural, industrial and commercial techniques. Change in the availability and the use of money is, for example, one of the keys to explaining the changing fabric of rural society, as well as of urban society, in the Middle Ages. The relevance of money to rural society in the Middle Ages is often ignored, to their cost, by early modern historians, who too readily assume that the rural use of money was a novelty of their own period. Change in the availability and the use of money is also one of the keys to explaining the changing nature of the framework of political activity in the Middle Ages. A knowledge of it greatly clarifies our understanding of a whole gamut of political structures, from the shreds of centralised organisation inherited by the barbarians from Rome, through the most decentralised forms of 'feudal' authority, to the earliest examples of the 'modern bureaucratic state' in the later Middle Ages. The study of money and its supply, therefore, has very wide implications as well as, more obviously, assisting the historian concerned with prices and wages, with the level and nature of rent, with interest rates, or with the profit and scale of trade.

Money has, of course, had different connotations at different periods, and changes in attitude towards it are extremely important. The virtues of *largesse* and of thrift are the very antithesis of one another. Poverty has been seen both as a condition to be embraced and as one to be relieved.

It is all too easy for the study of money in the Middle Ages to be focussed on the actual coins themselves. Coins were, of course, only a part of the money supply. In the earlier Middle Ages they were supplemented by a variety of other transferable objects, not only by uncoined precious metal, or valuable commodities such as pepper, but also by intrinsically valueless tokens like small squares of cloth made in a particular way. From the twelfth and thirteenth centuries, coins were already supplemented in some parts of Europe by holdings in the public debt and by bank deposits. These were transferable, by entry in the books of the bank or those of the officials of the *monte*, by bills of exchange, and, from the fourteenth century, by cheque.

However, the coins themselves, although not necessarily most important, have themselves survived in enormous quantities. The increased quantities of silver coins struck from the twelfth century onwards ran into millions and tens of millions and occasionally over a hundred million coins of the same type. In consequence coins are the most common object to survive from the later Middle Ages. Unlike most medieval artifacts they need not be confined to the collections of museums and of the very rich. It is possible for any teacher or student of medieval history to acquire a late-medieval coin. Coins can be the most vivid, as well as the most accessible, illustrations of the history of medieval Europe. To handle one of the deniers of Provins used to make payments at the Champagne Fairs, or one of the grossi struck to pay the wages of the shipwrights and mariners preparing for the Fourth Crusade, gives a very immediate contact with the events themselves. Gold coins are only a little less accessible. They were often minted by the hundred thousand. It is not difficult, or very expensive, to acquire a florin of Florence, as lent by the Bardi and Peruzzi to finance Edward III's purchase of allies to open the Hundred Years War. This tangible contact with past events has exercised an extraordinary fascination on many people over a long period of time. The collection and study of classical coinage, along with classical sculpture, began among the princely and patrician products of humanist education in the early Renaissance as ancillaries to their collection and study of classical texts. The fascination rapidly spread to coins of the Middle Ages. More than half a millennium of erudition has been expended on the study of the coins themselves. Numismatics has always been regarded as in some way ancillary to history, yet such has been the fascination of the study for its own sake, that the handmaid has given relatively little service to the muse.

Part of the problem lies in the fact that it is much rarer for the surviving coins to provide evidence for past events, over and above eloquent illustration of them. In the most extreme cases coins have provided evidence for the existence of otherwise unknown rulers, like the Anglo-Danish kings Cnut and Sigfrid, ruling at York from about 895 to about 903. The use of coins themselves as such direct evidence is most infrequent. It is less rare to be able to use coins indirectly as evidence. For example, it is possible to work out, from the coins themselves, and the hoards in which they have been found, that the late Anglo-Saxon kings of England regularly changed the whole circulating medium of the country. From this, indirectly, we can deduce something of the measure of control that these kings had over their kingdom.

Coins in an archaeological context are more useful than coins outside such a context. They are often the most narrowly datable of artifacts and provide the archaeologist with a more precise means of dating the layer in which they were found than any other. Coins in hoards are more useful as historical evidence than individual coins, although they can often pose problems of interpretation. The vast numbers of coins buried in ninth- and tenth-century Viking hoards are a case in point. They contain, as well as silver dirhams in quantity from Tashkent in central Asia, large numbers of silver pennies and pfennigs from Anglo-Saxon England and Ottonian Germany. The claims of piracy, legitimate trade and political tribute have all been advanced to explain the presence of these different coins in such quantities. The mere presence of coins from another country in an archaeological context is in itself evidence of commercial, ecclesiastical, political or military connection with the other country, but it is often difficult to determine which type of connection was involved.

It is this very sort of ambiguity that has so often deterred historians from using coins themselves as evidence. Nevertheless with the growth of economic and social history as a discipline in the past century or so, the realisation has become clearer that numismatics, let alone monetary history, ought to have an important role to play. The very vocabulary of numismatics, which has become even more esoteric in the past generation, has also been a deterrent. Until recently few economic historians have been sufficiently conversant with this 'language' to articulate it fully enough to treat the changing role of money in the European economy. They have therefore not, for example, been able to write with confidence of money as one of the keys to the developed market economy of Europe in the later Middle Ages; yet it deserves study as much as, or more than, the history of demography, technology or slavery.

One of the first to make a general study of money was Marc Bloch. He made a preliminary attempt to place the role of money in its true perspective in a series of lectures, published from his notes in 1954, a decade after his death, as an *Esquisse d'une histoire monétaire de l'Europe*. Carlo Cipolla, in a magisterial series of lectures, developed some of the most important themes in the history of money in the later Middle Ages and the early modern period. They were published as *Money, Prices and Civilization in the Mediterranean World* in 1956. Although there has been a lack of general studies, notable use has been made of monetary history by historians dealing with limited periods, for example by Peter Sawyer in his work on the Viking age. There have also been studies devoted to the monetary history of individual countries. For Italy, for example, there are Carlo Cipolla's excellent brief *Avventure della lira* and, more limitedly, his recent *Monetary Policy of Fourteenth Century Florence*. For France, there are studies by Landry, Rolland, Castaing-Sicard, Richebé, Fournial, Miskimin and Cazelles. Seminal books and articles by Van Werveke, De Roover, Lopez, Herlihy, Watson, La Roncière, Bisson, Prestwich, Sprandel and Day, have taken up particular themes in monetary history and made them accessible to economic historians. Many of these studies have appeared since I began writing this book. Meanwhile, eminent numismatists have also sought to make their intimate knowledge of coins available to a wider audience in their own languages. Kiersnowski has done so in Polish, Nohejlová-Prátová in Czech, Suhle in German, Porteous, Metcalf and Mayhew in English, and above all Grierson in a range of languages. This book is conceived on a more ambitious scale than any of these studies. I have attempted to treat the whole history of money in the Middle Ages, not merely the history of coinage. I have not limited myself to any one country, or any one period, or any one theme, but have tried to extract the most important elements for the historian from all these particular studies. How successful I have been in so broad an undertaking I leave the reader to judge.

I have arranged the book chronologically, rather than regionally, or thematically. A chronological approach reveals certain striking coincidences in time, for example between mining in one part of Europe and minting in another, even when no strict correlation of cause and effect can be demonstrated. I intend the book to present a picture of the many and changing roles played by money, in all its forms, in all parts of Europe throughout the Middle Ages. Some readers may be surprised to discover how early, how much used, and how familiar money, in many forms, was, not only to royalty and to the nobility, and to merchants and manufacturers, but also to the peasantry who so frequently paid taxes and tithes, rents and renders, and various amercements in cash down, besides being enmeshed in a network of rural credit.

PART I

Before the Commercial Revolution

1

Roman–Barbarian Discontinuity

The coinage that the barbarian peoples inherited from the late Roman Empire was naturally one that reflected the social and economic structure that they were taking over.

The late Roman Empire was primarily an agricultural society, predominantly organised in huge aristocratic estates, the largest of which extended over several thousand square miles. The senatorial aristocracy who dominated this society drew their revenues from their estates in gold, either by the bulk sale, for gold, of agricultural products raised by slave labour, or by rents paid, in gold, by their tenantry. The key coin for such men was the highly valued pure-gold solidus, which had been introduced by Constantine in 309, together with its half, the semissis, and its third, the tremissis or triens. The solidus was a coin only a little larger than a modern American dime or English penny, although, being gold, it was much heavier than either. In ancient terms it weighed 24 carats or siliquae,[1] or in modern terms, about 4½ grams. The quantity of solidi received by senators, particularly by those in the western provinces of the empire, could be enormous. Senators of middling wealth had incomes of 100,000 gold solidi a year, whilst the richest Roman senators had incomes of around 300,000 solidi a year in the fourth century. Incomes on this scale were still spectacularly large even after the heavy taxation demanded by the state had been paid. This small group of families could spend gold extravagantly on luxuries. Many of these came from the eastern provinces of the empire – linens, glass and papyrus for example, or from further east, Chinese silks, Indian spices, aromatics and jewels. They could buy slaves at 18 to 20 solidi a head and still had gold left over for investment. They spent it on extending their estates still further, by purchasing the lands of those lower down the social scale who were being crippled by the taxation system, the free peasantry in particular.

---

[1] Both the Greek κεϱατια and the Latin *siliquae* derive from the name of the carob or locust bean, *ceratonia siliqua* in Latin. Diamonds are still weighed in carats, and our system of measuring the fineness of gold in carats derives from the solidus. For centuries it was taken as the standard of pure gold, containing 24 carats of gold out of 24. Modern men and women are normally unaware that the diamonds and gold of their engagement and wedding rings are being measured in terms of ancient East Mediterranean locust beans.

For the state too the solidus was an admirable coin. In the course of the fourth century gold became more abundant, partially from Ilyrian and Armenian gold-mines and partially from the Sudan by way of Axum.[1] Taxation on land, which had hitherto been paid in kind, could consequently be converted to gold. In the fifth century the stock of solidi circulating within the empire went on being plentiful enough for taxation to continue to be paid in gold. The largest burden on the state's finances was the army. In the early fifth century it was still some 600,000 strong and by this time it was paid in gold. A private soldier received an allowance of 4 solidi a year instead of the food his predecessors had received when taxes had been paid in kind. He also received an allowance of 1 solidus for each of the garments that his predecessors had received from the state clothing-factories. This was in addition to his true pay, the donative of 5 solidi every five years, which had always been paid in coin.

The state equally used gold to maintain the court and the civil service, to keep up the public communications system and for the bulk purchase of food for free distribution to the favoured inhabitants of Rome and Constantinople. In 452 the butchers' guild provided some 3½ million pounds (1½ million kilograms) of pork for distribution in Rome at a price of 1 solidus for every 200 pounds (90.7 kilograms).[2]

Gold might be suitable for the purchases of the aristocrat or the state, but for the common soldier, the peasant and most particularly the city-dweller, smaller coins than those of gold were needed. The soldier needed to be able to exchange his gold solidi for a lower denomination to buy the food to live. The city-dweller needed to be able to buy a single pound of pork.

Apart from gold there was very little else except for low-value copper coins. The denominations of these frequently changed through the fourth century.[3] By the fifth century the standard unit of copper was the nummus, and in 445 Valentinian III decreed that the solidus was to be sold for 7200 nummi. This was not, however, a fixed relationship. By the end of the century, the number of nummi to the solidus had doubled, only to be brought back again to 7200 by Anastasius. It again crept upwards, to be brought back again once more to 7200 by Justinian in 539. However, by the end of Justinian's reign in 565, there were 12,000 nummi to the solidus.[4] The intermediate denominations between the nummus and the smallest gold coin, the tremissis, were surprisingly lacking. In the fourth century there had been sparse issues of silver miliarenses and these diminished in size as the century progressed. In Constantine's reign they had been worth a siliqua of gold (1/24 of a

[1] Evelynne Patlagean, *Pauvreté économique et pauvreté sociale à Byzance 4ᵉ–7ᵉ siècles* (Paris, 1977), p. 373.

[2] A. H. M. Jones, *The Later Roman Empire 284–602* (Oxford, 1964).

[3] Harold Mattingly, 'The monetary systems of the Roman Empire from Diocletian to Theodosius I', *Numismatic Chronicle*, 6th series, VI (1946), 110–20.

[4] Philip Grierson, 'The *Tablettes Albertini* and the value of the *solidus* in the fifth and sixth centuries A.D.', *Journal of Roman Studies*, XLIX (1959), 73–80.

solidus), but by the end of the century only half as much. In the eastern provinces of the empire they ceased altogether at the end of the century and no further silver was minted there until the early seventh century, apart from very limited issues of ceremonial coins. In Italy, however, miliarenses continued to be struck in small numbers, but even in Italy there was no denomination generally available between the copper nummus and the gold tremissis. To modern eyes this seems extremely inconvenient for retail trade. Not until the 470s did a fresh intermediate denomination appear. In 476 the mint at Rome began to strike heavy copper multiple nummi for the use of the people of the city. The largest of these, a 40-nummus piece, was an inch-and-a-half (3.8 centimetres) across and weighed nearly 17 grams, as large as a modern silver crown or dollar, but not so heavy. It soon became known as a 'follis'. Similar pieces were struck soon after at Carthage and by the end of the century at Constantinople. They were much more convenient for the everyday purposes of urban life than a currency consisting of single nummi had been. Prices were soon quoted in them. An atypical example comes from the famine years after 499, when eggs rose to as much as a follis each, and meat to $2\frac{1}{2}$ folles the pound. Early in the sixth century a building-labourer was paid 5 folles a day, instead of 200 nummi. By the middle of the sixth century, single nummi ceased to be used and the smallest denomination minted was the pentanummion, the 5-nummus piece.[1]

The collapse of the Roman Empire in the west was so prolonged a process that to expect to find any cataclysmic change in the coinage would be unreasonable. No such violent change or lengthy cessation of coinage occurred except in Britain. After the departure of the army and the breakdown of administrative contacts with the rest of the empire, no further coin entered Britain, and, within a generation, by about A.D. 435, coin ceased to be used there as a medium of exchange. Not for 200 years, until the seventh century, were coins again used in Britain as money, although many survived as jewellery, or were used for gifts or for compensation. Everywhere else in the area of the western empire the use of money was maintained, although its nature and functions gradually changed and, as they changed, slowly diverged from the differing evolution in the surviving eastern provinces under direct imperial rule.

The barbarian 'allies', although they had no tradition of coinage of their own, took over the Roman mints in the western provinces of the empire, and continued to strike coins at them in the names of the emperors. In Gaul this took place around A.D. 500, among the Franks probably under Clovis (484–511), and among the Visigoths probably under Alaric II (484–507). Over the next half-century gold solidi and trientes in the names of Anastasius, Justin and Justinian were issued by

---

[1] Jones, *Later Roman Empire*, p. 858, and Patlagean, *Pauvreté à Byzance*, pp. 407 and 414.

various Merovingian kings in northern Gaul, and by Visigothic kings, probably at Narbonne, without giving any indication of their real issuers.

At this stage the use of gold in the barbarian kingdoms in the west was much the same as in the provinces in the east remaining under the immediate rule of the empire. In the west the senatorial aristocracy retained many of their estates and continued to receive their incomes in gold. The taxation system survived more or less intact, and the barbarian kings received a revenue in gold as the Roman state had done. Indeed the Ostrogoth Theoderic (490–526) was rather more successful at collecting taxation in Italy than some of his weaker Roman predecessors had been. In addition, they received subsidies in gold from the emperors themselves. Chilperic, one of Clovis' grandsons, who ruled from Soissons, received 50,000 solidi from the Emperor Maurice Tiberius.

Although the barbarian kings were able to keep the minting of gold going in the west they were not so successful in keeping the copper coinage going. In Gaul the only copper was minted at Marseilles, the last functioning 'city' in Gaul where a succession of rulers, the Ostrogoth Athalaric, the Burgundian Godomar, and the Franks Childebert, Theodebert and Theodebald, managed to produce a rather poor series of small bronze coins that came to an end in the middle of the sixth century. Although no further bronze coins were minted in Gaul, they continued to circulate for some time.[1] In Italy, the Ostrogoths, and, after the sixth-century reconquest, the Byzantine administrators, managed to keep a feeble copper coinage going until the seventh century, when even that ceased. Save briefly in thirteenth-century Hungary, no further coins of bronze, or of pure copper, were struck in western Europe until the fifteenth century, except in Sicily, where the pattern of coinage fitted that of the central provinces of the Byzantine Empire. In Sicily an abundant copper coinage was maintained by the Byzantine administrators and passed down to their successors, even to the Norman conquerors of the island in the twelfth century. The prime function of a copper coinage is to provide for the enormous number of extraordinarily small payments that are a natural part of urban living, and play so much smaller a part in a thoroughly rural society. The countryman's transactions are far fewer and in general rather larger than the townsman's. The countryman buys and sells grain by the bushel, the townsman bread by the loaf, the countryman deals with whole beasts, the townsman with his meat in small joints. In a properly urban environment a great deal of small change of some sort is needed. It is perhaps a measure of the collapse of urban society that only in Sicily did the necessary copper coinage survive. Elsewhere in the west the great cities had

---

[1] Jean Lafaurie, 'Monnaies de bronze marseillaises du vɪᵉ siècle', *Bulletin de la Société Française de Numismatique*, XXVIII (1973), 480–2. Hoard evidence suggests that a small amount of copper coinage, including some from the empire, continued to circulate in Merovingian Gaul until about 630.

dwindled away, but in Sicily they continued to flourish, as they still did in the central provinces of the Byzantine Empire.

The barbarian rulers were only slightly more successful in keeping a silver coinage going. Theoderic was able to have a sequence of four denominations of silver minted in Italy in the names of the Emperors Anastasius and Justin. The largest of these was probably the equivalent in silver of 2 siliquae, or carats, weight of gold, the next the equivalent of a siliqua, the next of half a siliqua and the smallest of a quarter of a siliqua. Their issue was, however, so small that only single specimens of the two largest denominations survive.[1] A small series of poor copies of the silver coins of emperors ranging from Valentinian III to Anastasius was struck in northern Gaul at the end of the fifth century and the beginning of the sixth. They were probably intended to be worth half- or quarter-siliquae.[2] They have mostly been found between the Seine and the Rhine and were presumably struck, perhaps at Trier, for the last 'Roman' rulers at Soissons, Aetius and Syagrius, and for their frankish successor Clovis.

These nominally 'imperial' coins were followed by limited issues of silver coins struck in their own names by the barbarian rulers. In Italy silver 'siliquae' were struck in their own names at Rome, Ravenna and Pavia for the Germanic kings from Theoderic to Teja (552–3), the last Ostrogothic ruler before Justinian's reconquest. Justinian himself was able to strike a relatively abundant coinage of imperial 'siliquae' from his Italian mints. However, after the Lombard conquest of much of the Italian peninsula in 568–70, the silver coinage of Justinian's successors, from the remaining Byzantine mints at Ravenna and Rome, was very much sparser.[3] In their early years the Lombard invaders struck 'siliquae' that still bore the names of Justinian and of Justin II (565–78).[4] In Gaul the Merovingian kings of the Franks, from Theuderic of Rheims (511–34), the eldest son of Clovis, to Sigebert of Metz (561–75), continued in their own names the series of silver coins previously struck in the names of the emperors. These were also probably intended as 'quarter-siliquae', although the later ones imitated in type the much heavier 'half-siliquae' of Justinian. In the middle of the sixth century, copies in the name of Justinian were also being struck in the Rhineland, where his Italian 'siliquae', like their Ostrogothic precursors, had a certain circulation. The evidence of these silver

[1] Philip Grierson, 'Una moneta d'argento inedita di Teodorico il Grande', *Numismatica*, 2nd series, I (1960), 113–15.
[2] Surviving examples of the 'half-siliquae' weigh 0.9–0.97 grams, against prototypes that weighed 1.04–1.25 grams. Surviving examples of the 'quarter-siliquae' weigh from 0.5 grams down to as little as 0.2 grams (P. H. Mitard, 'Monnaies des ve/vi^e et viie siècles découvertes à Genainville (Val d'Oise)', *Revue Numismatique*, 6th series, XX (1978), 117–29).
[3] Philip Grierson, 'Monete Bizantine in Italia dal VII all' XI secolo', in *Moneta e scambi nell'alto medioevo*, Settimane di Studi del Centro Italiano di Studi sull'alto medioevo, VIII (Spoleto, 1961), pp. 35–55.
[4] Philip Grierson, 'The silver coinage of the Lombards', *Archivio Storico Lombardo*, 8th series, VI (1956), 130–40.

coins suggests that the balance of payments lay from south to north. Since political subventions were made in gold, the appearance of this silver implies commercial payments from south to north. In the sixth century the Austrasian Frankish rulers Theuderic and Theodebert successfully intervened in German tribal vendettas and were able to exact a tribute of livestock and slaves. Many of the latter were then sold.[1] The evidence of payments in silver from Italy northwards across the Alps suggests that, for a time at any rate, the value of slaves and other northern goods sent southwards through the Alps exceeded that of southern goods sent northwards, mostly commodities like textiles, which have long since perished. It is perhaps significant that the Rhineland was the key area in which these Italian silver coins have been found and imitations struck, for the Rhineland, formerly a frontier zone, was rapidly developing into a principal corridor for commercial activity through the midst of the barbarian peoples. The pattern of survival of durable objects from the Mediterranean, for which we can have archaeological evidence, such as Coptic bronze vessels from seventh-century Egypt, confirms the emergence of the Rhine as a major trade-route in Dark Age Europe.[2] (See Map 1.)

In the third quarter of the sixth century the issue of silver coins almost ceased throughout the area that had been the western half of the Roman Empire.[3] For nearly a century virtually no silver coin was struck at all in the west, and the west, unlike the east, was already without a copper coinage. What was left after the disappearance of both copper and silver was gold, and this was rapidly ceasing to be used as widely as it had been. This third quarter of the sixth century in many respects marks a distinct step away from the economic and political structure of the ancient world, and coinage too fits into this pattern.

Just as the barbarian kings moved from producing silver coinages in the names of the distant emperors to producing them in their own names, they also did the same with gold, but rather later. Procopius records how, after the Franks had taken over Provence, in 537, and occupied Marseilles, they made 'a golden coin from the product of the mines in Gaul, not stamping the likeness of the Roman emperor on this stater, as is customary, but their own likeness'. Procopius, in Constantinople, did not mind the barbarian kings making silver coins in their own names but he felt

---

[1] J. M. Wallace-Hadrill, *The Barbarian West 400–1000*, 3rd ed. (London, 1967), p. 75.

[2] Joachim Werner, 'Fernhandel und Naturalwirtschaft im östlichen Merowingerreich nach archäologischen und numismatischen zeugnissen', *Moneta e scambi*, pp. 557–618. Map 1 is derived from those prepared by Prof. Werner and appearing on pp. 566 and 582–3.

[3] Extremely limited issues of silver were struck in the late sixth century at Ravenna for Tiberius II and Maurice, and were imitated by the Lombards, and in the first half of the seventh century for Phocas and Heraclius (Philip Grierson, *Moneta e scambi*, pp. 35–55). In Constantinople silver coin was only struck for customary distribution on special state occasions, and there was not even always enough silver available for these purposes. In 578, for example, Tiberius II was unable to give the traditional accession largesse to the army partly in gold and partly in silver, and had to give it entirely in gold. Philip Grierson, *Catalogue of the Byzantine Coins in the Dumbarton Oaks Collection*, II (Washington, 1968), 18.

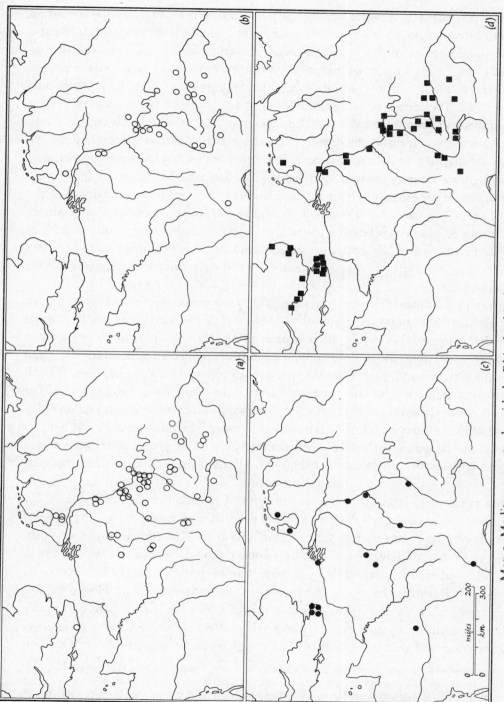

Map 1. Mediterranean trade with the Rhineland in the sixth and seventh centuries

a. Finds of silver coins from Ostrogothic Italy up to 552   b. Finds of silver coins from Byzantine Italy 555–578
c. Finds of gold coins from Visigothic Spain up to 575   d. Finds of bronze vessels from Egypt

that 'it is not considered right . . . for any . . . sovereign in the whole barbarian world to imprint his own likeness on a gold stater'. The earliest surviving solidi and trientes to bear the name of a Frankish king were struck for Theodebert of Austrasia (534–48), politically a figure of European importance, who occupied Marseilles for some years. He is almost certainly the man of whose effrontery Procopius disapproved. Procopius consoled himself by suggesting to his readers that such presumptuous issues were useless. 'They are unable to tender such a coin to those with whom they transact business, even though the parties concerned in the transaction happen to be barbarians.'[1] Procopius may even have been right, and Theodebert's gold may have been unacceptable, for, after his reign, issues of gold in the names of the emperors were resumed in Provence and continued down to the time of Heraclius (610–41). However, from the third quarter of the sixth century the minting of gold coins bearing the names of their true issuers became regular in both the Frankish and Visigothic kingdoms. In Gaul this began with the brothers Sigebert and Guntram, who began their reigns in 561, and in Spain, around 580, with Leovigild.

Barbarian solidi and trientes, whether issued in the names of the emperors or in those of their own kings, were, initially at any rate, as good as those struck in mints under direct imperial control. Their bronze and silver coinages, however, before they were given up in the middle of the sixth century, were often much poorer than their imperial prototypes, and would not have served well for any purpose in which the intrinsic value of the coin mattered. After the end of the bronze and silver coinages, even the gold coinage began to diminish both in quantity and quality. By the end of the century Frankish solidi were no longer acceptable in Italy.[2] What sort of an economy was it with only a diminishing gold coinage and neither silver nor copper? With the disappearance of urban life and the shrinking of trade, the role left for the gold coinage was becoming non-commercial.

Even taxes were ceasing to be paid in gold. The incoming kings had initially taken over the late Roman tax system, but it gradually broke down in the course of the sixth century, although it did not finally come to an end until the seventh. Gregory, Bishop of Tours from 573–94, observed the decline of the tax system. It had already partially collapsed by 579 when Chilperic, who ruled from Soissons, roused great animosity by trying to breathe new life into the system. However, it is not clear whether his attempted exaction of a tax in wine was instead of a tax in gold, or in addition to it. It certainly met with both passive and active resistance. Gregory observed that great numbers of people fled, because they could not, or

---

[1] Procopius, *History of the Wars*, Book VII, chapter xxxiii. I quote from the translation in the Loeb edition.

[2] 'Solidi Galliarum qui in terra nostra expendi non possunt'. From the register of the letters of Gregory I, pope 590–604, quoted by Robert Latouche, *The Birth of Western Economy* (1956; English trans., London, 1961), p. 128. The Frankish triens dropped in weight from 1.5 grams to 1.3 grams in the last quarter of the sixth century. See below, p. 19.

would not, pay, whilst in Limoges the inhabitants burnt the tax-collector's assessment-books and threatened his life. In the following year Chilperic gave up the attempt to collect the tax, ordered the tax-books to be burnt and promised that no fresh assessments would ever be made again.[1] This promise was not entirely kept, for his grandson, Dagobert, was still able to get some tax in gold from the Limousin in the next century.[2] When writing about Chilperic, Gregory reveals that some of the taxes collected by his father, Chlotar, had not yet been spent. Chilperic had a treasure-house still full of his father's gold, and Chlotar had died nearly twenty years before. This implies that the expenditure side of the state had collapsed already. There was no army or civil service to be paid regularly in gold. There was no state transport system to maintain, and there were no bulk purchases of foodstuffs for free distribution. Without state expenditure the gold could not get back into the hands of the tax-payers. It ceased to be recycled through the economy and was fossilised in great royal hoards, which were, according to Gregory, all too often seized by rival kings with great violence and bloodshed. The kings used their treasure-hoards, if at all, for prestigious gifts to their subjects, or for political payments to one another, like the payment to the Franks by Witigis, King of the Ostrogoths, of nearly 150,000 solidi, to prevent them from joining Belisarius in attacking Italy in 537.[3] The subjects who received gifts of gold were frequently royal relations, great noblemen, bishops or favoured monasteries. All of these hoarded rather than spent the gold. These noble and ecclesiastical hoards were also liable to violent theft or royal confiscation, often accompanied by brutal judicial murder. The pages of Gregory of Tours drip with blood and gold, but it was gold not in circulation and use, but clotted and hoarded.

In the Byzantine Empire the Avar and Persian conquests, at the end of the sixth century and the beginning of the seventh, brought about an abrupt reduction in the taxable base of the empire. As a result the government had far less gold at its disposal and experienced great difficulty in paying the armies ever more desperately needed for defence. Heraclius, who took over the government in 610 in the middle of a series of military catastrophes, changed the system of payment to a large portion of the native soldiers from gold to land. Large areas of imperial land in Asia Minor were divided up into smallholdings that were given to recruits on condition of hereditary military service. Their land provided the means whereby they were

---

[1] Gregory of Tours, *History of the Franks*, Book v, chapters xxviii and xxxiv. In Austrasia too, taxation had also become uncommon and difficult to collect. In 589 Chilperic's nephew, Childebert, attempted to collect a tax for the first time for at least fourteen years, but in 590 he too had to admit the difficulties of collecting and provide mammoth exemptions from it (Book IX, chapter x and Book X, chapter vii). Childebert's son, Theodoric II, also tried and also found difficulty in collecting taxes.

[2] Renée Doehaerd, *The Early Middle Ages in the West: Economy and Society* (1971; English trans., Amsterdam, 1978), p. 224.

[3] Procopius, *History of the Wars*, Book v, quoted by Philip Grierson, 'Commerce in the Dark Ages: a critique of the evidence', *Transactions of the Royal Historical Society*, 5th series, IX (1959), 132.

basically maintained and equipped, although they also received a very modest amount of fixed pay. The total monetary expenditure on the army was reduced to a half of that paid out in the sixth century.[1] In the barbarian kingdoms of the west there was no sudden drop in royal incomes, but a slow run-down of the taxation system. As a natural consequence the rulers gradually found that they were no longer able to pay their warriors, even when they wanted to do so, once they had distributed their hoarded gold, since they could no longer replenish their hoards from taxation. In times of war the payment of troops became a major problem. Although there was no systematic settlement of soldiers, as in the eastern empire, a gradual evolution in a similar direction took place in the west. Payment of warriors in land replaced payment in gold in the course of the seventh century. By the early eighth century so much royal land had been distributed, particularly in the civil wars within Frankia, that the Merovingians were utterly impoverished. The rising mayors of the palace faced the same problem and took the solution a step further. Pepin of Herstal (Mayor 680–714) and Charles Martel (Mayor 719–41), in particular, provided their military supporters with land by compelling the churches to grant them portions of ecclesiastical property. It was, however, not distributed directly to individual soldiers as smallholdings, but in estates to vassals who could thereby maintain and equip not only themselves, but also a group of armed dependants.[2] The ultimate genesis of feudal organisation is thus to be found in the lack of gold in the hands of the seventh-century Frankish kings and the impossibility of continuing to pay armies with money.

The class of great landlords was itself undergoing a fundamental change. It was still possible for Gregory of Tours to pick out members of old senatorial families from the Roman past. He himself belonged to such families on both sides. However, his was almost the last generation when it was possible to do so. Many of them were stripped of their lands, and lives, in the destructive wars brought about by the fratricidal strife among the descendants of Clovis, or the Lombard–Byzantine struggle for control of Italy after 568. Eventually, the remaining descendants of the Roman senatorial families were merged by marriage with the descendants of the conquering barbarian chieftains into one mixed nobility. It was a nobility that was able to draw less and less of its income in gold. The urban or state markets in which the produce of the estates could be sold in bulk for gold were in decline, and rents too were ceasing to be paid in gold. The earliest evidence that we have for its partial replacement by labour-rent comes from the Padua area in the middle of the sixth century,[3] and at the end of the century Pope Gregory I was

---

[1] George Ostrogorsky, *History of the Byzantine State* (1952; English trans., Oxford, 1956), pp. 86–90.
[2] F. L. Ganshof, *Feudalism* (1947; English trans., London, 1952), pp. 9–19.
[3] Philip Jones, 'Medieval agrarian society in its prime: Italy', in M. M. Postan (ed.), *Cambridge Economic History of Europe*, 2nd ed., 1 (Cambridge, 1966), 395–6.

taking rents in grain, even from Sicily, that had previously been paid in money.[1] Consequently the great landlords were compelled to live increasingly on the produce of their estates and to forgo many of the long-distance luxuries enjoyed by their predecessors. However, long-distance trade that used coin, even if radically diminished, never actually came to a standstill. It was still possible for Dagobert in the 630s to grant the abbey of St Denis 100 solidi a year to buy oil to maintain its lights out of the tolls of Marseilles and Fos.[2] Moreover the decline in the use of money cannot be used as an entirely satisfactory measure of the decline in trade, if by 'trade' is meant the transmission of goods from one place to another. There is considerable evidence that in the 'Dark Ages' goods were exchanged over quite long distances without the intermediary use of money at all. Before they entered the empire, the barbarian peoples had developed a tradition of 'gift-exchange', which was suited to a virtually moneyless society. This tradition of 'gift-exchange' survived after the barbarians had conquered the western provinces of the empire, and indeed lasted, in an extremely attenuated form, as late as the ninth century.[3]

Even if gold was losing its fiscal, rental and commercial functions, it was still used. It was, for example, the means of compensation, the payment of which played so significant a role in the laws of the barbarian peoples from the Lombards to the Anglo-Saxons. In the laws of the Salian Franks, which have come down in a basically sixth-century code, compensation payments were measured out in gold, starting with 200 solidi for the life of a free Frankish warrior and running down to compensation for the loss of a finger by a free Roman. Fines were also levied in gold. In a miscarriage of justice in the 570s, Albinus, Governor of Provence, fined the Archdeacon of Marseilles the immense sum of 4000 solidi, for alleged connivance in the theft of 70 jars of oil and wine from ships in the harbour of Marseilles.[4]

Gold too was used for what looks like wife-purchase. Gregory of Tours tells the story of an unsuccessful confidence trickster who tried to acquire a rich man's daughter by the pretended gift of 16,000 solidi.[5] Gold too was used for funeral purposes. The Sutton Hoo ship-burial of around 620 contained 37 trientes and 3 blanks of the same size for the pay of the 40 oarsmen, and 2 ingots, quadruple the size, for the captain and the pilot.[6] Here the lack of coin was made up with gold of equivalent weight, as in the Crondall hoard, in which 6 triens-size pieces of gold

---

[1] C. Wickham, *Early Medieval Italy* (London, 1981), p. 99.
[2] If the ninth-century author of the *Vita Dagoberti* can be accepted as evidence for the seventh century (Doehaerd, *Early Middle Ages*, p. 224).
[3] Grierson, 'Commerce in the Dark Ages', pp. 137–9.
[4] Gregory of Tours, *History of the Franks*, Book IV, chapter xliii.
[5] *Ibid.* chapter xlvi.
[6] Philip Grierson, 'The purpose of the Sutton Hoo coins' and 'The Sutton Hoo coins again', *Antiquity*, XLIV and XLVIII (1970 and 1974).

were used to make up a round 100.[1] The very fact that pieces of gold of the approximate size could be substituted for coins is another indication of how far the barbarians had travelled from the full use of coin.

It was not only the lack of order and the lack of coin that was running the economy down. There was also a critical lack of people. Historians argue about whether and by how much the population had already declined by the middle of the sixth century, and whether the *agri deserti* were merely vacant because of the tax-impelled flight of cultivators to other places, or whether there were already many fewer people, who were naturally concentrating on better land, and whether the deaths associated with disorder were compensated for by the new barbarian immigrants. There is, however, no doubt that, from 541, for just over two centuries, wave after wave of plague radically and repeatedly reduced the population of western Europe.[2] By the early eighth century the population of Italy, for instance, was at a lower point than at any other time in its recorded history.[3]

The quantities of gold in circulation in the west had been declining ever since the end of the fourth century. The west had little, except slaves, to offer for the silks and spices, the vessels of glass and bronze, and the oil, papyrus and indigo that Syrians, Greeks, and Jews were continuing to bring from the eastern Mediterranean. The imbalance of the shrinking trade with the east was therefore a perpetual drain on the gold available in the west, but so was hoarding. On the one hand there was hoarding by concealment in times of emergency, like the decades of invasion from 395 to 415, and the generation of continual wars in the later sixth century. On the other hand there was hoarding in the treasure-chests of kings, nobles and ecclesiastics. Either way, gold was taken out of circulation as coin. Between the middle of the sixth century and the end of the seventh the increasing dearth of gold in the west manifested itself in a number of ways. Trientes were minted rather than solidi, the number struck decreased rapidly, and the fineness of the gold from which they were minted deteriorated markedly.

In the second half of the sixth century it became more usual to strike the triens, the third part of a solidus, rather than the whole solidus. Solidi ceased to be struck by the Franks, except at Marseilles, and no whole solidi at all were struck by the Visigoths from the reign of Leovigild (568–86), at the latest. In seventh- and eighth-century Italy too, it was trientes that the Lombard kings struck from their mints in the Po valley and Tuscany. However, further south, the Lombard Dukes of Benevento, who were more strongly influenced by Byzantium, did strike whole solidi as well, as did the surviving Byzantine mints in Italy and Sicily.

---

[1] It has been suggested that the Crondall hoard, concealed around 640, was a compensation payment (Philip Grierson, 'La Fonction sociale de la monnaie en Angleterre aux VIIe et VIIIe siècles', in *Moneta e scambi*, pp. 341–62).

[2] J. N. Biraben and J. Le Goff, 'La Peste dans le Haut Moyen Age', *Annales*, XXIV (1969), 1484–1510.

[3] Jones, 'Medieval agrarian society', p. 343.

A further indication of the declining use of the solidus is provided by two hoards. A hoard from Seville, of the mid sixth century, contained at least 40 solidi and only certainly 18 trientes, whereas a hoard at Escharen, near Nijmegen, deposited half a century later, around 600, contained 44 trientes, but only 11 whole solidi.[1]

Although the solidus gradually ceased to circulate in the west, it still remained as a unit of account. Sums of money went on being expressed in solidi in codes of law, and in land transactions, but in practice the word 'solidus' had come to mean not one actual gold coin, but a unit of three tremisses or trientes.

By the seventh century the number of trientes struck was not very large. All the surviving specimens of the triens of the Bonn mint were struck from a single pair of dies, which suggests how small some of the issues were. From some mints no more than a few thousand trientes can have been issued. However, the number of mints had increased enormously since the fourth century. In the fourth century Gaul had been provided with a very large coinage from three enormous mints, Trier, Lyons, and Arles. Under the Merovingians the Franks had a much smaller coinage produced instead at a vast number of tiny mints.[2]

As well as being minted within what had been Roman Gaul, trientes were also struck in Frisia, preceded in the sixth century by cast derivatives of whole solidi, with runic inscriptions, which appear to have been more in the nature of amulets than coins. These Frisian trientes were the first coins struck outside the area in which money had been minted in antiquity. Otherwise, minting was still restricted to areas that had once been within the confines of the Roman Empire, and the circulation of coin, as shown by hoards and by finds of stray coins, barely extended beyond the old Roman frontiers.

The increasing dearth of gold in the west was also manifested in the deterioration of the quality of the coins. In the Visigothic kingdom the triens dropped to 18 carat gold as early as the reign of Leovigild (568–86). For much of the seventh century the fineness fluctuated between 14 and 16 carats, and at the very end of the century dropped even further.[3]

Among the Franks a lower weight standard, of approximately 7 siliquae, around 1.3 grams in modern terms, was used for the triens, alongside the original 8 siliquae standard, until the reign of Dagobert I (629–39). Thereafter only lighter-weight trientes were minted.[4] During Dagobert's reign the fineness also began

---

[1] Xavier Barral y Altet, *La Circulation des monnaies suèves et visigothiques. Contribution à l'histoire économique du royaume visigot. Francia*, supplement 4 (Munich, 1976), pp. 78–80. Jean Lafaurie, 'Le Trésor d'Escharen', *Revue Numismatique*, 6th series, II (1959–60), 153–210.

[2] See below, pp. 22–6.

[3] One triens of the Toledo mint, struck under Egica (687–98), has been found on analysis to be as poor as 11-carat gold, and later pieces were poorer still. At the same time the weight of the trientes, which had remained remarkably stable from Leovigild to Egica at 8 siliquae, or 1.5 grams, became totally erratic (Philip Grierson, 'Visigothic metrology', *Numismatic Chronicle*, 6th series, XIII (1953), 74–87).

[4] Jean Lafaurie, 'Le Trésor d'Escharen', 153–210. Metrology is discussed at pp. 168–71.

to decline. By the third quarter of the century they were only one third gold.[1]

The Anglo-Saxon trientes were all of the Frankish 7-siliquae weight standard, and in Britain the fineness of the gold used deteriorated markedly in the 660s.

In Italy, the same changes took place, but rather later. The Lombards did not begin to oust the Byzantine reconquerors of Italy until 568, a century and a half after the other barbarian peoples had invaded the empire. They kept the mints going, as other barbarian peoples had done, first in the names of the·emperors, whose representatives they were fighting, and then in their own names.[2] In the sixth century, and for most of the seventh, their issues remained as heavy and as fine as regular Byzantine issues. However the dearth of gold in the west eventually began to afflict both the Lombard mints and the surviving imperial mints in Italy, even those in Sicily. Although they were still able to go on minting with fine gold, both the Sicilian and the Lombard issues were reduced in weight towards the end of the seventh century. The Lombard kings even managed to maintain the same standards as the Byzantine provincial issues in Sicily until the reign of Liutprand (712–44).[3]

By the time of Liutprand gold had ceased to be minted elsewhere in western Europe. Outside Italy the issues of trientes had come to an end late in the seventh century, or early in the eighth. In most of Gaul, the mints ceased striking gold in the 670s. The latest royal triens to survive was struck for Dagobert II (674–9). In Provence the Marseilles mint probably went on striking gold for another decade. Hoard evidence suggests that the circulation of gold came to an end at more or less the same time.[4] By the beginning of the eighth century the disappearance of gold from Frankia seems to have been total. The hoarded gold so prominent in the pages of Gregory of Tours had been dispersed. Some of the gold had become jewellery, or been used to ornament shrines. Dagobert, in the first half of the seventh century, had given gold coin to his goldsmith, Eligius, for these purposes. However a century later new gold jewellery had itself ceased to be made; the gold had all been exported by then.

The Anglo-Saxons, who had only recently resumed the use of coin at all, and that

---

[1] Modern analyses have shown that up to the 620s the tremisses were still generally struck of gold at least 19 carats fine, but that in Dagobert's reign they were only between 12 and 17 carats fine, and fell further to between 10 and 12 carats fine in the years immediately after Dagobert's death. Jean Lafaurie has associated the drop in fineness with the activities of Eloi, the famous goldsmith, as a leading minister in Dagobert's reign and immediately after his death. (Eloi himself died in 660 and was later canonised as St Eligius.) ('Eligius Monetarius', *Revue Numismatique*, 6th series, xix (1977), 134–9.)

[2] There is some doubt about the earliest issue in the name of a Lombard king, but it is probably represented by surviving pieces of Cunincpert (679–700). That bearing the name of Aripert I (653–61) now seems to be a forgery.

[3] W. A. Oddy, 'Analyses of Lombardic tremisses by the specific gravity method', *Numismatic Chronicle*, 7th series, xii (1972), 193–215.

[4] Jean Lafaurie, 'Monnaies d'argent mérovingiennes des viiᵉ et viiiᵉ siècles', *Revue Numismatique*, 6th series, xi (1969), 98–219. The transition from gold to silver is discussed on pp. 115–22. The latest hoard, so far discovered, that contained trientes was concealed at Bordeaux around 700–5.

probably only in south-east England, stopped minting gold around the 670s, like their Frankish neighbours. In Spain the last Visigothic trientes of Achila II (*c.* 710–14) were succeeded only by a very sparse and short-lived issue of gold dinars by the conquering Ummayads. After A.H. 106 (A.D. 724/5) no further gold coins were struck in Spain until the tenth century.[1]

Minting of gold in western Europe in the eighth century continued only in Italy, which was still partially in the orbit of Byzantium. We have little evidence of its use, except for payments by rulers, although it is clear that, even in the eighth century, in the territories of the Lombards, gold coin was still used for capital outlay, such as the purchase of agricultural land, although the rents from such land were generally received in kind, or occasionally in services.[2] Even in Italy the general dearth of gold in the west made it impossible to continue to produce coins of fine gold throughout the eighth century. In Lombardy itself debasement began under Liutprand (712–44), and in Tuscany at more or less the same time. Nevertheless there was enough gold available in northern Italy to produce trientes of some sort for much of the century. Charlemagne even continued to issue them after his conquest in 773, but their circulation was forbidden by the Capitulary of Mantua in 781.

By the time the last issues were struck, the trientes had greatly deteriorated in fineness, from nearly pure gold to barely a quarter gold and three-quarters alloy.[3] There had still been direct Byzantine issues of gold coin in northern Italy as late as the middle of the eighth century, for Ravenna did not fall into Lombard hands until 751.

In central Italy the Byzantine issues of gold at Rome deteriorated at the same time as those of the Lombards further north. By the mid eighth century they were only about one-third gold and two-thirds alloy. In the 770s, just before Pope Adrian I took over the mint, the last Byzantine coins struck in Rome were only of gilded copper.[4]

In Byzantium itself the minting of gold solidi continued uninterruptedly, and even the original fourth-century standard of fineness and weight was maintained

[1] G. C. Miles, *The Coinage of the Ummayads of Spain* (New York, 1950). The first gold coins struck by the Arabs still had purely Latin inscriptions. They were followed in turn by a brief bilingual issue with inscriptions in both Latin and Arabic, and a final issue with entirely Arabic inscriptions, before the gold ran out. For the Latin issues (in Africa A.H. 84–98, and in Spain A.H. 93–8) and the bilingual issues (in Africa and Spain A.H. 97–9) see Anna M. Balaguer, *Las emisiones transicionales árabe-musulmanas de Hispania* (Barcelona, 1976) and 'Early Islamic transitional gold issues of North Africa and Spain', *Museum Notes*, XXIV (American Numismatic Society: New York, 1979), 225–41.

[2] Ernesto Bernareggi, *Il sistema economico della monetazione dei Langobardi nell'Italia superiore* (Milan, 1960), chapter 1.

[3] Oddy, 'Analyses of Lombardic tremisses'. Both documentary references and a hoard discovered at Ilanz, now in Switzerland, are evidence for their circulation in the 790s. Philip Grierson, 'Money and coinage under Charlemagne', in W. Braunfels (ed.), *Karl der Grosse: Lebenswerk und Nachleben*, I (Düsseldorf, 1965), 513–15.

[4] Philip Grierson, *Byzantine Coins* (London, 1982), pp. 168–70.

virtually unchanged until the eleventh century. In Sicily and the south of Italy, parts of which remained in Byzantine hands until the eleventh century, the use of gold coins also continued without any interruption. Otherwise the coinage of western Europe was minted exclusively of silver for the next 500 years, apart from a brief ninth-century interlude,[1] and a few altogether extraordinary pieces, issued by such rulers as Edward the Confessor of England, which were almost certainly intended only for prestigious royal alms-givings.

Alongside the last trientes the Merovingians and the Frisians also began to strike new denarii in the seventh century, of the same weight and module as the trientes, but in silver instead of gold. The future lay with the silver denarius, rather than the declining triens, for this denarius was the ancestor of the Carolingian denier and the whole range of medieval penny coinages.

Trientes and denarii were struck altogether in some 500 different places.[2] This in itself strikingly illustrates the way in which the economy and society of Gaul had fragmented and become extremely localised over the three centuries since the same area had been provided with a more abundant coinage by three very large mints. For some of these numerous mints we know of only a single *monetarius*.[3] For others we know of a whole sequence of them. Between trientes and the new silver denarii some 1500 different *monetarii* are known for the whole of Frankia.

In the Visigothic kingdom the same decentralisation took place, although not quite to such a marked extent. In the fourth century there had been no Roman mint in the Diocese of Spain. Its currency needs had been supplied from other provinces. By the time of the Arab invasions the Visigoths had minted at one time or another in nearly seventy different places. (See Map 2.)[4]

In northern Italy minting was not so localised, but even here there were a number of mints scattered throughout both Lombardy and Tuscany in place of a single Roman mint at Milan.

The mints were not quite as decentralised as these enormous numbers might lead one to believe at first sight, for a single *monetarius* was sometimes responsible for mints in more than one place, particularly when they were small or close together. Moreover it is probable that dies were cut in a relatively few regional centres, each serving a widespread group of mints. It has, for example, been suggested that a single goldsmith was responsible for engraving dies for mints as far apart as Cologne, Soissons and Strasbourg.[5] It is not even entirely clear that the craftsmen

---

[1] See below, pp. 50–2. [2] M. Prou, *Les Monnaies mérovingiennes* (Paris, 1892).
[3] I have deliberately not translated the term *monetarius* as 'moneyer' here so as to distinguish the public official responsible for the oversight of a local mint from the craftsmen whom he employed to actually make the coins. The *monetarius* was normally a substantial man in his own right. See R. S. Lopez, 'An aristocracy of money in the early middle ages', *Speculum*, XXVIII (1953), 1–43.
[4] Barral y Altet, *La Circulation des monnaies*, p. 61.
[5] H.-U. Bauer, in *Schweizer Münzblätter* (1951), as quoted by Werner, 'Fernhandel'.

Map 2. Visigothic mints

who actually minted may not also have come out from a limited number of central points in order to strike the coins, unless, alternatively, they struck them centrally and sent them out ready-made to the *monetarii* responsible for their issue. The fact that the same dies were sometimes used to produce coins issued from several different mints demands this sort of explanation. This identity of dies at different mints has been noticed for Lombard coins as well as for Frankish ones.

The extreme localisation of minting did not necessarily indicate the breakdown of central authority, although that was always at risk. Furthermore the absence of the names of the kings from the last Frankish trientes and the early deniers, by contrast with the Visigothic trientes on which the kings' names always appeared, must not be seen as evidence for a lack of royal control, but as a different expression of that control. The *monetarius*, as an official of the public fisc, gave a state authority to all coins on which his name appeared.

In the sixth century Theoderic, King of the Ostrogoths, when instructing his agents in Spain, included among the abuses that they needed to clear up the fact that '*monetarii*, who are specially established for public service (*in usum publicum*), have transferred themselves to the service of individuals'.[1] In seventh-century Italy his

---

[1] Letters of Cassiodorus, Book v, letter 39. *Corpus Christianorum (Series Latina)*, XCVI (1973), 213.

Lombard successor, Rothari, in his edict was still legislating against minting without royal authority: 'If any should work gold or strike money, except by order of the king, their hand should be cut off.'[1] Royal authority over minting was still being preserved but it was fragile. In the first years of the seventh century, Eloi, or Eligius, the celebrated goldsmith, was apprenticed to Abbo 'fabro aurifice probatissimo, qui eo tempore in urbe Lemovecina publicam fiscalis monetae officinam gerebat'.[2] In this case at least, running the mint was still a public function dependent on the royal fisc. Eloi himself went on to run the mints of Marseilles, Arles and Paris, the palatine mint and that of the scola palatina between about 625 and 641 when he was consecrated Bishop of Noyon.[3] He too struggled to maintain the royal authority over the coinage, and it was only after his elevation to a bishopric that royal control of the mints collapsed, in common with many other aspects of royal authority, in the years of Merovingian weakness after the death of Dagobert in 639. It was at this time that the landed aristocracy and the most influential ecclesiastics took over. Privileges of immunity from royal taxation and royal justice fortified these men in the usurpation of yet one more regalian right.[4] The greatest of these landed families was, of course, the Arnulfings, who eventually usurped the throne itself. When the *monetarius* ceased to be a public official and became the official of an immunist, his name ceased to be a worthwhile guarantee. It is at this point that the names of bishops and abbeys appeared on Frankish coins, and also at this point that they ceased to bear the name of an authenticating *monetarius*. Many eighth-century deniers have only the name of the place of issue without the name of any issuing authority whatsoever.

The implication of this is that minting was distributed much more widely than any breakdown of mint administration would account for. Indeed the multiplication of mint places came about before political control of the mints finally collapsed. In other words it was not for administrative reasons that minting was so localised. In tenth-century England, where the administration of the mints was thoroughly centralised, the equation of mint and market was made: every market town should have a mint.[5] I would suggest that this was also the case in seventh-century Frankia. The enormously wide distribution of mints would then be seen as a witness to a new vitality in local trade.[6]

Latouche emphasised that although land was still owned in great estates, the

---

[1] 'Si quis sine iussionem regis aurum figuraverit aut moneta confinxerit manus ei incidatur' (Wilhelm Jesse (ed.), *Quellenbuch zur Münz- und Geldgeschichte des Mittelalters* (Halle, 1924; repr. 1968), doc. 7).

[2] *Ibid.* doc. 11.

[3] Jean Lafaurie, 'Eligius Monetarius', pp. 111–51.

[4] The only charter specifically including coining rights in a privilege of immunity is, however, a forgery (Latouche, *Western Economy*, pp. 128–9).

[5] See below, pp. 87–9.

[6] Barral y Altet, *La Circulation des monnaies*, pp. 70 and 164, has similarly seen the proliferation of Visigothic mints as evidence for an internal trade within Spain that was very active although essentially local.

organisation of those estates was perpetually changing throughout the Merovingian period. The slave-run *latifundia* collapsed, and in its place the great estate came to have a myriad smallholding peasant tenants. Some were descendants of slaves, others of commended freemen and yet others of barbarian soldier-ploughmen, who had come in under conquering barbarian chieftains and cleared uncultivated areas alongside and between the existing settlements. Although the population of seventh-century Frankia was clearly lower than that of fourth-century Gaul, it seems to have been dispersed in a larger number of smaller settlements. The society that was emerging in the seventh century was one of peasant tenants, secure in tenures that made them semi-proprietors of the land that they and their families farmed, and hoped to go on farming for generations to come.[1] Such a society needed a different sort of marketing organisation from a city-focussed society, in which there had been continuous buying and selling every day, or yet again from that of great aristocratic estate-owners with their incomes in gold, who had been prepared to buy goods less often, but in large quantities and from the greatest distances, to meet their expensive tastes. There was instead a need for frequent markets at which the peasantry of a locality could buy or sell or exchange produce with one another all the year round. By the ninth century such markets were normally held weekly. In addition there was also a need for occasional fairs at which the typical products of a region could be sold or exchanged for products from outside. The Fair of St Denis was such a fair and dates from this period. Barter was quite obviously perfectly possible in such a peasant market of interchange, but it had its obvious limitations. It would only work if the objects to be exchanged were equally esteemed. It would not readily allow multilateral exchanges, and it would not easily allow for the situation in which one party had something to dispose of at one time of year and the other at a different time of year. All these limitations could be overcome with ingenuity, but in a society in which money, in some form, had been known for centuries, it was natural to use money as an intermediary for peasant market-interchange. Ninth-century documents quite clearly assumed that those at markets used deniers. How far then did the system of minting show that it was adapting to the transformation of society? The multiplication of local mints quite clearly fitted in with this sort of evolution. So did the evolution of the type of coin minted. Copper was too small for this sort of transaction, as large, pure-gold coins were too considerable. The triens was better than the solidus, particularly the poor triens of the mid seventh century, and the new denarius was, probably, even more useful.[2]

By its adoption of the new denier, and the multiplicity of mints, late Merovingian Frankia showed itself to have adapted to the new society, of a

---

[1] Latouche, *Western Economy*, Part II, chapters 1 and 2.
[2] For some agricultural prices see below, p. 35.

multitude of peasant proprietors attached to their soil, which had emerged, and which came to be the hallmark of the next centuries, in which the denier, and the localised minting of it, remained typical.

When gold coinage had finally disappeared outside Italy, western Europe was left with a new system of coinage, based on the silver penny, which was entirely unlike either that which survived in the east, in the Byzantine Empire, or that which had existed in the later Roman Empire. It was not that the barbarians had brought something new, and differently Germanic, into the Roman world, for they had had no coinage of their own, but that a transformation had taken place after the barbarian peoples were inside the Roman world. The break with antiquity was not a revolutionary break at a single instant, as when the Germanic peoples crossed the Rhine frontier in 406, but an evolutionary break, which had taken more than two centuries to work out. The disappearance of the coinage systems of antiquity, like the disappearance of the Roman senatorial aristocracy, took many generations. It was none the less complete.

2

The Appearance of the
Denier and the Revival of Trade

If the seventh century saw the final end of the economic structure of late antiquity in the west, it also saw the beginnings of a new economic structure. The silver penny, or denier, the minting of which began in this period, was, for over five centuries, not merely the characteristic coin of western Europe, but virtually the only coin in use.

The silver denarius of the late seventh century was modelled so exactly on the old triens, that they can sometimes only be distinguished from one another by the metal in which they were struck. Both were small coins, smaller than a modern British halfpenny or American cent. They were only a centimetre or a very little more in diameter, but relatively thick for their breadth. The same *monetarii* were responsible for their minting, and since the same die-cutters supplied them with dies for both, the strong similarity between them is not surprising. The Roman name 'denarius' was consciously revived for the new silver coins and, in order to distinguish them from the base-gold trientes, some of the earliest ones were inscribed with their denomination for a short period, LVGDVNO DINARIOS or DINARIO AVRILAI at Lyons and Orléans for example. In the same way, after a twentieth-century change, the new denominations in Britain were, for a few years, inscribed 'New Pence' until the public became accustomed to them. In the early eighth century the denomination name disappeared and their types were reduced almost entirely to legends and monograms.

As with the last trientes, the majority of silver deniers only bore the name of the place where they were issued and also, for a time, that of the *monetarius* responsible for them. Only one denier bears the name of a king. It is a very early issue, struck at Tours around 673–5, which bears the name of Childeric II of Austrasia. Other deniers bear the name of ecclesiastics or laymen who had been granted, or usurped, local authority. Among the earliest deniers are some struck by the authority of St Lambert, Bishop of Lyons from 678 to 684, of the abbeys of St Martin at Tours and of St Denis, at Catiliacus, near Paris. Early lay issuers include Ansebert and his successors as patricians, or governors, of Marseilles, and Ebroin, mayor of the palace of both Neustria and Burgundy. Professor Lafaurie believes that Ebroin, then the dominant personality in Frankish politics, was also the key figure in the introduction of the silver denier in the 670s.[1]

In Provence, where the minting of gold continued longest, the minting of the new deniers took place alongside the minting of the last trientes. In northern Frankia the minting of silver deniers took place after the minting of the basest of the pale-gold trientes, perhaps, at some mints, even after a short period when there was no minting at all. Many of the mints that had been striking gold closed at some point in the seventh century and did not reopen to strike the new deniers. Those that did strike silver mostly appear to have continued in operation into the Carolingian period without interruption. This may not have actually been the case, and the operation of these mints may have been sporadic in practice. We cannot tell, because we are not able to date their products with any degree of accuracy. Most often they have only the name of the place of issue. Apart from the earliest, they very rarely have an identifiable individual issuer. Even when the name of a *monetarius* is given this is of no help with dating, for he cannot be identified other than from his own deniers. The other named issuers are most often simply referred to by title, for example as the Bishop of Clermont or the abbey of St Maxentius, without any indication of who was bishop or abbot at the time of minting. Although our evidence for dating is so uncertain, it does not seem that silver deniers were minted in very considerable quantities before the final conquest of Frisia in the 730s.

Even before its complete conquest, Frisia seems to have been of crucial importance in the development of Frankish trade and coinage. The issue of silver deniers was concentrated in a corridor running between Provence, a region where trade had never entirely died, and northern Frankia, particularly the area closest to Frisia. In northern Frankia the largest number of known *monetarii*, responsible for the issue of either gold trientes or silver deniers, was at Verdun on the upper Meuse. There were seventeen of them. We know of twelve such *monetarii* for Huy and also for Maastricht, both lower down the Meuse.[2] This concentration of minting in the valley of the Meuse lay not only in the heartland of the Frankish people, but also on the key route northwards into Frisia, whose merchants were the leaders in the revival of trade.

The new pennies minted at the same time in Frisia and England were much more numerous than the early Frankish deniers.[3] They were minted in enormous

---

[1] Jean Lafaurie, 'Monnaies d'argent mérovingiennes des VIIe et VIIIe siècles', *Revue Numismatique*, 6th series, XI (1969), 120–1.

[2] Jean Dhondt, 'L'Essor urbain entre Meuse et Mer du Nord à l'époque mérovingienne', in *Studi in onore di Armando Sapori*, I (Milan, 1957), 75–7.

[3] These pennies or pennings are frequently called 'sceattas' or 'sceats' by numismatists. The sceatta is now understood to have been the weight of a barley grain, and the earliest pennies may well have had the same value in silver as a grain of gold (Philip Grierson, 'La Fonction sociale de la monnaie en Angleterre aux VIIe et VIIIe

quantities between the end of the seventh century and the third quarter of the eighth. It is not very easily possible to distinguish between pieces struck on the Frisian and Anglo-Saxon coasts of the North Sea. On the Anglo-Saxon side the earliest silver pennies seem to have replaced the last base-gold trientes in East Kent in the 670s, at the same time as the earliest deniers in Frankia. The first issues to be at all common have been associated with the reign of Wihtred, who was King of Kent between 691 and 725. Outside Kent there was, on the English side of the Channel, a steady coinage in the eighth century of rough pennies in East Anglia, sporadic coinages of them in London, Wessex, and Northumbria, but nothing at all in Mercia proper,[1] although stray finds of pennies struck elsewhere have been found there. However, the most common types, like the 'porcupine' type of around 720–40, which may have been minted in millions, appear to have been struck on the Frisian coast.[2] The stretch of coast then settled by Frisians reached from the mouth of the Weser in the north, to the mouth of the Zwin in the south, where Bruges was later to be built. By the early eighth century Frisian trade was well established. Their coastal trade already stretched southwards to Quentovic and the Seine in Frankia, and northwards to Jutland, to Norway, and even into the Baltic to Gotland. It also ran across the North Sea to Kent, London and Northumbria, up the Rhine to Cologne, Mainz and Strasbourg, and up the Meuse to Maastricht, Huy and Verdun. As such its focal point was the mouth of the Rhine and Meuse, where sea, coast and river traffic came together. The course of the principal branch of the Rhine was more northerly than at present, so that the focal point was not Europapoort-Rotterdam, but Dorestad or Duurstede, not far from Utrecht. Utrecht itself was the 'capital' of the dukes of the Frisians so long as they remained independent, and the see of the bishops of the Frisians after their conversion. Upstream 20 kilometres ($12\frac{1}{2}$ miles) from Utrecht, the houses and docks of Dorestad stretched for over a kilometre along the banks of the old Rhine, covering, around 800, more than 12 hectares (30 acres). It seems almost certain that the principal mint of the Frisians was in Dorestad itself. It was at Dorestad that the Frankish moneyers Remoaldus and Madelinus minted during the earlier, temporary, Frankish occupations under Dagobert and Pepin of Herstal. In the later eighth

siècles', in *Moneta e scambi nell'alto medioevo*, Settimane di studi del Centro Italiano di Studi sull'alto medioevo, VIII (Spoleto, 1961), pp. 341–62).

[1] Stuart E. Rigold, 'The two primary series of sceattas', *British Numismatic Journal*, XXX (1960), 6–53. There is great difficulty in determining the origins of these pieces with certainty since most were anonymous, although a few bear the names of moneyers, and even fewer those of kings, e.g. of Aldfrith of Northumbria, c. 700, and of Beonna of East Anglia in the 750s (Simon Keynes and Mark Blackburn, *Anglo-Saxon Coins* (Fitzwilliam Museum, Cambridge, 1985), pp. 7, 22–7). For a recent discussion of these early pennies see the papers in David Hill and D. M. Metcalf (eds.), *Sceattas in England and on the Continent*, British Archaeological Reports, British Series CXXVIII (Oxford, 1984).

[2] D. M. Metcalf, 'A stylistic analysis of the "porcupine" sceattas', *Numismatic Chronicle*, 7th series, VI (1966), 179–205.

century Dorestad appears, from the evidence of the surviving coins, to have been the most prolific mint of the Frankish kingdom, as it grew into an 'Empire', as well as its most important trading-centre.

There can be no satisfactory estimates of the size of the issues in either England or Frisia, or indeed in Frankia itself. Complex formulae have been proposed for estimating the number of dies used for striking them, from the number of coins that survive from different dies. These can produce a range of probabilities for the numbers of dies used.[1] This must be multiplied by a guess at the number of coins struck from a set of dies. The nearest evidence in date is from England under Edward I, over half a millennium later.[2] It is impossible to tell how much minting-technique had improved by the late thirteenth century, if at all. Whether one believes in a circulation of a few million deniers or of many millions depends on the difference of interpretation.[3] It is certain that there was sufficient coinage for more than merely notional use. The time of least coinage in circulation seems to have been that immediately before the introduction of the silver coinage.

One of the very real problems is how the west so suddenly came into possession of so much silver. It was perhaps a little less sudden than it appears, for the last issues of trientes contained twice as much silver as gold. It has been suggested that the silver was the same as that which had been available in much earlier centuries, that had been hoarded in the form of precious objects, which were only now dis-hoarded, melted down and minted. This I cannot believe. Evidence from the later Middle Ages suggests that hoarding and dis-hoarding can merely exacerbate a shortage or add to an increase in the supply of precious metals without changing the underlying trends. Such later evidence also suggests that political actions and payments can only make a considerable difference in the short run, but that long-term changes in the supply of precious metals were always a consequence of changes in the quantities mined and in commercial balances of payments.[4] It is therefore almost certainly necessary, for the seventh and eighth centuries also, to look for the radically increased supplies of silver either in local mining or in profitable trade with mining-areas.

---

[1] C. S. S. Lyon, 'The estimation of the number of dies employed in a coinage', *Numismatic Circular*, LXXXIII (1965), 180–1.

[2] Mavis Mate, 'Coin dies under Edward I and II', *Numismatic Chronicle*, 7th series, IX (1969), 207–18.

[3] Maximising estimates are provided by D. M. Metcalf, 'How large was the Anglo-Saxon currency?', *Economic History Review*, 2nd series, XVIII (1965), 479, who suggested that at the end of the eighth century 40 to 120 million deniers were circulating in the Carolingian Empire, concentrated in an area north and east of Paris. His reasoning has, however, been challenged. Philip Grierson, 'The volume of Anglo-Saxon currency', *Economic History Review*, 2nd series, XX (1967), 153–60, attacked Metcalf's argument in many particulars. Metcalf's reply 'The prosperity of North-Western Europe in the eighth and ninth centuries', *Economic History Review*, 2nd series, XX (1967), 344–57, reduced his earlier estimates, but still suggested a minimum of '6.7 million coins for Offa, a similar number for Pepin and even larger quantities for their successors.'

[4] See below, chapter 6, pp. 132–62.

There is no evidence of the mining of silver in eastern Kent, although this was where the minting of silver pennies, or sceattas, began. It seems that the silver had flowed from Frisia into Kent, rather than the other way round, and not only into Kent, but also into all the other kingdoms on the south and east coasts of England. Hoards of such pennies have been found all along these coasts from Dorchester in Wessex to Whitby in Northumbria, and all these coastal kingdoms began to mint silver pennies of their own at various times during the eighth century. Through the coastal kingdoms, silver penetrated inland, even ending up as far away as the territory of the Hwicce on the Severn,[1] as well as in Mercia.

It is, however, impossible to say why silver was imported into England with any degree of certainty. The Frisians were clearly exporting slaves from England captured in the internecine wars between the Anglo-Saxon peoples. In the middle of the seventh century St Eligius was buying them in batches of fifty and a hundred as they arrived in Frankish territory.[2] Bede also noted the presence of Frisian slave-traders in London in 679.[3] It also begins to seem clear that England was not only exporting wool or woollens in large quantities in the tenth century, but was already doing so in the eighth. But were all the *pallia fresonica*, the woollen cloaks sold to the Franks, made of Cotswold wool? They may have been, but we can never know. They could as well have been made from the fleeces of the sheep that fed on the rich marshland at the mouths of the Rhine, Meuse and Scheldt.[4] In return the Frisians, on archaeological evidence, brought pottery, brooches, and Coptic bronze vessels, and on documentary evidence, wine from the Moselle valley. Since the silver flowed from Frisia to England it implies both that the Frisians exported a greater value of slaves and wool, or woollens, than the manufactures and wine that they imported, and also that Frisians had some other source for silver.

The northern end of the Frisian trade showed the same imbalance as that with England, although not to so marked a degree. Silver did not reach Frisia from Scandinavia; instead, it trickled northwards. Earlier the imbalance had been more marked. In the early sixth century gold solidi had found their way from Byzantium through Italy, the Rhineland and Frisia to Scandinavia, where they had then been concealed, only to be rediscovered in modern times, particularly in Gotland, Öland and Bornholm. In the sixth century the Frisians had already also been carrying glass from the Meuse and Rhine valleys, bronze-work from northern France, and

---

[1] D. M. Metcalf, 'Sceattas from the territory of the Hwicce', *Numismatic Chronicle*, 7th series, XVI (1976), 64–74. It is impossible to prove, or disprove, Dr Metcalf's suggestions that the few discoveries of pennies lost in Hwiccian territory, from the 740s onwards, imply some use of coin in the area, and, since he believes them to be of London origin, that they represent payment for Cotswold wool and Worcestershire salt.

[2] Robert Latouche, *The Birth of Western Economy* (London, 1961), pp. 123–4.

[3] Dirk Jellema, 'Frisian trade in the Dark Ages', *Speculum*, XXX (1955), 17.

[4] Eleanora Carus-Wilson, 'The woollen industry', in M. Postan and E. E. Rich (eds.) *Cambridge Economic History of Europe*, II (1952), 363–6.

pottery to Scandinavia, but they obviously did not equal the value of the furs and other goods being carried southwards. However, in the seventh and eighth centuries the value of West European goods carried northwards more nearly matched the value of northern goods being brought back.[1]

The Frisians needed to receive continuous fresh supplies of silver from outside to enable them to carry silver outwards from Frisia westwards and northwards over long periods, for they had no sources of silver of their own. Silver-mines on the Frisian coast itself are even more geologically improbable than silver in East Kent. As yet we know little of Frisian trade eastwards with the Saxons, but there is at present no evidence to suggest that there was extensive silver-mining among them at this period. We can only conclude that the sources of Frisian silver must have been in Frankia. Trade between Frisia and Frankia was obviously complex and many-sided. The Frisians supplied the Franks with Anglo-Saxon slaves, Scandinavian furs and their own fish and cloth, particularly in the form of cloaks of many colours, and in return received corn and wine, metal-work, pottery and glass.[2] Payments in coin were obviously made in both directions, for coin hoards from Merovingian Frankia frequently contain Anglo-Frisian pennies, whilst those from Frisia contain Merovingian deniers. After the Frisians became subject to the Franks there was also a political element, as well as the purely commercial ones, in the balance of payments between the two peoples, and it is noticeable that silver became much more readily available in Frankia after the final conquest of Frisia in the 730s. It seems probable that until then the overall balance between the two peoples had been strongly in favour of the Frisians, and that, until the 730s, the Frisians had been receiving a high proportion of the silver being mined by the Franks. Among the commodities that the Frisians sent to the Franks, slaves, furs and textiles were all traditionally expensive ones.

We know of only one significant vein of silver being worked within Frankia itself, that at 'METULLO', Melle in western France, not far from Poitiers. It is not clear when silver-mines were first opened up there. The Melle mines were of argentiferous lead ore, so that there was also a considerable production of lead. In the second half of the ninth century the Melle mines were sending 8000 pounds (3630 kilograms) of lead every second year to the abbey of St Denis for roofing purposes. Hincmar believed that this was by grant from Dagobert I, but there is no reason to suppose that the mines were open as early as that.[3] There are very few Merovingian deniers known from Melle itself,[4] although in the Carolingian period it became one of the most prolific mints of the whole empire.[5] However, the

---

[1] Jellema, 'Frisian trade', pp. 17–21.
[2] *Cambridge Economic History of Europe*, II, 177, 365–6; Latouche, *Western Economy*, p. 135.
[3] Quoted uncritically, as evidence for the seventh century, by A. Richard, 'Observations sur les mines d'argent et l'atelier monétaire de Melle sous les Carolingiens', *Revue Numismatique*, 3rd series, XI (1893), 195.
[4] A. de Belfort, *Description générale des monnaies mérovingiennes*, II (1893), 343–7.
[5] See below, p. 61 n. 4, for the later history of these mines.

proliferation of mints in the Melle area suggests that there may already have been important silver-mines there at the end of the Merovingian period, even if their produce was not minted on the spot. There was an even greater concentration of mints in western France than in the trade corridor from Frisia to Provence, and the deniers minted there spread outwards to other parts of Frankia. In the coin hoard concealed at Bais about 735/40, on the borders of the lands occupied by the Bretons, and in that concealed about the same date at Plassac, near the mouth of the Gironde, there were larger proportions of deniers coming from the region of Poitiers than from anywhere else.[1]

At some date, presumably in Charlemagne's reign, mining began at a second place, as yet unidentified, in Frankish territory, for Charlemagne had deniers struck there inscribed EX ME(T)ALLO NOVO and METALL GERMAN. It was presumably called the 'new mine' to distinguish it from the older mines at Melle.[2]

Although silver deniers could and did travel very long distances from the places in which they were minted and were apparently interchangeable throughout Frankia, the majority of them stayed within a limited range, for the pattern of minting in the eighth century continued to be one of a very large number of mints designed to fit with a larger number of local markets.[3] An example of the proportion of coin with a purely local circulation and the proportion of coin with a circulation over a greater distance is provided by the hoard of nearly 2000 deniers concealed in Provence, at Nice-Cimiez, around 741. It contained no fewer than 1471 deniers minted locally at Marseilles, together with 142 deniers minted elsewhere within Provence; 139 deniers came from other mints in southern France and only 118 from further afield. Of these 53 deniers came from Paris, and there were 53 pennies that had travelled the whole distance from 'Frisia', including perhaps some minted on the English side of the North Sea.[4]

The relationship of 12 pence to the shilling dates from the earliest days of the minting of the silver denarius in Merovingian Frankia. In 745 Pope Zacharias in a letter to St Boniface took it for granted that a solidus was a shorthand method of saying a dozen deniers. However, by no stretch of the imagination could a good full-weight, fine-gold Byzantine solidus at any time ever have been worth only 12 pennies. When the denier was first introduced it should have been worth three times as much, or even more, depending on the relative values placed on gold and silver. However, at the time the new deniers were introduced, fine-gold solidi were

---

[1] Deniers of the Poitiers region made up 26% of the Bais hoard and 23% of the Plassac hoard (Lafaurie, 'Monnaies d'argent mérovingiennes', pp. 135–6).

[2] Philip Grierson, 'Money and coinage under Charlemagne', in W. Braunfels (ed.), *Karl der Grosse: Lebenswerk und Nachleben*, 1 (Düsseldorf, 1965), 521.

[3] See above, pp. 24–6.

[4] There were 1920 deniers in the hoard, of which the minting-places of 60 cannot be determined (Lafaurie, 'Monnaies d'argent mérovingiennes', p. 136). Grierson and Blackburn (1986) believe the Bais, Plassac and Cimiez hoards were concealed two decades earlier than the dates given here.

no longer in circulation in Frankia. What was in circulation were the last base-gold tremisses or trientes, and the solidus, enshrined in codes of law, land transactions and so forth, had become a unit of account, a shorthand way of saying 3 tremisses. It went on as an accounting-unit into the world of the new denier. The early eighth-century laws of the Alamanni express the transition with clarity: 'Tremissus est tertia pars solidi et sunt denarii quatuor.'[1] 4 new deniers to 1 old triens makes good sense for the late seventh and early eighth century. A ratio of 12 to 1 in the relative values of gold to silver would follow if the old trientes are taken to be one-third gold. Such a ratio is inherently likely, and many of the last trientes in the west were of 8-carat gold or thereabouts.[2] The solidus as a unit of account represented by 3 real trientes in this way became a unit of account represented by 12 real deniers.[3]

It has been suggested that, at the very beginning, in the 670s, 240 of the new deniers were struck from each pound weight of silver. Whether or not they actually *began* at this rate they were certainly struck for long enough at 240 to the pound for a pound-of-account, of 240 pence, to come into existence, and to survive in a fossilised form for the next 1300 years. However, in the chaotic years that culminated in the Arab invasion of Frankia, the weight of the denier was reduced, at first gradually, and then very rapidly.[4] Pepin the Short, as mayor of the palace, managed to stabilise the coinage, along with so many other Frankish institutions. Deniers were still being struck at 24s. (288) to the pound weight of silver when he ascended the throne as the first Carolingian king in 751.

Thus, by the early eighth century the familiar relationship of pounds, shillings and pence had arisen, which was almost universally employed in western Europe before the decimalisation of the last two centuries. The solidus, soldo, sueldo, sou, shilling or schilling had come to mean a dozen denarii, dinheros, deniers, pennies, or pfennigs, and the libra, lira, livre, pound, or pfund had come to mean a score of dozens.

The availability or scarcity of coinage, and of coinage in different metals, is reflected in the continuous transformation of the nature of various sorts of payments over long periods of time. The payment of rent is a very good example of

---

[1] *Leges Alamannorum*, cited by Wilhelm Jesse, *Quellenbuch zur Münz- und Geldgeschichte des Mittelalters* (Halle, 1924; repr. 1968), doc. 12.

[2] See above, pp. 19–21.

[3] In Anglo-Saxon England, where the last of the trientes, of extremely pale gold, had become even baser, the solidus, or shilling, had, temporarily at least, an even lower value in the new pennies. In Wessex it was a 5-penny unit of account, and in Mercia a 4-penny unit of account. The Frankish sense, that of a unit of 12 pennies, later became general in the Anglo-Saxon kingdoms as well.

[4] Deniers were next struck at 21s. (252) from the pound weight of silver, then by 730 their weight was reduced to 22s. (264) to the pound. In the 730s their weight declined very rapidly indeed, to 23s., 24s., and even 25s. (276, 288 and 300) to the pound in turn (Lafaurie, 'Monnaies d'argent mérovingiennes', pp. 144–8, based on the hoards concealed at St Pierre-les-Etieux (*c.* 731), Plassac (*c.* 735), and Nice-Cimiez (*c.* 741)). The most common weights of the coins found in the three hoards were 1.23 grams, 1.18 grams, 1.13 grams and 1.08 grams in turn, which correspond to striking at the rates of 22s., 23s., 24s. and 25s. to the pound respectively.

such successive transformations. At no period covered by this book was the form that rent payments took traditional and unchanging. I began in a period of transformation, the transformation of rents in kind to rents in gold in the fourth century. I have already touched on the transition from rents in gold back again, in some places, to rents in kind, and sometimes, in other places, to a new form of rent, labour-rent, or rent in service.[1] In 600 Gregory the Great took some rents in kind, but from other tenants he still took rents in gold, or at least expressed in gold, although a rent of 3 siliquae of gold, the eighth part of a solidus, due from one papal tenant could not possibly be paid in actual gold.[2] Eighth- and ninth-century evidence suggests that the newly achieved rents in kind and in service were no more static in form than any earlier or later forms of rent, and that they were transformed into silver as and when convenient to the landlords.[3]

Although the payment of rent did not often pass directly from payment in gold to payment in silver, payment for the purchase of land more frequently did so, in so far as it passed by purchase and was not inherited, seized by violence or subterfuge or received as a *beneficium*. References to land purchase by abbeys in Flanders passed directly from gold to silver. For example, payment for land purchased by St Peter's of Ghent between 625 and 650 was expressed in gold solidi, whereas that purchased by St Bertin between 704 and 778 was expressed in *solidi inter aurum et argentum*.[4] Amongst the Lombards the use of gold for land purchase continued into the eighth century.[5]

Wergilds seem to have passed through the same transformations as rents. The laws of the Ripuarian Franks, recodified in the late eighth or early ninth century, show layer upon layer of usage. The original assessments for compensation were fixed in gold, in solidi. To that was added a tariff of goods that could be used instead of gold. A cow instead of 3 solidi, a horse instead of 12 solidi, or a sword in a sheath for 7 solidi, are only a part of the list. Finally, to bring it more up to date a provision had at some stage been added that if payment is to be made in silver, it is to be reckoned at 12 deniers to the solidus, a rate that by 800 had already long been traditional.[6]

In the late seventh century silver coinage was revived only in Merovingian Frankia and on the Anglo-Frisian coasts. Other parts of western Europe had to wait until the eighth century and in eastern Europe the chronology was quite different. There were no issues of anything like the new deniers in Visigothic Spain. The

[1] See above, pp. 16–17.

[2] Renée Doehaerd, *The Early Middle Ages in the West: Economy and Society* (English trans. Amsterdam, 1978), p. 97.

[3] See below, p. 47.

[4] Fernand Vercauteren, 'Monnaie et circulation monétaire en Belgique et dans le nord de la France du VIe au XIe siècle', in *Moneta e scambi*, pp. 282–4.

[5] Ernesto Bernareggi, *Il sistema economico della monetazione dei Langobardi nell'Italia superiore* (Milan, 1960).

[6] Jesse, *Quellenbuch*, doc. 16.

silver that came from Melle and the Frisians did not penetrate Spain before the Arab invasions of the eighth century. Late Visigothic Spain and early Ummayad Spain had a shrinking gold coinage that finally came to an end in A.H. 106 (A.D. 724/5). This overlapped by two years with a silver coinage that began in A.H. 104 (722/3). However this was a very sparse coinage for a quarter of a century and did not become plentiful until after A.H. 150 (A.D. 767).[1] In other words, for a century there was a grave shortage of coin in Spain, very similar to that in Frankia, but slightly later in time. In late Visigothic Spain payment of taxes in coin was replaced in some cases by payment in kind,[2] whilst in early Ummayad Spain Arab authors comment on the temporary retreat to barter.[3]

In Lombard Italy, gold coinage continued until Charlemagne as the standard coinage, and the only silver coins issued were tiny pieces quite unlike the deniers. The Frankish deniers weighed 1 gram to $1\frac{1}{4}$ grams, whilst these tiny Lombard pieces weighed under $\frac{1}{5}$ gram. They are very rare. All the known specimens derive from two hoards concealed after 712.[4] The silver from Melle and the Frisians did not reach Italy until Charlemagne conquered the country.

In the eastern empire, increasingly Greek, although still calling itself Roman, and finally cut off from the west by the Slav invasions of the seventh century, a quite different pattern of coinage evolved, depending on quite different sources of precious metals. The eastern empire looked to Asia for precious metals, whilst the Latin west had basically to rely on its own resources.

In the eastern empire there had been a brief revival of silver coinage in the early seventh century, when no silver at all was available in the west. From 615 Heraclius had had large silver coins struck. They were known as 'hexagrams', since they weighed 6 Greek grams, approximately 6.8 modern grams. In other words they were 5 to 6 times the weight of the later silver deniers in the west. Heraclius first had them struck when extremely hard pressed in the prolonged and expensive wars with the Avars and with the Sassanian rulers of Persia. He used them, instead of gold, for paying his foreign mercenaries, still largely recruited from beyond the northern boundaries of the empire.[5] Although the only silver coined in the eastern empire for the previous two centuries had been of limited issues for ceremonial distribution, there does seem to have been a certain amount of hoarded silver within the empire. The Patriarch Sergius, in this desperate situation, put the resources of the churches at the disposal of the state to provide the silver for this

---

[1] George C. Miles, *The Coinage of the Ummayads in Spain* (American Numismatic Society, New York, 1950), pp. 39–40.

[2] Xavier Barral y Altet, *La Circulation des monnaies suèves et visigothiques. Contribution à l'histoire économique du royaume visigot. Francia,* supplement 4 (Munich, 1976), p. 75.

[3] Miles, *Coinage of the Ummayads,* pp. 39–40.

[4] They read PERT or PERX. Prof. Lafaurie has suggested that this derives from Cunipert or Aripert Rex. Cunipert and Aripert II ruled in turn from 679 to 712 (*Bulletin de la Société Française de Numismatique,* XXII (1967), 123–5).

[5] For payment of native troops in the same crisis with land instead of gold see above, pp. 15–16.

issue. The new hexagrams bore the appropriate legend 'Deus adiuta Romanis'. The striking of silver hexagrams, which had begun as a wartime emergency, was continued in large quantities after Heraclius' victory over Persia. The Sassanians had been issuing a plentiful coinage of silver direms continuously throughout the period when both western and eastern Europe were virtually without any silver coinage. They had access to silver-mines that showed no signs of depletion. For a very brief period the Sassanian rulers were reduced to a client relationship by Heraclius and enough silver reached Constantinople to maintain the minting of hexagrams. However, before he died in 641, Heraclius saw his victories undone. Arab armies overwhelmed the provinces he had regained from Persia, and other Arab armies were in the process of conquering Persia itself. As a consequence new silver was no longer available for minting in Byzantium. Under Constans II the coinage of hexagrams, although initially very considerable, diminished rapidly. By the 670s, when the new silver deniers were beginning to be minted in the west, the Byzantine state was again using silver coin only for ceremonial purposes.[1] Byzantine coinage once again consisted essentially of copper and gold. As the empire became increasingly Greek, its gold pieces were more frequently known by their Greek name, 'nomismata', rather than their Latin one, 'solidi'. I shall therefore refer to them as 'nomismata' from this point onwards.

The Arab conquerors, coming from a background in which coin was barely used, began by taking over the existing coinage systems in each of the areas that they conquered, without making any changes. In the provinces that they took from the Byzantine Empire the 'denarius aureus' (i.e. the nomisma or solidus) and the 'follis' continued to be minted as the gold 'dinar' and the copper 'fels'. In the Persian Empire, the Sassanian 'direm' continued to be minted as the silver 'dirham'. A common taxation system was soon imposed throughout the caliphate. Particularly important was the household tax on non-Muslims. From the time of the Caliph 'Umar (634–44) it was collected in gold-using areas at 4 dinars a year from rich households, 2 dinars from the moderately well-off and 1 dinar from poor households. In silver-using areas it was paid at a rate of 48 dirhams by rich households, 24 dirhams by the moderately well-off and 12 dirhams by poor households. Government spending, which was of course concentrated in the central provinces of the caliphate, was consequently undertaken in both gold and silver, so that the Arab world came to have an expanding core in which all three metals were used for currency, with diminishing areas to the west and east in which gold and silver respectively were the key medium for payments. (See Map 3.[2]) The Arabs took over the silver-mines that the Sassanians had enjoyed, and also the gold-mines

---

[1] Philip Grierson, *Catalogue of the Byzantine Coins in the Dumbarton Oaks Collection*, II (Washington, 1968), 17–21.
[2] Adapted from Maurice Lombard, *Études d'économie médiévale*, vol. I: 'Monnaie et histoire d'Alexandre à Mahomet' (Paris, 1971), pp. 152–3.

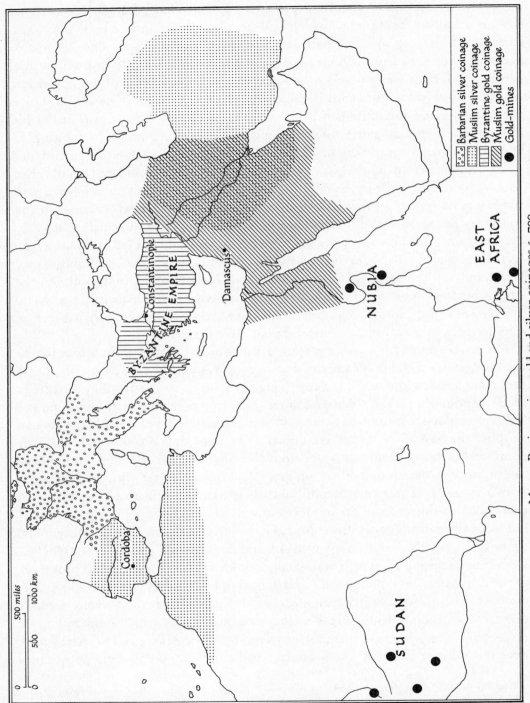

Map 3. Regions using gold and silver coinages c. 700

Legend:
- Barbarian silver coinage
- Muslim silver coinage
- Byzantine gold coinage
- Muslim gold coinage
- Gold-mines

Córdoba

Constantinople

BYZANTINE EMPIRE

Damascus

NUBIA

SUDAN

EAST AFRICA

500 miles
1000 km

500

500

0
0

of Armenia, which had lain on the Byzantine side of the disputed border with Persia. In addition fresh sources of silver were discovered in Armenia in the eighth century.[1] Since the Franks continued to import luxuries from the east, West European silver presumably replaced West European gold at the end of the seventh century for payments to the Middle East. Western coin has not yet been found in the Middle East from this period, but we do have the evidence of oriental goods continuing to arrive in the west. A charter of Chilperic II of Neustria in 716 in favour of the monks of Corbie gave them a regular supply of various commodities, including pepper, cummin, cloves, cinnamon, dates, figs, almonds, pistachio nuts, rice and papyrus, all imported through the Rhône delta port of Fos, and lying in the royal warehouses there.[2] Only slaves were worth sending in the opposite direction.

It was only at the very end of the seventh century A.D. that the Caliph ʿAbd al-Malik began the creation of an integrated monetary system for all the provinces of the caliphate. The weights and appearance of the coins were both changed. Their weights were adjusted to fit with the weight system in use in Arabia,[3] and, to fit in with Muslim teachings against graven images, the inherited iconographic Byzantine and Sassanian types for the gold dinar and the silver dirham began to be replaced by purely epigraphic types in A.H. 77 (A.D. 696–7) and A.H. 79 (A.D. 698–9) respectively. The new dinars that only carried inscriptions were known as dinars *manqûsh*, literally 'engraved dinars', as opposed to the older dinars *rûmî*, Roman, i.e. Byzantine, dinars.[4]

Sassanian coins were much broader and thinner than either Byzantine or western barbarian ones of the same weight. The Arabs preferred the Persian pattern. Much longer religious proclamations could be inscribed on the broader flans. In the course of the eighth century the broader flan was adopted by their neighbours. The Byzantine Emperor Leo III, the successful defender of Constantinople from the Arabs, used the thinner, broader flan for the new silver miliaresia that he introduced in 720. They were like the Ummayad dirhams in another way also, for they too carried inscriptions rather than pictorial types. Some of them were even overstruck on Arab dirhams. The Christian ιhsys xristys nica ('Jesus Christ conquers' in garbled Greek) thus emphatically and appropriately effaced Muslim declarations of faith.[5] In the west the Arab armies, after conquering Byzantine North Africa

---

[1] S. Vryonis, 'The question of Byzantine mines', *Speculum*, xxxvii (1962), 1–17.

[2] Latouche, *Western Economy*, p. 136; Doehaerd, *Early Middle Ages*, pp. 190–1.

[3] The dinar was reduced from 24 Byzantine carats (4.5 modern grams) to 20 Syro-Arabian carats (4.25 grams), and the dirham changed at the same time to 14 Syro-Arabian carats. Philip Grierson, 'The monetary reforms of ʿAbd al-Malik', *Journal of Economic and Social History of the Orient*, iii (1960), 241–64.

[4] Claude Cahen, 'Quelques problèmes concernant l'expansion économique musulmane au haut moyen âge', *L'Occidente e L'Islam nell'alto medioevo*, Settimane di studi del Centro Italiano di Studi sull'alto medioevo, xii (Spoleto, 1965), pp. 417–19.

[5] G. Miles, 'Byzantine miliaresion and Arab dirhem', *Museum Notes*, ix (American Numismatic Society, New York, 1960), 189–218.

moved on to take over Visigothic Spain, and were only brought to a standstill by the Franks under Charles Martel at Poitiers in 732. When the Ummayads began to strike silver in Spain in the 720s, it was in the form of broad, thin, silver dirhams.[1] In 754/5 the newly annointed Carolingian, Pepin, adopted the thinner, broader flan in his expanding kingdom of the Franks for his silver deniers, in place of the thick, dumpy flan previously used for the deniers of his Merovingian predecessors.

The broad, thin, 'hammered' flan, which was to be the typical format for coinage in Europe until the adoption of the coinage mill in the sixteenth and seventeenth centuries, came to the west, not from Rome, but from the Arabs, and, like many other Arab introductions to the west, had not been invented by the Arabs, but only transmitted by them. Just as 'Arabic' numbers were really Indian in origin, and the irrigation systems and vegetables introduced by the Arabs to the Mediterranean were really Punjabi, so the 'hammered' coinage introduced by the Arabs to the west was really Persian in origin.

Pepin's reform of the coinage in 754/5, as well as altering the appearance of the deniers, also increased their weight. He declared that in future no more than 22 sous (i.e. 264 deniers) should be made from the pound of silver instead of 24 sous. In other words he was aiming to restore the denier to the weight that it had possessed before the rapid decline of the 730s.[2] Pepin's reform applied primarily to the mints still under direct royal control. The immunists, mainly ecclesiastical, who controlled mints, also gradually turned from the issue of the smaller to the broader deniers, increased their weight, and began to add the royal title to their issues. In this way, although many of the mints were still locally controlled, there was at least a formal acknowledgement that the king had the ultimate authority in minting. This system continued until it was superseded in Charlemagne's reign by a much more centralised organisation under which identical coins were struck throughout the 'empire'.

In addition to the mints inherited from the Merovingian period, an increasing number of new mints was opened in the Carolingian era. The principal concentration of mints in the Carolingian Empire lay, not surprisingly, in the heartland of the Austrasian Franks, and coincided with the greatest concentration of Carolingian family property around the 'capital' at Aachen. As well as the palatine mint at Aachen itself, there were also prolific mints at Cologne and Bonn on the Rhine, and at Maastricht, Huy and Namur on the Meuse, and at a host of less important mints at such neighbouring places as Cambrai, St Trond, Tongres and Liège, and further

---

[1] See above, p. 36, and Miles, *Coinage of the Ummayads*, pp. 117–26.

[2] See above, p. 34. Of the 22 sous of deniers, 1 sou was to go to the moneyer. It is not clear if that was inclusive of all costs of minting and royal dues or exclusive of them. If the pound at this time weighed 327 grams, which is by no means certain, Pepin implied that he was raising the weight of the denier from 1.08 grams to at least 1.24 grams. However, surviving pieces suggest that a standard weight of 1.3 grams was aimed at.

up the Meuse, Moselle and Rhine at Verdun, Trier, Metz, Mainz and Strasbourg. The two most important mints of all were, however, outside this heartland, at Dorestad or Duurstede, previously the principal Frisian mint, and at Melle in Poitou, where silver was being extensively mined.[1] (Map 4.)

The issue of the broader, thinner deniers was not confined to Frankia. They were struck in the Spanish March at Barcelona and Ampurias, and by the 780s in Italy at such mints as Lucca, which had been very active as a mint for gold under the Lombards, at Milan, and above all at Pavia.[2] Deniers were also issued at Rome by the popes from Adrian I,[3] and by the Lombard princes in Benevento.[4]

The Germanic lands conquered to the east of the Rhineland were, however, not yet ready for coinage. There was no mint at all east of the Rhine until one was established at Regensburg on the Danube by Louis the Pious. This may be associated with his creation of his son Louis 'the German' as 'King of the Bavarians' in 817. It was in Regensburg that Louis set up his son. The royal residence at Regensburg was to continue as one of the principal palaces of the line of East Frankish rulers who descended from Louis the German. The output of the mint there was negligible,[5] and the mint, far from having commercial connotations, was presumably only there to supply coin for circulation in court and administrative circles.

In the larger part of England coin did not circulate as money in the eighth century. Its monetary use seems to have been limited to parts of the kingdoms on the southern and eastern coasts. In south-east England the dumpy Anglo-Frisian types of penny began to be replaced by new, broad pennies bearing a king's name in the 770s or possibly the 760s. It is not clear whether the earliest broad, signed pennies were struck for Offa of Mercia, or for Heaberht and Ecgberht, *sub-reguli* in Kent, at the mint at Canterbury.[6] It was this new, thin, broad penny, rather than the older smaller, thicker penny, that served as a model for the later pennies of all

[1] For Dorestad and Melle see above, pp. 29–30 and 32–3.

[2] In Lombardy, Charlemagne also struck deniers at Treviso; in Tuscany at Pisa; and as 'Patrician of the Romans' at Ravenna. The earliest documentary reference to deniers in Italy belongs to the mid-780s (Grierson, 'Money and coinage under Charlemagne', pp. 513–16).

[3] Independent issues of deniers by Adrian I and Leo III were succeeded after 800 by deniers struck jointly by Charlemagne and Leo III (Philip Grierson, 'The coronation of Charlemagne and the coinage of Pope Leo III', *Revue Belge de Philologie et d'Histoire*, xxx (1952), 825–33).

[4] First struck in the joint names of Grimoald III and Charlemagne between 788 and 792, and then in the name of Grimoald, and later of his successors, without any reference to a Frankish ruler (Grierson, 'Money and coinage under Charlemagne', p. 516).

[5] *Ibid.* p. 535.

[6] The 'orthodox' view, that the first broad pennies were minted at Canterbury by the *sub-reguli* around 775–80, is cogently presented by C. E. Blunt, 'The coinage of Offa', in R. H. M. Dolley (ed.), *Anglo-Saxon Coins: Studies Presented to F. M. Stenton* (London, 1961), pp. 39–62. Stewart Lyon has suggested that the first broad pennies were minted by Offa himself, perhaps a decade earlier, and possibly at London as well as, or instead of, Canterbury ('Historical problems of Anglo-Saxon coinage', *British Numismatic Journal*, xxxvi (1967), 218–21).

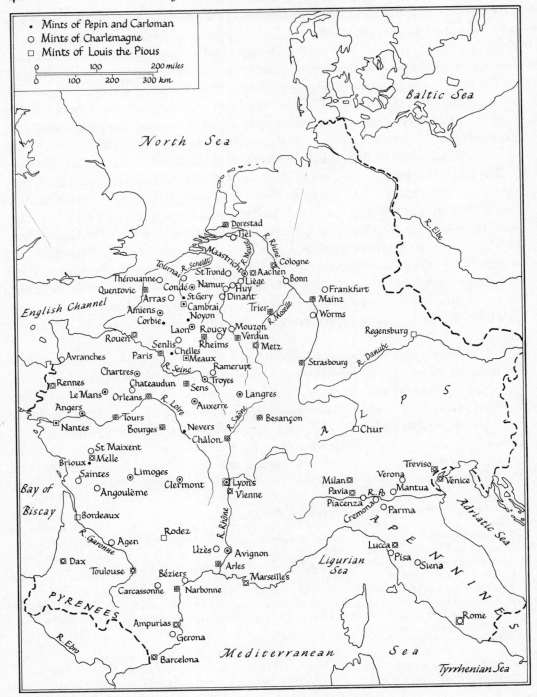

Map 4. Key Carolingian mints – Pepin to Louis the Pious

the Anglo-Saxon kingdoms, apart from Northumbria, where old-fashioned pieces of the smaller, thicker module curiously began to be minted again about the 820s.[1]

Around 792 Offa had increased the weight of his new, broad pennies to bring them into line with Charlemagne's deniers. However, almost immediately afterwards Charlemagne further increased the weight of his own deniers, as a part of his general reform of weights and measures. Universal acceptance of the new, heavier deniers was enjoined at the Council of Frankfurt in May 794. They were still of a very thin module, but even broader than their predecessors; instead of 15 millimetres (0.6 inch) they were about 20 millimetres (0.8 inch) in diameter, as broad as a current British penny or an American 5-cent piece. They were intended to weigh just over 1.7 grams, and 9 of the new deniers were to be worth 12 of the old.[2] It was to this standard that Charlemagne's successors tried to maintain their coinage through the ninth century.[3] It is from this standard that we can measure the different degrees by which the rulers in various parts of Europe allowed their coinages to fall away from a common standard which applied alike in western Germany and northern Italy, as well as Christian Spain and what is now France, whether their pennies were known as pfennigs or denari, dineros or deniers.

The degree of control over the coinage, after Charlemagne's reform of it, was reflected in the uniformity of the coinage throughout the empire. This was in marked contrast to the diversity that existed at the beginning of his reign. The earlier deniers, although acknowledging the king's authority, were crudely made, and give the impression of having been designed locally, according to the taste of the individual moneyers, and the skill of the smiths they could find to cut their dies. The reformed, heavy deniers are of careful design. The dies were obviously cut centrally and only differ from mint to mint in the mint name, and the use of the additional title of 'king of the Lombards' on deniers struck at Arles or in Italy. At one stage the idea was even entertained of centralising yet further by producing all the necessary coin at a single palatine mint at Aachen.[4]

Charlemagne's son, Louis the Pious, shortly after his accession, ordered that all the coin in circulation that had been minted during his father's reign should be brought in for reminting.[5] The evidence of coin hoards shows that this order was actually obeyed.[6] The success of such a proceeding was another measure of the

---

[1] H. E. Pagan, 'Northumbrian numismatic chronology', *British Numismatic Journal*, XXXVIII (1969), 1–15. Previous small, thick pennies had been minted in Northumbria, first anonymously, and then, from around 750 to the 780s, in the names of the kings, and of the Archbishops of York (C. S. S. Lyon, 'A re-appraisal of the sceatta and styca coinage of Northumbria', *British Numismatic Journal*, XXVIII (1955–7), 227–42).

[2] Instead of 1.3 grams, the weight to which Offa had just increased his pennies from 1.25 grams.

[3] Karl F. Morrison, 'Numismatics and Carolingian trade: a critique of the evidence', *Speculum*, XXXVIII (1963), 412–24.

[4] Grierson, 'Money and coinage under Charlemagne', p. 525.

[5] Jesse, *Quellenbuch*, doc. 41.

[6] The Belvézet and Veuillin hoards from early in Louis' reign contain 2 and no coins respectively of Charlemagne

degree of control over the coinage that Charlemagne had developed. In the 820s and 830s Louis the Pious only minted at some forty places throughout the whole empire. This degree of control lasted for one generation more. Map 5 shows the mints operated by Louis' four sons and two of his grandsons in the 840s and 850s.[1] Between 840 and 864 Charles the Bald minted at only about a dozen mints in his West Frankish share of his father's empire. In 864 he was still able to order a complete recoinage for West Frankia. The edict of Pîtres, in which this recoinage was ordered, also gives some details of how the recoinage was to be carried out.[2] Nine mints were named as being the customary places for minting, one in the palace, one at Rouen and Quentovic, formerly belonging to Quentovic, and others at Rheims, Sens, Paris, Orléans, Chalon-sur-Saône, Narbonne, and at the silver-mine at Melle.

Even if it is not clear to us precisely how the organisation worked, it is evident that there was a rigid centralised organisation at this stage, imposed in Charlemagne's reign on top of a tradition of multiple local outlets for coin, which had itself evolved over the previous centuries, to suit a society with intense, but very local, marketing arrangements.[3] In the tenth and eleventh centuries a similar centralised organisation of minting has been deduced for Anglo-Saxon England and Ottonian Germany.[4] Such an organisation made it possible from time to time to remint all the coin in a kingdom at the king's command, provided that the amount of coinage in circulation was still small enough for such a process to be physically possible. Even if the circulating medium was sufficiently small for periodical recoinages to take place, it was still much larger than it had been earlier. It reached a maximum in the middle of the ninth century, when the quantities available for payment to Viking armies as Danegeld were really quite large.[5]

As in the eighth century,[6] so in the ninth, the circulation of coin from these mints was predominantly, but not exclusively, local. In the first half of the century a hoard concealed around 817 at Veuillin, near Bourges in central France, contained 736 new deniers of Louis the Pious; 127 of them had been 'minted' at Bourges itself, but the remainder had been issued at 36 different mints, nearly all those working for Louis the Pious, including those as far away as Quentovic and Dorestad in the north, and in Spain and Italy in the south. The deniers had moved about as much as

　　out of 252 and 755 deniers (Grierson, 'Money and coinage under Charlemagne', p. 503). The extreme rarity today of deniers of Charlemagne's last type is a byproduct of this effective reminting in the ninth century.

[1] Based on Maps 8 and 9 in Hubert Frère, 'Le Denier carolingien, spécialement en Belgique' in *Numismatica Lovaniensa*, 1 (Louvain-la-Neuve, 1977), 125–236. The boundaries are those of the treaty of Verdun, 843.

[2] Partially printed in Jesse, *Quellenbuch*, doc. 43, and at greater length in Frère, 'Le Denier carolingien', doc. 29, pp. 96–100, and most recently discussed in Philip Grierson, 'The "Gratia Dei Rex" coinage of Charles the Bald', in Margaret Gibson and Janet Nelson (eds.), *Charles the Bald: Court and Kingdom*, B.A.R. International Series, CI (Oxford, 1981), pp. 39–51.

[3] See above, pp. 24–6.　　　　[5] See below, pp. 92–4.
[4] See below, pp. 61–4.　　　　[6] See above, p. 33.

Map 5. Mints of Louis the Pious' sons and grandsons 840s and 850s

this in the few years since the new coinage was introduced. In the second half of the century the free movement of coin was only slightly reduced. Of 493 deniers concealed at Glisy, near Amiens, around 881, that can be identified, 74 had been issued at Amiens itself and 113 at the great port of Quentovic just over 65 kilometres (40 miles) away. Altogether two thirds of the hoard came from a handful of mints in Picardy and the Île de France, within 120 kilometres (75 miles) of the place where they were eventually buried. The remaining third, however, came from 48 mints scattered over an immense area of northern Frankia from Orléans to Maastricht.[1]

This hoard evidence therefore suggests that free movement of coin about the empire was still a reality in the 880s.[2] How much this can be correlated with internal trade and the movement of goods is another matter. By then deniers were being carried about for reasons quite unconnected with trade. In the troubled years from the mid ninth century the roads bore streams of refugees fleeing in all directions, most often southwards and eastwards, carrying with them all that they held precious, whether the relics of saints like Philibert, or such coin as they possessed.

The capitularies of the Carolingians, however, assumed that, in normal times, there was a close correlation between money and marketing. When, in 833, Louis the Pious granted the right to open a 'moneta publica nostrae auctoritatis' at Corvey on the Weser it was 'quia locum mercationis ipsa indigebat'.[3] In the mind of the grantor at any rate, mint and market were firmly associated, and this seems to have been the case in practice in the Carolingian heartland. However, on the Weser a right to open a mint was not yet a useful one, as money was still hardly used east of the Rhine.[4]

The capitularies, as well as assuming a correlation between money and marketing, also legislated fiercely for the acceptance of royal coin, as if there was a certain reluctance to use coin to be overcome. This may have been caused by counterfeiting, and the capitularies again have much to say about this. Certainly the excellent preservation of many of the deniers that have come down to us suggests that they did not suffer a great deal of use, but this could equally be explained by the limited lifespan enjoyed by them, on account of the deliberate total recoinages. On the other hand excavations at Dorestad, and at Domburg on the island of Walcheren, another Frisian trading-port, have turned up such a number of stray deniers that it is quite apparent that money must have been there in common circulation for so many deniers to have been lost.

Dorestad and Domburg were, however, atypical. Carolingian Europe was a

---

[1] Vercauteren, 'Monnaie en Belgique', in *Moneta e scambi*, pp. 291–2.

[2] Morrison, 'Numismatics and Carolingian trade', suggests that even in the 890s in the basins of the Loire, Seine and Rhine, the deniers of Toulouse, Lyons and Arles circulated freely alongside those from northern mints.

[3] Jesse, *Quellenbuch*, doc. 44.　　　　[4] See above, p. 41.

very rural Europe. Frisian trading-ports were the exception. In the countryside the circulation of money, even in this false dawn of a 'money economy', was circumscribed socially. The polyptych of the abbey of St Germain-des-Prés compiled during the abbacy of Irminon (806–29) gives details of the revenues from the abbey's estates, which were largely situated in the Paris basin, an area in which money might be expected to have circulated as freely as anywhere in the Carolingian Empire. Only 3% of the revenue from servile *mansi* was received in silver, an average of no more than 2 deniers per *mansus*. The rest was in kind, or, above all, in services. On the other hand no less than 24% of the revenue from the free *mansi* was already received in money, an average of 2 sous, 24 actual deniers, per *mansus*.[1] Some of this was clearly in commutation of services rendered in the past. A free *mansus* at Villeneuve St Georges, for example, paid 4 sous in silver instead of military service.[2] In the Paris basin at any rate countrymen who held free tenures were increasingly using coin. The transformation of renders in kind or in service to renders at least partially in money is yet another instance of the extraordinary mutability of the forms of payment of rent. Carolingian polyptychs, as well as providing examples of the transformation of other forms of rent to money, also provide examples of new rents entirely in money. For example the Flemish abbey of St Bertin leased forty-seven *mansi* at Poperinghe, formerly part of its demesne, entirely for money-rent.[3]

Ecclesiastical landlords could thus expect to raise a certain amount of income from their tenants in ready money.[4] To obtain this the tenants obviously had to sell their own produce on the market for money. Alternatively the landlords could themselves raise money by selling produce, either that from the demesne, or renders in kind. When he needed to purchase new vestments Servatus Lupus (d. 862), the Abbot of Ferrières on the southern edge of the Paris basin, anticipated that he would have no difficulty in raising ready money to do so by selling the produce of the abbey's estates.[5]

What was the case at St Germain, St Bertin and Ferrières was not necessarily the case further from the economic and political heart of the Carolingian Empire. Outside the Carolingian heartland money was much less regularly available, and contracts and leases gave alternative means of payment as a matter of course. The abbey of St Gall lay not far from one of the main routes through the Alps into Italy,

---

[1] B. Guérard (ed.), *Polyptyque de l'Abbé Irminon* (Paris, 1844), pp. 892–7. The most recent discussion of this polyptych is by Emily R. Coleman, 'People and property: the structure of a medieval seigneury', *Journal of European Economic History*, VI (1977), 675–702.

[2] Quoted by Georges Duby, *Rural Economy and Country Life in the Medieval West* (Paris, 1962; Eng. trans., 1968), p. 368.

[3] Doehaerd, *Early Middle Ages*, p. 122.

[4] See also below, p. 64 n.1.

[5] Doehaerd, *Early Middle Ages*, p. 236.

and in the reign of Louis the Pious (814–40) there was a mint at Chur on this route.[1] Nevertheless, at this very time, in 836, a dependant of the abbey had the option of paying it each year '3 maldros sive 6 denarios vel precium 6 denariorum in ferramentis qualecumque ex his tribus facilius invenire possimus'.[2]

It has always to be remembered that even where money was most readily available, in the Paris basin for example, the abbey of St Germain took three quarters of its rents even from its free tenants in forms other than money. Because of the relatively low availability of money even here, there was consequently still a considerable emphasis on self-sufficiency. Great estates still maintained their own workshops, or demanded goods from tenants. St Germain-des-Prés received linen and woollen shirts as part of its rent-roll and so did the abbey of St Bertin.[3] Numerous great lords, lay and ecclesiastical, had their own salt-pans or brine-wells, sometimes in quite distant places, so that they could be supplied directly from them, without recourse to the market.[4]

The use of money in the first half of the ninth century was thus far from uniform throughout the Carolingian Empire; it could be very erratic, and varied from time to time as well as from place to place. The distribution of mints and of coin hoards suggests that the use of money was concentrated in Frisia, in the Frankish heartland, and in a 'Lotharingian' corridor leading to the Arelate and Lombardy.[5] At the north-west end of the corridor lay south-east England. It was to the east of this corridor that the use of money was particularly limited.[6] But even where money was not freely available, it was already being used as a measure of value. One of the tenants of the Bishop of Freising, in Bavaria, had the option of paying him 'sex denarios vel sex denariorum pretio in victu vel vestitu aut in cera, vel in pecudibus'.[7] In practice it was the goods that were paid. Even the great abbey of Fulda, in Hesse, on one occasion paid for some land with eight swords, five pieces of cloth, four cattle, a horse and two pairs of earrings.[8]

Even in the heart of the empire there was not enough money for taxation to be taken in coin. Taxation, in so far as there was taxation in the empire, still largely consisted of taxation in kind, *dona annualia*, and the levy of services, particularly military service.[9] The only dues levied in money were those imposed on trade, for example at the *cluses*, the customs points at the ends of the key alpine passes. Similar

[1] Arthur Suhle, *Deutsche Münz- und Geldgeschichte von den Anfängen bis zum 15. Jahrhundert*, 2nd ed. (Berlin, 1964), p. 36.
[2] Carlo M. Cipolla, *Money, Prices and Civilization in the Mediterranean World* (Princeton, 1956), p. 8.
[3] Doehaerd, *Early Middle Ages*, p. 131.
[4] *Ibid.* pp. 132–3.
[5] Grierson, 'Money and coinage under Charlemagne', pp. 503–5, lists the hoards for Charlemagne's coins.
[6] See above, p. 41.
[7] Doehaerd, *Early Middle Ages*, p. 237.
[8] *Ibid.* p. 239.
[9] Louis Halphen, *Charlemagne et l'empire carolingien* (Paris, 1947), pp. 167–79.

money dues were exacted at the great ports, like Quentovic or Dorestad, or the line of customs posts along the eastern frontier of the empire, like Magdeburg on the Elbe or Lorch on the Danube.[1] Although older foci of commercial activity still survived in the Rhône basin and in Italy, the major focus of commercial, as of political, activity was now in the basins of the Meuse and the Rhine, and new foci were beginning to develop in Saxony and along the Danube. External trade from the Carolingian Empire naturally connected with these foci, Provençal and Italian trade to the Middle East, Frisian trade to England and Scandinavia, and new routes to Slav Europe through Magdeburg and down the Danube from Regensburg.

The trade with the Middle East from the Arelate and from Italy had normally been one in which West European imports greatly exceeded exports. It was this trade that had sucked western Europe dry of gold by the end of the seventh century, and was carrying silver away for much of the eighth century. However, at the very end of the eighth century the balance changed, at least for a time. One of the natural consequences of the great Frankish expansion under the Carolingians was the availability of a great number of captives, who could be used as slaves within Frankia, or else sold onwards. For example, Charlemagne's campaigns between 793 and 800 brought in large groups of Saxon, 'Spanish' and Avar slaves in quick succession,[2] but these were only part of the continuous flow of slaves that were as much a corollary of Frankish conquests as they had earlier been of Roman conquests. In the ninth century the key area for expansion was on the eastern frontier at the expense of the Slavs. So many Slavs were reduced to slavery that the very word 'Slav' became synonymous with 'slave', and *sclavus* replaced *servus* as the standard term for a slave.[3]

By the end of the eighth century Verdun and Mainz, already considerable entrepôts for other goods, had added slaves to their wares, and became the key slave-markets of the west. The slaves primarily reached Verdun and Mainz after capture in the east, and were sold onwards to purchasers from the south. At the end of the eighth century St Sturm met slaves on the way to these slave-markets from the Thuringian frontier, and Paul the Deacon on his visit to Frankia in the 780s saw them on their way south.[4] Many were sold onwards from Frankia to the Arab world. Jewish traders under the protection of Louis the Pious were key intermediaries between Christian sellers of slaves and the eventual Muslim purchasers of them.[5] The overall numbers sold were so great that the 'normal' imbalance of payments between the Latin west and the Arab and Byzantine east was temporarily reversed, and gold and silver flowed for a time into Europe. It was because of the

---

[1] Latouche, *Western Economy*, pp. 169–72.
[2] J. M. Wallace-Hadrill, *The Barbarian West 400–1000*, 3rd ed. (London, 1967), p. 107.
[3] *Ibid.* p. 156.
[4] Doehaerd, *Early Middle Ages*, p. 198.
[5] Latouche, *Western Economy*, pp. 162–4.

export of human flesh and blood, the most profitable commodity in the world, that western Europe, empty of gold since the end of the seventh century, began to receive it again in limited quantities a hundred years later.[1]

From the 770s Byzantine nomismata and Arab dinars and dirhams all circulated to a limited extent in western Europe. Westerners mistakenly took the Arab adjective *manqûsh*, 'engraved', for a noun, and hence called the gold dinar *manqûsh* a 'mancus', rather than a 'dinar'.[2] The first mention of mancuses in western documents comes from a charter of the abbey of Sesto in Friuli dated to 778. In 786 they again appear in a contract made by the abbey of Farfa, near Orvieto in central Italy. Over the next eighty years further references to mancuses or to Arab gold were made in many parts of Europe, at Farfa again, at Subiaco near Rome, at Verona, in Istria, at St Gall, at Marseilles, at Narbonne, at Arras, at the abbeys of Cysoing and St Vaast (now in northern France), and at that of St Trond (now in Belgium), and even in Mercia.[3] After 870 they cease to appear in western documents for over eighty years, until after the reintroduction of a gold coinage into Arab Spain. A very limited number of Arab gold coins have been found from this period in western Europe. Around 820, for example, 11 dinars were concealed near Bologna, along with 28 Byzantine and Beneventan nomismata, and some 60 other gold coins, which were dispersed after their discovery in the last century without identification.[4]

There was enough Arab or Byzantine gold available for a very few western gold coins to be struck. Offa of Mercia produced a mancus that closely imitated a dinar of the Caliph al-Mansur dated A.H. 157 (A.D. 774) only inserting OFFA REX in Latin into the Arab inscription. It may not have been intended for normal circulation, but only for prestigious gifts, for after Offa's death in 796, Pope Leo III wrote to his successor, reminding him of Offa's promise to send 365 mancuses to Rome every year.[5] Other western gold coins both were more distinctively western and entered into commercial use. Under Charlemagne gold pieces were minted of the same weight as the Byzantine nomisma at Uzès in southern France and at AVRODIS, which has not yet been identified satisfactorily. They were possibly struck as early as the

---

[1] Some gold also came into the Carolingian Empire for political reasons. For example, in 812 Grimoald IV of Benevento paid 25,000 gold nomismata and promised a further 7000 annually as tribute (Philip Grierson, 'The gold solidus of Louis the Pious and its imitations', *Jaarboek voor Munt- en Penningkunde*, XXXVIII (1951), 1–41).

[2] See above, p.39

[3] Jean Duplessy, 'La Circulation des monnaies arabes en Europe occidentale du VIIIᵉ au XIIIᵉ siècles', *Revue Numismatique*, 5th series, XVIII (1956), 135–6; and Philip Grierson, 'Carolingian Europe and the Arabs: the myth of the mancus', *Revue Belge de Philologie et d'Histoire*, XXXII (1954), 1059–74. No work similar to Duplessy's has yet been done on the circulation of Byzantine coin in the west. It would be useful to compile a set of references to such items as the nomismata referred to in the will of a wealthy Venetian, Giustiniano Participazio, in 829.

[4] Duplessy, 'Monnaies arabes en Europe', pp. 121–4. Other dinars of this period have been found at Castel Roussillon in the Pyrenees, Venice and Eastbourne on the south coast of England.

[5] It was, perhaps significantly, in Rome that the sole surviving specimen was acquired by the Duc de Blacas early in the nineteenth century (Blunt, 'Coinage of Offa', pp. 50–1).

770s or 780s.[1] Early in his reign Louis the Pious also had struck gold pieces minted of the same weight. These were probably struck at the palatine mint at Aachen, and possibly also at Dorestad, and probably date from 816–18. From *c.* 830 to *c.* 900 these were extensively imitated in Frisia. Over eighty specimens have survived. Occasional English imitations were also struck, including the only imitation with an identifiable issuer, Wigmund, Archbishop of York from 837 to 854.[2]

It is perhaps significant that the Danegelds paid by the western Franks from the 840s onwards should have contained a little gold as well as a great deal of silver, although it is not of course clear whether or not this was coined gold.[3]

Arab silver dirhams also came to the west, but in much more limited quantities,[4] and the impact on the west was not so noticeable as the arrival of gold, for the west was virtually without gold. Because the west had silver and not gold it valued gold relatively highly, and this made it particularly attractive to Arabs and Byzantines to pay in gold, since they both had much more of it and consequently valued it less. In 862 Charles the Bald officially priced the pound of fine gold at 12 livres of deniers. This probably meant a gold–silver ratio of 1:12. In Byzantium, where gold was plentiful and silver scarce, gold was much less valued. In 739 the solidus was equivalent to 12 miliaresia of half its weight. It is not clear how it was valued after that, until the mid tenth century when it was still only equivalent to 14 miliaresia.[5] This gives a seventh-century ratio of 1:6 and a tenth-century ratio of 1:7. The Arab world nominally fell between the two; 10 dirhams weighed 7 dinars, and at the end of the ninth century the dinar was legally worth $14\frac{2}{7}$ dirhams. The legal value gives a gold–silver ratio of 1:10.[6] However the market values set on dirhams and dinars in the eighth, ninth and tenth centuries varied very considerably from the legal norm. It therefore always made sense to send gold from Byzantium to the west, and normally to send gold rather than silver from the Arab world. When the slave-trade diminished, the imbalance between east and west returned to normal, and gold

[1] Grierson, 'Money and coinage under Charlemagne', pp. 530–4. These pieces may be contemporary with Offa's mancuses.

[2] Grierson, 'Solidus of Louis the Pious', pp. 1–41. Louis the Pious and Lothar I also had heavier gold medallions struck for use as prestigious gifts, as Byzantine emperors did.

[3] The total for the period has been worked out as 685 lb. of gold and 43,042 lb. of silver (Peter H. Sawyer, *The Age of the Vikings*, 2nd ed. (London, 1971), p. 99, quoting P. Hauberg, *Myntforhold og Udmyntninger i Danmark indtil 1146* (Copenhagen, 1900), pp. 15–16).

[4] Duplessy, 'Monnaies arabes en Europe', pp. 121–4. Although Islamic Spain had a plentiful coinage of silver dirhams in the late eighth century and the ninth, it was not from this source that the few Arab silver coins to reach western Europe came. Instead it was from Africa and the Middle East, presumably more important as markets for slaves than Spain. Although the dirhams that circulated in the west indicate their source, they were only the few that escaped reminting into deniers in Italy. The flow of silver deniers from Italy into Frankia is most marked. Well over a third of the thousand deniers hoarded at Belvézet (near Uzès) and Veuillin (near Bourges) in the early years of Louis the Pious' reign had been minted in Italy. Most of these had come from Venice, through which so many slaves were exported.

[5] Grierson, *Dumbarton Oaks Collection*, III (Washington, 1973), 67.

[6] Cahen, 'L'Expansion économique musulmane', pp. 397–403.

again largely disappeared from the west, except for occasional surviving use among the Frisians, to whom a great deal of it seems to have gravitated. At the end of the century the Frisian merchants at Duisburg were still able to make an annual payment in gold, but it was measured in ounces, not in dinars ('mancusi') or nomismata ('bizanti').[1]

If southern trade, at least temporarily, brought coin into the Carolingian Empire, northern trade carried it out. Southern and eastern England acquired enough silver to maintain a number of regular coinages. The mint at Canterbury was still the most prolific in England through the first half of the ninth century. In the 820s it had a team of six moneyers working for the king and a further two for the archbishop. The East Anglian mint, which had had three or four moneyers under Offa, employed up to seven in the 820s, the mint at London employed three moneyers, and new mints were opened at Rochester around 810 and at Winchester in the 830s.[2] Minting began again in Northumbria, both for the king and for the Archbishop of York, in the 820s.

However, the main thrust of Frisian trade was northwards. The Frisians continued to carry pottery, bronze-work and glass to the north in increasing quantities in the eighth and ninth centuries, and in addition carried silver combs and other silver ornaments from Frankia, Frankish and Flemish swords, 'Frisian' cloth, of course, and such improbable objects as millstones from the upper Rhineland. All these have been found by excavators at the two leading trading-places in ninth-century Scandinavia, Hedeby (Sliaswich or Haithabu), on the isthmus across which traders went from the North Sea to the Baltic, where the Kiel canal is now to be found, and Birka in Sweden, whose traders took on the role formerly played by the men from Gotland.[3] There was a Frisian merchant colony at Birka, as at York. Nevertheless the value of goods imported from the north was greater still, and the Frisians carried silver northwards in increasing quantities, and even occasionally gold, for the Frisians drew Frankish gold to themselves. Frisian imitations of the gold pieces of Louis the Pious were more numerous than the originals. The hoard concealed at Hon, some 50 kilometres (31 miles) south-west of Oslo, in the 860s, contained some gold that had passed right through Europe: 20 coins, provided with loops for hanging on a necklace, included 9 Abbasid dinars, 3 Byzantine nomismata, and 2 Frisian imitations of the gold pieces of Louis the Pious.[4] By the time

---

[1] Renée Doehaerd, 'Impôts directs acquittés par des marchands et des artisans pendant le Moyen Age', in *Studi in onore di Armando Sapori*, I (Milan, 1957), 85.

[2] C. E. Blunt, C. S. S. Lyon, B. H. I. H. Stewart, 'The coinage of southern England 796–840', *British Numismatic Journal*, XXXII (1963), 1–74.

[3] Jellema, 'Frisian trade', pp. 25–32.

[4] Grierson, 'Solidus of Louis the Pious', p. 9; Kolbjørn Skaare, *Coins and coinage in Viking Age Norway* (Oslo, 1976), pp. 134–5.

they reached Norway these gold pieces had ceased to be used as coin, but in Denmark coin brought by the Frisians was perhaps beginning to be used as such, and coinage actually began to be minted on the Schleswig isthmus. By about 825 a mint, or mints, was in operation here, perhaps at Hedeby itself. This mint, or mints, did not even strike direct copies of Carolingian pieces, let alone an autonomous coinage of its own, but imitations of North Frisian imitations of Dorestad deniers, from pre-Frankish 'sceats', through the light and heavy deniers of Charlemagne, to those of Louis the Pious, including some with the distinctive 'trading-ship' reverse.[1] It is strange that it took place in such a roundabout way, for genuine deniers, even of the early part of Charlemagne's reign, circulated in this area. The hoard from Krinkberg, in Holstein, contained 91 deniers of Charlemagne, all struck before the reforms of 793/4. Although many were of the Dorestad mint and others from the mints of northern Frankia, some came from as far away as the Arelate and Lombardy.[2] About 834 a mint also appears to have been opened at Hamburg. The issues of Hamburg continued until about the middle of the century and then ceased. This beginning was not to lead to a continuous issue of coin in northern Germany, for in 845 the Danes under King Horik sacked Hamburg, and its mint ceased operations.[3] At about the same time the mint on the isthmus also closed down.[4] The real beginning of coinage in the north was to be much later.[5]

The second half of the ninth century saw in general a failure of minting in the Carolingian world, and not merely on its northern frontier. The opening-up of coinage in the seventh and eighth centuries was a false start in many ways, and the true start of medieval coinage was only found in the tenth century, if not later. The mint at Dorestad, so prolific under Frisian, Merovingian and Carolingian aegis, closed down about 875 after the repeated sack of the place for forty years by the Vikings.[6] The newly restarted coinage of the Northumbrian kingdom was cut short by the Vikings in the 860s after only forty years of existence.[7] Scandinavia itself had been on the verge of using coinage in the first half of the ninth century, but its raiders not only turned that possibility away, but also quite violently reduced the existing use of coinage in western Europe as a whole. Their impact could be felt as far away as the Mediterranean. The Vikings who sacked Pisa in 861 had ravaged

[1] Brita Malmer, *Nordiska mynt före år 1000* (Lund–Bonn, 1966), pp. 204–18.
[2] H. H. Völckers, *Karolingische Münzfunde der Frühzeit* (Göttingen, 1965), pp. 79ff.
[3] Gwyn Jones, *A History of the Vikings* (Oxford, 1968), p. 107.
[4] Malmer, *Nordiska mynt*, pp. 339–41.
[5] See below, pp. 83–5.
[6] H. Enno van Gelder, 'De Karolingische muntslag te Duurstede', *Jaarboek voor Munt- en Penningkunde*, XLVIII (1961), 15–42. It also suffered from the great inundations of 864, which diverted the course of the Lower Rhine away from Dorestad (Jones, *Vikings*, p. 210).
[7] Pagan, 'Northumbrian chronology'.

Provence in the previous year. Provence suffered particularly badly in the ninth century. Marseilles had been sacked by Saracens in 836, and in 888 other Saracens set up a permanent base at Fraxinetum. It is no wonder that the Rhône valley ceased to be a major artery of trade and that the formerly important mints at Marseilles, Arles, Uzès and Lyons either closed totally or minted very little.

3

'Feudal' Deniers and 'Viking' Dirhams

Although the earliest beginnings of 'feudal' society have been traced back to the late seventh-century collapse of the royal ability to pay for troops in Merovingian Frankia,[1] the key period for its development is generally regarded as having begun a century and a half later. The essential element in this development was the breakdown of imperial authority, assisted by the pressure of Scandinavian attacks. Carolingian imperial or royal officers, primarily the counts, began to treat the counties with whose care they had been charged for a limited period of time, as territories over which they ruled by right, and which they could pass on to their sons. The devolution of authority can be traced further, as comital officers, such as castellans, in their turn gradually became hereditary holders of fiefs, rather than temporary holders of offices. Eventually, by the eleventh century, a hierarchy of authority evolved in which personal ties, the holding of land, and the exercise of regalian authority became inextricably mixed. The fragmentation of the control of the minting of coined money was naturally involved at this period among other aspects of the fragmentation of regalian authority. Charlemagne had quite clearly re-established minting as an undoubted exercise of regalian authority,[2] and it was to be exercised through the counts. Around 820, Louis the Pious issued a capitulary on coinage on the explicit assumption that the care of his mints was already in the hands of his counts.[3] The edict of Pîtres of 864 reiterated the responsibility of counts for the running of the mints in Charles the Bald's kingdom.[4] Although the responsibility lay with the counts, the coinage was still essentially centralised at this date. However in the next few years political authority in the western half of the Carolingian Empire finally collapsed, and those counts who had a mint in their jurisdiction had to make their own arrangements for its survival. The counts, whose proper function was to protect imperial or royal interests, instead began to strike coins for their own advantage. Naturally they did not do so at first under their

---

[1] See above, p. 16. [2] See above, p. 40.

[3] Only surviving in fragmentary form. Printed in Wilhelm Jesse, *Quellenbuch zur Münz- und Geldgeschichte des Mittelalters* (Halle, 1924), doc. 40.

55

own names, nor, initially, did they allow their deniers to diverge much from the known and universal standards of weight and fineness that they were supposed to maintain. Later they did both.

Very many of these post- or sub-Carolingian deniers were anonymous, bearing neither the name of the emperor or king, nor that of the feudatory. From at least the early tenth century to the thirteenth the Counts of Auxerre, for example, struck deniers with a blank space where the name of the king should have appeared.[1] Others bore the name of some long-dead emperor or king, rather than that of a current ruler. The Counts of Poitou, for example, went on minting Melle deniers until the twelfth century, in the name of Charles the Bald, who had died in 877. Since coinage remained, in theory at least, an imperial or royal prerogative, it was natural that many lords who controlled the individual mints should for long periods refrain from using their own names on their deniers and should produce such anonymous or 'posthumous' pieces. Others, more boldly, began to declare on the coins themselves their usurpation of royal minting-rights. When they did so, some began by linking the name of the king with their own. It was in the first years of the tenth century that the names of the responsible counts began to appear. William the Young, Count of Mâcon and of the Auvergne from 918–26, issued deniers in both counties in his own name as well as that of Charles the Simple, King of the West Franks until his deposition in 922.[2] As late as 984–6 Heribert, Count of Vermandois, was still using the name of King Lothaire, with whom he was allied, on his deniers, as well as his own. However, by that date some counts were, more honestly, declaring that their deniers were in practice issued entirely by their own authority. Hugh, Count of the Lyonnais, was one of the earliest counts to do so. On deniers struck between 936 and 948 he omitted the king's name entirely, using only his name on them. At the same time, at the other end of France, the Norman ruler William Long-Sword did the same thing, as Count of Rouen, between about 936 and 940.[3] Soon afterwards Hugh Capet, or possibly his father Hugh the Great was issuing deniers at Paris and St Denis inscribed VGO DVX F and GRATIA DEI DVX.[4]

As with the earlier evolution of the independent coinages of the barbarian kingdoms in the fifth and sixth centuries, there was a considerable time-lag between the actual taking-over of the running of the mints and the formal acknowledgement of this act on the coins themselves. In these circumstances there

[1] Françoise Dumas-Dubourg, 'Le Début de l'époque féodale en France d'après les monnaies', *Bulletin du Cercle d'Études Numismatiques*, x (1973), 69–70, based on her *Le Trésor de Fécamp et le monnayage en Francia occidentale pendant la seconde moitié du Xᵉ siècle* (Bibliothèque Nationale, Paris, 1971).

[2] Dumas-Dubourg, 'L'Époque féodale', pp. 181–2, 254–8. The deniers struck at Mâcon bore the king's name and the count's initial, whilst those minted at Brioude in the Auvergne bore the king's monogram and the count's name.

[3] Dumas-Dubourg, 'L'Époque féodale', p. 70, and *Trésor de Fécamp*, pp. 72ff.

[4] Dumas-Dubourg, 'L'Époque féodale', pp. 71–2, and *Trésor de Fécamp*, pp. 138–47. These pieces began to be struck before 956–65, the dating attributed to the Soleure hoard in which one of them was found.

was a strong incentive to continue issuing the same types over long periods of time. This happened both in the barbarian kingdoms of the west in the fifth and sixth centuries, and in the 'feudal' society evolving between the Pyrenees and the Rhine from the ninth century to the twelfth. In order to maintain these static types, new dies were copied slavishly, and seemingly uncomprehendingly, from those previously in use. In the process gradual, degenerative change crept in. The monogram of the ruler, a typical Carolingian reverse type, continued to appear in gradually less and less recognisable forms on deniers from all parts of West Frankia until the eleventh or even twelfth century, whilst the obverse head became at times grotesque with repeated copying. It became the notorious *tête chartrain*, an abstract arrangement of lines and dots, on the deniers of Chartres and neighbouring mints of the eleventh century. Similarly the columned temple portico, another widely used Carolingian reverse, became transformed on the deniers of St Martin of Tours, first into a church porch flanked by towers, and then into a castle, by the time that the minting of deniers tournois was taken over by Philip Augustus in 1205.

The fragmentation of political authority by grant and usurpation over a period of three centuries, first amongst the successor kingdoms of the Carolingian Empire and eventually amongst a myriad of minor seigneurs, was not paralleled at all levels by a fragmentation of mint rights. They were fragmented certainly, but not so completely as some other aspects of political authority, like the administration of criminal justice.

All the successor kings naturally minted, and in the tenth century so did nearly all of the greatest feudatories of West Frankia; the Counts of Paris, who had become Marquesses of Neustria and then Dukes of the French; the Counts of Rennes, who had become Dukes of Brittany; the Counts of Poitou, who had become Dukes of Aquitaine; and the Norman Counts of Rouen who became in turn Marquesses and then Dukes of Normandy. However, at the next level of the 'feudal' hierarchy, the counts who did not achieve major importance, and were often vassals of their greater neighbours, relatively few operated mints. In the tenth century it depended very largely on whether or not there had been a regular Carolingian mint within their particular county and, apart from the exceptional circumstances of the last years of the reign of Charles the Bald, the number of regular Carolingian mints had been relatively restrained. In the 820s and 830s Louis the Pious had only minted at some forty places throughout the whole empire, whereas there were many hundreds of counties in it.[1] The tenth-century Counts of Meaux, of Verdun and of Bourges, for example, had regular mints to operate, as did the viscounts who took over the counties of Orléans and Narbonne, but most counts did not issue coins

[1] See above, p. 44.

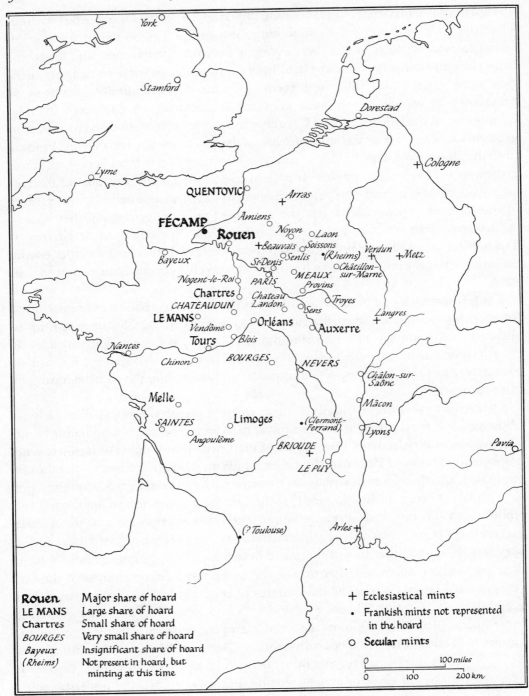

York

Stamford

Dorestad

Cologne

Lyme

QUENTOVIC

Arras

FÉCAMP

Amiens

Rouen

Noyon

Laon

Beauvais

Soissons

Verdun

Metz

Bayeux

St-Denis

Senlis

(Rheims)

Châtillon-sur-Marne

Nogent-le-Roi

PARIS

MEAUX

Chartres

Chateau Landon

Provins

CHATEAUDUN

Troyes

LE MANS

Sens

Langres

Vendôme

Orléans

Auxerre

Nantes

Tours

Blois

Chinon

BOURGES

NEVERS

Châlon-sur-Saône

Melle

Mâcon

Limoges

(Clermont-Ferrand)

Lyons

SAINTES

Pavia

Angoulême

BRIOUDE

LE PUY

(? Toulouse)

Arles

Rouen   Major share of hoard
LE MANS   Large share of hoard
Chartres   Small share of hoard
BOURGES   Very small share of hoard
Bayeux   Insignificant share of hoard
(Rheims)   Not present in hoard, but
           minting at this time

+   Ecclesiastical mints
•   Frankish mints not represented
    in the hoard
○   Secular mints

0   100 miles
0   100   200 km

Map 6. Mints represented in the Fécamp Hoard *c.* 980–985

before the eleventh or even the twelfth century, and many not even then.[1] Below the counts only a very limited number of lesser seigneurs were ever granted, or usurped, the right of minting. Their doing so did not, in any case, normally become apparent until the twelfth century, long after they had assumed many other rights. The Lords of St Pol or of Béthune in Artois are in this respect more typical of the limited number of castellans who minted,[2] than the quite exceptional, and otherwise unknown, Hugh the Dane, who minted in Normandy as castellan or 'Hvaleriv' at the end of the tenth century, at the very time that many other castellans were also achieving virtual autonomy, but not using it to mint.[3]

Alongside the lay hierarchy, a number of ecclesiastical feudatories also exercised the right of coinage. A very few of the regular Carolingian mints, like those at Strasbourg, Arles and Besançon, were entrusted to bishops rather than counts to administer and became attached to the sees as of right. However, as well as these, some totally new mints were opened under episcopal control as a result of specific individual royal grants. The earliest of these new mints was authorised in 864 by a grant to the Bishop of Châlons-sur-Marne at the time of the recoinage ordered by the edict of Pîtres.[4] The Bishops of Beauvais, Arras and Le Puy were among the small number of other bishops who received this favour at an early date.

In the troubled years of the late ninth century the abbots of some of the old-established monasteries attempted, by grant or usurpation, to resume the pre-Carolingian custom of independent minting by privileged immunist abbeys. Angilbert and Francon, successive abbots of the great seventh-century abbey of Corbie in Picardy, appear to be the first to have done so. As early as the 880s and 890s they briefly had deniers struck without any indication of royal authority. They used their own initials in place of the royal monogram. King Eudes protested against so blatant an assumption of independence, and by the end of the century Francon included the royal name on the deniers as well as his own. However, once the nominal royal authority had been acknowledged the usurpation of the right to mint was effectively condoned. Another great seventh-century monastic community, that of St Philibert, formerly on the island of Noirmoutier at the mouth of the Loire, but by the end of the ninth century dramatically driven by the Northmen to Tournus on the Saône, received a mint and its profits from Eudes in 889. In 915 Charles the Simple, lest the abbot should be tempted to follow the precedent of

[1] A comparison of Map 5, above, p. 45, showing the minting-places of the 840s and 850s and Map 6, p. 58 of the mints represented in the Fécamp hoard of c. 980–5 indicates the extent of the change.

[2] The Castellans of St Pol and Béthune made themselves virtually independent of the Counts of Flanders at the end of the tenth century. However, it was not until the third quarter of the twelfth century that their descendants began to mint (Claude Richebé, *Les Monnaies féodales d'Artois du Xe au début du XIVe siècle* (Paris, 1963)).

[3] Dumas-Dubourg, *Trésor de Fécamp*, pp. 100–3.

[4] Jesse, *Quellenbuch*, doc. 141. Discussed in Philip Grierson, 'The "Gratia Dei Rex" coinage of Charles the Bald', in Margaret Gibson and Janet Nelson (eds), *Charles the Bald: Court and Kingdom*, B.A.R. International Series, CI (Oxford, 1981), pp. 39–51.

Corbie, specifically required that the deniers of Tournus should bear his name. Despite the acknowledgement of ultimate royal authority, the running of another mint had effectively passed into the hands of an abbot. In 919 the even older community of St Martin's at Tours convinced Charles the Simple that they already possessed an ancient privilege permitting them to mint independently and persuaded him to confirm it.[1] It is not hard to see how the king was persuadable, for in 919 the abbot was not only a layman but the most powerful man in the kingdom, Robert, Marquess of Neustria, who was shortly to oust Charles from the throne itself. Although ostensibly a confirmation to an abbey, in reality this was yet another takeover of a royal mint by a great lay feudatory.

Thus either directly as counts, or much less frequently, as lay abbots or through bishops whom they appointed and controlled, the great lay feudatories took over the mints of the western parts of the Carolingian Empire. As well as a fragmentation of the authority by which coin was minted, the latter ninth century and the early tenth saw a very considerable decline in the use of money. As well as new mints being opened, some older mints closed, although these were mostly relatively unimportant mints like Dax. There was a reversion from the few large, centrally organised mints of the Carolingian period to the larger number of smaller, locally organised mints of the preceding period, and many of these small mints seem to have functioned very intermittently for much of the tenth century. At the same time the quantity of coin in circulation and the number of occasions on which men used money greatly declined. There was a retreat from the partially monetised rural economy revealed in some Carolingian polyptychs, to a society in which rural rent was again paid much more in goods and services and much less in money. Even the Carolingian heartland was affected. By 893 the abbey of Prüm in the Ardennes received only 1500 deniers from 2000 *mansi*. All the remainder of the rent was again being paid in the form of goods and services,[2] in marked contrast with the estates of St Germain, St Bertin and Ferrières in the first half of the century.[3] At Brescia in 905/6 the abbey of Santa Giulia was no longer receiving even its urban revenues in deniers, but in kind, in so many pounds of cheese or honey or so many *modii* of salt.[4]

The return to a low level of money in circulation once again demands some explanation. As was generally the case, up to the industrial revolution, there was an underlying imbalance of payments between western Europe and the east. The temporary reversal of the usual flow of payments came to an end with the slave-trade generated from Frankish expansion. As the Frankish conquests ceased, the

---

[1] For all these three abbeys see Dumas-Dubourg, 'L'Époque féodale', pp. 66–8, and *Trésor de Fécamp*, pp. 193–5.

[2] Renée Doehaerd, *The Early Middle Ages in the West: Economy and Society* (Amsterdam, 1978), p. 119.

[3] See above, pp. 47–8.

[4] Renée Doehaerd, 'Impôts directs acquittés par des marchands et des artisans pendant le Moyen Age', *Studi in onore di Armando Sapori*, I (Milan, 1957), 85.

opportunities for capturing slaves rapidly diminished. Although it did not cease, much less is heard of the export of slaves after the reign of Louis the Pious.[1] As a consequence, the payments of gold into Europe stopped. No 'mancuses' are mentioned in documents after 870,[2] and their import had presumably ceased a good while before that. As long as the ruling Frankish nobility could maintain the high standard of living to which they had become accustomed during the generations of expansion, they went on purchasing Eastern spices and perfumes, garments of silk or embroidered with gold, pearls and ivory. The clergy did the same. As late as 867 the monks of St Bertin were still regularly buying pepper and cummin, cloves, cinnamon and ginger.[3] Without adequate quantities of slaves or other products to send in return, the west had to pay in silver. Although the silver-mines at Melle continued to be worked,[4] their heyday had passed and they do not seem to have produced enough new silver to compensate for the losses from circulation. The failure of new mining of silver to match its export to the east would by itself have brought about a continual decline in the coinage available for use in western Europe. The decline was, however, aggravated and accelerated, by two factors – a quite extraordinary diversion of silver into church treasuries, and the Scandinavian invasions.

How far the Scandinavian invasions were responsible for the decline in coinage has been a matter of some controversy. Attention has been particularly focussed on the repeated payment of Danegeld as the way in which coin was taken out of circulation. However, some historians have suggested that, on the contrary, the need to pay Danegeld contributions caused so much plate to be turned into coin that the levying of Danegeld paradoxically mitigated the decline in money in circulation. It is, however, not even clear how much of these Danegelds were paid in coin. The Danes accepted these in terms of weights of silver, and apart from two occasions in the 860s when they were partly collected in coin, there is no reason to believe that the plate collected by the Frankish rulers was not actually handed over to the Danes as it was, without being minted.[5] By carrying off so much ecclesiasti-

---

[1] A stray reference in 870 reveals six ships crammed with slaves setting sail from Taranto for Alexandria, Tripoli and 'Africa' (Doehaerd, *Early Middle Ages*, p. 198).

[2] See above, pp. 49–52.

[3] Doehaerd, *Early Middle Ages*, p. 205.

[4] See above, pp. 32–3. In 848 the annalist of St Bertin thought it worth noting that the Northmen had destroyed the town by fire. The silver-mines that had presumably attracted them still made Melle sufficiently prosperous for it to be described as 'vicum populantes' (*Annales Bertiniani*, ed. G. Waitz (Hannover, 1883), p. 36). This was the end of their prosperity. Mining went on, however, and the mint continued to strike small quantities for a very long time. Three deniers have survived from the Carloman's reign (879–84), after which the Counts of Poitou ran the mint for themselves. In the tenth century the Counts of Poitou ceased to strike Melle deniers at Melle itself, so presumably the mines had been totally exhausted by then. See also above, p. 56.

[5] A failure to realise that the ninth-century Frankish Danegelds, unlike the tenth- and eleventh-century Anglo-Saxon payments, largely took the form of plate and not of coin has led some historians to seek for a solution to the non-existent puzzle of why the many millions of deniers that they thought had been paid as Danegeld did not turn up in Scandinavia. Professor Sawyer, for example, suggested that the raiders always had settlement in mind

cal plate the Danes made it impossible to return it to circulation in the west by reminting it into deniers, but they were not responsible for the original use of the silver as plate rather than coin. That was the act of innumerable pious laymen and clergy over the preceding years.

On the first occasion, when Charles the Bald bribed the Danish army under Ragner with 7000 pounds of silver to leave the Seine valley in 845, the sum was raised very rapidly, presumably largely from the royal treasure.[1] The small payment in 853 was presumably also available in the same way, but it was the large Danegeld of 5000 pounds in 861, that demanded the exaction of a general levy, for Charles the Bald no longer had large sums in hand. As well as imposing a levy on the treasures of churches, and on the property, particularly the plate, of merchants, a tax in deniers was levied on every *mansus* in the countryside. Direct taxation in coin had not been attempted for centuries. Even Charlemagne had not attempted it.[2] Collection was difficult, for the author of the *Annales Bertiniani* reckoned that 6000 pounds of gold and silver had already been taken in plunder over the previous five or six years. A further 6000 pounds was paid by the Marquess Robert of Neustria in 862, and then 4000 pounds by Charles the Bald in 866.[3] In 866 the collection of Danegeld was so difficult that it took five months to bring in. As usual, church plate bore the brunt of the collection, and merchants had also to hand over a tenth of all their possessions, but this time the magnates had to contribute as well, partly in silver and partly in wine. For a second time a tax was laid on the countryside, at first 6 deniers on a free *mansus* and 3 on a servile one, and then a further denier on every *mansus* to make up the sum required. Inferior holdings paid a denier or an obol each.

Philip Grierson has suggested that it was the collection of this Danegeld that caused Charles the Bald to resort to the temporary expedient of opening an unprecedentedly large number of mints. He has argued that the circulating medium was already so reduced that emergency minting of silver, presumably hitherto in the form of plate, became necessary to provide the coin to pay these taxes.[4] It is certain that instead of the nine central mints envisaged under the edict of Pîtres of 864, and the tenth mint conceded to the Bishop of Châlons-sur-Marne a few months later, a vast number of mints of some sort suddenly sprang into operation.

---

and that coin was accumulated by members of these raiding-bands until they had saved up enough capital with which to settle. He based this on a forced interpretation of 'feohleas', used by the Anglo-Saxon Chronicle for 896, as 'moneyless', rather than the more usual 'without stock' (Peter H. Sawyer, *The Age of the Vikings*, 2nd ed. (London, 1971), pp. 100–1).

[1] Grierson, ' "Gratia Dei Rex" coinage', pp. 45–6.
[2] See above, p. 48.
[3] Albert d'Haenens, 'Les Invasions normandes dans l'empire franc au IXe siècle', in *I Normanni e loro espansione in Europa nell'alto medioevo*, Settimane di Studio del Centro Italiano di studi sull' alto medioevo, XVI (Spoleto, 1969), pp. 272–3.
[4] Grierson, ' "Gratia Dei Rex" coinage', pp. 45–6.

The deniers struck at this time, with the new 'Gratia Dei Rex' formula, bear the names of no less than a hundred different places in West Frankia and a further twenty-five in Aquitaine. It is quite possible that deniers were only actually struck at the ten mints, and that the named places were effectively exchange points where new deniers could be acquired with bullion, or with old money. Alternatively teams of moneyers based on the ten original mints may have gone out, with centrally-cut dies, to work temporarily at the hundred 'mints'.[1] The next two Danegelds, 5000 pounds in 877 and 12,000 pounds in 884, were raised entirely from church treasures, perhaps an indication that the attempts to raise taxation in coin in the 860s were too difficult to repeat. If the dearth of coin in the countryside at large had made collection hard in 866, nothing had occurred in the meanwhile to make it any easier. However yet more Danegelds were to come, in 889, 897, 923/4 and 926, although we do not know how large they were, nor how they were raised. Nevertheless silver of some sort was still somehow raisable to make these payments. It was presumably not in the form of coin, for there was never again any resort to the extraordinary opening of large numbers of 'mints'. The 'Gratia Dei Rex' deniers of the 860s had, from the evidence of the surviving pieces, been the last considerable issue of the Carolingian period.[2]

The total of the Danegeld payments recorded in contemporary Frankish sources comes to around 40,000 pounds (18,144 kilograms) weight of silver. However, the sources are silent on the sums levied on numerous occasions, so that the real total may well have been two or three times this sum.[3]

What this meant in real terms is well exemplified by the abbey of St Riquier in Picardy, which in 831 had had 277 ciboria, chalices, patens, candelabra, lamps, crosses and reliquaries, mostly in silver, but some of gold or orichalcum and many set with precious stones. In addition to the church silver they had had domestic silver for monastic use, 64 silver plates and 18 silver dish covers, for example, and somewhat mysteriously 7 silver crowns. Professor Fossier believes that they had

[1] Either explanation would fit the evidence provided by the coins themselves. Coins of Charles the Bald minted with the same obverse dies have been noticed from Troyes and Mont Lassois, from Avallon and St Andoche d'Autun, from St Martin of Tours and St Maurice of Tours, and from the City and the Portus of Tournai. It has been suggested that the engraver at work at Châlons-sur-Marne was also responsible for the dies striking coins bearing the names of Nevers, Lyons, Vienne, Besançon, Dijon, Bar-sur-Aube and Avallon (Jean Lafaurie, *Bulletin de la Société Française de Numismatique*, XXIII (November 1968) and XXIV (July 1969)).

[2] Large issues of pennies continued a decade longer in Anglo-Saxon England, but only because the kings debased the coinage extensively, as an alternative method of raising the money needed to cope with the Viking raids. From the early 850s Burgred of Mercia and successive kings of Wessex gradually reduced the fineness of their pennies from over 90% silver to under 20% silver. When Alfred returned to minting good silver pennies in 879 it became apparent how much the stock of silver had diminished in England as well (D. M. Metcalf and J. P. Northover, 'Debasement of the coinage in southern England in the age of King Alfred', *Numismatic Chronicle*, CXLV (1985), 150–76).

[3] D'Haenens, 'Invasions normandes'. Both he and Grierson rely heavily on E. Joranson, *The Danegeld in France*, Augustana Library Publications, X (Rock Island, Illinois, 1924).

only about an eighth of this 'treasure' left by the end of the century. The other seven eighths had disappeared largely, although not entirely, for 'Danegeld'. Some had been stolen by unscrupulous Christians, and some had been sent in 896 to pay for building the new protective wall at Montreuil, the successor port to Quentovic.[1]

If the Scandinavian raiders did not directly denude western Europe of coin by carrying it off to Scandinavia, is it merely a coincidence that the raids were at their fiercest at the turning-point between a relatively abundant money supply and a relatively sparse one? Concealment of coin naturally took place, as at all times of disorder. We are only ever able to see the tip of this iceberg of concealment, in the form of hoards that were not reclaimed by their owners, but have been recovered in modern times.[2] Perhaps more important than the coins removed from circulation, either temporarily or permanently, was the slowing-down of the velocity of circulation. On a local level the destruction of towns reduced the scale of urban–rural interchange. The severe curtailment of the town market for the sale of rural produce radically reduced the means by which coin could reach the purses of the peasant tenant. On a broader scale the sack of every seaport between Hamburg and Bordeaux, some of them many times over, destroyed the Frisian trading-network. This, of course, affected not only western Europe, but Scandinavia itself. The immediate advantage of the raider worked to the disadvantage of his countrymen at home. A reduction of the flow of western coined silver into Scandinavia, rather than an increase, seems, ironically, to have been the consequence of the raids. Presumably as a further consequence, there seems to have been a lack of coined silver in Scandinavia itself at this time, if the absence of discovered hoards containing coins from the second half of the ninth century is more than accidental. West European silver coins had formed a part of Scandinavian silver hoards up to the middle of the ninth century, but when hoards containing coins began to be buried again in the 890s, West European coins were conspicuously absent.[3] It was not until the re-creation of the Frisian trading-network a century later that western coin again began to flow into Scandinavia.[4]

Our knowledge of the Vikings as traders is largely determined by archaeological evidence, and the abundant coin hoards of Scandinavia are amongst the more

---

[1] Robert Fossier, *La Terre et les hommes en Picardie jusqu'à la fin du XIIIᵉ siècle* (Paris-Louvain, 1968), pp. 237–8, 247–8. The treasure had been built up in a period when it had been possible to receive extensive revenues in silver deniers (cf. other abbeys, above, pp. 47–8); 2500 of its tenants had paid an annual *cens* of 12 deniers each. The surplus products of its workshops had sold for 12 pounds of deniers a year, etc. Altogether its abbot, Angilbert, estimated its cash income at 300 pounds a year. How much of this coin had been turned into the 'treasure' is not ascertainable.

[2] In the Netherlands alone sixteen ninth-century hoards have been recovered whose contents were of use to Dr Enno van Gelder in his discussion of the fate of the Dorestad mint ('De Karolingische Muntslag te Duurstede', *Jaarboek voor Munt- en Penningkunde*, XLVIII (1961), 40–1). In England hoards not recovered until modern times were particularly concentrated in the decade 865–75.

[3] Brita Malmer, *Nordiska Mynt före år 1000* (Lund–Bonn, 1966), pp. 335–6.

[4] See below, pp. 86–7.

dramatic forms which that evidence takes. Literary sources, at least in western Europe, give only an impression of raiders, and later of colonists. On the other hand the archaeological evidence provided by such excavations as those at Hedeby, on the Viking-age route from the Baltic to the North Sea just north of the modern Kiel canal, or at Birka, in Sweden on Lake Mälaren, presents a picture of active and wide-ranging trading communities.[1] In the deliberate excavation of these sites numerous coins have been found, but far more numerous are the coins that have been accidentally discovered in a great many places in the Baltic lands. Discoveries of such treasure hoards have been most numerous on the island of Gotland in the Baltic, but a large number have been unearthed in the area bordering on the eastern coast of southern Sweden and in the lake-filled region of central Sweden, west of Stockholm.

A generation after West European coins disappeared from them, Scandinavian hoards began, particularly from the 890s, to contain increasingly large numbers of Central Asian dirhams. They mark a new, eastward orientation in Scandinavian trade, following in the train of the Swedish expansion eastward into 'Russia' earlier in the century. These dirhams have been called 'kufic' from the script with which they are inscribed, and this term has been used to cover not only dirhams of the caliphate but also Samanid dirhams from Transoxiana, which was particularly prosperous in the tenth century. This prosperity depended in part on the exploitation of rich silver-mines in the Samanid provinces, particularly that at Shâsh, now Tashkent, and that at Pendjhir, now in Afghanistan, which were discovered in the second half of the ninth century. From Merv, Samarkand and Tashkent these coins passed to Scandinavia in the course of trade, by way of the Bulgars on the middle Volga and the Khazars on the lower Volga.[2] The Scandinavian 'Rus' collected sable and other kinds of fur, and also slaves in the north of what is today Russia, partially at least as tribute, and sold these for silver to Muslim merchants at Bulgar and Itil and also honey, wax, amber and furs from the Baltic area itself.[3] Of these commodities slaves were by far the most valuable. As well as slaves from northern Russia, other slaves were brought from the west. The Franks were now more likely to be taken as slaves, than to engage in slave-raiding.[4] However the Slavs again provided the largest group of slaves. Just as *sclavus* had earlier replaced *servus* in West European languages,[5] so in the ninth century a derivative of *sclavus*, *saqaliba*,

---

[1] See above, p. 52.

[2] See Map 7, p. 66. At the same time, from about 890, Kufic dirhams were also carried along the silk-road to China (Joe Cribb, 'An historical survey of the precious metal currencies of China', *Numismatic Chronicle*, 7th series, XIX (1979), 192–3) and also to India.

[3] Tadeusz Lewicki, 'Le Commerce des Sāmānides avec l'Europe orientale et centrale à la lumière des trésors de monnaies coufiques', in D. K. Kouymjian (ed.) *Near Eastern Numismatics, Iconography, Epigraphy and History: Studies in Honor of George C. Miles* (Beirut, 1974), pp. 219–33.

[4] J. M. Wallace-Hadrill, *The Vikings in Francia* (Reading, 1975), p. 18.

[5] See above, p. 49.

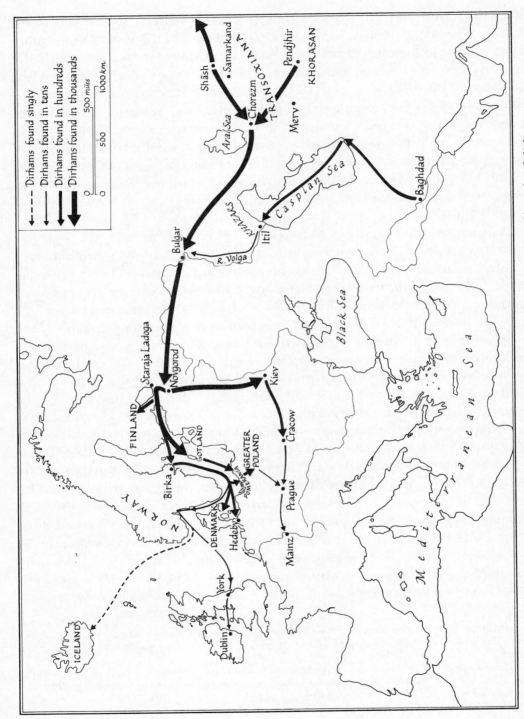

Map 7. Samanid–Viking silver-routes: reconstructed from the scale of hoards of dirhams

Legend:
- ----→ Dirhams found singly
- ——→ Dirhams found in tens
- ━━━→ Dirhams found in hundreds
- ━━━▶ Dirhams found in thousands

Scale: 500 — 1000 km.
0 — 500 — 1000 miles

became the general Arabic word for both Slav and slave. The great slave-market of Europe was now in Prague. It was because of this trade that these dirhams found their way to Scandinavian Russia, to Scandinavia itself, and to other lands bordering on the Baltic. Well over 200,000 dirhams have so far been found and recorded in hoards in northern, central and eastern Europe, including 60,000 in Gotland, 45,000 in the rest of Scandinavia,[1] and 25,000 in what is now Poland, principally along the Baltic in Pomerania. Most of the rest have been found in Russia itself. One single Russian hoard, that at Murom, about 240 kilometres (150 miles) east of Moscow on the Oka, a tributary of the Volga, on the route from Bulgar to the Baltic, contained no less than 11,077 dirhams besides 12 pounds of pieces of dirhams.[2] The origins of this trade go back to the very beginning of the ninth century when the Khazars on the lower Volga began to supply the Abbasid caliphate with furs and slaves from their East Slavic tributary peoples.[3] The dirhams brought to the Khazars to pay for these furs and slaves gradually worked their way northwards to pay for yet more furs and slaves until they reached the Ladoga region and the Baltic coast, where they attracted the attention of the Vikings, who violently muscled-in on the trade. The opportune discovery of the new Samanid silver-mines made it possible for the trade to expand enormously.

It was in the period after 890 that this trade was at its most considerable, and that Birka, looking eastwards to Russia from Sweden, was at its most prosperous. Kufic coins spread westwards from Sweden along the trade-routes, through Hedeby, and through Norway to the Norse parts of the British Isles. It is in this way that a hoard of 37 coins and of other silver objects at Goldsborough in Yorkshire, probably dating from *c.* 925–30, came to contain no less than 35 dirhams, of which at least 18 were of Samanid origin, struck at such mints as that at Samarkand between 895 and 911.[4] Many of the coin hoards, such as this one, in the Scandinavian world also contained silver in the form of ingots or ornaments or fragments of ingots and ornaments roughly cut to make up a fixed weight. It is therefore clear that silver was as yet only used as a means of exchange by weight by the Vikings and that coin was only regarded as one form of silver. This view is supported by the fact that no regular coinage was minted in Scandinavia itself until around the year 1000. Although these kufic dirhams were not used as coins in the strictest sense of the word in tenth-century Russia, Sweden, Denmark, Poland and northern England they nevertheless circulated in the furtherance of trade.

Ibrahim ben Ya'qub, a Jew from Tortosa on the Ebro in Muslim Spain,

[1] Swedish mainland 40,000, Denmark 4000, Norway 400.
[2] Sawyer, *Age of the Vikings*, p. 88.
[3] Thomas S. Noonan, 'Ninth-century dirham hoards from European Russia: a preliminary analysis', in M. A. S. Blackburn and D. M. Metcalf (eds.), *Viking-Age Coinage in the Northern Lands*, B.A.R. International Series, CXXII (2 vols., Oxford, 1981), pp. 51–3.
[4] J. D. A. Thompson, *Inventory of British Coin Hoards, A.D. 600–1500* (London, 1956), p. 64.

travelling through Mainz in 965, commented that as well as local grain and wine, Indian goods were on sale. 'It is extraordinary' he wrote 'that one can find at Mainz, at the extreme end of the West, perfumes and spices that only take their birth in the deepest end of the East.' As well as pepper, ginger, cloves and spikenard he found dirhams in use that had been struck at Samarkand in 913–14 at the beginning of the reign of the greatest of the Samanid emirs, Nasr b. Ahmad.[1] The perfumes and spices have long since been used up, but the dirhams survive as a witness to this strange long-distance trade. Dirhams at Mainz must, however, have been quite exceptional. Although the largest hoards in Russia and in Gotland contained dirhams in thousands, the largest hoards on the Swedish mainland, in Finland, Poland or Denmark rarely contain more than hundreds of dirhams. The largest groups found in Norwegian and Norwegian–British hoards can only be counted in tens, whilst no more than four have ever been found together in Iceland.[2] None have yet been found west of the Rhine or south of the Trent.[3] It is clear that, in a quite remarkable way, and for the only time in the Middle Ages, non-European coins circulated in Europe, although they can hardly be called a part of its currency.

The most difficult problem is to discover how these pieces were used in an area that did not have its own currency. The dirhams that Ibrahim ben Ya'qub encountered at Mainz have not been found in Rhineland hoards, and were presumably reminted in the Rhineland mints before passing further westwards. Others were reminted by Otto I, at Magdeburg, before they ever got as far west as Mainz, but what happened in Poland, or indeed in Scandinavia, or in Russia? It would be a reasonable assumption that, initially at least, members of a society that did not possess its own coinage would treat the currency of outsiders, Central Asian dirhams, as a commodity, either as a commercial commodity or as treasure, depending on whether the possessor was a 'merchant' or a chieftain of warriors. Hoards in which dirhams, fragments of dirhams, silver ornaments and ingots were mixed confirm this assumption and indicate that coin, like other silver, was a commodity to be accepted by weight.

At the far end of the route the Volga Bulgars were sufficiently close to the Arab world to use dirhams as coin amongst themselves, to such an extent that early in the tenth century they began to mint their own dirhams and went on doing so for much of the century. Many of their dirhams, of course, travelled north and west with the Samanid and Abbasid dirhams, and one has even been found in Norway.

However, in Russia, at the next stage on the route, the dirhams, and indeed all coin, seem to have been treated merely as silver, along with other silver objects.

[1] A. Miquel, 'L'Europe occidentale dans la relation arabe d'Ibrahim, b. Ya'qub', *Annales E.S.C.*, XXI (1966), 1059–60.

[2] Kolbjorn Skaare, *Coin and Coinage in Viking Age Norway* (Oslo–Bergen–Tromsö, 1976), pp. 48, 118.

[3] Jean Duplessy, 'La Circulation des monnaies arabes en Europe occidentale du VIIIᵉ au XIIIᵉ siècles', *Revue Numismatique*, 5th series, XVIII (1956), 125–8.

Silver, whether coined or uncoined, was seen as a commodity, albeit a very precious and prestigious commodity, and dealt in only by weight. When the Samanid dirhams became extremely irregular in weight, in the 930s,[1] the Rus had no hesitation in cutting or breaking them into fragments. The fragments were used to bring the weight of a quantity of irregular silver dirhams down to, or up to, a regular weight.[2] The fragments too passed on westwards and have very frequently been found in Scandinavia and Poland with whole dirhams.[3]

Treasure was patently central to the life of a chieftain among the Rus, and as such it was to be taken on into the afterlife for future enjoyment. An Arab visitor, Ibn Rustah, writing in the first half of the tenth century, described how, when one of their chieftains died, he was put into a house-sized grave with an abundance of coins, as well as clothing, food and drink and his favourite slave-girl.[4] In Scandinavia itself treasure was equally regarded as transportable into the afterlife. The untrustworthy thirteenth-century *Ynglinga Saga* incorporates the reputedly much earlier 'Law of Odin', which stated that the dead could enjoy any silver that they themselves had buried.[5] A society in which treasure was to be accumulated to be buried for enjoyment after death was very different from the West European or Arab societies, on either side, in which coin had for long been not only a store of wealth, but also a means of exchange and a measure of value.

Yet this was not a society without 'trade'. Without the slave- and fur-'trades' there could have been no silver-'trade'. Slave-girls and honey, furs and wax could be used to purchase not only 'treasure' from the Arabs, but also other enjoyable commodities. There is evidence that Indian perfumes and spices were carried to Sweden as well as to Mainz, together with Chinese silk and Persian glass.

Although dirhams were never more than a form of silver for the Rus, the problem remains as to whether they ever came to be used as coin in Scandinavia itself, or in Pomerania and Greater Poland. Historians have disagreed very considerably on this point.

Professor Kiersnowski, for example, said that, although it is clear that in Pomerania and Greater Poland dirhams were merely a commodity at the beginning

---

[1] They varied very widely indeed, from 2.7 to 4.5 grams each.

[2] V. L. Yanin, 'Les Problèmes généraux de l'échange monétaire russe aux ixᵉ–xiiᵉ siècles', in *Moneta e scambi nell'alto medioevo*, Settimane di studi del Centro Italiano di Studi sull'alto medioevo, VIII (Spoleto, 1961), pp. 485–505.

[3] Their existence has misled some historians into believing that fragments were deliberately made for small-trading purposes and has consequently conjured up an imaginary picture of vigorous, petty money-using exchanges in Sweden and Poland, e.g. Sawyer, *Age of the Vikings*, p. 193, or Ryszard Kiersnowski, *Pieniadz Kruscowy w Polsce wczesnosrednio-wieczney* (*Metal Money in Early Medieval Poland*) (Warsaw, 1960): I have relied on the English summary by Andrew S. Ehrenkreutz, 'The function of Muslim silver coins in the pre-Christian monetary history of Poland' (Conference Paper, c. 1966).

[4] As paraphrased by Gwynn Jones, *A History of the Vikings* (Oxford, 1968), p. 255.

[5] Paraphrased by Alfred E. Lieber, 'International trade and coinage in the northern lands during the early Middle Ages: an introduction', in Blackburn and Metcalf (eds.), *Viking-Age Coinage*, p. 27.

of the tenth century, he believed that they came to be used as currency in the course of the century. Basing his argument on the hoards found in modern Poland, predominantly along the Baltic in Pomerania, he suggested that a transformation took place. He argued that the earlier hoards of dirhams were mostly homogeneous in character, that is, that they contained coins closely related to each other by their place and date of minting. In other words, they had not circulated much after their arrival in Pomerania or Poland, were not far removed from the original payments for exports from Pomerania or Poland and had not been used for local monetary transactions. He pointed out that the later hoards contained dirhams from different periods and mints, and suggested that several transactions separated their burial from their first appearance on Slav markets.[1] From the second half of the tenth century the majority of hoards are of the latter sort. From this he concluded that by the middle of the tenth century the original attitude to dirhams as a commodity had disappeared and that they had become an accepted monetary medium circulating in Pomerania and Poland.

Kiersnowski went on to suggest that the possession and use of coinage ceased to be limited to 'export merchants' and chieftains. He pointed out that although most of the earlier hoards were larger (over one hundred coins), most of the later hoards were much smaller. Fifty-three out of the seventy-five eleventh-century Polish coin hoards of a known size had ten or fewer coins in them. Hoards of this size cannot by any stretch of the imagination be regarded as the 'treasures' of local chieftains, or 'capital' for large-scale commercial transactions. He suggested that by the middle of the tenth century the circulation of silver coinage had expanded beyond the closed circle of the group whom he chose to call a 'feudal and mercantile elite'. His tables were not constructed to show the tenth century divided into two halves, so that they do not provide a statistical backbone to this suggestion. However, his figures (Table 1) make it look probable by the eleventh century.

Ibrahim ben Ya'qub also visited Poland in 965 and said of its duke, Mieszko I, 'Tributa ab eo exacta e ponderibus mercatoriis (constant). Haec eius viris stipendio (sunt). In unumquemque mensem unicuique (eorum) certus numerus ex eis (datur).'[2] A money economy would appear from this to have sufficiently developed for some taxes at least to be paid in coin, rather than in goods and services, and for some wages to be paid in coin, by number. This reinforces Kiersnowski's

---

[1] Kiersnowski, *Pienadz Kruscowy* . . . (Ehrenkreutz, 'Muslim silver coins in Poland').

[2] Latin translation from Arabic in 'Relatio Ibrāhīm ibn Ja'kūb de itinere slavico, quae traditur apud Al-Bekrî', ed. T. Kowalski, *Monumenta Poloniae Historica*, new series, 1 (Cracow, 1946), 147. This passage presents some problems. The weights referred to are *mitkals*. The *mitkal* was the weight of the gold dinar and was sometimes used as a synonym for it, but there were patently no gold dinars in Poland in 965. The passage has been garbled in transmission by someone (al-Bekri?), who could not believe in dirhams in tenth-century Poland, and substituted dinars. But how much else has been changed?

Table 1. *Islamic coins in Polish territories, eighth to twelfth centuries*

hoards consisting of	number of hoards dating from:					
	eighth and ninth centuries	tenth century	eleventh century	twelfth century	?	total
stray finds	9	20	—	—	2	31
2–10 coins	3	22	53	—	—	78
11–100 coins	1	33	16	1	—	51
101–1000 coins	5	21	6	—	—	32
over 1000 coins	—	4	—	—	—	4
size unknown	—	30	27	2	—	59
Total	18	130	102	3	2	255

Ehrenkreutz, 'Muslim silver coins in Poland', p. 7, from Kiersnowski, *Pienadz Kruscowy* . . ., p. 105.

conclusions from the hoard evidence and suggests that by the second half of the tenth century dirhams were used as coins.

Dr Tabaczynski, on the other hand, did not believe that money was circulating widely by the middle of the tenth century and suggested that this stage in the development of the Polish economy did not occur until the mid eleventh century.[1] He pointed out that the hoards of the tenth century and earlier were not found in town excavations, but in isolated situations removed from human habitation, and that stray finds of individual coins do not occur in the archaeological excavations of town sites until the very end of the tenth century, as one would have expected if coin had been circulating relatively freely as a medium of exchange in local markets. Not until the middle of the eleventh century were townsmen using coin sufficiently freely to have the opportunity of losing many odd coins here and there for archaeologists to discover. He also pointed out that the very few stray coins found on town sites before the middle of the eleventh century were not dirhams, but western pieces, mostly German, but also English and Danish, and that balances and weights were also found in the same excavation. This would suggest that coin was still being used by weight on the rare occasions when it came into the hands of townsmen. Tabaczynski suggested instead that there was a long period of slow economic growth during which urban commerce developed on a basis of barter before the general body of inhabitants began to use coin for the local commercial exchange of the products of craftsmen and the foodstuffs of peasants. In some cases the use of coin was preceded or initially supplemented by some more primitive money to assist the process of barter. He also quoted Ibrahim ben Ya'qub, who was

---

[1] In other words at about the same time that a permanent native coinage began to be minted (Stanislaw Tabaczynski, 'Circulation monétaire dans les villes polonaises au haut moyen-âge vue à la lumière des recherches récentes', *Atti del VI Congresso Internazionale delle Scienze Preistoriche e Protostoriche* (1966), 208–10).

in Prague in 965, and found that western deniers were known there with a very high purchasing-power, but the inhabitants amongst themselves used a currency of squares of very fine cloth in which the value of all objects was reckoned.[1]

Ibrahim ben Ya'qub went on his great journey in 965, just as the 'trade' between central Asia and eastern and northern Europe was about to dry up. Its sudden cessation is rather mysterious, although attempts to explain it have been made in various ways. One explanation is in terms of Central Asian politics. The Samanids eventually lost control of Transoxiana to the Karakhanid Turks and the lands south of the Oxus to the Ghaznavids, who were descended from a Turkish mercenary leader. It has therefore been suggested that 'the new rulers, being themselves former Turkish military slaves, had no interest in continuing these imports [of Turkish slaves] for their own armies',[2] and so the slave-trade dried up for lack of customers. It is an appealing explanation, apart from the fact that the Karakhanids and Ghaznavids did not take over until the 990s and the flow of dirhams had stopped a generation earlier. And do societies really suddenly develop an aversion for slave-girls and honey . . .? Alternatively it has been suggested that it was the mines that were worked out and ceased production and that consequently there was no longer any means to pay for the slaves and the furs. More recent work has suggested that some of the mines were incredibly long-lived, and continued to be worked, sometimes even on an increased scale, up to the thirteenth century.[3] I do not doubt that small amounts of silver might be extracted over very long periods, but I am extremely reluctant to believe that these particular mines had a much longer lifespan than other mines, and that there would be anything really worthwhile to be taken out of a rich and vigorously-worked vein of silver after one century's mining, let alone three, even with the most primitive mining-technology. The most plausible explanation still seems to be that the links between Scandinavia and the Arabs were abruptly cut in the steppes themselves, and that, by the time that commercial relations could be resumed, the mints had gone into decline. By the early eleventh century the Islamic world was itself suffering from a shortage of silver.[4]

With a sudden decline of this trade with central Asia, there was a changed orientation in Scandinavian economic life. The flourishing 'Rus'-focussed market came to an abrupt end in the last third of the tenth century and at the same time Scandinavian coin hoards began to consist almost entirely of German and English pieces in place of Islamic dirhams. In Poland dirhams went on circulating until well into the eleventh century, and a few have even been found in three twelfth-century

---

[1] Paraphrased by Tabaczynski from *Monumenta Poloniae Historica*, I, 49.
[2] Lieber, 'International trade in the northern lands', p. 25.
[3] *Ibid.*
[4] See below pp. 97 and 148.

hoards, but during the second half of the tenth century the dirhams were overwhelmed by the influx of a great mass of West European coins, particularly German pfennigs. In northern, Novgorod, Baltic-orientated Russia, German pfennigs and Anglo-Saxon pennies occur increasingly in the first half of the eleventh century in hoards, but in southern, Kiev, Black–Sea-orientated Russia, they do not appear in hoards, and the rupture of the flow of imported dirhams in the 960s from the Samanid emirate eventually brought about a cessation in any sort of use of coined silver in the area from the early eleventh century. It was not resumed until the late fourteenth.

4

Saxon Silver and the Expansion of Minting

Over 70,000 German pfennigs and over 30,000 Anglo-Saxon pennies, almost all of the period 990–1050, have so far been found in Sweden. This indicates both the changed orientation in Scandinavian economic life, and also a considerable increase in prosperity in both Ottonian Germany and Anglo-Saxon England in the tenth and eleventh centuries. For Ottonian Germany the increased quantity of coin in circulation can be linked very closely with an increase in the mining of silver. A long series of pfennigs began to be struck in Saxony for the Empress Adelaide in conjunction with her grandson, Otto III, for whom she was regent from 991–95, and continued to be struck in their joint names for a further forty years after her death. Spectrographic analysis of the trace elements of various minor impurities in them has shown that the majority of them were minted from the silver mined out of the Rammelsberg above the town of Goslar in the Harz mountains.[1] This appears to be the mine whose discovery was recorded by the chronicler Widukind of Corvey, between 961 and 968.[2] It seems to be nothing more than a fortunate coincidence that mining of silver in Germany began at almost exactly the same time as access to the failing silver-mines of Transoxiana came to an end. Although silver-mining in the Harz began in the 960s, its development, at least as measured by the coins produced from it, seems to have been slow, until the 990s. It was only then that the considerable issues of 'Adelaide–Otto' pfennigs from the Goslar mint began. As well as the silver-mines in the Harz, of which the *Alte Lager* of the Rammelsberg was only the first, more silver was discovered and further mines were exploited elsewhere in Germany in the late tenth century and the early eleventh. In the southern Black Forest, for example, silver-mines were opened at Sulzbach, Kropbach and Steinbrunnen in the early eleventh century.[3] In this way the stock of silver available for minting in Western Europe increased enormously from the

[1] Emil Kraume and Vera Hatz, 'Die Otto–Adelheid-Pfennige und ihre Nachprägungen', *Hamburger Beiträge zur Numismatik*, new series XV (1961–3), 13–23 and appendices.

[2] Werner Hillebrand, 'Von des Anfängen des Erzbergbaus am Rammelsberg bei Goslar', *Nieder-Sächsischen Jahrbuch für Landesgeschichte*, XXXIX (1967), 103–14.

[3] E. Kraume, 'Münzprägung und Silbererz-Bergbau in Mittel-europa um die Jahrtausendwende (950–1050)', *Der Anschnitt*, XIII, 4 (1961).

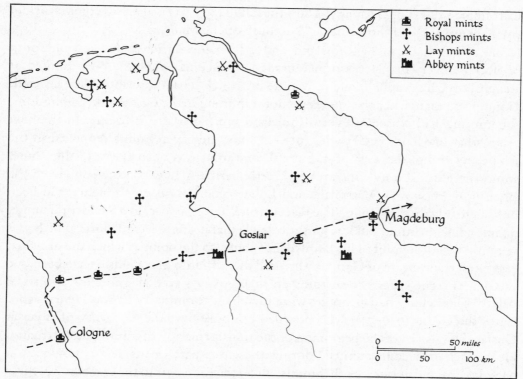

Map 8. New mints – Otto I to Otto III

second half of the tenth century onwards. No longer was it necessary, as it had been for Otto I, to melt down Central Asian dirhams to produce his own pfennigs at Magdeburg, for there was enough German silver available. The increased quantities of silver were immediately absorbed by the increased use of coin in trade. One of the striking phenomena of the tenth century in both Germany and England is the great number of new commercial centres deliberately created by imperial or royal fiat. These were not normally new settlements, but extensions in function of already-existing religious, military or administrative centres. The twin grants of the rights to hold a market and to operate a mint, added a new dimension to urban life, or at least gave regalian sanction and encouragement to such new developments. Mint and market went together. The market was not for barter, but for selling and buying with money, and to provide for this a mint was needed.[1] (See Map 8.)

Until the beginning of the tenth century there was no mint in Germany east of the Rhine except for the tiny 'palace' mint at Regensburg.[2] The last of the

---

[1] Cf. the similar development in Merovingian Frankia above, pp. 24–5.
[2] See above, p. 41.

Carolingian rulers of Germany, Louis the Child (899–911), also had coins struck in small quantities for a short time at Würzburg on the Main, as well as at Strasbourg, Mainz and Cologne in the Rhineland, and at Trier and Zurich to the west and south of it. However, his successor, Conrad of Franconia (911–18), only minted at Regensburg, his 'capital', and at Mainz, on which his family lands were centred. Conrad's reign marked the lowest point for minting in the East Frankish kingdom, for minting had ceased at every Rhineland mint apart from Mainz. In the next reign, that of Henry the Fowler (918–36), not only were mints reopened in the Rhineland and to the west of it, but a second mint was opened east of the Rhine, somewhere in 'Saxony', the area of North Germany between the Rhine and the Elbe, now known as Westphalia and Lower Saxony, of which Henry had been duke before he became king. The pieces struck at it, the so-called Sachsenpfennige, do not name the mint, but it is most probable that it was at Magdeburg, which was not only the focal point of his family lands, but also the point at which the principal east–west trade-route of Germany crossed the Elbe into Slav lands. It had been one of Charlemagne's frontier customs posts in 805. As well as a fortress and royal palace, Magdeburg had also a growing merchant community. It was Henry's son, Otto 'the Great' (936–73), who presided not only over the discovery of silver at Goslar, but also over the beginning of the transformation of minting in Germany. He himself had coins minted, during the latter part of his reign, not only at Magdeburg, but at twelve other mints, all on the Rhine, or to the east of it. Of these Cologne was the most important. As well as the mints that were worked in his own name, Otto I made a dozen or so grants to others of the right to operate a mint. Most of these grants were to abbeys and bishops and some of these were also east of the Rhine. Otto II (973–83) and Otto III (983–1002) opened some seventeen additional mints for themselves, and granted the right to others to open forty or so further mints. Most of these grants were still made to ecclesiastics, in contrast to the emphasis on comital mints in West Frankia. By the end of Otto III's reign more than eighty mints existed in 'Germany' instead of two under Conrad, only three generations earlier. A fairly high proportion of these new mints were east of the Rhine, and were concentrated in the area of Saxony along the main east–west trade-route from Cologne to Magdeburg. At Cologne this route crossed the Rhine into the area in which Carolingian minting had been most concentrated. It was also in this part of Saxony that the Saxon ruling house had its family lands. Important mints at Quedlinburg, Hildesheim, Dortmund and above all Goslar were opened here by the emperors themselves, whilst grants of mints were made to their favoured religious foundations, such as the abbey at Corvey or the abbey, later archbishopric, at Magdeburg. The archbishops of Magdeburg were not only given the profits of the royal mint at Magdeburg, but also the right to open mints at

Gittelde and Giebichenstein.[1] The abbey of Corvey acquired the right to mint at Meppen in the latter part of the tenth century, and at the same time was able at last to make use of its old right to mint at Corvey itself,[2] where the main route from Cologne and Aachen to Magdeburg crossed the Weser. An early example of such a grant is that by Otto I in 947, to the abbot and monastery of St Gall, of a mint and market at Rorschach. The grant explains that they were specifically to provide for the needs of merchants travelling to Italy, or those making the pilgrimage to Rome.[3] Mint and market are firmly linked together. Without money there can be no market. It is possible to believe that in the tenth century the circulation of coins for 'commercial' purposes began to be common, at least in parts of Germany. Some of the new mints were, of course, sited where a market already existed, but at least twenty-nine new markets were created by royal grants of privilege over the second half of the tenth century.[4]

The second half of the tenth century therefore saw a revival of minting and of the use of money in the Rhineland and its extension through Saxony to the Elbe. This, however, was only a part, although the central part, of a general revival and extension of minting in western Europe. The last years of the tenth century and the first half of the eleventh were in many ways the most significant period for the early growth of the use of coin in western Europe. One might almost think of this century as witnessing the real start of a money economy in western Europe. Although the foundations of the monetary system had been laid in the seventh and eighth centuries, they only survived into the tenth century in a severely attenuated form. The pattern of pounds, shillings and pence, of counting silver pennies in dozens and scores of dozens survived the period of contraction from the mid ninth to the mid tenth century, but there were not many silver pennies left to count, nor many mints left open to produce more.

The key to this growth in the use of money seems to have been the spread of silver from Saxony, largely through trade. (See Map 9.) If the number and geographical distribution of mints in operation, and the quantity of coin surviving from these mints, are taken as crude measures of the amount of coin that was used, a phenomenal increase and extension can be observed at this time.

From Saxony some silver travelled southwards. Minting therefore could revive not only in the middle Rhineland, but also in the upper Rhineland and, less appreciably, in northern Italy. From the upper Rhineland minting was extended permanently through Bavaria into Bohemia and Hungary, and German silver continued down the Danube to the Black Sea.

[1] Arthur Suhle, *Deutsche Münz- und Geldgeschichte von den Anfängen bis zum 15. Jahrhundert*, 2nd ed. (Berlin, 1964), pp. 46–58.
[2] See above, p. 46.
[3] Wilhelm Jesse (ed.), *Quellenbuch zur Münz- und Geldgeschichte des Mittelalters* (Halle, 1924), doc. 47, pp. 15–16.
[4] Robert Latouche, *The Birth of Western Economy* (London, 1961), p. 255.

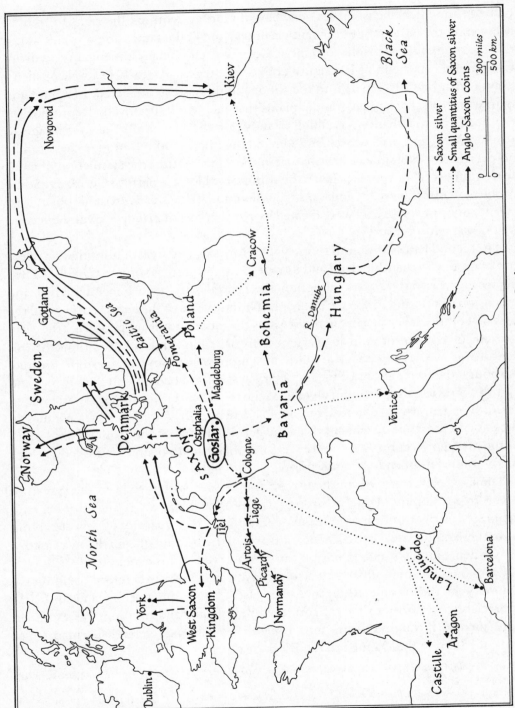

Map 9. Flow of silver from Goslar

From Saxony much silver travelled eastwards through Ostphalia to Poland, where minting began temporarily, and from Poland to Pomerania. A very large proportion of the 'Adelaide–Otto' pfennigs discovered in hoards have come from the area between the Elbe and the Vistula.

From Saxony a great deal of silver travelled northwards to Denmark, and through Denmark to Norway, Sweden, Gotland and the northern Rus. In Denmark, Norway and Sweden it provoked an indigenous coinage.

From Saxony a great deal of silver travelled westwards, to revive coinage in the Meuse valley and among the Frisians, and then across the North Sea to England, where minting was permanently extended from the south-east of the country to York and Chester, and eventually to Ireland.

Minting started rather hesitantly in Denmark and Norway, and soon stopped in Poland and Sweden, and after a longer time in Ireland. However, despite a further general contraction in the later eleventh century and the early twelfth, there was nevertheless a consolidation of minting at this time throughout Europe west of the Elbe, before the next leap forward in minting and the use of coin in the late twelfth century.

The chronology of the revival, or beginning, of minting on all sides of Saxony is remarkably similar. In Bavaria the dukes had taken over the mint at Regensburg in the first wave of 'feudal' devolution and had been minting there in their own names since Arnulf I (911–14 and 919–37).[1] It was this ducal coinage that was at the core of the expansion of coinage in Bavaria, and it was these Bavarian ducal pfennigs that also inspired the type and standard of the first indigenous coinage in Bohemia in the last years of Boleslav I. Ibrahim ben Ya'qub had observed German pfennigs in Prague in 965, although he made no mention of any minting by Boleslav, who was only to reign for a few years longer. What he did observe was the use of squares of cloth as a medium of exchange. The beginnings of coinage so early in the century fit in with the early involvement of the Czechs with the west, for they were the first of the Slav peoples to be tied in with western Europe. They had adopted Christianity in the previous generation, under St Wenceslas and, under Boleslav himself, acknowledged the suzerainty of Otto the Great. By the end of the century there were three mints in Přemyslid Bohemia and two others in the second Czech state, that of the Slavnics of Libice.[2]

---

[1] Walther Kienast, *Der Herzogstitel in Frankreich und Deutschland (9 bis 12 Jahrhundert)* (Munich–Vienna, 1968), pp. 358–9. The early devolution of coinage had been much the same in 'Germany' as in West Frankia. Arnulf had been the first magnate to issue a pfennig in his own name, without that of the king. A generation earlier, Bruno, Duke of the Saxons, had taken the preliminary step of issuing an obol in which he linked his own name with that of his king. The 'feudal' devolution of coinage in 'Germany' had, however, been arrested after these first stages, on the accession of the Saxon dukes to the throne. See below, p. 100.

[2] Stanisław Suchodolski, 'La Genèse de la monnaie indigène dans les pays slaves', *I Międzynarodowy Kongres Archeologii Słowiańskiej*, VI (Warsaw, 1968), 254–65.

The Magyars, having been one of the great scourges of the west for much of the tenth century, were much later in making positive links with it. It was not until St Stephen that they adopted Christianity, and not until his reign that they began to mint their own pfennigs, in 1001 at the earliest. Like the Czech coins, they were derived from the Bavarian type of pfennig, although, again like the Czech coins, they were lighter than their prototypes.[1] From Hungary a certain amount of western silver went on down the Danube. There are reports of it coming downstream to the Black Sea as early as the 970s.

Just as the coinage in Bohemia and Hungary derived from the Bavarian pfennigs, so the coinage of Poland, then focussed on Gniezno, derived from the Sachsen-pfennige minted immediately to the west. They began some time in the 980s, in the latter years of Mieszko I. As in Bohemia and Hungary, the beginning of coinage followed shortly after the adoption of Christianity. Mieszko was baptised in 966. Unlike the Czechs and Magyars the Poles do not seem to have yet been ready for an indigenous coinage. It was struck in very small quantities by Mieszko and his successor, Boleslav the Mighty, and petered out around 1010. Hoard evidence suggests that there was no lack of coins in Mieszko's Poland, first dirhams and then German pfennigs. The problem is to know how these coins were used. By the time that a permanent coinage was established in Poland, under Boleslav the Bold (1058–79), it is clear that coins were being widely used as such. Some historians believe, however, that coin was being used as coin, not merely as one form of silver, as early as Mieszko I.[2] If this was the case, the failure of the initial attempt at coinage is the more puzzling. A peculiarity of these early Polish coins, and perhaps one reason why they did not last, is that they were slightly heavier than their prototypes.[3]

German pfennigs do not seem to have travelled from Poland eastwards to Kievan Russia in large numbers. Nevertheless, at more or less the same time as the new coinages further west, very brief indigenous coinages of gold and silver were struck by Vladimir I in Kiev. As in Bohemia, Hungary and Poland this took place shortly after his conversion in 988. The inspiration for the Kiev coinages, however, came not from German pfennigs, but from the nomisma and the dirham.[4]

However, the main stream of Saxon silver flowed to the north. The Germans obviously bought enormous quantities of furs. Adam of Bremen wrote of 'strange furs, the odour of which has innoculated our world with the deadly poison of pride

---

[1] The weights of Bavarian pfennigs surviving from the end of the tenth century generally lie between 1.24 and 1.28 grams; of Czech pfennigs between 1.15 and 1.22 grams; and of Hungarian pfennigs between 0.75 and 1 gram.

[2] See above, pp. 69–71.

[3] The Sachsenpfennige weigh from 1.33 to 1.55 grams, the Polish derivatives 1.5 to 1.6 grams.

[4] I. G. Spasskij, *The Russian Monetary System*, 3rd ed. (Leningrad, 1962; English trans., Amsterdam, 1967), pp. 53–5.

. . . for right or wrong, we hanker after a martenskin robe as much as for supreme happiness'.[1] Although furs were also to be purchased in Poland and Bohemia, the main supplies came from and through the Baltic. Furs had, of course, been one of the two great staples of the trade with Central Asia that had brought so many dirhams into northern 'Russia' and the Baltic over the previous century. The Germans did not, on the other hand, provide an alternative market for slaves, an even more important commodity than furs in the Central Asian trade. Nevertheless, the quantity of German pfennigs to reach Scandinavian hoards, particularly between 990 and 1040, was on the same scale as the mass of dirhams that had reached Scandinavia between 890 and 965, and been hoarded there. The proportions hoarded naturally change with the distance from their sources. In Denmark, closest to Saxony, more pfennigs (9000) have been found than dirhams (4000), and the same in Norway, 3500 pfennigs against 400 dirhams. In mainland Sweden numbers were more equal: 35,000 pfennigs have been found against 40,000 dirhams. In Gotland, further from Germany and closer to the Rus, and still the place in which most silver was concealed, 40,000 pfennigs have been found against 60,000 dirhams.[2] Enormous numbers of pfennigs have also been found in the fur-producing areas of northern 'Russia' or on the routes to them. The largest hoard of all, some 13,000 West European coins and a single ingot, was found in a copper cauldron in the Ladoga area.[3] Gradually such enormous quantities of coin began to have an impact on attitudes towards it. It gradually ceased, particularly in Denmark and Norway, to be regarded merely as a form of silver like any other. For example, in hoards found in Skåne (then a part of Denmark, now a part of Sweden) coined silver came to exceed uncoined silver, gradually at first and then at the end of the tenth century increasingly rapidly.[4]

At the same time imitative coins began to be minted. After the cessation of minting in the mid ninth century, the next imitative deniers were struck in the Schleswig-Holstein area, probably at Hedeby/Haithabu, in small quantities from

---

[1] *History of the Archbishops of Hamburg-Bremen* IV, 18, trans. F. J. Tschan (New York, 1959), quoted by Gwynn Jones, *A History of the Vikings* (Oxford, 1968), p. 166.

[2] Alfred E. Lieber, 'International trade and coinage in the northern lands during the early Middle Ages', in M. A. S. Blackburn and D. M. Metcalf (eds.), *Viking-Age Coinage in the Northern Lands*, B.A.R. International Series, CXXII (2 vols., Oxford, 1981), p. 21, quoting A. E. Christensen, *Vikingetidens Danmark* (Copenhagen, 1969), p. 196.

[3] Spasskij, *Russian Monetary System*, pp. 57–8.

Hoards deposited between	Coined silver	Uncoined silver
900 and 950	15%	85%
950 and 975	30%	70%
975 and 1000	55%	45%
1000 and 1025	83%	17%
under Svend Estridson (1047–1074)	towards 100%	still a little scrap silver

Kirsten Bendixen, 'The currency in Denmark from the beginning of the Viking Age until *c.* 1100', in Blackburn and Metcalf (eds.), *Viking-Age Coinage*, p. 410.

the middle of the tenth century and in larger quantities from around 975. Unlike the earliest Bohemian, Hungarian or Polish imitations, these were not derived from contemporary German pfennigs. Instead, they were derived from much older coins, primarily from ninth-century Frisian imitations of Charlemagne's deniers struck at Dorestad. Despite the enormous numbers of dirhams that had arrived since, and the German pfennigs that were then arriving, the Hedeby merchant community's notion of what a coin traditionally and properly looked like had become fixed early in the ninth century. These late-tenth-century imitations may have looked 'right', but they were certainly not of the 'right' weight. The Carolingian prototypes had weighed around 1.3 grams; late-tenth-century Sachsenpfennige and Cologne pfennigs still weighed at least that amount; but these late-tenth-century Scandinavian imitations weighed only 0.2–0.25 grams, under a fifth of that weight.[1]

Such exceedingly thin and fragile pieces, not only extraordinarily light, but not even of a fixed weight, stand in stark contrast to the concurrent emphasis on silver as a commodity acceptable by weight. They can only have had a token value, like the contemporaneous pieces of cloth in Prague, divorced from their intrinsic value. As such they obviously had a role to play in local exchanges in Hedeby, although how they were used is not clear to us. They can have been of no use outside the locality until the idea of token coinage spread. Their issue continued through the German occupation of Hedeby, but was replaced soon after the Danes regained it in 983. They were succeeded at Hedeby by other pieces of the same light, fragile, module, although of a different type, like those which had already begun to be produced copiously elsewhere in the Danish kingdom, including Skåne, from Harald Gormsson's last years, *c.* 975–80 onwards. In the last years of the century similar flimsy pieces were also produced in Sweden, possibly in the Mälardal area.[2] This idea of token coinage, which was spreading from Hedeby in the last quarter of the century, was abruptly terminated around the year 1000 when much heavier coins began to be struck not only by Svein Fork-beard in Denmark and Olof Skotkonung in Sweden, but by Olaf Tryggvason in Norway as well. These, in complete contrast with their precursors, were heavier than the foreign coins then coming into Scandinavia, and, like the over-heavy Polish coins, only had a limited lifespan, perhaps for the same reason. In Denmark and Norway these coinages of the year 1000 follow soon after the official acceptance of Christianity by the same kings.

Since in so many kingdoms, Bohemia, Hungary, Poland, Kiev and Norway, the first minting of coins and, in Denmark, a fresh start to the coinage, followed so shortly after the official acceptance of Christianity, it begins to raise suspicions that

---

[1] Brita Malmer, *Nordiska Mynt före år 1000* (Lund–Bonn, 1966), pp. 135–55.
[2] *Ibid.*

this was no mere series of coincidences. The most reasonable hypothesis linking coinage and Christianity seems to be that, along with the official acceptance of Christianity, the rulers of these countries took leading missionaries into the circle of their intimate advisers, and that these men, coming out from societies in which coinage was an accepted and expected attribute of sovereignty, advised their new patrons that they too ought to strike coin. These new coinages also come at a point in time when kingship was being exalted, and contributed to it. Official Christianity and an official coinage both came soon after the first steps towards the making of a monarchical state out of hitherto tribal societies. Among the first coins of Kiev are ones that proclaim 'Vladimir on the throne', of Norway ones that say ONLAF REX NOR, 'Olaf King of the Northmen', and of Bohemia ones that proclaim BOLIZLAVS DVX INCLITVS, 'Boleslav the illustrious duke'; such inscriptions can surely be taken as a propaganda exercise, although how effective such propaganda could be is dubious, since it was written to an illiterate people in Latin, the language as yet only of the few, new, ecclesiastical advisers of the rulers. The early reverse types, even if borrowed, may have been more effective, and these were often propaganda for the Church, not the state: Christ pantocrator in Kiev, a Christian church building in Poland, and the cross, labelled CRVX, in Sweden.

Perhaps because it was a foreign graft, indigenous coinage did not always take. In Sweden it failed quite rapidly and seems to have lasted for an even shorter time than in Kiev or Poland. It was over a century before a permanent coinage was established in Sweden. In Denmark and Norway the early over-weight issues were very hesitant. It was not until Cnut, King from 1018 to 1035, that coinage was firmly established in Denmark and struck at a competitive weight at five well-organised mints. His son, Harthacnut, added three further mints. Nevertheless, foreign coin continued to circulate freely, for a hoard of 1400 coins concealed at Haagerup on the island of Funen in the middle of the century, still contained only 7% of Danish coins against 93% of foreign coins.[1]

As in Sweden the early indigenous coinage started in Norway by Olaf Tryggvason shortly before the year 1000 soon failed. However, unlike Sweden, a fresh start was made, after a pause, by Olaf Haraldsson. This too failed. After another twenty years, Harald Hardråde started minting again, and this time indigenous coinage was permanently established in Norway, around the middle of the eleventh century, struck on the coast at Nidarnes (Trondheim) and inland at Hamar (about 100 kilometres, or 62 miles, north of Oslo). Harald's pennies were of very variable silver content. Initially they were of good silver, up to 97% fine, like their ephemeral precursors, but by 1060 their standard had dropped and after that they were normally more than half copper and zinc and only 25% to 45% silver, and

---

[1] Bendixen, *loc. cit.* 'Currency in Denmark', p. 410.

sometimes even worse.[1] The decline in standard did not pass unremarked and the late sagas enshrine stories relating to this period. These, incidentally, are revealing of attitudes to coinage in a society which had only very recently adopted it.

The *Saga of Harald Hardråde* relates:

On the eighth day after Christmas the men were given their pay. This was called the *Haraldsslátta*, being mostly of copper. At its best it was half silver. When Halldórr (Snorrason) received his pay, he held the money in a fold in his mantle and gazed upon it. The silver did not look fine. He struck his fist with his other hand so that all the money fell down on the straw (floor).

(After Christmas when the king got ready for an expedition against Denmark, Halldórr showed no sign of joining. Bárd, another of the king's followers, tried to mediate between them.)

Halldórr said: 'Why should I serve him any longer, when I don't even get my pay unadulterated?' 'Don't talk about that,' Bárd said, 'you could well bear what noblemen's sons accept without grumbling. You did not behave decently, last time, when you threw the money down on the straw. You must understand, though, that the king regards this as an insult to him.' 'I don't think I have ever been so treacherous when following him, as he was in paying me,' Halldórr said. 'You are quite right,' Bárd said, 'yet wait and let me talk it over with the King!' Bárd actually went to the king again, and begged him to let Halldórr have his pay in good money, which he was surely worth. 'Don't you think it audacious of you,' said the king, 'to ask for other payment for Halldórr than that which sons of noblemen accept, after his contemptuous behaviour when he was last paid?' 'Sire, take into consideration,' Bárd said, 'what is far more valuable: his bravery, your long-lasting friendship – and your own magnanimity. You know Halldórr's harsh temperament, to honour him will be to your glory.' The king said: 'Let him have the silver!' This was done, and Bárd came to Halldórr and brought him 12 aurar (*öre*) of fine silver.[2]

Another story from this period, in the *Faereyinga Saga*, the saga of the Faroe Islanders, reveals that although the Norwegian king was happy to pay out poor coin, he was not happy to receive it.[3]

(Thrand had been gathering in tribute from the Northern Isles, that is, the Faroes and, I think, the Orkneys and Shetlands.)

Leif . . . then asked whether he had got in any tribute from the Northern Isles and how he had managed over the silver. Thrand answered, saying that it had not slipped his memory, and that the tribute should be paid over. 'Here is a purse, Leif, which you shall have, and it is full of silver.' Then Leif went over to Thrand, took the bag and carried it towards the door

---

[1] Kolbjørn Skaare, *Coins and Coinage in Viking Age Norway. The Establishment of a National Coinage in Norway in the XI Century* (Oslo–Bergen–Tromsö, 1976).

[2] *Ibid.* pp. 10–11. The øre, once a unit of weight, the Scandinavian ounce, became a unit of account with the transition from weighing to counting. It came to mean 30 penninger.

[3] Medieval governments frequently had such a double standard towards coin. In the eleventh and twelfth centuries the exchequers of England and Flanders made complex arrangements either to weigh and assay the coin paid in, or to add a surcharge in lieu of weighing and assaying, but paid out by counting.

of the tent, where there was some light. He poured out the silver on to his shield, stirred it about with his hand and called Karl to look at the silver. They examined it for a while and Karl asked what Leif thought of the silver. He said 'It is my opinion that every single bad coin in the Northern Isles has got here . . . I will not deliver this money to the king.'

(There is almost a fight, but finally Thrand offers money which he says his own tenants have brought him this spring.)

Leif took the bag and carried it to Karl. They looked at the money. Leif said: 'No need to look long at this silver. Each coin here is better than the last, and this money we will accept. Get a man, Thrand, to arrange for the counting.' Thrand said it would be best if Leif saw to it for himself. Then Leif and the rest went out a short way from the tent. They sat down and counted the silver.[1]

A story of the payment of a fine, from a generation earlier, points up the transition that had taken place from using silver by weight to using coin by counting. It comes from *Olafs Saga Helga*, referring to the time of St Olaf, King of Norway 1016–28.

Finn shouted to him to bring out the money. Thorir told him to go ashore and then he would bring it. Then Finn and his men went ashore and Thorir came to him and paid out silver. Out of one bag he produced ten marks by weight, and then he took out a number of purses. Some held a mark by weight, others half a mark or perhaps several *öre*.[2]

The flow of silver westwards from Saxony first reached the Rhineland, where the mint at Cologne, which had been closed, became one of the most prolific, if not the most prolific in 'Germany'. Further west, in the Meuse valley, in the Bishopric of Liège, there had been four Carolingian mints (Liège, Maastricht, Huy and Visé), all of which had stopped work by 908. They began to reopen in 983, and by 1006 they were all working again, together with two new mints.[3]

Very little of this silver appears to have gone on into northern France. The late tenth century and the early eleventh have not been particularly remarked as a time when minting noticeably increased or the circulation of money intensified in France.[4] There are a few slight indications that, even so, the new silver had a little impact in the north of the country. In Artois some deniers at least were minted at this time, by Baldwin IV of Flanders (989–1036), and they circulated with pennies of Aethelred II of England. Nothing else had been struck there earlier in the tenth

---

[1] *Faroe Islanders' Saga*, ed. George Johnston (Oberon, Canada, 1975), chapter 45. I am indebted to Dr Hilda Davidson for the translation of this passage.

[2] Snorri Sturluson, *Heimskringla*, 'The Saga of King Olaf the Saint', chapter 149 ('Finn Arneson's Expedition to Halogaland'), Everyman ed., trans. S. Laing (1914), ed. J. Simpson (London, 1964), p. 290.

[3] Hubert Frère, 'Le Droit de monnaie de l'évêque de Liège', *Revue Numismatique*, 6th series, VIII (1966).

[4] Only in the extreme south was the late tenth century and the early eleventh a key time for opening new mints, and this seems to have been through contact with Muslim Spain (Mireille Castaing-Sicard, *Monnaies féodales et circulation monétaire en Languedoc (X^e–XIIIe siècles)*, Cahiers de l'Association Marc Bloch de Toulouse, Études d'Histoire Méridionale, IV (Toulouse, 1961)). The Christian principalities of Spain began to mint their own dineros in the eleventh century; in the county of Barcelona early in the century, in Castille under Fernando I (1035–65), and in Aragon under Sancho Ramirez (1063–94).

century, and very little was to be struck again until after the accession of Philip of Alsace in 1168.[1] As a corollary there is some indication that by the 1020s there was again a little money in circulation in the countryside around Arras, Cambrai and Amiens, and in Vermandois. It has been suggested that it was the manufacture and sale of cloth that had drawn the silver in. The peasantry through whose hands it passed were able to spend some of it on the purchase of iron tools. Nevertheless it was evanescent, and by the end of the eleventh century there was again very little money in the Picard countryside.[2]

Although it barely touched France, the new silver of the late tenth century did much to revive Frisian trade. Near the mouth of the Rhine, the mint at Dorestad, the greatest Frisian port both in the independent Frisian period and under the Carolingians, had closed down in the 870s. Tiel took over its role as the principal Frisian port, but a mint did not open there until the 980s or 990s and only became of considerable importance in the first years of the eleventh century.[3]

The trade of Dorestad was renewed from the port of Tiel, although with a balance slightly different from before. The Frisians still traded up the Rhine, and their merchants could be found from Cologne to Worms, and they still exported Rhineland glass and pottery to Scandinavia. However, they also now traded with the newly-prosperous Saxons, and their merchants could also be found all along the road to Magdeburg, in Dortmund, Soest, Hildesheim and Brunswick. For both Saxony and the Rhineland they were primarily import merchants bringing in merchandise from the Baltic and from England. The balance of trade with the Baltic was grossly in favour of the north. The imports of honey, wax and above all fur greatly exceeded the value of the exports. As a consequence Frisian and Rhenish coins were taken by Frisians in enormous numbers to the Baltic, not only to Sigtuna on the east coast of Sweden, where there was a Frisian merchant guild in the eleventh century, but also to Riga, where there was a Frisian trading-settlement at this time.[4] Riga was a convenient port of entry to reach Smolensk, a central point in the communications system among the northern Rus. The Frisian coins taken to pay for north Russian furs still survive in north Russian hoards in enormous numbers. By themselves they make up a third of the German coins in these hoards, and with the issues of Cologne and Utrecht, a half of them.[5] The other main thrust

[1] Claude Richebé, *Les Monnaies féodales d'Artois du Xᵉ au début du XIVᵉ siècle* (Paris, 1963), pp. 35–46.

[2] Robert Fossier, *La Terre et les hommes en Picardie jusqu'à la fin du XIIIᵉ siècle* (Paris, 1968), pp. 251 and 446. For some evidence of increased circulation in Normandy see Françoise Dumas, 'Les Monnaies normandes (Xᵉ–XIIᵉ siècles)', *Revue Numismatique*, 6th series, XXI (1979), 84–5.

[3] Gert Hatz, 'Tieler Denare des 11 Jahrhunderts in den Schwedischen Münzfunden', in N. L. Rasmusson and L. O. Lagerqvist (eds.), *Commentationes de Nummis Saeculorum IX–XI in Suecia repertis*, II (Stockholm, 1968), 95–190.

[4] Dirk Jellema, 'Frisian trade in the Dark Ages', *Speculum*, XXX (1955), 34–6.

[5] Peter Ilisch, 'German Viking-age coinage and the north', in Blackburn and Metcalf (eds.), *Viking-Age Coinage*, p. 138.

of Frisian trade was with England, and the availability of a greatly increased purchasing power on the part of the Frisians' customers greatly increased the scale of imports from England, so much so that Professor Sawyer has suggested that it was in the late tenth century that England began to take the primacy in European wool production that it was to hold for so many centuries. The large-scale export of wool and cloth from England naturally brought large quantities of German silver into the country.[1] England, at least southern and eastern England, unlike Scandinavia, had been using coin for centuries. The silver from Germany did not, therefore, circulate in England as German coin, but was reminted into English coin. The law that 'there shall run one coinage throughout the realm', which was first promulgated by Athelstan in 930[2] and frequently reiterated, was enforced for centuries as an effective barrier to the circulation of foreign coin in England. As a consequence, instead of a surge of German coin into England, as there was throughout the Baltic, there was a surge in the minting of English coin. The tenth century saw the extension of minting from the south and east into the west of England and into the Midlands even as far as Chester in the north-west, and the resumption of minting at York. The last years of the century saw the very considerable intensification of minting, associated, as in Germany, with 'boroughs' and markets,[3] so that by the early eleventh century money was as commonly in circulation throughout lowland England as in the Rhineland or in Saxony itself. The increase in the number of mints in England was parallel to that in Saxony and, as in Saxony, accelerated at the end of the century. Before the reform of the coinage attributed to Eadgar in 973 there were already over twenty-five mints at work in England. By the end of the century there were seventy. (See Maps 10A and 10B.[4])

The question remains of who was using money by the early eleventh century in Germany and England, and it seems impossible to avoid the conclusion that, in parts of these countries at least, all sections of the community were using coin to a certain extent.

In England the frequent collection of geld, based on land, necessitated the regular accumulation of coin by its payers, which they could only do by selling their agricultural produce for money, or by exacting part of the rents from their tenants in coin. The tenants, in their turn, would need to have sold some of their agricultural produce for money. For example the Berkshire section of the Domesday inquest tells us that whenever a geld was taken in the reign of Edward

---

[1] Peter H. Sawyer, 'The wealth of England in the eleventh century', *Transactions of the Royal Historical Society*, 5th series, xv (1965), 145–64. See above, pp. 28–30 and 52–3, for early Anglo-Frisian trade.
[2] *English Historical Documents*, I, ed. Dorothy Whitelock (London, 1955), 384.
[3] H. R. Loyn, 'Boroughs and mints, A.D. 900–1066', in R. H. M. Dolley (ed.), *Anglo-Saxon Coins: Studies presented to F. M. Stenton* (London, 1961), pp. 122–36.
[4] The maps are derived from those in R. H. M. Dolley and D. M. Metcalf, 'The reform of the English coinage under Eadgar', in Dolley (ed.), *Anglo-Saxon Coins*, pp. 136–68.

Map 10A. English mints, Athelstan to 973. The circles are of 15-mile radius (24 kilometres) to show the areas within market distance of a mint.

Map IOB. English mints 973–1066

the Confessor (1042–66), each hide of land paid 7 pennies in 2 half-yearly instalments.[1] The *Rectitudines Singularum Personarum*, a compilation on the management of an unknown great estate, probably made during the reign of Edward the Confessor, describes how the ordinary unfree, peasant tenant-farmer, the *gebur*, not only rendered labour services to his lord, and paid rent in kind, but also paid 10 pennies at Michaelmas as *gafol* (payment in coin).[2] Various surveys of known estates, such as those of Hurstbourne Priors, Hampshire (*c.* 1050) and Tidenham, Gloucestershire (*c.* 1060), confirm that the Anglo-Saxon peasant was ordinarily paying part of his rent in coin, although not yet, at this period, the major part of it.[3] The measure of the monetary changes of the late tenth century in England, seems to be that by the first half of the eleventh century the minting and circulation of coin had spread to all parts of England, that markets and regular sales for money had come to supplement, if not yet to replace, barter as the normal means of disposing of agricultural surpluses, and that the ordinary peasant in this way had some coin with which to pay at least a part of his rent, and the landholder some coin with which to pay his geld.

Conditions in the Rhineland and Saxony seem to have been comparable with those in lowland England, but it is not clear how far the use of money had developed in other parts of Germany. In Bavaria, for example, the evidence is ambiguous. The survey made in 1031 of the estates of the abbey of St Emmeran, at Regensburg on the upper Danube, where the earliest mint east of the Rhine had started striking two centuries before, superficially suggests that the use of money in early eleventh-century Bavaria was perhaps slightly less widespread than in the Paris basin in the early ninth century.[4] 600 *mansi* on 33 estates produced only 5 pounds, 1200 pfennigs, in coin. This was made up of trifling sums that arose from such peripheral activities as the closing-down of estate workshops for making woollen cloth, and the consequent commutation of the women's workshop services. The abbey still received its 'rent' in kind or in services. At first sight this seems to imply that money barely circulated at the level of the ordinary peasant. On the other hand it could also be a matter of preference for goods and services on the part of the abbey. On an outlying estate, from which it was less convenient to transport produce, the abbey found no difficulty in commuting the rents into money. It received 12 pounds (2880 pfennigs) a year from that estate. Its *censuales* (*cens*-paying dependants) were equally able to raise an annual *chevage* (capitation) in money, and paid the abbey 15 pounds (3600 pfennigs) between them.[5]

From England large quantities of silver pennies were transported to Scandinavia. Part of this no doubt went because of trade, since the English were not averse to

---

[1] *English Historical Documents*, ed. D. C. Douglas and G. W. Greenaway, II (London, 1959), 866.
[2] *Ibid.* p. 814. [3] *Ibid.* pp. 816–18. [4] See above, p. 47.
[5] Philippe Dollinger, *L'Évolution des classes rurales en Bavière* (Paris, 1949), pp. 150 and 145.

wearing Baltic furs, but a larger part was transferred for political rather than commercial reasons. Intermittently from 991 to 1018 the English paid large sums in tribute to the Danes, rising, according to the *Anglo-Saxon Chronicle*, from a payment of 10,000 pounds in 991 to one of 82,800 pounds in 1018. In 1012 King Aethelred II of England began the levy of *heregeld*, a tax used for the maintenance of a standing army of Scandinavian mercenaries to defend the country. It was levied by successive kings at the rate of some 5000 pounds a year until 1051. Thus, if the *Anglo-Saxon Chronicle* is to be believed, something in the region of 200,000 pounds was paid to the Danes as tribute, and a similar sum as wages over a total period of 60 years. If this was all paid in coin, a total of about 100 million pennies was handed over. This seems to be far more than the total amount of coin circulating in England in the first half of the eleventh century,[1] and one must postulate that a great deal of this money was not transmitted across the North Sea, but remained in England. Even if only a proportion of this vast tribute and these continuously paid wages was sent or carried back to Scandinavia, it would easily account for the quantities of English coin found there, without taking any account of trade.

The change of scale between the tribute payments made by the ninth-century Franks and those made by the eleventh-century English is noticeable,[2] particularly as most of the Frankish payments consisted of plate, and most of the Anglo-Saxon of coin. Such a change reflects the great increase in the amount of money in circulation in western Europe, in particular in England.

The end result of these geld payments is that Anglo-Saxon pennies are just under half as common in Scandinavian coin hoards as the pfennigs that had come directly from Germany.[3] Anglo-Saxon pennies passed on with German pfennigs into Pomerania and Poland, as well as into northern 'Russia'. The pennies of Aethelred II provided the prototypes for the new coinages of the year 1000 in Scandinavia, and even vied with German pfennigs as prototypes for some of the coins struck by Slav rulers. At the same time Anglo-Saxon pennies came to circulate freely amongst the Norse settled in other parts of Britain, particularly Ireland. An imitative coinage began to be struck in Dublin under Sihtric Anlafsson, shortly before the year 1000, and continued, eventually in a very degraded form, for a century and a half.[4] Long after the geld payments had ceased, the English went on importing Irish marten-skins and other furs through Chester, and paid for them in silver.

---

[1] In his debate with D. M. Metcalf, Philip Grierson, *Economic History Review*, 2nd series, XVIII (1965) concluded (p. 159) that 'a circulating medium of £60,000–£80,000 looks quite reasonable' about the year A.D. 1000, i.e. 1½–2 million pennies. Metcalf believed it to be much greater.

[2] See above, pp. 61–3.

[3] In Norway, which had the strongest contacts with Britain, 3000 Anglo-Saxon pennies have been found, against 3500 pfennigs; in Denmark 4000 pennies against 9000 pfennigs; in mainland Sweden, 10,000 pennies against 35,000 pfennigs; and in Gotland, 25,000 pennies against 40,000 pfennigs (Lieber, 'International trade in the northern lands', p. 21).

[4] R. H. M. Dolley, *The Hiberno-Norse Coins in the British Museum* (London, 1966).

The silver from Saxony thus set in motion a great chain reaction. The Saxons acquired not only furs from the north and the east and cloth from the west, but also wine from 'France' and from the banks of the Rhine, the Moselle and the Danube, glass and pottery from the Rhineland, salt from various places and 'corn, wax and honey from almost everywhere'.[1]

In all the places to which Saxon silver penetrated the chronology is remarkably similar; a small preliminary expansion in the 970s soon after the discovery of the Harz silver, and then a major expansion from the 990s, reaching a peak around 1025. This pattern is not surprisingly seen most clearly in the arrival of German pfennigs in Scandinavia directly from Saxony. It is only with the arrival of large numbers of Adelaide–Otto pfennigs, first minted around 991, that the flow of silver to the north became really considerable.[2]

In late Anglo-Saxon England the coinage was more closely controlled than anywhere else in Europe. The coinages of the various other Anglo-Saxon kingdoms had come to an end during the Scandinavian onslaught of the ninth century and the coinage of Wessex remained alone, apart from a variety of Danish and Hiberno-Norse penny coinages of not dissimilar type in northern England. With the West Saxon reconquest a uniform coinage was imposed on the whole of England, with only slight regional deviations, as for example in the mints of the north-west. The mint towns had originally been few in number and the bulk of the coinage had been issued at Canterbury and London, but during the tenth century the number of mints increased greatly. In 930 Athelstan stipulated that every borough should have a mint. This did not imply extreme decentralisation, for the dies were cut for the whole country either in a series of regional workshops or in London, and very strict royal control over the coinage was maintained. Over the next two generations the number of mints increased prodigiously, although the extreme of one mint to every borough was never quite achieved.[3] From the 980s, royal control over the coinage was tightened still further. In about 973 Eadgar undertook a general reform of the coinage, which included a complete recoinage of all the old pennies then current, in much the same way that the Carolingians had intermittently carried out similar recoinages.[4] However, about six years later the advisers of the new young king, Aethelred II, carried out a fresh recoinage, and from that time onwards the complete currency was totally reminted at more or less regular intervals and the previous issue demonetised.[5]

---

[1] Latouche, *Western Economy*, p. 256.

[2] Only 171 German pfennigs have been found in Scandinavian hoards buried before 991, but 3322 pfennigs have been found in hoards buried between 991 and the end of the century (Ilisch, 'German Viking-age coinage', pp. 135–6).

[3] See above, p. 87.

[4] See above, pp. 43–4.

[5] Professor Michael Dolley firmly believed that these recoinages were deliberately intended to take place on a fixed

The coins themselves naturally make it clear that a system of renewal was being practised. When such a system was in operation, each successive type had to be clearly and distinctly different from the last, so that the ordinary user could tell whether he had current coin in his hand or not. In Anglo-Saxon England the type of pennies changed quite clearly.[1] The large bulk of the coin in the country should have been reminted fairly soon after a new type was introduced, and in consequence, when the system worked, the stock of money in men's hands was very homogeneous, as the hoard evidence shows. Of thirteen hoards so far discovered that were concealed in the Anglo-Saxon kingdom between about 975 and about 1042, no less than eight contained only pennies minted in one coinage period, whilst the other five contain pennies primarily minted in one period with only a few from the immediately preceding period.[2]

When the coinage was renewed the king took a considerable profit. It seems that on each such occasion the royal moneyers gave out only three new pennies for every four old ones taken in.[3] Such a system of regularly renewed coinage was therefore equivalent to a regular tax of 25% every six years on capital held in the form of coin. It is no wonder that greedy and insecure kings were tempted to renew the coinage more frequently. Harold I did so in 1038 only three years after Cnut had done so, and Harthacnut in 1040 only two years later.[4] From this point onwards the lifetime of a coinage was permanently reduced to two or three years.

It is not clear what effect such a form of taxation had on the economy but it is

six-year cycle. He strongly propounded this theory in Dolley (ed.), *Anglo-Saxon Coins*, pp. 136–87, and in his *Anglo-Saxon Pennies* (British Museum, London, 1964) and defended it in 'Some Irish evidence for the date of the *crux* coins of Aethelred II', in Peter Clemoes (ed.), *Anglo-Saxon England*, II (1973), 145–54. Dr Bertil Petersson believes that they were intended to take place on a seven-year cycle (H. Bertil A. Petersson, *Anglo-Saxon Currency: King Edgar's Reform to the Norman Conquest* (Lund, 1969), p. 87). Professor Grierson, in a presidential address to the Royal Numismatic Society, *Numismatic Chronicle*, 7th series, II (1962), ix–xiv, expressed disbelief in the regularity of the recoinages. C. S. S. Lyon, 'The significance of the sack of Oxford in 1009/1010 for the chronology of the coinages of Aethelred II', *British Numismatic Journal*, XXXV (1966), 34–7, believes that they only gradually became regular.

[1] The 'reform' coinage of Eadgar introduced (using Professor Dolley's chronology) in 973 was distinguished by a small cross. Aethelred's first replacement in 979 was distinguished by the 'hand of God'; the coinage of 985 by a different type of hand; of 991 by a cross separating the word CRVX; of 997 by a long cross; of 1003 by the king wearing a helmet; of 1009 by a small cross again. After an interval of eight years, not six, Cnut introduced a coinage in 1017 with a quatrefoil reverse; in 1023 with himself in a pointed helmet; in 1029 with a short cross; and at the end of his reign in 1035 with a jewelled cross (Gay van der Meer, 'Some corrections to and comments on B. E. Hildebrand's catalogue of the Anglo-Saxon coins in the Swedish royal coin cabinet', in Dolley (ed.), *Anglo-Saxon Coins*, pp. 185–6).

[2] Dolley and Metcalf, 'Reform of coinage under Eadgar', pp. 156–8. How abnormal this was may be gauged by contrasting this situation with that four centuries later. In a hoard concealed at Attenborough in Nottinghamshire around 1420, a quarter of the coins were a century or more old. *British Numismatic Journal*, XXXVIII (1970 for 1969), 50–83.

[3] Petersson, *Anglo-Saxon Currency*.

[4] Whether it was a byproduct of political instability or of the subjects' resistance to too-frequent renewals of the currency is not clear, but at about this time it ceased, temporarily, to be possible to get all the old coin reminted, and a few hoards contain coins of more than two coinage periods (Dolley and Metcalf, 'Reform of coinage under Eadgar', pp. 156–8).

clear that it was one of the contributory factors to the strength of the late Saxon and Norman monarchy in England.[1] It is equally clear that such a system was only applicable in a country which already had a strong governmental organisation to enforce it, and which had a sufficiently developed money-using economy, but a sufficiently small stock of coin for it to be practicable, and in which no foreign coin was allowed to circulate. Such a set of preconditions was not often met with. Apart from the Byzantine Emperors the Anglo-Saxon Kings were unique in their control of their currency at this period. No other rulers, not even the Ottonian Emperors, had so much ability to manipulate the coinage. The large number of mints in England proved invaluable for these frequent total remintings, and there is some evidence to suggest that an attempt was made to ensure that no one should be more than 15 miles (24 kilometres) distant from a mint. A very considerable measure of royal authority is also implied by the way that Anglo-Saxon pennies were of token value rather than intrinsic value. They fluctuated quite considerably in weight and fineness from one issue to the next and yet their value remained constant, since it derived not from their intrinsic worth, but from the word of the king.[2] Elsewhere in western Europe the value of the denier generally depended on its silver content or its supposed silver content. Coin certainly had a premium over uncoined silver, but this premium did little more than cover minting-costs and give a very modest profit to the ruler.

The Normans adopted the Anglo-Saxon system in its entirety. It continued to function, with its profitable remintings at frequent intervals and its basis on royal credit, albeit with a declining number of mints, until the early years of Stephen's reign.[3] The 'anarchy' that followed saw, for the only time in England, the emergence of a feudal coinage and the shattering of royal credit. The feudal coinage was on a very limited scale and the only permanent survival from it became the national coinage of Scotland. After Stephen's reign it was no longer possible to validate the coinage by the authority and credit of the monarchy. Henry II did not try to revive the old system of coinage with its frequent and profitable remintings. Instead he began the series of coinages of fixed types each lasting for many years. He saw to it that, if the coinage had to be based on the intrinsic value of the penny, it should be good, known and stable. He was assisted in this by the vastly increased quantities of silver available in England for coinage from the 1170s.

---

[1] James Campbell, 'Observations on English government from the tenth to the twelfth century', *Transactions of the Royal Historical Society*, 5th series, xxv (1975), 39–54.

[2] Dr Petersson believes that the late Anglo-Saxon penny was 'overvalued in relation to its metal content by $33\frac{1}{3}$%. The conclusion is evident for the entire period between King Edgar's monetary reform and the Norman Conquest' (*Anglo-Saxon Currency*, p. 101).

[3] Edmund King, 'The anarchy of King Stephen's reign', *Transactions of the Royal Historical Society*, 5th series, xxxiv (1984), 148, associates the breakdown of Stephen's control of the coinage with his capture at the battle of Lincoln in February 1141.

Meanwhile a number of other countries had taken up the system of coinage renewal. Around 1075 Harald Hen reformed the coinage of Denmark and attempted a thorough recoinage of all the old and foreign coin circulating in the country, and like Eadgar's reform in England a hundred years before, this was followed by a regular sequence of renewals of the coinage.[1] At about the same time Vratislav II, the first ruler of Bohemia to be dignified as 'king', and Solomon of Hungary reformed their coinages, and regular renewals of the coinage followed. In Poland Boleslav III (1102–38) reformed the coinage, and his successors embarked on the system of *renovatio monetae* and so did a number of German colonial principalities, after the breakdown of imperial control, in the twelfth and thirteenth centuries.[2] In all four kingdoms there was a relatively strong central authority, monarchy having succeeded directly to tribal organisation, a developing market structure (perhaps as many as a hundred weekly markets in twelfth-century Poland), and a relatively small coinage (perhaps as few as a million pfennigs in twelfth-century Poland).[3] Some of the same features can be seen as earlier in Anglo-Saxon England. The greed or need of the ruler reduced the length of time between renewals, sometimes quite remarkably. In 1118 the Kings of Bohemia began to renew their coinage every six months, and in 1267 they were still doing so.[4] Such frequent renewals brought complaints and petitions. In 1276 the Archbishop of Magdeburg, on request, agreed not to renew his coinage more than once a year.[5] By these standards the Teutonic Knights who promised, when they introduced the system of renewal in 1233, only to renew the coinage every tenth year, seem extremely moderate, particularly as they promised to give as many as 12 new pfennigs for 14 old ones on renewal. The contrast is dramatic between the variety of types of pennies produced in sequence in these countries on the margins of Europe and the immobilised types produced for long periods in what were becoming 'Germany', 'the Netherlands' and 'France', 'Italy' and 'Spain', as well as in England after Henry II.

The flow of silver from the Harz was relatively short-lived. It reached a peak around 1025 and diminished rapidly after 1040, although a very little silver-mining was still being carried out near Goslar over a century later. The effects were

---

[1] Bendixen, 'Currency in Denmark', pp. 412–13. She bizarrely calls this the introduction of 'feudal' coinage, although the very fact of complete recoinage implies that the apparatus of the state lay in the hands of the king and was not devolved into the hands of feudatories. 'Feudal' coinage is typified much more by the immobilised coin-type than the frequently renewed coin-type.

[2] Stanisław Suchodolski, 'Renovatio Monetae in Poland in the 12th century', *Wiadomości Numismatyczne*, v (1961), 57–75.

[3] A relatively small coinage meant that a recoinage could be undertaken very rapidly. In Hungary in 1271 six weeks was allowed for a recoinage; in the bishopric of Merseburg in 1255 four weeks; and in thirteenth-century Poland it was supposed to be done 'per tria fora', in three consecutive weekly markets.

[4] Jesse, *Quellenbuch*, doc. 131.

[5] *Ibid.* doc. 134.

naturally first felt on the spot. The distinctive pfennigs minted in the name of the Empress Adelaide and her grandson Otto III since 991 ceased to be struck around 1040. The impoverishment of Saxony after a half-century of prosperity no doubt contributed to the disorders that marked the second half of the eleventh century in Saxony. The decline in imperial revenues from mining and minting served to underline the weakness of Henry III and Henry IV compared with their predecessors.

The shrinkage of supplies of new silver from Saxony had a contracting effect on all sides. No longer was there a strong pole of attraction for consumer goods among the Saxon nobility.

The lack of silver to the south of Saxony can be seen in the inability of the Dukes of Bavaria to continue minting pfennigs after Heinrich VII (who died in 1047) for three quarters of a century.[1]

The lack of fresh silver supplies flowing to the east became visible as the dearth of coin in Poland towards the end of the eleventh century. It was not for another century that adequate supplies of coin were to be available for 'town–country relations to be saturated with coin'.[2]

In the north the demand for furs must have dwindled away in the middle of the century, for the quantities of German pfennigs arriving in Scandinavia and the other Baltic lands slowly decreased after 1040, if hoard evidence is to be believed.[3] It has been suggested that the marked deterioration in the silver content of the Norwegian penny under Harald Hardråde, beginning before 1060, was caused simply by the inability to acquire enough silver to mint better coins.

To the west the lack of silver was soon felt in the Rhineland. Although the Cologne mint, the most prolific in Germany in the first half of the century after that at Goslar, did not close, unlike many other mints, it struck very little from the archbishopric of St Anno in the 1070s until that of Archbishop Philip of Heinsberg, in the 1170s.[4]

If silver was lacking in the Rhineland, it also began to disappear in the Meuse valley and further west. At the abbey of St Trond the faithful no longer brought offerings of money, but offerings of goods, 'animalia, palefridos, boves et vaccas, verres, arietes, oves . . . linum et caera, panes et casei', so much so that the custodians were utterly worn out with coping with the offerings that were being received. The author of this description optimistically estimated that these offerings were then, sometime between 1055 and 1082, worth 100 pounds a week.[5]

---

[1] Kienast, *Der Herzogstitel in Frankreich*, pp. 358–9.
[2] See Stanislaw Tabaczynski, 'Circulation monétaire dans les villes polonaises au haut moyen-âge vue à la lumière des recherches récentes', *Atti del VI Congresso Internazionale delle Scienze Preistoriche* (1966), 210.
[3] Ilisch, 'German Viking-age coinage', p. 140.
[4] See below, p. 95.
[5] Quoted by Fernand Vercauteren, 'Monnaie et circulation monétaire en Belgique et dans le nord de la France du

However, it was the Frisians who suffered most from the renewed collapse of trade. The short-lived revival focussed on Tiel came to an end, and the pfennigs minted at Tiel declined sharply both in numbers and in silver content after 1040.[1] When revival came again at the end of the twelfth century, it passed by Tiel, and the Frisians were overshadowed by merchants from the newer centres of Flanders and the Hanse, and by the merchants of Cologne, who then dominated the lower Rhine and sent vessels overseas directly from Cologne.

The collapse of Frisian trade cut off the supplies of new silver to England and the sagging demand for wool and cloth brought about a general malaise in English commerce that has sometimes been misconstrued as a nefarious side-effect of the Norman conquest of the country, rather than as part of a general North European recession. In England the decline in the availability of money began around the 1070s and is most marked. A tentative estimate of the circulating medium in England around the year 1000 was in the order of 20 million pennies and rising rapidly despite geld payments to the Danes. A similar tentative estimate of the circulating medium around 1158 was of the order of 10 million pennies.[2]

Outside the area directly affected by the rise and fall of Goslar silver there was also a general retreat from silver. The Central Asian mines, from which the Scandinavians had been cut off in the 960s, soon afterwards went into decline. As a consequence the Muslim states of the Middle East gradually gave up minting silver coin. In the Byzantine Empire, which at this period largely relied on the Muslim world for its silver,[3] the striking of silver coin was much reduced. Miliaresia of the tenth century are today very common, but those of the eleventh century are rare. Byzantine emperors reduced in turn the output, the weight and the fineness of the miliaresion until, in the 1090s, Alexius I abandoned the striking of silver altogether. After 1092 the miliaresion was only a unit of account, one twelfth part of a nomisma.[4]

It is not clear whence Italy drew its silver at this time, and there are contradictory indications about what was happening there. In some areas of activity the use of money was increasing in Italy when it was decreasing elsewhere. For example, in the hinterland of Genoa and Lucca rents in kind gave way to rents in money in the course of the eleventh century, and in the Campania the exploitation of estates began with labour hired for money wages.[5] Yet a group of North Italian charters

---

VIᵉ au XIᵉ siècle', in *Moneta e scambi nell'alto medioevo*, Settimane di studi del Centro Italiano di Studi sull'alto medioevo, VIII (Spoleto, 1961), p. 302.

[1] Hatz, 'Tieler Denare', pp. 119–27.   [2] See below, pp. 196–7.

[3] Although it had some silver-mines of its own in the north-eastern parts of Asia Minor (S. Vryonis, 'The question of Byzantine mines', *Speculum* (1962), 1–17).

[4] Philip Grierson, *Catalogue of Byzantine coins in the Dumbarton Oaks Collection*, vol. III (Washington, 1973), pp. 67–8.

[5] Philip Jones, 'Medieval agrarian society in its prime: Italy', in *Cambridge Economic History of Europe*, 2nd ed., I (Cambridge, 1966), 400.

suggest that the use of money was disappearing there as elsewhere. Between 1075 and 1140 there are frequent references to money substitutes that can be used to fulfil contracts instead of coin. Equivalents for the sum to be paid are stipulated in cattle or in goods, including pepper in Lombardy and gold in Tuscany. Yet even at the lowest point of the movement away from money, over 40% of contracts only specified payment in silver denari.[1] Northern Italians, even at a low point in the use of money, in their own terms, were still using coin a great deal more often than other Europeans. This slight retreat from the use of money has been interpreted as a reaction to inflation, itself a result of too much poor money from Pavia, rather than as a reaction to a dearth of money. On the other hand, evidence from central Italy, from Rome and Latium, shows no retreat from the use of money to money substitutes there. Such means of payment were extremely rare.[2] Italy's foremost place in the use of money is not in doubt, but whether it was advancing or retreating in the late eleventh and early twelfth century is not at all clear.

It was just at this time that a new means of draining Europe of coin was developed, the crusade. The cost of crusading was crippling. Just as a national war could empty a single country like England of a large part of its, by then plentiful, coinage under John or Edward I, so a crusade could do it for a whole continent, particularly at a time when the currency was not being renewed by vigorous mining of silver. The efforts to raise the money to participate in the First Crusade were prodigious. In order for the great hero of the First Crusade, Godefrey of Bouillon, to go on it at all, he had to sell his allodial estate of Bouillon itself. The Bishop of Liège agreed to buy it for 1300 marks of silver and 3 marks of gold, but the bishop did not himself have such a sum. He had to go round the abbeys of his diocese seeking for this amount. He could not raise it in money, as there was no longer this amount of money circulating in the area, so he was reduced to pillaging shrines, even ripping the gold plates off the reliquary of St Lambert himself, the patron saint of Liège. A lesser northern noble, Baldwin of Ghent, also wishing to go on the First Crusade, mortgaged his *curtis* of Ootegan to a local abbey for 42 marks – and again this had to be raised, in part out of silver plate, and with difficulty. To mount an undertaking as large as the First Crusade in an era when money was in such short supply was unendingly beset with difficulties. The larger part of the proceeds of these sales and mortgages was carried out of Europe, never to return. The scouring of Europe for coin and plate in the 1090s for the First Crusade was only the beginning of the cost. The maintenance of the Christian states in the Holy Land was a perpetual drain on western resources. The military

---

[1] David Herlihy, 'Treasure hoards in the Italian economy, 960–1139', *Economic History Review*, 2nd series, x (1957–8), 1–14; but see below, pp. 201–2.

[2] Pierre Toubert, *Les Structures du Latium médiéval . . . du IXᵉ à la fin du XIIᵉ siècle*, Bibliothèque des Écoles françaises d'Athènes et de Rome ccxxi (Rome, 1973), pp. 602–8.

orders acted as funnels into which money, if it could be had from rents, or the sale of demesne produce, was continuously poured from their estates in the west. In the 1140s and again in the 1180s the widespread sales and mortgages of estates began again for the participants in the Second and Third Crusades. Between the crusades individual men went on expeditions to the East and had to do the same. There were lesser nobles like Odo of Hellain, who raised only $5\frac{1}{2}$ marks on mortgage to take on his visit to Jerusalem in 1162, or great men, like Godfrey III, Duke of Brabant, who mortgaged his fief of Herstal to the Bishop of Liège for 300 marks before his departure for Jerusalem in 1171.[1] All this reduced the circulating medium in the west to the point at which very many of the mints of the 'Ottonian' period were closed for long periods and the use of money was in retreat.

Some of the coin taken overland by crusaders never reached the Holy Land. It was nevertheless withdrawn from circulation in western Europe. In 1147, French and German participants in the Second Crusade left a trail of deniers from Normandy and Champagne, and pfennigs from the Rhineland, Franconia, Bavaria and Austria, along their route. They have been found in what was then the kingdom of Hungary at Esztergom and Zombor on the Danube, and in the Byzantine Empire in the Maritza valley near Adrianople, and in Thrace and on the south coast of Asia Minor at Antalya and Side.[2]

From the 1160s onwards there were renewed supplies of silver available in Europe and on the basis of these a total transformation took place of practically every facet of the economy and of society in which money was involved.[3] The coinages that the new Europe inherited in the 1160s were not, however, the same as the coinages of the 860s. In the intervening centuries the use of money in society had not merely contracted, expanded and contracted again within the same framework. The remarkable geographical expansion in the use of coined money was one way in which the framework had changed at the point when the building of new states, a second great surge of missionary activity, and a temporary outpouring of abundant supplies of newly-mined silver had coincided. Another way in which the framework had changed was by fragmentation. The political fragmentation by feudal devolution in West Frankia in the ninth and tenth centuries was only a part of this general fragmentation. At the beginning of the ninth century coin had been struck throughout western Europe by no more than two authorities, that of Charlemagne and that of Offa, and the deniers and pennies that they had minted were intended to be of the same standard of weight and fineness

---

[1] Hans van Werveke, 'Monnaies, lingots ou marchandises? Les instruments d'échange aux XIe et XIIe siècles' (1932), and 'Le Mort-Gage et son rôle économique en Flandre et en Lotharingie' (1929), reprinted in *Miscellanea mediaevalia* (Ghent, 1968), p. 200 and pp. 169–72.

[2] Philip Grierson, 'A German crusader's hoard of 1147 from Side (Turkey)', in T. Fischer and P. Ilisch (eds.), *Lagom* (Munster, 1981), pp. 195–203.

[3] See the next seven chapters.

throughout, whether in the Spanish March or in Frisia, in Rome or in Canterbury.

By the middle of the twelfth century it was quite otherwise. Not only had the mints in France fallen generally into the hands of counts, and in some cases bishops and abbots, but in Germany the authority to mint had also become widely dispersed. In Germany, apart from that in the hands of the Duke of Bavaria, such mints as went on working were in imperial or royal hands until the latter part of the tenth century. It was only in the middle of the tenth century that Otto I began to give away imperial mints and grant the right to open new mints. His successors, particularly Otto III, continued the process more rapidly.[1] The beneficiaries were very often abbeys or bishops, and only very occasionally laymen. In this way the fragmentation of minting in Germany took on a peculiarly ecclesiastical complexion that it did not do in France. This, of course, fits in with a general preference to delegate authority to ecclesiastics rather than laymen by the Ottonian rulers, in an attempt to prevent an overstrong, hereditary, lay, feudal hierarchy developing. Charges given to bishops or abbots were likely to remain public offices longer than those granted to laymen, which they tended to treat as heritable private property. The imperial–papal clashes of the later eleventh century weakened imperial control over German churchmen and so over the public offices that they held. Minting therefore largely ceased to be an imperial concern by the end of the eleventh century. Imperial pfennigs continued to be struck in a limited number of imperial towns, but were lost in the great variety of German pfennigs struck by an enormous diversity of mints, mostly under some sort of ecclesiastical control. The initial fragmentation of coinage in Germany, therefore, took place much later than in France and was much more ecclesiastical than 'feudal' in its flavour. In Italy imperial control remained strong for a much longer period. In 1100 there were still only four mints in Italy north of Rome. They were at Milan, Pavia, Lucca and Venice, and all of them had been in more or less continuous operation since Carolingian times, although they had often produced only very minute quantities. It was only in the twelfth century, when centralisation was under way in France, that fragmentation began to take place in Italy. The new mints in Italy were not, however, generally in the hands of either lay feudatories or ecclesiastics as they were in France and Germany respectively. Instead they passed directly to the towns, a natural reflection of the different political and economic structures developing there. This was a very late development and really fits with the next period of expansion. In Tuscany, for example, the old imperial mint at Lucca gradually passed into communal hands, but it was not until 1151 that a second mint was opened in Tuscany, that at Pisa, the seaport of Tuscany.[2]

In England, apart from the brief 'feudal' episode in Stephen's reign, there was no

---

[1] See above, pp. 76–7.
[2] See below for the continuation of this development, p. 189.

real fragmentation of minting. The Archbishops of Canterbury and York, the Bishop of Durham and the Abbot of Bury St Edmunds had the right to mint, but they always did so in the King's name, using dies engraved by royal die-cutters. Only the profit went to the bishop or abbey.

The political fragmentation of the right to mint made no difference to the use of the money minted in itself, but a variety of issuers tended to adjust the standards of weight and fineness to suit their own interests, so gradually breaking up the uniformity of the coinage and producing different standards, sometimes amazingly different, for coins that were still all nominally the same. Until the developments of the thirteenth century all the enormous variety of pieces struck were still nominally pennies, by one name or another – deniers, pfennigs, or denari – but there was now a seemingly infinite variety of types and a wide range of weights and fineness. No longer was a denier in one place equal to a denier in another. No longer was a livre, i.e. 240 deniers, in one place equal to a livre in another. It became necessary to specify the currency in which a sum was being expressed, money of Pavia, or Cologne or Toulouse, not merely to express it as an unlabelled sum of pounds, shillings and pence. This took place only gradually. For example in Latium large sums were expressly called money of Pavia in the mid eleventh century, whilst small ones were still expressed in denari without qualification.[1]

The process of divergence that lay behind this need to label currencies naturally went back to the very moment of the first usurpation of the right of minting by the greatest Carolingian feudatories. (See Table 2.)

By the time that the Rennes hoard was concealed in the 920s, there was already considerable divergence from the 1.7 gram standard set by Charlemagne in 794. The norm was now 1.5 grams, but the deniers of Saint Denis still weighed 1.64 grams, whilst those of Orléans now weighed only 1.34 grams. Sixty years later the Fécamp hoard shows how the divergence from the Carolingian standard had increased. The norm was now 1.25 grams, but the deniers of Sens still weighed 1.45 grams, whilst the denier of Paris weighed only 0.99 grams. The next twenty years saw very little deterioration. The norm for deniers in the Le Puy hoard was still 1.2 grams and the heaviest deniers in the hoard were those of Limoges at 1.44 grams and the lightest those of Arles at 0.92 grams. But the divergence from weight standard was only a part of the story. Analysis of the 'Gratia Dei Rex' coins struck after the edict of Pîtres in 864 shows that they were struck of 93% to 94% fine silver. Analysis of coins in the Fécamp hoard, 120 years later, shows that they were normally of silver 70% to 75% fine, but the best ones, which included some of the heaviest ones, like the deniers of Limoges and Bruges, were over 80% fine, whilst the worst ones, which included some of the lightest ones, like the deniers of Paris

---

[1] Toubert, *Latium médiévale*, p. 578.

Table 2. *Weight and fineness of deniers, tenth to twelfth centuries*

N.B. Charlemagne's deniers 794 onwards weight 1.7 grams (0.96 fine).

	920s	980s	first half of eleventh century	c. 1050–1075	c. 1125–1130	c. 1160	c. 1200
English mints	1.33 grams	1.26 grams				1.46 grams (0.925 fine)	1.46 grams (0.925 fine) [1.35 grams fine]
Limoges		1.4 grams (0.8+fine)	1.44–1.25 grams				
Saint Denis	1.64 grams	1.23 grams					
Cologne		1.18 grams	1.3 grams	1.4–1.2 grams	1.46 grams	1.4 grams (0.925 fine)	[1.3 grams fine]
Tiel			1.3 grams	0.92 gram			
Trier					0.97 gram (0.83 fine)		
Toulouse							1.14 grams (0.58–0.5 fine) [0.66–0.57 gram fine]
Milan					[0.6 gram fine]	imperiali 1 gram (0.5 fine)	1 gram (0.5 fine) [0.5 gram fine]
Rouen		1.21–1.13 grams (0.5+ fine)	0.96–0.7 gram				
Paris		0.99 gram (0.5+ fine)				1.28–0.85 gram!	1.04 grams (0.375 fine) [0.39 gram fine]
Melgueil					1.1 grams (0.42 fine)		1.12 grams (0.33 fine) [0.37 gram fine]
Jacca (Aragon)						1.08 grams (0.33 fine)	
Provins							1.09 grams (0.33 fine) [0.36 gram fine]
Flanders			<1 gram				0.42 gram (0.83 fine) [0.35 gram fine]
Fulda (bracteate)						0.83 gram	

Table 2. *cont.*

	920s	980s	first half of eleventh century	*c.* 1050– 1075	*c.*1125– 1130	*c.* 1160	*c.* 1200
Tours (royal mint)							0.95 gram (0.35 fine) [0.33 gram fine]
Tours (abbey mint)							0.95 gram (0.33 fine) [0.31 gram fine]
Barcelona				1.14 gram (0.33 fine)		0.66 gram (0.2 fine)	0.92 gram (0.33 fine) [0.3 gram fine]
Provence							0.92 gram (0.303 fine) [0.28 gram fine]
Pavia	1.47 grams	1.4–1.27 grams			[0.68 gram fine]	[0.22 gram fine]	[0.22 gram fine]
Lucca					[0.65 gram fine]	0.6 gram (0.6 fine)	0.25 gram (0.7 fine) [0.18 gram fine]
Verona					[0.35 gram fine]	[0.1 gram fine]	[0.1 gram fine]
Venice					[0.35 gram fine]	[0.05 gram fine]	[0.05 gram fine]
Le Puy					1 gram+ (0.19 fine)		

Weights expressed in grams.
Fineness in parentheses. Pure silver=1.
Weight of silver in denier in square brackets, in grams of fine silver.

and Rouen, were between 50% and 60% fine. By the middle of the eleventh century the Rouen deniers weighed only 0.7 grams and were under 50% silver.[1]

By the end of the eleventh century the heaviest and finest deniers, like those of Maine and Toulouse, were worth 2 deniers of neighbouring counties. The deniers of the county of Maine were double those of the counties of Anjou or Touraine, the deniers of Toulouse double those of Melgueil. The worst deniers, like those of the Bishop of Le Puy, 'pougeoises', were worth a half of most of their neighbours' deniers, like those of Melgueil, and consequently a quarter of some, like those of

[1] Dumas, 'Monnaies normandes', pp. 30–45.

Toulouse. As a consequence 'pougeoise' became a name for the farthing. The difference was not so much in weight as in fineness. Around 1125–30 the deniers of Le Puy were only 2¼d. fine (19% silver), those of Melgueil 5d. fine (42% silver), and those of Toulouse 10d. fine (83% silver).[1]

In Germany the same sort of divergence began rather later. From the moment that minting revived in the tenth century and that mints were granted out, the process began. By 1030 the pfennigs of Cologne, Tiel and Westphalia still weighed 1.3 grams, but pfennigs of Mainz weighed only 1.0 grams, and those of Bruges and Utrecht even less. The monetary uniformity created by the reforms of Charlemagne was long since lost both in France and in Germany.[2] The so-called 'period of regional pfennigs' had begun. A century later the divergence within the empire had gone even further. Local rulers in the southern and western parts of the empire (Italy, the Rhône valley, Bavaria, Lorraine, the Rhineland, Frisia and parts of Franconia and Swabia) continued to issue ordinary silver deniers. On the other hand, from around the 1130s, local rulers in the east (along the Baltic, and in Saxony, Thuringia and the remainder of Franconia and Swabia) struck paper-thin pfennigs or deniers commonly called bracteates. They were struck on very thin silver wafers. They had only an obverse design, the reverse being hollowed out to match the obverse type. They are considerably lighter than the normal pfennigs and of very slight intrinsic value. In Poland, Silesia and Bohemia, the minting of bracteate denars also replaced that of the heavier denar in the last quarter of the twelfth century and the first years of the thirteenth. Bracteate denars similarly replaced the heavier denars in Hungary under Béla IV (1235–70) and in Sweden at the same time. In many places the issue of bracteate pfennigs was associated with a regular renewal of the complete currency at intervals, not unlike that in late Anglo-Saxon and Norman England. As then, it was a symptom of a relatively strong central control over a not very highly-developed economy. The bracteate pfennigs' lack of intrinsic value was therefore of little importance, since their local value was a token one. For long-distance transactions silver was carried about in the form of ingots. The fragility of the bracteate pfennigs was also of little importance, since they were designed to circulate only over a limited area and for a limited period. In the most extreme cases the coinage was totally renewed after circulating for only six months.

In Cologne at the end of the twelfth century 160 pfennigs were being minted from the mark weight of silver, whilst in the 'bracteate' area, 320 pfennigs were often being struck from a marked weight.[3] In others words they were only half the weight of the Cologne pfennigs and rapidly getting lighter, whilst the Cologne pfennig retained its weight.

---

[1] See Appendix 1, pp. 397–8 for medieval methods of expressing fineness.
[2] Ilisch, 'German Viking-age coinage', p. 131.   [3] Suhle, *Deutsche Münz- und Geldgeschichte*, pp. 86ff.

Whereas in the areas where the *renovatio monetae* was practised it was essential that only one coinage should circulate, elsewhere a mixture of currencies circulated. In southern France, the Rhineland or the southern Netherlands the mixture was extraordinarily broad; some currencies were conveniently worth double others, but less convenient relationships also existed. In 1156, 15 sous of the money of Narbonne were worth 12 sous of the money of Melgueil. The deniers were remarkably similar and circulated together on the coastal plain of Languedoc.

Taking a view right across Europe, the heaviest coinages on the eve of the great expansion of the late twelfth century were the sterling pennies of England and the pfennigs of Cologne weighing 1.4 grams each, of silver 92% fine, whilst at the other extreme the poorest coinages were the dineros of Barcelona, weighing only 0.66 grams and only 20% fine; the denari of many North Italian cities, which were slightly lighter, but half silver; and the bracteates.

The new silver thus came into a society that was not only thoroughly fragmented politically, but was using a thoroughly fragmented and regional currency, with only rudimentary attachment to the currency that had been equally valid all over Carolingian Europe. One of the first results of the new silver was an enormous increase in the number of 'rulers' minting. The heyday of 'feudal' coinage was not at the time when political authority in West Frankia was most dispersed and devolved, at the end of the tenth century, but in the late twelfth and early thirteenth century, when the new supplies of silver allowed every minor baron of the Gard hills or the Limburg heathlands to run a mint. Such a total devolution of the rights of coinage lasted, however, very briefly indeed, for royal power was rapidly increasing in France at this very time. In the course of the thirteenth century successive kings of France did their best to ensure that royal coinages should oust feudal coinages wherever possible. The coinage inherited by the new Europe of the long thirteenth century, therefore, looked to be rapidly becoming more and more fragmented and localised, but in fact, although at first accelerated, the trend was soon to be reversed, and national and international coinages were soon to dominate the scene.

PART II

---

*The Commercial Revolution
of the Thirteenth Century*

5

New Silver c. 1160 – c. 1330

The German humanist, Georgius Agricola, writing on the spot, but in the 1540s, related the traditional story of the discovery of the first major new source of silver in Europe since that at Goslar:

It came about by chance and accident that the silver mines were discovered at Freiberg in Meissen. By the river Saale . . . is Halle . . . famous and renowned for its salt springs . . . When some people were carrying salt from there in wagons . . . they saw lead ore (*galena*) in the wheel tracks, which had been uncovered by the torrents. This lead ore, since it was similar to that of Goslar, they put into their carts and carried to Goslar, for the same carriers were accustomed to carry lead from that city. And since much more silver was smelted from this ore than from that of Goslar, certain miners went at once to that part of Meissen in which is now situated Freiberg, a great and wealthy town; and we are told by consistent stories and general report that they grew rich out of the mines.[1]

According to Agricola, this happy accident had taken place some 380 years earlier, in other words in the 1160s, in the reign of the Margrave Otto of Meissen.

In 1189, towards the end of his reign, Otto, nicknamed, unsurprisingly, 'the Rich', had the contents of his treasury seized by the Bohemians. A contemporary annalist estimated that it contained more than 30,000 marks of silver.[2] Most of this presumably took the form of thousands of mark bars of silver.[3] Had it been minted into the very light bracteate pfennigs struck for Otto in his numerous mints, it would have made some 10 millions of them.[4] This was only the residue of Otto's dramatically increased silver revenues after very considerable war expenditure. Otto does not appear to have deliberately accumulated treasure. On the contrary he had invested vast sums, specifically recognised by contemporaries as derived from his mining-wealth, in extensive land purchase in Thuringia, so much so that he had antagonised the Count of Thuringia, who had seized Otto in 1182 and only let him

---

[1] Georgius Agricola, *De veteribus et novis metallis* (Basle, 1546), p. 397. Translation adapted from that in notes to Georgius Agricola, *De re metallica*, trans. and ed. H. C. and L. H. Hoover (London, 1912), pp. 35–6. And see Map 11, p. 110.

[2] 'Annales Pegavienses', *Monumenta Germaniae Historica*, Scriptores, XVI (Hanover, 1859), 266–7.

[3] See below, pp. 209–24.

[4] Otto's bracteate pfennigs weighed just under a gram each, so that more than 300 were struck from every mark.

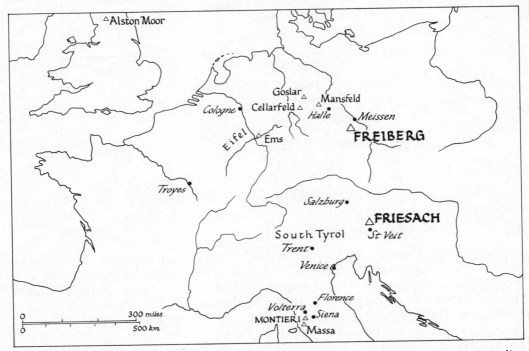

Map 11. European silver-mines *c.* 1170 – *c.* 1230. Places connected with mines are in italic.

go at the injunction of the emperor. Not only had he invested silver in land, he had also spent it freely for the good of his subjects and the good of his soul. For his subjects he had, *inter alia*, financed the building of new town walls at Leipzig, Eisenberg, Oschatz and Weissenfels, as well as Freiberg itself. For his soul he had deposited 3000 marks of silver at the monastery of Zella to be divided, after his death, among the churches around.[1] And still, in the middle of a war, he had 10 million pfennigs-worth of silver in his treasury. His share of the silver mined was probably a tenth of the declared product of the mines, as it was later to be for his successors. Therefore 10 million pfennigs-worth in the treasury by itself represented 100 million pfennigs-worth of silver mined. How many hundreds of millions of pfennigs-worth of silver had been mined over the previous twenty years we cannot tell. Every 100 million pfennigs-worth of silver represented an average annual production of around 4 tons of silver. From its impact it is likely that in its heyday the production from the mines at Freiberg was comparable with that from the mines at Kutná Hora in Bohemia, or at least that from the mines of Schwaz in the Tirol, in their turn the richest in Europe. At the beginning of the fourteenth century the Kutná Hora mines were producing between 20 and 25 tons of silver a year, and at the end of the fifteenth century those at Schwaz were producing some 11 tons of

[1] Walther Herrmann, 'Bergbau und Kultur', *Freiberger Forschungshefte*, series D, II (1953), 22.

silver a year.[1] It is not likely that the Freiberg mines were even more productive, although Professor Bolin in one case was prepared to accept a higher estimate for the production of silver from medieval mines. He believed that those at Shâsh (Tashkent) in Transoxiana produced as much as 30 tons of silver a year in the early ninth century.[2]

What difference was made to the circulating medium of Europe over a period of twenty years by the addition of silver worth hundreds of millions of pfennigs? We have as yet no idea at all of the quantity of coin already circulating in Europe as a whole in the 1160s. It has been suggested that some 10 million pennies, admittedly nearly twice as heavy as the Meissen pfennigs, were recoined in England in 1158, and that this was then the larger part of the circulating medium of a country peculiarly rich in coinage.[3] These hundreds of millions of pfennigs-worth of new silver were, however, only a beginning. Professor Nef has guessed that, from the 1160s to the 1320s, there were few decades in which the production of precious metals in Europe did not increase.[4]

The traditional source of silver in Europe, the mines in the Rammelsberg near Goslar in the Harz, had been producing less and less silver since the 1040s, and by the time that the Freiberg silver was discovered, they were nearly exhausted.[5] Although payments were still being specified in Cologne in the 1170s in ingots of silver from Goslar (*examinati argenti, quod Ramisberch appellatur*),[6] the Goslar mines were as much known in the twelfth century for their copper as their silver,[7] and when the famous German Dominican scholar Albertus Magnus was writing his *Book of Minerals* in the mid thirteenth century he regarded Goslar only as a source for copper.[8] In the intervening years, the once prolific mines of Goslar, which had formerly been the prime European source of silver, had been totally superseded by those of Freiberg. In fact the only source of silver that Albertus considered worth mentioning by name was Freiberg,[9] although he was clearly conscious of other sources, for he wrote of silver ore found in four forms, and only when he came to the fourth sort of ore did he specify: 'And it is found in earth as a sort of vein purer

[1] See below pp. 124–5 and p. 363.
[2] Sture Bolin, 'Mohammed, Charlemagne and Ruric', *Scandinavian Economic History Review*, I (1953), 21.
[3] See below, pp. 136–7.
[4] 'Mining and metallurgy in medieval civilization', in *Cambridge Economic History of Europe*, II (1952), 437.
[5] See above, pp. 95–7.
[6] Werner Hillebrand, 'Der Goslarer Metallhandel im Mittelalter', *Hansische Geschichtsblätter*, LXXXVII (1969), 34, quoting from R. Hoeniger, *Kölner Schreinsurkunden des 12 Jahrhunderts*, I, Publikationen der Gesellschaft für rheinische Geschichtskunde I (Bonn, 1884), 124–5; no. v.2, 3.
[7] E.g. by Otto of Freising writing *c.* 1143–6, or the *Annalista Saxo, c.* 1150, both quoted by Werner Hillebrand, 'Von den Anfängen des Erzbergbaus am Rammelsberg bei Goslar', *Niedersächsisches Jahrbuch für Landesgeschichte*, XXXIX (1967), 111.
[8] Albertus Magnus, *Book of Minerals*, trans. and ed. Dorothy Wyckoff (Oxford, 1967). Certainly written after 1248, probably between 1254 and 1262.
[9] There is no doubt that this is Freiberg, and not Freiburg, for he commented on the name of the place: 'Vurieberg, quod sonat liber mons' (p. 181).

than any found in stone; for in the place called Freiberg it is sometimes found as soft as a firm mush; and this is the purest and best kind of silver.'

Modern historians believe that Agricola's date for the discovery of silver in Meissen was correct, and that it took place in 1168. The readiness of Saxon miners to leave Goslar in that year for Meissen may be accounted for not only by the higher quality of the new ore, but by the interruption of mining around Goslar itself by the troops of Henry the Lion, who were besieging the city.

The discovery took place in the lands with which the Margrave Otto had very recently endowed his new monastery of Zella, which was still in the course of building and not yet occupied by monks. Otto's appreciation of the potentialities of the discovery is revealed by the way in which he rapidly arranged for the territory of the three villages affected by the discovery to be given back to him.[1] The financial advantages gained by Otto himself have already been discussed, and they are reflected by the tremendous upsurge in the striking of silver pennies by the margrave's mint at Leipzig, but the margrave's share was not, however, the major part of the silver. This fell to the miners themselves, and it is little wonder that the twelfth-century equivalent of the later Californian gold-rush or the Potosi silver-rush took place. We know that the population of California rose from approximately 14,000 in the summer of 1848 to 224,000 at the census of 1852,[2] and that the population of Potosi grew from nothing when the silver was discovered in 1545 to 120,000 when the Spanish Governor of Peru took a 'census' in 1572.[3] Jachymov (Joachimsthal) in Bohemia, grew in population from 1050 to 14,072 in the 10 years 1516 to 1526.[4] We do not, of course, have comparable figures for Freiberg, but the influx of miners, particularly from Saxony, was such that the village of Christiansdorf, where the initial discovery was made, growing haphazardly like the mining-camps of the Californian gold-rush, soon became known as Sachstadt, 'the town of the Saxons'.

In 1185 the Margrave Otto deliberately turned this mining-camp into a chartered town, to which he gave the name of Freiberg ('free mountain') presumably in allusion to the freedoms enjoyed by the miners (*Bergmänner*). The period of rapid growth seems to have gone on into the early thirteenth century, and two very considerable extensions to the town were made (1210/18) under Margrave Dietrich, which more than tripled the area of Otto's Freiberg, by now known as the Altstadt. After these initial fifty years of expansion there seems to have been

---

[1] This took place in 1169 or 1170 and provides the clearest evidence for the dating of the discovery itself. Walther Herrmann, 'Bergbau und Kultur', pp. 7–22.
[2] R. W. Paul, *California Gold* (Cambridge, Mass., 1947), pp. 23–5.
[3] L. Hanke, *The Imperial City of Potosi* (The Hague, 1956), p. 1.
[4] R. Mols, 'Population in Europe 1500–1700,' in *Fontana Economic History of Europe*, II, 40, quoting from P. Jancarer, 'K problematice demografickeho vyvoje Jachymova v dobe piedbelohorske', *Historicka Demografie*, II (1968), 18.

relatively little further growth in the town, which more or less remained the same size as under Margrave Dietrich, circumscribed by its walls.[1]

This period of rapid growth appears to have been followed, as at Potosi,[2] by a long period in which, although not growing much, Freiberg maintained its size and importance. It was during this period of Freiberg's maintained pre-eminence that Albertus Magnus was writing on minerals. A few years later, in November 1265, the Italian merchant and banker Andrea de Tolomei, in writing a report home to his business colleagues in Siena from Troyes in Champagne, gave the current exchange rates at the fair there and the prices of various commodities. Before the price of gold, he quotes that for unminted silver: a mark of 'Ariento di Friborgho buono' was for sale at 57s. 6d. provinois (the money of Champagne).[3]

However, at this date the effective period of dominance of the Freiberg mines was about to come to an end, and this is hardly surprising, for the mines had by then already been worked for nearly a hundred years. One of the pioneers of economic history in Germany, Gustav Schmoller, on the basis of a detailed examination of silver-mines opened in the fifteenth and sixteenth centuries, observed that there was only a limited lifespan to any mining enterprise, given the state of technology that confined the exploitation of ore-deposits to those on the surface and relatively near it, and the inevitable exhaustion of such deposits within a circumscribed period. He pointed out that there was a lifespan of only two or three generations for new mines of the fifteenth and sixteenth centuries[4] and postulated that the earlier mines of Freiberg fitted into the same pattern and that their importance only lasted until about 1300.[5]

[1] Manfred Unger, *Stadtgemeinde und Bergwesen Freibergs im Mittelalter*, Abhandlungen zur Handels– und sozial-geschichte v (Weimar, 1963), map at end (derived from J. Langer (1934)).

[2] Hanke, *Potosi*. The population of Potosi, according to the 'census' of 1572, was already 120,000. and according to that of 1650 still no more than 160,000.

[3] C. Paoli and E. Piccolomini (eds.), *Lettere volgari del secolo XIII scritte da Senesi* (Bologna, 1871), p. 57. Text of letter translated by R. S. Lopez and I. W. Raymond in *Medieval Trade in the Mediterranean World* (New York, 1955), pp. 392–4, where they identify 'Friborgho' as Freiburg in Breisgau without comment. However A. Schaube in his lengthy commentary on this letter in *Zeitschrift für Social- und Wirtschaftsgeschichte*, v (1897), 248–308, identified 'Friborgho' as Freiberg in Meissen and this seems more logical in view of other evidence. Freiburg in Breisgau was not of importance as a silver-market until the fourteenth century; see below, pp. 126 and 130. There is a slight problem of interpretation. 'Ariento di Friborgho buono' is preceded by 'Isterlino', also quoted by the mark. Later in the century, and probably at this date, sterling by the mark meant ingots of silver of sterling fineness, not English coin, see below, pp. 218–19. 'Ariento di Friborgho' could similarly have come to mean silver of Freiberg quality, not necessarily from Freiberg. In the same way, the silver at Cologne in the 1170s cited above, p. 111, could have been of Rammelsberg fineness, rather than from Goslar.

[4] Gustav Schmoller, 'Die geschichtliche Entwicklung der Unternehmung, x, Die deutsche Bergwerksfassung von 1400–1600', *Jahrbuch für Gesetzgebung, Verwaltung und Volkswirtschaft im Deutschen Reich*, xv (Leipzig, 1891), 963–4.

[5] Later writers, either at first or second hand, have mostly adopted Schmoller's tentative suggestion as a firm fact. M. M. Postan, for example, has written 'The highly important mining industry of Freiberg . . . reached the farthest limit of its development by the beginning of the fourteenth century' (*Cambridge Economic History of Europe*, II (1952), 202), and Unger, *Stadtgemeinde und Bergwesen Freibergs . . .*, has followed Postan.

The frequently repeated pattern of production from a major group of mines naturally began with the discovery of some ore. This was usually accidental, but was sometimes a consequence of deliberate prospecting. After a longer or shorter period the really rich seams began to be discovered, production then expanded very fast to reach a high level, accompanied by active prosperity in the vicinity, which disclosed the whereabouts of most of the ore and its limits. Production remained at a very high level for a relatively short period whilst the richest seams were being worked out, and then sank to a much lower level. Mining of the less productive veins then continued at a low and generally diminishing level of output for a relatively long period, until everything had been extracted that could profitably be taken out with the available technology.

As technology improved, successive deposits of the same scale could be worked out more rapidly. Without much technological innovation, it seems as though the Freiberg mines lasted for much the same length of time as those at Melle and Goslar. However with the rapidly improving mining-technology of the fifteenth and sixteenth centuries the Schwaz mines lasted less time than those at Freiberg, and the Joachimsthal mines less than those at Schwaz.[1] With the next leap forward in mining-technology in the nineteenth century, the Californian gold-mines lasted less time than the silver-mines at Joachimsthal.[2] The same pattern of production was repeated again and again, but over a shorter and shorter timespan.

In the absence of any precise production figures before the second half of the fourteenth century, it is impossible to date the decline of the Freiberg mines, but it is probable that production had shrunk to a low level rather earlier than Schmoller thought, quite possibly well before the end of the thirteenth century. By the apogee of the medieval European commercial expansion, the Freiberg mines, which had sustained so much of this expansion, had gone into decline and been surpassed by more recent discoveries. The Freiberg mines were not, however, abandoned and in the fourteenth century continued to produce silver in quantities that were small only in relation to what had been produced earlier. In 1353, 550 kilograms of silver (just over half a ton), was minted at Freiberg,[3] and by that date this probably represented by far the larger part of the silver mined.

---

[1] Mining began at Schwaz in the Tirol in 1448. In 1483, 48,097 marks of silver were produced; in 1525, 77,875; in 1564 only 17,518; and after 1570 only 2000 marks. At Joachimsthal, where mining began in 1516, nearly a quarter of a million talers-worth of silver were produced in 1533, but only 50,000–60,000 talers-worth between 1545 and 1554 and only 16,000–25,000 between 1570 and 1575 (Schmoller, 'Die geschichtliche Entwickelung . . .'; also see below, p. 363).

[2] Gold was found at Sutters Creek in California in 1848; gold production rose to over 80 million dollars-worth in 1852; but by 1857 it was down to 44 million dollars-worth and never after 1865 did it exceed 20 million dollars-worth (Paul, *California Gold*, p. 345).

[3] Karel Castelin, 'Grossus Pragensis', *Arbeits- und Forschungsberichte zur sächsischen Bodendenkmalpflege*, XVI–XVII (1967), 667, based on figures printed in H. Ermisch (ed.), *Urkundenbuch der Stadt Freiberg*, II, 'Bergbau, Bergrecht, Münze', Codex Diplomaticus Saxoniae Regiae XIII (Leipzig, 1886).

At about the same time as, or perhaps even a little earlier than, the discovery of silver at Freiberg, the silver deposits in the Colline Metallifere of Tuscany began to be exploited vigorously. During the later Middle Ages small veins of silver were discovered in a large number of places in these hills, at Batignano, at Prata and at Monte Ciriota for example.[1] However only in the area around Montieri (at Gerfalco, Fosini, Travale and Montieri itself) was the ore available in quantities to make the mining of it really worthwhile. Rising to 1051 metres (nearly 3500 feet) the Poggio di Montieri is one of the highest and bleakest hills in this desolate region. Medieval miners sank pits into it right to the very top. It stands not far from the point where the *contadi* of Volterra, Siena and Massa meet. In the twelfth century, from being a backward and forgotten land its lordship suddenly became the object of intense concern. In 1137, although some silver-mines were already in existence there they were still so insignificant that the Lord of Volterra, its bishop, could happily give away half of Montieri to the Bishop of Siena in exchange for some other lands.[2] Over the next forty years the miners grew in importance. Meanwhile the Emperor Frederick I during his frequent visits to Italy had disturbed the whole pattern of regalian rights in both Lombardy and Tuscany. By 1171 the regalian rights over the mines of Montieri were divided between the Bishop of Volterra and the emperor's nominee, the Marquess of Tuscany. When the Marquess of Tuscany ceded the imperial rights over the mines to the commune of Siena in 1180 they were sufficiently valuable to raise vigorous protests from the Bishop of Volterra. Three years later the dispute was resolved by an agreement by which the Bishop of Volterra was to collect all the mining-royalties, but to pay the Consuls of Siena 215 lire a year in compensation for relinquishing their share, a quarter. By implication the net value of the regalian rights was between 800 and 900 lire a year at this stage. At around this time the gross royalties were fixed at the rate of one basketful of ore out of every four mined. Between 1204 and 1221, during the dispute between the Bishop of Volterra and his chapter over the tithes of the mines, the yield of the mines was reckoned to be between 600 and 800 marks a year 'ad pondus Montieri'. A little later Ildebrandino Orrabile, one of the *Consules et Rectores* of Montieri in 1235, reckoned that the mines were yielding 1600 marks a year, then worth 8000 Pisan lire. Although large by most standards, this was small by comparison with Freiberg. Nevertheless, on the strength of the mines, Montieri had grown from a village to a town and had become a commune in 1219.

As with many other mines, the productive period lasted around a century. At Montieri mining remained profitable until the 1250s and then collapsed quite

---

[1] G. Volpe, 'Montieri: costituzione politica, struttura sociale e attivita economica d'una terra mineraria toscana nel XIII secolo', *Vierteljahrschrift für Social- und Wirtschaftsgeschichte*, VI (1908), 317–21, where he lists a large number of silver deposits.

[2] A. Lisini, 'Notizie delle miniere della Maremma toscana e leggi per l'estrazione dei metalli nel medioevo', *Bullettino Senese di Storia Patria*, n.s. VI (1935), 244.

suddenly. In 1241 the emperor, Frederick II, through his vicar general for Tuscany, took the regalian rights into his own hands. They were still sufficiently valuable for him to be able to raise 11,000 Pisan lire, for the siege of Viterbo, from the Davanzati of Florence in return for farming the mines of Montieri and a number of tolls to them for 2½ years. At the expiry of that time he obtained a further 3000 marks, to pay his Tuscan garrisons, from Sienese bankers in return for farming the mines. After Frederick's death the Bishop of Volterra reclaimed the mining-royalties, but only managed to vindicate his claim with some difficulty. Having done so in 1252 he promptly raised 6000 marks, on the strength of them, from the Bonsignori and Tolomei, two of the leading banking-houses of Siena. However, the mines were soon to decline radically in output and the Tolomei never recovered their money from the mines. In 1265 mining-royalties came only to 45 marks. In 1287 the miners petitioned to have the rate of mining-royalties, the *ius monte*, halved, 'cum fructus et proventus ipsarum fovearum sint adeo diminuti'. It is hardly surprising that under these circumstances the Bishops of Volterra, never regular payers at best, altogether ceased to pay their annual 215 lire to the commune of Siena. In 1326 a group of lawyers declared that the commune of Siena, whose troops were already occupying Montieri, was entitled to appropriate it on account of the prolonged non-payment of the annual 215 lire.[1] For some time the city of Siena went on spending money trying to revive the silver-mines of Montieri, but the accounts of the commune show no receipts from successful exploitation.[2] The mines of Montieri, the 'profondissime fosse, donde gli antichi nostri trassero notabilissima somma d'argento', were exhausted.[3]

In the eastern Alps, in Styria and Carinthia, silver-mining may have begun as early as 1072,[4] and mint rights in this area can be traced back to the mid tenth century. However, the distinctive coinage of the area, the Friesacher pfennigs struck at Friesach for the Archbishops of Salzburg, only went back to around 1125–30.[5] Although both mining and minting were of long standing by the late twelfth century, neither was yet very considerable, even though the pfennigs of Friesach were marked out for dominance. The period of the really large production of the mints of this area, and presumably of the mines, did not begin until about 1195. In this year the Archbishop of Salzburg thought it necessary to obtain a privilege from the Emperor Henry VI confirming the alleged custom of carrying silver mined in

---

[1] Volpe, 'Montieri', pp. 321–423.

[2] W. Bowsky, *The Finances of the Commune of Siena 1287–1355* (Oxford, 1970), pp. 24–5 and 62–3.

[3] So described by Jacopo Tondi in his report on developing the commerce and industry of Siena, 1334 (Lisini, 'Notizie delle miniere della Maremma tuscana', p. 217).

[4] E. Kraume, 'Münzprägung und Silbererz-Bergbau in Mitteleuropa um die Jahrtausendwende (950–1050)', *Der Anschnitt*, XIII, 4 (1961), p. 142.

[5] Arthur Suhle, *Deutsche Münz- und Geldgeschichte von den Anfängen bis zum 15. Jahrhundert*, 2nd ed. (Berlin, 1964), p. 142.

the mountain to the mint of the archbishop for minting.[1] The necessity for such a privilege implies that new silver had recently begun to be mined in large quantities, and was not being carried to the archbishop's mint as he thought it ought to be. The large-scale minting that began around this date only lasted until 1230, barely more than a single generation. In that space of time, the Friesach mint, for Eberhard II of Salzburg (archbishop 1200–40), and the associated mint at St Veit for Bernhard of Carinthia (duke 1202–30), issued a vast number of pfennigs. It was not only a large coinage, but also a carefully regulated one, issued under a monetary convention between the archbishop and the duke. Regular renewal of the coinage was practised, probably every four years, from 1200 to 1220, and every two years, from 1220 to 1230.[2] Despite the archbishop's privilege, large amounts of silver were taken to other mints in the vicinity, mostly to the south and east, from Laibach (Ljubljana) in Slovenia to Graz in Styria. (See Map 14.) The miners presumably received a better price for their silver there than the archbishop and the duke were prepared to give. To compound the injury to the archbishop, the silver was then minted into pfennigs closely resembling those struck for him at Friesach. The principal issuers of such imitative pfennigs were the Lords of the Krain, Henry IV of Andechs-Meran (margrave 1205–28) and his successor Frederick II of Styria and Austria (1229–43). Henry IV minted at Stein (Kamnik), Windischgraz (Slovenj Gradic), and Gutenwert (Hrvatski Brod).

After 1230 the quantity of Friesacher pfennigs, both legitimate and imitative, diminished very rapidly. The exhaustion of the richest seams in the mines was no doubt responsible for this.[3] The tight control previously exercised over the legitimate mints seems to have collapsed at the same time, even though the monetary convention between the archbishop and the duke went on being renewed up to 1286. Small quantities of Friesacher pfennigs continued to be struck until the mid fourteenth century, presumably reflecting the small quantities of silver still being mined. During this last stage of silver-mining, the associated minerals took on a greater importance. Here, as at Goslar, it was copper that was principally found with the silver. In 1318 Nicholas of Friesach carried copper rather than silver to Venice.[4]

[1] 'Ut argentum, quod a montibus et villis (*sic? recte*, vallis) et aliis quibuscumque locis ad monetam archiepiscopi Salz. defferi consuetum, secundum consuetudinem illius deferatur' (*Steiermark Urkundenbuch*, II, no. 8, cited by Adolf Zycha, 'Zur neuesten Literatur über die Wirtschaft . . . des deutschen Bergbaus', *Vierteljahrschrift für Sozial- und Wirtschaftsgeschichte*, v (1907), 266).

[1] For most of what follows see Egon Baumgartner, 'Die Blütezeit der Friesacher Pfennige', *Numismatische Zeitschrift*, LXXIII (Vienna, 1949), 75–106; LXXVIII (1959), 14–57; and LXXIX (1961), 28–63. A numismatic synopsis of Baumgartner's articles is provided for English readers in D. M. Metcalf, *The Coinage of South Germany in the Thirteenth Century* (London, 1961), pp. 50–60.

[3] The same pattern as elsewhere; see above, pp. 113–14.

[4] Henry Simonsfeld, *Der Fondaco dei Tedeschi in Venedig und die deutsch-venetianischen Handelsbeziehungen*, I (Stuttgart, 1887), doc. 54.

The profitable discovery of the rich silver ores of Freiberg, and even to a lesser extent those of Montieri and Friesach, set off a sort of silver-mining mania in many parts of Europe by way of a chain reaction. The Margraves of Meissen were so patently enriched by their silver mines, just as governments are today of countries in which oil is found, that silver then came to be sought for as widely as oil is now. Even the slightest deposits of argentiferous ore were seized upon avidly and worked eagerly in the hope of emulating the Bishops of Volterra or the Arch-bishops of Salzburg, if not the Margraves of Meissen themselves.[1]

In the Harz mountains strenuous efforts were made to find alternative sources of silver to the worked-out ore of Goslar, and silver was indeed found near Cellerfeld in the Oberharz shortly after 1200[2] and rediscovered at Mansfeld in the Mittelharz at about the same time;[3] but it proved of very little significance at this period, although the Mansfeld mines were to become very important with the improvements in technology in the fifteenth century.

Very shortly after the discovery of silver ore at Freiberg, other, much less important, deposits were found in the Alps. Silver began to be mined in the southern Tirol from about 1185 when Albrecht, Bishop of Trent, brought in 'Silbrarii' to work it.[4] The Tirolese mining-laws were clearly derived from those of Goslar, which suggests that many of these miners, like those at Freiberg, Cellerfeld and Mansfeld, had come from the declining mines of Goslar.[5]

There is no clear evidence that former Goslar miners were involved in any of the other attempts at exploiting silver ore in Germany or Italy at this period, although they may well have been. It has been suggested that the term used for the silver-miners at Montieri, *guerchi*, may be German in origin, from *Werk*, as *Guelph* from *Welf*.[6] Even if it is true, no connection can be made with any particular part of Germany, nor has any particular affiliation been claimed for the earliest mining-code from Massa, which dates from around 1200.[7] The mines of Massa probably

[1] See Map 11, p. 110, for some of these minor mines.

[2] Kraume, 'Münzprägung und Silbererz-Bergbau', p. 5.

[3] Karl Mieleitner, 'Geschichte der Mineralogie im Altertum und Mittelalter', *Fortschritte der Mineralogie, Kristallographie und Petrographie*, VII (1922), 479, describes the Mansfeld mines as twelfth-century. C. J. Singer *et al.* (eds.), *A History of Technology*, II (Oxford, 1956), 65, say they were opened in 1215. Kraume, 'Münzprägung und Silbererz-Bergbau', p. 6, contents himself with being no more specific than 'the thirteenth century'.

[4] Schmoller, 'Die geschichtliche Entwicklung . . .'; Kraume, 'Münzprägung und Silbererz-Bergbau', p. 8; and Aloys Schulte, *Geschichte des mittelalterlichen Handels und Verkehrs zwischen Westdeutschland und Italien mit Ausschluss von Venedig* (Leipzig, 1900), p. 146.

[5] Bertrand Gille, 'Les Problèmes de la technique minière au Moyen Age', *Revue d'histoire des mines et de la métallurgie*, I (1969), 282, quoting N. von Wolfstrigl-Wolfskron, *Die Tiroler Erzbergbau (1300–1665)* (Berlin, 1899).

[6] Volpe, 'Montieri', pp. 370–1, where he also discusses a number of other Tuscan mining-terms, possibly of German extraction.

[7] L. Simonin, 'De l'exploitation des mines en Toscane pendant l'antiquité et le moyen âge', *Annales des mines*, 5th series, XIV (1858), 557–615.

ranked second in Tuscany to those of Montieri in the first half of the thirteenth century.

Silver lodes in the Lahn–Rhine–Mosel area had been worked by the Romans, and litigation between the Archbishops of Trier and the Counts of Nassau provides evidence of the reopening of one of them, near Ems on the Lahn, as early as the mid twelfth century. Mines in that area continued to be worked, but without much evidence of profit, into the thirteenth century. Another at Mechernich in the Eifel, which had also been worked by the Romans, was also reopened in the thirteenth century.[1]

It was presumably the products of such mines as these that provided Albertus Magnus with his descriptions of three forms of silver ore less pure and good than that found at Freiberg.[2]

More important than any discovery since those at Freiberg and Friesach was that about 1220/30 at Jihlava (Iglau) on the borders of Bohemia and Moravia, which attracted miners from Freiberg, in the same way that the Freiberg and Alpine discoveries had attracted miners from Goslar half a century earlier. It is therefore hardly surprising that the mining-laws of Jihlava were based on those of Freiberg, which in their turn had been based on those used in Goslar since the tenth century.[3] Nor is it surprising that the King of Bohemia opened a mint at Jihlava, which rapidly became the busiest in his kingdom.

Ottokar II, king from 1253 to 1278, drew some 2000 marks in one year from the silver-mines in Bohemia, primarily these at Jihlava. Assuming that the royal share was an eighth of the total mined, as it was later, this probably represents a total annual production of some 4 tons of silver.[4]

At about the same time that the mines at Jihlava were replacing those of Freiberg and Friesach as the principal silver-mines of central Europe, those of Iglesias in Sardinia were replacing those of Montieri as the principal silver-mines of southern Europe.

In 1257 a Pisan ship returning from Sardinia was seized by the Genoese, with whom the Pisans were again at war. According to some chroniclers it was carrying 20,000 marks of silver, about 5 tons. According to others there were no less than 28,000 marks on board. The silver was applied by the Genoese to the extension of their Arsenal.[5] Even if these figures are exaggerated we may feel confident that the

[1] Kraume, 'Münzprägung und Silbererz-Bergbau', p. 7; F. H. Beyschlag et al., *The Deposits of Useful Minerals and Rocks: Ore Deposits* (1909; English trans., London, 1914–16), p. 702.
[2] See above, pp. 111–12.
[3] Gille, 'Problèmes de la technique minière', p. 282, and see Map 12, p. 120.
[4] Balint Homan, 'La circolazione delle monete d'oro in Ungheria dal x al xiv secolo e la crisi europea dell'oro nel secolo xiv', *Rivista Italiana di Numismatica*, 2nd series, v (1922), 132.
[5] C. Baudi di Vesme (ed.), *Codex Diplomaticus Ecclesiensis*, Historiae patriae monumenta xvii (Turin, 1877), Introduction, pp. lxxxvi ff.

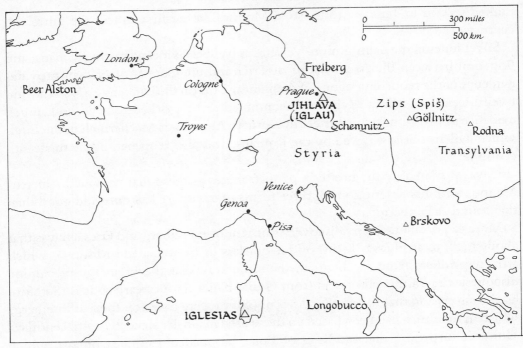

Map 12. European silver-mines *c.* 1230 – *c.* 1290. Places connected with mines are in italic.

silver-production of Sardinia had become quite appreciable by the 1250s. The principal silver-mines were in the south-west of the island. This area lay firmly in the Pisan sphere of influence, and its lords were the Counts of Donnoratico, the leading noble family of Pisa. The whole district became known, from its silver-mines, as Argentiera. As it grew in importance, the counts followed the normal Tuscan pattern of delegating their authority to a *podestà*, the 'Potestatem argenterie'. He had charge of the whole mining-area and of Villa di Chiesa di Sigerro, now Iglesias, the fast-growing boom town at its heart. It is not clear when *podestàs* began to be appointed, but the earliest surviving nomination of an individual *podestà* only dates from 1282.[1] By then Villa di Chiesa was already large and prosperous, for in the next year it was rich enough to purchase its first charter of liberties, giving it a degree of self-government under the *podestà*. In 1302 the commune of Pisa took over the direct rule of the area from the Donnoratico and governed it through two rectors. Large numbers of Pisans settled there and considerable investment from Pisa also followed. Pisa also granted further privileges to Villa di Chiesa,[2] and set up a branch mint there which struck grossi aquilini

[1] *Ibid.* pp. 318–19.
[2] F. Artizzu (ed.), *Documenti inediti relativi ai rapporti economici tra la Sardegna e Pisa nel medioevo*, Publicazioni dell'Istituto di storia medioevale e moderna dell'Universita degli studi di Cagliari, 1 (Padua, 1961), introduction by Alberto Boscolo, pp. xl–xli.

from the local silver, very similar to those of the main mint of Pisa itself, but inscribed 'Facta in villa eclesie p(ro) com(mun)i pisano'.[1] As at Freiberg, there was a half-century or so of continuous growth at Villa di Chiesa, followed by another half-century or so of consolidation before the mines began to decline. It was during the period of expansion that the renown of the mines of Argentiera spread far and wide. The anonymous North African author of *Zohri*, writing in the 1270s or 1280s, praised them. Sardinia, he wrote, 'contains a silver mine of which the ore is very rich, since pure metal makes up a third of it'.[2] Although the mines were flourishing and the Pisans were drawing considerable revenues from them, the city of Pisa was foundering politically. In the thirteenth century it had ranked with Genoa and Venice as one of the three leading maritime powers of Italy, and indeed of the Mediterranean. After the crushing defeat of La Meloria at the hands of Genoa in 1284, Pisa slipped from its position of pre-eminence. Its loss of control of Sardinia was a consequence of its military weakness in the fourteenth century. The Aragonese conquered the south-west of the island in 1323–4. At the time of the conquest the mines were still very flourishing. As recently as 1321 a large partnership of Pisans had invested no less than 15,000 lire di piccoli of Pisa in the 'argenteries de Sardinea'.[3] The renewed confirmation of the city charter of Villa di Chiesa, shortly after the conquest, contains, in the liberties granted to the mining community, very considerable detail of the operation of the mines. The regulation of the mines and miners in the hills around the city under elected *maestri del monte* reads very like the regulation of German mining communities. Some of the pits, like 'La Bergamastra' in Monte Barla, even had names that were patently German in origin.

The mines began to decline in the 1330s, for Don Raimondo della Valle, who took a lease of the royal rights, in the silver-mines, in the mint and in the city, for three years from 1332, surrendered the lease after two years, since the profits were declining. A royal ordinance of 1334 also speaks of the Villa di Chiesa being in decline to the great damage of the king and the whole island. Count Baudi di Vesme attributed the decline to the enfeoffment of the island to rapacious Aragonese and Catalans, who did not understand the free mining communities and circumscribed their activities, but it is more inherently probable that the silver just began to run out in the natural order of things. One example of the greater regulation of the miners at this time, perhaps as a response to the decline in direct royal revenues from the mines, was the introduction of a rule that compelled the miners to have their silver minted at the royal mint in Villa di Chiesa. As a consequence the number of grossi affonsini struck at the mint increased at a time when the mines

---

[1] Baudi di Vesme (ed.), *Codex Diplomaticus Ecclesiensis*, pp. ccxxvii ff.
[2] Cited in E. Fagnan, *Extraits inédits relatifs au Maghreb* (Algiers, 1924), pp. 24–5.
[3] Artizzu (ed.), *Documenti relativi ai rapporti economici tra la Sardegna e Pisa*, II (1962), xvi and doc. 59.

were becoming less productive, leaping to a peak of over 900,000 a year in 1337–9.[1] From 1340 however, the decline in mining can be seen in the continuous reduction of the quantity compulsorily minted from it. Villa di Chiesa was destroyed by fire in 1355 and suffered heavily in the prolonged civil war between the supporters of the Kings of Aragon and those of the Counts of Arborea during the second half of the century. In 1365 the mint closed finally and by the fifteenth century there was no longer any sign of mining activity.[2] The exploitation of the mines of Iglesias had lasted just over a century.

At some much earlier date silver had been mined in Nurra in the north-west of the island, in another Monte Argentiera. These mines had long been exhausted but in the 1250s, when the Pisans were beginning to do so well out of the Iglesias mines, a modest company with a capital of 200 Genoese pounds was set up in Genoa to attempt to revive the Nurra mines. Orlando Paglia, a Lucchese financier living in Genoa, and three associates, engaged two 'toeschi', Friedrich and Consolino son of the late Konrad, to go with them to buy 'mines, furnaces or veins for the production of silver'. Although members of two families surnamed Todeschi were in Genoa at this time, Roberto Lopez suggests that these 'toeschi' were in fact Germans (*tedeschi*), and were Transalpine mining-experts,[3] such as were evidently present at the other end of the island, at Iglesias, by the early fourteenth century. Nothing further is known of the venture, so it presumably met with little success.

As well as the new, leading mines at Jihlava and Iglesias, a large number of other attempts to open up silver-mines took place in Europe in the latter half of the thirteenth century. In all of these German miners were involved, as they were in Sardinia. Men from Jihlava itself participated directly in the generally fairly successful mining-ventures to its south and east, but a certain amount of unsuccessful, or marginally successful, prospecting and mining took place elsewhere, in the Alps, in southern Italy, in western Germany, and even in England. (See Map 12.)

Miners from Jihlava (Iglau), itself a German enclave in a Slav land, went out southwards and eastwards to find new ores. Sometimes this was at the specific invitation of rulers like Uros, King of Serbia, who in 1254 invited 'Saxon' miners to open up a mine for him at Brskovo.[4] Wherever they went, German miners took their own mining-laws with them and set up a German mining community in a strange land. The mining-code of Brskovo, and indeed of all the later Serbian and

---

[1] Mint accounts, now in the Archives of the Crown of Aragon in Barcelona, abstracted by John Day, to whom I am grateful for this information.

[2] Baudi di Vesme (ed.), *Codex Diplomaticus Ecclesiensis*, pp. ccliv ff.

[3] R. S. Lopez, 'An aristocracy of money in the early middle ages', *Speculum*, XXVIII (1953), 6–18. The text of the agreement is on pp. 7–8. A translation into English appears in Lopez and Raymond, *Trade in the Mediterranean World*, pp. 194–5.

[4] Desanka Kovacevic, 'Dans la Serbie et la Bosnie médiévales: les mines d'or et d'argent', *Annales, Économies, Sociétés, Civilisations*, XV (1960), 248–58.

Bosnian mines, was based on that of Jihlava. So was that granted by Béla IV of Hungary, king from 1235 to 1270, to the miners of Schemnitz, now Banská Štiavnica, the mother town of all the 'Hungarian' mining-towns.[1] One must conclude that, at an early stage in their exploitation, the mines of Brskovo and Schemnitz were largely worked by men who had previously been at Jihlava.

Of the new 'Hungarian' mines, those at Schemnitz were the most successful. By the time of Georgius Agricola, who was the town physician there for over twenty years (1533–55), their continued eminence had conferred upon them a traditional date of discovery in the seventh century. They were in fact already being exploited to a certain extent before Béla IV. In 1217 King Andrew II drew 300 marks from his share of the production of the mine, which suggests an annual production in the early thirteenth century of some 600 kilograms (12 cwts.) of silver. After Béla IV's introduction of miners from Jihlava, production seems to have increased rapidly and reached its highest point in the second half of the thirteenth century.

Miners from Schemnitz also opened up a considerable number of other silver-mines in the surrounding hills, further east in Zips, now Spiš, which became a 'German' enclave in Slovakia, and even in Transylvania, all then in the kingdom of Hungary. Of the many daughter mines of Schemnitz, the two most important groups in the thirteenth century seem to have been at Rodna in Transylvania and Göllnitz (Golniczbánya) in Zips. The former were already open by 1241, but the latter were still only producing about 200 kilograms (4 cwts.) of silver a year in 1280.

Elsewhere prospecting went on, sometimes with some success. Silver-mining in the Alps continued, although in a much quieter and less dramatic way than earlier. Some new ore was found. At some date before 1265 new mines were opened at Ziering in Styria, for example, which were quite flourishing in the second half of the thirteenth century.[2]

Although the mines of Montieri were dead, silver-mining did not cease in Italy. Charles of Anjou, the conqueror of the kingdom of Sicily, arranged for prospecting for silver to be undertaken in his new kingdom, which resulted in the discovery of silver at Longobucco in Calabria in 1274. The royal share of the proceeds came to several hundred pounds of silver every year,[3] and the mines there were still sufficiently productive for Pegolotti to mention them as a source of silver in the first half of the fourteenth century.[4]

---

[1] Most of these 'Hungarian' silver-mines were in Slovakia, then a province of the kingdom of Hungary, but now in Czechoslovakia. This and most of what follows on Hungarian silver-mines is derived from Homan, 'La circolazione delle monete d'oro in Ungheria', pp. 134–5.

[2] Kraume, 'Münzprägung und Silbererz-Bergbau', p. 8.

[3] Émile G. Léonard, *Les Angevins de Naples* (Paris, 1954), p. 86.

[4] Francesco Balducci Pegolotti, *La pratica della mercatura*, ed. Allan Evans, Medieval Academy of America (Cambridge, Mass., 1936), p. 291.

In western Germany attempts to mine silver in the hills on either side of the Rhine continued, and in 1250 Konrad von Hochstadt, Archbishop of Cologne, was actually making some profit from silver-mines at Lüderich in the Berg Hills, which he spent on the rebuilding of his cathedral.[1]

An almost new area for silver-mining was England.[2] In 1262 silver ore was apparently accidentally found in Devon. First the Sheriff of Devon was ordered to prevent anyone digging it. Then, early in 1263, two Englishmen were sent down to take charge. Within two months the English king, Henry III, began optimistically assigning debts to be paid out of the first issues of the mine, before ever any work was done, and ordering the construction of a good, strong house with a stone tower to keep the hoped-for treasure. All this, six months before Reiner Advocatus and his fellows, presumably Germans, arrived in England to carry on the mines and prospect for more. Three years later they were joined by further miners, who came from Germany at the King's expense.[3] After this there is no further reference in the patent rolls for thirty years. The initial optimism proved ill-founded. 'Birland' (now Beer Alston) was no Freiberg or Iglau; the stone tower for treasure was a gross over-provision, except for a short period in the 1290s.[4] Until then mining went on intermittently on a very small scale.

At the very end of the century, the most prolific mines of the whole period were opened up at Kutná Hora (Küttenberg) in Bohemia.[5] It appears to have been miners from the Tirol who were responsible for opening them up, for Kutná Hora was provided with a mining-code based on the Tirolean one.[6] Silver was discovered at Kutná Hora in 1298, in lands belonging to the abbey of Sedletz.[7] Just as Otto of Meissen had rapidly retrieved the future Freiberg from the abbey of Zella when silver was discovered there, so the King of Bohemia, Wenceslas II, now did precisely the same. By 1300 Kutná Hora was in royal hands and very opportunely so, for Wenceslas II is reputed to have said that, when the discovery was made there, the silver-mines at Jihlava and elsewhere in his kingdom were almost all exhausted.[8]

---

[1] Kraume, 'Münzprägung und Silbererz-Bergbau', p. 6; Beyschlag *et al.*, *Useful Minerals*, p. 696.

[2] In the 1160s and 1170s a small seam of argentiferous lead ore had been worked at Alston Moor in the Cumbrian hills, and in the 1190s an even smaller seam had been worked at 'Carreghova' on the Welsh border.

[3] *Close Rolls 1261–1264* (London, 1936), pp. 187 and 227; *Calendar of Patent Rolls 1258–1266* (London, 1910), pp. 249, 253, 304; *Calendar of Liberate Rolls 1260–1267* (London, 1961), p. 246.

[4] See below, pp. 127–8.

[5] I have referred to this place by its Czech name, Kutná Hora, although, since the mines were of German origin, they themselves called it Küttenberg. I have similarly referred to Jihlava, above, p. 119, by its Czech name, although it was known to the miners as Iglau. I have, inconsistently, referred to Schemnitz, above, p. 123, by its German name, rather than by its Slovak name, Banská Štiavnica, or its Magyar name, Selmecbánya.

[6] Gille, 'Problèmes de la technique minière', p. 282.

[7] For most of what follows see Castelin, 'Grossus Pragensis', pp. 665–75.

[8] Homan, 'La circolazione delle monete d'oro in Ungheria', p. 132, citing Adolf Zycha, *Das Böhmische Bergrecht des Mittelalters* (1900), pp. 174–5.

The wealth of the Kutná Hora mines provided the basis for a radical reform of the coinage of Bohemia. Hitherto minting had taken place not only at Prague and Iglau, but at fifteen other towns in Bohemia as well. Now all seventeen mints were centralised at Kutná Hora, in one vast establishment built to house the seventeen different coining-workshops. Hitherto there had been a free trade in precious metal, in the form of bar silver, now there was a royal monopoly. In theory the silver from the Kutná Hora mines should only have passed into circulation through the Kutná Hora mints. In the first years the quantity was enormous. From 1300 to 1305, 6.4 to 6.7 tons of silver were minted annually in the Kutná Hora mints. In practice this was still only a part of the silver mined, for Wenceslas II's share of the silver mined rose first to 5000 and then to 10,000 marks a year,[1] and, if his share was an eighth, this corresponds to an annual production of silver rising to about 20 tons of silver a year. In Vienna at the beginning of the fourteenth century, Albert, Duke of Austria and, from 1298 to 1308, King of Germany, believed that the Bohemian royal share had amounted to 80,000 marks over a period of 6 years.[2] If true, this suggests an annual production of as much as 25 tons of silver, in which case as little as a quarter of the silver may have actually been minted even in Wenceslas' own reign. The rule that all the silver mined should pass through the mints naturally fell into abeyance when the mints were closed during the troubled years after the early death of Wenceslas II's young son, Wenceslas III, in 1306. In the 8 years after the mints were reopened in 1311 for the new king, John of Luxemburg, only about 1½ tons of silver a year were minted, and later in his reign the quantities were even smaller. The miners had obviously resumed their traditional freedom in the disposal of their silver and bypassed the royal mints. Chroniclers suggested that 95,000 marks of silver, about 24 tons, left the country each year in the 1320s, although the quantity minted was minimal. In 1338 the annual production of the mines may still have been at the rate of 22 tons of silver.[3]

The silver found at Kutná Hora was the last, as well as the greatest, discovery of silver ore of the 'long thirteenth century'. The last years of the thirteenth century and the first half of the fourteenth also saw mining continuing on a large scale in Sardinia, and on a small scale in the kingdoms of Hungary, Serbia and Naples (see Map 13), as well as attempts to find new sources of silver in Tuscany and the Rhineland, and attempts to exploit already known silver-bearing ore more vigorously in the Black Forest and England.

In the silver-bearing hills of Tuscany numerous tiny mines went on being

[1] Homan, 'La circolazione delle monete d'oro in Ungheria', p. 132, quoting from Emler, *Regesta Diplomatica Bohemiae*, II (Prague, 1855), 1018–19.
[2] Homan, *ibid*.
[3] On the basis that eight weeks' royal revenue from the mines was reckoned at 2000 sexagene of silver, and assuming a royal share of an eighth, and a consistent production throughout the year (*ibid.*).

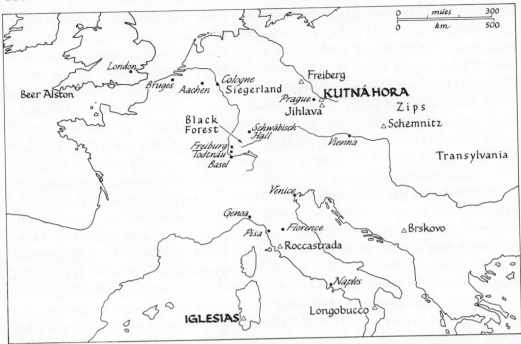

Map 13. European silver-mines *c.* 1290 – *c.* 1325. Places connected with mines are in italic.

worked hopefully into the fourteenth century. Those at Roccastrada, where silver was found in 1304, had a certain ephemeral success and for a time attracted unemployed miners from the worked-out mines of the Montieri district nearby.[1]

In the Rhineland also tiny mines went on being worked hopefully, and prospecting continued. Some new silver was found. In 1298, Adolf, King of the Romans, invested his relatives, the Counts of Nassau, with a new silver-mine at Ratzensheid in Siegerland, as a potential source of profit, but whether the potential was realised is not clear.[2] Some of the Black Forest silver-mines did have a brief period of prosperity at the very end of the thirteenth century and the beginning of the fourteenth, when the Duke of Austria's mint at Todtnau, near one of the mines, had an evanescent importance as a producer of bracteate pfennigs. Early in the fourteenth century Freiburg-im-Breisgau became a considerable market for silver, and at the same time the denarii hallenses, or hellers, of Schwäbisch Hall, which had been struck in small quantities since the late twelfth century, began to be struck in large numbers and were widely imitated. They provided the small change for everyday use throughout southern Germany and even as far away as Bohemia and

[1] Volpe, 'Montieri', pp. 389ff.
[2] Kraume, 'Münzprägung und Silbererz-Bergbau', p. 7. Ratzensheid is at Landeskrone bei Wilnsdorf.

Aachen.[1] They were commonly used as half-pfennigs, since they contained half as much silver as the Cologne pfennigs which dominated the currency of Germany.

The English mines exemplify very well the amount of effort expended and the scale of return generally achieved in the lesser mining-ventures. In the 1290s Edward I made a vigorous attempt to make the mines discovered in his father's reign at Beer Alston in Devon productive and profitable. Two radical changes were made in the 1290s. First, the normal system of free mining was abolished. By this system miners had worked on their own account and paid over a proportion of their production as royalty to the king. The mines were now taken into the king's own hands, and miners were paid as hired men at piece-work rates. This brought in a large number of men who would not otherwise have been prepared to work in such uneconomic mines. Secondly, a great deal of money was laid out on digging drainage adits, which, according to the King's Treasurer, Walter Langton, in 1298, had doubled the yield of the mines. This seems to have been true. Between 1292 and 1296 the mines yielded an average of just over 700 pounds weight of silver a year. In 1296–7 just over 1100 pounds weight of silver from the mines was delivered to the mint, and in 1298 the mines yielded over 1400 pounds weight of silver.[2] In 1299 the great Italian merchant banking-company of the Frescobaldi was cozened into taking over the mines in the expectation of making a notable profit and so reducing the king's debt to them. Far from making a profit, they found that the costs of operating the mines, of refining the silver and of transporting it to London for minting exceeded the value of the silver produced. They consequently gave up the mines after only one year and demanded recompense from the king for their losses. Obviously the details of such a claim must be treated with reserve. They said, for example, that the mines were abandoned when they took them over, which is hardly credible. They also said that they brought out 3600 loads of ore worth only 10s. a load, at a production cost of 13s. 4d. a load.[3] This is partially corroborated by the London mint's account, which records the receipt from them of some 1900 pounds weight of silver. The mines reverted to direct royal exploitation, and the king presumably bore the loss of running them. For the next few years they appear to have yielded about the same quantity of silver. In 1305 it was just under 1800 pounds weight. Although the Devon mines seem to have been uneconomic to operate and only to have brought a financial loss to the king, they did, on the other

---

[1] A. Engel and R. Serrure, *Traité de numismatique du moyen âge*, III (Paris, 1905; repr. 1964), 1234–5; F. von Schrötter (ed.), *Wörterbuch der Münzkunde* (Leipzig, 1930; repr. 1970), pp. 259–61; and Eberhard Gothein, *Wirtschaftsgeschichte des Schwarzwaldes und der angrenzenden Landschaften*, I (Strassburg, 1892), 648.

[2] L. F. Salzman, *English Industries of the Middle Ages*, 2nd ed. (Oxford, 1923), pp. 52–63. This is reckoning in the Tower pound of approximately 350 grams, from which approximately a pound value of coin was minted. From 1279 to 1335 a Tower pound of silver was made into 243 pennies, 486–94 halfpennies, or 976–1000 farthings (quarter-pennies).

[3] *Ibid.*; and Armando Sapori, *La compagnia dei Frescobaldi in Inghilterra* (Florence, 1947), pp. 19–20, 39ff.

hand, increase the stock of silver in England, particularly over a period of about fifteen years, up to 1305 or 1306. This was obviously thought to be worth while for its own sake, for it to have continued for so long. Attempts to find more mineable English silver were also made at this time, for example in Guernsey.[1] However, eventually the loss outweighed the advantage and an attempt was made at about this time to cut production costs at the miner's expense.

In 1307 it was reported that, of 700 miners previously working there, all but 60 had gone away in a state of discontent. This was the end of the mines as effective producers of silver, although they lingered on for years operated by only a handful of men. In 1347 they were still open, but only 70 pounds weight of silver were produced.[2]

It is worth asking how significant was a supply of silver in Edward's England, which rose from 700 pounds a year to some 1800 pounds a year. It was obviously small in comparison with the estimated yields from such successful mines as those at Freiberg or Kutná Hora, but probably provides a more typical model of what happened elsewhere. It is difficult to make a fair comparison with the amount of money minted, since between 1295 and 1305 the annual production of the English mints fluctuated wildly, but averaged some 30,000 pounds a year.[3] Set against this scale of minting, the Devon mines, even at their most successful, did not make a significant contribution to the supply of money in England, let alone Europe.

The contrast is very marked between such tiny mines as these and the handful of really successful large mines of central Europe.

The share of the proceeds of mining that accrued to the prince varied enormously from place to place, according to local custom, which was not in itself unchangeable. Looked at retrospectively, from the dubious perspective of Agricola's time, the princely share of the mines in German principalities seems generally to have been a tenth – the *Bergzehnten*. In Bohemia the kings received an eighth of the silver, and the Kings of Hungary not surprisingly followed this example.[4] In Italy the practice was very varied. At Montieri in the twelfth century the Bishops of Volterra took a quarter of the ore, although this was reduced to an eighth in the thirteenth century when the mines were becoming exhausted.[5] In the thirteenth century the Counts of Savoy took a tenth, an eleventh and a fortieth from mines in different places, whilst the Patriarch of Aquileia took an eighth.[6] When the mines at Iglesias were opened up, the city of Pisa took a twelfth part of the silver, and in the

---

[1] Michael Prestwich, *War, Politics and Finance under Edward I* (London, 1972), p. 217.
[2] Salzman, *English Industries of the Middle Ages*, pp. 52 and 64.
[3] C. G. Crump and C. Johnson, 'Tables of bullion coined under Edward I, II, and III', *Numismatic Chronicle*, 4th series, XIII (1913), 208–11, 228–9, 232–5.
[4] Homan, 'La circolazione delle monete d'oro in Ungheria', pp. 133 and 135.
[5] See above, pp. 115–16.
[6] Volpe, 'Montieri', p. 364.

fourteenth century the Kings of Aragon took the same proportion.[1] The same system continued into early modern times. The King of Spain took an imperial fifth of the silver from the mines of Potosi in the sixteenth and seventeenth centuries.

This was not, however, all that the miners had to pay out. They also had to make payments to the actual surface-owners. In the Black Forest area, for example, as well as the standard *Bergzehnten* to the Bishop of Basel, the abbey of St Trudpert or the Count of Freiburg, as prince and thus owner of the *Bergregal* or mining-royalties, the miners also made payments that varied according to individual agreements between mine-owners and landowners. Generally the thirtieth or thirty-first pfennig was paid here, although from a good mine the twentieth pfennig might be paid, or from a poor one the fortieth pfennig, or from a very unproductive mine only the hundredth pfennig.[2] At Friesach, at the end of the twelfth century, the miners paid a ninth to the monastery of Admont,[3] which seems rather a high proportion for a landowner. In some cases the prince and the surface-owner were one and the same. The Margraves of Meissen at Freiberg, the Bishops of Volterra at Montieri, and the Kings of Bohemia at Kutná Hora made sure that they should be.

On top of these payments to prince and landowner there were, of course, ecclesiastical tithes to be discharged, and the costs of smelting had also to be met.[4] Nevertheless the bulk of the silver remained in the hands of the mine-owners, to dispose of as they liked.

In most places the miners were themselves the mine-owners. Medieval miners were generally self-employed men working in small groups. Each partnership owned and operated its own pit or gallery and the silver they took from it was entirely their own once they had paid the prince, the landowner, the church and the smelters. This tradition of the 'free' miner was an extremely strong one and very widespread. In some places it lasted through into modern times, and the early Californian gold-miners were still staking out their claims to mine on their own account in this tradition. In Italy, however, investment by non-miners in mining appeared at a very early date. At the beginning of the thirteenth century a complex early capitalist form of organisation had already developed in Tuscany. There there were shareholders, *partiarii*, who formed *Le compagnie di fatto d'argentiera* at Montieri, or the *communitates fovee* at Massa. They employed mine-managers, *magistri*, who took on the actual miners, the *guerchi* or *laboratores*, as hired men, who worked for wages, not for themselves. There even seems to have been some division of labour amongst the workmen.[5] When the Pisans opened up the mines at

---

[1] Baudi di Vesme (ed.), *Codex Diplomaticus Ecclesiensis*, introduction.
[2] Gothein, *Wirtschaftsgeschichte des Schwarzwaldes*, I, 630–1.   [3] Volpe, 'Montieri', p. 364.
[4] In some places there were, in addition, peculiar local dues, like the *ius corbelli* paid at Montieri to the Tinacci family, who had a hereditary monopoly of weights and measures there.
[5] *Ibid.* p. 370.

Iglesias later in the century, they took much the same organisation with them, and investment in mining was treated in just the same way as investment in any other profit-making activity. For example, the notarised inventory of the property of a rich Pisan orphan, drawn up by his guardian in 1318, showed that, amongst other investments, he held shares in no less than six different mines in the vicinity of Iglesias.[1] Not until the fifteenth century did this sort of capitalist investment in mining take place north of the Alps. Edward I's attempt to exploit the Beer Alston mines directly, appears to be a unique experiment, and he soon called in outside contractors to run the enterprise for him.

Until the fifteenth century most of Europe's miners were their own masters, fiercely maintaining the extensive 'liberties' enshrined in their mining-codes and with a real chance of becoming, at least temporarily, wealthy men, if they discovered a rich vein of ore.

In the twelfth and thirteenth centuries there seems to have been no compulsion to pass the silver through a local mint. The attempt to do so at Kutná Hora in 1300 has already been seen as an innovation, and a not very successful innovation at that. At about the same time, minting may also have been compulsory in England. The Frescobaldi claimed the cost of transporting silver to the mint in 1299–1300 as an expense inherent in mining. Even if it was only a specious plea to get more money out of Edward I, it is interesting that it could be advanced. The notion of compelling miners to have their silver minted immediately was obviously under discussion at this time in other places besides Bohemia and England, for in the first years of the fourteenth century the miners of the *contado* of Siena took the trouble to obtain confirmation from the city of their traditional liberty to carry their unminted silver wherever they liked.[2] It was not until later in the fourteenth century that further attempts were made to make immediate minting compulsory. At Freiberg the first attempt to compel the miners to have their silver minted took place in 1339. It was also in the 1330s that compulsory minting was introduced at Iglesias. Pegolotti records, as if it were something distinctive, that Sardinian silver was not available in plates, since it all had to be minted into grossi affonsini, or 'anfrusini' as he calls them. These were first minted in 1326/7, but were only struck in considerable quantities in the late 1330s, which suggests that the new regulation was actually enforced.[3] In the Black Forest area, mining and smelting remained separate undertakings, and it was the smelters who disposed of the metal. In 1369 silver-smelters could still sell their silver in bar form at Freiburg-im-Breisgau. In the toll-roll of that year the town took a toll of 4d. per mark on unminted silver. It

---

[1] Artizzu (ed.), *Documenti relativi ai rapporti economici tra la Sardegna e Pisa*, II, 78–80.

[2] Volpe, 'Montieri', p. 365.

[3] Philip Grierson, 'The coin list of Pegolotti', in *Studi in onore di Armando Sapori*, I (Milan, 1957), 489. Also see above, pp. 121–2. The novelty of the regulation is borne out by Pegolotti's note (*La pratica della mercatura*, p. 182), that in 1331 Sardinian silver had been exported to Tunis in bar form. The regulation was renewed in 1354 (Volpe, 'Montieri', *ibid.*).

was only in 1399, after the formation of the great monetary union of the upper Rhine, the *Genossenschaft der Rappenmünze* or *Rappenmünzbund*, that any attempt was made to force smelters to have their silver minted.[1]

It was not, however, any amount of legislation by the princes in whose lands the mines were to be found, but a quite different cause, that brought an end to the widespread circulation of silver in the form of bars and plates. This was the widespread changeover in the fourteenth century to the use of gold coin for many of the purposes for which bar silver had previously been used.[2] It only then became normal for silver mined in Europe to be rapidly minted into coin.

Even if there was no compulsion in the twelfth and thirteenth centuries to have newly mined silver minted, it was nevertheless often useful to have a proportion of it minted. For the convenience of the people, as well as the profit of the prince, a new mint therefore usually opened close to a successful silver-mine, after a longer or shorter delay. The Margraves of Meissen opened a new mint at Freiberg as well as their existing one at Meissen, the Archbishop of Salzburg at Friesach as well as at Salzburg, the Bishops of Volterra at Montieri as well as, or perhaps instead of, at Volterra, the Kings of Bohemia at Jihlava as well as at Prague, the commune of Pisa at Iglesias as well as in Pisa. In the same way, at later periods, Count Sigismund moved his mint to Hall am Inn to be near the silver-mines at Schwaz, the King of Castille opened a mint at Potosi, and the United States government at San Francisco, on the insistent demand of the inhabitants of California.

Despite the opening of these new mints the larger part of the precious metal left the mining-areas in an unminted state. In the mid nineteenth century in California, gold dust was used, uncoined, by miners to purchase their supplies and equipment from the many 'Yankee' and German shopkeepers there, and from the ubiquitous Jewish clothing-merchants.[3] As late as 1869, when the Union Pacific Railroad was opened, it advertised in San Francisco that fares could be paid in uncoined gold dust. In the sixteenth century, ingots as well as coin crossed the Atlantic from Spanish America and, at the end of Elizabeth's reign, silver in both forms reached the English mint in London.[4] In the twelfth and thirteenth centuries and well into the fourteenth, ingots as well as coin were similarly used for large payments throughout Europe, and many of the payments outwards from Europe were also made in silver that was still in the form of ingots rather than coin.[5] It is however, in my opinion, more important to examine how and why the newly mined silver was so rapidly conveyed away from the regions in which it was mined, than to know whether it was used in the form of coin or of ingots.

---

[1] Gothein, *Wirtschaftsgeschichte des Schwarzwaldes*, I, 648.
[2] See below, pp. 267–88.
[3] Paul, *California Gold*, p. 80.
[4] Christopher E. Challis, 'Spanish bullion and monetary inflation in England in the later sixteenth century', *Journal of European Economic History*, IV (1975), 381–92.
[5] See below, pp. 209–24.

6

The Balance of Payments
and the Movement of Silver

Much has been written about the flow of income from California and Australia in the nineteenth century, and even a certain amount of attention has been paid to the way in which specie flowed from Potosi after 1545. At first historians concentrated on the royal 'fifth' of the silver mined. A large part of this could clearly be seen returning to Spain, after the considerable expenses of South American administration had been deducted. It could then be seen passing on from Spain through royal expenditure to other parts of Europe, for example to the army in Flanders or to the royal bankers in Genoa. More recently greater attention has been paid to the much greater proportion of the new silver that remained in private hands.[1] How the silver was taken out of the hands of the miners themselves may be judged by the estimates that about 1600 there were not only 14 dance-halls and a theatre in Potosi, but also 36 gambling-houses, where the miners might be fleeced by between 700 and 800 professional gamblers, besides the 120 licensed and the innumerable unlicensed prostitutes. Gold-rush San Francisco was much the same, and it is not hard to believe that Freiberg, and Montieri, Friesach and Jihlava, Iglesias and Kutná Hora had, in their time, had the same free-spending carnival atmosphere. Was it as true there as in nineteenth-century California that 'the great profits went to the merchant, the hotel keeper, the transportation company and the gambling house proprietor'[2] or at least to their medieval equivalents?

The miners themselves, together with the gamblers, the prostitutes and all the myriad other hangers-on of a successful mining community spent lavishly on goods as well as pleasures. Suppliers moved in to meet this demand with extraordinary speed. Within two years of the discovery of silver, Potosi was the most considerable market for luxuries in the Americas, and continued to be so more and more despite the attempts of the Governor of Peru to restrain what he considered as waste.[3] Silver therefore not only changed hands very fast within

---

[1] This was more than four-fifths, since the royal 'fifth' was not taken from the ore mined on Sundays, which were consequently the busiest days in the mines.

[2] H. V. Faulkner, *American Economic History*, 8th ed. (New York, 1960), p. 192.

[3] Gwendolin B. Cobb, 'Supply and Transportation for the Potosi Mines, 1545–1640', *The Hispanic American Historical Review*, XXIX (1949), 26–7.

Potosi, but soon left it to pay for an extraordinary range of commodities. Fortunes were made in Potosi from dealing in

. . . silks of all sorts, and knitted goods from Granada; stockings and swords from Toledo; clothes from other parts of Spain; iron from Viscaya; rich linen and knitted goods from Portugal; textiles, embroideries of silk, gold, and silvers, and felt hats from France; tapestries, mirrors, elaborate desks, embroideries, and laces from Flanders; cloth from Holland; swords and steel implements from Germany; paper from Genoa; silks from Calabria; stockings and textiles from Naples; satins from Florence; cloths, fine embroideries, and textiles of excellent quality from Tuscany; gold and silver braid and rich cloth from Milan; sacred paintings from Rome; hats and woollen textiles from England; crystal glass from Venice; white wax from Cyprus, Crete and the African coast of the Mediterranean; ivory and precious stones from India; diamonds from Ceylon; perfume from Arabia; rugs from Persia, Cairo and Turkey; all kinds of spices from the Malay Peninsula and Goa; white porcelain and silk cloths from China; Negro slaves from the Cape Verde Islands and Angola.[1]

Fortunes were to be made in the supply of basic necessities as well as of luxuries, for in sixteenth-century Potosi, as in nineteenth-century California, the prices of ordinary foodstuffs reached incredible heights.

It would be splendid for medieval historians if a thirteenth- or fourteenth-century chronicler had made a similar list of the goods that flowed to Freiberg, Jihlava or Kutná Hora. We can do little more than assume that these places, each in its own heyday, had the same magnetic attraction for the luxuries of Europe, as well as for very considerable quantities of food. Only for Iglesias do we have a small glimpse of the luxuries flowing to a medieval mining-town, silks and linens as well as woollen cloth, olive oil and Greek wine. The swollen population of Argentiera required necessities as well as luxuries. The mining-boom provoked a considerable expansion of agriculture in the hinterland, but even this proved inadequate to feed the multitudes drawn by the mines. In the twelfth century Sardinia had been an exporter of grain, but in 1295 the commune of Iglesias had to make a large bulk purchase of Sicilian grain to keep the people alive.[2] When in 1318 the city of Pisa ordered Sardinian grain to be shipped to the Italian mainland to feed the mother city, the community of Iglesias protested vigorously that they were importers of foodstuffs not exporters: 'homines . . . intendunt magis in laborerio argenterie quam grani et ordei, ita quod de sua recollecta non possent vivere xv diebus nisi aliunde portaretur eis blada'.[3]

Chaunu has been able to examine in detail the exports and imports of sixteenth-century Seville, and to provide precise quantities for a large part of the range of

[1] The chronicle of Orsúa y Vela, quoted by L. Hanke, *The Imperial City of Potosi* (Hague, 1956), p. 28.
[2] C. Baudi di Vesme (ed.), *Codex Diplomaticus Ecclesiensis*, Historiae patriae monumenta xvii (Turin, 1877), Introduction, pp. ccliv ff.
[3] G. Volpe, 'Montieri: costituzione politica, struttura sociale e attività economica d'una terra mineraria toscana nel xiii secolo', *Vierteljahrschrift für Social- und Wirtschaftsgeschichte*, vi (1908), 363.

goods passing through the city. He has thus been able to explore and explain the changes in the scale and nature of goods going to the New World.[1] Domenico Sella has neatly summarised the impact on European industries of this demand and the flow of income involved in it.[2] There are, unfortunately, no statistics for the goods bought at the Champagne Fairs, which passed eastwards through Cologne and Frankfurt to Meissen and Bohemia in the thirteenth century, nor is there any means of showing whether the thirteenth-century expansion of European industries, for example the textile industry in Flanders, can be closely related to demands generated in Meissen or Bohemia.

Although we do not have very much direct information on the link between silver-mining and the development of trade and industry, we have a certain amount of indirect information, particularly about specie flows, which, at later periods, are so clearly connected with the demands in mining-areas for goods and services.

In 1968, Raymond de Roover wrote: 'As yet, very little is known about specie flows in the Middle Ages except for scattered bits of information which it would take years to collect and to assemble in a synthetic picture, a job which ought to be done, but has not yet been attempted.'[3]

This chapter is a first attempt at making such a synthetic picture.

It has been compounded not only from merchants' notebooks, but also from random references from official, chronicle and literary sources, backed up by the evidence, provided by coin hoards or by lists of coins used on specific occasions, for what coins were in circulation in particular places. At other periods additional information is provided by chemical analysis of impurities that have linked particular coins to particular mines, by official orders to permit specific foreign coins to circulate, by the survival of coins from one place countermarked for use in another. The evidence provided by the imitation of coins of one country in another can be ambiguous, but is also usable from time to time. Nevertheless a great deal needs to be done to fill in the picture.

Patently the silver from the mines flowed outwards in all directions, but in some directions the flow of silver was much more evident than in others.

From the mines at Friesach, for example, silver flowed predominantly eastwards and southwards.

The pfennigs struck at Friesach and St Veit, together with the numerous imitations struck immediately to the south and east, have been found in enormous quantities in Hungary. These large hoards concealed at Detta, Abapuszta and Érszodno in eastern Hungary between about 1220 and 1241 consisted almost

---

[1] H. and P. Chaunu, *Séville et l'Atlantique 1504–1650* (8 vols., Paris, 1955–60).

[2] D. Sella, 'European industries 1500–1700', in *The Fontana Economic History of Europe*, ed. Carlo M. Cipolla, II (1974), 360–5.

[3] R. de Roover, *The Bruges Money Market around 1400* (Brussels, 1968), p. 46.

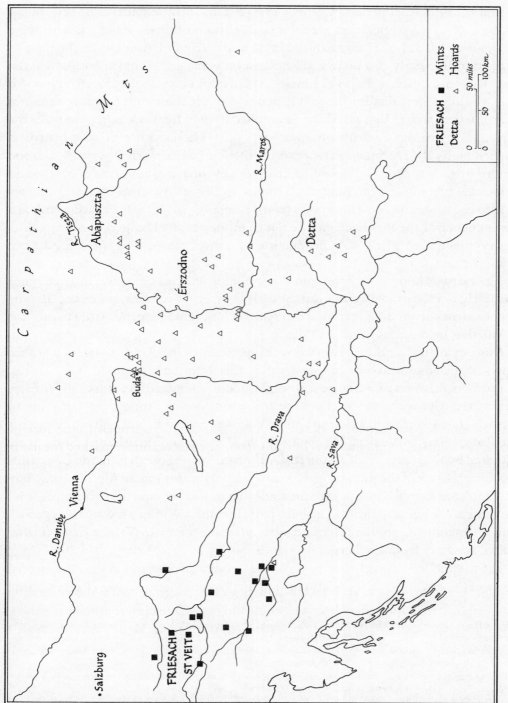

Map 14. Friesacher pfennigs in Hungary

entirely of Friesacher pfennigs. Out of 18,112 coins in these 3 hoards no fewer than 17,690 (98%) were Friesacher pfennigs or imitations of them. If these hoards were in any way typical of Hungarian currency in the reign of Andrew II, then it was made up very nearly completely of Friesacher pfennigs. It is not surprising that the next King of Hungary, Béla IV, himself had pfennigs struck of a Friesach type. All this would suggest that for the first generation of the thirteenth century the mines near Friesach and St Veit provided an ample currency for a whole region from the eastern Alps to the Carpathians (See Map 14.)[1] The evidence of coin hoards is backed up by the repeated reference to the pfennigs of Friesach in written sources. Andrew II, for example, specified that money due to him should be paid in Friesacher pfennigs.[2] The counterpart of this immense flow of specie into Hungary was an enormous increase in exports from Hungary, particularly of cattle, and, as a consequence of the increased circulation of money in the Hungarian countryside, the flourishing of small-scale production of manufactured goods for local rural consumption.

The eastward flow of specie from other mining-centres of central Europe is not so clearly demonstrable again until the early fourteenth century, when the 'Prague groats' struck from the silver mined at Kutná Hora came to form a large part of the circulating medium of southern Poland.

More evident than the eastward flow of specie from these mining-areas were the flows of specie southwards and westwards. (See Map 15.)

From its discovery on a large scale at the end of the twelfth century, silver from the eastern Alps seems to have been the prime commodity brought by 'Germans' to Venice. The silver from Friesach and St Veit was carried in large quantities across the Tarvis Pass to Venice. On their way to Venice the Friesacher pfennigs were imitated by the Patriarch of Aquileia. By the time of the Fourth Crusade Bernardus Teotonicus, one of the merchants who brought silver from these Alpine mines, had accumulated so much profit from the trade that he had become the richest foreigner in Venice. On his death in 1213 he left a huge fortune.[3] Within a few years a Munich bullion-merchant, another Bernard, was bringing silver to Venice from further afield, possibly from Freiberg.

In 1228 the Venetians began to build the *Fondaco dei Tedeschi* in the commercial heart of the city, next to the Rialto bridge, to provide 'German' merchants visiting

---

[1] Egon Baumgartner, 'Die Blütezeit der Friesacher Pfennige', *Numismatische Zeitschrift*, LXXIII (Vienna, 1949), 75–106; LXXVIII (1959), 14–57; and LXXIX (1961), 28–63; I. Gedai, 'Fremde Münzen im Karpatenbecken aus den 11–13 Jahrhunderten', *Acta Archaeologica Academiae Scientiaram Hungaricae*, XXI (1969), 111–31. See also Map 14, based on those by Baumgartner, p. 80, and Gedai, p. 145.

[2] The written sources on the circulation of Friesacher pfennigs in Hungary are gathered together in B. Homan, *Magyar Pénztörténet [Hungarian Monetary History]* (Budapest, 1916), pp. 276–313.

[3] Frederic C. Lane and Reinhold C. Mueller, *Money and Banking in Medieval and Renaissance Venice*, I (Baltimore, 1985), 136–8.

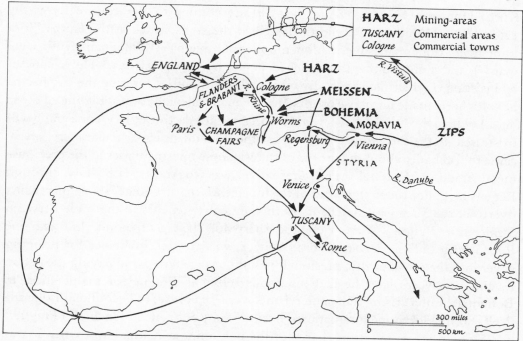

Map 15. General movement of Central European silver in the thirteenth century

Venice with lodgings and warehouse facilities. It was a means both of encouraging a trading group who had already become important to the city, and of regulating their activities.[1]

Venetian documents of the 1260s and 1270s show that 'German' silver was then dominant there. Its import was taxed, and consequently continued to be stringently regulated. In 1268 German merchants coming to the *Fondaco* were told that, within two days of their arrival, they had to register what they had brought with them with the *Vicedomini*, the officials appointed by the city to supervise the *Fondaco*. If they disposed of more than a single mark of silver or coin before registering it they became liable to penalties. By 1270 German merchants were liable to a tax of a fortieth on all the goods that they brought in, including 'argentum et platas argenti'.[2]

Around 1320 the Venetian da Canal notebook still contained a note that the mint of Venice was supplied with 'L'arçento che vien d'Alemagna'.[3] 'Germany' of course included Bohemia. Unminted Bohemian silver, from Jihlava, before the

[1] Frederic C. Lane, *Venice, A Maritime Republic* (Baltimore, 1973), p. 61.
[2] Roberto Cessi (ed.), *Problemi monetari veneziani. Documenti finanziari della Repubblica di Venezia*, 4th series, I (Padua, 1937), docs. 14 and 15.
[3] Alfredo Stussi (ed.), *Zibaldone da Canal, manoscritto mercantile del secolo XIV*, Fonti per la Storia di Venezia, V (Venice, 1967), p. 7.

Kutná Hora ore was discovered, was already coming to Venice as early as the 1260s.[1] The Florentine, Pegolotti, described the coins struck at the Kutná Hora mint from Bohemian silver as 'buenmini dalla magna' ('Bohemians from Germany'), and indicated that they reached Venice by way of Vienna.[2] The Viennese, by insisting on their *Stapelrecht*, by which all commodities entering the city had to be sold there, made immense profits. They equally alienated and antagonised those on all sides who might have wished to carry goods through Vienna but were frustrated. In the early fourteenth century the Bohemians in particular increasingly came to feel badly about the profits of the Viennese intermediaries in the precious-metal trade with Italy.[3] The alternative was to trade with Italy through Regensburg. For the first quarter of the fourteenth century Regensburg merchants overtook the Viennese merchants as the key entrepreneurs in the trade between Venice and Prague. Some were too sharp for their own good. In 1322 one Regensburg bullion-dealer, Konrad Spitzer, was arrested in Venice for bringing silver into the city illegally, presumably without registering and paying the tax on it, and two years later he had his goods seized in Prague for malpractices in Bohemia.[4] Enterprising Italian merchants were, of course, to be found in Bohemia itself. Some Florentine international business houses opened branches in Prague,[5] and Florentines were put in charge of the new mint at Kutná Hora when it was opened.

The da Canal notebook also reveals that around 1320 the Venetian mint was supplied with silver from Hungary as well as Germany. In 1270 Hungarians had already been bringing silver to Venice for some time, and customarily paid '14 soldi per centenaria' on it.[6]

As well as the silver that was carried from Styria and Meissen, Bohemia and Hungary directly to Italy, there was an almost equally important specie flow from the mining-areas of central Europe westward to the Rhineland, the Low Countries and eastern France.

In the Rhineland, Cologne was already established as the leading commercial centre, and furthermore, had been the principal bullion-market of Europe in the period of dominance of Goslar's silver-mines. In the Low Countries, the textile industries, particularly the manufacture of woollen cloth, were growing rapidly in response to the demand generated by the newly increasing money supply. From

---

[1] Josef Janáček, 'L'Argent tchèque et la Méditerranée (xive et xve siècles)', in *Mélanges en l'honneur de Fernand Braudel*, I (Toulouse, 1973), 246.

[2] Francesco Balducci Pegolotti, *La pratica della mercatura*, ed. Allan Evans, Medieval Academy of America (Cambridge, Mass., 1936), p. 147.

[3] Balint Homan, 'La circolazione delle monete d'oro in Ungheria dal x al xiv secolo e la crisi europea dell'oro nel secolo xiv', *Rivista Italiana di Numismatica*, 2nd series, v (1922), 125.

[4] Janáček, 'L'Argent tchèque', pp. 247, 249.

[5] Homan, 'La circolazione delle monete d'oro in Ungheria', p. 139.

[6] Cessi (ed.), *Problemi monetari veneziani*, doc. 16.

the late twelfth century to the early fourteenth, the different cities of Artois, Hainault, Flanders and Brabant dominated the woollen-cloth industry in turn. In eastern France in the twelfth and thirteenth centuries the fairs at the four great fair-towns of Champagne (Troyes, Provins, Bar-sur-Aube and Lagny), were the key points of exchange between north-western Europe and Italy, and between central Europe and the growing Capetian kingdom of France.

This specie flow began almost as soon as the Freiberg mines were opened up, and newly mined silver was already to be found in Champagne, Cologne and Flanders in the 1170s.[1] Throughout the thirteenth century references to new silver continue to be found in all these places. In 1224, for example, unminted silver, presumably from Freiberg, was passing westwards through Worms on its way to the Champagne Fairs,[2] and in 1265 the price of unminted silver, specified as from Freiberg, was being quoted in Champagne at the Troyes Fairs.[3] In Cologne in the 1250s Albertus Magnus was writing about Freiberg silver,[4] and at Bruges at the end of the century, silver from Bohemia and Hungary was generally available.[5]

All the evidence suggests that throughout the thirteenth century silver continued to be carried to the Rhineland, the southern Netherlands and Champagne, whether travelling by land along the *Hochstraat* of Europe, or through Vienna, up the Danube and then down the Rhine, or down the Vistula and round through the Baltic and North Seas. (See Map 15, p. 137.) Equally, merchants from Flanders and Cologne are found carrying goods, primarily cloth, in the opposite direction to Bohemia, and from France, the Rhineland and the southern Netherlands to Hungary and, for example, attending the fairs at the mining-town of Golniczbánya (Göllnitz) in Spiš (Zips).[6]

The silver that had been carried across Germany to the Rhineland, the southern Netherlands and Champagne did not remain there. Much spread out into France for the purchase of foodstuffs. It reached the Île de France from the 1190s.[7] Some was carried away by sea by Hanseatic merchants into and through the Baltic.[8] Some was transported to England, and a great deal was taken, either by land, or, increasingly from the end of the thirteenth century, by sea, to Italy. From the 1180s the evidence for the import of newly mined silver to England is very clear. It possibly began in the 1170s,[9] and from the mid thirteenth century the individual importers and their places of origin can frequently be identified. For example,

---

[1] See below, pp. 195–7   [2] See below, pp. 214–15.
[3] See above, p. 113.   [4] See above, pp. 111–12.
[5] A list of commodities generally available in Bruges is printed in Konstantine Höhlbaum (ed.), *Hansisches Urkundenbuch*, III (Halle, 1882–6), 419–20.
[6] Homan, 'La circolazione delle monete d'oro in Ungheria', pp. 134 and 140.
[7] See below, pp. 197–9.
[8] Rolf Sprandel, *Das mittelalterliche Zahlungssystem nach Hansisch-Nordischen Quellen des 13–15. Jahrhunderts* (Stuttgart, 1975), pp. 97–123.
[9] See below, pp. 196–7.

around 1242 the exchange in London expected to receive silver in the form of plate from Flanders, from Brussels and Malines in Brabant, and from 'Germany' amongst other places, and in the form of foreign coin from a number of places including Brussels and Cologne.[1] In 1257–8 purchases of silver by the exchange at London were recorded from ten foreigners – nine from the southern Low Countries, from Ghent, Ypres and Douai in Flanders, and from Malines, Brussels and Louvain in Brabant, together with one from Cologne. In 1266–9 purchases of silver were recorded from ten merchants from the southern Low Countries; from Bruges and Ghent in Flanders, from Malines and Louvain in Brabant, and from Dinant on the Meuse in the bishopric of Liège, and also from nine merchants of Cologne, from one of Kempen, and from one merely called 'Henricus le Alement'. In 1287–8 the London mintmaster purchased silver from numerous merchants from Malines, two from Brunswick, and probably from Dortmund, and three merely called 'de Alemannia'.[2] Werner Hillebrand, writing on the Goslar metal-trade, believed that the Brunswick merchants indicate that this was still Goslar silver, whilst Manfred Unger, writing on Freiberg, believed that this was Freiberg silver.[3] It was not necessarily either, but it is clear that for at least these three decades of the thirteenth century, silver was primarily being brought to England by merchants from Flanders, Brabant and Cologne. In 1299 the rulers of Flanders and Brabant took advantage of this, by regulating the export of silver for their own profit.[4] In return, increasing quantities of English wool, and decreasing quantities of English cloth, moved in the opposite direction.[5]

    Throughout the thirteenth century there seems generally to have been an adverse balance of trade between the north-western parts of Europe and Italy. The northerners in general seem to have bought more goods from Italian merchants than they sold to them. In the latter half of the twelfth century and for much of the thirteenth, the Flemish merchants had to take silver as well as cloth to the Champagne Fairs, despite the enormous expansion in the amount of cloth that they sold there.[6] Hanseatic merchants, who sold Baltic wares in Flanders on the way, then carried Flemish merchandise as well as Baltic goods to the Champagne Fairs,

[1] Mint documents published with Nicholas Oresme, *De Moneta*, ed. with English trans. by Charles Johnson (London, 1956), pp. xxiv–xxv and pp. 50–1.

[2] K. Kunze (ed.), *Hanseakten aus England 1275–1412*, Hansische Geschichts-quellen VI (Halle, 1891), pp. 3, no. 2, and 24, no. 5.

[3] Werner Hillebrand, 'Der Goslarer Metallhandel im Mittelalter', *Hansische Geschichtsblätter*, LXXXVII (1969), 34; Manfred Unger, *Stadtgemeinde und Bergwesen Freibergs im Mittelalter*, Abhandlungen zur Handels- und Sozialgeschichte V (Weimar, 1963), p. 70.

[4] See below, p. 215.

[5] E. Miller, 'The fortunes of the English textile industry in the thirteenth century', *Economic History Review*, 2nd series, XVII (1965), 64–82; and T. H. Lloyd, *The English Wool Trade in the Middle Ages* (Cambridge, 1977), and *Alien Merchants in England in the High Middle Ages* (Brighton, 1982).

[6] Henri Laurent, *Un grand commerce d'exportation au Moyen Age. La draperie des Pays-Bas en France et dans les pays mediterranéens (XIIe–XVe siècle)* (Paris, 1935), pp. 83–114.

but they, too, frequently bought more than they sold and had to use silver acquired in Flanders to make up the difference. As late as 1294 Philip IV was trying to compel Lübeck merchants, who were doing this, to pass through his tolls at Bapaume.[1] Merchants trading between England and Champagne also had to bring silver as well as goods with them. Sterling could consequently be acquired by Italian merchants at the Champagne Fairs.[2] As a result, English pennies sterling found their way south to Italy, through Champagne, for much of the thirteenth century. As early as 1202 they were already available in Venice.[3] They reached Italy in such quantities that sterling came to be the principal standard of fineness for silver in the Mediterranean. In 1233 the goldsmiths of Venice were swearing not to work silver of less fineness than the English penny sterling. In 1288, when Pisa and Genoa made peace, the war indemnity to be paid by Pisa to Genoa was stipulated in sterling.[4]

Most silver was, however, carried from Champagne to Italy either as ingots or plates of still-unminted silver, or else in the form of the current coins of Champagne. In the latter part of the twelfth century and the first half of the thirteenth these were the deniers struck for the Counts of Champagne at Provins.[5] These 'deniers provinois' consequently circulated widely in Italy, beginning in the 1160s, and were known there as 'provisini'.[6] They were so common that they were even imitated in Rome, at least as early as 1184, possibly even by 1177.[7] Towards the end of the thirteenth century the kings of France acquired Champagne, and, at about the same time, a change in the methods of doing business gradually shifted the commercial focus away from the Champagne Fairs. Instead of visiting the fairs, Italian merchants maintained permanent agents in Paris.[8] The royal takeover of Champagne, combined with the growing commercial importance of Paris, meant that French royal money came to play a similar role to that formerly played by the deniers provinois in the trade with Italy. At the end of the century French royal money was consequently to be found in large quantities in Italy instead of the money of Champagne. The papal collectors' accounts for the twelve dioceses of Tuscany in 1296 reveal that over a tenth of the money that they collected there had come from France. In three of the dioceses, including that of Pisa, French royal money formed a third of the value of the tax collected.[9]

---

[1] P. Dollinger, *The German Hansa* (1964; Eng. trans., London, 1970), doc. 5, pp. 383–4.
[2] Its price was quoted by Andrea de Tolemei at the Cold Fair at Troyes in 1265 (C. Paoli and E. Piccolomini (eds.), *Lettere volgari del secolo XIII scritte da Senesi* (Bologna, 1871), p. 57).
[3] See below, pp. 160–1.
[4] See below, p. 218.
[5] See below, p. 197.
[6] Pierre Toubert, 'Une des premières vérifications de la loi de Gresham: la circulation monétaire dans l'état pontifical vers 1200', *Revue Numismatique*, 6th series, xv (1973), 180–9.
[7] See below, pp. 201–2.
[8] And also at Bruges and London. See below, p. 252.
[9] John Day, 'La Circulation monétaire en Toscane en 1296', *Annales, Économies, Sociétés, Civilisations*, XXIII (1968), 1054–66.

Fifteen years later, when the Emperor Henry VII issued a monetary ordinance for Pavia, French royal gros tournois were put first amongst the 'foreign' grossi to which he wished the circulation there to be limited, apart from gold and his own imperial grossi and parvi.[1] A few years later still, Pegolotti included French coin as a source of silver for the Naples mint.[2]

Some Italian city governments quite deliberately took measures to enhance the flow of specie to Italy. In 1273, for example, Venetian merchants trading with Marseilles, Aigues Mortes and Montpellier were forbidden to purchase goods to a greater value than those they sold. They were not permitted to take or send any means of payment from Venice whether minted or unminted silver or gold or bills of exchange. Those buying cloth in France, i.e. in Champagne, were likewise forbidden to pay with minted or unminted silver or gold, but were permitted to pay by bill of exchange.[3] The possibility of using bills of exchange regularly depended on other merchants wishing to remit equal or greater sums from Champagne to Venice. The del Bene company of Florence, who specialised in cloth-finishing, regularly bought unfinished French and Flemish cloth at the Champagne Fairs, for finishing in Florence, for resale either in Florence or in Naples. Their accounts survive from 1318 to 1323, and during that period they never needed to carry silver or gold, minted or unminted, to France. There were always plenty of Florentine merchants whose agents had sold more than they bought in Champagne, and consequently had ready money available there, who were glad to sell the del Bene bills of exchange in Florence and so reduce the need for their agents to remit precious metals.[4]

By the end of the thirteenth century the overland routes from north-western Europe to Italy were being supplemented by the newly-opened sea-route around Spain. Galleys were sent first by Genoa, and then by Venice and Pisa, direct to Flanders and England. These too brought specie from the north-west to Italy and their departures from Bruges in June and December were marked by *strettezza*, a scarcity of money. On the other hand there was *larghezza*, that is, money was easy to find, in Bruges, in August and September, when merchants from Germany arrived in Bruges and brought in a flow of specie.[5]

Thus two principal streams of silver flowed from Central Europe through most of the countries of Europe in the thirteenth century and irrigated their economies in the process. Until the springs dried up in the fourteenth century it did not really

[1] All the other permitted grossi were from other parts of Italy, all but the Sicilian grossi from within 320 kilometres (200 miles) of Pavia (Wilhelm Jesse, *Quellenbuch zur Münz- und Geldgeschichte des Mittelalters* (Halle, 1924), pp. 157–8).

[2] Pegolotti, *La pratica della mercatura*, p. 182.

[3] Cessi (ed.), *Problemi monetari veneziani*, docs. 21 and 18.

[4] Armando Sapori, *Una compagnia di Calimala ai primi del Trecento*, Biblioteca Storica Toscana VII (Florence, 1932).

[5] Raymond de Roover, *Money, Banking and Credit in Medieval Bruges* (Cambridge, Mass., 1948), pp. 66–7.

matter how much of the silver flowed out of any particular country, so long as there continued to be more to flow in. The long-distance flows of silver from place to place were, of course, primarily inter-urban flows, since the demands for goods over long distances were primarily for urban goods and from city to city, but from each urban centre silver flowed out in eddies of demand into the surrounding countryside, so that a radical change in the rural as well as the urban use of coin took place between the late twelfth and the early fourteenth century. In this way not only was the superficial urban economy irrigated by these streams of silver, but the habit of using money a great deal more than in the past soaked down to the very roots of the fundamental rural economy.[1]

An overall picture of the flows of silver from various directions into Italy is provided for the early fourteenth century by the notebook of Francesco Pegolotti.[2] It is however sometimes difficult to know how precisely to use the evidence provided by a man such as Pegolotti, as it is not always clear to what date it refers. His well-known *Pratica della Mercatura*, finally compiled in the 1340s, has been described as 'not so much the practical handbook of an active man of business, as a compilation of the notes, which a retired merchant has at one time or another copied out in the hope that they would sometimes be useful, and which now, in his old age, he cannot bring himself to jettison'.[3] These notes span the whole of the period in which Pegolotti served the famous Florentine merchant and banking-house of the Bardi, from before 1310 until after 1340, and some even go back to about 1290, perhaps when the young Pegolotti was beginning his career, or perhaps incorporated by him from some earlier, now lost, 'handbook for merchants'.

Such a compilation naturally reflects the places in which Pegolotti himself worked. He was manager in turn of the Bardi branch offices in Antwerp (1315–17), London (1317–21) and Famagusta in Cyprus. At no time was Pegolotti himself in Germany or eastern Europe, nor did the Bardi ever have any branches there. For Pegolotti Germany was only a source of fox-furs, copper from Goslar sold at Bruges, wool sold at Venice, salt sturgeon sold at Antwerp and blue carbonate of copper sold at Alexandria.[4] This lack of direct contact with Germany, Bohemia or Hungary meant that he did not give any list of different sorts of Central European silver like those he gave for different qualities of wool from England or of alum from Asia Minor.

On the other hand he did insert into the coin list at the end of the handbook a short section of fourteen items of 'argento in pezzi e in verghe'. It has been suggested that this coin list is a part of the compilation that dates back to 1290,

---

[1] See below, pp. 241–7.   [2] See p. 138, n. 2.

[3] Philip Grierson, 'The coin list of Pegolotti', in *Studi in onore di Armando Sapori*, I (Milan, 1957), 492.

[4] Pegolotti, *La pratica della mercatura*, pp. 298, 381, 141, 253 and 70.

although with later additions.[1] This list might reasonably be supposed to relate to Florence itself. In addition, under Naples, Pegolotti also lists six sorts of silver likely to be brought to the mint there. This part of the compilation may date from the 1330s. Unminted German silver, coming from the north, appears as such in his early bullion list for Florence, strangely described as 'Argento di strabocco di Stanborgo della Magna'. 'Stanborgo' has not yet been identified to my knowledge. Central European silver, as such, does not appear forty years later in his list of silver coming to the Naples mint. It is, however, there under the guise of Venetian silver, described more fully in his Florentine bullion list as 'della bolla di Vinegia', in other words bars of silver sealed by the Venetian mint as of guaranteed and specified fineness. Such silver we have already seen to be of Bohemian or 'Hungarian', i.e. Slovak, origin at this date.

Silver that had come round to Italy indirectly through France is represented in Pegolotti's Florentine bullion list by the 'verghe della Bolla di Genova', the bars of silver sealed by the mint of Genoa, and 'argento in piastre lavorato in Genova'.[2] In the Genoese section itself Pegolotti refers to silver in the context of Genoese connections with Marseilles, Nîmes, Montpellier, the papal curia then at Avignon, Paris and Bruges. One of the last stages of the journey of this Central European silver to Florence by way of France and Genoa is described by Pegolotti in a short section on the cost of carrying silver from Genoa to Porto Pisano, by then the port of Tuscany. Carriage, duties and fees for loading and unloading and weighing added together to something like 4% of the value of the bullion transported.[3]

The silver coming into Tuscany from central Europe, however indirectly, joined the stock of silver already there from more local sources. In the twelfth and earlier thirteenth centuries this had come from Montieri and the other silver-mines of Tuscany itself, but in the later thirteenth and earlier fourteenth centuries from Sardinia.[4] 'Argento sardesco' heads Pegolotti's Florentine bullion list. After the Aragonese conquest of Sardinia and the introduction of compulsory minting there, Pegolotti inserted 'Affussini di Sardigna' as an additional item in his Florentine bullion list. Before the Aragonese conquest a large share of the Sardinian silver was attracted to Pisa, not only by way of the commune's twelfth part of the silver mined, and by the dividends paid by the mines to individual Pisan shareholders who had invested in them, but also by way of payment for the supplying of both necessities and luxuries to the mining community of Argentiera.[5] Presumably the

[1] Grierson, 'Coin List of Pegolotti', p. 489.
[2] Robert H. Bautier, 'L'Or et l'argent en Occident de la fin du XIIIᵉ siècle au début du XIVᵉ siècle', *Académie des Inscriptions et Belles Lettres, Comptes Rendus des Séances* (1951), 171 suggests that the bars sealed in the Genoese mint were not merely bars that had travelled around Europe and been assayed and guaranteed in Genoa, but rather that they were actually made in Genoa out of coin that had come from France and been melted down.
[3] Pegolotti, *La pratica della mercatura*, p. 220.   [4] See above, pp. 119–22.
[5] See above, p. 133. A Pisan-Aragonese agreement of 1309 valued the Pisan commune's revenue from the island at

larger part of this silver came to Pisa in the form of ingots, for the production of coin at the Iglesias mint seems to have been insignificant before the Aragonese conquest. From Pisa it spread out into Tuscany and further afield. Some of it was carried, for example, to Venice, still uncoined, by men of Lucca. In 1270 the Venetians exempted the men of Lucca from the bullion tax on the 'argentum et platas argenti' that they brought with them when purchasing goods in Venice.[1] Much of it, however, was transformed into coin in Pisa, and, as 'grossi aquilini', circulated widely in Tuscany. When the papal tenth was collected in Tuscany in 1296 grossi aquilini were only surpassed in value by gros tournois, which had come by way of trade from France, and by the grossi of Volterra minted from the silver mined in Tuscany itself.[2] After the Aragonese conquest of Sardinia, a large part of· the silver went to Naples, where in 1326 the number of moneyers had to be increased 'ex argenti copia quae in dicta sicla auxit et auget assiduo incremento monetae argenti'.[3] It is not surprising that 'argento sardesco' also headed Pegolotti's Neapolitan bullion list.

Northern Italy and Tuscany were not, however, the final resting-place of the silver from the mines of Freiberg and Montieri, of Friesach and Jihlava, of Iglesias and Kutná Hora. Much did, of course, accumulate there, since the profits of the middlemen in any trading-enterprise are traditionally the highest, and this concentration of liquid assets in northern Italy and Tuscany did much to ensure the dominance of their inhabitants in the commercial revolution of the thirteenth century.[4] These Tuscans and northern Italians were great adders of value to the commodities that passed through their hands, not merely by buying cheap and selling dear, but also by the processing of the commodities they handled. The Lucchese, for example, were great manufacturers of silk cloth, without any considerable local production of silk; the Florentines and other Tuscans were great manufacturers of woollen cloth, without any considerable local production of wool, besides finishing cloth made elsewhere; and the Milanese were great manufacturers of metal and cotton goods, without any considerable local mining of iron and no local production of cotton whatsoever. But from the very beginning of

60,000 florins, of which the Iglesias mines by themselves provided 15,000 florins, a quarter of the whole value. If this at all approximates to the commune's twelfth, it implies an annual output of 180,000 florins worth of silver (Rosalind P. Brown, 'Social development and economic dependence: Northern Sardinia, *c.* 1100–1330' (Ph.D. Thesis, University of Cambridge, 1985), pp. 89–90 and 267.

[1] Cessi (ed.), *Problemi monetari veneziani*, docs. 15 and 16.

[2] Papal collectors in the twelve Tuscan dioceses collected 21,047 lire di piccoli of Florence, of which 8692 lire was in florins, 10,664 lire in grossi and only 1682 lire in piccoli. Of the sum collected in grossi, over 54% was in Tuscan grossi, primarily Volterran grossi (21%) and Pisan aquilini (15%). Gros tournois made up 21% of the sum, and Venetian grossi made up 11%. They did not collect significant sums in any other sort of coin (Day, 'La circulation monétaire en Toscane', pp. 1054–66).

[3] Philip Grierson, 'La moneta veneziana nell' economia mediterranea del Trecento e Quattrocento', in *La civiltà veneziana del Quattrocento* (Fundazione Giorgio Cini, Florence, 1957), pp. 77–97.

[4] See below, pp. 258–9.

the new supplies of silver in the second half of the twelfth century, silver can also be seen passing on southwards and eastwards from northern Italy and Tuscany. As early as the 1140s and 1160s Dr Abulafia reckons that the Genoese could not pay for their imports from Sicily and southern Italy with the industrial products of northern Italy and transalpine Europe and had to pay for the majority of their imports in silver. Indeed the privilege of William I (the Bad) to the Genoese in 1156 anticipated that they would be bringing silver with them, since the dues to be paid on landing at Messina were expressed in silver, although silver did not yet have any currency function in the south. It was merely a commodity. In 1156 the coinage of the Regno still consisted entirely of copper and of gold tari.[1] They were nevertheless to pay 12 silver denari per man and 24 silver denari *per apotheca* (?load).[2] The export dues in the same privilege of 1156 were expressed in tari. Stocks of silver in the south built up gradually and came to be used as currency alongside gold and copper. Payments in provisini, the deniers provinois of Champagne, which had begun in Rome in the 1150s and in southern Latium in the 1160s,[3] were also made further south later in the century. In the 1180s and 1190s charters expressed payments in provisini not only in Campania, but also in Apulia, and a hoard of several hundred of them, which possibly dates from the very end of the twelfth century, has been discovered in Basilicata.[4]

At the same time as the expansion of North Italian and Tuscan trade with southern Italy and Sicily, there was a general expansion of North Italian and Tuscan trade with Constantinople, Palestine and Egypt. At the same time as the Genoese, Pisans and Venetians were setting up *fonduks*, hospices, consular houses, harbours and even churches in Naples, Messina and Palermo, they were also acquiring quarters in Constantinople (the Genoese in 1155, the Pisans and Venetians earlier still), markets and harbours in Acre and *fonduks* in Alexandria. With most of these places the trade was unbalanced, and European silver had to be exported.

In Constantinople itself, however, there was no immediate impact on the currency of the presence of western merchants. Constantinople had not had a silver coinage since the eleventh century[5] and insufficient western silver reached the city to provoke a fresh coinage of silver there until the end of the thirteenth century. The Mongol 'peace' allowed the opening-up of a trans-Asian route with its western termini on the northern shores of the Black Sea at Caffa in the Crimea and Tana on the Sea of Azov. Western merchants increasingly took advantage of this route in the last quarter of the thirteenth century. From the end of the thirteenth century they carried silver, largely in the form of ingots, through Constantinople into the Black

---

[1] See below, p. 167, n. 1.
[2] David Abulafia, *The Two Italies* (Cambridge, 1977), pp. 92, 219, 223.   [3] See above, p. 141.
[4] Pierre Toubert, *Les Structures du Latium médiéval . . . du IXe à la fin du XIIe siècle*, Bibliothèque des Écoles françaises d'Athènes et de Rome CCXXI (Rome, 1973), pp. 583–4.
[5] See above, p. 97.

Sea, and then on through Caffa and Tana into the western steppes in prodigious quantities. Much of this remained in the form of ingots,[1] but a certain amount was minted. In the 1280s the Khans of the Golden Horde began a prolific coinage of dirhams, known to Italian merchants as 'aspri', or 'aspers'. In the early fourteenth century aspers became the common currency all round the Black Sea, not only at Caffa and Tana, on the north coast, but at the mouth of the Danube and also on the south coast in the Byzantine outpost of Trebizond and among the Seljuks of Rum in central Asia Minor. They were, of course, carried eastwards and could also be found at Tabriz under the Il-Khans. This surge of West European silver through Constantinople in the late thirteenth century enabled the restored Palaeologi to mint a silver coinage there for the first time for nearly three centuries. The silver basilicon began to be struck there from at least 1304, if not a few years earlier.[2]

Although West European silver did not reach Constantinople itself in considerable quantities until the late thirteenth century, it was available in Asia Minor and in Greece much sooner. In Asia Minor the alum-mines attracted western merchants, who carried away alum to supply the fast-growing manufacture of woollen cloth in western Europe. It was paid for in western silver and the Seljuk rulers were enabled to begin minting a silver coinage of their own at their capital, Konia (Iconium), as early as 1185–6 and at Kaiseri in 1199–1200. In Greece the Fourth Crusade brought West Europeans into control of much of the country. In the thirteenth and fourteenth centuries Greece provided abundant supplies of oil, wine and grain for the cities of Italy, paid for, of course, in West European silver coins, which circulated there widely and inspired derivative coinages there.[3]

In the thirteenth century the principal western imports were English sterlings (mainly introduced before 1274), French deniers tournois (mainly introduced *c.* 1230–65) and Venetian grossi. From the 1260s to the 1340s imitative deniers tournois were struck by various princes in Frankish Greece itself, so that, although fresh deniers tournois were no longer being brought from the west, tournois continued as the principal currency of Greece along with Venetian grossi. From the mid fourteenth century, when other Greek issues of deniers tournois were coming to an end, the Venetians began to mint them for their Greek colonies – Negroponte (Euboea), Crete, and various places in the Peloponnese. These deniers passed under the name of torneselli, and were struck in Venice specifically for export to Greece. At around the time that the first torneselli were struck, considerable quantities of soldo coins, soldini, were also being sent out from Venice.[4]

---

[1] See below, pp. 211 and 220–1.

[2] D. M. Metcalf, *Coinage in South-Eastern Europe 820–1396*, 2nd ed. (Royal Numismatic Society, London, 1979), chapter 11.

[3] See below, p. 155.

[4] Alan M. Stahl, *The Venetian Tornesello. A Medieval Colonial Coinage*, Numismatic Notes and Monographs CLXIII (American Numismatic Society, New York, 1985).

In the Middle East silver had been rare since the stocks of it had shrunk rapidly at the end of the tenth century.[1] In Egypt after the reign of al-Hakim, who was murdered in 1021, the Fatimids had only managed to mint small quantities of very poor black dirhams, or dirhams *waraq*. Outside Egypt the minting of silver had ceased altogether by A.H.418 (1027–8). In the 1170s the amount of silver rapidly rose to the point where the minting of silver could be resumed. It began first in Damascus in 1174/5. By the end of the century there were at least nine mints striking silver coins in the Middle East (see Map 16A, p. 150), and in Egypt Saladin had enough silver by 1188 to attempt a restoration of the dirham to half silver.[2] The speed with which the silver of Freiberg and Montieri reached Syria and Egypt in quantities large enough to provoke its minting is quite astonishing. The continued supply of silver from Europe is reflected by the striking of dirhams from it at more and more mints further and further into Asia over the course of the thirteenth century (see Maps 16B and 16C, pp. 150–1). The shortage of money that marked the declining years of the Abbaside and their successors right to the end of the Seljukid period, was suddenly transformed in Syria under Saladin (1169–93) and his Ayyubid successors, and in Irak under an-Nasir (1180–1225) during the revived caliphate in Baghdad. Not only were dirhams minted again, but they were minted in such large quantities that Professor Ashtor has described the Ayyubid period as a veritable 'age of silver'. Silver was so freely available that the fineness of the dirhams could even be increased from around one-half silver in Saladin's reign to two-thirds silver in 1225. In addition to the vast amount of European silver available in the form of coin, the use of silver for inlaid metalwork began at exactly the same time in the late twelfth century as the revival of minting of silver dirhams. In eastern Persia and in Upper Mesopotamia, such metalworking became a flourishing industry, particularly at Mosul and in cities to which the silversmiths of Mosul migrated.

In the middle of the thirteenth century the Middle East was divided sharply into two by the Mongol invasions. Irak, and parts of Syria, fell under the overlordship of the Mongol Il-Khans based in northern Persia at Tabriz, whilst Egypt and the remainder of Syria remained outside Mongol control under the Bahrite Mamluk sultans. Contacts between the two parts were extremely limited. European merchants, however, traded with both parts of the Middle East, although the contacts with Mamluk Egypt were nominally limited by papal prohibitions. Trade with Mongol Irak and Persia prospered through Christian Armenia, which

---

[1] This section, to p. 152, is largely derived from E. Ashtor, *A Social and Economic History of the Near East in the Middle Ages* (London, 1976), pp. 175, 216, 234, 239–248; and Andrew M. Watson, 'Back to gold – and silver', *Economic History Review*, 2nd series, xx (1967), 1–34.

[2] P. Balog, 'History of the dirhem in Egypt from the Fātimid Conquest until the collapse of the Mamluk Empire', *Revue Numismatique*, 6th series, III (1961), 109–46, although M. Balog doubts the effectiveness of Saladin's restoration.

acknowledged Mongol overlordship, and considerable quantities of European silver consequently continued to find their way through Armenia, which itself had a prolific silver coinage, into Irak and Persia. Here it merged into a rapidly increasing stock of silver, which was also apparently being supplied from the reopened silver-mines of central Asia. In Turkestan, Ferghana and Bukhara are supposed to have enjoyed a brief revival of their earlier prosperity of the ninth and tenth centuries. There is no evidence that this revival of silver-mining in central Asia, and even on a very modest scale in Asia Minor,[1] owes anything to the example of European mining, but it is singular that it happened at a time when contacts with Europe were more considerable than ever before, and when extra-ordinarily widespread prospecting for silver was taking place in Europe.

This increase in the quantity of silver from the late twelfth century to the early fourteenth century was a direct consequence of the increasing volume of exports and re-exports by Italians to Europe. The Pisans, Venetians and Genoese, established at Alexandria, Damietta and Aleppo, together with those in the Christian states of the Holy Land, particularly at Acre, carried away increasing quantities of North Syrian cotton for manufacture in Lombardy, as well as the whole range of spices from India and Arabia that passed through the Levant. The transit trade, as in North Italy and Tuscany, greatly enriched the wholesale spice-traders through whose hands it passed. The number of merchants increased generally, and some groups became particularly wealthy, such as the Karimis, a loose association of rich shipowners trading under Ayyubid protection, who brought Indian spices to Egypt and the Yemen, or the Iraki traders of Damascus, who brought spices overland from the caliphate. European silver, in the guise of a European demand for Levantine and oriental products, brought about a commercial revival in the Middle East almost as rapidly as it had done in Italy, as well as a stimulus to certain branches of agriculture and industry. The growing of cotton, for example, increased greatly, as did both the growing of sugar cane and the refining of sugar, and so did the manufacture of glass in northern Syria, until the Venetians developed their own glass industry enough to supply the European market directly. In its initial stages European demand was quite simply a stimulus to the economy of the Middle East, but fairly rapidly Italian ingenuity provided substitutes for many of the manufactured goods of the Middle East. Not only was glass manufactured and sugar refined in Venice rather than Syria, but linens and cottons were woven in Lombardy rather than Syria or Egypt, and even silks were manufactured in Tuscany. At the height of the expansion of Italian trade and industry in the early fourteenth century, Italian textiles, primarily linens, had not

---

[1] In 1332 Ibn Battuta visited silver-mines at 'Kumish', in Anatolia, some 60 kilometres (40 miles) south of Trebizond (H. A. R. Gibb (ed.), *Travels of Ibn Battūta 1325–54*, Hakluyt Society, 2nd series, CXVII (1962), pp. 436–7).

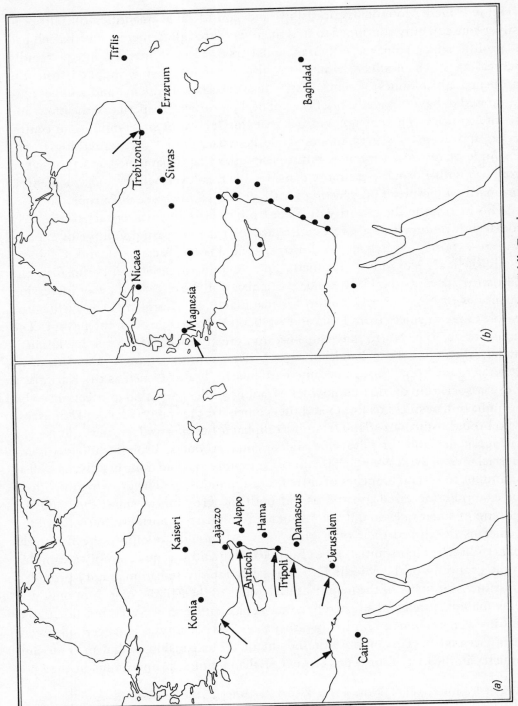

Map 16A. Mints striking silver coins in the Middle East by 1200
Map 16B. Mints striking silver coins in the Middle East by 1250

Tiflis

Erzerum

Baghdad

Trebizond

Siwas

Nicaea

Magnesia

(b)

Kaiseri

Lajazzo

Aleppo

Hama

Damascus

Antioch

Tripoli

Jerusalem

Konia

Cairo

(a)

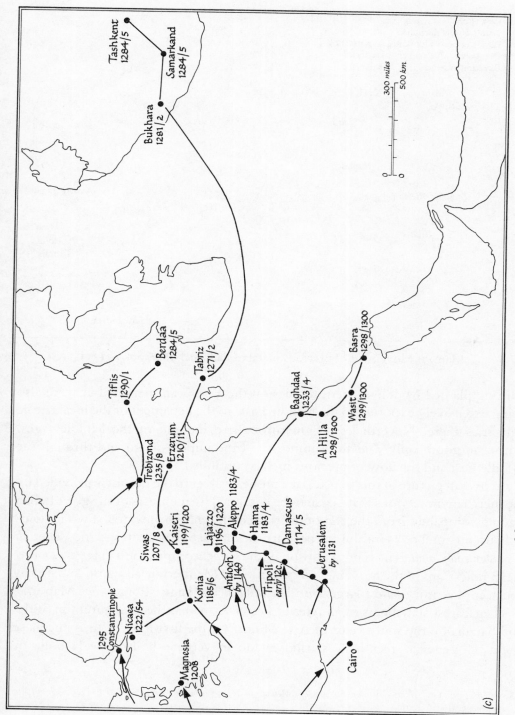

Map 16c. Mints striking silver coins in the Middle East by 1300

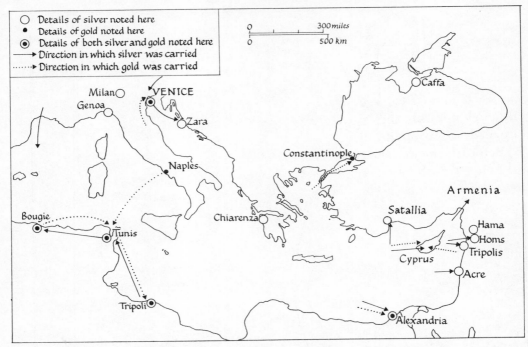

Map 17. Movement of precious metals – da Canal notebook *c.* 1311

only supplanted Middle-Eastern textiles on the European market, but were also being extensively exported to the Middle East, to the detriment of the local textile industries there. Nevertheless, right through to the end of the Middle Ages, European goods only paid for a minority of the imports from and through the Middle East and the flow of precious metals continued.[1]

An overall picture of this transfer of European silver to the Levant is provided by the merchant notebooks that began to be compiled by members of the great Italian trading companies from the end of the thirteenth century onwards. Two particularly useful notebooks for this purpose are the *Pratica* of Pegolotti and the Venetian *Zibaldone da Canal*. The central portion of the latter, compiled in 1311, gives a few clear indications of the movement of silver in the Mediterranean world in the early fourteenth century, and a larger number of less clear suggestions.[2] (See Map 17.)

The clearest statements of all refer to Lesser Armenia, the Hama mint in Syria, and Satallia on the south coast of Asia Minor. Of the first it says: 'In Armenia se porta da Venexia arçento de sterllin gitado in verge e bollade de la bolla de

---

[1] See below, pp. 342–56, and Eliyahu Ashtor, *Les Métaux précieux et la balance des payements du Proche-Orient à la Basse Époque* (Paris, 1971).

[2] See p. 137, n. 3.

Venexia',[1] of the second it says: 'La çecha si da a çaschun che porta arçento de sterllin in Aiman . . . deremi de çecha chuniati'.[2] Of Satallia it says: 'E si tu portis gss[i] de Venexia elli . . .'[3]

At Alexandria and Acre the sale of sterling silver is noticed, and at Tripoli and at Limassol in Cyprus the use of gros tournois from France, and at Zara in Slavonia the use of grossi from Venice.[4] Local silver coin is naturally referred to repeatedly, although it is only at Hama that it is possible to see that the dirhams in circulation are made of European silver.

Before the memoranda on exchange and on weights and measures written down in August 1311, the earlier part of the manuscript, which Frederic Lane reckons to be of about the same date, contains a series of arithmetical problems for a young man taking up a business career. The second sum set is about exchangers in Venice dealing with silver of different finenesses. 'L'inchanbiadori da Venexia conpra l'arçento che vien d'Alemagna e d'Ongaria le quelle nonn é afinà, çerto e puo' lo fasse afinar.' The silver that came in may not have been of a fixed fineness, but that which went out certainly was: 'Li marchadanti de Venexia porta per lo mondo arçento de sterllin.'[5] This Venetian sterling silver, in sealed bars, has already been noticed as far away as Syria and Armenia. The latter example is repeated in one of the supplementary sections at the end of the manuscript, which Professor Lane reckons was added shortly after 1320.[6] The rate is given at which the Armenian mint at Sis is bound to accept sterling silver in bars.[7]

The material collected by Pegolotti in his *Pratica della Mercatura* spans at least four and possibly five decades. Pegolotti spent most of the earlier part of his career in the Low Countries and England and the material collected at this period has already been used in discussion the flow of silver within western Europe.[8] However, from 1321 until he finished the compilation, about 1340, he was either in charge of the Bardi's branch in Cyprus, or else attached to their head office in Florence. His information on the flow of precious metals within the Mediterranean therefore relates primarily to the 1320s and 1330s and follows on from the da Canal notebook material of 1311 and 1320.

Pegolotti equally presents a picture of silver being carried southwards and then

[1] 'To Armenia is carried from Venice sterling silver cast into bars and sealed with the seal of Venice' (*Zibaldone da Canal*, fo 38r; Stussi ed., p. 62).

[2] 'The mint there gives to each person who carries sterling silver to Hama . . . dirhems coined in the mint' (*Zibaldone da Canal*, fo 40v; Stussi ed., p. 67). Pegolotti's editor, Allan Evans, identified 'Aiman' as Amman, but W. Heyd identified it as Hama, which makes more sense.

[3] 'And if you carry Venetian grossi thither . . .' (*Zibaldone da Canal*, fo 42v; Stussi ed., p. 71).

[4] *Zibaldone da Canal*, fos 41v, 42r, 39r, 34r and 33v; Stussi ed., pp. 68, 70, 64, 55 and 54.

[5] 'The changers of Venice buy the silver which comes from Germany and Hungary which is not of a fixed fineness and can have it refined'; 'The merchants of Venice carry throughout the world silver of sterling fineness' (*Zibaldone da Canal*, fos 1r and 2r; Stussi ed., pp. 6 and 7).

[6] *Zibaldone da Canal*, Intro. to Stussi ed., p. lv.

[7] *Zibaldone da Canal*, fo 63r; Stussi ed., p. 108.

[8] See above, pp. 143–5.

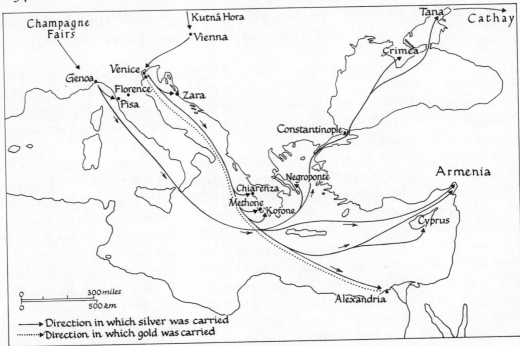

Map 18. Movement of Central European silver – Pegolotti notebook *c.* 1321–1340

eastwards, from central Europe either directly through Vienna to Venice, or indirectly through the Low Countries and France to Italy, and from there to Cyprus and the Levant, and onwards, by way of Lesser Armenia to the Mongol world. (See Map 18.)

He listed the fourteen different sorts of silver that came to the Famagusta mint in Cyprus, presumably when he was there from 1324 to 1329 or later, or on his return in 1336, and the nine sorts of silver to be expected at the mint at Lajazzo in Lesser Armenia, where the Bardi had a sub-branch that he visited in 1335 or 1336. By this time it is quite clear that this is Bohemian silver, primarily from the Kutná Hora mines, for in the bullion lists of both the Famagusta and the Lajazzo mints there appear 'Bracciali cioe buenmini', and 'braccali coniati',[1] in other words Bohemian groschen, better known now as Prague groats, minted at Kutná Hora, largely from the silver mined there.

Like the compiler of the da Canal notebook, Pegolotti explained that it was necessary for a merchant to know how to alloy silver correctly to make ingots 'per portare d'uno paese in uno altro',[2] and this silver in ingots appears alongside coin in Cyprus and Lesser Armenia. In both places silver cast into plates and bars sealed in Venice featured prominently, followed in the case of Famagusta by 'grossi di

---

[1] Pegolotti, *La pratica della mercatura*, pp. 81 and 60. [2] *Ibid.* p. 342.

Vinegia coniati'. In the section on Alexandria, both 'ariento in verghe di Vinegia' and 'grossi nuovi coniati di Venegia' have a place, and it is clear that balances from Venice to Alexandria were settled in silver, either in bars or in grossi.[1] Within Constantinople and Pera (the commercial port of Constantinople) Venetian grossi circulated alongside Byzantine coins and the imitative deniers tournois of Frankish Greece, whilst western bar silver was recast there into fresh bars, *sommi*, of a different fineness (11oz. 17dwt. fine, or 0.98 fine by modern reckoning), suitable for Asiatic trade, which were carried across the Black Sea to Gazera (the Crimea) and Tana on the Sea of Azov.[2] The mints of Cyprus and Armenia also both expected to receive from the west 'grossi tornesi' or silver 'a lega di tornesi grossi' and 'sterlini' or silver 'di lega di sterlini'. Although the gros tournois were clearly French and represented the continuation eastwards of the flow of silver southwards from France into Italy,[3] it is not clear that sterling was English any longer. Sterlings had once been current in Greece and the Aegean[4] and were still a money of account in Frankish Greece at Chiarenza, Istiva, Negroponte, Methone and Korone, but Pegolotti makes it clear that in these places Venetian grossi or local imitative deniers tournois were actually in use in his time.[5] The impression from the da Canal notebook is that sterling had become the normal description for the Venetian standard of fineness for silver.[6] It is interesting to observe that Pegolotti nowhere mentions Genoese coins outside Genoa, despite the vast scale of Genoese trade with the eastern Mediterranean. There is no hint that Genoese coin circulated in the way that Venetian grossi did or French gros tournois. It would seem that the Genoese traded almost exclusively with silver in the form of bars. Under his description of Genoa Pegolotti included a sub-section on the costs of transporting silver by weight, in armed galleys, from Genoa to Pera, which was then the principal Genoese overseas trading-post.[7] Bar silver sealed in Genoa occurs in both his Famagusta and his Lajazzo bullion lists.

Pisa, by the time that Pegolotti was making his notes, no longer counted in the same league as Venice and Genoa, but the Sardinian silver, on which Pisan prosperity had once been based, still appears, alongside Central European silver, in Pegolotti's notes on the eastern Mediterranean. In his description of Sardinia Pegolotti describes how its silver was carried in various directions, particularly to Naples and Cyprus.[8] In his bullion lists for the Cypriot and Armenian mints 'argento sardesco' commanded the highest prices, and Sardinian silver at second hand, as Neapolitan coin, also appeared, as 'gigliati coniati' and as silver 'a lega di gigliati'. (See Map 19.)

---

[1] *Ibid.* pp. 74–5.
[2] *Ibid.* pp. 40–1 and 25.
[3] See above, pp. 141–2.
[4] See below, p. 161 n. 6.
[5] Pegolotti, *La pratica della mercatura*, pp. 116f, 119, 149, 153.
[6] See above, p. 141.
[7] Pegolotti, *La pratica della mercatura*, pp. 219–220.
[8] *Ibid.* p. 120, and see above, p. 145.

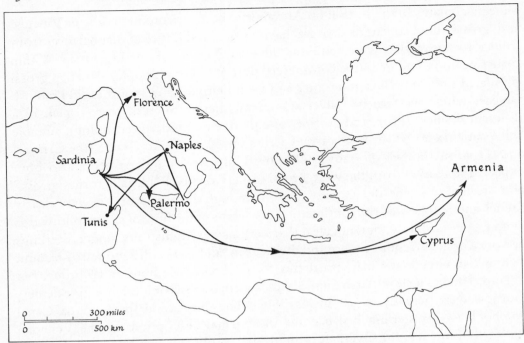

Map 19. Movement of Sardinian silver – Pegolotti notebook *c.* 1321–1340

It seemed clear both to an early-fourteenth-century Venetian, and to his slightly younger Florentine contemporary, that the silver of Germany and Bohemia, of Hungary and Sardinia, flowing through France and Genoa, Venice and Naples, was largely ending up in Lesser Armenia and the Crimea, in Syria, Cyprus and Egypt, arriving there primarily in the form of bars of silver sealed in Venice or Genoa, but also as gros tournois, Venetian grossi, or Neapolitan gigliati.

From the Middle East the silver went on eastwards. Not only did the Karimis carry it to India, but also it travelled overland towards China. Pegolotti reported that Italian merchants, whom he knew, carried Italian linens to Urgenj, south of the Aral Sea, which they sold there for silver *sommi*, and then took the silver with them to China, where it was exchanged for paper money at the frontier, which they then used for the purchase of silks for the return journey to Europe.[1]

Silver mined in Europe thus eventually ended up paying for the primary products enjoyed and used by Europeans, even if they were produced in extremely distant places, like the silk of China, the spices of the East Indies, the precious stones and spices of India, and the pearls of the Persian Gulf, as well as those coming from less distant places, like the furs of Russia, the alum of Asia Minor and the wool of England.

[1] *Ibid.* p. 23.

Trade balances provided the basic and overwhelming reasons for normal and continuous flows of specie both within thirteenth-century Europe and outside it. They were not the only reasons. Religious and political factors also played a part in the movements of bullion. In the short run these could sometimes have much greater effects on the flow of specie than trade balances, although in the long run trade was always far more important.

Throughout the period from the 1160s to the 1320s there were three major religious reasons for the movement of bullion. These were the workings of the papacy, pilgrimages and the Latin presence in the eastern Mediterranean. All these were regular and continuous, and in general, tended only to accentuate the concurrent trade-based movements of bullion about Europe. From the late twelfth century onwards successive popes developed an extensive taxation system that reached into every corner of Latin Christendom. As the papal financial administration established more and more complex and widespread means of tapping the increasing liquid wealth of the Church for its own needs it aroused greater and greater animosity towards its exactions amongst churchmen throughout Europe. In the second half of the twelfth century the papacy had at once begun to take advantage of the quantities of silver newly available in the hands of churchmen, and highly articulate protest very soon followed. Before the end of the century the cupidity of the curia was being ridiculed in the scathing parody *The Gospel according to Marks of Silver*. In 1199 Innocent III began the direct taxation of the Church to finance his new Crusade, the Fourth. He repeated this in 1215, for the Fifth Crusade.[1] His successors continued the system for the ordinary support of the papacy. The stream of clerical invective continued.[2] This income from papal taxation maintained the central bureaucracy of the papal monarchy, and enabled many of the popes to exert considerable political pressure. Until the early fourteenth century the popes generally lived somewhere in the papal states in central Italy, although not necessarily in Rome itself. The flow of payments to the papal chamber therefore only contributed to the general movement of silver to Italy. In the early fourteenth century the popes were in, initially reluctant, exile from Italy and gradually became established at Avignon.

At Avignon, John XXII (1316–34) overhauled the taxation system thoroughly. The revenues of John XXII averaged 228,000 Florentine florins a year.[3] This was less than the revenue of the city government of Florence and less than half the

[1] Louise and Jonathan Riley-Smith, *The Crusades: Idea and Reality 1095–1274* (London, 1981), pp. 144–8 and 124–9.

[2] The *Besant de Dieu* and the *Roman de Carité* are only two examples of the stream of literate protest of the first half of the thirteenth century. Excerpts are printed in M. W. Baldwin, *Christianity through the Thirteenth Century* (New York, 1970), pp. 389–93.

[3] Yves Renouard, *Les Relations des papes d'Avignon et des compagnies commerciales et bancaires de 1316 à 1378*, Bibliothèque des Écoles françaises d'Athènes et de Rome, CLI (Paris, 1941), pp. 3–39.

income of any of the contemporary Kings of France, Naples or England. However, unlike these revenues, which came from a relatively limited area, the papal income was drawn from all parts of Europe. Although this flow of payments went in the first instance to Avignon, rather than Italy, a large proportion of it still ended up in Italy. John XXII's reforms were made in order to be able to maintain an army to reconquer the papal states, and most of his income was therefore immediately transferred to Italy to pay his troops. Of the remainder, spent in Avignon, a major part was expended on the upkeep of the papal court. The members of this then spent their income on goods and services provided by North Italian entrepreneurs who sent agents to Avignon or settled there themselves in large numbers. Papal revenue therefore largely ended up in North Italy, whether the popes themselves were residing in central Italy or the Rhône valley. In addition to the amount that passed through the *camera apostolica*, the papal curia also drew a great deal more money to itself. The cardinals shared in the proceeds of papal taxation, but they also held the strings of benefices scattered through Europe from which they drew revenues. Lesser members of the curia did the same on a smaller scale. The income accounted for by the *camera apostolica*, therefore, represented only a half, or even less, of the total amount of money sent to the Curia. Nevertheless, even this sum, when compared with some of the sums involved in international commerce, was still relatively small. Shortly after the papacy of John XXII the workshops of the Florentine *Arte della Lana* were producing 1,200,000 florins worth of woollen cloth a year for export.[1] In other words the members of one guild in one city (admittedly one of the more important guilds in one of the more important cities) had a much greater effect on the flow of bullion in early fourteenth-century Europe than the whole of the papal curia.

The effect of pilgrimages on the flow of bullion is impossible to measure. The two greatest resorts of pilgrims were naturally Rome and the Holy Land itself. Money spent by wealthy pilgrims on the journey to either only reinforced the commercial flows of silver to Italy and the Levant. On a smaller scale foreign pilgrims to the shrine of St Thomas Becket at Canterbury only added, and not very extensively at that, to the flow of silver that was in any case coming to England to pay for its wool and its tin. Some pilgrimage routes, however, did run against the prevailing flow of specie. French pilgrims, for example, carried silver to St James at Compostella, although trade was drawing Spanish gold into southern and western France in the late twelfth and early thirteenth centuries.[2]

The effect of the first two crusades and the maintenance of the crusading principalities in the Holy Land has already been seen as a great drain of silver out of Europe, which helped to create the bullion famine in the west in the first half of the

---

[1] Giovanni Villani, *Cronica*, Book XI, chapter xciv, referring to the period 1336–8.
[2] See below pp. 180–2.

twelfth century.[1] After silver-mining began again on a significant scale from the 1160s, and the European stock of silver began to increase again, the drain of silver to the Holy Land became much less significant in terms of its effect on the stock of silver in the west. But even though it was less significant in its effect, the scale on which money was sent to the east actually became greater. Indeed there is reason to suppose that after Saladin's victory at the Horns of Hattin in 1187 the crusader states in the Levant became much less self-supporting and more dependent on the west. After the Fourth Crusade there was the Latin Empire in Constantinople and Frankish Greece to maintain as well.[2] Such payments from the west to the east went on continuously throughout the thirteenth century. Year after year, the crusading orders, chiefly the Templars and Hospitallers, drew increasing revenues from their larger and larger landholdings in the west and remitted them, along with alms collected from the faithful, to the eastern Mediterranean.[3] On a lesser scale the orders of the Teutonic Knights and of the Sword remitted the revenues from their smaller landholdings to the eastern shores of the Baltic. In addition to the continuous flow of money to the east year in and year out, the preaching of crusades time and again called forth efforts of prodigious expense from 1187 to 1274 and less frequently thereafter. The involvement of the three greatest monarchs of the west in the Third Crusade ensured that it was the costliest expedition to date. The participants in the Fourth Crusade found even the expense of their passage to the east in Venetian shipping more than they could afford and had to allow themselves to be diverted to Zara and then to Constantinople. St Louis' first crusade had to bear the cost of ransoms, principally St Louis' own, after the expense of crusading had already strained the resources of many of the participants.[4] Only a few crusades, like those of Frederick II or of Edward I of England, did not overstrain the resources of the participants. All alike added to the flow of precious metals to the east, or at least to places like Venice on the way to the east.

International politics within western Europe, particularly war and preparation for war, involved much larger payments than any religious activity except the most

---

[1] See above, pp. 98–9.

[2] In the first half of the thirteenth century silver sent from the west to support the new Frankish rulers of Greece largely took the form of English 'short-cross' pennies (see below, p. 161, n. 6) and, from the middle of the century, of French deniers tournois. Throughout the thirteenth century Venetian grossi also found their way to Greece, but this was more likely to be the consequence of trade than of subsidies from the west (Metcalf, *Coinage in South-Eastern Europe*, pp. 247–66).

[3] D. M. Metcalf, 'The Templars as bankers and monetary transfers between West and East in the twelfth century', in P. W. Edbury and D. M. Metcalf (eds.), *Coinage in the Latin East* (Oxford, 1980), pp. 1–18. He discusses the thirteenth century as much as the twelfth.

[4] After his release by the Egyptians in 1250, St Louis himself spent no less than 1,053,476 livres parisis in the Holy Land over the next three years, all of which had to be sent from France. An English translation of his accounts for these years is printed in Riley-Smith, *The Crusades*, pp. 148–52. For a discussion of them, and of other payments involved, see André E. Sayous, 'Les Mandats de Saint Louis sur son trésor et le mouvement international des capitaux pendant la septième croisade 1248–1254', *Revue Historique,* CLXXVII (1931), 254–304.

expensive of crusades. Many of the spectacularly large 'abnormal' payments associated with war and the preparation for war, were in fact made in the same direction as commercial payments, and only a few ran counter to 'normal' commercial payments. The ones that ran counter to the 'normal' flows of specie can be more easily seen in their effects.

The whole sequence of 'imperial' expeditions to Italy, from Henry VI to Charles IV, carried yet more silver from Germany to Italy. For example, in 1194, Henry VI's invasion of the kingdom of Sicily, carried out in the name of his wife Constance, the heiress of the Norman Kings, and partially financed by the ransom of Richard I of England, brought a vast amount of transalpine silver into southern Italy and Sicily. This sudden political injection of silver, on top of a generation of gradual accumulation of silver in the south through trade, made it possible for Constance and Henry, soon after their invasion, to break with the 'Sicilian' tradition of only minting gold and copper, and to launch a coinage of silver in Apulia for the first time. Their denari, although quite unlike anything minted in the south before, fit comfortably into the whole range of penny coinages generally minted from Rome to the Irish Sea over the previous generation.

Imperial expeditions were not the only ones. In the fourteenth century much of the royal share of the silver of Kutná Hora paid for the Italian adventures of John the Blind, King of Bohemia, between the 'imperial' expeditions of his father, Henry VII, and of his son, Charles IV. From France, too, expensive expeditions were sent to Italy. In the 1260s Charles of Anjou, St Louis' brother, spent vast sums in Italy from France and Provence to wrest the kingdom of Sicily from Manfred and Conradin.[1] In the next century his great-nephew, Charles of Valois, brother of Philip IV, and the richest magnate in France, also came on an expensive, but less successful, adventure into Italy. All these carried silver in the same direction that it was flowing naturally.

The Kings of England, however, ruled over a kingdom that, because of natural resources, was normally a recipient of silver throughout the period from the 1160s to the 1320s. Their foreign involvements carried coin in exactly the opposite direction to the commercial flows of specie. Richard I's crusade, and then his ransom, and his support for Otto IV, carried enormous quantities of short-cross pennies out of England.[2] One of the effects of these enormous payments of sterling by Richard was that sterling became freely available in many parts of the continent for making payments. Because they were made of good silver (0.925 fine) the sterlings were not melted down but used again and again. They were used

---

[1] One effect of this vast transfer from France to Italy was an increase in the price of gold florins at the St Ayoul fair at Provins in 1265 from 7s. 9d. provinois to 8s. 1d. provinois 'per chasione de la crociera' (for Charles' invasion was nominally a crusade) (Paoli and Piccolomini (eds.), *Lettere volgari*, p. 57).

[2] H. Fichtenau, 'Akkon, Zypern und das Lösegeld für Richard Löwenherz', *Archiv für Österreichisches Geschichte*, CXXV (Vienna, 1966), 11–32; and see below, pp. 390–1.

internally in the areas to which they were sent, as for example in 1198 when Baldwin IX, Count of Flanders, having received large subsidies from Richard, was able to give *his* allies and vassals 'infinitam pecuniam denariorum esterlingorum', according to Lambert of Ardres.[1] They were also used internationally, as for example in October 1202 when, in preparation for the Fourth Crusade, Baldwin IX, together with Louis Count of Blois, the Marshal of Champagne and other barons agreed to pay 118 marks and 3 ounces of silver in Venice. They did so in sterling.[2]

King John's continued support for Otto IV, his brother-in-law, in his attempt on the imperial crown, sent more sterling out of England, and so did his financing of the Bouvines campaign in 1214.[3] The same pattern can be seen in John's as in Richard's reign, internal use in the area to which it was sent, followed by long-distance use away from that area. In 1207 John sent 6000 marks, nearly 1 million short-cross pennies if all in coin, to Otto IV. Short-cross pennies circulated freely in the Rhineland and have been found in hoards concealed there at this period.[4] In 1214 when the Archbishop of Cologne sent 500 marks to Rome, he sent 'marcis bonorum novorum et legalium sterlingorum'.[5]

A generation later, in 1235, Henry III's marriage of his sister Isabella to the Emperor Frederick II took large, but not such large, quantities of silver into Germany. Henry sent 30,000 marks dowry, nearly 5 million short-cross pennies if all in coin, with his sister.[6] His brother Richard of Cornwall's attempt on the imperial crown after the death of Frederick II carried new long-cross pennies to the Rhineland.[7]

---

[1] As quoted by Hans van Werveke, 'Monnaies, lingots, marchandises? Les instruments d'échange aux XIe et XIIe siècles', *Annales d'Histoire Économique et Sociale*, IV (1932), 452–68, collected in *Miscellanea mediaevalia* (Ghent, 1968), pp. 194 and 202.

[2] *Bilanci generali della Repubblica di Venezia*, vol. I, part 1, Documenti Finanziari della Repubblica di Venezia, 2nd series (Venice, 1912), doc. 8, pp. 24–5.

[3] See below, pp. 247–8.

[4] Otto IV himself also struck imitative short-cross pennies in the Rhineland, and so did Frederick II, after his victory over Otto IV (S. Rigold, 'The trail of the Easterlings', *British Numismatic Journal*, VI (1949), 31–55).

[5] Walter Hävernick, *Der Kölner Pfennig im 12. und 13. Jahrhundert*, Vierteljahrschrift für Sozial- und Wirtschaftsgeschichte, supplement XVIII (Stuttgart, 1930), p. 132.

[6] Imitative short-cross pennies were struck by a dozen different rulers in Westphalia in the 1230s and 1240s (Rigold, 'Easterlings'). Payments continued to be made from northern Europe to southern Europe in sterling, and sterling became one of the key standards for fineness for measuring silver in the Mediterranean (see below, pp. 218–19). Short-cross pennies themselves continued to circulate widely in the Mediterranean for some time. In Greece, for example, sterlings formed a large part of the circulating medium in the middle of the thirteenth century. Ian Stewart, 'A hoard of sterlings from the Aegean', *Coin Hoards*, V (1979), 141–2, suggests that this hoard, reputedly concealed on Naxos in the 1260s, was largely made up of short-cross pennies that had left England in the 1230s and 1240s. Even after sterling ceased to circulate in Greece, it remained a money of account there (Metcalf, 'Easterlings', pp. 261–6).

[7] For Richard's expenditure in the Rhineland between 1259 and 1268 see N. Denholm-Young, *Richard of Cornwall* (Oxford, 1947). It was presumably some of this coin that was available at Troyes in 1265, unless 'sterling' was being used as a term for a fineness of silver in ingots at the Champagne Fairs as well as in the Mediterranean at this date (Paoli and Piccolomini (eds.), *Lettere volgari*, p. 57).

A generation later still, Edward I spent some £750,000 on war between 1294 and 1298, much of it sent abroad, partially to pay troops, to defend Gascony against Philip IV, but also to purchase a great alliance of princes on the northern and eastern frontiers of France. The German King, Adolf of Nassau, the Archbishop of Cologne, the Duke of Brabant, the Count of Holland, the Count of Flanders, the Count of Bar, and the leagued nobles of Franche Comté were all promised subsidies. Once again the export of English pennies provided a large part of the circulating medium for a whole area of Europe.[1] As well as their effects abroad, the transport out of the country of such sums made a radical difference to the amount of money in England. In between, of course, the continually favourable balance of England's trade ensured that England's stock of silver was not only replenished, but even increased between each of these great bursts of foreign expenditure.[2] Even political expenditure on this scale could only temporarily reverse the effects of the balance of trade or the flow of specie.

[1] They were used consistently for long enough to become a money of account and were again widely imitated by the rulers of the region, not only by such considerable princes as the Duke of Brabant, the Count of Flanders, the Count of Holland and the Count of Luxemburg, but also by a host of minor rulers. Some of their pieces were honestly made of good weight and fineness, clearly differentiated from English sterlings, although equally clearly derived from them. Others, mostly, although not entirely, struck by the lesser rulers of the region, were fraudulent imitations, short in weight or fineness or both, intended to deceive and make a profit for their issuers. Imitations, both honest and deceptive, flowed back into England, for the balance of trade continued to be in England's favour. There is even reason to believe that, in the 1290s, silver that would earlier have been sent to England in the form of ingots and minted on arrival at London or Canterbury was deliberately minted into imitative sterlings on the continent before it was sent across the Channel. The imitative sterlings not unnaturally caused considerable disruption in England. Between 1300 and 1302 the recoinage of over £250,000 of foreign silver removed most of the worst of these imitation sterlings from circulation in England, but many continued to circulate for another half century (Mavis Mate, 'Monetary policies in England 1272–1307', *British Numismatic Journal*, XLI (1972), 34–79; N. J. Mayhew (ed.), *Edwardian Monetary Affairs (1279–1344)*, British Archaeological Reports XXXVI (Oxford, 1977); and N. J. Mayhew, 'The circulation and imitation of sterlings in the Low Countries', in N. J. Mayhew (ed.), *Coinage in the Low Countries (880–1500)*, B.A.R. International Series LIV (Oxford, 1979), pp. 54–68; and N. J. Mayhew, *Sterling Imitations of Edwardian Type* (London, 1983)).

[2] After adding up the amount of silver coming into the country to be minted, C. G. Crump and A. Hughes ('The English currency under Edward I', *Economic Journal*, V (1895)) believed that the stock of silver in Edward I's reign (1272–1307) increased fourfold. They took no account, however, of the political movement of silver. More recently Michael Prestwich ('Edward I's monetary policies and their consequences', *Economic History Review*, 2nd series, XXII (1969), 406–16; and *War, Politics and Finance under Edward I* (London, 1972)) suggested that the stock of coin in the country was rising in the 1280s; reaching a total of around £800,000 on the eve of Edward's military and diplomatic expenditure of £750,000 between 1294 and 1298; rising from a low level with the flowing into the country of imitative sterlings, particularly after the peace of 1298; and increasing further with the revival of the wool-trade, from 1300 to 1307, to reach a level at the end of the reign little higher than that at the beginning. See also below, pp. 202–5.

7

European Silver and African Gold

At the same time as the stock of silver was increasing so rapidly in Europe, the stock of gold was increasing in Africa. The process had begun very much earlier than the European discoveries of silver at Freiberg and Montieri, for a little gold was already crossing the Sahara in the eighth century. It began to do so in considerable quantities at the end of the tenth century, and continued to do so, almost uninterruptedly, until the fifteenth century.

Trans-Saharan trade was very unevenly balanced. From the north, traders carried both Egyptian and, later, European textiles, glass, particularly glass beads, spices and sometimes copper. On the most westerly route they were able to purchase the all-important salt at Taghaza on the way, and on the easterly routes they could pick up further copper at Takedda. On returning to the north, the trans-Saharan caravans took with them ivory, ebony, sometimes copper from Takedda, and from the fourteenth century, malaguetta pepper (or grains of paradise). They also took with them large numbers of slaves who had been seized by the rulers of the successive savannah kingdoms of Ghana[1] and of Mali in raids on their southern forest-dwelling neighbours. Ibn Battuta, on his return to the Maghreb in 1353, travelled with a slave-trader who was crossing the desert with 600 women. The northern goods were so highly prized that in the markets of the south they greatly exceeded the value put on local commodities. Salt was particularly esteemed, and in some places was literally worth its weight in gold. It is little wonder that the gold of the western Sudan flowed to North Africa and to Muslim Spain and Sicily in much the same way as the silver of central Europe flowed to northern Italy.[2]

The gold itself came from 'Takrur' and 'Wangara', according to al-Idrisi in the twelfth century, and these have been identified as Bambuk, an area on the upper Senegal, and Bure, on the upper Niger, respectively.[3] By the eighth century the rulers of Ghana between the upper Senegal and the upper Niger had established a

---

[1] Medieval Ghana was not at all where modern Ghana is to be found. Instead it lay in an area that is now western Mali and southern Mauretania.
[2] E. W. Bovill, *The Golden Trade of the Moors*, 2nd ed. (Oxford, 1968), pp. 92–105.
[3] *Ibid.* pp. 119–31.

general overlordship over both these areas. In 773 al-Fazari referred to Ghana as 'the land of gold'. Their rule was broken by an extraordinary invasion across the desert in 1062 by the Almoravids, who succeeded in establishing an empire south of the Sahara, although it only lasted for a quarter of a century. In the twelfth century no single people dominated the western Sudan, but in the thirteenth century the Mali built up a vast savannah kingdom between the desert and the tropical rain-forests, which stretched from the mouth of the Senegal eastwards beyond the Niger.

Mines in the same places seem to have gone on for centuries and are still not entirely exhausted. There were no sudden changes like those found in Europe – the discovery of new silver-mines, their rapid exploitation and their consequent exhaustion. What did change in Africa was the routes by which the gold was carried northwards across the Sahara from the western Sudan. Consequently different cities of North Africa, and of Muslim Spain and Sicily, were enriched in turn by the trans-Saharan trade. At the end of the tenth century, the key route ran due north across the western Sahara from the goldfields of Bambuk and Bure to Sidjilmasa, and then through the Atlas Mountains to Fez, in modern Morocco, and finally to the caliphate of Cordoba in southern Spain. Sidjilmasa had been founded in the eighth century when trans-Saharan trade was opening up. At the end of the tenth century, Ibn Hauqal estimated that its ruler drew 400,000 dinars in gold from the trade through his city each year. By the middle of the eleventh century the most important route ran north-eastward across the Sahara to Kairouan, the capital of the Zirid state in modern Tunisia, and thence on to Muslim Sicily. With the emergence of the Almoravids in the second half of the eleventh century the western route through Sidjilmasa resumed its predominance, although a large number of other routes were also used, and gold reached the North African coast at a series of ports from Sale, Tangier and Ceuta in modern Morocco, through Oran and Bougie in modern Algeria, and Tunis and Mahdia in modern Tunisia, to Tripoli in modern Libya.[1] In addition a certain amount of trade followed a route south of the Sahara to the upper Nile valley. By the fourteenth century the trans-Saharan trade was largely concentrated on two routes. According to Ibn Khaldun, writing in the second half of the century, an annual caravan of 'twelve thousand' camels travelled from Mali to Egypt, crossing the desert between Takedda and Ouargla, or Wargala, in Algeria. Even so the western route from Timbuktu to Sidjilmasa surpassed it in importance. In the kingdom of Mali, Timbuktu on the middle Niger came to be the great focal point for trade at this time, and the rulers of Mali became spectacularly wealthy from their control of its trade. It was a wealth flaunted before North Africa and the Middle East by the pilgrimage of Mansa Musa to Mecca in

[1] C. Vanacker, 'Géographie économique de l'Afrique du Nord du IXe siècle au milieu du XIIe siècle', *Annales E.S.C.*, XXVIII (1973), 659–80.

1324–5. He reputedly took with him 80 to 100 camel-loads of gold, besides the gold staves carried before him by 500 slaves.[1]

The trans-Saharan trade was in large measure responsible for the general revival in prosperity of the Maghreb and of Muslim Spain in the late tenth century. The changing routes of the trans-Saharan trade were later reflected in the varying prosperity of the particular cities of North Africa at which they terminated. For example, the eleventh-century heyday of Kairouan, and its port, Mahdia, coincided with the importance of the routes leading to it. Their prosperity did not survive the Almoravid conquest of the Zirid state in the 1050s and 1060s. In 1087 the Pisans, Genoese and Amalfitans dropped their differences to combine to find a means of breaking in on the Almoravid monopoly of the trans-Saharan trade. It is therefore surprising that they picked on Mahdia, as if it were still the key to the trade, and tried to seize it as a base for their operations.[2]

Apart from a little that was cast into ingots at Timbuktu, the gold crossed the Sahara in the form of dust. Much of it remained as dust, although some more was cast into ingots at Sidjilmasa or Wargala. A large part of it, however, was minted into dinars in the mints of North Africa, and the relative importance of the production of the different mints at different times is another indicator of the changing scale of trade on the different routes. (See Map 20.)

At the time of the Almoravid conquests in the 1050s and 1060s Kairouan and Mahdia suddenly ceased to be among the leading mints of North Africa, leaving Sidjilmasa, the stronghold of the Almoravids, as the sole significant mint in North Africa for thirty years. By the end of the century the major mints producing gold dinars were all clustered along the western route across the Sahara. Sidjilmasa remained the most important, although rivalled by new or reopened mints at Aghmat and Nul (which, like Sidjilmasa itself, prospered where the gold-bearing caravans left the desert), at Fez and Marrakesh on the northern side of the Atlas Mountains, and at Almeria, Seville and Granada in southern Spain. The mints in these cities remained the most important issuers of gold dinars in the twelfth and thirteenth centuries, apart from those at Aghmat and Almeria, which declined earlier.[3]

In the same way the North Italians passed on to the Middle East the silver that they had accumulated from Central European mines, the inhabitants of the cities of North Africa passed on their gold to the Middle East, for they too had an unfavourable balance of trade with the Levant. As a consequence, Egypt and Syria were able to maintain a prolific currency of gold dinars throughout the Middle

---

[1] Bovill, *Golden Trade*, pp. 86–8.
[2] David Abulafia, *The Two Italies* (Cambridge, 1977), p. 52.
[3] Harry W. Hazard, *The Numismatic History of Late Medieval North Africa*, Numismatic Studies VIII (American Numismatic Society: New York, 1952).

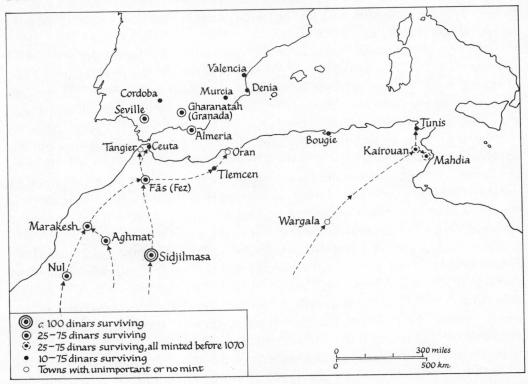

Map 20. Trans-Saharan routes, and mints striking gold in Maghreb and Spain 1047–1439

Ages. By the fourteenth century both Egyptian merchants and Egyptian textiles travelled the whole length of the routes to the western Sudan. Ibn Battuta commented on their presence when he was at Timbuktu in 1352–3.

Further east, in Irak for example, gold for minting remained plentiful as long as trade was possible with Egypt and Syria, but after the Mongol conquests of the 1250s commercial contacts were radically reduced, and gold dinars were minted in much smaller quantities and were partially replaced by silver dinars.[1]

Although the larger part of the gold from West Africa passed through Muslim Spain and North Africa to the Muslim Near East, a certain amount overflowed into some neighbouring Christian lands. In Christian Catalonia, for example, this happened remarkably soon after the sudden increase in the quantity of gold available in the caliphate of Cordoba.[2] In the Cordoban state the previous dearth of gold suddenly came to an end between 965 and 975. Amongst the many other uses to which they put the gold, the Muslim rulers of Spain were now enabled to pay

[1] E. Ashtor, *A Social and Economic History of the Near East in the Middle Ages* (London, 1976), pp. 291 and 254–5.
[2] This passage is largely derived from Pierre Bonnassié, *La Catalogne du milieu du Xe à la fin du XIe siècle. Croissance et mutations d'une société* (2 vols., Toulouse, 1975–6), I, 363–432.

Catalan mercenaries with it. The first recorded use of dinars by the inhabitants of Barcelona appears as early as 981, and by the last decade of the century their use was so common that more than half (57%) of the few land transactions of which record survives in and around Barcelona, were expressed in gold, to the value of over 1000 'mancusos' (dinars). It is sometimes clear that the dinars concerned were those of Sidjilmasa and Ceuta. This extraordinary growth continued for another 20 years. By the second decade of the eleventh century the vast majority (87%) of such transactions were in gold, to the value of over 3000 mancusos. By this time mancusos were to be found in the countryside, as well as in the town, in the hands of relatively ordinary people, village smiths, country priests and the owners of insignificant allods. It was at the end of this decade that the Countess of Barcelona began to have dinars struck in the city. In the late 1030s the mint of Barcelona was being supplied with African gold in the form of ingots shipped from Ceuta. The regular use of gold did not, however, spread beyond Catalonia, and even in the inland county of Urgel its use was much less common than on the coast. On the far side of the Pyrenees, in Narbonne, only one payment in gold is known between 990 and 1050. Far from going further into Christian Europe, the gold that was paid to the Catalans flowed back into Muslim Spain instead. The inhabitants of Catalonia used it to purchase Andalusian silks and carpets, and even Syrian fabrics or North African furs. In so far as dinars left Catalonia for other Christian countries at this period it was in tiny amounts, as prestigious, pious gifts – 6 mancusos to Compostella, or 10 to Rome.

At about the same time that the Countess of Barcelona began minting Christian dinars in Catalonia, the Lombard princes of Salerno in southern Italy began minting Christian *rubā'i* or quarter-dinars, which they called 'taris'. By the middle of the century their near neighbours, the Dukes of Amalfi, were also minting gold taris,[1] and when the Norman Duke of Apulia conquered Sicily a few years later, he too began minting Christian quarter-dinars. The gold taris of Robert Guiscard, minted at Palermo, after he captured the city in 1072, followed the *rubā'i* of al-Mustansir, minted immediately beforehand, without a break. Until 1278 the Norman, Swabian and Angevin rulers of Sicily went on minting taris, from their mints in Palermo and Messina, with inscriptions in Arabic and later in a combination of Arabic and Greek.[2] During two centuries of Christian rule, fresh gold to

---

[1] The earliest documentary references to Christian taris being struck in Salerno and Amalfi date from 1012 and 1057 respectively (Philip Grierson, *Later Medieval Numismatics* (London, 1979), addenda and corrigenda, pp. 1–2). In calling these pieces 'tari' or 'tarenus' the Lombards mistook the adjective for the noun. In Arabic it was *rubā'i* that meant a 'quarter' (dinar), whilst *tari* meant only 'new'. The mistake goes back at least to the early tenth century. An Amalfitan contract of 922 used 'tari' for quarter-dinar (*Codice diplomatico-amalfitano*, ed. R. Filangieri di Candida (1917), p. 3). It is parallel to the eighth-century error confusing *manqûsh* and *dinar*. See above, p. 50.

[2] P. Grierson and W. A. Oddy, 'Le Titre du tari sicilien du milieu du xiᵉ siècle à 1278', *Revue Numismatique*, 6th series, xvi (1974), 123–34.

mint these taris continued to come from Africa. Some came by way of tribute, for Christian rulers from Roger II to Charles of Anjou claimed, and from time to time managed to enforce, overlordship over parts of the North African coast. Tunis alone was supposed to pay 34,300 dinars yearly. Some came by trade. In the 1180s, for example, the Genoese were carrying on a triangular trade, exporting European goods to Tunis, carrying African gold to Sicily, and importing Sicilian goods to Genoa.[1]

West African gold obviously also reached Constantinople in the eleventh century, for when, in 1092, Alexis I reformed the gold coinage of the Byzantine Empire, he fixed on 20½ carats as the fineness for his new 'hyperpyron'.[2] This was the natural fineness of the gold from West Africa. Nineteenth-century analyses showed that the gold dust then being obtained from the upper Senegal area contained just over 20½ carats of gold.[3] The hyperpyron went on being minted at the same fineness from its introduction in 1092 until the reign of John III Vatatzes, who ruled, in exile from Constantinople, at Nicaea from 1222 to 1254.[4] They became known to Italian merchants as 'perperi'.

At the same time as the Normans were advancing on Sicily, the Christian rulers of Spain were gradually encroaching on the lands of their Muslim neighbours. They thus acquired Muslim subjects who had for long been accustomed to the use of gold coins, as well as receiving tribute in gold from those whom they had not yet conquered. After the conquest of Toledo by Alfonso VI of Castille in 1085, the surviving Muslim rulers called in the Almoravids from North Africa to defend them. After the defeat of Alfonso VI by the Almoravid Yusuf ben Texufin in 1086, all Muslim tribute to Alfonso naturally ceased. Nevertheless the inhabitants of the Christian kingdoms of northern Spain continued to use a certain amount of Muslim gold throughout the Almoravid period. The dinars of the Almoravids were known to the Christians as 'morabetinos'. When the last of the Almoravids, Mohamed ben Saad, stopped minting dinars in Murcia in 1170, the lack of freshly minted dinars was so keenly felt in Castille that, in 1172, Alfonso VIII began to have his own gold morabetinos, or maravedis, struck at Toledo. They copied the format of the last Almoravid dinars, but replaced the specifically Muslim inscriptions by Christian ones, whilst still retaining their Arabic script. They too were of the West African fineness of 20½ carats. Leon and Portugal soon followed the Castilian example and

---

[1] Abulafia, *The Two Italies*, p. 156.

[2] The previous version of the nomisma, the histamenon, had been frequently debased over the preceding half-century and had sunk to around 8-carat gold on the eve of the reform. In comparison the new hyperpyron lived up to its name, which means 'ultra-pure'.

[3] That is, 870 thousandths of gold and 105 of silver (R. S. Lopez, 'Settecento anni fa; il ritorno all'oro nell'occidente duecentesco', *Rivista Storica Italiana*, LXV (1953), 31).

[4] Philip Grierson, 'The origins of the Grosso and of gold coinage in Italy', *Numismatický sborník*, XII (1971–2), 41.

for the next fifty years Christian gold morabetinos were minted in the three kingdoms.[1]

In the 1240s these Christian gold dinars of the old-fashioned Almoravid type were at last succeeded by Christian gold double dinars, or 'doblas', of the type that had been issued by the Almohad successors to the Almoravids for the whole time that the Christians had, conservatively, been striking gold maravedis. The dobla was to become the standard gold coin of Castille from the thirteenth-century reconquest onwards, throughout the later Middle Ages, although it was not initially minted in large numbers, for the very fact of reconquest did much to dry up the flow of gold into Spain from Africa.[2]

A decade before the introduction of the dobla into Castille, the Emperor Frederick II, as King of Sicily, also had a double dinar struck. Frederick II was supposed to receive 34,330 dinars a year as tribute from the Hafsid Emir of Tunis, and this was paid sufficiently frequently for Frederick to be able in 1231 to strike his own double dinars. In addition his subjects benefited greatly from the security to trade extensively with North Africa, provided by the treaties with Tunis, made in 1221 and 1231.[3] They principally exported Sicilian grain. In the year 1240, when there was dearth in North Africa, grain shipments from Sicily to Tunis brought in 20,000 Sicilian ounces of gold. Gold consequently became much more plentiful in Sicily. Enough gold also reached the mainland of Italy for Frederick II to mint his double dinars at Brindisi as well as at Messina. The Hafsid double dinars were of $20\frac{1}{2}$-carat gold, the fineness of the gold of *paiola* or *pagliola*, as Italians called the gold that arrived from West Africa. Frederick II's double dinars were of the same weight and fineness,[4] but totally different in appearance. They bore an idealised portrait of Frederick II as a Roman Emperor, consciously derived from classical prototypes, and entitled him Caesar Augustus. They were consequently known as 'augustales'.[5]

As well as the African gold that came into Christian hands from tribute and conquest, or the sale of grain, a further amount passed through the hands of

[1] Octavio Gil Farres, *Historia de la moneda española*, 2nd ed. (Madrid, 1976), pp. 194–8 and 322–4.

[2] *Ibid.* pp. 327ff. The Portuguese only began to mint dobras and the Aragonese to mint florins in the middle years of the fourteenth century. At the same time Castillian doblas began to be minted in much larger numbers. See below, p. 288.

[3] *Monumenta Germaniae Historica*, Legum IV, Constitutiones et acta publica, II (Hanover, 1896), 187ff.

[4] They were only worth $7\frac{1}{2}$ rather than 8 of the tiny, traditional Sicilian quarter-dinars (taris), which were continuing to be struck, since the Sicilian and Tunisian coinages had diverged since the eleventh century. Tunisian gold coins had been reduced in weight, and Sicilian in fineness. The taris of al-Zahir, struck at Palermo and in Tunisia in the 1030s, and those of al-Mustansir, struck at Palermo in the 1050s, had also been of a West African fineness, but al-Mustansir had debased them extensively before the Norman conquest of his island. It was his last debased, $16\frac{2}{3}$-carat taris that had been emulated by his Christian successors (Grierson and Oddy, 'Le Titre du tari sicilien'). By the thirteenth century $16\frac{2}{3}$-carat gold was known in Italy as 'tari' gold.

[5] H. Kowalski, 'Die Augustalen Kaiser Friederichs II', *Revue Suisse de Numismatique*, LV (1976), 77–150.

enterprising North Italian merchants who were acting as intermediaries between Muslim Spain and North Africa on the one hand, and the Muslim Near East on the other. Part of the trade to the Near East went to Egypt along the North African seaboard, but much of it went by sea, and it was into this seaborne trade that the Italians managed to insert themselves.

The registers of Giovanni Scriba in the 1150s and 1160s, and those of later notaries, suggest the importance for the Genoese of this trade by the second half of the twelfth century. Silks, dyestuffs, paper and carpets were being carried by Genoese middlemen from Alexandria and other Near Eastern ports to Bougie and Ceuta in what are now Algeria and Morocco.[1] Ceuta was the main port at which gold crossing the Sahara on the western route through Sidjilmasa was available. It was the principal North African port that was dealt with by the Genoese from the 1170s to the 1220s.[2] Some of the gold used to pay for these Near Eastern goods naturally stuck to the hands of the middlemen. By the end of the twelfth century a certain amount of gold was available in Genoa, partially from this transit trade, and partially from trade with Sicily. Notarial documents of the 1180s and 1190s distinguish payments within Genoa both in tari gold from Sicily and in *paiola* gold from Africa.[3]

By the end of the twelfth century, West African gold was in use as coin in Christian Sicily and the Christian parts of Spain. West African gold, not necessarily coined, was also becoming available in Genoa, and presumably also in Pisa, whose merchants were engaged in the same range of commercial activities as the Genoese. Elsewhere in western Christendom gold was no more than a rare and particularly highly-valued and desirable commodity.

One of the effects of Europe having become a major silver-producing continent, whilst Africa remained a major gold-producing continent, was that the two metals were differently valued on the northern and southern coasts of the western Mediterranean.

In the last quarter of the twelfth century gold was sufficiently plentiful in Tunis for any given quantity of it to be worth only six and a half times the amount of silver.[4] In Genoa, from the 1160s to the 1250s gold was generally valued at between eight and nine times the amount of silver.[5] From the 1220s Tunis replaced Ceuta as the main North African port with which Genoese merchants traded.

---

[1] J. K. Hyde, *Society and Politics in Medieval Italy* (London, 1973), pp. 66–8, drawing on E. Bach, *La Cité de Gênes au XIIe siècle* (Copenhagen, 1955).

[2] Robert H. Bautier, 'Les relations commerciales entre l'Europe et l'Afrique du Nord et l'équilibre économique méditerranéen du XIIe au XIVe siècle', *Bulletin philologique et historique du Comité des Travaux Historiques et Scientifiques* (1955), 399–416.

[3] Abulafia, *The Two Italies*, pp. 267–73.

[4] Andrew M. Watson, 'Back to gold – and silver', *Economic History Review*, 2nd series, XX (1967), 27.

[5] Calculated from tables 18 and 19 of G. Pesce and G. Felloni, *Le monete genovesi* (Genoa, 1975), pp. 337–44.

As a consequence of the different values put on the two metals on the opposite coasts of the western Mediterranean, it was naturally in silver that commercial payments were made between Christian Europe and Africa or Muslim Spain, sent out in large quantities from every port on the European coastline from Barcelona to Pisa. The balance of trade was almost entirely in favour of the Maghreb. Europeans consumed far more of the products of Africa than Africans did of European products. The transhumant shepherds, from the Atlas Mountains westwards as far as Libya, provided skins and wool for Europeans in enormous quantities. The notable Pisan leather industry, for example, relied heavily on North African hides. The apiculture of what is now Algeria provided honey, and, more particularly, beeswax, in sufficiently large amounts for the principal port of this region, Bougie, to give its name to wax candles in French. In addition there was olive oil from what is now Tunisia, and cotton and sugar from what is now Morocco, besides ivory, ebony and other trans-Saharan products that were available in the ports of North Africa. Because of the much higher value placed on silver in North Africa all these goods seemed relatively cheap to the European merchants who brought their silver across the Mediterranean to buy them. This cheapness of African goods, when paid for in silver, made commerce with North Africa very profitable, and encouraged the European merchants, who dominated the trans-Mediterranean trade, to expand their operations constantly.

The silver arriving from Europe into the countries dominated by the Almohads, or Muwaḥḥidūn, was transformed by them into distinctive square dirhams and half-dirhams. These were minted, anonymously, throughout North Africa and Andalusia in enormous quantities. Since they are anonymous it is not possible to distinguish between rulers, either of the Almohad dynasty, or of the Hafsid dynasty that succeeded them in Tunisia after 1230. They therefore cannot be dated with any certainty, but it is believed that their issue began before the death of Yusuf I in 1184.[1] In other words, the silver from the new mines of Europe was being minted in North Africa as rapidly as it was in Syria.[2] As well as the Hafsids, the other North African successors to the Almohads, the Hudids, the Marinids and the Ziyanids, also went on striking them through the thirteenth century and into the fourteenth. There was thus a common silver currency, of European origin, struck at Seville, Cordoba, Granada and eight other mints in Muslim Spain, as well as at seven major, and half a dozen minor, mints in North Africa, from Ceuta to Tunis on the coast, and even inland as far as Sidjilmasa itself, where the caravans arrived bearing gold from across the Sahara. (See Map 21.)

These distinctive square silver coins were known to West Europeans as 'millares', 'milliarenses', 'miliaresi' or 'miglioresi'. By the middle of the thirteenth

---

[1] Hazard, *Numismatic History of North Africa*, pp. 66–7 and 267–76.
[2] See above, pp. 148–50.

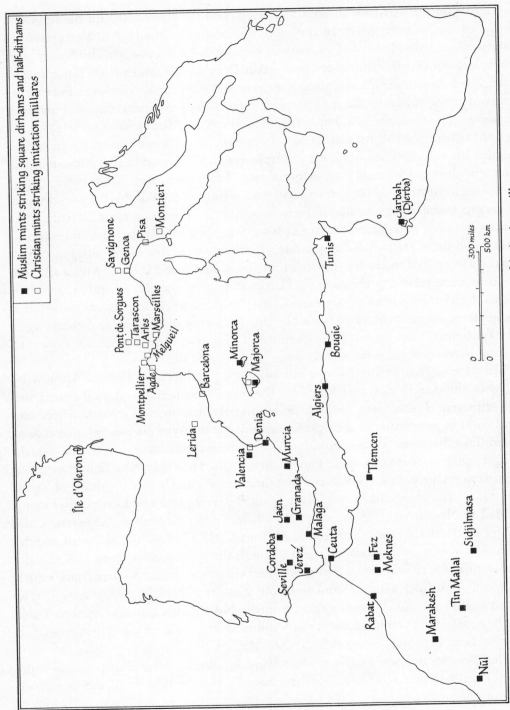

Savignone
Genoa □
Pisa □
□ Montieri

Jarbah
(Djerba) ■

Tunis ■

Pont de Sorgues □
Tarascon □ Arles □
□ Marseilles
Montpellier □
Agde □ Melgueil □
Barcelona □

Minorca ■
Majorca □

Bougie ■

Algiers ■

Lerida □

Denia ■
Murcia ■

Valencia ■

Tlemcen ■

Jaen ■
Granada ■
Malaga ■
Ceuta ■

Cordoba ■
Seville ■
Jerez ■

Fez ■
Meknes ■

Sidjilmasa ■

Île d'Oleron ■

Rabat ■

Marrakesh ■

Tin Mallal ■

Nūl ■

300 miles

500 km

Map 21. Main mints striking square dirhams and imitative millares

century West European merchants, as well as carrying silver to North Africa in bar form, were also taking counterfeit millares with them, minted for trade purposes in or near their home ports. In the 1250s and 1260s counterfeit millares were being minted at a vast number of points along the whole of the northern coast of the western Mediterranean from Pisa around to Valencia (see Map 21),[1] itself only relatively recently reconquered from the Almohads, and probably as far away as the Île d'Oleron at the mouth of the Gironde as well.[2]

It is not clear how early this counterfeiting had begun. The earliest certain indication of it taking place was in 1253. The Fieschi, who were one of the greatest Genoese noble houses, then granted a consortium the right of minting miliaresi in their castle at Savignone on the principal land-route to Genoa over the Apennines. The consortium was headed by the Bonsignori of Siena, the leading commercial company of the day, trading between Italy and the Champagne Fairs, so presumably the silver was coming from these fairs. The miliaresi were certainly destined for Genoese overseas trade.[3]

The state mint of Genoa was also minting miliaresi by that year. In December 1253 a group of merchants bought a cargo of North African sheepskin from a certain Guglielmo de Campa, and agreed to pay him 6060 'bisanti di migliaresi' of the Genoa mint.[4] Other notarised contracts of 1253 refer to merchants purchasing 'miliarenses argenti de ceca Ianuae vel de ceca Thuxiae' for export from Genoa to North Africa.[5]

Notarial registers in Marseilles in 1248 and in Genoa in 1250 already refer to the purchase of millares in those cities for export.[6] There is a strong presumption that they were locally-minted ones. However, the problem is to know how much earlier than 1248 millares were minted in Christian Europe. Blancard and following him, Watson, believed that Christian minting of counterfeit millares had been going on since the earliest years of the century. The evidence that they have

---

[1] Watson, 'Back to gold – and silver', pp. 11–14, based on Louis Blancard, *Le Millarès* (Marseilles, 1876). I have not been able to find a copy of this, but have had to rely on Watson, and on Blancard's own summary in his *Essai sur les monnaies de Charles Ier comte de Provence* (Paris, 1868–79), pp. 480–93. Jean Duplessy, 'La Circulation des monnaies arabes en Europe occidentale du viiie au xiiie siècles', *Revue Numismatique*, 5th series, xviii (1956), 142–3, reprinted the relevant parts of five of the key documents referring to 'millares' between 1257 and 1267.

[2] In 1268 moneyers from the Île d'Oleron were buying bullion at La Rochelle to mint 'falsam monetam Sarracenorum' (Duplessy, *ibid.* p. 144).

[3] R. S. Lopez, 'Contribute alla storia delle miniere argentifere di Sardegna', *Studi economico-giuridici dell'Università di Cagliari*, xxiv (1936), 12.

[4] Pesce and Felloni, *Le monete genovesi*, p. 341. 'Bisanti di migliaresi' was the European equivalent of *dīnār darāhim*, the 'dinar of dirhams'. Ten miliaresi or dirhams were reckoned to the besant or dinar of account.

[5] Lopez, 'Miniere argentifere', p. 12. The 'ceca Thuxiae' was presumably that operated by Tuscans for the Fieschi at Savignone, although it could have been a miliaresi-producing mint in Tuscany, such as those at Pisa or Montieri.

[6] Blancard, *Essai sur les monnaies de Charles I*, pp. 491–2, and Pesce and Felloni, *Le monete genovesi*, p. 339.

produced is unfortunately not conclusive.[1] However, by 1253 at latest, and almost certainly by 1248, Christian mints were producing millares.

It was not only great commercial cities and their leading citizens who were involved in this production of imitative millares, but also lay princes, who used their regular mints for this purpose. It was even more a cause for scandal that bishops did so, since the millares bore a sequence of specifically Muslim legends including 'There is no God but God' on the obverse and 'Mohammed is our messenger' on the reverse. It was not until 1266 that Pope Clement IV, provoked by St Louis, wrote to Berengar, Bishop of Maguelonne, who for at least three years, and probably many more, had been using his vast mint at Melgueil, outside Montpellier, for striking *moneta miliarensis* as well as the Melgorien deniers that were the standard coin for much of southern France and northern Spain.[2] Clement IV told Berengar, in no uncertain terms, that he was 'injuring the King of Glory by having his coinage struck with the title of Mahomet, . . . which is displeasing to God and is contrary to the profession of a bishop'.[3] As well as persuading the pope to put pressure on the offending bishops, St Louis wrote equally forthrightly to his own brothers, Alfonse, Count of Poitiers and Toulouse, and Charles, Count of Anjou and Provence. He reproached the former with having minted, in the Venaissin, presumably at Pont-de-Sorgues, on the east bank of the Rhône, 'Moneta miliarensis in cujus superscriptione fit mencio de nomine perfidi Machumeti et dicatur esse ibi propheta Dei'. Alfonse was persuaded to desist, but Charles, far from giving up, not only continued, but even extended, his minting of them. The mint at Marseilles had already been striking millares before he took it over in 1257. Charles continued to do so and, in addition, gave the right to strike millares in 1272 to the farmers of his mint at Tarascon.[4]

From 1262 at latest, James I of Aragon was making notable profits from striking millares at his mint at Montpellier. For example, between mid-December 1266 and mid-April 1269 he received the substantial addition to his revenues of 1362 li. 14s. melgorien by way of seigniorage on the striking of 54,509 marks weight of millares. This quantity of silver made over 9 million millares.[5] If a single mint was striking millares at the rate of nearly 4 million a year, the total quantity produced

[1] In 1234 a number of Genoese ships had been attacked in the harbour of Ceuta. Their owners claimed that they had lost 55,000 millares on this occasion. However, at Ceuta these might very well have been genuine millares, since its mint was one of the major producers of them. In 1212 millares were evaluated at Marseilles, but there is no indication that these were locally produced. In 1228 the export of 'miliareses' from Venice was forbidden (Roberto Cessi (ed.), *Problemi monetari veneziani*. Documenti finanziari della Repubblica di Venezia, 4th series, I (Padua, 1937), doc. 11), but there is again no indication that these were locally produced either.

[2] See below, pp. 191–2.

[3] Faustin Poey d'Avant, *Les Monnaies féodales de la France*, II (Paris, 1860), pp. 289–90.

[4] Blancard, *Essai sur les monnaies de Charles I*, pp. 483–6.

[5] The square Almohad dirhams weighed by Hazard, *Numismatic History of North Africa*, averaged 1.41 grammes. Blancard, *Essai sur les monnaies de Charles I*, p. 488, attributed an average weight of 1.36 grammes to the imitations from the Marseilles mint. The Montpellier mark weighed 239 grammes.

for transport to North Africa at the multitude of mints from Valencia to Pisa must have been truly staggering.

It is not altogether clear why Christian mints should have produced millares. That those who ran the mints made a handsome profit is clear, but why should merchants have suffered the inconvenience of carrying enormous numbers of millares instead of taking their silver in bar or plate form, as was normal for long-distance trade? The different value set on gold and silver on the northern and southern shores of the western Mediterranean is an inadequate explanation.[1] The only plausible solution is that, for the time being, coined money had so large a premium over uncoined silver in North Africa that it was worth while going to the considerable trouble and expense of having millares minted at home before setting out, as well as having the inconvenience of carrying a multitude of tiny coins across the Mediterranean. Unfortunately the surviving North African evidence is inadequate either to substantiate or to disprove this supposition. However, at some date before 1262, perhaps in the 1240s, the fineness of the Hafsid dirham was reduced, although the weight and value remained the same.[2] This reduction in fineness could have provided the necessary premium on coined silver to provoke the European imitations. Certainly the millares minted at Montpellier between 1265 and 1269 were only 9d. fine, whilst those minted in Majorca from 1268 were to be 'ad illam legem quam voluerint mercatores qui eam emere voluerint'. In other words the merchant purchasers of millares were left to determine what fineness would make it worthwhile carrying coin, rather than ingots, to North Africa. The end of the Christian imitation of millares in the 1270s coincided with the introduction by the Hafsid mints of a new dirham, the dirham *jadid*, with a better alloy.[3] When this bizarre episode came to an end, European merchants reverted to carrying their silver to Africa in unminted bars and plates. The quantities remained as large as ever. In an undated memorandum presented to Philip IV, the general master of his mints, Bettino Calcinelli, a Lucchese, surveying the export of silver from France at the end of the thirteenth century declared roundly that 'L'on a bien trait en la terre des sarrasins 400,000 marcs et plus.'[4] That this was no improbably large and wild guess can be verified by comparison with the scale of minting of millares at Montpellier, in the 1260s, when silver was leaving France in that form.

Whilst silver in enormous quantities was being exported from Europe to North

---

[1] See above, pp. 170–1, and below, pp. 178–9, for the different value set on gold and silver. This only points out that it was commonsense to send silver from Europe to Africa, not the form that the silver should take.

[2] In 1262 patently anti-Semitic accusations were made that it was the Jewish melters in the mints who had, at some time in the not too distant past, been responsible for the deterioration of the dirham (Robert Brunschvig, 'Esquisse d'histoire monétaire almohado-hafside', *Mélanges offerts à William Marçais* (Paris, 1950), pp. 63–94).

[3] *Ibid.*

[4] Guilhiermoz, who printed the memorandum, dated it before 1292, and probably before 1287, but Armand Grunzweig has associated it with the ban on the export of silver from France in April 1295 ('Les Incidences internationales des mutations monétaires de Philippe le Bel', *Le Moyen Age*, LIX (1953), 118).

Africa, such payments as had to be made in the opposite direction were naturally made in gold. Apart from payments to Sicily for foodstuffs, African gold was also sent to Genoa, although it is not clear how much of this came from the Genoese share of the transit trade between the Maghreb and the Levant, and how little in direct payments for European textiles and other goods. In the late twelfth century some West African gold was already to be found in Genoa.[1] In the first half of the thirteenth century similar references to the gold of *paiola* appear more frequently in Genoese records.[2] After 1210, the references to African gold in Genoese notarial registers often specify the fineness of it, usually 21 or 20½ carats. After 1229 they refer to it in stamped *virgis* and by 1237 they reveal that the stamping is official and local. The gold rods have been 'sealed with the stamp of the commune of Genoa'. As well as the *paiola* gold that had come immediately from Africa, there was also gold from Sicily and southern Italy in Genoa. In the first half of the thirteenth century the Genoese notarial registers refer as frequently to gold in tareni or taris as to the gold of *paiola*.[3] Outside of the favoured ports of Genoa and Pisa gold seems to have gradually acquired some sort of irregular but widespread circulation in the second quarter of the century throughout central and northern Italy. Frederick II's attempts to subdue both central and northern Italy helped to introduce a certain amount of South Italian and Sicilian gold into the area in payment for his campaigns. Frederick was not alone in this. For example, when papal troops were attacking Viterbo in 1243 it was possible for Innocent IV to pay them in gold. He paid them 2500 ounces of it,[4] presumably in Sicilian taris at 30 to the ounce (*uncia*), or even in his opponent's new augustales, at 4 to the ounce.

By 1252 there was enough gold in, or passing through, Genoa and Florence for these cities to commence striking gold coins of their own. In Genoa the genovino and in Florence the fiorino d'oro were both struck for the first time within a few months of one another. Professor Lopez has underlined the particular circumstances of the Genoese issue. He believes that there is enough evidence to show that in 1252 Genoese commerce was in a particularly expansionist phase, which had begun around 1248.[5]

[1] See above, p. 170.

[2] P. F. Casaretto, *La moneta genovese in confronto con le altre valute mediterranee nei secoli XII e XIII*, Atti della Società Ligure di Storia Patria LV (1928), pp. 186–7.

[3] Pesce and Felloni, *Le monete genovesi*, pp. 343–8. In the Mediterranean both tari and *paiola* gold were measured by the local ounce, as silver was elsewhere by the local mark or pound. Whether in the form of coin or dust or nuggets, gold was frequently to be found in sealed leather ounce bags. Such sealed leather bags went back at least to the eleventh century in Egypt, and probably earlier in Byzantium. The Norman kings of Sicily sealed up their tari in ounce bags, each worth 30 tari, and from the end of the thirteenth century the commune of Florence continued the tradition by sealing up its own gold florins 'in petiis corii' (S. D. Goitein, *A Mediterranean Society*, I (Berkeley, 1967), 231–3, 237; Mario Bernocchi, *Le monete della repubblica fiorentina*, III (Florence, 1976), 275–6).

[4] T. C. Van Cleve, *The Emperor Frederick II of Hohenstaufen* (Oxford, 1972), p. 466.

[5] Lopez, 'Settecento anni fa', pp. 19–55 and 161–98, particularly pp. 187ff. This important article, which was separately reprinted in Naples in 1955, gathers together a great deal of information on the use of gold in Italy in the thirteenth century. An English summary appeared as 'Back to gold, 1252', *Economic History Review*, 2nd series, IX(1956), 219–40.

Unlike the Christian Spanish gold maravedis and doblas and the Christian Sicilian taris or tareni, the new genovini and fiorini were not derived from preexisting Muslim pieces, not even at one remove like Frederick II's augustales. The size of the Florentine florin was dictated instead by the existing currency system of Tuscany. It was made of enough gold to be worth exactly a lira, or twenty soldi, in the money of account not only of Florence, but also of the other leading cities of Tuscany – Pisa, Lucca and Siena.[1] The size of the genovino was equally dictated by the existing currency of Genoa. A convenient size of gold piece for the Genoese was one worth eight of their soldi, but since the existing money of Genoa had not been debased as much as the Tuscan coinages this produced a coin of almost exactly the same weight as the Florentine florin – 3.53 grams against 3.54 grams.[2] There is no evidence of any agreement between the two cities, although it is singular that as well as being of almost exactly the same weight, both were also of pure gold, rather than the normal West African 20½ carat standard, which was then prevalent around the Mediterranean. Although ostensibly they were valued for domestic use in Liguria and Tuscany, the immediate international use of both the genovino and the florin underlines the merchant interests that brought them into being.[3] In the thirteenth century the genovino and the florin both circulated much more in the Levant than in the west.[4] They were both used initially for that part of the transit trade between the Maghreb and the Levant in which the Italians acted as middlemen, and they have turned up in considerable numbers in the Near East. Professor Grierson has even suggested that florins soon replaced the local 'bezants' as the gold currency of the few surviving crusader states. In a hoard concealed at Aleppo and believed to consist of part of the loot from the capture of Acre in 1291, some 600 out of 630 gold coins were Florentine florins.[5]

Since Venice was not so closely linked with North Africa as Genoa and Pisa, the

---

[1] Although written three-quarters of a century later, the chronicle of Giovanni Villani provides the clearest description of the introduction of the florin. As well as being a careful and accurate chronicler, Villani was head of a great Florentine merchant house, and charged with a great range of municipal offices, including the oversight of the mint. He wrote: 'I mercatanti di Firenze per onore del comune, ordinaro col popolo e comune che si battesse moneta d'oro in Firenze; e eglino promisono di fornire la moneta d'oro . . . e allora si comincio la buona moneta d'oro fine di ventiquattro carati, che si chiamano fiorini d'oro, e contavasi l'uno soldi venti. E cio ful al tempo [as *podestà*] del . . . messer Filippo degli Ugoni di Brescia, del mese di Novembre gli anni di Cristo 1252. I quali fiorini, gli otto pesarono una oncia, e dall'uno lato era la'mpronta del giglio, e dall'altro il san Giovanni' (*Cronica di Giovanni Villani*, Book VI, chapter 53). The most recent description of the Florentine gold florin is in Mario Bernocchi, *Le monete della repubblica fiorentina* (4 vols., Florence, 1974–8).

[2] The near contemporary *Annales Ianuenses* recorded simply 'Eodem anno nummus aureus Ianue fabricatus'. The most recent description of the genovino is in Pesce and Felloni, *Le monete genovesi*, although the chronology of the early issues that they propose is not acceptable to the present author, who is convinced by the alternative chronology proposed by Professor Lopez, 'Settecento anni fa'. A quarter-genovino was also struck, worth two soldi, and even a tiny gold soldo.

[3] Villani specifically emphasises the role of merchants in promoting the gold florin. See above, note 1.

[4] It was not until the fourteenth century that the Florentine florin had a wide circulation in western Europe and became the prototype for so many other European gold coinages. See below, pp. 267–88.

[4] Philip Grierson, 'La moneta veneziana nell' economia mediterranea del Trecento e Quattrocento', in *La civiltà veneziana del Quattrocento* (Florence, 1957), pp. 82–3.

quantity of gold there did not accumulate so soon to the point where it became worth minting it. It was nevertheless growing in the mid thirteenth century, reaching Venice much more frequently from southern Italy and Sicily than directly from North Africa. In 1269 the Great Council decreed that gold sold in Venice had to be of a fixed fineness (23¼ carat = 0.979 fine) and had an official refinery for gold set up near the Rialto. Presumably its products were marked with a guarantee of fineness like the gold sealed with the stamp of the commune of Genoa a generation earlier, and like the ingots of silver marked in a wide variety of cities, including Venice itself. It was not until 1284 that the official manufacture of bars from gold was largely replaced by that of ducats.[1] When authorising the striking of the first ducats, the Great Council specified that they should be 'tam bona et fina per aurum vel melior ut est florenus'.[2] At 72 to the Venetian mark they were essentially the same weight as the Florentine gold florin and the Genoese genovino. To be so they had to be given a value that did not fit at all neatly into the pre-existing Venetian money of account. They were valued at 18 grossi or 39 soldi a grossi. So bizarre an initial value implied that the prospective internal use for the new ducats was expected to be subordinate to their external use. The following year the Great Council explicitly gave preferential minting terms to those who wished to carry their newly coined ducats to Apulia or outside the Adriatic.[3]

By the 1280s the continual growth for over a century of the stock of silver in Europe had begun to have a cumulative effect on the relative values placed on gold and silver. Whereas for a hundred years up to the 1250s a given weight of gold had generally been purchasable in Europe for eight or nine times its weight in silver, the continuing supplies of fresh silver mined in Europe pushed the value of gold further upwards in the second half of the thirteenth century. In the 1260s gold in Genoa was worth over ten times the amount of silver. By the 1280s the relative value of silver had so dropped that a given weight of gold was now only purchasable for eleven times its weight in silver. For another half-century the value of gold in terms of silver went on increasing, or, rather, that of silver in terms of gold went on diminishing. In the first years of the fourteenth century gold in Genoa was worth over thirteen times the amount of silver, and that was in a city where gold was more plentiful than in any other commercial city in Europe. Elsewhere in Europe gold was more highly valued still, and in the early years of the fourteenth century was purchased by fourteen, fifteen, sixteen or even more times the amount of silver.[4]

---

[1] The official manufacture of gold bars did not entirely cease (Cessi (ed.), *Problemi monetari veneziani*, doc. 41, p. 52).

[2] Wilhelm Jesse (ed.), *Quellenbuch zur Münz- und Geldgeschichte des Mittelalters* (Halle, 1924; repr. 1968), doc. 209, p. 87.

[3] *Ibid.* doc. 210, p. 87.

[4] Based primarily on Watson, 'Back to gold – and silver'. For a general discussion of European gold–silver ratios, see below, pp. 271–5 and Graph, p. 272 and also p. 354.

The quantity of silver that had crossed the western Mediterranean was so great, that a drop in the value of silver began to be felt in North Africa as well, particularly in Tunis. In 1278 silver was so plentiful there that it had dropped to less than a ninth of the value of an equivalent weight of gold. In 1272 al-Mustansir, the Hafsid ruler of Tunis, had sought to pay his tribute to Charles of Sicily, recently increased after the Tunis crusade, in silver rather than gold, although Charles still preferred to receive gold.[1] In general, however, the value of silver remained higher in North Africa than in Europe, and it consequently normally remained worthwhile to send any remittances from Europe to Africa in silver and from Africa to Europe in gold.

The Venetian da Canal notebook gives tantalising hints of a complex flow of precious metals in the western and central Mediterranean in 1311. Some of it is straightforward enough. There is a description of the rates of payment for gold at the Venice, Alexandria and Constantinople mints. The gold was reaching Alexandria and Constantinople from Venice, and at Constantinople it was specifically described as 20 carat, in other words, West African.[2] Other parts of the notebook are less straightforward. There is a detailed description of the Barbary coast from Bougie to Tripoli. The values of gold 'massamutini' or 'dopla' (double dinars) are given in silver miliares for six towns along this coast. It is apparent that the value of gold increased going eastwards from Bougie, and that of silver going westwards from Tripoli and Tunis. The compiler notes that a profit of $4\frac{1}{2}$ miliares per dopla, some 13%, is to be made by carrying gold from Bougie to Tunis, or silver in the opposite direction.[3] Bougie, of course, lay closer to the great West Saharan trade-route through Sidjilmasa, which brought the most gold to the Mediterranean. Tunis and Tripoli were, by implication, where European silver was most easily found. However the notebook goes on, paradoxically, to describe the receipt not of silver, but of gold from Europe. It was by now of interest for a Venetian to know the rates offered for gold at the Tunis mint, the customs dues to be paid on importing gold by weight from Venice, and the exchange rates in Tunis for coined gold from Europe, not only Venetian ducats, but also Florentine florins and Neapolitan carlini, the Angevin successors to the augustales.[4] The value set on gold in Tunis was then so high, at least temporarily, that Tunis was drawing in not only fresh West African gold, but also gold that had been to Europe before coming back to North Africa.

A little later Pegolotti's notebook perhaps gives a slight clue to the unravelling of the paradox. The author of the da Canal notebook had pinpointed the export of

[1] Brunschvig, 'Histoire monétaire almohado-hafside'.
[2] Alfredo Stussi (ed.), *Zibaldone da Canal, manoscritto mercantile del secolo XIV*, Fonti per la Storia di Venezia v (Venice, 1967), fos 42v, 43r, 41r, 41v and 42r, on pp. 71, 68 and 70. Coined gold (Venetian ducats and Neapolitan carlini) was also being carried east from Europe to Cyprus (fo 35r, on pp. 56–7).
[3] *Ibid.* fo 30r; Stussi ed., p. 49.
[4] *Ibid.* fos 27v and 31r; Stussi ed., pp. 43 and 51.

gold to Tunis from Naples, amongst other places. Pegolotti notes its corollary, the import of silver from Tunis to Naples. However he also explains that Tunis received its silver in plates directly from the mines of Sardinia. The solution to the paradox seems therefore to be that Sardinian silver was so plentiful in Tunis in the early fourteenth century that, in terms of gold, it was even cheaper and more undervalued there than it was in Naples and Venice. Although the particular exchange at this time may have been of silver from Tunis to Naples and of gold from Naples to Tunis, the general flows of the precious metals were still normally in the opposite directions. As late as 1343 the problem in Venice was still of how to help the mint to cope with the enormous quantities of gold being imported into the city from overseas.[1]

By the beginning of the fourteenth century the traditionally gold-using areas of Europe, southern Italy, Sicily and Spain, all formerly Byzantine or Muslim, had been joined by northern and central Italy, where a mixture of older South Italian and newer North Italian gold coins were in circulation. In a hoard of coined gold buried at Pisa in the last decade of the thirteenth century the larger number of coins were still taris that had come from the south, many of them minted at the beginning of the century, whilst the more recent florins from neighbouring Florence, although less numerous, were much greater in value.[2]

The real problem is to know how much further the use of gold had spread.

Some gold was certainly available in the mid thirteenth century in the south of France.

When Alfonse, Count of Poitiers, set off on crusade in August 1249 to join his brother, Louis of France, in Egypt, he took over 100,000 livres tournois with him. This prodigious sum turned out to be inadequate. By the next April his chaplain, Philip, who was administering his finances in his absence, had scraped together all the extra money that he could obtain for his master, and sent it to him, together with a consignment of cheeses, wines and herrings that he had asked for. The extra money totalled more than 17,000 livres tournois and was listed in detail when it was shipped out from Aigues Mortes in May.[3] Of this some 1700 livres tournois, almost exactly a tenth, was in gold. The gold sent out, apart from a single mark of uncoined gold, and 3½ marks each of Byzantine perpers and South Italian or Sicilian augustales, consisted overwhelmingly of anfuris, the gold morabetinos minted in Castille up to 1221. There were no fewer than 3900 of them, together with 300

---

[1] F. Thiriet, *Délibérations des assemblées vénitiennes concernant la Romanie*, vol. 1 (Paris, 1966), docs. 496 and 497, p. 201.

[2] From the south: 137 pieces – 119 taris and multiples, 16 augustales and one half-augustale, and one three-centuries-old solidus – with a combined total value of around 42 florins. From Tuscany: 92 florins – 91 Florentine, and one equivalent piece from Lucca (Giuseppe Castellani, 'Il ripostiglio di Pisa', *Bolletino d'Arte*, xxx (1937), 476–84).

[3] Alfonse was captured, with his brother Louis, at Mansurah on 6 April and released on 6 May. The request for money was therefore made before his capture, and arrived after his release.

obolis, weighing nearly 65 marks and worth well over 1500 livres tournois.[1] How this extra money had been raised is not clear. Since Alfonse's Poitevan lands had been squeezed to the limit the previous year, it seems probable that a large part of it had come from the newly inherited territories of his recently deceased father-in-law, Raymond of Toulouse. Even if it is not certain which territories provided the gold, it is clear that a considerable amount of it could be found in some parts of southern France if diligently sought out. It is also apparent that the gold involved was rather different from that to be found in northern Italy. It was not primarily *paiola* gold, straight from Africa, or tari gold that had come through Sicily. Instead it was gold that had seeped in rather slowly through Christian Spain where it had been minted at least thirty years before. There are other indications of the circulation of gold from Spain in southern France, although nothing on so large a scale.[2] At the beginning of the thirteenth century the consuls of Montpellier had promised to pay Innocent III and his successors 2 marks of gold annually, to be reckoned at 100 masamutinis to each mark. Du Cange cited a payment of 1211 of a gold mark of 'oblorum massabitinorum'. In 1247 the Lord of Agantico, near Maguelonne, agreed to pay a *cens* of 3 'marabutinorum anfusinorum'.[3] When Alfonse died, and his counties reverted to the crown, in 1271, a description of his revenues included two items traditionally paid in gold, a marobotin from a fief in the Agenais and an obole d'or from land in the Toulousain.[4] Such pieces as have been found in southern and western France all emphasise the Spanish connection.[5] By the middle of the century, when the mints of southern France were active in sending out imitative silver millares, rather more African gold had come into the area, not only, although principally, through Spain, but also including small quantities of North African coin, of unminted gold, of taris and augustales from southern Italy, and of hyperpyra from Byzantium. This mixture could be found in Provence.[6] Some of its components were also present in Gascony in 1254,[7] and even as far north as Tours, where, in 1255, the Jewish community agreed to pay the archbishop 5 gold obols for the use of a cemetery.[8]

Yet further north, in Champagne, a certain amount of gold was to be found at the

[1] E. Cartier (ed.), 'Or & argent, monnoyés ou non monnoyés, envoyés en Palestine à Alfonse comte de Poitiers, frère de Saint-Louis, dans l'année 1250', *Revue Numismatique* (1847), 120–2.

[2] Duplessy, 'Monnaies arabes en Europe', pp. 139–44, reprinted the relevant parts of twelve documents referring to 'marobotins' between *c.* 1120 and 1268, and of three documents of the early thirteenth century referring to masamutinis. All but one of these came from southern France.

[3] Cartier, 'Or & argent envoyés en Palestine dans l'année 1250', pp. 133–4.

[4] Yves Dossat (ed.), *Saisimentum Comitatus Tholosani* (Paris, 1966).

[5] Duplessy, 'Monnaies arabes en Europe', pp. 128–33, gives details of three hoards and two stray finds of Almoravid dinars, and of two hoards of Almohad dinars, from the twelfth century and the first half of the thirteenth.

[6] Blancard, *Essai sur les monnaies de Charles I*, quoted by Watson, 'Back to gold – and silver', p. 14.

[7] See below, p. 185.

[8] Cartier, 'Or & argent envoyés en Palestine dans l'année 1250', p. 135.

fairs. A letter home to Siena in 1265 quotes the values for the gold of *pagliola*, for tari gold, for augustales and for the new florins from Florence.[1] All these were found by the agent of the Tolomei at the Cold Fair at Troyes, available in limited quantities, as commodities. Northern France was not yet ready for gold as coin. When St Louis tried to start a gold coinage in the following year it was without success. His gold écus had a short life and a limited circulation. Nevertheless the amount of gold in France was increasing, albeit very slowly. In the second half of the century additional gold came from Italy rather than from Spain. The gold to be found at the Champagne Fairs in 1265 had more in common with that available in northern Italy than with that previously available in southern France. It already included gold florins. They were gradually to be found in other parts of France as well, at Beaune in 1274, at Chalon in 1275, at Dijon in 1285 and in Forez by 1295.[2] When Philip IV attempted to introduce a gold coinage to France he had rather more success than his grandfather. His first attempt, in 1290, was to mint a piece that, significantly, had the same size, weight and fineness as a florin. It was at his second attempt that he achieved a moderate success, with the masse d'or, a double florin, which he introduced in 1296. The price offered for gold at French mints was so attractive that a bi-metallic flow between France and Italy may have been triggered off. In 1299 the mark of gold was officially worth fourteen of silver in France, in 1309 it was worth sixteen, and in 1311, nineteen marks of silver.[3] This was much higher than in Genoa. It would not have been surprising if in the last years of the thirteenth century, and the first years of the fourteenth, ingots from Montpellier had been carried from Montpellier to Marseilles and Genoa, and gold brought back in exchange to feed the French mints in southern France. The evidence for the export of silver is clear, but that for the import of gold is not. As the export of silver had been banned since 1295, prosecutions were brought before the royal courts against a number of men accused of melting down hundreds of thousands of marks of deniers to make ingots for export. The focus of this activity was Montpellier, the principal trading-port of southern France.[4] It is not, however, clear if this silver was improperly exported to purchase gold, or merely sent to North Africa to maintain the traditional import trade in African goods, or even sent to Italy to pay for Italian goods. With Italy there had also for long been an unfavourable balance of trade from southern France. Already in the 1250s bars of silver sealed in Montpellier had been noticed in Genoa.[5] Nevertheless, whether in direct exchange for French silver

[1] C. Paoli and E. Piccolomini (eds.), *Lettere volgari del secolo XIII scritte da Senesi* (Bologna, 1871; repr. 1968), p. 57.

[2] Henri Dubois, *Les Foires de Chalon-sur-Saône et le commerce dans la vallée de la Saône à la fin du moyen âge* (Paris, 1976), p. 21.

[3] Watson, 'Back to gold – and silver', pp. 26.

[4] Robert H. Bautier, 'L'Or et l'argent en Occident de la fin du XIIIe siècle au debut du XIVe siècle', *Académie des Inscriptions et Belles Lettres, Comptes Rendus des Séances* (1951), 170. Bautier, like Watson, finds the evidence for the exchange of silver for gold conclusive. I am not convinced that the evidence necessarily bears this interpretation.

[5] Pesce and Felloni, *Le monete genovesi*, p. 341.

or otherwise, Italian gold coins did appear in France, and the French mints were able to mint limited quantities of gold coins of their own. France, or at least the south of it, had thus become accustomed to some use of gold coinage by the time that Pope John XXII settled at Avignon in 1316. The arrival of the pope set the seal on the use of gold in southern France. Papal revenues, rising rapidly under John XXII's hard-pressed administration to pay for the cost of war, averaged 228,000 florins a year during his reign and were largely received and spent in gold. Although the larger part was spent in Italy, enough was used to purchase provisions for the papal court to increase the quantity of gold circulating in the Rhône valley quite appreciably. Gold was spent for grain and wine as far away as Burgundy.[1] Gold florins even began to be minted by John XXII himself in 1322, by the Dauphin of Vienne in 1327, and by the Duke of Burgundy at Auxonne in the same year, but they are all very rare today, and we can therefore probably deduce that the numbers struck were tiny.[2] Nevertheless, even if these issues were small, they are a significant indicator of the rising use of gold coin in the Rhône valley. At the same time the issue of gold agnels between 1311 and 1326 proved to be the first really successful coinage of gold by the Kings of France.[3] Sub-Saharan gold thus penetrated the Midi in the first quarter of the fourteenth century, as it had done northern Italy in the thirteenth century. It is still not clear, however, how much northern France was affected by the influx of gold at this stage.

Just as in France, a certain amount of gold coin was available in England in the mid thirteenth century, and, as in France, it was treated as a commodity and not yet as a part of the currency. Instead it was used for such strictly uncommercial purposes as prestigious alms-giving by the king.

Those gold coins that were used as royal alms at once ceased even to be objects of commerce. They were given on the great festivals of the Church and ended up, along with similar offerings by other great men, in the treasuries of monasteries and cathedrals, or attached to shrines, such as that of St Thomas at Canterbury, or those of St Lawrence and St Ethelbert in London. They remained there until they were melted down and turned into ornamental goldsmith's work.

Royal accounts reveal that, apart from a few 'gold pennies' of his own striking, Henry III used gold coins from a variety of very distant places. A few hyperpyra of Byzantium were the only Christian gold pieces. The rest, and during his reign Henry III managed to purchase several thousand pieces through his agents in

---

[1] Henri Dubois, 'Commerce international, métaux précieux et flux monétaires aux confins orientaux du royaume de France XIIIᵉ–XVᵉ siècles', in *La moneta nell'economia europea, secoli XIII-XVIII* (Prato, 1982).

[2] Jean-Baptiste Giard, 'Le Florin d'or au Baptiste et ses imitations en France au XIVᵉ siècle', *Bibliothèque de l'École des Chartes*, CXXV (1967), 94–141.

[3] At the Paris mint alone over half a million agnels were struck in 1316–18. H. A. Miskimin, *Money, Prices and Foreign Exchange in Fourteenth Century France* (New Haven, Conn., 1963), has guessed that, between them, all the mints of France struck nearly half a million agnels yearly in the second decade of the fourteenth century.

London, came from Muslim sources. They were mostly dinars and double dinars of the Almohad rulers of Spain and the Maghreb, known in England as 'oboli' and 'denari de musc',[1] but there were some even more prestigious multiple dinars amongst them, possibly from as far away as Ghazni in Afghanistan, where such pieces were struck by the last Ghurid rulers in the first decade of the century.[2]

How such distant coins reached England is not clear. The bringing of courtesy gifts by foreign embassies, or the carrying home of souvenirs by pilgrims returning from the Holy Land or Compostella, have been suggested as means by which some such coins may have reached England, along with the looting of gold by successful crusaders. Most of it, however, was gold that was deliberately purchased and imported for goldsmiths working in England. Almohad Spain was the most accessible part of the Muslim world for merchants coming from England. It would seem from the evidence that a certain amount of the gold was purchased already minted into coins, instead of as gold leaf or even as gold dust. Either dust or leaf was an equally usable alternative to coin for goldsmiths, but for alms-giving pieces of gold were much more appropriate, even if inscribed with the, admittedly unreadable, tenets of a strange religion.

Around 1200 West African gold was worth six and a half times its weight in silver in Tunis. It was presumably slightly dearer in Almohad Spain, but a substantial profit was to be made by the merchant who carried it to England, despite his expenses, for in the first half of the century gold leaf was normally sold for ten times its weight in silver.[3] The price of gold naturally fluctuated from time to time like any other commodity, according to supply and demand. In 1267 Henry III had to pay 24 pence a piece for 'gold pennies' minted in his own name.[4] Since they weighed exactly twice the ordinary silver penny used as currency, this puts the price of gold in that year as high as twelve times its weight in silver.

Henry III mostly employed the goldsmith Edward Fitz Otto, the hereditary engraver of the mints, to purchase gold for him, whether for alms-giving or plate. He purchased it for the king from such men as Solomon le Evesque, a London Jew, who, on one occasion, provided 85 marks weight of gold, largely in gold leaf, but partially in Almohad dinars or 'besants'.[5] Whether Solomon was actually the importer of the gold is not clear. Although goldsmiths, and presumably gold, were heavily concentrated in London, it was already surprisingly possible to obtain gold from Spain in provincial England. The accounts for the Bishop of Winchester's

---

[1] Philip Grierson, 'Oboli de Musc', *English Historical Review*, LXVI (1951), 75–81.

[2] Philip Grierson, 'Muslim coins in thirteenth century England', in D. K. Kouymjian (ed.), *Near Eastern Numismatics, Iconography, Epigraphy and History. Studies in Honour of George C. Miles* (Beirut, 1974), pp. 387–91.

[3] According to evidence given at the exchequer in 1257, *Cronica Maiorum et Vicecomitum Londoniorum*, quoted in Jesse, *Quellenbuch*, doc. 207, pp. 85–6.

[4] Charles Oman, *The Coinage of England* (Oxford, 1931), p. 154.

[5] Charles Johnson, Introduction to Nicholas Oresme, *De Moneta* (London, 1956), p. xxx, quoting *Calendar of Close Rolls 1250–9*, p. 459.

West Country manor of Taunton for 1256/7 include the surprising sum of no less than 1529 Almohad 'denari auri musc'.[1]

Gold had as yet no currency function in England, as the rapid failure in 1257 of Henry III's own 'gold penny' coinage clearly demonstrated. In the end it was to be European gold, coming through Italy, that was to give England a gold coinage,[2] but in the mid thirteenth century gold from Italy was not yet to be found in England. It was not worthwhile specifically purchasing gold in Italy, for import to England, for, in the 1250s, gold was as dear in Florence as it was in England, if not dearer.[3] It was much cheaper to buy gold in Spain. The only Italian gold coins to reach England were odd ones such as the few augustales, brought in with some 'besants', as part of a transfer of royal treasure from Gascony in 1254.[4] The treasure consisted mostly, of course, of gold in the form of gold leaf and gold dust.[5]

Only two of these thousands of Muslim Spanish and North African gold coins have survived in England. This is not surprising, since they were not destined for currency, but for use by goldsmiths. If they happened to be used also as royal or noble alms-gifts, this was merely an intermediate stage on the way to the melting-pot in a goldsmith's workshop. That this was one of the traditional uses of gold in society before it was used as currency is illustrated by the way that the shrine of St Lawrence in the cathedral church in London had a gold coin of the Almoravids already attached to it in 1295 as well as gold pieces of the Almohads. Almoravid rule in Spain had finally come to an end in 1171, so that the piece was at least 120 years old in 1295. How much of this stretch of time it had been immobilised in St Paul's Cathedral, or when it was brought to England, is impossible to tell, but the implication may well be that the import from Spain of West African gold for English goldsmiths to work on was no novelty in the reign of Henry III.

This sort of pre-coinage use of gold can be paralleled at this time elsewhere, and also at other times. In 1254 Louis IX offered 28 besants to St Denis for the 7 years that he had been away on crusade, because he and at least his two predecessors as Kings of France had been in the habit of going annually to the martyr's shrine and acknowledging his role as protector of the king and kingdom by a gift of gold. 'Dominus Rex quando ivit ad sanctum dyonisium iiii bizantios' appears in the accounts for the royal jewels under Philip Augustus.[6]

Although minted in the same generation that saw the creation of commercial gold coinages in Florence, Genoa and Venice, the gold pennies of Henry III and the

[1] Grierson, 'Muslim coins in England', pp. 387–91.
[2] See below, pp. 281–2.
[3] See Graph II, p. 272.
[5] Grierson, 'Muslim coins in England', p. 390.
[1] Almoravid dinars found in London (Duplessy, 'Monnaies arabes en Europe', p. 133).
[2] Gabrielle M. Spiegel, 'The cult of Saint Denis and Capetian kingship', *Journal of Medieval History*, I (1975), 60–1. A charter in the name of Charlemagne, forged in the mid twelfth century, records that Charlemagne offered four besants to St Denis, so that the custom may well go back to the date of forgery.

gold écus of Louis IX belong much more to the world of prestigious alms-giving, which reached backwards in time to the gold pennies of Edward the Elder in tenth-century England or Louis the Pious in ninth-century Frankia. In some parts of Europe, this tradition continued very much longer. In the late fifteenth century, in the Muscovite state, not yet an area in which gold was used as coin, imitations of Hungarian ducats were struck in Ivan III's own name for him to use on the occasion of royal pilgrimages.[1] It was to this sort of world that the England of Henry III and northern France of St Louis belonged, rather than that of the contemporary kingdoms of Castille and Sicily, or the city states of Florence or Genoa, where doblas and augustales, florins and genovini had functions as coins.

[1] I. G. Spasskij, 'Gold coins and coin-like gold in the Muscovite state', *Numismatic Chronicle*, 7th series, xix (1979), 165–84.

8

New Mints

A great increase in the amount minted was the most obvious consequence of the vast quantities of new silver being mined in Europe from the 1160s onwards. Although large amounts of silver did circulate in uncoined bars, even larger quantities were turned into coin year by year until the 1320s. As more and more silver was carried about Europe, there was an ever greater need in all parts of the continent to turn uncoined silver into coined silver, foreign coin into local coin and, every so often, old coin into new coin.

At first this meant a reopening of mints that had been closed, and an increase in the activity of those that had remained open. It also entailed the opening of more and more mints to cope with the demand for coin to be easily available everywhere. However, after a certain point had been reached, it became more practical to manage the increasing quantity of coinage by using fewer, larger mints rather than more and more tiny, local mints. In other words, the initial stages of the expansion merely resulted in more of the same sort of small, workshop mint that had been inherited from the 'Viking' and 'feudal' period. However, the later stages of the expansion resulted in the creation of minting 'factories' involving considerable division of labour, with hundreds of workmen, run for rulers by profit- and cost-conscious entrepreneurs, often Tuscans, who treated them as large-scale business ventures. The qualitative change in the way minting was carried out followed on when the quantity of coin to be minted passed the critical volume to justify the division of labour required. The improvement of communications and the centralisation of government also contributed to this transformation. In some parts of Europe minting remained dispersed in an immense multitude of tiny mints, right through to the fourteenth century and beyond, either because government remained highly decentralised or because the scale of coinage did not pass the critical volume. When the scale of coinage remained small the system of frequent renewal of the coinage often survived, and for this purpose a large number of local mints was most convenient.

For the convenience of the people, as well as the profit of the prince, there usually came to be a mint place close to a new silver-mine, after a longer or shorter delay,

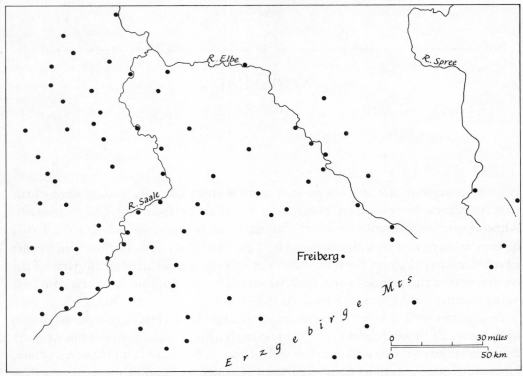

Map 22. Multiplication of mints around Freiberg *c.* 1170 – *c.* 1200

even if, in the twelfth and thirteenth centuries, there was no compulsion to use it.[1]

New mints were set up not only at the key point of discovery and mining of silver, but wherever it flowed, first in the vicinity, and then further afield. For example in an area around Freiberg bounded by the Saale on the west, and the Spree in the east, there were only nine mints around 1130, before the discovery of the Freiberg silver. By 1197, after thirty years of silver-mining there, there were twenty-five mints in the same area, and no less than forty by about 1250.[2] (See Map 22.)

In Tuscany the new silver-mines at Montieri and elsewhere in the Colline Metallifere had much the same effect. Around 1135 there had been only a single mint in Tuscany, that at Lucca, which had been working more or less continuously since the Lombard period. Before 1151 a new mint had opened at Pisa, and another around 1155 at Volterra, on the edge of whose *contado* Montieri lay. Clear

---

[1] See above, pp. 130–1.

[2] Manfred Unger, *Stadtgemeinde und Bergwesen Freibergs im Mittelalter*, Abhandlungen zur Handels- und Sozial-geschichte v (Weimar, 1963), p. 92. In the whole of Germany there were perhaps 60 mints operating tenuously around 1170, but around 220 by 1200, and about 580 by 1270. The map and catalogue of mints in Ulrich Klein, 'Münzstätten der Stauferzeit (etwa 1140–1270) in Deutschland und Italien', *Revue Suisse de Numismatique*, LVI (1977), 171–278, replace those in Arthur Suhle, *Deutsche Münz- und Geldgeschichte von den Anfängen bis zum 15. Jahrhundert*, 2nd ed. (Berlin, 1964), p. 142.

documentary evidence of the operation of the Volterran mint exists, but no distinctive denari of it can be identified. It seems most probable that they were identical with the denari of Pisa. Certainly 'Pisan' denari, whether minted at Pisa or elsewhere, were minted in large numbers and, in the 1170s when the mines were becoming very productive, replaced the denari of Lucca as the standard coinage of Tuscany.[1] Around 1180 a new mint was opened at Siena, in whose *contado* so many of the minor silver-mines lay. Mining was at the basis of Siena's prosperity and lay behind the surprisingly precocious flowering of its trading and banking companies. Arezzo had a mint before 1196, and Florence around the end of the century. The Bishop of Volterra was running a mint at Montieri itself early in the next century, but for how long it had been in existence is not clear.[2] The denari struck at Florence, Arezzo and Montieri are unidentifiable and were presumably subsumed in the general mass of 'Pisan' denari in circulation.

Some Tuscan silver crossed the Apennines to northern Italy, but this was *par excellence* the region to which 'German' silver flowed, either directly over the Alps, or by way of a long passage through the Rhineland, the Low Countries and Champagne. Here there was a similar multiplication of mints. Around 1135 there were still only three mints operating in the whole of the vast region between the Alps and the Apennines in which vigorous commercial life was so rapidly emerging. They were at Milan, Pavia and Verona, and were all mints that had been in more or less continuous operation since Carolingian times. Other former mints, like those at Venice or Ravenna, had fallen into decay. By 1200 not only were these older mints working again, but new mints had been opened at Genoa (1138), Asti and Piacenza (*c.* 1140), Cremona (*c.* 1155), Ancona (before 1170), Brescia (*c.* 1184), Bologna (after 1191), and at Ferrara and Mantua (before the end of the century).

Whereas there had been only four mints north of Rome in 1130, by 1200 there were twenty-six, and a mint was being worked at Rome itself as well. The numbers of mints went on increasing in the thirteenth century, albeit more slowly, and by 1250 there were thirty-seven in operation north of Rome. (See Map 23.[3])

In Italy and eastern Germany it is fairly easy to trace the multiplication of mints at this period, because they were new, chartered foundations; but in France and western Germany it is a great deal more difficult, since what is involved is often the

[1] David Herlihy, 'Pisan coinage and the monetary development of Tuscany, 1150–1250', *American Numismatic Society Museum Notes*, VI (1954), 143–68.

[2] Nor is it clear whether this may not have been the existing episcopal mint transferred from Volterra because of civil disturbances. What is clear is that in 1218 arbitrators were called in to settle a dispute between the bishop and the Cavalcanti company of Florence, who had by then been running a mint for him at Montieri for some time (G. Volpe, 'Montieri: costituzione politica, struttura sociale e attività economica d'una terra mineraria toscana nel XIII secolo', *Vierteljahrschrift für Social- und Wirtschaftsgeschichte*, VI (1908), 340–1).

[3] Largely based on Lucia Travaini, 'Mint organization in Italy between the XIIth. and XIVth. centuries: a Survey', in Peter Spufford and Nicholas Mayhew (eds.), *Mint Organization in Medieval Europe*, B.A.R. (Oxford, 1987).

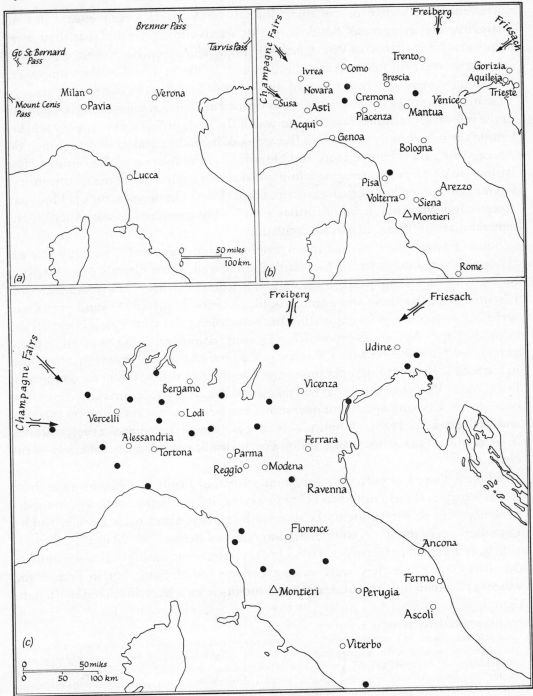

Map 23. Multiplication of mints north of Rome *c.* 1135 – *c.* 1250

A. Mints operating *c.* 1135   B. Mints operating *c.* 1200   C. Mints operating *c.* 1250

revival of very ancient mint rights, or the usurpation of such rights, without any written mandate, by semi-independent rulers. The great period of 'feudal' money in France was not, strangely enough, at the time when political authority was most widely dispersed and 'feudalised' in the tenth and eleventh centuries, but in the late twelfth and early thirteenth centuries when, although political authority was much less decentralised, there was a growing need for minted coin throughout France and a growing availability of silver to meet that need.

In the small county of Artois in north-eastern France, for example, Philip of Alsace, count from 1168 to 1191, struck coins at no less than 6 mints. Only that of St Omer had been in regular use during the previous 100 years. Although the mints at Arras and Lens had clearly struck coins in the eleventh century, they had no history of continuous operation, and were effectively new mints. His mints at Aire, 'Favrebie' and 'Chirisi', of which the two latter have not yet been identified with any certainty, were entirely new. Not only did Philip of Alsace himself open 5 new mints in Artois in the last quarter of the twelfth century, but his vassal, Robert IV, Count of Béthune, also struck coins at new mints at Béthune and Saint Venant of the same types as those of his overlord. Another vassal, Anselm, Count of St Pol, already had a mint in operation at the accession of Philip of Alsace, as did the abbey of St Bertin at St Omer. The number of mints operating in Artois was thus increased during Philip's reign from 3 to 10, although it must be admitted that it is far from clear that all 10 mints were ever in operation at one time.[1] The same sort of thing seems to have been taking place in other parts of France from the last quarter of the twelfth century. In the west, for example, new mints seem at this time to have been established in turn in the adjacent counties of Angoulême, Perigord and La Marche by 1211 at the latest, all of which struck very similar deniers to each other.

The next stage in the process of expansion was the domination of the money of a region by the coinage of one mint. An example of this is the domination of the process of buying and selling in the coastal plain of Languedoc by the Melgorien deniers issued by the Bishops of Maguelonne, as Counts of Melgueil. These not only became the official coinage of the nearby city of Montpellier, but were so successful that independent coinages ceased to be issued at Béziers and Carcassonne in the west, and in the east at Uzès, Nîmes and St Gilles at the mouth of the Rhône. All these had stopped being minted by the early thirteenth century. In the thirteenth century, the deniers struck at Narbonne, once the most important royal mint in southern France, were almost supplanted by those of Melgueil. (See Map 24.[2]) The Melgorien deniers also crossed the Pyrenees to become the key silver currency of

---

[1] Claude Richebé, *Les Monnaies féodales d'Artois du Xe au début du XIVe siècle* (Paris, 1963).
[2] Mireille Castaing–Sicard, *Monnaies féodales et circulation monétaire en Languedoc (X^e–XIIIe siècles)*, Cahiers de l'Association Marc Bloch de Toulouse, Études d'Histoire Méridionale IV (Toulouse, 1961).

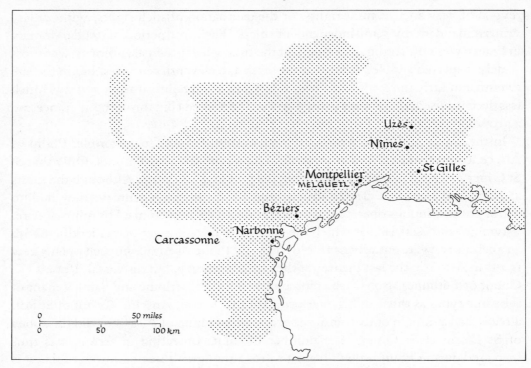

Map 24. Area of circulation of money of Melgueil

northern Spain at the end of the twelfth century and in the early thirteenth.[1]

In the same way, the deniers tournois of the abbey of St Martin at Tours came to dominate large areas of western France. The Parisian deniers of the kings came to dominate the Île de France, and the deniers provinois of the Counts of Champagne, from the great Fair town of Provins came to dominate large parts of eastern France.[2]

In Germany the coins produced in a few mints also came to dominate the circulation over large areas. The domination of the currency of the Rhineland from Frankfurt to the North Sea by the pfennigs of Cologne in the thirteenth century is the best example of this process in Germany.[3]

---

[1] C. E. Dufourcq and J. Gautier-Dalché, *Histoire économique et sociale de l'Espagne chrétienne au moyen âge* (Paris, 1976), p. 86.

[2] See below, pp. 197–200.

[3] Walter Hävernick, *Der Kölner Pfennig im 12. und 13. Jahrhundert*, Vierteljahrschrift für Sozial- und Wirtschafts-geschichte, supplement XVIII (Stuttgart, 1930), particularly Map II. On a smaller scale the pfennigs of Augsburg came to dominate the currency of a large part of Bavaria in the second half of the thirteenth century (Norbert Kamp, 'Münzprägung und Münzpolitik der Staufer in Deutschland', *Hamburger Beiträge zur Numismatik*, V (1963), 517–44).

In Flanders, too, the multiplication of mints was followed by the concentration of minting in a few larger mints. In the second half of the thirteenth century minting there was concentrated on Bruges and Ghent.[1]

This concentration in fewer, larger mints might take place as a result of purely commercial factors, as with the money of Provins, Melgueil, Cologne or Bruges, or it might be bound to political expansion, as with the money of Paris or Tours.

In an already centralised country such as England, where almost all the mints were royal, it was possible to concentrate the coinage in two large mints, at London and at Canterbury, and to close all the others (apart from those of the abbots at Bury St Edmunds and the bishops at Durham), except in times of recoinage. Sixteen strategically placed mints were opened for the recoinage of 1248–50, and six mints for the recoinages of 1279–81 and 1300–2. On each occasion they were closed again once the recoinage was over.

In southern Italy, in the mainland half of the centralised kingdom of Sicily, it was possible to concentrate minting at Brindisi. Even on the occasion of a recoinage it was only necessary to organise a multiplicity of outlets for exchanging coin, rather than to operate a multiplicity of mints. In 1269 the masters of the Brindisi mint were ordered to find 'distributores nove monete' in each of the thirty or so administrative districts (*justiciarates*) into which the country was divided, who would take in old coin and give out new in exchange.[2]

The gradual multiplication of mints in Bohemia, as more and more silver became available, and then their ultimate centralisation at Kutná Hora also exemplifies the two stages of the expansion of minting. When the mints were concentrated at Kutná Hora, exchanges probably remained in the seventeen towns from which the mints were moved.

Unlike the primitive money-making workshops of an earlier period, these new large mints were veritable factories with a large and complex organisation. They had extensive buildings, and permanent officers in their wardens, whose function was to keep a continual oversight, in the interests of the prince, on the succession of masters who came to take leases of the mint for limited periods to operate it for their own profit. Frequently there was also a permanent comptroller, or counter-warden, whose function was to protect the interests of the public, or rather the merchant community, from the masters, who were naturally tempted to increase their profits at the expense of the public if not at that of the prince also. In addition, permanent assayers and engravers were frequently appointed and, like the wardens and comptrollers, were paid a regular annual salary and provided with a house and

---

[1] Only six mints remained open in Flanders in the second half of the century (J. Ghyssens, *Les Petits Deniers de Flandre du XII*^{e} *et XIII*^{e} *siècles* (Brussels, 1971), p. 142). Earlier in the century, when the focus of the textile industry had been further to the south, Lille had been the most important mint, and earlier still, Arras, but minting had not been monopolised by either Lille or Arras.

[2] Eduard Sthamer, *Das Amtsbuch des sizilischen Rechnungshofes* (Burg, n.d.), pp. 264ff.

garden within the confines of the mints. The masters themselves tended to be entrepreneurs who had already made their mark in other businesses and saw this sort of industrial enterprise as just one more means of making a profit.[1]

The development of mint factories on this scale first took place in Italy,[2] and it is therefore not surprising that by the end of the thirteenth century many of the more successful mintmasters throughout Europe were Italian businessmen. In 1300 the great new Kutná Hora mint was set up by Tuscan merchant bankers. At about the same time other Florentines took over the mint of Hall in Swabia and the coinage that it issued, the heller, was rapidly transformed from a minor local currency to one that dominated southern and western Germany.[3] In 1306 the Count of St Pol called in a Lucchese businessman to run his mint and in 1305 the Count of Perigord called in two Florentines.[4]

In England the English branch of the great Florentine merchant banking house of the Frescobaldi took over both the exchanges and the mints during the recoinage of 1300–2.[5] Edward I's earlier and greater recoinage of 1279–81 had been farmed out, not to Italian entrepreneurs, but to William de Turnemire of Marseilles. The scale of organisation that these entrepreneurs provided may be gauged by the fact that for Edward I's smaller recoinage of 1300–2, over 400 additional skilled workmen were brought over from France and the Low Countries.[6]

Apart from the Tuscans, the other main group of Italian businessmen to spread their activities across Europe at this time came from upper Lombardy, from such towns as Asti. In 1285 the Count of Flanders, when reorganising the mint of Namur, called in an entrepreneur from Asti to run it. In 1300 the mint of Geneva was run by another businessman from Asti.[7]

It is natural to ask if any evidence exists for an increasing overall scale of output, first from the multiplication of old-fashioned, small, workshop mints and later from the fewer new, large, factory mints. There are unfortunately no statistics of production from the twelfth century to indicate with any precision whether there

---

[1] After this sudden change in the thirteenth century, mint organisation only evolved slowly over the next two centuries. For a description of the way 'factory' mints were run in the fifteenth century see Peter Spufford, 'Mint organisation in the Burgundian Netherlands in the fifteenth century', in C. N. L. Brooke, B. H. I. H. Stewart, J. G. Pollard and T. R. Volk (eds.), *Studies in Numismatic Method presented to Philip Grierson* (Cambridge, 1983), pp. 239–61.

[2] E.g. in Venice (Frederic C. Lane, *Venice, A Maritime Republic* (Baltimore, 1966), p. 161).

[3] Aloys Schulte, *Geschichte des mittelalterlichen Handels und Verkehrs zwischen Westdeutschland und Italien mit Ausschluss von Venedig* (Leipzig, 1900), pp. 331–2, and H. Ammann, 'Vom Lebensraum der mittelalterlichen Stadt', *Berichte zur deutschen Landeskunde*, XXXI (1963), 284–316.

[4] Faustin Poey d'Avant, *Les Monnaies féodales de la France* (3 vols., Paris, 1858–62), II, 55.

[5] Armando Sapori, *La compagnia dei Frescobaldi in Inghilterra* (Florence, 1947), pp. 21–2.

[6] Michael Prestwich, 'Edward I's monetary policies and their consequences', *Economic History Review*, 2nd series, XXII (1969), 412. For Edwardian mint organisation in general see Mavis Mate, 'Monetary policies in England 1272–1307', *British Numismatic Journal*, XLI (1972), 34–79.

[7] Schulte, *Geschichte des mittelalterlichen Handels*, pp. 333 and 335.

was a marked and measurable increase in mint output in the last quarter of the century following on the opening of the Freiberg mines and the proper exploitation of those at Friesach and Montieri and the consequent increase in the flow of silver through Europe. However, if subjective impressions are anything to go by, I believe that I can discern such a marked increase in output from the mints of Cologne, Flanders and Artois, England and northern France, as well as from those of Venice, Pisa and Rome.

The new silver from Freiberg can thus be seen not only in the mass-produced, poorly designed bracteate pfennigs of Otto the Rich of Meissen himself,[1] but also in the pfennigs of Philip of Heinsberg as Archbishop of Cologne. The pfennigs that he had minted there in the 1170s were the first to be struck at Cologne in considerable quantities since those of St Anno in the 1070s.[2] As early as 1174 it was possible for Philip of Heinsberg to mortgage the income from his mints for a year for 1000 marks. Dr Elisabeth Nau has suggested that this implies an annual output of at least 13,000 marks, reckoning on a maximum seigniorage of 1 shilling per mark.[3] In terms of actual coins struck this meant a minimum of 2 million pfennigs a year.[4] From negligible activity to 2 million pfennigs a year is a remarkable transformation, and surviving coins suggest that the high level of mint activity that began so suddenly in the 1170s continued unabated at Cologne until the end of the thirteenth century.[5]

Philip of Heinsberg was chancellor to the Emperor Frederick I, Barbarossa, and his nominee at Cologne. His newly prolific Cologne pfennigs were clearly modelled on those struck for Barbarossa at Aachen. It seems that minting there also enormously increased in the 1170s.[6]

The flow of ingots westwards into the Netherlands was accompanied by considerable quantities of these pfennigs. For example the hoard concealed in Flanders, at Beveren in the Waasland, west of Antwerp, shortly after 1181 contained 1500 pfennigs of Frederick I out of around 6000 coins, besides numerous pfennigs of Philip of Heinsberg from Cologne. The wide circulation in Flanders of these numerous new German pfennigs had already been foreseen and regulated by an agreement between Frederick and the Count of Flanders, Philip of Alsace, in 1173.[7]

---

[1] See above, p. 112.   [2] Hävernick, *Der Kölner Pfennig*.

[3] E. Nau in the catalogue of the exhibition *Die Zeit der Staufer*, III (Stuttgart, 1977), citing the Frankfurt dissertation of G. Gattermann. I owe this reference to N. J. Mayhew, who discusses Philip of Heinsberg's coinage further in 'Coinage and inflation in England 1180–1220' in John Day (ed.), *Études d'histoire monétaire XIIe–XIXe siècles* (Lille, 1984), pp. 159–77.

[4] 13,000 Cologne marks weigh 2730 kilograms (nearly 2¾ tons). The pfennigs of Philip of Heinsberg each weigh just under 1.4 grams.

[5] Hävernick, *Der Kölner Pfennig*.

[6] J. Menadier, 'Die Aachener Münzen', *Zeitschrift für Numismatik*, xxx (1913), 321–422 and plates LX–XVI.

[7] Ghyssens, *Les Petits Deniers de Flandre*, pp. 49–57.

In Flanders itself, and in Artois in the 1170s, a prolific coinage of small-module deniers, many with the name of the mintmaster, 'Simon', probably of Arras, succeeded the sparse issues of the earlier part of the century. No fewer than 2500 of the deniers minted by Simon's authority were found in the Beveren hoard.[1] The importance of the Arras mint was to be even greater at the end of the century.[2] Documentary evidence confirms the new abundance of coin in this area. In 1186, for example, Baldwin V of Hainault reckoned that his debts from his recent campaigns came to a total of 41,000 'libras Valcenceniensium denariorum'. Within seven months he had raised almost the whole amount in small sums by crushing his subjects with impositions. In other words he had managed to extract some 9 million deniers from them. At around the same date the Lord of Ardres, wishing to transform the village of Ardres into a chartered town, was able, rather ostentatiously, to give his lord, the Count of Guines, a *modius* 'plenissimo denariis' for permission to do so.[3]

From the Netherlands much silver was sent to England. In England the scale of minting dramatically increased in the 1180s at the beginning of the issue of short-cross pennies by Henry II. Mr Mayhew has recently suggested that the first four types of short-cross pennies struck for Henry II, Richard I and John between 1180 and 1204 reached a total value of half a million pounds. He has calculated this from the evidence of die studies of the coins of the Lincoln and Carlisle mints.[4] Such a figure of half a million pounds could have been made up from an initial recoinage of some 20 million pennies followed by a normal annual minting of some 4 million pennies. Some evidence from the Pipe Rolls has been adduced to suggest that the scale of minting in this period was of the same magnitude as in the 1220s,[5] when the combined output of England's two principal mints, those at Canterbury and at London, was in the region of 4 million pennies a year.[6] Dr Metcalf, using the same sort of evidence, had earlier calculated that the total production of the cross and crosslets coinage of 1158 to 1180 was of the order of 20 to 30 million pennies.[7] This could have been made up from an initial recoinage of around 10 million pennies, followed by a normal annual coinage that averaged half to three quarters of a million pennies produced in 20 different mints. In other words, although the stock

---

[1] *Ibid.*

[2] See below, pp. 197–8.

[3] Chronicles of Gislebert of Mons and Lambert of Ardres quoted by Hans van Werveke, 'Monnaies, lingots ou marchandises? Les instruments d'échange aux xiᵉ et xiiᵉ siècles', *Annales d'Histoire Économique et Sociale*, IV (Paris, 1932), 463.

[4] Mayhew, 'Coinage in England', pp. 5–12.

[5] *Ibid.* p. 3.

[6] See below, p. 202.

[7] D. M. Metcalf, 'A survey of numismatic research into the pennies of the first three Edwards', in N. J. Mayhew (ed.), *Edwardian Monetary Affairs (1279–1344)*, British Archaeological Reports, xxxvi (Oxford, 1977), pp. 26–31 and 6–7.

of coin in England was already very gradually increasing in the 1160s and 1170s, an abrupt change took place around 1180. After that date the normal coinage of new coin, principally from bullion brought into the country, seems to have been 6 to 8 times what it had been before.

In commercially precocious Champagne, where the Sienese agent of the Tolomei was later to quote the sale price of Freiberg silver at the fairs,[1] the increase in the scale of minting of deniers provinois seems to have taken place in the 1170s at the same time as in Cologne and Arras. The Champagne deniers, of traditional types struck intermittently since the earlier revival of coinage in the tenth century, seem only to have been struck in considerable quantities with the growth of the Champagne Fairs from regional to international importance in the second half of the twelfth century, particularly from the reign of Henry I the Liberal onwards. (He was count from 1152 to 1180.) They appear to have been struck in their largest numbers, and to have had their greatest importance, in parallel with the Fairs, in the first half of the thirteenth century. Two of the four Fair towns, Lagny and Bar-sur-Aube, did not contain mints, and the mint at Troyes was gradually outstripped in importance by that at Provins, so that the denier of Provins formed the basis of the money of account that became the standard not only at Provins, but for the whole of Champagne and all its fairs, and even for the Chalonnais, the Barrois and Lorraine.

In the Île de France and Picardy large issues of deniers did not begin until the 1180s or even the 1190s. The denier of the distinctive type known as the parisis, struck for the kings of France at Paris, from Louis VII onwards, had been initially, and remained for some time, an urban coin for use only in and around Paris itself. In the same way Louis, in the course of his long reign, from 1137 to 1180, had sparse issues of different deniers struck in nine other towns under direct royal control for use in and around those towns. Even under his vigorous successor, Philip II Augustus, distinctive local deniers continued to be minted at Bourges and Sens, and for a time at Montreuil-sur-Mer. However, it was under Philip II that the parisis became the denier not merely of Paris, or even of the Île de France only, but of much of northern France, and that it came to be minted on a considerable scale. The key to the transformation of the role of the denier parisis was the inheritance by Philip II of Artois and Peronne in 1191. The textile industry of the southern Netherlands was then focussed on Arras, and the financiers of Arras had an international importance. Philip II did not continue the local coinage of small Flemish deniers, but instead set the already-important mint of Arras to work at minting parisis together with the lesser mints at St Omer and at Peronne in Vermandois. At the same time he brought to an end his own coinage of distinctive

[1] See above, p. 113.

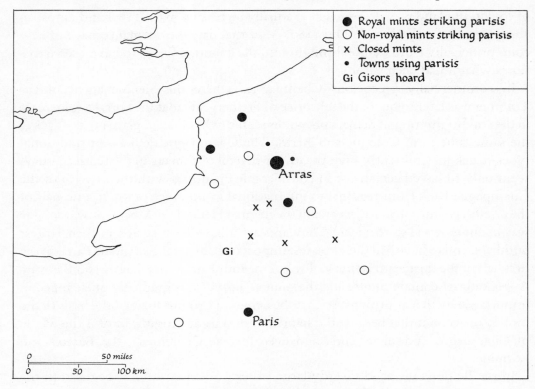

Map 25. Spread of money parisis, first quarter of the thirteenth century

urban deniers at the key port of Montreuil-sur-Mer. This was the successor to Quentovic. The main trade-route from Cologne and Aachen through the Mosan metal-working region and the rapidly growing textile areas of Hainault and southern Flanders reached the Channel there until early in the thirteenth century.[1] From Artois the deniers parisis spread southwards to become the common currency of much of northern France (see Map 25).[2] In response Eleanor, Countess of Vermandois from 1183 to 1214, had imitative parisis struck at her mints at St Quentin in Vermandois and at Crépy in Valois, itself important as a toll-station on

[1] So much was Montreuil *the* port for textiles, that a greater value of textiles was sold at Genoa in 1197 with Montreuil as its declared place of origin than from any of the actual textile-producing towns (R. L. Reynolds, 'Market for northern textiles in Genoa 1179–1200', *Revue Belge de Philologie et d'Histoire*, VIII (1929), 831–51).

[3] Françoise Dumas, 'Comparisons between the political, the economic and the monetary evolution of the north of France in the twelfth century', in N. J. Mayhew (ed.), *Coinage in the Low Countries 800–1500*, British Archaeological Reports, International Series LIV (Oxford, 1979), pp. 25–48.

the road system. Reckoning in the money of St Quentin ceased around 1205. Hugh IV, Count of St Pol from 1174 to 1205, also struck them at his mint of St Pol in Artois. So did Renaud de Dammartin, Count of Boulogne from 1191 to 1214 at Boulogne; and also William III, Count of Ponthieu from 1191 to 1221, and his successors, at Abbeville. To the west of Paris imitative parisis were struck at Dreux for a Count Robert, but whether Robert II, count from 1184 to 1218, or Robert III, count from 1218 to 1234, or both, is not clear. At the same time the Archbishops of Rheims altered their deniers to be of the same weight, fineness and value as the deniers parisis.

Meanwhile Philip II also arranged for a number of mints to be closed. He made agreements with the Abbot of St Peter at Corbie in Picardy, with the Bishops of Noyon and Laon, also in Picardy, and with the Bishop of Beauvais in the Île de France, which brought all their hitherto independent coinages to an end before 1220. He acquired the mint town of Amiens himself in 1186, but did not mint there. It is not surprising that by the end of the twelfth century occasionally, and at the beginning of the next generally, payments were made and accounts reckoned in money parisis as far north as Arras, Béthune and St Omer in Artois, at Boulogne and even at Douai in Flanders.[1] The cumulative effect of the spread of the use of deniers parisis can be seen from the hoard concealed at Gisors in the Norman Vexin shortly after 1244. Out of 11,375 identifiable deniers, 9183 were royal deniers parisis. These were dominated by the issues of Philip Augustus. There were hardly any pieces of an earlier date. By far the largest group of parisis were those from Arras, emphasising the importance of that mint. The parisis of Paris ranked second in importance and those of Montreuil ranked third. Among the 1289 'feudal' deniers by far the largest place was taken by those of the Archbishops of Rheims, of the parisis standard, whilst there were over a hundred each of the imitative parisis of Boulogne, Abbeville, St Quentin and Dreux. The only significant number of non-parisis were the 824 English short-cross pennies, but they only formed 7% of the whole hoard.[2]

In the last quarter of the twelfth century the deniers struck by the abbey of St Martin of Tours were probably the most successful of the five types of deniers that were circulating together in increasing quantities in the continental dominions of the Plantagenet Kings of England, who were at the same time Dukes of Normandy and Counts of Anjou, Touraine and Maine. The others were the short-cross pennies struck by the Plantagenets as Kings of England, the mansois and angevin deniers struck by them as Counts of Maine and Anjou respectively and the

---

[1] Richebé, *Monnaies d'Artois*, pp. 124–32; Robert Fossier, *La Terre et les hommes en Picardie jusqu'à la fin du XIIIᵉ siècle* (Paris, 1968), p. 94; Ghyssens, *Les Petits Deniers de Flandre*, pp. 21–2.

[2] F. Dumas and J. D. Brand, 'The British coins in the Gisors (1970) hoard', *British Numismatic Journal*, XL (1971), 22–43.

guingampois deniers struck by the neighbouring Counts of Penthièvre on the borders of Brittany. All are represented in varying proportions in the large number of hoards buried at about the time of the French royal conquest of these lands in the first years of the thirteenth century.[1] They all found a place in the ordinance of 1204 made by Philip Augustus to regulate the currency of the newly conquered Duchy of Normandy.[2] Normandy had shared in the general decline of coinage in western Europe in the late eleventh century. Its attenuated coinage finally came to an end in the mid twelfth century. Strangely enough, it did not share in the revival of coinage in the late twelfth century. Instead it used coin struck by its rulers in their other dominions, particularly the money of Anjou.[3] In 1204, Philip Augustus did not seek to impose the denier of Paris on these newly conquered lands, but put his authority behind the denier of Tours, as the most successful of the existing coinages in this region of France. He brought the coinage of mansois and angevin deniers to an end, and, after a transitional stage in which they were struck in the joint names of the abbey of St Martin and of the king, the deniers of Tours became a royal coinage. In 1226 Philip II's son and successor, Louis VIII, declared that only royal coin was to circulate freely throughout the whole realm and that the circulation of 'feudal' coin was to be limited to the fief of issue.[4] In many parts of France this was no more than a pious hope for some considerable time, but in the west this policy had a very remarkable success. Less than a quarter of 1% of a hoard buried in Brittany between 1251 and 1266 consisted of anything but native breton deniers and tournois deniers struck for successive kings, or earlier for the abbey of St Martin at Tours.[5] This was despite the fact that St Louis' brother Charles, to whom the Counties of Anjou and Maine had been granted in appanage, had by then resumed the striking of angevin and mansois deniers. It is not clear how many mints, if any, besides that at Tours itself, struck the tournois type of deniers for Philip II, Louis VIII and Louis IX, since individual mint names were not used to differentiate them.

In 1210, or possibly 1224, the dominant coin of eastern France, the provinois denier of the Counts of Champagne, struck for them in the internationally important Fair town of Provins, was deliberately altered to bring it into conformity with the tournois denier.[6]

[1] F. Dumas, 'La Circulation monétaire dans les domaines Plantagenêts', *Bulletin de la Société Française de Numismatique*, XXIV (1969), 467–9. In their county of Poitou and their duchy of Aquitaine, however, the currency was completely separate and dominated by deniers minted by the Plantagenets in Aquitaine itself (Albert Bronfenbrener, 'Le Trésor de Guitinières', *Revue Numismatique*, 6th series, XI (1969), 271–88).

[2] See A. Dieudonné, 'L'Ordonnance de 1204', *Mélanges Schlumberger*, II (1925), 328–37.

[3] Françoise Dumas, 'Les Monnaies normandes (X^e–XIIe siècles)', *Revue Numismatique*, 6th series, XXI (1979), 84–103.

[4] Harry A. Miskimin, *Money, Prices and Foreign Exchange in Fourteenth Century France* (Newhaven, Conn., 1963), p. 51.

[5] Jacques Yvon, 'Le Trésor de Bouvron', *Revue Numismatique*, 6th series, X (1968), 236–49.

[6] A. Blanchet and A. Dieudonné, *Manuel de numismatique française* (4 vols., Paris, 1912–36), vol. IV: 'Monnaies féodales françaises', p. 133.

The commencement of minting of this western stream of silver ingots can be paralleled in Italy for the southerly flow of silver. Here too there seems to have been a very sudden increase, in a very short time, in the amount of money available. Here too there had been a late-eleventh and early-twelfth-century dearth of coin, after the supplies of silver made available in the tenth century had run out.[1] This had been brought about partially through wear and tear and partially through immobilisation in hoards and in gifts to shrines and churches, but largely through the gradual and persistent drain of silver to the east. In Venice, for example, there seems to have been very little money in circulation in 1168, when the Freiberg silver was discovered. The evidence of the surviving coins leads one to suppose that, when and if it was working, the Venetian mint was only issuing minute quantities of the traditional denari in the name of the Emperor 'Henry', which it had started producing a century earlier. The revival of minting began during the reign of Vitale II Michiel, who was doge from 1156 to 1172. New denari were struck with the name of the ruling doge, but since few of them survive today, it is likely that the revival began near the end of his reign. However, having begun, the revival of minting continued strongly. The surviving pieces give the impression that considerably more denari were minted over the next twenty years, during the reigns of Sebastiano Ziani and Orio Malpiero, than over the previous century.[2] Then at the end of the next reign, that of Enrico Dandolo, doge from 1192 to 1205, the first grossi, or large silver coins, in Europe were struck.[3] In only thirty years, one generation, there had been a transformation of the amount of money circulating in Venice, from nearly nothing to enough to warrant the minting of much larger coins. In the following quarter-century, during the reign of Pietro Ziani, more of the new, larger coins, the grossi, were struck than of anything else.

In Tuscany, where there was the silver from Montieri as well as that from north of the Alps, the revival of minting began earlier and the increase was rather slower. Nevertheless the 1170s were a key decade in Tuscany as well, for it was at that time that the denari of Pisa began to be minted in large numbers and to dominate the whole region.[4]

In central Italy there was no mint open at all in 1170, and the whole area was reliant on outside sources for its sparse currency. However, enough silver reached Rome during the 1170s for the senate, by agreement with the pope, to open a mint,

---

[1] See above, pp. 97–8.

[2] Eighty-six varieties of denari are listed in the *Corpus Nummorum Italicorum* (Rome, 1910–61) for the reigns of Ziani (1172–8) and Malpiero (1179–92), compared with only fifty-two varieties of denari in the name of the Emperor 'Henry', which I suspect are mostly eleventh-century rather than twelfth. No work on the dies used for these denari, comparable with that done on the cross and crosslets and short-cross pennies of England, has yet been done, so that it is not yet possible to estimate original production from the survivals.

[3] See below, pp. 225–7.

[4] D. Herlihy, 'Pisan coinage and the monetary development of Tuscany', *Museum Notes*, VI (American Numismatic Society, 1954), 143–68.

which soon supplemented the deniers provinois, which had then recently begun to flood into the area from Champagne, with a plentiful supply of imitative denari provisini.[1]

Whether one looks at Venice or Cologne, at commercially developed Champagne, Artois and Tuscany, or rural Anjou, Touraine and England, one gets the impression of a sudden change in the quantity of silver passing through the mints in the 1170s, 1180s and 1190s, which inaugurated a continuously growing increase in minting that was sustained right through the thirteenth century. In its beginnings the evidence for this growth is heavily based on the surviving coins, but there is more solid documentary evidence from the thirteenth century, of which the best surviving material is for the output of the two principal English mints, those of London and Canterbury.

The earliest surviving evidence for production in English mints so far published is from the period 1220–2. At the London mint, over a period of two years and three months 9013 tower pounds of silver (over 3000 kilograms, or 3 metric tons) was struck into over 2 million short-cross pennies, and at the Canterbury mint, during the same period, 34,027 tower pounds of silver (nearly 12 tons) was struck into over 8 million short-cross pennies.[2] These are the earliest certain statistics of mint output yet available. All earlier figures are only estimations.[3] The Canterbury mint was the more productive because the mint and exchange of Canterbury was designed to cope with the foreign coin and bullion coming into England through the Cinque Ports on the south-east coast, and ensure that all the foreign coin, and as much as possible of the bullion, was converted into English pennies before being spent by foreigners on English goods. This represents an average rate of production in the London and Canterbury mints of just under 1 million, and well over 3 million, pennies a year respectively. A combined account for the two mints together for the four years 1225 to 1229 indicates that minting of pennies was then continuing at approximately the same rate. We may conclude that it was normal for a combined total of 4 million pennies a year to be struck at the 2 principal mints of England in the 1220s. There were, however, also 4 minor mints still in operation,[4] so that it is far from clear how many more than 4 million pennies were actually being minted throughout England at this time. We have even less means of guessing how much coin was in circulation in the country.

From the mid-1230s onwards we have an almost continuous sequence of figures for mint production from the London and Canterbury mints. This information appears as Graph 1, p. 203. It will be seen that, from 1234 up to the eve of the long-

---

[3] The mint was probably opened in 1176/7 (Pierre Toubert, *Les Structures du Latium médiévale . . . du IXe à la fin du XIIe siècle*, Bibliothèque des Écoles Françaises d'Athènes et de Rome CCXXI (Rome, 1973), pp. 552–624).

[1] C. E. Blunt and J. D. Brand, 'Mint output of Henry III', *British Numismatic Journal*, XXXIX (1970), 61–6.

[3] E.g. above, pp. 196–7.

[4] At Durham and Bury St Edmunds, and, until 1223, at York and Winchester.

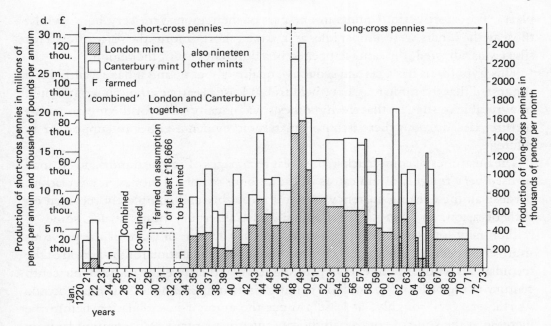

Graph I. English mint production – reign of Henry III. The height of the columns gives the rate of striking per annum. The area of the columns gives the amount struck per annum. Derived from figures printed by Blunt and Brand, 'Mint output of Henry III' and C. G. Crump and C. Johnson, 'Tables of bullion coined under Edward I, II, and III', *Numismatic Chronicle*, 4th series, XIII (1913), 200–45.

cross pennies in 1247, the two principal mints together were generally striking in the region of 10 million pennies a year; usually rather more in the 1240s, and rather less in the late 1230s. There would thus appear to have been another marked increase during the earlier 1230s, in the amount minted, followed by a slighter, but continued, increase up to 1247. After the end of the recoinage in 1251 only the 2 major mints were normally open, apart from those of the abbot at Bury St Edmunds and the bishop at Durham, so that the known figures for London and Canterbury from then onwards cannot be far short of the overall total minted in England. In the 1250s some 15 million pennies or, in other words, well over 20 tons of silver, were generally minted each year, a further increase on the amount struck in the 1240s. However, after that, the figures grow much more erratic. It has been plausibly argued by Professor Miskimin that between 1334 and 1384 the mints of northern France, Flanders and England should be looked at as a single group. In this way the erratic behaviour of single mints within the group may be explained in terms of the deliberate movement by speculators of a great deal of silver from one part of the region to another, according to the price offered for silver by the different mints. The same coin was consequently frequently reminted in different places. For short periods mints in one part of the region were very busy, whilst those in the others were almost idle, and, after a short time, as the price offered for silver was adjusted, the same happened in a different part of the region.[1]

This hypothesis has a certain seductive quality about it, and it has recently been suggested that the same may have held true at least as early as the 1290s.[2] It would be agreeable to suggest that the hypothesis was equally valid for the previous two or three decades, but there is unfortunately no evidence either to support or to refute it.

The quantities of coin struck in the great recoinages of 1247–50 and 1279–81 may be used very roughly as indicators of the amount of coined money in circulation, because all the existing currency was so thoroughly and completely recoined on each occasion. In 1247–50 the London and Canterbury mints struck some 70 million new long-cross pennies, some £300,000 worth, in place of the previous short-cross pennies, and there were 18 other mints in operation for the period of the recoinage. It would not be excessive to suggest that there were in the mid thirteenth century in the order of 100 million pennies circulating in England, some £400,000 worth, or, very roughly, at least 5 times the amount in circulation before the increase in the scale of coinage in the late twelfth century.[3] A generation later, in 1279–81, the London and Canterbury mints between them struck some 120 million new pennies, £500,000 worth of 'sterlings', in place of the previous long-cross pennies, and there were also 8 extra mints in operation for the period of the recoinage. The situation was perhaps now more complex than 30 years before, for some foreign coin and bullion may have been attracted to England simply in order to be reminted into the new pennies and straightaway exported again. I would therefore be more tentative in suggesting that the coined money in England by 1279–81 had reached the order of 150 million pennies, over £600,000, although this is quite possible.[4] It ought to be borne in mind that, in the following decade, there was enough silver in the country for Edward I to be able to spend no less than £750,000 in the years 1294 to 1298 to pay for his wars against Philip IV of France.[5] In fact only about half of this was spent on the direct costs of the war, particularly the payment of troops, and is likely to have been in coin, whilst the other half was

[1] Miskimin, *Money in Fourteenth Century France*, pp. 100–16.
[2] Prestwich, 'Edward I', particularly p. 414; Miskimin, *Fourteenth Century France*, pp. 107–8.
[3] See above pp. 196–7, for estimates of 10 million and 20 million pence for the recoinages of 1158 and 1180 respectively. This remarkable increase had taken place despite the vast quantities of coin that had been exported at intervals for political purposes. See above, pp. 160–1.
[4] The availability of coin in late-thirteenth-century England can be illustrated from the case of Adam de Stratton, who was chamberlain of the exchequer and was convicted of fraud in 1290. He had no less than 3,040,051 pence in his house at the time of his fall, all in coin (N. Denholm-Young, *Seignorial Administration in England* (Oxford, 1937), pp. 83–4).
[5] See above, p. 162.

spent on lavish subsidies to foreign princes to maintain a system of alliances stretching along the French frontiers from Flanders to Savoy.[1] This could more conveniently have been transmitted in the form of ingots, but whether any of it was actually sent in bars instead of coin is not clear.

The partial recoinage of 1299–1301 was designed to remint into English coin the continental imitative pennies known as 'crockards' and 'pollards' that had been imported into England over the previous decade. Rather under 50 million pennies were struck at the London and Canterbury mints. From this occasion some accounts survive for the 6, out of 8, provincial mints, specially opened for the recoinage. Their relative scale of operation may be judged from the fact that between them they struck some 13 million pennies, making an overall total for the partial recoinage of over 60 million pennies. Again it is not clear how much of this may have been brought into the country simply because of the recoinage itself. What is striking is the enormous quantity of silver coin circulating in England during the thirteenth century. The quantity shrank progressively during the fourteenth century, particularly rapidly during the second decade, for reasons to be discussed later. It is astonishing to realise that the weight of silver generally minted each year in thirteenth-century England was not regularly exceeded until after the Napoleonic Wars. As far as recoinages were concerned, even the weight of silver passing and repassing through the mints during Henry VIII's great debasement of 1545–51 did not exceed that passing through the mints in the partial recoinage of 1299–1301, let alone the major recoinages of 1279–81 and 1247–50. In the second half of the thirteenth century England appears to have had a more plentiful silver currency, admittedly all in pennies, than it was to have again for 500 years. It is moreover quite possible that the quantities of coin available in the sixteenth century were no greater than those available in the thirteenth. It was certainly so for England. Dr Challis has estimated the stock of coin in England at the end of the reign of Queen Elizabeth in 1603 at around 3 million pounds sterling in silver and half a million pounds sterling in gold, in other words 1 million tower pounds' weight of silver coin and the equivalent of another sixth of that in gold.[2] In 1309, at the end of the reign of Edward I, there were around 1¼ million tower pounds' weight of silver pence in circulation in England.

It is difficult to evaluate the fragments of information available from other parts of Europe against the background of this continuous record, since it is usually far from clear whether the figures that survive represent a normal output, a major recoinage, or even very slack working of the mint.

The earliest surviving French royal mint account to survive is no earlier than

---

[1] Prestwich, 'Edward I', p. 411.
[2] C. E. Challis, *The Tudor Coinage* (Manchester, 1978), pp. 246–7.

1254. It is not clear to which mint it refers, or how long a period of time it covers. It is therefore of little use to know that it accounts for the striking of over 2 million deniers.[1]

Probably the next in sequence is an account from the mint of Poitou at Montreuil-Bonnin. Its exact date is uncertain, although it is obviously from the period after the death of Alfonse of Poitiers in 1271 when Poitou was once more in royal hands. The account is for the striking of slightly under 12½ million deniers, and nearly 2½ million mailles, or half-deniers, over a period of 8 months. In other words, it indicates striking at the rate of some 21 million pieces a year. This is a higher annual rate of production, in terms of the numbers rather than value of pieces minted, than had been achieved at either the London or the Canterbury mint separately in any recorded year up to then, even in the recoinage of 1247–50. It has therefore been plausibly suggested that it records the immediate recoinage of poitevan deniers into tournois deniers in 1272, the very next year after Alfonse had died.[2]

The next surviving accounts are for the striking of great coins, or gros, of the tournois type. From the mint of Vermandois, at St Quentin on the Somme, comes an account for 10 months in 1278–9, recording minting at the rate of over 3 million gros a year. Since the tournois gros was, at this date, worth 12 of the old, small tournois deniers, this had the same value as minting at an annual rate of almost 40 million of the small tournois deniers.[3] From the mint of Tournai comes an account for 7 months in 1285, which records minting at the rate of 4½ million gros a year. Another account from the Paris mint, for 8 months of the same year, records minting at the much more modest rate of some 1,300,000 tournois gros a year, together with over 800,000 tournois deniers a year.[4] Regular series of French royal mint accounts do not survive from before the middle of the fourteenth century. A considerable number of isolated accounts are known for individual years before that, particularly a group from the period 1309–12, towards the end of Philip IV's reign, when royal power was at its strongest in France. Even this group of accounts is far from complete, and there are considerable gaps in the information for the 8 mints covered during these 4 years. There were also 3 other royal mints operating in those years for which no accounts survive. It is impossible to know which of the gaps represent occasions when the mints were shut, and which have simply resulted from the failure of the mint accounts to survive. As a minimum, the accounts record the minting over the 4 years of 298,180 troy marks of silver into

[1] N. de Wailly, 'Système monétaire de Saint Louis', *Memoires de l'Institut de France. Académie des inscriptions*, XXI, 2 (1857), 145.

[2] A. Dieudonné, 'Compte de fabrication de tournois par Philippe III à Montreuil-Bonnin (1272)', *Revue Belge de Numismatique*, LXVI (1924), 9–28.

[3] De Wailly and Delisle (eds.), *Recueil des historiens . . . de la France*, XXII (Paris, n.d.), 756.

[4] *Ibid.* p. 666.

Table 3. *Output of French mints open 1309–1312 according to the surviving accounts*[1]

	Out of 48 months, accounts survive for:	In livres tournois	
		total minted:	per month:
Paris	22 months	291,000	13,200
Montreuil-Bonnin (Poitou)	25 months	174,000	7,000
Toulouse	30 months	142,000	4,700
Sommières/Montpellier (Languedoc)	39 months	176,000	4,500
Rouen (Normandy)	19 months	77,000	4,000
St Pourçain (Bourbonnais)	25 months	76,000	3,000
Troyes (Champagne)	under 26 months	73,000	2,800
Tournai	23 months	52,000	2,300

[1] Derived from the table in Miskimin, *Money in Fourteenth Century France*, pp. 161–5.

coin worth 1,063,000 tournois pounds or livres. If all the gaps in our information are the result of the failure of mint accounts to survive, rather than because the mints were not being worked, and, if these lost accounts showed the mints working at the same rate as is shown by the surviving accounts, then the amount actually minted in these 4 years was about double the amount recorded in the surviving accounts. In other words it is quite possible to believe that coin worth some 2 million tournois livres was struck in these 8 mints from some 600,000 troy marks of silver. This would have been an average weight of 150,000 troy marks a year, or getting on for 40 tons of silver or, for comparative purposes, it might be more reasonable to equate it to a weight of 110,000 tower pounds a year. From Graph 1 (p. 203) it will be seen that, except in the immediately preceding years, this scale of operations was only reached by the 2 principal English mints together at times of recoinage. On the other hand, this represents the output of no less than 8 of the new factory-type mints for a country much larger in area, population and wealth than England. At the rates of striking recorded in the surviving accounts, only the Paris mint was then operating on a scale comparable with that of either the London or the Canterbury mints. The relative scale of operations of the other mints may be judged from Table 3.

The royal coinage of France was, of course, only a part, although an increasing part, of the total coinage in France. For the non-royal coinages the only quantitative evidence that survives is in the form of those leases of mints to mintmasters which specify the minimum quantities of coin that the master of the mint was expected to have struck during his tenure of office. The lease of the mint of Poitou, at Montreuil-Bonnin, in 1253, by St Louis' brother, Alfonse, Count of Poitiers, provided for the minting of 8 million deniers. The lease of the mint of Provence, in 1262, by another brother, Charles of Anjou, provided for the minting of 30 million deniers of the tournois type over a period of 5 years.[1] The lease of the mints of Burgundy in 1282 provided for the minting of 4½ million deniers.[2] As late as 1305 the lease of the mint of Perigord by the count to two Florentine entrepreneurs, provided for the minting of 20,000 marks of alloyed silver into perigord deniers within three months. This weight of metal would have produced some 4 or 5 million deniers.[3] These are not negligible quantities, and the 30 or so non-royal mints that were still operating at the beginning of the fourteenth century were continuing to make a considerable contribution to the currency of France alongside that of the 8 royal mints.

It is unfortunate that we only have continuous records of the amounts of coin minted for England in the thirteenth century, and that elsewhere in Europe we have to rely on piecing together an impression from fragments, whilst for some of the most important mints of all, like Venice, there is no statistical information at all.[4]

---

[1] A. Engel and R. Serrure, *Traité de numismatique du moyen âge* (3 vols., Paris, 1891–1905), p. 779.

[2] De Wailly, 'Système monétaire de Saint Louis', p. 146.

[3] F. Poey d'Avant, *Les Monnaies féodales de la France* (3 vols., Paris, 1858–62), II, 55.

[4] A few further early fourteenth-century statistics are referred to in John Day, 'The question of monetary contraction in late medieval Europe', *Nordisk Numismatisk Årsskrift* (1981), 12–29.

9

Ingots of Silver

Even if we had fairly detailed statistics of the increase in coined money minted in several countries of Europe during the thirteenth century, we would still not know how much money was in circulation, not only because of the problems posed by repeated reminting, but, much more, because major payments, both locally and internationally, continued to be made not in coin, but in silver ingots. Coin was only a part of the silver in circulation, and it is quite impossible to gauge how large or how small a part.

The use of ingots for large payments was by no means new in the twelfth century, but at the end of the century their availability and use naturally increased enormously, both in proportion to the overall increase of silver in circulation and also in parallel with the quantities minted into coin. For large payments, unminted silver, provided its fineness was known, was obviously more convenient than minted silver, which had to be counted out, or weighed, in the form of thousands, or even tens of thousands of separate coins.

This unminted silver travelled from the mining-areas of Europe to the more economically advanced areas in bars or ingots of a standard fineness. There is some evidence to suggest that they were also frequently of a standard weight, the mark, although the mark weight itself, of course, varied from place to place. In the spring of 1204 Bishop Wolfger of Passau set out for Rome. His chamberlain brought with them a supply of silver bars to exchange along the route into local currency to pay for the needs of the bishop's party. The weights of the bars exchanged were normally, although not always, in round numbers of marks. He changed 3 marks at Tarvis, crossing the Alps into Italy, a single mark at Padua, 4 marks at Ferrara, then 2 more marks there, and yet another 2 before they moved on to Bologna, where he exchanged an odd weight of silver into Bolognese denari. Across the Apennines in Florence, he exchanged a round 5 marks, but an odd weight in Siena. In Rome itself, on all the 5 occasions when he exchanged bars for currency, complete numbers of marks were involved, first 11 marks, then another 11, then 16, then 3 and finally another 3 before they started the return journey.[1] In other words in 11

---

[1] Wilhelm Jesse (ed.), *Quellenbuch zur Münz- und Geldgeschichte des Mittelalters* (Halle, 1924), doc. 370, p. 251.

transactions out of 13 the chamberlain was offering silver bars that weighed a complete number of marks, which strongly suggests that most of the bars that he was carrying weighed a mark or an exact multiple.

At the beginning of the fourteenth century Pegolotti noted, in his perhaps anachronistic section on the Champagne Fairs, that 'Argenta si vende in fiera a marco.'[1] Even if he copied this passage into his own notebook from an earlier merchant's notebook, compiled before the fairs went into decline, it is clear that at the heart of the overland trade of the twelfth and thirteenth centuries, silver had been available in quantity in ingot form. In 1265 Andrea de Tolomei had quoted the value of silver, by the mark, at one of the Troyes Fairs.[2]

At the end of the thirteenth century, Bruges in part succeeded to the financial and commercial role of the Champagne Fairs. It is not surprising that 'argent en plate' was then available there, although its origin was curiously described as Poland and Hungary.[3]

One of the most persistent and increasing movements of precious metals from the twelfth century, throughout the thirteenth century and into the fourteenth century, was, of course, that to the papal curia from all parts of Christendom. This papal magnetism for the silver of Europe was already so pronounced by the end of the twelfth century as to be satirised in the *Gospel According to Marks of Silver*.[4] In practice it was normal for papal collectors to receive some of the larger sums due to them in ingots, as well as the smaller ones in coin. In 1282, for example, the papal collector for Denmark, Sweden and Rügen, as well as collecting small sums amounting to over 70,000 marks in pence, also collected over 1000 marks in larger payments in ingots.[5] As late as 1317, Peter Durandi, papal collector in Germany, received quantities of mixed coinages in the archdiocese of Salzburg, along with a few ingots. The Bishop of Gurk, for example, acquitted himself of his share of the papal subsidy with 40 'Marchas argenti quod dicitur crematum'. Other sources speak of such 'burnt' silver as 'cocti argenti', 'marca combusta', or 'brandsilber'.[6] Durandi was then faced with the problem of conveying what he had collected to Avignon. He would have preferred to send it in gold, but no gold was yet to be had in those parts of Europe: 'Quas siquidem predictarum pecuniarum et marcharum quantitates . . . quia in illis partibus nummum auri cambium poterat inveniri, portari fecimus ad civitatem Venetorum per magistrum Stephanum Pistoris,

[1] Francesco Balducci Pegolotti, *La pratica della mercatura*, ed. Allan Evans, Medieval Academy of America xxiv (Cambridge, Mass., 1936), p. 236.

[2] C. Paoli and E. Piccolomini (eds.), *Lettere volgari del secolo XIII scritte da Senesi* (Bologna, 1871), p. 57, discussed above, p. 113.

[3] See above, p. 139.

[4] C. H. Haskins, *The Renaissance of the Twelfth Century* (Cambridge, Mass., 1927), pp. 185–6.

[5] Rolf Sprandel, *Das mittelalterliche Zahlungssystem nach Hansisch-Nordischen Quellen des 13.–15. Jahrhunderts* (Stuttgart, 1975), p. 101.

[6] F. von Schrötter (ed.), *Wörterbuch der Münzkunde* (Berlin–Leipzig, 1930), pp. 60–2.

nostrum fidelem notarium, qui de predictis pecuniis et marcharum quantitatibus ibidem in cambio habuit et nobis assignavit . . . 1477 floreni auri.' In this particular case silver in ingot form was only transported from Carinthia to Venice, but, even at this time, a certain amount of silver was still conveyed in the form of ingots all the way to the curia. In 1334, on the death of John XXII, the papal treasurer reckoned up all the receipts that had come into the apostolic camera during John's pontificate. Over the years since 1316 a large proportion of the papal income had reached Avignon in gold, having been converted into florins on the way, but a not-inconsiderable amount came in the form of silver coin from all parts of Christendom. Nevertheless, even at as late a date as this, a surprisingly large amount came as uncoined silver. More than 4800 marks, or rather over 1 metric tonne, had been received in this form, during these 18 years.[1]

In the first half of the fourteenth century Pegolotti took it for granted that commercial payments outwards from Europe to the Near East would also normally be made in the form of ingots of European silver, and actual commercial contracts show how this had been working in practice. On 22 March 1291, for example, four contracts were made in Genoa for payments to be made in Caffa in the Crimea in 'argento buono in verghe' within fifteen days of the arrival of a specified galley from Genoa.[2] When entering the Black Sea, Europeans melted down their mark bars, which had been suitable for European use, and recast them into *sommi*, silver bars suitable for Asiatic use. Surviving contracts vividly illustrate the use of such ingots. In 1360–1, Antonio di Ponzo, a notary at the Genoese colony at Kilia, at the mouth of the Danube, entered in his register contracts for the import of wine and salt, for the export of wheat and of Bulgarian honey and wax, and for the re-export of slaves, mostly Mongol girls of twelve or thirteen. Payment for all of these was predominantly made in 'virge sommorum argenti'.[3]

Other payments outwards from Europe were also frequently made, at least in part, in ingots. In 1250 when Philip, the treasurer of St Hilary's at Poitiers, wished to send around 17,500 livres tournois to Alfonse of Poitiers, then on crusade with his brother St Louis, he only sent a third of it in money normally current in France. He first bought up as much gold as he could acquire, some 17,000 livres worth. He then laid out the remainder, nearly 10,000 livres, on acquiring in more or less equal portions, English sterlings, then very acceptable in the Near East, and silver in ingot form, as the most suitable means of conveying so large a sum to Egypt.[4]

---

[2] Accounts of papal collector and treasurer printed in Jesse, *Quellenbuch*, docs. 376 and 375, pp. 257–9. Translated, inadequately, in W. E. Lunt, *Papal Revenues in the Middle Ages* (2 vols., New York, 1934), docs. 77 and 13. Prof. Lunt was unfortunately not aware of the meaning of all the monetary terms he was translating.

[1] G. Pesce and G. Felloni, *Le monete genovesi* (Genoa, 1975), p. 342.

[2] Octavìan Iliescu, 'Nouvelles éditions d'actes notariés instrumentés au XIVe siècle dans les colonies génoises des bouches du Danube', *Revue des Études Sud-Est Européennes*, xv (1977), 113–29.

[4] Document ed. E. Cartier, *Revue Numismatique* (1847), 120–2. See below, pp. 213 n. 3 and 218–19.

Europeans, as well as sending silver in ingots to the Near East, from the Crimea to Egypt, also sent it out to the south-west and the north-east. North Africa was supplied not only with ready-made milliarenses, but also with silver bars. Pegolotti reported that in 1331 the mint at Tunis began to strike coins from Sardinian silver that had been sent there in the form of thin bars.[1] At the other end of Europe, however complex the patterns of payment within the Hanseatic trading-area, one thing was clear, that throughout the whole of the later Middle Ages there was a perpetual imbalance of trade with Novgorod that resulted in the continuous payment of bar silver to Russia.[2]

It was, then, normal for silver to be carried from place to place in the form of ingots rather than coin. It did not always happen that it was transformed into coin when it came to rest. It continued to be used in ingot form for larger local payments from the latter twelfth century onwards, for longer or shorter periods, according to differing conditions in the various parts of Europe.

The local use of ingots can be followed along the routes by which bullion was diffused from the mining-areas of Europe. The bullion that flowed westward and provoked the enormous increase in the minting of pfennigs at Cologne from the 1170s was also available in the Rhineland for larger local payments in the form of ingots of *puri argenti, probabilis argenti, argenti ponderati*.[3] West of the Rhine, in the Aachen region, ingots were similarly used for larger transactions. In 1263, for example, the Count of Isenburg mortgaged his estate at Mühlheim to the Count of Berg, against an advance of 73 marks of 'pure silver'.[4] Further west the principal abbeys and churches of the Meuse valley and of Flanders commonly accumulated considerable quantities of silver ingots in their treasuries from the 1160s onwards. They were then able to make advances to princes, to noblemen and even to non-noble freemen when they needed large sums for special purposes, like participating in the Third Crusade. In return for sums that were sometimes as considerable as 1600 *marcas puri argenti, pondo Coloniensi* they then mortgaged lands and revenues to the abbeys.[5] In the last third of the twelfth century and the first half of the thirteenth, in the towns of this region, St Omer, Arras, Béthune, Douai and Hesdin, smaller sums were also paid in marks and fiertons of 'pure silver'.[6] A fierton was a quarter of a mark.

---

[1] Pegolotti, ed. Evans, *La pratica della mercatura*, p. 133.

[2] Sprandel, *Das mittelalterliche Zahlungssystem*, pp. 106–12.

[3] Walter Hävernick, *Der Kölner Pfennig im 12. und 13. Jahrhundert*, Vierteljahrschrift für Sozial- und Wirtschafts-geschichte, supplement XVIII (Stuttgart, 1930), pp. 30–1.

[4] J. Menadier, 'Urkunden und Akten zur Aachener Münzgeschichte', *Zeitschrift für Numismatik*, XXXI (1914), doc. 8a.

[5] Hans van Werveke, 'Le Mort-gage et son rôle économique en Flandre et en Lotharingie', *Revue Belge de Philologie et d'Histoire*, VIII (1929), 53–91; 'Monnaie, lingots ou marchandises? Les instruments d'échange aux XIᵉ et XIIᵉ siècles', *Annales d'Histoire Économique et Sociale*, IV (1932), 452–68; both reprinted in *Miscellanea mediaevalia* (Ghent, 1968), pp. 159–208.

[6] Claude Richebé, *Les Monnaies féodales d'Artois du Xᵉ au début du XIVᵉ siècle* (Paris, 1963), pp. 117–21. 'Pure silver'

At the opposite end of France, in Languedoc, the use of ingots for large, local transactions increased enormously at much the same time as in Flanders and Artois. Here, too, it was the expansion of an already-existing pattern of payments. As early as 1137, the cellarer of the abbey of Gellen, when buying land at Adelaiz, had paid for it in a mixture of coin and ingots, 20 sous of the new money of Melgueil and 20 marks of silver. Such payments became common at the end of the century. As in Flanders, it was abbeys and prelates who very commonly had ingots at their disposal. They used them most frequently for the purchase of property, although they also used them in more ordinary transactions. The richer lords of the Midi also had ingots at their disposal. They used them for payment of ransoms, or as dowries for daughters who were not given land. In 1172 the Lord of Montpellier left 100 marks of silver in his will as dowry for one daughter, and a further 20 marks in silver for her younger sister.[1]

In the Rhône valley great lords were also using silver as a substitute for land, as both dowry and dower. In 1222 the Lord of Beaujeu promised 1000 marks as dowry with his daughter when she married a son of the Count of Forez, and in 1205 the Count of Auvergne promised a dower of 2000 marks to his prospective bride, the daughter of the previous Count of Forez. A yet earlier Count of Forez had accepted 1100 marks of silver from the Archbishop of Lyons as compensation when they made peace in 1173. This was at the point in time when enough silver was first commonly available for making such large payments.[2] Ingot silver was easily available in parts of France in 1250, when 1772 marks of 'argenti in plata' was acquired by the treasurer of St Hilary's of Poitiers for sending to Alfonse of Poitiers.[3]

Ingots also found their place in Italian transactions. In Tuscany agreements between communities could involve payments by the mark. In 1202 when the men of Montepulciano submitted themselves to the protection of Florence they agreed to pay 10 marks of silver annually to Florence. However they also agreed that, whenever the Florentines preferred, they would pay in good denari of Pisa instead of ingots. A similar agreement with Citta di Castello involved the latter in paying

---

was not always specified, and it is sometimes not clear if a sum expressed in marks and fiertons was paid in ingots, or in coin by weight. However Professor van Werveke believed that these large advances were generally made in the form of ingots rather than by weighing out enormous quantities of small deniers.

[1] Mireille Castaing-Sicard, *Monnaies féodales et circulation monétaire en Languedoc (X^e–XIIIe siècles)*. Cahiers de l'Association Marc Bloch de Toulouse, Études d'Histoire Méridionale IV (Toulouse, 1961), 60–4.

[2] Etienne Fournial, *Les Villes et l'économie d'échange en Forez aux XIIIe et XIVe siècles* (Paris, 1967), pp. 499–500.

[3] See above, p. 211. It was acquired in 4 consignments; the 2 largest, of 712 marks, and of 460 marks, were acquired with tournois money, presumably in western France itself, where Alfonse's principal resources were to be found. Two smaller consignments were acquired with parisis money, and had presumably been brought in from Paris or northern France. The consignment of 460 marks was described as 'marchis aquilatorum', a term that I find hard to interpret. It could have been Sardinian silver, as used by the Pisans for striking aquilini, but it would have been surprising to find this in western France. Its price, 53s. 9d. tournois the mark, indicates that it was silver as good as sterling.

the Florentines 30 marks of silver. Again, there was an option of payment by ingots or in the denari of Pisa. In 1245 this was brought up to date. Thenceforth the tribute could alternatively be paid in the new grossi of Florence or Lucca or Siena. The original payments, presumably, had actually been made in ingots.[1]

On a much larger scale the peace treaty made in 1288 between Genoa and Pisa, after the catastrophic defeat of the latter at the battle of Meloria, involved the payment to Genoa of 20,000 marks.[2] For sums of this size, payments in denari or even grossi were useless.

As well as finding a local use in the west and the south, ingots were also used in northern and eastern Europe. In 1224 Waldemar II of Denmark agreed to give 45,000 marks, as ransom for himself and his sons, to Count Henry of Schwerin,[3] and at least 25,000 marks of silver were actually paid.[4] In the Baltic area, as elsewhere, ingots were used not only for royal and princely ransoms, but also for dowries and land purchase.[5] In Poland written sources of the thirteenth century frequently refer to the use of uncoined silver, usually described as *argentium purum*. Indeed the obligation to use the coins minted by the dukes who then ruled the various disunited parts of Poland was limited to transactions not exceeding the eighth part of a mark.[6] In Hungary also, silver circulated internally in ingot form from the twelfth century onwards.[7]

Initially there was no attempt to regulate ingots as a means of payment. Gradually, however, the combination of the fiscal interests of rulers and the commercial interests of merchants ensured that regulation crept in. As early as 1224 the Bishop of Worms, eager to see that his mints were as profitably busy as possible, brought a petition to the imperial diet against the free movement of silver in ingot form through Worms. The diet ruled that anyone who wished to spend silver that he had brought into the city in ingot form had first to take it to the bishop's mint to have it transformed into pfennigs. Moreover, he was not to be allowed, on pain of forfeiture, to take it out of the city again unminted, to the Champagne Fairs, or indeed anywhere else, except on pilgrimage.[8] In 1231 Henry, King of the Romans, generalised the ruling in the Worms case and declared that

---

[1] Mario Bernocchi, *Le monete della repubblica fiorentina*, vol. III: 'Documentazione' (Florence, 1976), pp. 131 and 135.

[2] Pesce and Felloni, *Le monete genovesi*, p. 341.

[3] Jesse, *Quellenbuch*, doc. 118, and notes p. 289.

[4] Sprandel, *Das mittelalterliche Zahlungssystem*, p. 81.

[5] Sprandel, *ibid.*, provides thirteenth- and fourteenth-century examples of the use of ingots for ransoms, pp. 81–2, for dowries and dowers, pp. 71–2, and for the purchase of lands and rights, pp. 68–70.

[6] Ryszard Kiersnowski, 'Srebro czyste i najczystsze w Polsce średniowiecznej', *Archeologia Polski*, XVI (1971), 667–76, with English summary, pp. 676–7.

[7] Balint Homan, 'La circolazione delle monete d'oro in Ungheria dal X al XIV secolo e la crisi europea dell'oro nel secolo XIV', *Rivista Italiana di Numismatica*, 2nd series, V (1922), 113–14 and 119.

[8] 'Sententia de Argento Vendende', *Monumenta Germaniae Historica*, Legum IV, Constitutiones et acta publica, II (Hanover, 1896), no. 283.

anywhere in Germany where a mint was established 'Nemo mercatum aliquod facere debeat cum argento, sed cum denariis proprie suae monetae.'[1] Later in the year Henry's father, the Emperor Frederick II, backed up this decision in much the same terms: 'Nec mercimonia nec victualia alique argenti pondere emantur seu vendantur, praeter quam illis denariis qui cuilibet civitati vel oppido sunt communis.'[2] This insistence on the use of local pfennigs for trading should have ruled out the use of ingots in Germany, for all local payments except land purchase, noble dowries and other transactions on that scale, and should have ensured that when they came to rest ingots were converted into local pfennigs. As with so many regulations, this proved ineffectual. In 1258 the Archbishop of Cologne tried to give teeth to regulations against using ingots. He not only ordered that any merchants coming into the district of Cologne ought to exchange their silver at the Cologne mint, but added that, if they did not do so, they were liable to arrest by the archbishop's men and not to be released until their silver had been exchanged for pfennigs at the mint.[3] Despite such restrictions ingots were still needed for inter-regional trade, and continued to reach the Low Countries and Champagne from the empire.

At some stage in the thirteenth century the town authorities of Dortmund recognised that they could not interfere overmuch. They allowed their citizens to acquire unminted silver 'quantumcumque necesse habet ad mercandisas suas vel ad peregrinationes'.[4] At the end of the century the rulers of Flanders and Brabant also recognised that it was necessary to have silver in ingots for export, particularly to England, but tried to ensure that they took a share of it by imposing a mint monopoly on dealing in ingots. In 1299 they specified that all uncoined silver coming in had to be brought to the mints, and that ingots for export could only be obtained from the mints.[5] A similar regulation had already been made in Venice in 1273.[6]

It is only at this date that attempts began to be made to ensure that silver was minted as soon as it was mined. In the English case, where the mines were small and in the hands of the crown, or leased to a single entrepreneur, this seems to have been enforceable,[7] but at Kutná Hora, despite the presence of the mint on the spot,

---

[1] 'Sententia de Cambio', *ibid.* nos. 301 and 302.

[2] 'Edictum Contra Communi Civium', *ibid.* no. 156.

[3] Hävernick, *Der Kölner Pfennig*, p. 24. At some date a similar sanction was introduced in Naples, for Pegolotti, *La pratica della mercatura*, p. 182, records that by the time he was compiling his notebook, silver in plates and bars brought to the city had to be taken to the mint on pain of confiscation.

[4] Hävernick, *Der Kölner Pfennig*, p. 24.

[5] Victor Gaillard, *Recherches sur les monnaies des Comtes de Flandre . . . jusqu'à l'avènement de la maison de Bourgogne*, 2nd ed. (Ghent, 1857), doc. XIII. See also above, p. 140.

[6] Roberto Cessi (ed.), *Problemi monetari veneziani*, Documenti Finanziari della Repubblica di Venezia, 4th series, I (Padua, 1937), doc. 19, p. 13. This regulation was confirmed with modifications again and again, for example in 1278 (doc. 26), 1290 (doc. 54) and 1295 (doc. 62).

[7] See above, p. 130.

compulsory minting seems to have been totally ineffective, and large quantities of silver were still leaving the area in the form of ingots in the 1320s and 1330s.[1] It was in the 1330s that compulsory minting was introduced at Iglesias and seems to have been relatively effective, but in the context of rapidly declining production.[2]

Even if silver was transformed from ingots into coins, either at source or at some later point on its journey through Europe, it did not necessarily remain in the form of coin. It could equally be transformed from coin back into ingots. The Flemish regulations in 1299 imply that coin might be turned into ingots for re-export. In England internal transactions seem, exceptionally, to have been exclusively carried out in coin,[3] but external transactions could be carried out with ingots, as in other places.[4] By the 1327 charter of the Goldsmiths' Company the old prohibition was reiterated against merchants bringing 'coined money into this land, but only fine silver in plate'. In addition regulations were made that 'silver in plate' could only be acquired for export in London at the royal exchange or from goldsmiths selling it openly in the 'Goldsmythery' in Cheapside. 'Silver in plate', presumably ingots in the form of flat plates, was carefully distinguished from vessels of silver. The charter explicitly refers to melting down the latter to make 'silver in plate' for export. By implication coin was also melted down to make such ingots.[5]

Ingots were also made from coin in fourteenth-century Italy. Professor Bautier believed that many of the ingots cast in Genoa had been made from French coin,[6] and Giovanni Villani described how Florence was lacking good silver coin by 1345 because it had been melted down into ingots for export overseas.[7]

Ingots, then, far from being made only by refiners working directly from new ore, were made all over Europe. Initially the ingots do not seem to have been marked in any way but, at some point, probably in the mid thirteenth century, they began to be marked. It was a simple matter to check on the weight of an ingot, but to be certain of its fineness was far from simple. It was, therefore, of direct use to merchants that ingots should carry some mark to indicate and guarantee their fineness. The earliest reference that I yet know to such a mark is the acknowledgment, before a Genoese notary in December 1253, of a loan to be repaid before the following Easter in 'argento buono e *bollato* della lega di Montpellier'.[8] In Genoa

---

[1] See above, p. 125.   [3] See above, pp. 121–2 and 130.

[3] See above, p. 204, n. 4, for Adam de Stratton, who had over 3 million pence in his house in 1290 and no ingots.

[4] R.-H. Bautier, 'L'Or et l'argent en Occident de la fin du XIIIᵉ siècle au début du XIVᵉ siècle', *Académie des Inscriptions et Belles Lettres, Comptes Rendus des Séances* (1951), 171, citing the Patent Rolls between 1298 and 1300 for examples of the export of silver from England in ingot form by Lombards and Brabançons.

[5] T. F. Reddaway, *The Early History of the Goldsmiths' Company 1327–1509*, ed. Lorna E. M. Walker (London, 1975), pp. 222–4. Pegolotti, *La pratica della mercatura*, p. 255, also refers to the purchase and sale of silver in London both in plates, in *piatte*, and in bars. He was in charge of the London branch of the Bardi company from 1318 to 1321.

[6] Bautier, 'L'Or et l'argent en Occident', p. 171.   [7] Giovanni Villani, *Cronica*, Book XII, chapter liii.

[8] Pesce and Felloni, *Le monete genovesi*, p. 341. From the value put on this silver, the 'alloy of Montpellier' was 11 oz. 14d. fine, the same as that of Venetian grossi and the older Genoese grossi.

itself, it was the mint that sealed bars of standard fineness. It did so with coin dies.[1] In Venice it was also done at the mint, and, at least from 1273 to 1362, the dies used for striking grossi were used for this purpose.[2] Silver, in plate form, was also marked in Lucca, but whether or not this was also done with coin dies is not apparent.

Coin dies were also used in England. A large part of what appears to have been an English mark bar has in fact survived. It is an ingot stamped with both the obverse and reverse dies of a London long-cross penny around 1278/9.[3] It is not clear whether coin dies continued to be used, or if the 'pounceon ove la teste de leoparde' referred to in the 1327 charter of the London goldsmiths came to be used to guarantee 'silver in plate' as well as vessels of silver.[4]

In the agreement that the Count of Flanders made in 1299 with the cities of Ghent, Ypres and Douai for the regulation of the currency a reference appears to 'le cambre fondoire, ou se font l'argent de la ville'.[5] Other sources of this period indicate that the *chambres fondoires* or *barnecameren* of Bruges, and at least four other Flemish cities, not only refined and assayed silver, but also issued silver bars bearing an assay stamp as a guarantee of fineness. In 1305 Bruges paid 10s. to Janne 'den Zeghelmakere' for a die for this purpose. It had the arms of the city on it.[6]

In the Empire both documentary and hoard evidence attest the stamping of bars with civic emblems of guarantee. Thus, 162 marks of silver, described as 'puri et *examinati*', were involved in a transaction at Osnabrück in 1277, and the record of the transaction gives some insight into what *examinati* might mean: 'Quam fecimus examinare de voluntate nostra per Nicholaum Eufelarium civem osnaburgensem ad monetarium osnaburgensis cuius pecie signum est quinque pungtorum sextum in medio quasi rosa.'[7] The mint was here also involved in the verification and stamping of bars, as it was in Aachen in 1334. The city accounts for that year record a payment for the 'malleo monete cum quo Jo. de Royde argentum signare debebat'.[8] Some of the fourteenth-century ingots that have been found in North Germany bear civic emblems, from places such as Brunswick, stamped into them to guarantee their fineness.[9]

---

[1] Pengolotti, *La pratica della mercatura*, p. 291; see also above p. 144.

[2] Cessi (ed.), *Problemi monetari veneziani*, docs. 19, 20, 54, 125 and 140.

[3] It is now in the royal mint collection. Its origin is unknown. In the nineteenth century it was classified as a trial plate, although it is quite different in shape from any known trial plate, and did not come from among the trial plates at Westminster Abbey used for the trial of the pyx. Dr Christopher Challis, who has recently recognised its true nature, will shortly be republishing it, with its new identification, in the forthcoming catalogue of the royal mint collection. I am much indebted to him for drawing my attention to it.

[4] Reddaway, *The Goldsmiths' Company*, pp. 222–4.   [5] Gaillard, *Les Monnaies des Comtes de Flandre*, doc. XI.

[6] Georges Bigwood, *Le Régime juridique et économique du commerce de l'argent dans la Belgique du moyen âge*, I, Mémoires de l'Académie Royale de Belgique, Classe des Lettres et des Sciences Morales et Politiques, Collection in 8°, 2nd series, XIV, i (Brussels, 1921), 422–5.

[7] Hävernick, *Der Kölner Pfennig*, p. 31.

[8] Menadier, *Urkunden und Akten*, doc. 86.   [9] See below, pp. 220–1.

The finenesses guaranteed by these marks were not, however, universally the same. Pegolotti noted, for example, that silver from the mines at Longobucco in Calabria was 10 oz. 22d. fine (0.910), whilst Roman silver was 11 oz. 12d. fine (0.958) and some of the ingots marked in Venice were 11 oz. 14d. fine (0.965), like the Venetian grossi. It was presumably this fineness that was marked with the grossi dies. The silver 'in piastre di Lucca' was yet finer still at 11 oz. 20d. fine (0.986) whilst ingots straight from Sardinia were the finest silver of any that he noted, at 11 oz. 21½d. fine (0.991).[1] He also noted down that an expert, 'uno conoscitore d'ariento', could estimate the fineness of silver bars both blanched and unblanched, by eye.[2]

Despite this apparent diversity there were some international standards for silver. The most used of these was the sterling standard. The four contracts made in Genoa in March 1291 involving payments at Caffa in marked ingots described them as 'verghe marcate dalla zecca di Genova alla lega sterlinorum'.[3] English sterlings (pennies) were 11 oz. 2d. fine (0.925). It was this fineness that Pegolotti ascribed both to 'verghe della bolla di Genova' and to 'verghe della bolla di Vinegia'.[4] It is not at all clear when and how the fineness of English pennies had come to be adopted as the standard of fineness for silver in the two principal European seaports of the Mediterranean. The use of a sterling standard in Genoa can only be traced back a few years earlier. A contract notarised in 1287 involved 'argento bianco in verghe marcate alla lega degli sterlini', and the 20,000 marks indemnity to be paid to Genoa by Pisa in the following year were also to be 'argento di sterlini'.[5] In Venice the mint was already casting bars of sterling standard by 1274, for in that year the fee to be paid at the mint for having them cast was reduced.[6]

These references are quite clearly to a standard for unminted silver in bar form, but what are we to make of it when in 1265 Andrea de Tolomei quoted from one of the Troyes Fairs: 'Isterlino, al chanbio, cinquanta e nuove s. la marca'? Was this also an example of the sterling standard for ingots, or was it evidence for the availability of English money in Champagne?[7] What are we to make of the purchase for Alfonse of Poitiers in 1250 first of 'iiij c. marchis stellingorum' with money of Poitou, then of 'iiijcl marchis stellingorum' with parisis money, and finally of 'mille marchis stellingorum' with tournois money? Were these really 300,000 English

---

[1] Pegolotti, *La pratica della mercatura*, p. 291.

[2] *Ibid.* pp. 359–60.

[3] See above, p. 211.

[4] Pegolotti, *La pratica della mercatura*, p. 291. However, *argenti bullati* was also used for silver of grosso fineness; see above, and below, p. 222 n. 6.

[5] Pesce and Felloni, *Le monete genovesi*, p. 341.

[6] Cessi (ed.), *Problemi monetari veneziani*, doc. 22, pp. 14–15. New mint regulations of 1278 also include a clause, 74, on the alloying and stamping, 'ligare et bullare', of bars 'ad ligam de sterlino' (doc. 25, pp. 15–34).

[7] See above, p. 113 n. 3.

pennies or were they yet more ingots of a sterling standard?[1] The time when sterlings had circulated widely in Europe had been at the end of the twelfth century and the beginning of the thirteenth.[2] It was presumably at this period that 'sterling' became attached to a fineness of silver in ingot form, although we have no direct evidence of the use of the word in this way until 1274. In the first half of the fourteenth century the distinction between sterling as coin and sterling standard ingots was clear. John XXII's treasurers listed separately '319 march. 4 unc. sterling. arg. ponderis curie' received in ingots, and a smaller amount in English pennies '83 libr. 14 sol 11 den cum dim. sterling.'[3]

As well as the sterling standard of Mediterranean Europe there were other widely used standards. In the Black Sea area the standard used was that of the *sommi*. Pegolotti describes how in Constantinople most bars of silver were of this standard, 11 oz. 17 dwt. fine (0.98). It was really an Asiatic standard, and western ingots of silver, such as those of the Mediterranean sterling standard, had to be melted down and recast, for example at Pera or Galata, the Italian merchant suburbs of Constantinople, into fresh bars of this higher fineness and of a suitable weight for Asiatic trade. These *sommi* were carried from Constantinople to all parts of the Black Sea region, but particularly to the Crimea and to Tana on the Sea of Azov, and thence across Asia to China, at whose frontiers silver *sommi* were eventually exchanged for paper money.[4] *Sommi* were also cast at the mints in Venice and Genoa for the Black Sea trade.[5]

A third widely used standard prevailed in northern Europe. This was so-called *lötiges silber* or *wêrsilber*. It was this silver that was stipulated for the ransom of Waldemar II of Denmark in the 1220s. It was then described as 'pura praeter lotonem', in other words one lot, or a sixteenth part, short of pure (0.94 fine).[6] In origin it may have been the silver of Lübeck, and its use extended to the whole of the Hanseatic trading-area.[7] This widespread northern standard was contrasted with *argentum usuale* or *argentum commune*. When it was referred to, *argentum usuale* was generally qualified by the name of a place, as 'marcae argenti usualis Brunsvicensis ponderis et valoris'. In other words it was the common silver only of a particular locality, and seems to have been the same standard as was currently being used there for minting pfennigs.[8] Such local *argentum usuale* could sometimes have a

---

[1] See above, p. 211.
[2] See above, pp. 141 and 160–1.
[3] Jesse, *Quellenbuch*, doc. 375.
[4] Pegolotti, *La pratica della mercatura*, pp. 21, 23, 25, 40–1, 53, 150, 223.
[5] Cessi (ed.), *Problemi monetari veneziani*, doc. 140 (1362); and Michel Balard, *La Romanie Genoise*, II (Rome, 1978) 663.
[6] See above, p. 214.
[7] Wilhelm Jesse, *Der wendische Münzverein* (Lübeck, 1928), pp. 159–60. Dr Jesse referred to it as 'lötiges lübeckisches Silber'.
[8] Von Schrötter, *Wörterbuch der Münzkunde*, pp. 60–2.

slightly wider circulation when leagues of cities agreed to accept one another's ingots. As with agreements to mint common coin, such arrangements arose out of leagues for general political and economic co-operation. For example, seven members of the Saxon town league, and five other associated towns, agreed in 1382 that they should make ingots of a common fineness and that, in addition to their own town symbols, they should stamp them with a crown so that they could be recognised and accepted in the other towns of the league. In this case their *argentum usuale* was to be 12¾ lot fine (0.80), well below *lötiges silber*.[1]

In thirteenth-century Poland the same distinctions were made. On the one hand there was *argentum purum, purissimum, purificatum, fusum, examinatum, probatum, bonum, optimum,* or *mundum,* which appears not to have actually been pure silver, but rather something very like, if not actually the same as *lötiges silber.* On the other hand there was *argentum commune, usuale, currens, nigrum,* or even, significantly, *denariatum,* which, like its German counterpart, was of the same standard as the denars.[2]

In the same way that much of the sterling silver of the Mediterranean ended up being recast into *sommi* for Asiatic trade, so much of the *lötiges* silver of the Baltic ended up being recast into fresh ingots in Novgorod for use in Russia. Novgorod silver thus provided the fourth major standard for ingots in the commerce in which West Europeans participated.

A limited number of ingots have been found in various parts of Europe. Many of them conform to one of the major weight standards and confirm the deduction from the Bishop of Passau's narrative that ingots generally, although not always, weighed a mark or a multiple of a mark in western Europe. The mark itself, as a weight, varied enormously from place to place.[3] Presumably the comment made by Pegolotti about the *sommi* in use around the Black Sea could be applied to all these ingots: 'i detti sommi sono verghe d'argento che non sono iguali di peso, ma quale pesa più e quale meno come vengone gittate'.[4] The 92 *sommi* concealed in the 1330s at Uzanbaïr, near Tulua on the Danube delta, show just this lack of uniformity. Their weights ranged from 172 to 219 grams. However 70 of them weighed between 197 and 205 grams, as if a weight of around 200 grams were being aimed at.[5] There were local standards for the *sommo,* as there were for the mark, and

---

[1] Jesse, *Quellenbuch,* doc. 306.

[2] Kiersnowski, 'Srebro czyste . . .'

[3] Weight standards for eighty-eight different places are listed in A. Luschin von Ebengreuth, *Allgemeine Münzkunde und Geldgeschichte,* 2nd ed. (Berlin and Munich, 1926), pp. 166–70.

[4] 'The said sommi are bars of silver which are not equal in weight, but some weigh more and some less depending on the casting' (Pegolotti, *La pratica della mercatura,* pp. 40–1).

[5] They were concealed with 159 gold hyperpyra, 23,440 silver aspers, eleven chunks of rough silver and a little jewellery. These *sommi* were of sterling fineness, not of the higher standard described by Pegolotti (Octavian Iliescu and Gavrilă Simion, 'Le Grand Trésor de monnaies et lingots des XIIIe et XIVe siècles trouvé en Dobroudja septentrionale', *Revue des Études Sud-Est Européennes,* II (1964), 217–28).

these were what was aimed at. Sometimes the makers of *sommi* ingots were much more successful at achieving their aim, as may be judged by the weighing in 1373 at Licostomo, also at the mouth of the Danube, of 32 *sommi* bars. They were found to weigh 31 *sommi*, 37 *saggi* and 19 carats,[1] so that the overall weight of the bars was accurate within ½% of the local standard weight for *sommi*.

The numerous ingots in Russia generally conform very accurately to two different weight standards. The so-called 'Kievan' *grivnas*, hexagonal ingots of the pre-Mongol period, have a constant weight of 160 grams, whilst the Novgorod *grivnas*, formed as bars, weigh 200 grams, a weight standard very close to some West European marks and to the *sommi*. These *grivnas* were always cast in open moulds. Since none of those that survive show any sign of extra silver being added or removed to make the weight correct, it follows that the exact amount must have been poured into the moulds in the first place. Ladles for pouring liquid metal of the same capacity as a Novgorod *grivna* bar have been unearthed in excavations in Novgorod.[2] Presumably similar ladles were used for ensuring that *sommi* bars in the Black Sea region and mark bars and plates in western Europe could be cast very close to the size required.

Just as Novgorod *grivnas* and 'Kievan' *grivnas* had distinctive shapes, the ingots of other regions were also presumably distinguishable by their shapes, as well as by the symbols stamped on them.[3] Unfortunately we do not have enough surviving ingots to be able to generalise. Only one ingot survives from England, and none at all from Italy, France, the Low Countries, the Rhineland or, after the eleventh century, from Poland. Although written evidence clearly indicates that they once existed in large numbers, it very rarely indicates the form that they took. Pegolotti wrote of the bars of Sardinia that they were 'piu sottili che quelli dell'ore che si fanne in Firenze'.[4] He also distinguished bar-shaped ingots from Genoa or Venice from plates from Lucca, and refers to plates as well as bars from London. Some of the surviving ingots from northern Germany are very irregular, whilst others are hemispherical. All of the surviving German ingots that have been analysed have proved to be of various poor qualities of *argentum usuale*. No ingots of good, *lötiges*, silver have yet been identified. However, by an extraordinary chance we do have an example of the ingots specified by the Saxon town agreement of 1382, one from Halberstadt, marked with a crown, as stipulated, as well as the civic mark for Halberstadt.[5] The places from which ingots have survived are mostly those where

[1] 'Virge sommorum argenti triginta duas, que erant sommi XXXI, sagii XXXVII et charati XVIII'. There were 45 *saggi* to 1 *sommo* (Iliescu, 'Actes notariés dans les colonies génoises', p. 126).

[2] I. G. Spasskij, *The Russian Monetary System*, 3rd ed. (Leningrad, 1962; English trans., Amsterdam, 1967), pp. 64–9.

[3] The *sommi* found at Uzanbaïr were in the form of thin flattened bars, half an inch wide and deep, and 5½–6 inches long (1½ centimetres by 14–15¼ centimetres).

[4] Pegolotti, *La pratica della mercatura*, p. 133.

[5] A. Loehr, 'Probleme der Silberbarren', *Numismatische Zeitschrift*, LXIV (1931), 101–9.

ingots remained in use longest. Elsewhere bars, plates and hexagonal or hemi-spherical ingots have disappeared. At some point in their journey through Europe or Asia most were turned into coin, or goldsmith's work, and were never recast into ingots, but minted and re-minted, or fashioned and re-fashioned into different objects of silver over and over again. Nevertheless some hoarded ingots have presumably been found in modern times, but not recognised as having any historical interest, and therefore melted down without any records being made of them. This very lack of recorded examples has meant that the use of ingots in commerce has been severely underestimated. It has even caused some writers, such as Hävernick, to be extremely sceptical about their use on a large scale, in their own areas of expertise.

The use of ingots was already as normal for the payment of large sums as the use of deniers was for small ones when the succession of new mines from the 1160s enormously increased the circulating medium of Europe. The amount of silver in ingot form increased in parallel with that in the form of deniers. How long ingots remained in circulation for larger payments varied from place to place. In Languedoc ingots were used less frequently for local transactions as the thirteenth century progressed, and their later use there is only clear for the very largest sums.[1] In Forez and in Artois large sums were normally expressed in livres rather than marks from the 1220s and 1230s onwards, and this suggests a shift towards the use of coin rather than ingots for local transactions there also.[2] In Germany legislation from 1231 attempted to limit the use of ingots for local transactions, but with singular lack of success.[3] For inter-regional transactions ingots remained one of the normal means of payment, until the fourteenth century. Pegolotti still took their use for granted, but their use rapidly declined in his own lifetime as the new gold from Hungary became available in such large quantities in the 1330s and 1340s as to drive ingots out of circulation in many parts of Europe.[4] The use of ingots came to an end in Hungary itself, and in Italy and France, at more or less the same time. John XXII still received payments in mark bars, but the future was already indicated by the single Hungarian ducat that came into the *camera apostolica* at the end of his reign.[5] The use of ingots ceased so suddenly and so completely in Italy that it seems almost anachronistic to find repeated as late as 1356 the injunction to the celebrant at St Peter's that he should hand over to the *camera* any ingots offered at the main altar of the church.[6] In the Low Countries nothing more is heard of *chambres fondoires*

---

[1] Castaing-Sicard, *Monnaies féodales en Languedoc.*
[2] Fournial, *Les Villes en Forez*, and Richebé, *Monnaies d'Artois.*   [3] See above, pp. 214–15.
[4] See below, pp. 267–88.   [5] Jesse, *Quellenbuch*, doc. 375.
[6] Lunt, *Papal Revenues*, doc. 574. The last reference to payment with ingots in Venice was in a regulation of 1362 evaluating them in gold: 'quelibet marcha argenti bullata de bulla S. Marci computari debeat in omnibus contractibus et solucionibus mercacionum . . . s. xi. gross. vi in auro' (Cessi (ed.), *Documenti monetari veneziani*, doc. 140).

soon after the sudden arrival of gold coin in large quantities at the end of the 1330s.[1] In northern Germany and the Baltic area, where gold did not penetrate in the mid fourteenth century, the use of mark ingots continued for much longer.[2] In Saxony it was still worth making arrangements for the stamping of bars in the 1380s, when their use had ceased in southern Europe.[3] In Lithuania and in northern Russia *grivna* bars continued to be used in the fifteenth century. In the Black Sea area the use of *sommi* increased rather than diminished in the fourteenth century, as the circulation of Byzantine gold came to an end at more or less the same time as its use increased so enormously in the west.

Whilst the mark was in use as a unit of weight and applied to ingots, it could also be applied to coin. In the later Middle Ages mint ordinances in many parts of Europe specified the weight of coins to be struck by stipulating the number to be struck from a mark weight of the appropriate metal. Like the pound, the mark was also gradually transformed into a unit of account. Unlike the pound, whose transformation into a unit of account came at a time when western money was relatively homogeneous, the mark became a unit of account at a time when the deniers of Europe were marked by extreme diversity. The mark as a unit of account therefore came to mean different things in different places. In England and Scotland the mark or merk came to mean 13s. 4d. (160 pence), in Cologne it came to mean 12s. (144 pfennigs), and by extension it was used to mean 144 pfennigs in neighbouring cities, such as Aachen or Duisburg. In Lübeck, and thence in many other Hanseatic cities, it came to mean 16s. (192 pfennigs). However in Bremen it meant 32s. (384 pfennigs). In Denmark, Norway, Sweden and Gotland the mark was divided into 8 öre and 24 örtug, but the number of pence to the örtug varied. In Denmark and Norway there were 10, but in Sweden 8 and in Gotland 12. In Prussia the mark was divided into 24 skot, each of 30 pfennigs, making 720 pfennigs in all.[4] Each of these meanings for the mark as a unit of account derived from a period when this many actual pence or pfennigs had been struck from a mark weight of silver. Such a period had to be long enough for the relationship to become customary. It was then fossilised for accounting purposes long after the real number of pence or pfennigs to the mark weight had eventually changed. Although the mark, particularly the mark of the Champagne Fairs, that of Troyes, continued to be used to weigh silver in France and the Low Countries, the number of deniers to the mark was never constant for long enough for the mark to become a permanent accounting unit there. The occasional document might reckon in marks, as in one at St Omer in 1250, which referred to 'marcs de 35 s. parisis',[5] but

---

[1] Bigwood, *Le Régime du commerce de l'argent dans la Belgique*, p. 425.
[2] See below, pp. 282–3. [3] See above, p. 220.
[4] Rolf Sprandel, *Das mittelalterliche Zahlungssystem*, Appendix II, pp. 194–202.
[5] Richebé, *Monnaies d'Artois*, pp. 117–21.

this was a mode of accounting that was too soon overtaken by a change in the denier parisis to become established.

The same happened later in Russia, with the Novgorod *grivnas* or *roubles*. After they ceased to exist as ingots they came to be used for accounting purposes as fixed numbers of coins.

In England reckoning in marks finally died out in the eighteenth century, but in many German principalities the long-term debasement of the pfennig, of which the mark was a multiple, meant that it eventually became practical to strike mark coins, and in Russia rouble coins, long after the circulation of mark- or rouble-weight ingots had been forgotten.

10

New Money

At about the same time that the expansion in the quantities of coin minted affected the nature of minting and brought about the transformation from the numerous, older, workshop mints to the few, large, newer, factory mints, there was a similar qualitative change in the nature of the money minted. The natural first stage in the expansion was to produce more of the same sorts of coins, the traditional pennies of varying types. The second stage was to produce different and larger coins. This change took place at varying dates between the early thirteenth and the mid fourteenth century depending on the economic needs of the different parts of Europe. The natural place for this stage to begin was northern Italy, not only because it was by far the most commercially advanced area of Europe, and because it was the area to which so much of the newly-available silver tended to gravitate, but also because the traditional pennies here had become much slighter in silver content than in many other parts of Europe. Whereas the prototypical denier of Charlemagne's reforms had weighed 1.7 grams, the denari of Pavia and Venice in the 1170s contained only 0.2 gram and 0.1 gram respectively.[1] By way of contrast the English penny still contained over 1.3 grams of silver. A fairly obvious solution to the problem of the diminished silver content of the coinage was simply to attempt to replace the old denari by better, new denari. One attempt of this kind was made between 1155 and 1161 by the Emperor Frederick I, who caused new and better denari imperiali to be struck in Lombardy. These were to contain no less than 0.5 gram of silver, and were thus worth twice as much as the pre-existing denari of Pavia and Milan. Although the new, imperial denari fairly rapidly replaced the older denari, this was not the radical solution that was required. It merely brought the Lombard denari up to the same approximate level as the Tuscan ones.[2]

The occasion for the initiation of the radical change that was required was the

---

[1] Philip Grierson, 'The origins of the Grosso and of gold coinage in Italy', *Numismatický sborník*, XII (1971–2), 35. The denari of Verona were still worse, with a silver content of 0.08 gram around 1185.

[2] A similar solution was adopted in Pisa later in the century when denari novi were introduced, at some point before 1192, to compensate for progressive debasement of the Tuscan denari over the previous thirty years (David Herlihy, 'Pisan coinage and the monetary development of Tuscany, 1150–1250', *American Numismatic Society Museum Notes*, VI (1954), 143–68).

Fourth Crusade. In 1201 the crusaders, mostly from north of the Alps, bargained to pay the Venetians 85,000 marks of silver for their transport by sea the following year.[1] It was spent in advance on the pay of shipwrights and other *arsenalotti* for constructing additional ships,[2] and after that for provisioning the fleet and for the wages of mariners.

Bars of silver were the natural method of making payments of large sums to a single recipient or a small number of recipients, but what was required here was the payment of a large number of small sums to a large number of recipients in easily divisible amounts. Had the whole 85,000 marks of silver been minted into the then current Venetian denari, it would have made about 230 million of them. To make so many coins would have been immensely time-consuming and inconvenient, but probably just within the bounds of the possible. Instead the doge, Enrico Dandalo, ordered the striking, probably in the spring or early summer of 1201,[3] of great coins, or 'grossi', each of which was to be worth no less than twenty-four of the older denari. This was no mere replacement of old denari by new ones, since the older denari, which by contrast were called 'piccoli', 'little ones', went on being struck alongside the new grossi. What had happened was that a complete new tier had been added to the monetary system. The new pieces not only weighed about 2.18 grams each, which was heavier than any silver coin struck in western Europe since antiquity, but were also struck of almost pure silver, 965/1000 fine, unlike the

---

[1] The negotiators only paid 2000 marks in 1201, itself borrowed in Venice, and, since the crusaders were many fewer than anticipated, they only managed to bring 49,000 marks more the following year. However, the Venetian state had spent the whole sum stipulated in preparing a larger fleet than was actually required and made the repayment of the remaining 34,000 marks a first charge on the wealth of Constantinople when it was captured (John Godfrey, *1204 The Unholy Crusade* (Oxford, 1980), pp. 49, 41, 73 and 112).

[2] 'Mesire Henric Dandle, li noble dus de Venise, mande venir li charpentiers, et fist erraument apariller et faire chalandres et nes et galies a planté; et fist erraument faire mehailles d'argent por doners as maistres la sodee et ce que il deservoient: que les petites que il avoient ne lor venoient enci a eise: et dou tens de monseignor Henric Dandle en sa fu comencié en Venise a faire les nobles mehailles d'argent qu l'en apele ducat, qui cort parmi le monde por sa bonté' (Martin da Canal, *Les Estoires de Venise*, Part I, chapter xxxvii, written some sixty-five years later, most recently ed. A. Limentani (Florence, 1972), p. 46). L. B. Robbert, 'Reorganisation of the Venetian coinage by Doge Enrico Dandolo', *Speculum*, XLIX (1974), 48–60, has disputed this report and suggested that the new grossi were far too large for use as wages. Instead she has suggested that the new obol, or half-denaro, $\frac{1}{52}$ grosso, minted at approximately the same time, was the coin struck for paying wages. Unfortunately no information about Venetian wage-rates survives from this period, so that she cannot prove her case. The earliest surviving Venetian wage-rates come from much later. At the beginning of the fourteenth century ordinary seamen were being paid 2½ to 3 grossi a day, and even widows on pensions were receiving more than 1 grosso a day (Frederic C. Lane, 'Diet and wages of seamen in the early fourteenth century' (1963), reprinted in his collected essays, *Venice and History: Collected Papers* (Baltimore, 1966), pp. 263–8). In other words, by 1300 the grosso was most certainly a useful coin for paying wages. Between 1202 and 1300 the grosso had not been debased or reduced in weight, so that essentially the same coins were available for use in 1202 and in 1300. This makes it look highly probable that grossi rather than obols were suitable for paying wages in 1202, unless of course Venetian wage-rates, in terms of silver, had rocketed fifty-fold in the course of the thirteenth century! This is beyond credibility in a century remarkable for the pressure exerted in a contrary direction by the enormous rise in population.

[3] This dating is suggested by Donald E. Queller, 'A note on the reorganisation of the Venetian coinage by Doge Enrico Dandolo', *Revista Italiana di Numismatica*, LXXVII (1975), 167–72.

poor-quality piccoli, which contained only one quarter silver and three quarters alloy.

The type of these new grossi was derived from that of the leaden *bulla* or seal of the doge, with Christ enthroned on the obverse and St Mark and the doge standing on the reverse. This had been the traditional type for the doges' *bulla* for the previous seventy years and had itself been derived early in the twelfth century from Byzantine prototypes.[1] The popular name for the new Venetian grossi, 'matapans', appears to have been derived from the Arabic *mantaban*, meaning 'seated king', which had earlier been applied to the old Byzantine hyperpyron of a similar type. These silver grossi were also known as 'ducats', probably from the prominent word 'dux' on the reverse legend, but possibly from their vague general resemblance to the early-twelfth-century silver coins issued by the Norman kings of Sicily in their *duchy* of Apulia, which had also been called 'ducats', and which had also been derived from a Byzantine prototype.[2]

Venice's greatest rival in Mediterranean trade, Genoa, also struck grossi within the first decades of the thirteenth century,[3] and similar pieces were struck at Marseilles, which was closely associated with Genoa, from 1218.[4] In the 1220s and the 1230s the striking of grossi spread rapidly, to Verona, for example, which had only been recently eclipsed as a minting-place by Venice, and was still the key mint city for much of north-eastern Italy, and to Milan, Parma, Bologna, Ferrara and Reggio north of the Apennines.[5] South of the Apennines, Siena, then the second city of Tuscany, coined a grosso by 1231. Pisa, then the largest city and the port of Tuscany, followed suit a few years later, and the fast-growing boom town of Florence, which was to surpass both Siena and Pisa well before the end of the century, also struck silver grossi or fiorini, from 1237 onwards, and so did Lucca, Arezzo and, above all, mine-owning Volterra, at about the same time.[6]

These Tuscan grossi seem to have been of a common weight from the beginning, but further north the grossi were not uniform in weight between one city and another, although they were all of one general size and were distinctly different in scale from the piccoli that were already circulating in northern Italy. They were all, initially at least, of good silver, and their weights ranged from the 1.4 to 1.5 grams

[1] Agostino Pertusi, 'Quedam regalia insignia', *Studi Veneziani*, VII (1965), 3–123.

[2] Philip Grierson, 'La moneta veneziana nell'economia mediterranea del Trecento e Quattrocento', *La civiltà veneziana del Quattrocento* (Fundazione Giorgio Cini, Florence, 1957), p. 80.

[3] The first documentary reference is in 1222. See R. S. Lopez, 'Prima del ritorno all'oro nell'occidente duecentesco: i primi denari grossi d'argento', *Rivista Storica Italiana*, LXXIX (1967), 174–81; but there is a Genoese tradition of dating them much earlier. G. Pesce and G. Felloni, *Le monete genovesi* (Genoa, 1975), for example, do so.

[4] Henri Rolland, *Monnaies des Comtes de Provence, XIIᵉ–XVᵉ siècles*. Histoire monétaire, économique et corporative (Paris, 1956), pp. 113, 201.

[5] Grierson, 'La moneta veneziana'.

[6] Herlihy, 'Pisan coinage'.

of the grossi of Genoa, Bologna and Ferrara, through the rather heavier grossi of Verona and the Tuscan cities to the 2.2 grams of the Milanese and Venetian grossi. Their values in terms of pre-existing piccoli equally varied from city to city, depending, of course, not only on the weight of the new grossi, but also on the weight and fineness of the piccoli. In Genoa the grossi were initially only worth 4 of the older Genoese denari, and in Marseilles, 6 of the older deniers royaux coronats. In Tuscany the grossi were circulating in the 1240s as pieces of 12 denari. In other words the Sienese, the Pisan and the Florentine soldi had become, temporarily at least, real coins rather than merely convenient accounting-multiples.[1] Most of the new grossi were not changed in weight or fineness over long periods of time, unlike the older denari. In Venice, for example, the matapan remained unchanged from 1201 to 1379. Meanwhile the piccoli continued to be debased from time to time, particularly from the second half of the thirteenth century, and as a consequence the grossi increased in value in terms of piccoli. When the matapan was introduced it was probably designed to be worth a neat 2 soldi, or 24 piccoli, and during the first half of the thirteenth century it stood for long at 26 piccoli.[2] However, in the second half of the century it rapidly rose in value in terms of piccoli. In 1265 it was valued at 27 piccoli, in 1269 at 28 piccoli, and in 1282 at 32 piccoli.[3]

Thus between 1201 and 1237 every important Italian mint north of Rome began to strike grossi of about 2 grams in weight. But these 2-gram grossi were not destined to be the standard-sized silver coins of the later Middle Ages. Yet larger coins (also called grossi) were to appear, of about double the size. The first such piece appeared in Rome in 1253 during the rule of Brancaleone d'Andolo. It too began as a soldo, a piece of 12 Roman denari or provisini. These grossi or 'romanini' were continued by the Senate after his death, and then by Charles of Anjou (senator 1263–6, 1268–78, 1281–4).[4] After his temporary loss of control over Rome in 1278, Charles struck pieces of a similar size, known as 'carlini', at Naples, by then the capital of his kingdom, and when Constance of Hohenstaufen and her husband, Peter of Aragon, recaptured Sicily from him in 1282 they too struck heavy grossi, known as 'pierreale', for the island. Both carlini and pierreale had very long lives, and they continued to be minted until the close of the Middle Ages. Even in northern Italy itself, the home of the smaller grosso of the early thirteenth century, these larger grossi began to be struck at Milan at about this time, where

---

[1] C. M. Cipolla, *Le avventure della lira* (Milan, 1958), pp. 37–8.

[2] The silver content of the grossi and piccoli was initially in the ratio of 1:26.1. However a value of 2 soldi would take into account the cost of the alloy of the piccoli and the greater cost of labour in making 24 coins instead of 1.

[3] G. Luzzatto, 'L'oro et l'argento nella politica monetaria veneziana dei secoli XIII–XIV', *Rivista Storica Italiana* (1937), reprinted in *Studia di storia economica veneziana* (Padua, 1954), pp. 261–3.

[4] Philip Grierson, 'I grossi "senatoriali" di Roma, parte I, del 1253 al 1282', *Rivista Italiana di Numismatica*, LVIII (1956), 36–69.

they were known as 'ambrosini' from the seated figure of St Ambrose on the obverse.

Among the smaller grossi of the early part of the century, only the Venetians with their enthroned Christ had a seated figure as the obverse type, but it was to be common on these larger grossi which began in the third quarter of the century. Not only was there St Ambrose seated on the ambrosini, but also a personified 'Roma' on the earlier romanini, and Charles of Anjou's successors showed themselves enthroned as kings on the later carlini, or gigliati, of Naples, as did the kings of Cyprus, on the similar grossi that they issued from the Famagusta mint from Henry II (1268–1324) onwards.

The use of larger coins in other parts of Europe spread very gradually, even though Charles of Anjou's elder brother, (St) Louis IX, had begun to strike 4-gram coins for France as early as 1266, as Charles himself had also done in Provence at about the same time. Apart from a few earlier 2-gram pieces from Marseilles, the French 'gros tournois', as they were called, were the first 'great' coins of any sort to be struck outside Italy, but they do not seem to have had a very wide circulation at first. They had an initial value, as at Rome, of 12 of the pre-existing deniers. For 2 decades the gros tournois was thus the sou tournois. However, in 1290 Philip IV brought this equivalence to an end by reducing the weight of the denier tournois, whilst keeping the gros unchanged. He consequently revalued the gros tournois at $13\frac{1}{8}$ deniers tournois. He soon changed the denier tournois again, and he and his successors did so repeatedly, so that, from then onwards, the gros tournois, which continued to be struck in France until 1364, had a very variable value in the French tournois and parisis moneys of account, which continued to be based on the frequently changing, and usually deteriorating, deniers tournois and parisis. Many of the gros tournois travelled south to Italy, as the sterlings and provinois had done before them since the twelfth century.[1]

As against the large numbers of gros tournois that were taken southwards to Italy, very few of them were carried northwards into the 'Benelux' area, because specie continued to flow from this area into France, as in the period of the deniers parisis.[2]

The southern Netherlands remained the second most commercially advanced area of Europe, developing in parallel with North Italy. The state of the currency there in about 1264, on the eve of the first coinage of gros tournois in France, is illuminated by the hoard of over 140,000 silver deniers found at Brussels, then in Brabant. This hoard, weighing over 100 kilograms (2 hundredweights), is the largest single hoard of medieval coins yet discovered, and illustrates the huge

[1] See above, pp. 141–2 and 155.
[2] See above, pp. 197–9.

number of coins that men were prepared to handle in the era before the introduction of the gros. The two major constituents of the hoard were pennies of England, and deniers of Brabant itself. The pennies of England at this date still weighed 1.46 grams, which was as heavy as the lightest of the new Italian grossi. To a certain extent there was, therefore, not the same pressing need for a larger coin that there had been in Italy. However, larger coins were minted in the Netherlands, and as in Italy the progression to the use of larger coin came in two stages.

Within, at most, five years of the first striking of the gros tournois in France a new, indigenous, range of coins of a higher denomination than the existing deniers was created in the Netherlands. These were the baudekins or pillewilles known to visiting Italian merchants as baldacchini. They were equivalent to two of the commonly circulated English pennies, or two thirds of the recently introduced French gros tournois. They weighed about 2¾ grams. The earliest, known as 'baudekins a keval', from the obverse type of a knight on horseback, were first struck between 1267 and 1271 at Valenciennes for Margaret of Constantinople as Countess of Hainault. At about the same time she also had other baudekins struck for her at Alost as Countess of Flanders. Pegolotti distinguished these as 'baldacchini coll'aquila' from the two-headed eagle of their obverse type and those of John I, Duke of Brabant, he called 'baldacchini cogli angioli', since they showed the archangel St Michael. By 1272, Nicholas, Bishop of Cambrai had begun the issue of tiestars, similar pieces with a mitred head on the obverse. The initial striking of baudekins of all sorts lasted for a decade, or maybe rather longer, and then continued intermittently for the next forty-five years. They were widely imitated by minor rulers in the Netherlands, from Artois to Frisia.[1]

The baudekins travelled southwards into France, as did the gros tournois minted in the area in very large numbers for the King of France at St Quentin in Vermandois in 1278–9 and at Tournai in 1285.[2] Indeed, although so many were minted in the area, the gros tournois had a very slight circulation in the southern Netherlands for a long time. In Artois, payments reckoned in gros tournois in the 1280s seem to have been confined to commercial transactions over long distances and the count's dealings either with his Italian bankers in Siena, or with the King of France.[3] It is possible that a large, 4-gram gros was still too big for internal circulation.[4]

---

[1] J. Duplessy, 'Chronologie et circulation des "Baudekins à cheval" ', *Revue belge de Numismatique*, CXVII (1971), 169–234.

[2] See above, p. 206.

[3] Claude Richebé, *Les Monnaies féodales d'Artois du Xe au début du XIVe siècle* (Paris, 1963), pp. 132–5.

[4] This certainly seems to have been the case in England, where in 1279 Edward I attempted to introduce an even larger great coin, the groat. This weighed nearly 6 grams and proved to have no practical value for internal use in England, although a small number were to be found in commercial circles in Paris at the end of the century (Duplessy, ' "Baudekins à cheval" ', pp. 174 and 213–16). None have been found in England itself except in the 'foreign' hoard at Dover (*British Numismatic Journal*, XXVIII (1957), 147–68).

In the 1290s the emphasis in the Low Countries was once more on English pennies or sterlings, known there as 'esterlins'. They came into the area in enormous numbers in the course of the Anglo-French war.[1] They were then imitated in even larger numbers by the Dukes of Brabant, the Counts of Flanders, Hainault, Holland and Luxemburg, and a host of minor rulers.[2] Nicholas Mayhew has reckoned that in this decade some 90 million esterlins were struck in the Netherlands, particularly the southern Netherlands, as opposed to only 9 million sterlings struck in England itself.[3] Much of this coin was playing an international as well as a purely local role. Mayhew has reckoned that by 1301 half the esterlins struck in the Netherlands over the previous decade had ended up in England for wool-purchases.[4] Another large group of them followed the baudekins into France. In Paris they formed the larger part of the foreign coin compulsorily withdrawn from circulation in 1299.[5] Philip IV had even gone as far as producing, in 1295, his own sterling-size coin, one-third of his gros tournois.[6] International payments by coin did not yet supplant payments by ingot; they only supplemented them.

The Anglo-French war of the 1290s, together with the attempts of Philip IV of France to subjugate Flanders in the following decade, eventually brought the gros tournois into internal circulation in the Netherlands. As early as 1298 the Count of Flanders was paying his troops in gros tournois,[7] but hoards discovered in the Netherlands do not contain an appreciable proportion of gros tournois until as late as 1310, and then rarely pieces issued before the reign of Philip IV (1285–1314).[8] Meanwhile imitative groten of the type of the gros tournois had begun to be struck in smallish quantities from the late 1290s by Florence V in Holland (count 1256–96), John II in Brabant (duke 1294–1312), Hugh of Chalon in Liège (bishop 1295–1301), and John II d'Avesnes in Hainault (count 1280–1304). The striking of groten in

---

[1] See also p. 162.

[2] For a detailed description of these European esterlins see J. Chautard, *Les Imitations des monnaies, au type esterlin* (Nancy, 1871), and for a brief list A. Engel and R. Serrure, *Traité de numismatique du moyen âge* (3 vols., Paris, 1891–1905), pp. 1427–31. For an up-to-date summary see N. J. Mayhew, *Sterling Imitations of Edwardian Type* (London, 1983).

[3] N. J. Mayhew, 'The circulation and imitation of sterlings in the Low Countries', in N. J. Mayhew (ed.), *Coinage in the Low Countries*, B.A.R. International Series LIV (Oxford, 1979), p. 61.

[4] *Ibid.*

[5] This was forbidden money seized in Paris by the serjeant of the Chatelet following the monetary ordinance of 31 December 1298. Of the first 722 foreign coins seized in small lots from 43 separate persons, no less than 547 were esterlins. By implication both English and Netherlandish esterlins were involved. The second most frequently seized coin was the baudekin, but only 39 of them were taken in these first 43 lots. Further small sums seized after Candlemas consisted entirely of esterlins. In addition, large sums of esterlins were delivered direct to the mint by Lombards, for example Bonaventura Jacobi brought in 98 marks and an ounce of esterlins (account of seizures partially printed by Duplessy, ' "Baudekins à cheval" ', pp. 212–16).

[6] Jean Lafaurie, *Les Monnaies des rois de France* I (Paris, 1951), nos. 222 and 223.

[7] Richebé, *Monnaies d'Artois*, pp. 132–5.

[8] *Revue Suisse de Numismatique* (1963), 67.

Flanders was provided for by the monetary agreement with Brabant of April 1300, but none have survived earlier than the regency of John of Namur (regent 1302–3). On the other hand, joint groten of Namur and Brabant still exist, without any surviving trace of a formal written agreement for their striking.[1]

At about the same time the baudekin types were revived, as half-groten, and initially proved much more popular than the whole groot. Striking probably began in Hainault in 1297, and in Flanders the next year, whilst by June 1299 half-groten were also being struck in Brabant and Liège that were interchangeable with those of Flanders. Finally the tiestar type of baudekin was revived in Cambrai by Philippe de Marigny (bishop 1306–9). By 1312 imitations of the baudekins of the great princes of the Netherlands were again being struck by petty lords with mint rights from Artois to Frisia. In addition, their circulation southwards along one of the main land-routes across eastern France was soon marked by further imitations. They were minted in the valley of the Meuse, in Lorraine and at Toul, and for a short time after that even down the Saône–Rhône valley as far as Dauphiné and Orange.

A multi-tier system had thus gradually come into existence with two or three denominations being struck at any one time, for the old deniers continued to be struck alongside the new esterlins, baudekins, and gros. The old deniers were gradually debased and soon became suitable only for petty purchases and alms, whilst the larger, good silver was more suitable for wages and rents. In the Flemish–Brabançon agreement of April 1300, provision was made for striking deniers noirs in Flanders, of which 18 were to be worth a gros, and for petits deniers in Brabant, of which 9 were worth a gros. The intermediate denomination, a third of a gros, was thus worth 6d. in Flanders and 3d. in Brabant.[2]

The idea of striking grossi also percolated gradually through the Alps into the Germanic lands beyond. The 2-gram-size grossi of Verona provided the prototypes for pieces struck along the trade-route that ran to it from the Brenner Pass down the Etsch or Adige valley. Using the silver mined in the Tirol, the Bishops of Trent, from the 1230s, and the Counts of Tirol, by 1271, struck grossi or groschen at Bozen and Meran (Bolzano and Merano) valued at 20 Veronese piccoli. They continued to strike them until the middle of the fourteenth century. Issued on a linguistic frontier, they were known by many names, such as 'zwainziger' or 'vigintiarii' from their value, or 'tirolini' from their source, but also in Italy as 'aquilini' from their reverse type of an eagle, and in Germany as 'kreuzer' from their obverse type of the double cross. They were much imitated in what are now

---

[1] In the names of John II of Brabant (duke 1294–1312) and John I of Namur (count 1298–1331). A. De Witte, *Histoire monétaire des comtes de Louvain, ducs de Brabant*, I (Antwerp, 1894), 107–8, suggested a date of *c.* 1302–5 for these pieces.

[2] Victor Gaillard, *Recherches sur les monnaies des Comtes de Flandre . . . jusqu'à l'avènement de la maison de Bourgogne*, 2nd ed. (Ghent, 1857), doc. XIV.

Austria, Switzerland and southern Germany as well as in north-eastern Italy, to which most of them were carried.[1]

In the fourteenth century the smaller groschen, the kreuzers, also began to be supplemented in the southern German lands by larger groschen. The first and most prolific of these were the Prague groschen of Bohemia, struck at Kutná Hora from 1300 onwards. Here the introduction of the new, large factory mint coincided exactly with the introduction of the new, large denomination of coin. The new Prague groschen, or 'grossus pragensis', with a weight of about 3.8 grams,[2] fitted into the general pattern of 4-gram grossi and gros already being struck in Rome, Naples, Milan, and Paris and other French royal mints. It was valued initially at 12 of the pre-existing pfennigs, thenceforwards naturally known as 'parvi'. Pieces of a similar size were soon issued at Freiberg for the Margrave of Meissen, and, from 1329, a generation later, for the King of Hungary, who also had his own silver-mines. Although the Bohemian and Meissen groschen circulated to a certain extent in such neighbouring lands as Silesia, Lausitz and Brandenburg, this part of Europe was not yet ready for such coins, outside the silver-mining districts themselves, and this perhaps partially explains why so large a part of the silver mined in Bohemia was not minted into groschen.[3] Even the Dukes of Austria did not attempt to mint such large groschen at this time, despite the large amounts of silver passing into Italy through Vienna. The mid-fourteenth-century attempt of Casimir the Great to do so at Cracow in Poland failed, and his successors had to be content with the limited issue of kwartniks, which were of the size of the smaller grossi, as the Polish economy still had no real use for the larger pieces. On the other hand even if they were not of much use in eastern Europe, the Prague groschen do seem to have flowed freely southwards through Vienna into Italy, where they were much more usable, and were known to Pegolotti as 'bohemians'.[4]

At the other end of Germany, pieces of the scale of the gros tournois, many of them direct derivatives, began eventually to be minted in the Rhineland in the course of the fourteenth century,[5] but their minting did not spread further into Germany than this. Even the Hanseatic cities of the north never produced them apart from a brief and abortive issue by Lübeck in the 1360s. The scale of their

---

[1] Arthur Suhle, *Deutsche Münz- und Geldgeschichte von den Anfängen bis zum 15. Jahrhundert*, 2nd ed. (Berlin, 1964), pp. 157–8. Aquilini were struck in Italy at over a dozen different mints including Vicenza, Padua and Mantua.

[2] Karel Castelin, 'Grossus Pragensis', *Arbeits- und Forschungsberichte zur sächsischen Bodendenkmalpflege*, XVI–XVII (1967), 667.

[3] See above, pp. 124–5.

[4] See above, pp. 153–4.

[5] The gros tournois themselves were established in the Rhineland about the same time as in the Netherlands, in the first decade of the fourteenth century (W. Hess, 'Das Rheinisches Münzwesen im 14 Jahrhundert', *Der deutsche Territorialstaat im 14 Jahrhundert*, Vorträge und Forschungen XIII (Sigmaringen, 1970), pp. 257–323). The earliest hoard discovered in Westphalia that contains gros tournois dates from 1313 or shortly after (Peter Ilisch, *Münzfunde und Geldumlauf in Westfalen im Mittelalter und Neuzeit* (Münster, 1980).

commercial activity and urban life did not warrant it. Not until the middle of the fourteenth century did they progress far enough even to mint witten, pieces no larger than an English penny. Up to then the currency in the Baltic area, apart from bar silver, had still consisted primarily of extremely light pfennigs of the bracteate type. The hoard deposited at Kirial in Denmark in the 1360s gives a good impression of Baltic currency in the period immediately before the extensive issue of witten after the formation of the Wendish monetary union of Hanseatic cities in 1379. It contained over 73,000 German bracteate pfennigs, principally from Hamburg, Lübeck, Mecklenburg and Lüneburg, together with about 4500 further such pfennigs cut in two for smaller change. The only larger pieces were some 2700 heavier pennies, English and imitative sterlings and a mere handful (25) gros tournois.[1] Over a century and a half after the introduction of the first grossi in Venice, the currency in the Baltic still consisted almost entirely of pfennigs that happened to be lighter than those which made up the Brussels hoard in the 1260s. After a century and a half there were only 25 gros amongst 80,000 coins! This makes it abundantly clear how very different the timing of the progression from pennies to groats was in different parts of Europe. It immediately poses the question of what conditions determined the readiness of an area for the use of coins of a larger denomination than the penny. Sometimes the attempt was made before the area was ready, as it was by Edward I in England, Casimir the Great in Poland, or the city of Lübeck, and it failed. It is necessary to inquire what conditions were lacking in England in the late thirteenth century, or in Poland and even in the chief city of the Hanseatic league in the mid fourteenth century, that were present in northern Italy in the early thirteenth century, central Italy in the mid thirteenth century, southern Italy and the Low Countries in the late thirteenth, or England and the Rhineland in the mid fourteenth century.

It might be instructive to look at the case of England, where groats failed in 1279 and succeeded in 1351. What change had taken place in these seventy years? The volume of coined money in England in 1279 was probably in the region of 150 million pennies,[2] so that there was no general dearth of money at that time. Indeed there was probably a lesser total volume of coined money in England in 1351,[3] so that the sheer quantity of money in circulation does not seem to have been the efficient cause of change. It is not possible to estimate the total volume of England's external trade accurately. The quantities of raw wool, England's prime export commodity, sent overseas are, however, mostly known. They fluctuated violently between 1279 and 1351. Although short-term trends can be seen, no general long-term trend is discernible, for the fluctuations all fell within the broad, general band of an annual export of 30,000±10,000 sacks of wool. Neither in the 1280s nor the

---

[1] *Nordisk Numismatisk Årsskrift* (1970), 37–168.
[2] See above, p. 204.   [3] See below, p. 341 n. 1 and p. 348.

1350s did English cloth exports seem of much importance compared with those of wool. English overseas trade may have fluctuated over these seventy years, but it did not at any point increase so much as to change its order of magnitude, so that the sheer volume of international transactions does not seem to have been the efficient cause of change, and indeed this leads one to question the often-made assumption that great coins, grossi, gros, groschen or groats, were primarily struck for long-distance trade. On the contrary, when in the 1280s the gros tournois was still of a scale only to be usable in the Low Countries for long-distance transactions, it was not much used and did not catch on.[1] Until the reappearance of a gold coinage, large long-distance transactions seem primarily to have been settled in bar silver, if it was not possible for payments to be carried out entirely in paper.[2] The key change must therefore have been an internal one, and I would suggest that the key lies in the relationship between the size of the basic coin available and the consequent number of such coins needed for the most frequent transactions for which coin was necessary, and in the volume of such frequent transactions. I would further suggest that the payment of, and spending of, wages were the key transactions – and even from this I would exclude the vast majority of wages, those annual money-wages paid to the rural labourer, which were supplements to the board and lodging that were the real wages for such people. This leaves the urban wage-earner, the journeyman who received day-wages, possibly actually paid by the day, although more probably by the week, the peripatetic wage-earner such as the building-craftsman or labourer, who moved from job to job and whose wages were in terms of days worked, as were the seasonal labourers who performed such functions as helping to gather in the harvest, and the soldier whose pay was similarly reckoned by the day. Among these the urban wage-earners and possibly the soldiers seem to have been of critical importance. The growth of towns or armies beyond a certain point meant a need for coins of the right size to be readily available for the payment and spending of wages. In the 1280s the wages of building-labourers in southern England were 1½d. a day, or 9d. for a six-day week, if paid weekly. Groats, worth 4d. in the 1280s, were not of much use to such men. In the 1350s their wages were in the process of doubling. In 18d. weekly pay, a groat was marginally acceptable.[3] One might cite the modern analogy of the £5 note. In 1950 average, gross, weekly pay in Britain was £7 10s. 5d. and over three quarters of British wage-earners had weekly after-tax take-home pay between £3 and £10. The £5 note was then still a rare denomination. Under 400,000 were in circulation. In 1964 the average, gross, weekly pay-packet was £19 11s. 9d. and over three quarters of British wage-earners

---

[1] See above, p. 230.

[2] See below chapter 12, and above, chapter 9.

[3] Initially half-groats (2d. pieces) may have been more popular than groats. A small hoard concealed in Coventry around 1365 contained nearly twice as many half-groats as groats. It also contained twice as many pence as half-groats (*Coin Hoards*, III (1977), no. 332, p. 131).

had weekly after-tax take-home pay between £10 and £40. The £5 note had become common. Over 1000 million were in circulation. In the 1960s the £5 note was of some use to ordinary wage-earners when it represented under a third of the weekly, take-home pay. In the 1950s it had not been, when it represented over a half of the weekly, take-home pay.

The level of prices of everyday commodities seems to have been rather less relevant. In England most of the thirteenth-century price-rise had occurred by 1279. Although prices in the 1350s were higher, they were not very much higher. The need to pay soldiers must also be borne in mind. Although 1279 was itself a year of peace, Edward I was frequently at war. The ordinary foot-soldiers in his main armies in Wales or Scotland were paid 2d. a day, and pence were adequate. In 1351 and subsequent years, considerable payments of soldiers' wages for Edward III's French war were needed, and from then on it became normal for soldiers to be paid their wages in groat-size coins.

If enough thirteenth- and fourteenth-century wage-data were accumulated, it would be possible to test my hypothesis that the need for a larger denomination of coin was only reached when and where there was sufficient urban growth for there to be a large enough number of people living primarily on money-wages, and when those money-wages, in terms of the existing denari or deniers, required an inconveniently large number of coins to be paid over on each of a large number of occasions.

According to the chronicler Martin da Canal, admittedly writing sixty-five years after the event, the first grossi of Europe had been minted specifically for the purpose of paying the wages of the shipwrights who were building and fitting out the ships for the Fourth Crusade. They were presumably still being used for paying wages in the Venetian Arsenal in da Canal's own day.[1] The pattern of the introduction of grossi suggests that da Canal's specific report of the primary use of the first grossi can be generalised, and that grossi were normally introduced and extensively used for urban wages. In the first forty years of their issue grossi were limited to the urban centres of Italy north of Rome in which large wage-earning groups existed. The next most highly urbanised area of Europe, the southern Netherlands, did not adopt coins of this size until the late 1260s, when the baudekins of Margaret of Constantinople, as Countess of Hainault and Flanders, and similar pieces issued by other princes in the area, began to fulfil the same role for paying wages in their commercial and industrial cities. In large parts of Europe, the whole Baltic area for example, urbanisation and the payment of day-wages in money was not extensive enough even in the fourteenth century for such larger coins to be much needed. The attempt to strike groschen in Lübeck in the 1360s proved abortive.

---

[1] See above, p. 226 n. 2.

The new, large coins of good silver of the thirteenth century were thus, in the first place, most suitable for paying urban wages, and consequently for other medium-scale payments of urban living, house-rent for example.

They also soon found a use in another area associated with urban growth, the purchase of food from the countryside. Good, silver coins were the most convenient form for the great seasonal flows of money from town to countryside.[1] Grossi, gros or groten were convenient for purchasing whole beasts from the peasantry and grain by the *setier* or *muid*, and wine or oil by the skin. They were then usable for the payment of rural rents and taxes and in due course returned to the cities.

Many types of grossi or groten, although not all, thus had a circulation that was geographically restricted. The grossi of the Tuscan cities, whose economies were so intermeshed, circulated freely between themselves and in their dependent *contadi*, but rarely further afield. Similarly, geographically restricted areas of circulation existed for the groten issued by the principalities of the Netherlands, and for the grossi issued by the Italian cities north of the Apennines, none of which were much used outside the Netherlands or the Po basin respectively, except for the grossi of Venice.

Meanwhile the deniers that were already being struck at the end of the twelfth century continued to be issued. However, many of them were rapidly debased in the course of the thirteenth century, in contrast to the new grossi, which largely retained their initial weight and fineness for long periods of time. These debased denari and deniers, in some places known as 'piccoli' in contrast to the new 'grossi', or in others as 'monnaie noire' from their low silver content in contrast to the new 'monnaie blanche', also had a specific role to play in the new urban economy. Whereas the large coins of good silver were suitable for purchasing grain by the bushel, whole beasts and skins of wine or oil, the everyday preoccupations of townsmen were with buying bread by the loaf, meat by the joint, and wine and oil by the *pinte*. In their new, debased form many of the small deniers were admirably adapted for this scale of purchase.

Two examples may serve to illustrate the different uses of denari and grossi. In 1332 in Florence the principal coins in circulation were piccioli, which were heavily debased denari made only one twelfth of silver and eleven twelfths of copper, and grossi, known as 'fiorini guelfi', made of almost pure silver, with only one twenty-fourth part of copper in them to harden them. The grossi were then worth 30 piccioli (2s. 6d.). Wages for master craftsmen in the building-trades were then generally 7s. a day, nearly 3 grossi, and for ordinary workmen 4s. 6d. a day, nearly 2 grossi. The loaf of bread cost 4 piccioli, and in neighbouring Pistoia, which also used Florentine coin, mutton then had a maximum price of 7 piccioli a pound, ox-

[1] See below, pp. 382–5.

beef of 8 piccioli a pound, pork of 9 piccioli a pound, and veal of 14 piccioli a pound.[1] In Venice in 1343–4 the principal coins in circulation were base piccoli and good, silver grossi, then worth 32 piccoli (2s. 8d.). The domestic account-book of the Morosini, a patrician household of eight people, survives for six months. It was an affluent enough household to bake its own bread, so it bought wheat by the *staio* at 22 grossi the *staio*. It could also afford to buy oil in bulk, at 15 grossi the *miro*, but even affluent households had to buy meat in small quantities twice a week. They paid 12 piccoli a pound for beef and 16 piccoli a pound for pork. They bought vegetables, invariably cabbages or turnips in the winter, daily, and spent only 4 or 5 piccoli a day on them. Other minor items of domestic expenditure also appear in the accounts. Boys' haircuts, for example, cost 4 piccoli a time.[2] These domestic accounts make it quite clear that vegetables and haircuts were paid for in piccoli, like loaves of bread and pounds of meat, whilst grossi were used for wheat by the *staio* and oil by the *miro*.

When and where the deniers were not, or not yet, small enough, halves and quarters were created to cope with the minutiae of everyday living. In Venice, for example, under Doge Enrico Dandolo half-denari or oboli were struck for small change at the beginning of the thirteenth century, although later in the century the denaro was itself sufficiently small for all purposes. In England in 1279 and 1280 Edward I began to have quarter- and half-pence minted. The half-penny 'wastel'-loaf of white bread then weighed just under a kilo (about 2 pounds) and the half-penny loaf of coarse bread was twice the weight. There were smaller loaves priced at a farthing (the quarter-penny).[3]

Where the deniers had become very small, low multiples of them were also minted. By the mid fourteenth century the coin most commonly struck in Florence was the quattrino or 4-denari piece, which was the standard payment for a loaf of bread. In Florence, as in England, loaves of bread varied in size according to the price of wheat. It would have been impossible to charge a variable price for a fixed size of loaf, since there were no coins in circulation sufficiently small to accommodate the gradations in price involved.[4]

Even where deniers had become too small for making purchases by themselves, they could still be useful for making up payments of odd prices in conjunction with larger coins, or used alone for charitable purposes. The denier parisis eventually became known as the 'denier de l'aumesnerie'. Urban charity, which had earlier

[1] Mario Bernocchi, *Le monete della repubblica fiorentina* (Florence, 1974–8); Charles M. de la Roncière, *Florence, centre économique régional au XIVᵉ siècle* (5 vols., Aix-en-Provence, 1976), pp. 295 and 344–5; David Herlihy, *Medieval and Renaissance Pistoia* (New Haven, Conn., 1967), p. 127.

[2] Gino Luzzatto, 'Il costo della vita a Venezia nel Trecento', *Ateneo Veneto*, cxxv (1934), reprinted in *Studi di storia economica veneziana* (Padua, 1954), pp. 285–97.

[3] Alan S. C. Ross, 'The assize of bread', *Economic History Review*, 2nd series, ix (1957), 332–42.

[4] For further discussion of the functions of small change in late medieval towns, see below, pp. 328–32.

consisted of gifts in kind, in the course of the thirteenth century came to be given in money. Even charity adapted to the new economy.

The transformation from a currency consisting of a single denomination to one consisting of a multiplicity of denominations was the natural corollary to the extreme complexity of urban transactions that developed over the thirteenth century.

11

The Place of Money in the
Commercial Revolution of the Thirteenth Century[1]

Just as Fernand Braudel wrote of a 'long sixteenth century', there seems also to have been a 'long thirteenth century', stretching from the 1160s to the 1330s. It is within this 'long thirteenth century' that fundamental changes took place in the methods of doing business that have been dignified with the title 'the commercial revolution'. Dramatic changes certainly also took place in the physical form of the coinages of western Europe during this long century of the commercial revolution and it is these that have generally attracted the attention of historians and numismatists alike.[2]

Although these changes in the physical forms of the currency were so dramatic, and can be seen so vividly by handling the surviving coins, they were not in my opinion fundamental, nor were they directly linked, as is so frequently repeated, simply to the increasing scale of international trade.[3] The purpose of this chapter is to suggest that these changes were only the visible counterpart of a range of complex and important developments that represent the true role of money in the commercial revolution of the thirteenth century.

The quantity of money in circulation, the use to which it was put, and the attitudes to it, seem to me to be more important than the forms in which it circulated. From the 1160s there was a continuous sequence of large-scale producers of silver within Europe until the Villa di Chiesa mines went into a sharp decline in the 1330s and 1340s and those of Kutná Hora a little later.[4] The silver produced by this sequence of mines vastly surpassed that produced by the mines of the Harz in the tenth century and rivalled that produced by the mines of central Europe at the beginning of Braudel's long sixteenth century itself.

In my opinion the changes brought about by this mass of silver were greater than those effected by either tenth- or sixteenth-century silver-mining. The scale of mining in the tenth century was never great enough to bring about the qualitative

---

[1] An earlier version of this chapter appears in John Day (ed.), *Études d'histoire monétaire XIIᵉ–XIXᵉ siècles* (Lille, 1984), pp. 355–95.
[2] For the new grossi see the previous chapter, pp. 225–34, and for the new gold coins see above, pp. 176–8.
[3] For the actual, local, use of grossi see above, pp. 234–9.
[4] See above, pp. 109–31, and below, pp. 343–9.

changes that occurred in the thirteenth century, and the sixteenth-century revival of the stock of European silver operated on an economy already transformed in the thirteenth century. It is moreover quite possible that the quantities of coin available in the sixteenth century were no greater than those available in the thirteenth.[1]

As money increased in quantity it could be used more freely for a wide range of activities in which it had previously played a minimal role.

In the countryside money-rent could oust both labour-rent and rent in kind as the dominant form of peasant rent.

In Picardy, in northern France, for example, in a 'labour-rent' area of Europe, Professor Fossier found that rent services were entrenched up to around 1170, although, of course, even here, there was also a considerable element of payment in kind in the rents that tenants owed their landlords, besides a light *cens* in money – a few deniers a year. As increasing quantities of money came into the area after 1170, more and more land was let on terms whereby money replaced the hitherto-dominant labour element in the rent. By the period 1220–50 he was able to conclude that the possibility of paying a money-rent was liberating for the richer peasants with extensive farms, who were able to sell their produce for sums greatly in excess of the rents demanded of them. For their poorer neighbours, money-rent was burdensome, for it was not possible for them to sell enough produce to pay their rent, and they were consequently compelled to find outside work, paid by money-wages, to meet the financial demands put on them. The poorest peasants could not by any means raise the necessary money and still continued to pay the rent for their tiny plots of land with their own labour. Meanwhile the produce element in the rent, which here was normally in grain (for Picardy was a predominantly cereal-growing area), remained unchanged until the second quarter of the thirteenth century. It then also very rapidly gave way to payments in cash. Fossier's whole description of rural Picardy in the mid thirteenth century is of a society in which money had become common. For produce to be sold for money had become normal. For wages to be paid in money had also become normal. Payment of rent by work had become an abnormal survival, which was to disappear there totally by the end of the century.[2]

When, in 1931, Marc Bloch wrote about 'the great metamorphosis which overtook the seigneurie between 1100 and 1200', he believed that the attenuation in services and the shrinking of the demesne were peculiar at this period to France.[3] It has now for long been apparent, largely on account of the studies provoked by Bloch's own work, how much more widespread such an attenuation of services had been, where, that is, labour rent had ever been important.

[1] See above, p. 205.

[2] Robert Fossier, *La Terre et les hommes en Picardie jusqu'à la fin du XIIIe siècle* (Paris–Louvain, 1968), pp. 588ff, 723ff, and 405.

[3] Marc Bloch, *French Rural History* (1931; English trans. 1966), pp. 93–9.

In much larger areas of Europe rent in kind was, by the twelfth century, traditionally far more important than work-rent. Professor Toubert's study of Latium, in central Italy, provides an excellent example of the alternative tradition. There labour service was light or non-existent in the twelfth century. There was also a light *cens* in money there, but the bulk of the rent consisted of payments in kind – a third of the grapes or olives grown, or a quarter or a fifth of the cereals. However, here too the arrival of money in large quantities in the area had the same effect as in Picardy, and at the same time. The existing pattern of rent payments, however different, was transformed into payment in money.[1] A series of other studies, like Slicher van Bath's for the Netherlands or Dollinger's for Bavaria, show the same transformation from rents in kind to money-rents for large areas of Europe in the late twelfth and early thirteenth centuries. In Bavaria a rather late example is provided by the abbey of Baumburg. At the end of the twelfth century, neither its dependent *mansi* nor the outlying parcels of field and vineyard that it possessed yet provided the abbey with anything but agricultural products. Half a century later, in 1245, 90% of the minor holdings and 75% of the *mansi* were farmed out exclusively for cash-rents. The abbey of Baumburg was not in the forefront, for other Bavarian examples of money-rents, like those paid to the abbey of Asbach, go back to the 1170s, to the very beginning of the new wave of silver.[2]

In all these cases the initiative was the landlord's, but it was not possible for the transformation to take place fully until there was a market, and money available for the peasant to obtain by selling his produce. For example, in parts of northern France when landlords wished to reduce their labour services and lease out parts of their demesnes in the middle years of the twelfth century they could not yet do so for money. Instead they had to lease them out for a proportion of their yield (*champart*).[3] When money was available at the end of the century and the beginning of the next, *champart* gave way to money-rent.

Fossier has shown how payment in money rather than in work was an increased burden on all but the most prosperous tenants. To have his labour returned to him and to be expected instead to provide a money- or goods-rent out of the produce of a holding that he had hitherto farmed to sustain himself and his family, without the size of the holding being increased, meant the handing-over or compulsory sale on the market of a large proportion of the produce that he and his family had

---

[1] Pierre Toubert, *Les Structures du Latium médiéval . . . du IXe à la fin du XIIe siècle*, Bibliothèque des Écoles Françaises d'Athènes et de Rome CCXXI (Rome, 1973), pp. 502 (labour services 3–8 days a year), 537–9 (*cens* 2d.– 6d. a year) and 545 (rent in kind).

[2] Philippe Dollinger, *L'Évolution des classes rurales en Bavière* (Paris, 1949), pp. 145–50.

[3] Bloch, *French Rural History*, pp. 93–9; by contrast, in southern England, the other area in which labour-rent had been strongly entrenched, there was still enough coin left over from the previous monetary expansion of the tenth and eleventh centuries for it to be possible to begin to transform labour-rent directly into money-rent in the middle years of the twelfth century and to farm out demesnes for money even before the stocks of new silver started to reach the country.

previously consumed, and so a radical diminution of their standard of living. Tenants who had traditionally paid their rents largely in produce did not necessarily find the substitution of money-rents such a burden, although a fixed money-rent did mean that the tenant, rather than the landlord, took the risks of poor harvests or, alternatively, of low sale-prices. The initiative and the advantage was the landlord's, and he was able to impose his will on his tenants because of the pressures of population. Although there are no statistics that can be used with any certainty outside very limited localities, the impression strongly held by historians is that when the flood of new silver became available in the late twelfth century Europe was already in the grip of a population explosion, which continued, in parallel with the expanding stocks of silver, throughout the course of the thirteenth century. Estimates of when the rise in population came to an end vary not only with the area of Europe considered, but also with the predilections of the individual historian. However it seems clear both that the population increase had begun before the increase in the supply of bullion, and that it had come to an end before the supply of bullion diminished in the fourteenth century. Already, in the middle of the twelfth century, the increase in population and the competition for tenancies meant that landlords could alter the conditions of tenancy to their own advantage. However it was not until adequate supplies of money were available at the end of the century that this advantage could be turned to practical account.

The transition to an economy in which money was the measure of all things, from one in which money had had a relatively minor role, was not, however, without its difficulties even for landlords. As has been seen, rent in money, already common by the end of the twelfth century in some parts of Europe, went on to supplant surviving rents in kind and labour-rents as the thirteenth century proceeded. The thirteenth century was, however, subject to strong inflationary pressures, primarily because the increased population put pressure on the agricultural resources and caused the price of basic foodstuffs to rise, but partially also, no doubt, because of the increased money supply itself, and partially because of the diminution of the silver content of the individual coins. This diminution was generally only the necessary reduction in weight at longish intervals to compensate for wear and tear, but sometimes took the form of violent debasements to help meet the financial emergencies of the rulers.[1] Inflation, from whatever cause, meant that the real value of money-rents diminished and that only those that had been most recently commuted gave any real advantage to the landlord.[2] Landlords dealt with, or failed to deal with, the problem of the decline in rents in a variety of different ways. In southern England and Tuscany, for example, landlords were faced with the problem in a peculiarly acute form. In southern England, where the

---

[1] See pp. 289–318.
[2] Georges Duby, *Rural Economy and Country Life in the Medieval West* (Paris, 1962; English trans. 1968), pp. 237–9.

coinage was not debased, the problem has been associated with the sudden surge in the money supply at the end of the twelfth century and the beginning of the thirteenth, when a greater quantity of silver entered the country than the economy was ready to absorb.[1] The price of wheat doubled, from 1s. 6d. to 3s. a quarter between 1190 and 1210, and that of cattle tripled over the same period of time from 2s. to 6s. a head.[2] The reaction of many landlords was to attempt to benefit directly from the market price for agricultural goods, which continued to rise, although not so rapidly, throughout the thirteenth century under the twin pressures of rising population and rising bullion stocks. Many landlords therefore took back into their own hands the demesnes that had already been leased for money. When the demesnes had been leased, villein tenures for labour-rent had naturally been transformed into tenancies for money-rent at the same time, since the labour had no longer been needed. Landlords who took their demesnes back into their own hands varied in their treatment of their villein tenants. In some cases instead of entirely reimposing the old labour services on their villein tenants they took advantage of the freer use of money to employ *famuli*, full-time workers for money-wages, to cultivate their demesnes round the year, and only reimposed on the tenants of villein land the obligation to perform boon-works, to labour on the demesne at the busiest seasons of the agricultural year, at lambing-time, at haymaking, or at the harvest, for example. In other cases they nominally reimposed the whole range of labour services, but in practice demanded cash on an *ad hoc* basis instead of a variable and often large proportion of the services each year, according to that year's particular needs. In yet others, work-rent was not reimposed at all and the demesnes were entirely worked with wage-labour. In general, services permanently disappeared north and west of the line from the Wash to the Severn, and were reimposed to some extent to the south and east of this line.[3] However the surviving Hundred Rolls, from 1279, covering a considerable part of this area, show that by then money-rent still, or again, predominated over labour-rent in southern England.[4] In these ways, landlords were able to maximise their advantages – rising prices for demesne produce sold on the market for money, produced by the labour of *famuli* who were paid decreasing real wages, together with the services, where needed, of villein tenants, who were still paying most of their rent in money. The system was excellently adaptable to changing circumstances.

In Tuscany, where there was no tradition of labour services and no demesne, landlords reacted differently to bouts of inflation largely induced by the declining

---

[1] See above, pp. 139–40.
[2] P. D. A. Harvey, 'The English Inflation of 1180–1220', *Past and Present*, LXI (1973), 3–30.
[3] Edward Miller and John Hatcher, *Medieval England. Rural Society and Economic Change 1086–1348* (London, 1978), pp. 121–8 and 213–24.
[4] E. A. Kosminsky, *Studies in the Agrarian History of England in the Thirteenth Century* (1947; English trans. Oxford, 1956), pp. 152–96.

silver content of the denaro. Even in the twelfth century landlords switched between fixed money-rents and leases for fixed quantities of agricultural produce as opportunity arose and circumstances demanded, frequently reverting to leases for agricultural produce in periods of monetary instability. In the thirteenth century long leases were replaced, when they came up for renewal, by shorter and shorter leases, and if money-rent was preferred, it was increased each time to match the inflation. Eventually, by the end of the thirteenth century, landlords began to abandon fixed rents altogether, and leased their land for half its produce or rather, unless they happened to wish to consume the produce, for the prevailing market price of half the produce. This new system, *mezzadria*, enabled Tuscan landlords to share directly in the rising prices of foodstuffs in an inflationary situation.[1] The widespread rural use of money, despite occasional difficulties, could thus always be turned to the landlords' advantage with imaginative adaptation to changing circumstances.

The landlords' initiative in demanding money-rents was part of a whole revolution in attitudes towards money. Just as cultivable land ceased to be regarded simply as a source of immediately consumable produce and came to be seen as a source of money, so other resources came to be judged in terms of the money that they would produce. Forests ceased to be seen merely in terms of hunting for pleasure or food and were valued in money terms. In Champagne, for example, in the 1170s under Count Henry the Liberal, good timber began to be treated as a cash crop to be cultivated and sold for building, whilst scrub was to be cleared and transformed into cultivable land. Such new assarts paid money-rents from the start. The same count deliberately invested in building mills, both for grinding corn and for fulling cloth, and in having ovens and winepresses constructed for the money income that they would produce.[2] His contemporary, Philip of Alsace, Count of Flanders from 1168, whose mints, like Henry's, were among the first to actively provide more coin at this very time,[3] treated his forests and fens in the same way, as a source of money. He invested in drainage schemes to reclaim fresh land for cultivation and sold his reserves of peat for fuel. It is not surprising that the same count and his brother Matthew, Count of Boulogne, were among the earliest founders of new towns for profit. They included Calais, Dunkirk, Nieuwpoort, Damme and Gravelines.[4] Their subjects rapidly added to the investment. Quick-

---

[1] P. J. Jones, 'An Italian estate 900–1200', *Economic History Review*, 2nd series, XII (1954), 18–32; Philip Jones, 'Medieval agrarian society in its prime, Italy', *Cambridge Economic History of Europe*, 2nd ed., I (Cambridge, 1966), 340–431; P. J. Jones, 'From manor to mezzadria: a Tuscan case-study in the medieval origins of modern agrarian society', in N. Rubinstein (ed.), *Florentine Studies* (London, 1968), pp. 193–241.
[2] Jean Longnon, 'La Champagne', in Ferdinand Lot and Robert Fawtier (eds.), *Histoire des institutions françaises au moyen âge*, I, 'Institutions seigneuriales' (Paris, 1957), pp. 123–36.
[3] See above, pp. 196–7.
[4] A. Verhulst, 'Initiative comtale et développement économique en Flandre au XIIᵉ siècle', *Miscellanea mediaevalia in memoriam Jan Frederik Niermeyer* (Groningen, 1967), pp. 227–40.

ened by the profit motive, the men of Bruges and St Omer almost at once organised the cutting of channels suitable to bring sea-going vessels inland from the new coastal towns of Damme and Gravelines respectively.[1] Not only ruling princes and townsmen were involved in this investment for profit. Vast numbers of lesser landlords invested on a smaller scale with the monetary returns clearly in mind, and even began to employ professional managers and accountants to get the most out of their resources. By the early thirteenth century the chapter of Amiens reckoned to make 20s.–40s. a year from a winepress, 12s. from an oven, and 24s. from a mill,[2] whilst the bakers and millers themselves made so much profit that they joined the village élites of the richer peasants, who were hard to distinguish from impoverished knights.

The richer peasants, who gained from the new opportunities presented by a market for their produce, and welcomed the new cash-rents as freeing them to have more time to spend on the cultivation of their land, also benefited from the labour-saving winepresses and mills provided by their landlords, whilst their poorer neighbours continued to wear themselves out milling their grain by hand. They very soon acquired the new outlook towards money themselves and bought tenancies and bits of tenancies from their poorer neighbours as well as allodial land. Fossier began to find such peasant land-purchases for money around 1175 in Picardy. They became much more common there after 1225, and even more so after 1250.[3] Well-to-do peasants, as well as purchasing the land of some of their poorer neighbours outright, also invested surplus cash in purchasing rent-charges on the lands of others, and so increased their money income yet further.[4]

Kings and princes, as the greatest landlords in their territories, stood to gain, like other landlords, from the increased possibilities of compelling their tenants to pay rents in money. Many other traditional sources of 'income' in goods and services were equally transformed into money. The Counts of Flanders, for example, had systematically imposed this conversion to money by 1187, and in royal France a similar transformation was largely brought about early in the thirteenth century by Philip Augustus.[5]

In addition, the widespread availability of money in the hands of a numerous peasantry also allowed for the imposition of direct taxation in money on a much larger scale than anything attempted since antiquity.[6] In the thirteenth century the

---

[1] Alain Derville, 'Le Marais de Saint Omer', *Revue du Nord,* LXII (1980), 73–93.

[2] Fossier, *La Terre et les hommes en Picardie*, p. 621.

[3] *Ibid.* p. 577. Paul R. Hyams, 'The origins of a peasant land market in England', *Economic History Review*, 2nd series, XXIII (1970), 18–31, suggests a similar development in East Anglia by 1240 at the latest.

[4] Fossier, *La Terre et les hommes en Picardie*, p. 604. Rent-charges became common in Picardy after 1210. They were very rare before that date.

[5] Bryce Lyon and Adriaan Verhulst, *Medieval Finance* (Bruges, 1967).

[6] See below, p. 383. The tenth-century expansion of the use of money had allowed for some direct taxation, for

burden of direct taxation on the countryside was frequently much greater than that of indirect taxation in the town. In the 1280s the countryside of Pistoia supported a tax burden six times as high as that paid by the city. This excessive tax burden was only a part of the sucking-dry of the *contado* by the city at this period. In Tuscany, payments from the country to the city greatly exceeded payments from the city to the country. The countryside fell into a state of endemic debt to the city. Repeated and continuous loans from the city to the countryside, and the purchase of rent-charges on the countryside by city-dwellers, only made the situation worse. *Contadini* were compelled to concentrate on cash crops rather than their own needs, and a cycle of deprivation was set up not unlike that in parts of the Third World today.[1]

Such enormously increased money incomes of cities, princes and kings quickly affected the conduct of war and politics. The use of money in politics and war is well illustrated by the 40,000 marks of silver that John of England sent to pay for the Bouvines campaign of 1214.[2] Indeed their enlarged money incomes allowed kings and princes the possibility of running their states and maintaining power by the payment of regular salaries in money, without prejudicing the future by grants of land to maintain officials or soldiers.

In the last quarter of the twelfth century money-fiefs, *fiefs-rentes*, *feoda de bursa*, very suddenly became common in the Low Countries. From 1190 the same swift increase in such grants took place in England, and from 1200 in France and Germany. They were not new. The earliest-known example comes from the end of the tenth century, when the church of Utrecht in 996 enfeoffed a knight, Frethebald, not with land, but with 12 livres of deniers, payable annually. However, only half a dozen similar cases are known from the eleventh century and not many more from the first three quarters of the twelfth century. It was only when rulers regularly had enough money in hand that money-fiefs could replace enfeoffments with land as the normal means of paying knights and also, occasionally, other officials.[3] This was at the same time that it became normal to pay salaries in money to the general run of non-military officers in the service of the rulers of western Europe. The availability of adequate and regular money incomes allowed for a revolution in the government of states.

Castellans and knights paid with money did not become hereditary as their land-

example the English Danegeld, but this had ceased in the late eleventh and early twelfth century when money became scarcer again.

[1] David Herlihy, *Medieval and Renaissance Pistoia* (New Haven, Conn., 1967), pp. 143–4; David Herlihy, 'Santa Maria Impruneta: a rural commune in the late Middle Ages', in Rubinstein (ed.), *Florentine Studies*, pp. 266–7. After the mid fourteenth century the burdens were reversed.

[2] Georges Duby, *Le Dimanche de Bouvines* (Paris, 1973), p. 39. The sum of 40,000 marks is quite within the bounds of possibility. If coined as sterling, it was 6.4 million pennies. The total amount recoined in 1205 had been around 40 million pennies, and that had not been a total recoinage.

[3] Bryce D. Lyon, *From Fief to Indenture* (Cambridge, Mass., 1957).

paid predecessors had done, nor did 'civil servants' paid with money. Henry the Liberal was able to reorganise the local administration of his county of Champagne into twenty-nine *prévôtés*, each administered by a *prévôt* who was paid in money, not land.[1] Thus the first post-feudal states could emerge.

· As well as such annual payments of regular money-fiefs to castellans or knights, the greater availability of ready money allowed rulers to make irregular supplementary payments to knights in cash when actually on campaign. Writing in the context of the Bouvines campaign, Professor Duby suggested that by the opening of the thirteenth century such payments on campaign were normal, and were the vital element that kept knights from drifting away from the host and going home after their 'feudal' service had been done. Most of the knights at Bouvines, he pointed out, had received money for being there, or expected to do so, over and above their income from land or money-fiefs.[2]

In the eyes of contemporaries there was no scandal in that. The scandal lay in paying non-noble mercenaries. Such mercenaries were not entirely new in the second half of the twelfth century, but the increasing availability of money allowed them to be hired on a scale never known before. Henry the Liberal of Champagne appears again as one of the earliest rulers who could afford to employ such men. It was in the 1170s that non-noble mercenaries proliferated. They were much hated for their brutality and were frequently described pejoratively as 'Brabançons', presumably from the place of origin of some of the most notorious of them. It was as 'Brabançons' that they were condemned by the Third Lateran Council in 1179. Some 700 of these hated 'Brabançons' in John's pay were slaughtered mercilessly by the victorious French after their victory at Bouvines.[3] So brutality breeds brutality. By the 1180s such mercenaries were already to be found in organised companies with leaders sufficiently well known for their names to feature in chronicles. Such companies could be extremely expensive to employ and strained the resources of even the wealthiest princes at the end of the twelfth century. In 1183, shortly before his premature death, the young King Henry, son of Henry II of England, had to resort to desperate measures at Limoges to keep his mercenary troops in his service. He exacted a forced loan of 1000 livres from the citizens and seized a similar sum from the treasury of St Martial. Such acts by desperate princes caused Professor Duby to describe these mercenary companies as marvellous agents of the *déthésaurisation* that nourished and increased the stock of circulating money from the last quarter of the twelfth century onwards. They also, of course, 'dethesaurised' a considerable amount of silver by straight-forward looting. One chronicler was scandalised that a camp of mercenaries at Dun-le-Roi in Berry in 1183 was not only full of whores, but also full of chalices and *ciboria*.[4]

---

[1] Longnon, 'La Champagne'.   [2] Duby, *Le Dimanche de Bouvines*, p. 103.
[3] *Ibid.* p. 64.   [4] *Ibid.* pp. 105–10.

It was in the thirteenth century that the problem of financing post-feudal war began to be solved. When the size and regularity of their money incomes was sufficiently assured, and when banking had evolved to an adequate scale,[1] rulers were able to use their regular incomes as security for borrowing large lump sums. Such possibilities of anticipating their regular incomes gave rulers a much greater freedom of action in emergencies. In this way post-feudal armies could be paid in wartime, just as post-feudal administrations could be paid in peacetime. Sienese bankers gave this sort of help to Frederick II, Florentine bankers to Charles of Anjou, and a variety of Tuscan bankers to both Edward I and Philip IV in their wars with one another.

As well as being freer than their predecessors to hire and fire non-hereditary officials and troops, rulers had also become freer, from the second half of the twelfth century, to choose where they would live. Hitherto they had had to perambulate incessantly between places to which the produce of their estates could conveniently be brought for consumption. When the proportion of the produce of their estates received in money rather than in kind increased rapidly, it became much easier for them and their courts and administrators to remain static for long periods. In this way each of the patchwork of formerly feudal states that made up twelfth-century 'France' was able to develop a 'capital' in which its ruler, or at least his administration, was permanently to be found – for example at Ghent, Paris, Provins, Poitiers or Toulouse.

This same liberation from the necessity of living in the countryside was also experienced by the landowning classes in general. Many of them chose to spend at least part of the year 'at court', living in newly built, noble town houses in or near the capital of their ruler. At Provins, the *hôtels* of some of the nobility of Champagne still survive in the upper town beside the palace of their count. Such noblemen brought their rural incomes with them, or had them remitted to them there by their stewards. Their time 'at court' was a time for great spending, on, for example, conspicuous extravagance to emphasise political importance, or on foreign luxuries only available in such cities. The flow of silver around Europe from the mining-areas to the ports by which it left Europe for the Levant was thus not a simple flow, but one with complex eddies of diffusion into the countryside and re-concentration into the towns. The places on which it concentrated were primarily those of political importance where the nobility increasingly congregated.

When, in the course of the thirteenth century, the kings of France acquired so many of these twelfth-century states, Paris came to absorb the attributes of their lesser capitals into itself. Paris thus became the greatest single focus in France, not

[1] See below, pp. 252–6.

only for political activity, but also for consumer demand, whilst Provins and Toulouse died as capital cities. The greater landlords, lay and ecclesiastical, from all the principalities ruled directly by the kings of France came to maintain *hôtels* in Paris. Similarly the higher clergy and greater nobility of England came to build inns in London or Southwark near to their king's capital at Westminster. The failure of central monarchy in the Empire meant that, apart from Prague and Rome, no single major capital developed there. In Germany the minor princely capitals, which largely vanished from France in the thirteenth century, survived and flourished. In Italy too the nobility increasingly chose to live in the cities, whether under republican or signorial constitutions. Indeed some of the cities obliged the nobility of the *contado* to spend a certain proportion of each year within their walls. Grim, noble tower houses dominated the cities of North and Central Italy in the first half of the century, only giving way to more spacious aristocratic *palazzi* at the end of it. In Sicily and the Regno the monarchical capitals of Palermo and Naples attracted the nobility to build their own *alberghi* around the palaces of their Hohenstaufen, Angevin and Aragonese rulers. The papal monarchy too, which no longer merely survived on goods and services from the Patrimony of St Peter, but drew a money income from all parts of Christendom, developed a capital for itself, first at Rome and then at Avignon. The palaces of the cardinals, and other papal 'nobility' were to be found there, scattered around the Lateran in the ruins of ancient Rome, and later clustered about the new palace at Avignon, or facing it across the Rhône from Villeneuve-lès-Avignon.

The nature of the goods in demand in these capital cities is one of the commonplaces of medieval economic history. There was a rapidly expanding clientele for luxury foods such as sugar in place of honey, or for pepper, cloves and other Asiatic spices to give a superior flavour to local food, as well as for luxury drinks such as the finer wines of the Rhineland, Burgundy or Bordeaux instead of the poor, local *vins ordinaires*. The largest market of all was for clothing and furnishing, for luxury woollen clothes from Flanders and Tuscany, rather than local homespun, for high-class linen from Artois, Champagne and Lombardy, for superior leather from Pisa, for high-quality furs from Ireland or northern Russia, for tapestry, damask, brocade, cloth of gold and for the most expensive silks from Lucca, Sicily, Byzantium and even China. There was also a prodigious demand for conspicuous display articles such as gold and silver plate, often made in the capital cities themselves, or bronze and enamel from the Meuse valley, the Rhineland and Limoges, or pearls from the Persian Gulf, and diamonds, rubies and other gems from India. In addition, there was a huge market for commodities specifically related to the noble way of life of a still very military aristocracy, for high-class war horses from Lombardy or Hungary, and for arms and armour from Solingen and Toledo, and, later, from Milan. The dramatic increase in the popularity of the tournament, dating, significantly, from the 1170s and 1180s,[1] was both an expression of the new ability of landowners to indulge in conspicuous expenditure and a cause for channelling much of that expenditure into prestigious armour and horses. There was also, of course, a continuous demand for the services of whole armies of prestigious, and less prestigious, hangers-on, from accountants to cooks, from armed retainers to peaceable valets, who thronged the *hôtels*, inns, *palazzi* or *alberghi* that the nobility had erected in the new capital cities. All these too needed feeding, clothing and housing, as did the suppliers of goods and services, grocers and lawyers, whores and tailors.

The increase in the demand for luxury goods, backed up by the newly liberated quantities of ready cash, arising from the revolution in rents, brought about an enormous quantitative change in the volume of international trade. Moreover, as the amount of business focussed on a limited number of particular places, or rather along a limited number of routes between those places, passed a critical mass, qualitative changes in the nature of commerce began to take place as well as merely quantitative ones. Such qualitative changes in the ways of doing business, have been dignified with the title 'commercial revolution' on the analogy of the title 'industrial revolution' for changes in the organisation of manufacture. This vital transformation could only take place when the concentrated supply of money, and consequently of trade, rose beyond a certain critical point.

Until the critical scale of operations was reached, on any particular route, all that occurred was an increase in the volume of trade within the traditional framework. Italian merchants, for example, merely added extra mules loaded with goods to the mule-trains that accompanied them when they ventured northwards across the Alps. However, once the critical volume was reached, the scale of enterprises allowed for a division of labour.

When that point was reached, businesses became large enough and continuous enough to maintain three separate parties: the sedentary merchants remaining full-time in northern Italy, who specialised in the financing and organisation of import–export trade; the specialist carriers, whether *vectuarii* by land or shipowners by sea, who took the goods from the principals to their agents; and thirdly the full-time agents themselves, resident overseas or beyond the Alps, who devoted their energies to sales or procurements according to the instructions sent to them by their principals.

Such a three-fold division of labour naturally took place first on the routes along which demand was most concentrated at an early date, along which the quantity of trade first passed the critical point at which qualitative change became possible. This occurred first on those routes which ran from the ports of northern Italy to the

---

[1] Duby, *Le Dimanche de Bouvines*, pp. 110–28.

Levant. Colonies of resident Venetian, Genoese and Pisan agents came to live permanently from the twelfth century at Acre, Alexandria and Constantinople. Only a little later, similar North Italian colonies began to be found in Rome, Naples and Palermo and at the Fairs of Champagne, as well as colonies of agents from other cities within the cities of North Italy itself. Later still, by the end of the thirteenth century, they were to be found in the northern capitals, at Paris and London, and also at some of the greater ports with wealthy hinterlands, such as Bruges, Seville, Barcelona and Montpellier.

This transformation of commerce, by which the peripatetic merchant moving about western Europe and the Mediterranean with his goods was replaced by several different men with specialised functions, only became possible in turn in those areas in which a sufficient amount of money and a sufficient scale of demand came to be concentrated. The lack of an effective central monarchy in Germany meant that, since there was no single great capital, demand was too diffused for any single route to carry enough trade to warrant the new commercial division of labour. As a consequence the trade of the Hanseatic cities, northwards and eastwards from Bruges, did not reach this critical volume at this period, and that of the South German cities was still equally primitive in its organisation. Germany and central Europe, with one exception, was not yet ready for the commercial revolution. Only at Prague, where the last Přemyslid and the first Luxemburg kings of Bohemia ran a centralised monarchy, as well as enjoying mining-revenues, was there a capital large enough for the scale of demand generated in it to warrant even a small resident Italian business community. It was much later, in the second half of the fourteenth century, that the Angevin monarchs of Hungary, supported by the new gold from Kremnica, managed in the same way to make Buda a focal point for the nobility of Hungary and hence also for Italian business-men. The fourteenth-century kings of Poland never succeeded in drawing in their nobility to Cracow in this way, despite their attempts to do so.

The byproducts of this revolutionary commercial division of labour have been increasingly understood by historians since the Belgian businessman and scholar Raymond de Roover first pointed out the essential elements of this vital transform-ation at a meeting of the American Business Historical Society in 1941.[1] Partner-ships and financing, which had previously lasted only for a single voyage, took on a more permanent aspect, lasting for terms of several years at a time, often renewed at the end of the term, on a similar basis, for a further period. In Tuscany, in

---

[1] 'The commercial revolution of the thirteenth century', *Bulletin of the Business Historical Society*, XVI (1942), 34–9, repr. in F. C. Lane and J. C. Riemersma (eds.), *Enterprise and Secular Change* (London, 1953), pp. 80–5. He expressed this insight more fully in his chapter on 'The organization of trade' in the *Cambridge Economic History of Europe*, III (1963), 42–118. It has since become part of the stock-in-trade of medieval economic historians, although the specific role of the money supply in the transformation has not been explored until now.

particular, partnership was extended enormously. The capital of one of the largest companies, the Bardi of Florence, when renewed for 21 years in 1310, was divided into as many as 56 shares.[1] Such shares were transmissible within the lifetime of the company without breaking up the partnership. They were held not only by members of the families of the founders of a company, and by its principal employees, who were encouraged to put their own savings into their own company, but also by other rich men. These were investors not at all concerned with the actual running of the company. In addition to the *corpo*, that is, the capital raised by the shareholders when a company was formed or re-formed, additional capital could be put in later, by shareholders, by employees and by outsiders. Such *denari fuori del corpo* carried fixed rates of interest, like modern debentures. The sedentary merchant at home was no longer a simple individual capitalist; as head of a company he was a manager responsible to his shareholders. As well as the expansion of the scale of firms at home, which mobilised such large amounts of capital, there was an equivalent expansion of the scale of enterprise abroad. It was perfectly possible to repeat the principal–agent relationship over and over again, with agents of the same principal in many different places. The earliest such multi-branched companies, such as the Chiarenti of Pistoia, or the Cerchi of Florence, came into existence in the middle years of the thirteenth century.[2] Commercial correspondence, which had been unnecessary when the merchant had his own goods under his own eyes and struck personal bargains with sellers and buyers, became much more prolific, and regular courier services developed between the main commercial centres. Commercial accounting, which had been rudimentary and largely unnecessary for the same reasons, came to be much more complex, as business firms had to deal with shareholders, suppliers, customers, multiple branches and associated companies over long distances and long periods of time.[3] At about the same time the trade along some routes passed the critical volume at which tolls exacted on it became large enough to finance what has been called a road revolution.[4] As well as a straightforward resurfacing of roads, new bridges were built, new Alpine passes were opened, new hospices for travellers were founded where major routes passed through uninhabitable mountains and forests, new

---

[1] Armando Sapori, *La crisi delle compagnie mercantili dei Bardi e dei Peruzzi* (Florence, 1926), pp. 227–81.

[2] For multi-branched companies in Pistoia, see Herlihy, *Pistoia*, pp. 165–6; a former student of mine, Dr Clare Baggott, is at present engaged in a study of the early Cerchi and hopes to be able to publish an article on them shortly.

[3] Double-entry book-keeping was the most significant of these advances in accounting (Raymond de Roover, 'The development of accounting prior to Luca Pacioli according to the account books of medieval merchants', in A. C. Littleton and B. S. Yamey (eds.), *Studies in the History of Accounting* (London, 1956), pp. 114–74, repr. in *Business, Banking, and Economic Thought in Late Medieval and Early Modern Europe. Selected Studies of R. de Roover*, ed. Julius Kirshner (Chicago, 1974)).

[4] Johan Plesner, *Una rivoluzione stradale del Dugento*, Acta Jutlandica (Copenhagen, 1938).

harbour-works were undertaken, and new lighthouses constructed. All of these made the work of the professional carriers easier and safer. For the calamities that could not be avoided, particularly at sea, insurance was invented.

A further consequence of the regularity and scale of trade was the growth of mutual confidence amongst international merchants, and between them and their suppliers and customers. On the basis of this confidence credit sales could take place, so effectively anticipating and increasing the supply of money.

The most important consequence of this mutual confidence between merchants was the use of various instruments of payment out of which the bill of exchange was gradually perfected. No longer did every prospective purchaser or returning vendor need to carry with him large and stealable quantities of precious metals, whether in coin, or in marks of silver or ounces of gold, depending on the trading-area. Instead the static manager could send and receive remittances from his factors and agents by bills of exchange. The bill of exchange seems to have evolved into its definitive form by the end of the thirteenth century. Its evolution had begun over a hundred years earlier with the notarised *instrumentum ex causa cambii*. The surviving Genoese notarial registers include some such instruments from the late twelfth century, mostly involving transactions between Genoa and the Champagne Fairs. In the thirteenth century the Champagne Fairs were not only the principal bullion-market of Europe but also the principal money-market as well, and the forcing-house for the development of the bill of exchange. By the first half of the fourteenth century it had become normal to make commercial payments by bill of exchange between a wide range of cities in western Europe. The merchant-banking network was focussed on the great trading cities of North Italy, particularly of Tuscany. It extended westwards to the papal curia when it was at Avignon, to Montpellier, Barcelona, Valencia, Seville and sometimes Lisbon; northwards to the Champagne Fairs, until they faded from importance, and to Paris, Bruges and London; and southwards to Naples and Palermo.[1]

Even between these cities, although the majority of transactions could be carried out by bill of exchange, any eventual imbalance had ultimately to be settled up in gold or silver. When an imbalance between two banking-places became too great, the rate of exchange rose (or fell) to such an extent that it passed one of the specie points. In other words it temporarily became cheaper, in one direction, to transport bullion with all its attendant costs and risks, than to buy a bill of exchange. The net quantity of silver transported from Bruges to London or Paris to Florence, or of gold from Seville to Genoa did not diminish as a result of the development of bills

---

[1] Raymond de Roover, *L'Évolution de la lettre de change (XIVᵉ–XVIIIᵉ siècles)* (Paris, 1953), and numerous other writings, the most important collected in *Business, Banking and Economic Thought*. Most, but far from all, the exchange rates collected in Peter Spufford, *Handbook of Medieval Exchange*, Royal Historical Society (London, 1986), fall within the geographical area outlined above.

of exchange, but the amount of business that it represented was increased out of all proportion. The bill of exchange enormously multiplied the supply of money available for international transactions between these cities.

Although bills of exchange were developed by merchants for merchants, they very quickly came to be used by non-merchants as well. Successive popes were the most considerable non-commercial users of bills of exchange. Papal collectors in England and the Low Countries, northern France, the Spanish kingdoms and Italy normally used bills of exchange to transmit the money they had collected to the apostolic *camera* at Avignon in the first half of the fourteenth century.[1] Bishops travelling to the curia no longer needed to ensure that their chamberlains were loaded down with an adequate quantity of mark bars of silver.[2] Noblemen, whether on pilgrimage or representing their princes on embassies, could also avail themselves of bills of exchange. There were, however, limits. Certain international political payments, such as wages to keep whole armies in the field for protracted periods, subsidies for expensive allies, or royal ransoms and dowries, could easily prove too large for the normal commercial system to handle, and so had to be transmitted largely, or wholly, in silver, or gold.[3] Nevertheless a very large proportion of normal payments within this network of cities was made by bill of exchange by the early fourteenth century.

However, outside this range of banking-places, even ordinary international payments had still to be made primarily in bullion. Nevertheless credit, when extended from buyer to seller, or vice versa, still stretched the money supply here too, by deferring payment and so enabling a greater volume of business to be transacted. Where there was a large and continuous imbalance of trade, as there was between the mining-centres of Europe and the commercially advanced areas, a bill-of-exchange system had little chance of developing. In the fourteenth century, papal collectors in Poland still had to take bullion to Bruges or Venice before they could make use of the West European banking-system by acquiring bills of exchange to remit to the curia.[4] Until the fifteenth century even the most prominent trading-cities of Germany, such as Lübeck, basically remained outside this network of exchanges.

Between Christian Europe, Muslim North Africa and the Levant, the use of bills

---

[1] Yves Renouard, *Les Relations des papes d'Avignon et des compagnies commerciales et bancaires de 1316 à 1378*, Bibliothèque des Écoles Françaises d'Athènes et de Rome CLI (Paris, 1941), and see below, pp. 392–5.

[2] See above, pp. 209–10.

[3] For example, when John XXII needed to pay 60,000 florins to the papal army in Lombardy in the summer of 1328, he had to send it in coin. It is an excellent example of the risks involved in carrying coin, for, despite a guard of 150 cavalry, the convoy was ambushed and over half the money lost on the way (Giovanni Villani, *Cronica*, Book X, chapter xli). The political payments discussed in the conclusion, below, pp. 390–2, all had to be made in silver or gold.

[4] Armando Sapori, 'Gli Italiani in Polonia fino a tutto il quattrocento', in his *Studi di storia economica medievale – secoli XIII, XIV, XV*, III (Florence, 1967), 149–76.

was little developed. This was so even though the scale of trade was very large, and the division of labour between manager, carrier and factor developed early, for here there were not only chronic imbalances of trade, but also decided differences in the values given to gold and to silver in the three areas concerned. Since Europe was a silver-producer and Africa a gold-producer, silver was less valued in Europe than Africa, and gold less valued in Africa than Europe. When this disproportion in value was sufficiently great to overcome the risks and costs of the voyage across the western Mediterranean, it occasionally became worthwhile to take European silver to Africa in order to purchase African gold. Much more frequently it was commonsense to carry additional silver southwards and gold northwards along with other more ordinary merchandise.[1] The balances both between Christian Europe and the Levant, and between Muslim North Africa and the Levant, were strongly in favour of the Levant, and were consequently settled by sending enormous quantities of European silver and African gold.[2] The Near East itself had a generally unfavourable balance with the Middle and Far East, so that much African gold and European silver continued further into Asia.[3] Such circumstances were the very antithesis of the more balanced trading-conditions in which the bill of exchange evolved.

In addition, local banking developed at the same time as international banking. Within certain of the leading commercial cities money-changers extended their activities from manual money-changing to taking deposits, and then to transferring sums from one account to another on the instructions of the depositors. In Genoa, the most precocious centre for such local banking-activities, the notarial register of Guglielmo Cassinese (1190–2) indicates that local payments could be made not only by transfer between accounts within the same bank, but also by transfer between accounts in different banks in the city.[4] This was possible because the bankers maintained accounts in each others' banks. In this way interlocking banking-systems came into existence. The largest of these was that at Florence,

---

[1] Andrew M. Watson, 'Back to gold – and silver', *Economic History Review*, 2nd series xx (1967), 1–34; and R. S. Lopez, 'Back to Gold, 1252', *Economic History Review*, 2nd series, ix (1956), 219–40.

[2] As a consequence of the chronic imbalance between the Maghreb and the Levant, all payments from one to the other were made in coin, although a number of banking-instruments had already evolved within the central countries of the Muslim world. The *suftadja* there was the equivalent of the European bill of exchange, and the ṣakk of the cheque. Although the *suftadja* and ṣakk evolved some two centuries before their western counterparts, there is no convincing evidence that they had any direct influence on European developments, apart from the possible derivation of the word 'cheque' from ṣakk. Indirect influence is probable, but too nebulous to pin down, for considerable numbers of eleventh- and twelfth-century Italian merchants must have become aware of the banking-instruments used, between themselves, by the Muslim merchants with whom they traded in the cities of the eastern Mediterranean (Eliyahu Ashtor, 'Banking instruments between the Muslim East and the Christian West', *Journal of European Economic History*, 1 (1972), 553–73).

[3] Eliyahu Ashtor, *Les Métaux précieux et la balance des payements du Proche-Orient à la Basse Époque* (Paris, 1971).

[4] Raymond de Roover, 'New interpretations of the history of banking', *Journal of World History*, II (1954), 38–76, repr. in his *Business, Banking, and Economic Thought*, pp. 213–19.

where there were reputedly as many as eighty banks by the early fourteenth century.

By the fourteenth century it had become customary amongst merchants within a limited number of cities to make payments as far as possible by assignment on their bank accounts (*per ditta di banco*). Such assignment was initially normally made by oral instruction by the account-holder in person at the bank. In the course of the fourteenth century, written instructions, or cheques, supplemented and eventually supplanted oral instructions.[1] By 1321 it was apparent that some Venetian bankers were reluctant to pay out cash, instead of making transfers between accounts, for in that year the Great Council had to legislate that bankers were to be compelled to pay out cash within three days if asked to do so.[2] By allowing overdrafts and thus letting their cash reserves fall below, and often well below, the total of their deposits, such local deposit-bankers were not only facilitating payments, but also effectively increasing the money supply.

In Venice, to which so much unminted silver came in the course of the thirteenth century, it had become normal practice by the fourteenth century for merchants to be paid for the bullion that they brought to the city by crediting them with its value in a bank account. Its importers could then immediately pay for their purchases of spices and other merchandise by assignment in bank.[3]

As well as these current accounts, on which no interest was paid, these money-changer banks also ran deposit accounts on which interest accumulated. These were suitable for sums of money that were not required for several years, the dowries of orphan girls for example, and could therefore be invested by the banker in long-term enterprises. Some Venetian bankers invested directly in trading-voyages. A complete round trip, from Venice to the Levant, back to Venice, onwards to Flanders, and back to Venice again, took two years. To make an investment in such a voyage the banker had to be certain that his depositors would not call for their money suddenly.

Such transfer banking developed in other cities much more slowly than in Genoa. In Venice, for example, the earliest direct evidence of a money-changer

---

[1] Two Pisan cheques of 1374 are illustrated as doc. 155 in Federigo Melis, *Documenti per la storia economica* (Florence, 1972). See his sections on banking in that book, pp. 75–104 and 463–96, and also his *Note di storia della banca pisana nel Trecento*, Pubblicazioni della Società Storica Pisana 1 (Pisa, 1955). On the use of cheques in fourteenth- and fifteenth-century Florence see Marco Spallanzani, 'A note on Florentine banking in the Renaissance: orders of payment and cheques', *Journal of European Economic History*, VII (1978), 145–65. Similar written orders to pay came into use in Genoa and Barcelona, but Venetian banks continued to insist on the presence of the payer, or of an agent with a notarised power of attorney, to give oral instructions (Reinhold C. Mueller, 'The role of bank money in Venice 1300–1500', *Studi Veneziani*, new series, III (1979), 47–96).

[2] Reinhold C. Mueller, *The Procuratori di San Marco and the Venetian Money Market* (Ph.D., Johns Hopkins, 1969; printed Arno Press, New York, 1977), p. 188. Another habit, of which the bankers' account-holders complained in Barcelona and Genoa as well as Venice, was to send them to other banks to look for cash (Mueller, 'Bank money', p. 75).

[3] *Ibid.* pp. 61–7.

running bank accounts is as late as 1274, and then it is not clear if they were current or deposit accounts. Indirect evidence, however, suggests that such banking activities had by then already been going on for several years.[1] Outside Italy the earliest evidence is a little later still. The Privilege of Barcelona in 1284 implies that current-account banking, with credit transfer between accounts, already existed there at that date, and the register of the treasurer of Aragon for 1302–4 shows that it then also existed at Valencia and Lerida.[2] The evidence for money-changers acting as local bankers in Bruges also begins around 1300.[3] Later evidence suggests that they were also acting in this way in the course of the fourteenth century in Liège, Strasbourg and Constantinople.[4]

Bank accounts were quite clearly part of the money supply by the end of the long thirteenth century, and legislation was introduced to protect those who used them. In Venice a guarantee of 3000 lire was required in 1270 before a money-changer banker was allowed to set up in business.[5] In Barcelona, from 1300, book entries by credit transfer legally ranked equally with original deposits among the liabilities of bankers. Those who failed were forbidden ever to keep a bank again, and were to be detained on bread and water until all their account-holders were satisfied in full. In 1321 the legislation there was greatly increased in severity. Bankers who failed and did not settle up in full within a year were to be beheaded and their property sold for the satisfaction of their account-holders. This was actually enforced. Francesch Castello was beheaded in front of his bank in 1360.[6]

International banking and local banking soon came to be combined, where that was possible. Thus bills of exchange could be bought by debiting a bank account and their proceeds credited to a bank account.[7]

It can be argued that the money supply was also increased in the thirteenth century, again in a limited number of cities such as Genoa, Florence and Venice, by the creation of negotiable paper, such as shares in the *monte*, the public debts of the cities. In Venice for example, where forced loans had been exacted since 1164, the

---

[1] Mueller, *The Procuratori di San Marco*, pp. 163–4.

[2] A. P. Usher, *The Early History of Deposit Banking in Mediterranean Europe*, I (Cambridge, Mass., 1943), 239 and 256–7.

[3] Raymond de Roover, *Money, Banking and Credit in Medieval Bruges* (Cambridge, Mass., 1948), pp. 171ff.

[4] De Roover, *La Lettre de change*, pp. 24ff.

[5] In 1318 this was increased to 5000 lire to compensate for the decline of the lira (Mueller, 'Bank money', p. 73).

[6] Usher, *Deposit Banking*, pp. 239–42.

[7] Raymond de Roover has described how this was done in Bruges and Barcelona; Reinhold Mueller in Venice ('Bank money', pp. 57–9) and Jacques Heers in Genoa. Heers gives a late but vivid example of how important this combination of the two forms of banking became. Between 1456 and 1459 an account-book of the Piccamiglio records the receipt of payments from abroad by bills of exchange totalling 159,710 Genoese lire. Of these only 11,753 lire's-worth of bills were paid to them in cash. All the rest, over 92½% of them, were met by transfer in bank (*Gênes au XVe siècle*, abridged ed. (Paris, 1971), p. 90).

rights to their repayment became negotiable in 1262. In the meanwhile, the purchaser became entitled to the interest.[1]

It will be apparent that bank money and other additions to the money supply did not develop where the money supply was generally poor, but, on the contrary, in some of the places where the money supply was already most abundant. The silver mined in Europe largely ended up in Asia. Much of it passed on the way through wide areas of the European countryside and through the capital cities of the west, but a great deal of it concentrated in its passage through Europe in the great commercial cities. It was the middlemen of these cities who took the largest profits and added most to the value of the goods passing through their hands. In consequence, it was in their cities, and in certain areas of primary production, like wool-growing England, that the largest accumulations of silver were to be found. The middlemen of the Middle East did not seem to have the same success as their West European counterparts, particularly the Italians, in detaining a large proportion of this silver on its way to India or China. It was therefore only in a limited number of cities, mostly in North Italy, that the money supply built up to an adequate level for giro banking to develop. Once it did so, it increased the money supply still more and allowed further developments to take place.

Once certain levels of monetary activity had been reached, quantitative changes thus led on to qualitative changes in commercial methods, which themselves increased the money supply and the scale of business still further.

Among the natural consequences of this revolution in the use of money and the increased possibilities of productive investment was a radical change in attitudes towards lending. Coin and ingots, instead of being hoarded for safety, or only lent reluctantly at rates of interest that were very high, to compensate for the risks involved, were commonly mobilised for investment. A great dethesaurisation of previously hoarded precious metals added further to the supply of money and its velocity of circulation.[2] In Italian cities it is easy enough to find examples of investment rather than hoarding. When a moderately well-to-do Genoese nobleman, Guglielmo de Castro, died in 1240, his executors discovered that, apart from his house and domestic goods, all his assets, some 1100 Genoese lire and 440 bezants, had been invested by him and his wife over the previous six years in two dozen separately notarised *commenda* contracts.[3] A generation later, in 1268, the

---

[1] G. Luzzatto, 'Il debito pubblico nel sistema finanziario veneziano dei secoli XIII–XV', *Nuova Rivista Storico*, XIII (1929), repr. in *Studi di storia economica veneziana* (Padua, 1954), pp. 211–24.

[2] H. van Werveke, in his 'Le Mort-gage et son rôle économique en Flandre et en Lotharingie', *Revue Belge de Philologie et d'Histoire*, VIII (1929), 53–91, illustrates the way that ecclesiastical treasure was put into circulation, particularly in the late twelfth and early thirteenth centuries.

[3] Inventory printed in R. S. Lopez and I. W. Raymond, *Medieval Trade in the Mediterranean World* (New York, 1955), pp. 92–4.

executors of the extraordinarily rich Venetian doge, Ranieri Zeno, discovered that he had no less than 22,935 Venetian lire di piccioli invested in 132 *colleganza* contracts, compared with only 3388 lire in actual coin.[1] Less than 7% of his enormous wealth was liquid, whilst 46% was invested in the commercial enterprises of others.

The same phenomenon of wide investment is equally striking when seen from the other end, and on a much smaller scale. The executors of a Genoese businessman, Armano, who died in Bonifacio in Corsica in 1239, found that he had managed to persuade twenty-six men and women to finance his business by commending small investments to him, to a total of 1201 Genoese lire. He also had a partner who had put 400 lire into the business.[2] By the end of the century small investors, rather than putting their money directly into business ventures, were in some cities alternatively able to deposit it in greater safety in banks, which took the risk of the eventual commercial investments. By combining investments, some very small indeed, in this way, quite enormous sums could be mobilised. A striking, although rather late, example of this is provided by the Aiutamicristo bank of Pisa, which was able to lend 100,000 florins of its depositors' money to the Sancasciano company of Pisa, for purchasing cloth, between 1354 and 1371.[3] Large investors, on the other hand, continued to invest directly in business ventures.[4]

As commercial loans became an ordinary part of North Italian economic life, so North Italian canonists reworked the ecclesiastical doctrine of usury to make the payment of interest acceptable under certain circumstances. The old approach condemned loans at interest, with biblical and classical precedents, because in a largely non-commercial age such loans had primarily been consumption loans and trapped the borrower in a downward spiral of misery. A new approach was needed to cope with productive loans that enabled the borrower to expand the scope of his business. The key to the new approach was *lucrum cessans*, the profit the lender would have made himself if he had kept the money to trade with, but had in fact forgone in order to lend it to the borrower so that he could trade with it instead. The most significant of the early writers along these lines was the Lombard canonist Henry of Susa.[5] In 1271 he wrote: 'If some merchant, who is accustomed to pursue trade, and the commerce of the fairs, and there profit much, has . . . lent (me) money with which he would have done business, I remain obliged from this to his *interesse*.'[6]

---

[1] In addition he had 6500 lire in negotiable state bonds (G. Luzzatto, 'Il patrimonio privato di un Doge del secolo XIII', *Ateneo Veneto*, XLVII (1924), repr. in his *Storia economica veneziana*, pp. 81–7).

[2] Inventory printed in Lopez and Raymond, *Medieval Trade*, pp. 95–8.

[3] Melis, *Banca pisana*, pp. 147–61.

[4] See above, p. 253.

[5] Better known as Hostiensis, since he became Cardinal Bishop of Ostia.

[6] Hostiensis, *Commentaria super libros decretalium*, v, 'De Usuris', as quoted by Barry Gordon, *Economic Analysis*

• As men felt freer to invest rather than hoard, commercial interest rates dropped, particularly in those places where the money supply was most plentiful, like the cities of northern Italy, to a level at which a great many undertakings could be profitably financed that would have been impossible at higher rates of interest.

In Genoa in 1200 bankers were making commercial loans at 20% per annum,[1] in Florence in 1211 at 22%,[2] and in Venice Pietro Ziani, doge from 1205 to 1229, lent at 20%.[3] Commercial interest rates were still at the same rate as personal loans. The loans on the security of land in central Italy in the third quarter of the twelfth century were also at 20% per annum.[4] A hundred years later things were very different. In the first half of the fourteenth century commercial loans in Genoa could sometimes be obtained for as little as 7%, although they were generally rather higher. In Florence the Peruzzi bank in the first quarter of the century was paying its depositors 8% and charging 2% more for loans.[5] In Pisa in the 1350s the Aiutamicristo bank was still lending to the Sancasciano company at this same average rate of 10%.[6] In Venice money was cheaper still. In the 1330s, the banker Francesco Cornairo was only paying his depositors 5% and 7%,[7] whilst loans were being made to shopkeepers and craftsmen at 8%.[8] Late-thirteenth- and early-fourteenth-century cities paid their own citizens for forced loans at even lower rates,[9] but had to pay the market rate when they wished to attract voluntary loans.[10] Princes, noblemen and other private individuals, all bad risks, still had to pay high rates, whether to loan sharks, or even to reputable bankers who sometimes extended their operations into these grey areas.[11] The differential between commercial and non-commercial loans is clearly illustrated in the cor-

before Adam Smith (London, 1975), p. 157. The standard work on the evolution of the doctrine of usury is J. T. Noonan, *The Scholastic Analysis of Usury* (Cambridge, Mass., 1957).

[1] Sidney Homer, *A History of Interest Rates* (Rutgers, New Brunswick, 1963), p. 91.

[2] De Roover, 'Accounting prior to Pacioli', pp. 116–17.

[3] As his father had done before him. Funds accumulated in the hands of pious foundations and lent to those engaged in the Levant trade had also paid 20% in the twelfth century (Frederic C. Lane, 'Investment and usury', *Explorations in Entrepreneurial History*, 2nd series, II (1964), repr. in *Venice and History: Collected Papers* (Baltimore, 1966), p. 63).

[4] Toubert, *Latium medievale*, p. 614.

[5] Homer, *Interest Rates*, p. 94.

[6] Melis, *Banca pisana*, pp. 147–61.

[7] Mueller, *The Procuratori di San Marco*, p. 175

[8] 8% was the standard rate for *colleganza* within the city in 1330, but rates were still dropping. They were down to 5% after 1340. Pious foundations had only been getting 5% on funds invested in the Levant trade since the previous century (Lane, 'Investment and usury', p. 60).

[9] Nominally 5% in Venice from 1262. Since this was well below the market rate, the shares in the public debt changed hands at well below par. Between 1285 and 1316 their price fluctuated between 60% and 78%, giving a return of 6½% to 8⅓% on the market price. When the rate of interest on bank deposits fell to 5% in the 1330s the shares rose to par (Luzzatto, 'Il debito pubblico nel sistema veneziano', in his *Storia economica veneziana*, pp. 213–14).

[10] The Venetian government, through the Ufficio del Frumento, offered 8% to 12% in the late thirteenth century, but this rate too dropped to 5% or under by the mid fourteenth century (Mueller, 'Bank money', p. 78).

[11] For the effect of loans to princes see above, p. 249.

respondence of the Vicente company in 1260. 'Money here', they wrote from Siena, 'is priced at five and six denari per lira between merchants, and for those who are not merchants at ten and twelve denari per lira.'[1] The dropping of commercial interest rates in the principal cities of Italy in the course of the thirteenth century from 20% per annum and upwards to 10% per annum and below is a very clear indication of the change in scale of the money supply.[2]

In the thirteenth century the return on money invested in land also fell significantly, although it was always lower than the return on loans. In Picardy, Fossier found that land purchase gave 9% to 12% in rent before 1200, but only a mean of 5% after 1260.

Another clear indicator of the change of scale of the money supply is provided by the share of it that passed through the coffers of the state. This is most clearly seen in the case of the Italian city states. For example, the chamberlains of the city of Florence in 1240 accounted for revenues received at the rate of 26,000 Florentine lire a year, whilst a century later in 1343, they received 942,000 lire.[3] Even allowing for the falling value of Florentine petty money, this represented an eleven-fold increase in the revenue of the Florentine state in terms of gold. Can one hazard that the means of payment available in Florence increased in the same proportion? For comparison, both public revenue, and the means of payment, in Great Britain, only increased seven-fold in the century of industrialisation from 1811 to 1913.

Numismatists, and historians who have concentrated on the physical form of the coinage, have hitherto made much of the return to using gold coin in the west. However, in my opinion, a much more radical change than the convenience of using gold coin rather than uncoined gold, as far as international trade was concerned, was the evolution of the bill of exchange for transactions between the major international banking-centres of Europe.

Historians who have emphasised the new multi-denominational nature of everyday currency, after the creation of the silver grosso, have not, hitherto, adequately linked this with the growing complexity of life within the great cities of the west. Just as the introduction of the bill of exchange was more significant than that of gold coinage for international trade, so, within some of these great cities, the evolution of transfer banking and the creation of bank money was a more significant change than the creation of a multi-denominational currency. The bill of

---

[1] 'Chè Sapi ch'é denari ci sono valuti, da uno merchatante ad altro, cinque d. e sei libra, e altri che ne siano merch[at]anti sono valuti diece d. e dodici in chorsa' (Siena to Provins, 5 July 1260) (C. Paoli and E. Piccolomini (eds.), *Lettere volgari del secolo XIII scritte da Senesi* (Bologna, 1871), p. 16). They regarded the commercial rate that they were quoting as abnormally high on account of the war with Florence.

[2] The decades when interest rates dropped have not yet, to my knowledge, been pinpointed. It is, however, noticeable that the dei Boni only paid 7% at Pistoia on money invested with them *fuori del corpo* as early as 1259 (Herlihy, *Pistoia*, p. 164).

[3] David Herlihy, 'Direct and indirect taxation in Tuscan urban finance *c.* 1200–1400', *Finances et Comptabilité Urbains du XIIIᵉ au XVIᵉ siècle*, Pro Civitate, Collection Histoire in 8°, VII (Brussels, 1964), 385–405.

exchange and the oral precursor of the cheque, rather than the florin or the grosso, were the really radical and important developments in the means of payment associated with the commercial revolution of the thirteenth century.

The increase in the supply of money may not have been directly a cause of that commercial revolution, but it was a necessary pre-condition for it. Without an adequate money supply available in the countryside, albeit seasonally, the landlords could not have taken advantage of the pressure that growing population was enabling them to put on their tenants and bring about the revolution in rents that they desired. Without such a revolution in rents the landlords could not have achieved an enhanced standard of living and obtained a variety of choice of purchases that had not been available before. The demand generated in the mining-areas may have initiated commercial and industrial expansion, but it was the strong and sustained demand from the rulers and landowners that acted as the stimulus to continuous commercial and industrial growth almost uninterruptedly for a century and a half. Without the concentrated force of that demand in capital cities, rather than scattered between rural castles throughout western Europe, merchants could not have operated on an adequate scale for the revolutionary division of labour in commerce to take place, with all its ancillary changes.

An example that elegantly ties together a number of these strands is provided by the accounts of the Trésor du Louvre. Philip IV of France, in need of money for his war with Aragon, was granted permission to tax the revenues of the French clergy by Pope Nicholas IV. In 1289 one of the largest international business houses in Florence, the company of Musciatto and Albizzo di Guido di Figline, commonly known as the 'Franzesi' on account of the amount of business they did for the King of France, were nominated as receivers of this tax, a tenth, in the Auvergne. The company sent out three men, led by Noffo Dei, their resident agent at the Champagne Fairs, to collect it. Having collected it in ready cash, they transported it by cart to the May Fair at Provins, where the coin was used for loans and the purchase of goods.[1] At one stroke coin was drawn out of rural Auvergne directly into the mainstream of international banking and trade.

From rural rent to courtly living, from banking and international trade to public revenue and military service, the long thirteenth century of the commercial revolution witnessed a series of fundamental transformations, each associated with a complete change in the scale of, and attitudes to, the use of money. The whole period from this commercial revolution to the industrial revolution of the eighteenth and nineteenth centuries possessed an economic unity, the basis of which was established by these radical transformations arising from the new uses of money in the long thirteenth century.

---

[1] Quoted by R. Davidsohn, *Storia di Firenze* (1896–1927; Italian trans. 1956–68), VI, 628–9.

PART III

The Late Middle Ages

12

The Victory of Gold

The first half of the fourteenth century saw the transformation of Europe from an area that primarily used silver for currency, to one that primarily used gold. Gold coinage had already been minted in western Europe from the mid thirteenth century, but its use had been largely limited to Mediterranean lands and the ultimate source of the gold lay outside Europe.[1] However, the last great sources of precious metal to be exploited on a large scale in the expansive 'long thirteenth century' were the Hungarian gold deposits around Kremnica (Kremnitz or Körmöczbánya) in Slovakia, which were opened up about 1320.[2] (See Map 26.)

The mining of gold in Hungary was not new in 1320, but the scale of operations changed radically at that point. Occasional direct references to gold-mining in Transylvania go back to the very beginning of the thirteenth century. The earliest reference to the transit of gold up the Danube through Vienna is slightly earlier still, in 1196, so that some mining must have taken place as early as this. Other Viennese documents suggest that a small but frequent quantity of gold passed through the city to Passau, Regensburg, and Swabia throughout the thirteenth century. By the end of the century Magyar gold was to be found in Bruges.

A certain amount of Magyar gold was also sent southwards in the thirteenth century. As early as 1217 the King of Hungary, Andrew II, when he was bargaining over the cost of hiring Venetian galleys for his part in the Fifth Crusade, also negotiated that Hungarian gold should be exempt from customs duties in Venice. In return he exempted from his own customs duties certain Venetian goods brought to Hungary in exchange for his gold. In the course of the thirteenth century Venetian merchants began to visit Hungary, as well as Hungarian merchants to visit Venice.[3]

In 1269 the Great Council decreed that gold sold in Venice had to be of a fixed fineness ($23\frac{1}{2}$ carats=97.9%), and had an official refinery for gold set up near the

---

[1] See above, pp. 176–83.
[2] Štefan Kazimír (ed.), *Kremnická mincovňa 1328–1978* (Kremnica, 1978).
[3] Balint Homan, 'La circolazione delle monete d'oro in Ungheria dal x al xiv secolo e la crisi europea dell'oro nel secolo xiv', *Rivista Italiana di Numismatica*, 2nd series, v (1922), 128–31.

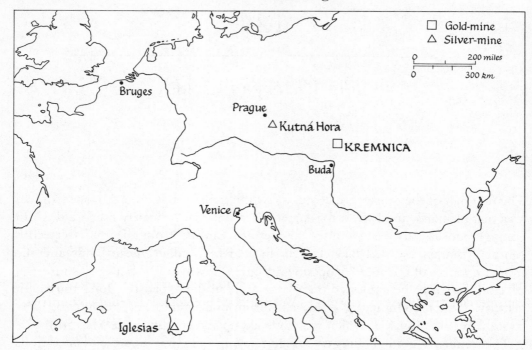

Map 26. Mining after *c.* 1325

Rialto. Most gold at this period still came from West Africa. It reached Venice through southern Italy and Sicily, Barbary and Byzantium, or even the Levant, but a small amount came across the Alps. In 1284 the official manufacture of bars from gold was replaced by that of ducats, and the mint records frequently refer to the supply of gold from 'Germania'.[1] By the early fourteenth century enough Hungarian gold was available in Italy, outside Venice, to be recognisable as Magyar in origin in Florence in 1315.[2]

Although the quantities of Hungarian gold available before 1320 were still insignificant in comparison with West African gold, by 1328 there was enough gold being produced at Kremnica for the King of Hungary, Charles Robert of Anjou, to commence the first successful minting of gold coins beyond the Alps there. They were pieces of almost the same weight and fineness as the Florentine florin and the Venetian ducat,[3] and the first issues even imitated the Florentine florin in type as well.

---

[1] F. C. Lane, 'Le vecchie monete di conto veneziane ed il ritorno all' oro', *Atti del' Istituto Veneto di Scienze, Lettere ed Arti,* CXVII (1959), 59.

[2] Homan, 'La circolazione delle monete d'oro in Ungheria', p. 131.

[3] *Ibid.* p. 120. New Florentine florins should have weighed 3.54 grams, Venetian ducats 3.56 grams and Hungarian florins 3.56 grams (69 were to be minted to the mark of Buda). In practice 87 Hungarian florins of Charles Robert and his son Louis the Great weighed by Homan averaged 3.55 grams. All were nominally of pure

At the same time enough Hungarian gold had already been exchanged for Bohemian silver for the King of Bohemia, John the Blind of Luxemburg, also to begin minting gold florins.[1] In 1327 the two kings and their treasurers had met together to discuss coinage. They agreed upon an identical florin–groschen system for both countries, drawing on Bohemian silver and Hungarian gold. As a consequence Charles Robert recruited moneyers in 1328 from Kutná Hora, the seat of the Bohemian mints and still the most important mining-town of Bohemia, to go to Kremnica, which the recently-discovered gold had already made the most important mining-town in the kingdom, to work in the new mint there. They were employed to mint silver groš as well as gold florins. The issue of silver groš began in 1329.[2] This Hungarian–Bohemian monetary alliance was renewed and extended to a general commercial treaty in 1335 in which the King of Poland also joined. Both agreements were aggressively directed against Habsburg Vienna, which had in the thirteenth century become the prosperous intermediary in both Hungarian–German and Bohemian–Italian trade, particularly the precious-metal trade, and had come to be resented by both Czechs and Magyars.[3] As a result of this commercial treaty, trade through Vienna was boycotted by both countries.[4] Hungary virtually ceased to trade with Germany and directed its trade and its gold towards Italy, whilst Bohemia virtually ceased to trade with Italy and directed its trade, and its silver, through Germany to the Low Countries.[5] Hungary's trade to the west in future was to be through Bohemia or Poland.[6] (See Map 27.) These discoveries of gold generated an enormously increased purchasing-power in Hungary and a greatly increased flow of commodities to the country, focussed on the fairs of Buda. Most of these commodities came across or around the Alps from Italy, rather than from Poland or Bohemia. There was consequently a reciprocal flow of gold to Venice. Doge Giovanni Soranzo, during whose reign (1312–28) the

gold. In practice the Florentine florin and the Venetian ducat were 99.7% fine and the Hungarian florin 98.9% fine ($23\frac{3}{4}$ carats).

[1] Although tiny deposits of gold were mined in Bohemia their production was too small to be of any significance. The Bohemian minting of florins therefore depended on imported gold, and they were only minted as a matter of prestige and had negligible economic importance (Josef Janáček, 'L'Argent tchèque et la Méditerranée (xive et xve siècles)', in *Mélanges en l'honneur de Fernand Braudel*, 1 (Toulouse, 1973), 252).

[2] The new groš were modelled on the grossi or gigliati currently being minted in very large numbers on the other side of the Adriatic by the king's uncle, Robert, in Naples. For the wide use of Neapolitan gigliati, see below, pp. 284–5.

[3] Homan, 'La circolazione delle monete d'oro in Ungheria', pp. 123–5.

[4] Both Hungarian and Bohemian gold florins did nevertheless begin to circulate in Austria from the 1330s. At the same time gold-panning began hopefully in Alpine streams. This was followed by gold-mining in the Gastein and Rauris valleys of the High Tauern, which produced just enough gold for the Dukes of Austria and the Counts of Görz to strike their own florins (Bernhard Koch, 'Die Anfänge der Gold- und Groschenmünzen in der Österreichischen Alpenländern 1250–1350', *Numismatický Sborník*, xii (Prague, 1971–2), 245–53).

[5] See below, pp. 341–2.

[6] Even the routes were specified from Buda through Esztergom, Holič and Brno to Bohemia and from Buda, through Košice, and Zips, to Poland.

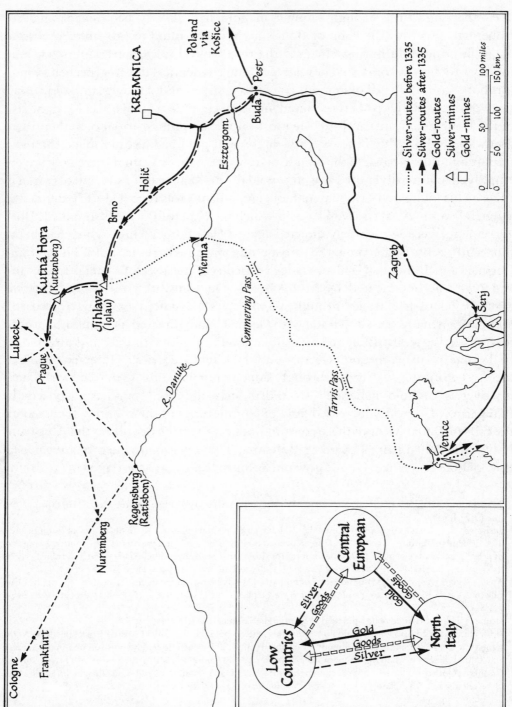

Map 27. Trade-routes from Hungary and Bohemia as altered by the 1335 treaty

great discoveries of gold took place, emphasised that Hungarian merchants had become accustomed to bring gold to Venice.[1] The enhanced prosperity of the 'German' merchants there is witnessed by the ease and splendour with which the *Fondaco dei Tedeschi* was rebuilt on a much grander scale after a disastrous fire. In return some of the major business houses of Florence opened branches in Buda for the sale of their goods.[2]

The price of gold in terms of silver had been rising in Italy ever since the introduction of the florin and the genovino in 1252. Suddenly gold was available in Italy in large enough quantities to meet the demand for it, and direct supplies of silver ceased at the same time. The price of gold, in terms of silver, began at last to fall, after rising for three quarters of a century. In Venice itself gold reached its highest value in terms of silver in 1328 and then began to fall, and had fallen quite considerably by 1335. In Genoa the highest point was reached in 1326–7, in Florence between 1326 and 1331, in Siena in 1329, and in Naples in 1326–7.[3] The mint reforms of 1328 mark the point at which Venice moved from a silver standard to a gold standard.[4] From then onwards the minting of gold ducats greatly exceeded in importance the minting of silver grossi. The quantity increased so much that in 1343 a commission advised the setting up of a duplicate mint organisation.[5]

It was obviously a great deal more convenient to carry very much smaller quantities of gold than much larger quantities of silver to obtain the same purchasing power. On the eve of the great influx of gold from Hungary, it needed just over fourteen times the weight of silver to have the same purchasing power as a given weight of gold in Venice. Because silver has a much lower specific gravity,[6] this larger weight of silver took up no less than twenty-six times the volume of the equivalent value of gold. And that was in Venice, where gold was already much more available than in most parts of Europe. Elsewhere the weight and volume ratios between equal values of gold and silver were even higher at this time. As late as 1318, the papal collector for the diocese of Salzburg was complaining that he had

---

[1] Homan, 'La circolazione delle monete d'oro in Ungheria', p. 131.

[2] *Ibid.* p. 139.

[3] Lane, 'Le vecchie monete di conte veneziane', pp. 72–5, and see Graph II, p. 272.

[4] See below, pp. 283–4.

[5] Antonio Lombardo, *Le deliberazioni del consiglio del XL della repubblica di Venezia*, I, Monumenta Storici, new series, IX (Venice, 1957), docs. 173–7. Professor Lane has pointed out that this enlargement of the mint was a response to the quantity of gold waiting to be coined in December 1342. It could not, therefore, be related to the import of African gold through Egypt, as has been sometimes supposed, since trade with Egypt was banned by papal order at this date, and the appeal to the pope to lift the ban was not even formulated until after the arrival of news in October 1343 that the Venetians had been driven out of Tana (Azov). He therefore believes that the principal supplies of gold in 1342 and 1343 were those brought to Venice by 'German' merchants from Hungary (Frederic C. Lane, 'The Venetian galleys to Alexandria, 1344', *Beiträge zur Wirtschaftsgeschichte*, IV (1978), 431–40).

[6] The specific gravity of pure gold is 19.3, whilst that of pure silver is only 10.5.

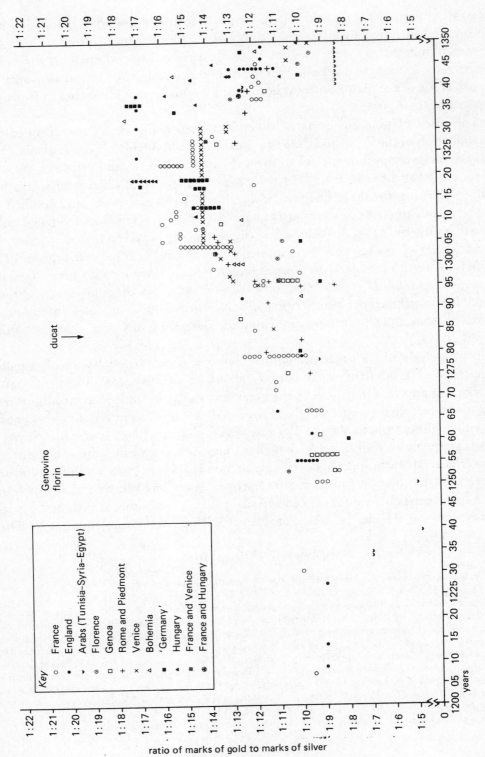

Graph II. Gold–silver ratios *c.* 1250 – *c.* 1350

to carry all that he had collected to Venice in bulky silver, before he could have it exchanged into gold.[1] Soon after the opening of the new mines in the 1320s, ingots of silver stopped being transported to Italy and being featured in Italian merchant notebooks or commercial correspondence. It was of course preferable to carry merchandise in both directions, and so make a double profit, rather than to carry either silver or gold on the southward journey only. In 1376, for example, two Florentines, Buonaccorso Pitti and Matteo Tinghi, went to Hungary, where there was, by then, a flourishing Florentine colony. Tinghi took a great quantity of saffron, which he bought for 1000 ducats in Venice and sold for 2000 in Buda. Pitti returned with Magyar horses, which he resold in Italy for a handsome profit.[2] Normally, however, there was a gross imbalance between the northwards and southwards trades in favour of the south, which had to be settled in precious metals. As a consequence of gold replacing silver on the road to Italy the quantities of gold available there expanded enormously from the 1320s onwards.[3] As early as the end of the next decade Giovanni Villani was able to boast that the mint of Florence was accustomed to strike no less than 350,000 gold florins every year, and sometimes 400,000.[4]

Gold came to replace silver for large-scale transactions within Hungary itself rather more slowly than on the road to Italy, perhaps because the Italians had already been in the habit of using gold coins for three generations or more, so that gold was just that much more readily acceptable. Gold coin was not a novelty there, and there were no conservative feelings to be overcome. In Hungary itself ingots of silver did not begin to fall out of use until the 1340s.[5] In Bohemia, apart from one stray reference in 1341, silver in bars ceases to be heard of after 1336.[6]

Because of the agreement between the kings of Hungary and Bohemia, gold did not travel along the other principal trade-route from central Europe, the so-called 'cloth road' across Germany to the Rhineland, Brabant, Flanders and ultimately England. This route remained under the domination of Bohemian silver.[7] It was therefore from quite a different direction that gold eventually reached north-western Europe in any appreciable quantity.[8]

The political and military activities of kings and princes were not the only causes

[1] Koch, 'Die Anfänge der Gold- und Groschenmünzen', p. 247.

[2] G. Brucker (ed.), *Two Memoirs of Renaissance Florence* (New York, 1967), pp. 25–7.

[3] For the large quantities available and the widespread use of florins in and around Florence from the 1320s to the 1370s, see C. M. de la Roncière, *Florence centre économique régional au XIVᵉ siècle*, II (Aix en Provence, 1976), pp. 505–47.

[4] *Cronica*, Book XI, chapter xciv.

[5] Homan, 'La circolazione delle monete d'oro in Ungheria', p. 122.

[6] Analysis of references to bar silver in *Regesta Diplomatica nec non Epistolaria Bohemiae et Moraviae* in L. Nemeškal, 'Die Veränderung des Präger Groschens und des Böhmischen Florens in der damaligen Währung in Böhmen', *Numismatický Sborník*, XII (1971–2), 128–9.

[7] See below, pp. 341–2.

[8] See below, pp. 277–80.

of dramatic short-term movements of coin. Wherever and whenever both gold and silver were in use as currency there was always the possibility that the ratios between the two metals would move sufficiently far apart in two countries to make it worth while to export silver from one country to the other in return for gold. The difference had to be sufficiently wide not only to pay for the costs of transport and usually also the costs of reminting, but also to provide a reasonable return, as against other commercial investments, on the considerable capital necessary to make such a speculation at all possible, and to overcome the very considerable risks involved in carrying precious metals over long distances. Every sensible merchant normally avoided moving gold or silver about from place to place, unless he could not help it, and tried to use bills of exchange wherever possible. There always, of course, had to be those who carried gold or silver wherever there was an imbalance of trade, or imperfectly developed exchange arrangements. Which metal they chose to carry was dictated by the relative values of the two metals at the ends of their journey. However, from time to time the relative values of the two metals were sufficiently far apart not only to dictate which metal was to be carried in ordinary commercial dealings, but to make the coinages themselves objects of commerce. It has already been suggested that this sort of bi-metallic flow may have existed between the Christian and the Muslim shores of the Mediterranean during the thirteenth century and the early fourteenth, and that this was how Mediter- ranean Europe came to be possessed of a sufficient stock of African gold to enable the return to gold coinage to take place.[1] With the extension of gold coinage to other parts of Europe the possibility of bi-metallic flows between countries was greatly extended. Such flows usually involved very large quantities of coin over very limited periods. The very fact of the flow outwards of one metal and the flow inwards of the other in itself tended to bring the market values of the two metals towards those in the other country involved. Any reasonably flexible government normally caused the mint price of the two metals to respond accordingly, and the bi-metallic flow then ceased as abruptly as it had begun, once the difference in ratios became sufficiently small for there not to be an adequate profit left, after meeting the costs of transport and reminting, to justify the risks involved.

In the case of France it has already been seen that St Louis had attempted, without much success, to initiate the coinage of gold; and that his successors, with varying degrees of success, strove to emulate him. France was, therefore, the only European country before the Hundred Years War that was likely to be involved in bi-metallic flows with Italy. Such flows do seem to have taken place from time to time particularly in the latter part of the reign of Philip IV. The net effect of many of his changes in the coinage was to raise the value of gold in terms of silver even higher than in Italy. As a consequence, silver flowed out of France and gold,

---

[1] See above, pp. 175–8.

particularly Florentine florins, flowed in from Italy.[1] When the price of gold in Italy began to drop in the late 1320s, as a result of the influx of Hungarian gold, it again became worthwhile to export gold from Italy to France, where the price remained high, and to import silver in exchange. This time the whole of France seems to have been involved. All the mints throughout France were closed from October 1329 to September 1330 and again from March 1334 to February 1336 from sheer lack of silver. At the same time Italian, or rather Hungarian, gold came to large areas of central and, more particularly, northern France, in which gold coin had hardly been known before outside the capital. It was the foreign gold that had accumulated in this way over the previous decade that Philip VI was able to draw on in 1337 when he began his enormous issues of écus. Philip VI was financed in the opening phases of the Hundred Years War by his own subjects and not by Italian backers, and by this stage his own subjects could provide him with resources in gold. It was thus that his subsidies to his allies in the Low Countries could be paid in his own gold écus. The accounts for all the eleven royal mints in France survive only for the five months from December 1338 to May 1339 and just for that one short period it is possible to catch a glimpse of the relative importance of the different mints of France. It is, of course, impossible to tell how typical these accounts are, but when plotted on a map the minting-pattern that can be made from them is very suggestive. (See Map 28.) Even now there were large areas of France in which gold coin was relatively scarce, as well as those in which its use was a novelty. Although a few florins had already been struck then in the 1320s, the minting of gold only really began in the principalities of the Rhône valley in the 1340s.[2] This coincided with the lavish spending of gold by Clement VI, pope from 1342 to 1352, who not only used up his considerable annual income, but also dispersed the large treasure accumulated by his austere and pacific predecessor Benedict XII, and even ended up in debt. Large parts of France must therefore be included among the areas to which the use of gold coin spread for the first time in the 1330s and 1340s.

A certain, limited amount of gold coin, primarily Florentine florins, had begun to reach the Low Countries in very small numbers from the very end of the thirteenth century onwards in the course of trade with Italy,[3] and small quantities

[1] See above, pp. 182–3. The exile of the popes in Avignon also brought very considerable quantities of gold from Italy to the Rhône valley, although, until 1334, most of it was sent back to Italy to pay the papal armies there.

[2] In the 1340s and 1350s florins were struck in the Rhône valley by the Counts of Provence, the Archbishops of Arles, the popes themselves, the Princes of Orange, the Lords of Montelimar, the Counts of Valence, the Dauphins of Vienne, and the Counts of Savoy at Pont d'Ain (Jean-Baptiste Giard, 'Le Florin d'or au Baptiste et ses imitations en France au xive siècle', *Bibliothèque de l'Ecole des Chartes*, cxxv (1967), 94–141). Further north, the Archbishops of Besançon acquired the right to mint gold at this time, although they did not use it (Maurice Rey, 'La Monnaie estevenante des origines à la fin du xive siècle', *Mémoires de la Société d'Émulation du Doubs*, new series (1958), 35–66).

[3] Peter Berghaus, 'Umlauf und Nachprägung des Florentiner Guldens nördlich der Alpen', in *Congresso Internazionale di Numismatica*, vol. ii: 'Atti' (Rome, 1965), pp. 595–604.

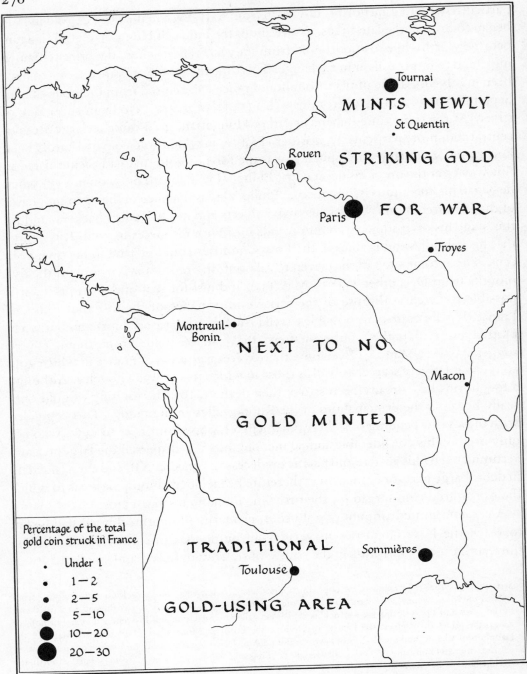

MINTS NEWLY

STRIKING GOLD

FOR WAR

NEXT TO NO

GOLD MINTED

TRADITIONAL

GOLD-USING AREA

Tournai

St Quentin

Rouen

Paris

Troyes

Montreuil-
Bonin

Macon

Toulouse

Sommières

Percentage of the total
gold coin struck in France

·   Under 1

·   1 — 2

•   2 — 5

●   5 — 10

⬤   10 — 20

⬤   20 — 30

Map 28. Minting of gold in France 1338–1339

of uncoined gold from Poland, Bohemia and Hungary were available in Bruges from about the same period.[1]

In England a certain number of foreign gold coins had been available in the thirteenth century, but these had been treated more as a commodity than as a part of the currency, and had been used for such strictly uncommercial purposes as prestigious alms-giving by kings and other great men.[2] In 1307 the papal collectors were still unable to turn the money that they had collected in England into gold for transmission to the curia and had to carry £4000 in sterling as far as Paris before they could exchange it for florins.[3] However the amount of gold in England began to increase over the next few decades. Since a higher value was set on gold in England than on the continent,[4] it made sense for Italian merchants to import florins into England. An inquiry in 1314 revealed that the king's Genoese banker, Antonio Pessagne, had passed on 50,000 Florentine florins in England, and ten years later the leading Florentine business houses, the Bardi and the Peruzzi, had florins available at their London branches with which to repay deposits of £2000 sterling left with them by the younger Despenser.[5] Successive kings quite deliberately wished to prevent this gold becoming part of the internal currency of England. In 1331 Edward III insisted that no gold money should be received in payment in his kingdom and set up official exchange tables at Dover and other ports to prevent any more coming into the country. Over the following five years sterling was actually given in exchange at these tables for Florentine florins and French gold royals.[6] In England royal action combined with the public's perception of foreign gold coins as not having quite the full attributes of money. In 1336 the monks of Canterbury Cathedral priory still regarded 440 florins that they had stored away, not as the direct means of making a payment, but as a valuable commodity against which they could raise a loan of £60, with which to make a payment.[7]

It was not until the late 1330s that any considerable quantity of gold entered north-western Europe, and then for political rather than commercial reasons. Both Edward III of England and Philip VI set about purchasing allies in 1336 in preparation for war. In the following year they spent even more heavily on buying 'friends'. To do so, Edward borrowed over 1½ million florins from Florentine bankers, particularly the Bardi and Peruzzi, and much of this was conveyed in gold from Florence to the royal paymaster at Valenciennes. The most expensive ally, the

[1] See above, p. 139 n. 5.

[2] See above, pp. 183–4.

[3] W. E. Lunt, *Papal Revenues in the Middle Ages* (2 vols., New York, 1934), I, p. 251.

[4] See Graph II above, p. 272.

[5] Michael Prestwich, 'Early fourteenth century exchange rates', *Economic History Review*, 2nd series, XXXII (1979), 476.

[6] Mavis Mate, 'The role of gold coinage in the English economy 1338–1400', *Numismatic Chronicle*, 7th series, XVIII (1978), 126–41.

[7] Prestwich, 'Exchange rates', p. 477.

Duke of Brabant, was promised in the region of 360,000 florins. The Emperor, Lewis IV, of Bavaria, was promised 300,000 florins, to serve with Edward with 2000 men for 2 months. Other subsidised allies included Edward III's father-in-law, the Count of Hainault and Holland; his brother-in-law, the Count of Guelders; the Margrave of Juliers; the Count Palatine; and the Counts of Berg and Loos.[1] Philip VI was no less active in the same area, and subsidised the Count of Flanders, the Bishop of Liège and the Count of Luxemburg, John the Blind, who was also King of Bohemia. He sent his subsidies largely in the form of gold écus, which he began to mint in large quantities from 1337. Both Edward and Philip had to go on paying out subsidies, as far as they could, to keep their allies, when the hostilities proved much more protracted than could have been expected. Much of this was in gold, and continued to be drawn northwards from the Mediterranean area, quite contrary to the normal balance of payments. For example, in the first four months of 1348 the pope, Clement VI, sent 450,000 florins towards Philip VI's continued war expenditure.[2]

As a consequence of these vast payments of political subventions, north-western Europe came to use gold coins rather than silver ingots for large payments. In the Low Countries the mint of Flanders, which had already struck a very small number of gold royals the previous year, began minting considerable numbers of gold coins for the first time in 1336.[3] The mints of Brabant, Hainault, Cambrai and Guelders all began to mint gold for the first time in 1336 and 1337. In type these followed either the Florentine florin or the French écu, the two coins in which the English and French subsidies entered the area. (See Map 29.)[4] The politically inspired deluge of gold florins and écus brought the quantity of coined gold in the area over the threshold that made it usable as money rather than as a precious commodity. This triggered off the minting, or reminting, of the gold coin and dust that had been gradually accumulating in the area since the thirteenth century. As a corollary the system whereby the cities of Flanders had ingots of silver cast and marked with a guarantee of fineness ceased to be heard of after the middle of the century.[5]

[1] May McKisack, *The Fourteenth Century* (Oxford, 1959), pp. 119–22, and E. B. Fryde, 'Financial resources of Edward III in the Netherlands, 1337–40', *Revue Belge de Philologie et d'Histoire*, XLV (1967), 1142–216.

[2] J. B. Henneman, *Royal Taxation in Fourteenth Century France* (Princeton U.P., 1971), p. 233. This was only a part of the contribution made by Clement VI and his brother Guillaume Roger, Count of Beaufort, to Philip VI's war finances. Their contribution amounted in all to some 3,517,000 florins, but most of this was made up of papal taxation of the French clergy, which was diverted to royal use, and so consisted of money that was already in France, and did not involve mammoth international movements of gold coin.

[3] H. Enno van Gelder, 'De munten van Vlaanderen onder Lodewijk van Nevers en Lodewijk van Mole', *Jaarboek voor Munt- en Penningkunde*, XXXIII–XXXIV (1946–7), 122–31, and M. de Marchéville, 'La Monnaie d'or de Louis de Crécy, comte de Flandres', *Congrès International de Numismatique 1900. Procès Verbaux et Mémoires* (Paris, 1900), pp. 301–15.

[4] The first wave of florin imitations followed directly after Edward III had sent such large numbers of Florentine florins into the area. A second wave of florin imitations followed a decade later, when the florins sent, from 1345 onwards, by the pope, on Philip VI's behalf, reached the area.

[5] Georges Bigwood, *Le Régime juridique et économique du commerce de l'argent dans la Belgique du moyen âge*, I,

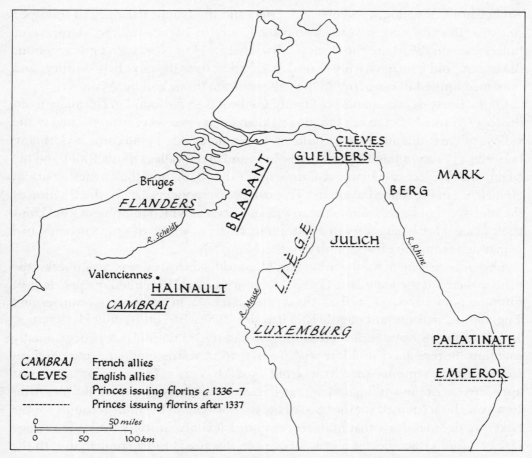

Map 29. Florin imitations in the Low Countries and the Rhineland *c.* 1336–1337

The use of gold up the Rhine and the Main followed soon after. The earliest hoards containing gold coins yet found in Germany were buried in the vicinity of Koblenz, at Limburg on the Lahn and at Vallendar shortly after 1338. These contained both Florentine florins and French écus, the former greatly outnumbering the latter.[1] Florins appeared for the first time in the city accounts of Aachen in 1338, and écus in Cologne in 1340.[2] Not surprisingly, in view of the enormous subsidy he had received from Edward III, Lewis of Bavaria was the first to commence the minting of gold coins in 1339. The four great Rhineland electors, the

Mémoires de l'Académie Royale de Belgique, Classe des Lettres et des Sciences Morales et Politiques, Collection in 8°, 2nd series, XIV (Brussels, 1920–1), 425. At Ghent the revenue from the municipal *barnecamer* dropped radically from 1337 to 1338 and stopped in 1343.

[1] P. Berghaus, 'Die Ausbreitung der Goldmünze und des Groschens in Deutschen Ländern zu Beginn des 14. Jahrhunderts', *Numismatický Sborník*, XII (Prague, 1971–2), 213 and 223–5.

[2] *Ibid.* p. 214.

Archbishops of Cologne, Mainz and Trier, and the Count Palatine, all followed suit over the next fifteen years, as did the Count of Cleves and the Margrave of Juliers and, on the Main, the Bishop of Bamberg.[1] However, with one exception, the use of gold coinage hardly spread any further over the next half-century, and remained limited in Germany to the valleys of the Rhine and the Main.

Of the thirty-seven hoards containing gold coins so far found in Germany from the forty years *c*. 1338 to *c*. 1378, no less than thirty-two were concentrated in the valleys of the Rhine and Main. Of the sixteen mints striking gold coins in Germany between 1339 and 1386, fifteen were to be found in the valleys of the Rhine and the Main, the farthest east being at Bamberg on the Main, and the farthest south at Heidelberg in the Rhine Palatinate. This close correspondence in the distribution of the find-spots of hoards and of the towns and cities in which minting of gold coins took place, clearly suggests to what a limited area the use of gold currency had penetrated from the Low Countries. (See Map 30.)

The only German mint striking gold outside this area was at Lübeck, the principal city of the Hanseatic League, to which Lewis IV granted the privilege of minting gold coins, as well as silver, in 1340.[2] As in the Low Countries and England, a small amount of gold coin had already reached the leading Hanse cities. Bonds and wills of Lübeck merchants who had traded with Flanders occasionally mention 'floreni aurei de Florencia' from 1316 onwards, and similar references survive from Hamburg merchants from 1308.[3] In 1341 a Tuscan mintmaster was appointed to the new mint, and in 1342 he began to issue gold Lübeck florins. After two years he accounted for the issue of 68,509 florins, and the mint accounts for the next two decades show that minting continued at approximately the same average rate of some 35,000 florins a year.[4] For scale this needs to be compared with the issue of some 100,000 florins during each of the first 2 years that gold was minted by the Flemish mint at Ghent in 1336–8, also, incidentally, under an Italian mintmaster.[5] It should also be compared with Villani's boast that 350,000 gold florins or more were struck each year in the mint of Florence at the same period. The quantity of Lübeck florins issued was thus about a third of that struck at Ghent and a tenth of that minted in Florence. This does not seem to be very far from reflecting the relative size and commercial importance of these three cities.

The gold for minting does not seem to have reached Lübeck by political means, but to have been deliberately acquired by purchase in Flanders at Bruges. A

[1] *Ibid*. p. 216.
[2] Wilhelm Jesse (ed.), *Quellenbuch zur Münz- und Geldgeschichte des Mittelalters* (Halle, 1924), doc. 213, p. 89.
[3] G. Hatz in discussion at conference on E. Nohejlova-Pratova (ed.), 'Les Commencements de la grosse monnaie et de la monnaie d'or en Europe Centrale (1250–1350)', *Numismatický Sborník*, XII (Prague, 1971–2), 243.
[4] Berghaus, 'Umlauf und Nachprägung des Florentiner Guldens', II, 601.
[5] Mint account published by Victor Gaillard, *Recherches sur les monnaies des Comtes de Flandre . . . jusqu'à l'avènement de la maison de Bourgogne*, 2nd ed. (Ghent, 1857), doc. 19, pp. 46–50.

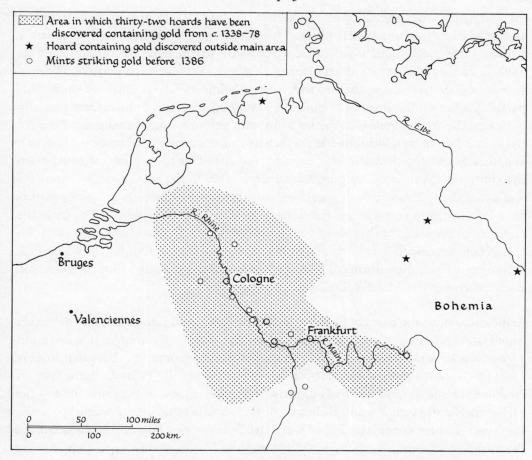

	Area in which thirty-two hoards have been discovered containing gold from *c.* 1338–78
★	Hoard containing gold discovered outside main area
○	Mints striking gold before 1386

Map 30. Circulation of gold in 'Germany' *c.* 1338 – *c.* 1378

memorandum of about 1350 survives, which shows that some difficulty was experienced in obtaining gold, since the sellers were reluctant to part with it, except at very high rates, in return for the proffered silver coins, some of which had been brought specially from Lübeck for the purpose, and the rest received in Bruges from the sale of Hanseatic products, such as beer.[1]

Some of the increased quantities of gold available in the Low Countries in 1336 and 1337 were attracted to England by the higher value set on gold there than on the continent.[2] Under such circumstances it was natural for English wool to be paid for in gold. However, the import of gold and the considerable concurrent export of silver, for Edward's war expenditure, brought down the value of gold abruptly in 1338. Nevertheless, the accumulated stock of gold in England, and the example of

[1] Printed by Jesse, *Quellenbuch*, doc. 215, pp. 89–90.
[2] See Graph II, above, p. 272.

his near neighbours on the continent, induced Edward III also to engage Florentines as mintmasters to strike gold for him. The first attempt, early in 1344, was to strike a florin-sized piece, which was called a 'leopard', together with its double and its half. Since they were overvalued in terms of silver, they drew over 200,000 florins' worth of gold to the mint before they ceased being struck six months later. This partially reflected the amount of gold already accumulated in England and partially indicated the attractiveness of the London mint price to continental gold. Edward III replaced them by a 'double-écu', which he called a 'noble', together with its half and quarter. After a slow start these too proved attractive to continental gold, when the continental valuation on gold sank even further in the late 1340s. In the 1350s and 1360s they were struck in enormous numbers as the ransoms and other profits of a successful war were remitted back to England in gold, along with the continuous proceeds of the sale of English wool. In 1361, when the ransom of John II was being received, over 600,000 nobles were minted, each of which was worth well over 2 Florentine florins. The noble remained the standard English gold coin until the end of the Middle Ages.

In the more outlying parts of Europe the transition to gold came later, in some cases much later. Although David II attempted to have gold coins minted in Scotland in 1357, they were not a success, and it was not until two generations later that Robert III (1390–1406) was able to establish a gold coinage.[1] In Poland, there was an ephemeral issue of gold florins at Cracow in the late 1320s, at the same time as the earliest issues of Hungary and Bohemia. It was so small that only a single specimen survives. Similar ephemeral issues were struck in several Silesian duchies around the middle of the century. However, although gold florins continued to be carried into the country from Hungary, in exchange for Polish salt, gold for long continued to be regarded primarily as a commodity in Poland, and the real beginning of gold coinage there did not take place until 1528, almost exactly two centuries later.[2]

In those areas of northern Europe to which the use of gold coin did not spread in the 1330s and 1340s the traditional use of ingots of silver for large payments naturally survived much later. Indeed Luschin von Ebengreuth considered that the use of such 'getekneten Usualmarken' in northern Germany was at its most extensive in the second half of the fourteenth century.[3] Despite the issues of gold florins in Lübeck in the 1340s it was not until the 1420s and 1430s that the circulation

[1] I. H. Stewart, *The Scottish Coinage*, 2nd ed. (London, 1955), pp. 26, 37–8.

[2] R. Kiersnowski, 'Florins et gros cracoviens au 14ᵉ siècle', *Numismatický Sborník*, XII (Prague, 1971–2), 196–7, and 'Złoto na rynku polskim w xii–xiv w' ('Gold on the Polish market in the thirteenth and fourteenth centuries'), *Wiadomości Numizmatyczne*, XVI (1972), 129–56, with English summary.

[3] A. Luschin von Ebengreuth, *Allgemeine Münzkunde und Geldgeschichte*, 2nd ed. (Munich, 1926; repr. 1969), p. 182, and see above, pp. 220–1, for the agreed common marking of ingots by members of the Saxon town league from 1382.

of silver marks generally gave way to rhinegulden in the Baltic.[1] An agreement between the Queen of Denmark and the Hanse cities in 1424 implied some slight circulation in Denmark as well as the Hanse cities of gold coins from England, France, the Rhineland and the Low Countries.[2]

Even if Scotland, Scandinavia, Poland and parts of northern Germany continued to use silver ingots for large purchases, they fell out of use in the second quarter of the fourteenth century over much larger, more densely populated and commercially advanced areas of Europe. They ceased to be used not only in Hungary, Bohemia and Austria, but also in France, the Low Countries, England and the Rhineland. Silver became what it was to remain for centuries, the metal for local transactions, the payments of wages, rents etc.[3] For these purposes it had to be coined, and it seems that a much larger proportion of the silver of Europe was in the form of coin after the middle of the fourteenth century than it had been earlier. After the middle of the century silver was not used for large, political payments and consequently silver coins were no longer imitated over wide areas in the same way that they had been earlier.[4] That fate was now reserved for gold, which was to remain the prime metal for international transactions, whether commercial or political, and indeed for all considerable payments, for the purchase of land, for example. Uncoined silver, of course, did remain available in large quantities in the hands of the well-to-do, but no longer in the form of ingots; rather in the form of plate, which had a domestic use as well as being a store of wealth. Such domestic plate was rarely directly usable as a means of payment, but had normally first to be sent to a mint to be turned into coin. However, there is some evidence that silver drinking-cups, made to weigh precisely a mark, were sometimes used as a means of payment in early fifteenth-century Toulouse.[5]

A difficult situation very rapidly began to develop in Venice as a consequence of gold replacing silver in the 1320s and 1330s as the principal means of payment across the Alps, for Venice was already traditionally the leading exporter of silver from Europe to the Levant. The situation was not helped by the inflexibility of the Venetian Senate. It obdurately refused to alter the weight or fineness of either the gold ducat or the equally prestigious silver grosso. Even more surprisingly, it refused to change the relationship between them, which had only just been fixed, in 1328, on the eve of the great influx of gold and the diminution of silver supplies. As a consequence, the officially maintained ratio between gold and silver in Venice increasingly diverged from the realities of the market. Silver poured out of Venice

---

[1] Rolf Sprandel, *Das mittelalterliche Zahlungssystem nach Hansisch–Nordischen Quellen des 13.–15. Jahrhunderts* (Stuttgart, 1975), pp. 68–82.

[2] Jesse, *Quellenbuch*, doc. 313, pp. 182–3.

[3] See below, pp. 323–8.

[4] For imitations of deniers provinois see above p. 141, of deniers tournois, p. 147, of pennies sterling, pp. 161–2, of baudekins, p. 232, of gros tournois, pp. 231 and 233, and of gigliati see over p. 284.

[5] See below, p. 348.

to 'Romania' and the Levant, and in the 1340s gold even came in from the east by sea! By 1355 the Venetian mint had entirely ceased to strike grossi, and had struck very few for the previous twenty years. Venice had virtually passed from a silver standard to a gold standard, with its accounts expressed in 'lire', 'soldi' and 'denari di grossi a oro' in which the grosso was no longer the real coin, but the notional one twenty-fourth part of the real ducat.[1]

As late as 1343 and 1344, the Venetian convoys sent past Constantinople to Tana and Trebizond, and those sent to Cyprus, still carried enormous quantities of silver to cover the difference between the goods exported from Venice and the much greater quantities imported.[2] It soon, however, became impossible to send silver, and gold was sent instead.

A very clear example of the way that gold replaced silver in payments from Italy eastwards is provided by the financing of two wars in the Aegean – the so-called Crusade of the Aegean of 1344 and the Venetian–Genoese war of 1350–5, most of which was fought out in the Aegean. In the 1340s the principal coins expended were silver gigliati or carlini of Naples, the silver for which was largely drawn from the Sardinian mines. For some time the Neapolitan grosso or gigliato had rivalled the Venetian grosso or matapan as the principal trading coin of the eastern Mediterranean and, since the failure of the Venetian grosso in the 1330s, briefly supplanted it. It was, moreover, a very convenient coin for the payment of wages to sailors and troops. In the next decade, the 1350s, the principal coins expended were no longer silver, but the gold ducats of Venice, which were just becoming the principal trading money of the eastern Mediterranean.[3]

The dividing line between the era of silver and the era of gold in the Aegean obviously fell around 1350. The sudden accumulation of silver gigliati in the area in 1344 provoked the minting of imitative gigliati, not only by the crusaders, like the knight-hospitaller rulers of Rhodes or the Genoese after their capture of Chios, but also by the very Muslim enemies against whom the crusade was launched, the Turkish Emirs of Sarukhan, Mentesche and Aydin, at Magnesia, Miletus, and Theologos, the ancient Ephesus, who had obviously acquired a great deal of the silver brought out by the Christians. Less than a decade later, at the time of the

---

[1] Gino Luzzatto, 'L'oro e l'argento nella politica monetaria veneziana dei secoli XIII–XIV', *Rivista Storica Italiana* (1937), repr. in *Studi di storia economica veneziana* (Padua, 1954), p. 270. The Florentines similarly came to express their accounts in gold-based 'lire', 'soldi' and 'denari affiorino'. For fuller details of these accounting systems see Peter Spufford, *Handbook of Medieval Exchange* (Royal Historical Society, London, 1986), and see below, pp. 412–13.

[2] In 1343 three round ships carrying out silver were escorted by the war galleys of the Captain of the Gulf as far as the Dardanelles, and in 1344 four commercially operated galleys were specially commissioned to carry silver only to Constantinople and Cyprus. At the same time, Nicolo Zeno, the envoy sent to the Soldan of Egypt, to negotiate the re-opening of direct trade, was given instructions emphasising that the Venetians were ready to pay in silver (Lane, 'Venetian galleys to Alexandria').

[3] See below, p. 354.

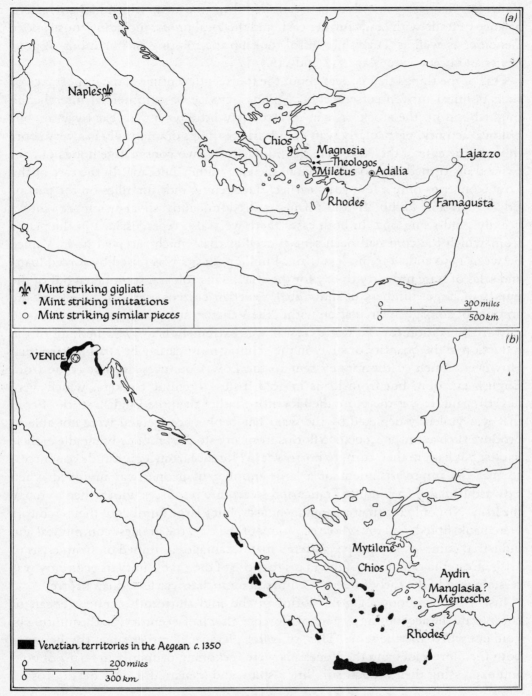

Map 31A. Gigliati and imitations in the 1340s
Map 31B. Aegean ducat imitations in the 1350s

Venetian–Genoese war, silver had vanished from the area, which had a negative balance of trade with lands further east, and the local mints, including those under Genoese, as well as Turkish, control took up the minting of imitations of gold Venetian ducats. (See Maps 31A and 31B.)

One of the things that is clear about the fourteenth century is the importance of such political movements of coin. Mining activity or commercial interchange might build up the stock of coin in a country little by little, year by year, but political activity, particularly war, could change things dramatically in a very short time. In the case of the Aegean in the mid-century two consecutive floods of coin twice transformed the stock of coin in the area within a decade. In the case of the Low Countries only a few years earlier, the opening bids for allies on the part of Edward III and Philip VI transformed a predominantly silver-using area into a heavily gold-using one. In both cases there were also repercussions in the places from which the coin had been sent as well as that which received it. In Venice between 1350 and 1355, no less than $2\frac{1}{4}$ million ducats was raised by forced loans and sales of state property to pay for the war.[1] This colossal sum, taken out of the purses of large numbers of individual Venetian citizens, seriously depleted the amount of coinage in circulation within the Venetian state. In England, from 1336 onwards, taxation for the war overseas was extremely heavy. Something of the reduction in the quantity of silver in the country must clearly be attributed to this. However, much of the money sent to the Low Countries did not come from English taxation, but from loans in gold from Florentine bankers, which were never repaid. It was therefore the Florentine rather than the English stock of coin that was violently depleted by the war. The bankers concerned were not able to produce such a sum as 1,600,000 florins from any stock of money lying idle in their vaults, but had, in their turn, to borrow it in Florence from a multitude of sources, so that the impoverishment of a large number of people was involved when Edward III failed to conquer France and so acquire resources with which to repay the loan. Not only the major banking-houses, but a large number of their creditors were bankrupted, and the whole economy of the city, the greatest commercial and industrial complex in Europe, suffered major damage. It limped on from crisis to crisis, from the calamities of the 1340s to those of the 1370s, until its economy was re-stabilised in the early fifteenth century at a much lower level than before.

Just as the minting of gold florins in the mid thirteenth century began to complicate the accounting system of Florence after half a century, so the minting of gold elsewhere did the same. This, of course, happened rather later. By the 1320s both the Florentines and the Venetians were reckoning primarily in terms of gold and expressing their accounts in 'lire', 'soldi' and 'denari affiorino' or 'di grossi a

[1] G. Luzzatto, *Il debito pubblico della republica di Venezia* (Milan, 1963), pp. 96ff, 125, 283 and 286.

oro'. In this way the lack of silver grossi in Venice from the 1330s, and fluctuations in the silver coinage in Florence in the middle of the century, made no difference to the scale of debts, or the real magnitude of payments, provided that they were originally expressed in money 'affiorino' or 'di grossi a oro', since the florin and the ducat both remained unchanged. It is no wonder that these two moneys of account were the most popular in fourteenth-century Florence and Venice.

Elsewhere in Europe reckoning in gold also followed the widespread use of gold coin. In much of southern France, for example, accounting from the mid-1340s to the mid-1360s was frequently carried out in florins and gros. The florin used as the basis for this system of accounting was not the Florentine florin, but the imitative florin of Dauphiné. The gros was reckoned as one twelfth part of these florins.[1] In the 1360s, this system of accounting partially gave way to reckoning in francs and gros. The franc was the franc à cheval struck by the kings of France from 1360 onward, and the gros was a notional, one-sixteenth, part of the franc. In parallel with these new gold-based systems of accounting, the older systems of reckoning, in livres, sous and deniers parisis and tournois, survived, based on the actual, poor, silver deniers tournois. However, a gold-based system became very attractive to particular groups in society, in a period when the silver currency was being debased. Some seigneurs, in upper Dauphiné for example, managed to preserve the value of their rents by insisting that they should be expressed in florins.[2] The initial transforming surge of gold-mining in Hungary took place in the 1320s and 1330s, but the production of gold continued throughout the next century and a half, often at much higher levels than those of the first two decades, important though those were. Some indication of the high points of gold-mining is provided by the fact that the largest numbers of gold florins were minted in Hungary under Louis the Great (1342–82), Sigismund (1387–1437), and Matthias Corvinus (1458–90). It is no wonder not only that the Hungarian ducat remained the favourite means of payment of all central Europe, but that in the last century and a half of the Middle Ages most countries of western Europe usually had an adequate stock of gold currency, however debased and however diminished their silver currency might be.

African gold, although now overshadowed by Hungarian gold, still continued to be transported across the Sahara. It seems that in the fourteenth century trade

---

[1] The florin and gros system of accounting began being used in Dauphiné around 1337; it spread to the Lyonnais by 1342, Franche Comté by 1344, Forez by 1345, Savoy by 1350, Toulouse and Burgundy by 1356, and was in Lorraine by 1360 and in Perigord by 1365. It stopped being used officially by the count's administration in Forez in 1360, but continued in use by private individuals in Toulouse to the 1390s and in Forez, in the Lyonnais, in Savoy and in Dauphiné itself well into the fifteenth century (Étienne Fournial, *Les Villes et l'économie d'échange en Forez aux XIIIe et XIVe siècles* (Paris, 1967), pp. 571–614; and Philippe Wolff, *Commerces et marchands de Toulouse (vers 1350–vers 1450)* (Paris, 1954), pp. 322–5).

[2] P. S. Lewis, *Later Medieval France* (London, 1968), p. 58.

switched back from the eastern to the western route across the Sahara, through Sidjilmasa to Morocco. In the latter part of the century Ibn Khaldun recognised its greater importance, and Ibn Battuta had travelled along it in 1352–3. Merchants of Tlemcen such as the al-Makkari brothers, were involved at this time in trading both with Walata, south of the Sahara, and with Europe.[1] This shift westwards of caravan routes may go back to the alliance made between the Merinid Sultan of Fez and Mansa Musa of Mali, before he died in 1332. It would explain why Spain was suddenly able to acquire gold again in a way that it had not been able to do for over a century, whilst Sicily and southern Italy, which had benefited from the greater use of the more easterly route to Tunis in the thirteenth century, had very little gold in the mid fourteenth century. The gold of *paiola*, gold dust carried across the Sahara in little leather bags, rather than Hungarian gold, therefore presumably lay behind the flourishing minting of Castilian doblas and Aragonese florins in the second half of the fourteenth century.[2] Merchants' notebooks suggest that trade between Spain and Italy was imbalanced in favour of the latter and that gold had to be transported from Spain to Italy. Aragonese florins were similarly transported into southern France. In this way gold from south of the Sahara joined Hungarian gold in Italy and France. The European and North African goods carried south across the Sahara, in exchange for gold, ivory and slave-girls, included improbably, amongst other things, a bronze ewer and jug bearing the badge of Richard II of England and the proverb:

> 'He that will not spare when he may,
> he shall not spend when he would'

It was still in an Ashanti war shrine in Kumasi in 1896.[3]

[1] E. W. Bovill, *The Golden Trade of the Moors*, 2nd ed. (Oxford, 1968), pp. 89–97, and see above, pp. 164–5.

[2] Castilian doblas, although struck in small quantities for a century (see above, p. 169), did not become common until the 1340s. Also in the 1340s Pedro IV, King of Aragon, began striking florins, once again in imitation of the florentine, at Perpignan, on the 'French' side of the Pyrenees. In the 1360s the striking of florins expanded enormously on both sides of the Pyrenees. On the French side they were minted in Béarn and by the Count of Poitiers, as lieutenant of the king, at Toulouse and Montpellier (Giard, 'Le Florin en France au XIVe siècle'), and on the Spanish side in Navarre, and in the various kingdoms of the crown of Aragon, at Zaragoza in Aragon itself, at Barcelona and Tortosa in Catalonia, in Valencia and eventually in the Balearic Islands, on Majorca (Octavio Gil Farres, *Historia de la moneda española*, 2nd ed. (Madrid, 1975), pp. 238, 273, 288 and 296). Meanwhile in Portugal, Pedro I, 1357–67, had begun the minting of gold dobras.

[3] Jack Goody, 'Economy and feudalism in Africa', *Economic History Review*, 2nd series, XXII (1969), 395.

13

The Scourge of Debasement

Much has been written on the problem of population in the fourteenth century, on changing marriage patterns, on the severe and killing famines, particularly those of the second and fifth decades, and on the continent-wide epidemics, particularly of bubonic plague, which recurred frequently from the fifth decade onwards. The questions have been discussed at length of how soon population began to decline in different parts of Europe, and of how soon that decline made enough of an impact on the gross overpopulation of Europe to produce any significant changes in the economic and social structure. Much has also been written on the extraordinarily widespread war and disorder of the century. There were civil wars in France, Castille, Naples and Prussia, inter-city wars by land, and by sea, between the states of northern Italy, the ravages of *routiers* and *condottieri* in times of nominal peace, the 'social' revolts of peasantry in England and France, or of artisans in the cities of the southern Netherlands and northern Italy, the dissolution of strong central government and the imposition of crushing tax burdens. All this happened against a background of deteriorating climate and progressive soil-exhaustion.

It would have been well if even one factor could have remained stable in such a period, but in many parts of Europe the currency too was remarkably unstable, and marked by violent debasements and equally violent attempts to return to 'strong' money. Debasement was, of course, generally a byproduct of war.

When a ruler engaged in debasement for the sake of profit he considerably reduced the metal content of new coins, by reducing the fineness of the metal from which they were made, or their weight, or both. This enabled him to make many more coins from every mark or pound of precious metal. He could therefore pay a higher mint price, per mark or pound, for precious metal brought to the mint, including of course the currency already in circulation. He thus made it seem profitable for all of his subjects who had precious metal or currency to bring it to the mint to be recoined. This sort of debasement for profit must be distinguished from the occasional minor downward adjustments in the weight of new coins dictated by the state of wear of the coinage already in circulation.

When a ruler returned to 'strong' money, he began to mint coins with a weight and fineness approximating to that before his debasements. In order to make the new money acceptable he proclaimed a disproportionate reduction in the face value of the debased coins in circulation. All those who had debased coin in their hands made an immediate loss, which they could slightly mitigate by taking the debased coin to the mints for recoining into better coin. The debased coin was usually totally demonetised after a period of time.

Both sudden debasements and sudden strengthening of coinages had markedly destabilising social effects. Sudden debasements impoverished those who lived on fixed incomes, in particular landowners with fixed money-rents. Since these included the most powerful men in society, they responded with vigorous political action. Sudden strengthenings of coinage were generally accompanied by wage and price regulations and by new taxes. The burden of the new taxes, the uneven application of wage and price regulations, and the sudden restoration in 'strong' coin of old levels of fixed payments, all afflicted the poor and weak in society. Without political muscle they could only respond by riot and disorderly violence.

One measure of the overall effects of these changes is provided by international exchange rates. Throughout the fourteenth and fifteenth centuries international banking was largely run by Tuscans, who thought in terms of Florentine florins. Consequently a fairly considerable number of exchange rates survive for all the major European currencies, and for many of the minor ones, against the Florentine florin. Throughout the fourteenth and fifteenth centuries the Florentine florin remained essentially the same in weight and fineness.[1] It is, therefore, an effective yardstick against which to measure the deviations in other currencies.

Table 4 gives a selection of exchange rates against the Florentine florin at fifty-year intervals. Such a table must be used with extreme caution. Even in times and places of monetary stability, when the exchange rates stayed approximately the same for decades on end, they were not entirely static. As now, there were normally minor changes from one day to the next according to the demand for different currencies. Map 32 shows the whole range of currencies for which quotations survive.

There were also more considerable, but still limited, seasonal changes geared to regular calendared patterns of trade, to an annual cycle of fairs, for example, or to the arrival or departure of galley fleets. In times of rapid monetary changes, the exchange rates for one year cannot be applied even to the next year. The effects of the debasements that financed Philip IV's wars against England and Flanders, or the debasements to pay for the first phase of the Hundred Years War, mean that the figures given for the value of Florentine florins in French tournois money in 1300

---

[1] When first struck in 1252 new florins were supposed to weigh 3.54 grams. In the course of the fourteenth and fifteenth centuries they never dropped lower than 3.33 grams. This was less than 6% below the original weight, and they were generally struck within 2% of it. In 1500 they were being issued at 3.53 grams (Mario Bernocchi, *Le monete della repubblica fiorentina*, vol. III: 'Documentazione' (Florence, 1976), p. 66).

Table 4. *Rates of exchange against Florentine florins 1252–1500*

	1252	1300	1350	1400	1450	1500
Tuscany						
Florence						
(gold florin in piccoli of Florence)	20s.	46s. 6d.	64s.	77s. 11d.	96s.	140s.
Lucca						
(gold florin in money of Lucca)	20s. veteri	38s. 6d. novi (1292)				
Pisa						
(gold florin in money of Pisa)	20s.	46s. 4d. (1299)	64s.	70s.	(Pisa under Florence)	
Siena						
(gold florin in money of Siena)	20s.	50s. (1302)	63s.	78s.	95s. (1451)	128s. 8d. (1499)
Italy outside Tuscany						
Sicily						
(gold florin in pierreali)		10 (1298)	$11\frac{1}{2}$ (1344)	12 (1403)	14	$25\frac{1}{3}$ (1506)
Naples						
(gold florin in gigliati or carlini)	12 (1280)	$13\frac{1}{2}$	12	10 (1404)	10	12 (1497)
Rome						
(gold florin in provisini of the Roman Senate)	20s.	34s.	47s.	73s. (1403)	98s. 8d. (1452)	130s.
Bologna						
(gold florin in money of Bologna)	24s. (1264)	40s. (1298)	32s.	36s. (1392)		
(gold bolognino in money of Bologna)				36s.	49s.	70s.
Venice						
(gold ducat in piccoli of Venice)	48s. (1284)	64s.	64s.	93s.	116s. (1452)	124s.
Verona/Tirol						
(gold ducat in grossi or kreuzer)		33 (1303)	36 (1356)	36 (1411)	49	80
Milan						
(gold florin in imperiali)	? 10s.	17s. 3d.	32s.	36s.	65s.	91s.
Genoa						
(gold genovini in money of Genoa)	8s.	17s. 2d. (1302)	25s.	25s.	43s.	64s. (1498)
Savoy						
(gold florin in viennois)	12s. 6d. (1275)	18s. (1298)	24s. (1349)	36s. 6d. (1384)		

Table 4. – *cont.*

	1252	1300	1350	1400	1450	1500
Outside Italy						
Iberia						
Barcelona						
(florin in money of Barcelona)	11s. (1276)	11s. (1310)	12s.	15s. 3d.	17s. 1d. (1447)	23s. (1480)
Aragon						
(Florentine florin in money of Jacca)	9s. (1280)	11s. 6d. (1320)	11s.			22s. (1479)
(Aragonese florin in money of Jacca)				10s. 4d.	10s. 9d.	16s.
Castille						
(florin in maravedis and dineros) (maravedi=10 dineros)		5m. 8d. (1291)	25m. (1358)	66m.	150m.	375m. (1497)
France						
Paris						
(florin in Tournois money) (£4 parisis=£5 tournois) (£1 tournois=£1 provinois of Champagne)	8s. (1265)	10s.	25s.	22s. (1398)	31s. 3d.	38s. 9d.
(florin in gros tournois)	9 (1274)	11½	12	14 (1390)		
England						
London						
(florin in sterling) (mark sterling=13s. 4d.)	2s. 6d. (1277)	3s. 1½d. (1301)	3s. ½d.	3s. (1405)	3s. 9½d.	4s. 7d.
Low Countries						
Flanders (Bruges)						
(florin in Flemish groten and miten) (1 groot=24 miten) (1 stuiver=2 groten)		13gr. 3m. (1317)	16gr. 20m. (1348)	33gr. 12m.	49gr. (1453)	80gr.
Empire						
Cologne						
(florin in money of Cologne) (Cologne mark=12s.)	2s. 6pf. (1277)	6s. 8pf. (1301)	22s. 5pf. (1349)	42s.	61s. (1454)	112s.
Lübeck						
(Florentine florin in money of Lübeck)	8s. (1288)	12s. (1317)	8s. (1345)		28s. (1460)	

Table 4. – *cont.*

	1252	1300	1350	1400	1450	1500
(Lübeck florin in money of Lübeck) (Lübeck mark=16s.)			8s. 6d.	15s. 6d. (1402)	32s. (1449)	32s. (1483)
Swabia/Nuremburg (florin in heller) (1 schilling=12 heller)	10s. (1265)	12s. (1308)	17s. 6h. (1351)	25s.	26s.	28s.
Bohemia (florin in Prague groschen) (1 schock=60 groschen)		12	13	20	31	30
Austria (florin in money of Vienna) (here 1 pfund or talent=8 schillings) (1 schilling=30 pfennigs)	60pf. (1262)	66⅔pf. (1298)	94pf. (1354)	150pf.	222pf.	330pf. (1498)

Unless otherwise specified all the accounting systems in this table used the relationships: 12 denari, deniers, pennies or pfennigs=1 soldo, sou, shilling or schilling and 20 soldi, sous, shillings or schillings=1 lira, livre, pound or pfund. When reading the table it should therefore be borne in mind that although most of the rates are quoted in soldi or shillings, they are based on denari or pennies, so that a value for the florin of 77s. 11d. could equally be expressed as 935 denari or as 3li. 17s. 11d. For further details of money of account in the later Middle Ages see Appendix II below, pp. 411–14.

Where no quotations are available for the exact year, a quotation is given for the nearest year and its date added in parentheses.

The values given here are drawn from the *Handbook of Medieval Exchange* (Royal Historical Society, London, 1986), compiled by the author with the support of the Economic and Social Research Council of Great Britain.

The table is arranged in the same geographical order as in the *Handbook*, starting with exchange in Florence itself; then the rest of Tuscany; then the rest of Italy, from south to north; then the rest of Europe working clockwise from Italy.

and 1350 cannot be taken as general indicators for exchange rates over several decades. When the debasements or strengthenings of a currency were very large, the exchange rates, as with modern devaluations, altered radically within weeks or even days. Some general indications of the variety of experience in different countries may, nevertheless, be gathered from the table. The experience of Castille, where the maravedi in 1500 only retained one sixty-fifth of its 1300 value, against the Florentine florin, was patently very different from the experience of its neighbour Aragon, where the money of Jacca was still worth over a half of its value

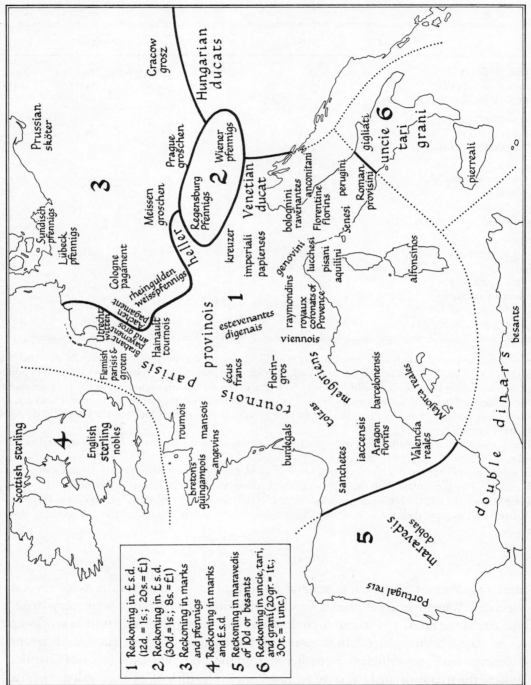

Map 32. Principal currencies of late medieval Europe

The map contains the following labels:

Region 3:
- Prussian sköter
- Sundisch pfennigs
- Lübeck pfennigs
- Meissen groschen
- Cologne pagament
- Cracow grosz
- Prague groschen

Region 2:
- Hungarian ducats
- Wiener pfennigs
- Regensburg Pfennigs
- heller
- kreuzer
- Venetian ducat

Region 1:
- rheingulden
- weisspfennigs
- Aachen pagament
- Utrecht
- Brabant payments & groten
- Hainault tournois
- Flemish parisis & groten
- provinois
- Parisis
- Tournois
- estevenantes digenais
- écus francs
- florin-gros
- roumois
- mansois
- angevins
- bretons
- guingampois
- burdegals
- viennois
- imperiali papienses
- genovini
- raymondins
- royaux coronats of Provence
- melgoriens
- tolzas
- sanchees
- iaccensis
- florin-gros
- bolognini
- ravennantes
- anconitani
- lucchesi
- pisani
- aquilini
- Florentine florins
- Senesi
- perugini
- Roman provisini
- gigliati
- alfonsinos
- Aragon florins
- Valencia reales
- Majorca reales
- Barcelonensis

Region 6:
- uncie
- tari
- grani
- pierreali

Region 5:
- maravedis
- doblas
- double dinars
- besants
- Portugal reis

Region 4:
- Scottish sterling
- English sterling nobles

Legend:
1. Reckoning in £.s.d. (12d. = 1s.; 20s. = £1)
2. Reckoning in £.s.d. (30d. = 1s.; 8s. = £1)
3. Reckoning in marks and pfennigs
4. Reckoning in marks and £.s.d.
5. Reckoning in maravedis of 10d. or besants
6. Reckoning in uncie, tari, and grani (20 gr. = 1t.; 30t. = 1 unc.)

Table 5. *Long-term changes in twelve major currencies 1300–1500*

	c. 1300	c. 1400		c. 1500		1300–1500
Castille	5m. 8d.	66m.	(× 11.4)	375m.	(× 5.7)	(× 65)
Cologne	6s. 8pf.	42s.	(× 6.3)	112s.	(× 2.7)	(× 16.8)
Flanders	13gr. 3m.fl.	33gr. 12m.fl.	(× 2.6)	80gr.fl.	(× 2.4)	(× 6.1)
Austria	66⅔pf.	150pf.	(× 2.3)	330pf.	(× 2.2)	(× 5)
France	10s. tourn.	22s. tourn.	(× 2.2)	38s. 9d. tourn.	(× 1.8)	(× 3.9)
Rome	34s. prov.	73s. prov.	(× 2.1)	130s. prov.	(× 1.8)	(× 3.8)
Florence	46s. 6d. pic.	77s. 11d. pic.	(× 1.7)	140s. pic.	(× 1.8)	(× 3)
Hanse	12s. lub.	15s. 6d. lub.	(× 1.3)	32s. lub.	(× 2.1)	(× 2.7)
Bohemia	12gr.	20gr.	(× 1.7)	30gr.	(× 1.5)	(× 2.5)
Venice	64s. pic.	93s. pic.	(× 1.5)	124s. pic.	(× 1.3)	(× 1.9)
Aragon	11s. 6d. jac.	15s. 1d. jac.*	(× 1.3)			(× 1.9)
(Aragonese fl.)		10s. 4d. jac.		16s. jac.	(× 1.5)	
England	3s. 1½d. sterl.	3s.	(× 1.0)	4s. 7d.	(× 1.5)	(× 1.5)

* Value calculated from other rates.

It will be realised that all the currencies involved in these tables were based on silver coins, and that exchange rates between these currencies and gold florins therefore incorporate the different relative values placed on gold and silver in each place at each date. However both Tables 4 and 5 and Graph III have, for simplicity, been constructed without taking changing gold:silver ratios into account. Gold:silver ratios were certainly not constant throughout Europe in the fourteenth and fifteenth centuries. Graph II, on p. 272, illustrates how some gold:silver ratios changed in the first half of the fourteenth century, and Table 7, on p. 354, indicates how the Venetian gold:silver ratio changed over the next 150 years. The overall effect of the changes in the ratios between the two metals is that Tables 4 and 5 slightly underestimate the degree of debasement in the fourteenth century and slightly overestimate it in the fifteenth century. The small extent of this underestimation and overestimation can be illustrated from the sterling currency of England. New English pennies struck in 1300 should have contained 1.44 grams of sterling silver, those struck in 1400 should have contained 1.17 grams, and those struck in 1500 0.78 grams. Therefore the actual decline in the silver content of the penny should have raised the exchange rate between sterling and the florin by a factor of 1.2 in the fourteenth century, by 1.5 in the fifteenth century, and by 1.8 over the two centuries combined. However, the decline of the value of gold in terms of silver in the fourteenth century meant that the exchange rate actually rose only by a factor of 1.1, whilst the increase in the value of gold in the fifteenth century made no significant difference to the exchange rate. Over the two centuries together, the exchange rate actually rose by 1.7.

for 200 years earlier. Table 5 shows the long-term change of a dozen currencies, in order from that of Castille, the least stable, to those of Aragon and England, the most stable. Where, as in France, the post-war strengthening of a currency attempted to counteract the wartime debasements, the cumulative effect is barely apparent in the table, but where, as in Castille, the post-war strengthening of the maravedi was negligible, the cumulative effect was enormous. Graph III is designed to show both the long-term trends and the short-term debasements and strengthenings of the twelve currencies.

The aristocratic reaction to debasement is best summed up by the *De Moneta* of Nicholas Oresme. This became the key treatise on the constitutional place of money in late medieval Europe. When Oresme wrote it in the middle of the fourteenth century, he was already one of the most famous nominalist writers in the University of Paris, and was, at the time, Master of the College of Navarre.

In this treatise Oresme began by citing the existing 'royal' theory that he was

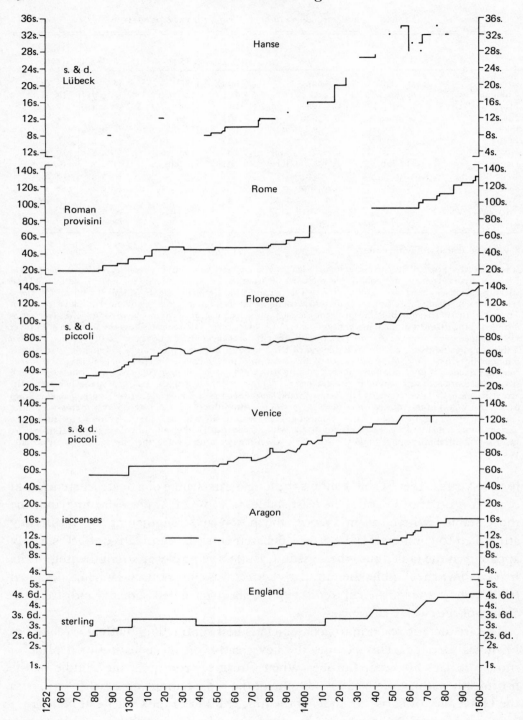

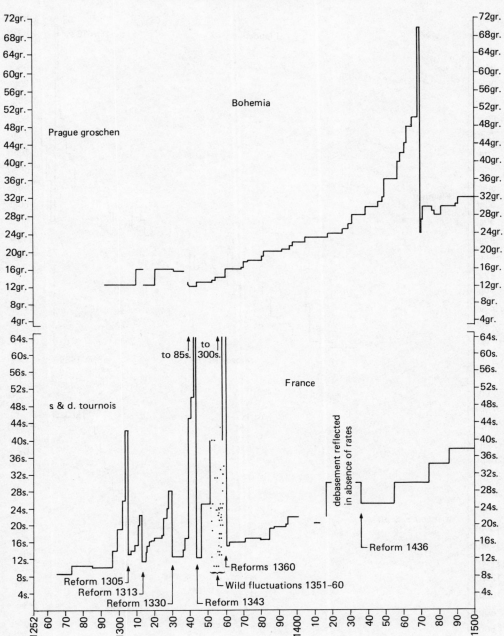

Graph III. Changes in the value of the florin and the ducat in twelve currencies 1252–1500.

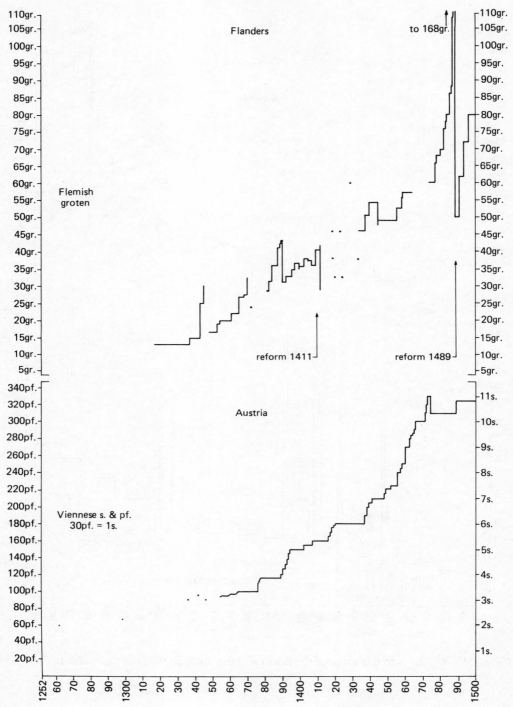

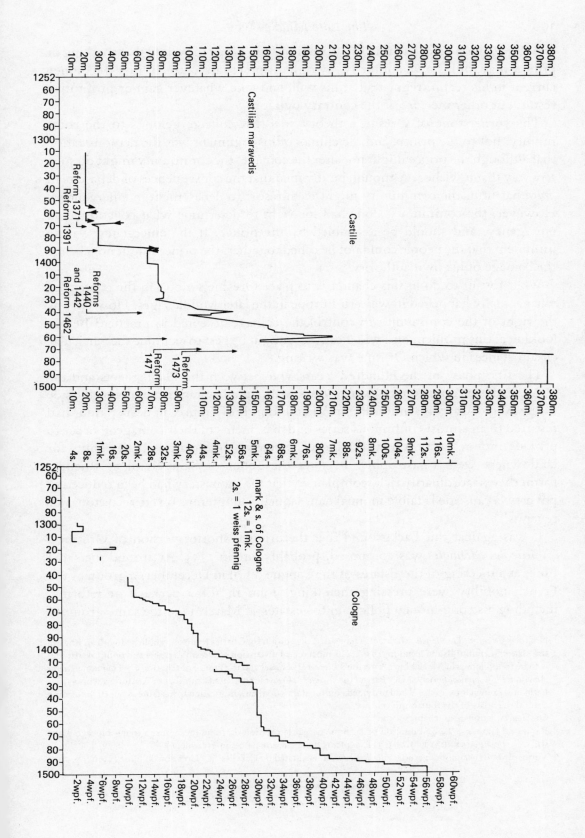

arguing against, before setting out to demolish it: 'Some men hold that any king or prince, may, of his own authority, by right or prerogative, freely alter the money current in his realm, regulate it at his will, and take whatever gain or profit may result: but other men are of the contrary opinion.'[1]

The cornerstone of Oresme's theory was that coinage belongs to the community, not to the prince; and the climax of his argument was the demonstration that although the prince might not alter the coinage, the community might do so in any way that it wished. Although he affirmed that the consequences of debasement were harmful, the community might even resort to debasement in emergencies. However, the community alone had the right to determine what constituted an emergency, and should be assembled by the prince. If the emergency was so imminent that the people could not be called together, the prince might not change the coinage of his own authority.[2]

What I want to do in this chapter is to place Oresme's views in the context of what actually happened in western Europe in the later Middle Ages. How far was the right of the community to control the coinage accepted in practice? Before looking at this problem on a wider canvas it might be best to examine the particular circumstances in which Oresme was writing.[3]

The first phase of the Hundred Years War between the Plantagenets and the Valois had been going on for twenty years, with the advantage generally on the side of the Anglo-Gascon armies. Philip VI and John II of France, in desperation, had resorted to an almost continuous series of debasements of their coinage in order to provide money to meet a succession of expensive emergencies. The results for landowners were catastrophic. In 1354 the abbot of Saint-Rémi at Rheims, formerly extraordinarily rich, complained that the monastery had been reduced to poverty 'à cause de la faible monnai dans laquelle, longtemps on été reçus tous nos revenus'.[4]

It was against this background that the original shorter version of Oresme's *Traictie des Monnoies* was composed, probably late in 1355. At around the same time, at a meeting of the Estates of the Langue d'Oil in December, a group of the French nobility were pressing their king, John II, for a package of reforms, including a strong money policy. In the estates of March 1357 the same group of

[1] Nicholas Oresme, *De Moneta*, chapter 1. I have used the edition by Charles Johnson, published with an English translation (Edinburgh and London, 1956). The most recent discussion of Oresme's career and political attitudes is to be found in Susan M. Babbitt, 'Oresme's *Livre de Politiques* and the France of Charles V', *Transactions of the American Philosophical Society*, LXXV Part 1 (1985), 1–158. Oresme translated a number of Aristotle's works from Latin into French for Charles V and provided commentaries on them, in addition to his fame as one of the leading natural scientists of the fourteenth century.

[2] *De Moneta, passim*, esp. chapter XXIV.

[3] Raymond Cazelles, 'La Stabilisation de la monnaie par la création du franc (décembre 1360) – blocage d'une société', *Traditio*, XXXII (1976), 293–311, explains these circumstances in great detail.

[4] Varin, *Archives administratives de la ville de Reims*, II, 664, cited by Cazelles, 'La Création du franc (1360)', p. 294.

'reformers', drawn from the upper clergy and the nobility, again demanded the same reforms from the Dauphin Charles, who was acting as regent whilst his father, John II, was a prisoner of war in England. The next meeting of the estates, in January 1358, was dominated by a quite different group of men, led by Etienne Marcel, who wanted a very different set of policies. After the regent left Paris, he was joined by the group of great landowners who had led the opposition to John II in 1355 and to himself in 1357. It was their voices that were dominant in the rival assembly called by the regent at Compiègne to support him in May 1358. It was probably about this time that Oresme produced the longer, definitive, Latin text of the treatise, the *De Moneta*. From 1358 this group of men, led by Guillaume de Melun, Archbishop of Sens, and Jean de Melun, Count of Tancarville, provided key counsellors of Charles as regent. After his father's death he became king, as Charles V, and they continued as his principal advisers right through to 1380. Their policies, including a strong money policy, became the policies of government. Oresme's treatise, originally written as a tract for the opposition, in its revised form became the new orthodoxy, and a standard text for government policy in France. As a spokesman of the government he had his reward and became Bishop of Lisieux.

On closer inspection Oresme turns out, therefore, not to be an idealistic, ivory-towered thinker, but a party man writing a tract for the times. Nevertheless his views became a new orthodoxy for the next two centuries and replaced an older orthodoxy that, since the twelfth century at least, had held that a prince, and particularly a king, had an exclusive right to do whatever he liked with the coinage without any interference. In the twelfth and early thirteenth century a sequence of bargains had been struck between princes and their subjects in France, the Low Countries and Spain. By these the princes, for specified periods, gave up their undoubted right to change the coinage at regular intervals and received, in return, grants of alternative taxes, hearth-taxes, or tallages on bread and wine, frequently called *monetagium*.[1] Such bargains could only be made on the assumption that the ruler could change the coinage at will. In the thirteenth century Innocent III and Thomas Aquinas both held that coinage belonged to the ruler, and indeed it was a view sanctified by Holy Scripture for had not Christ himself said of the Roman denarius that it was Caesar's?

However, at the beginning of the fourteenth century this view began to be questioned in practice.[2] In 1295 Philip IV of France, after a century of stable royal coinage, which in retrospect came to be called the good money of St Louis, began

---

[1] Thomas N. Bisson, *Conservation of Coinage, Monetary Exploitation and its Restraint in France, Catalonia and Aragon c. 1000–1225 AD* (Oxford, 1979), explored these bargains in great detail.

[2] This section summarises Peter Spufford, 'Assemblies of estates, taxation and control of coinage in medieval Europe', in *Studies Presented to the International Commission for the History of Representative and Parliamentary Institutions*, XXXI (Louvain–Paris, 1966), 115–30.

to debase the coinage radically to pay for his unsuccessful, but expensive, attempt to conquer Gascony from Edward I of England.

Debasement of the coinage, although not new in the 1290s, had not been practised for a very long time, largely because of the sequence of agreements to replace renewal of the coinage by alternative forms of taxation in the twelfth century. Certainly the scale on which Philip IV indulged in it was quite novel. Apart from the necessary downward modifications of the weight of new coinage circulation,[1] the thirteenth century was a century of remarkably stable coinages in most of western Europe. Outside Italy most of the older penny coinages were not much worse at the end of the thirteenth century than at the beginning, whilst the newer 'great' coinages, introduced in the course of the thirteenth century, were mostly still made of nearly as high a weight and fineness as when they were first minted. The ritual of frequent *renovatio monetae* was still practised in parts of eastern Europe, where the currency involved was much smaller. However, the nominal weight and token value of the ultra-thin bracteate pfennigs made them suitable only for internal transactions.[2] What really mattered were the currency bars used for large transactions and for long-distance trade, and these were not to be tampered with.

It is against this background of century-long stability, outside Italy, that Philip IV's debasements of the coinage must be seen. Unlike Edward I, he had no long tradition to draw on of direct taxation, voted by a national assembly, which could tap the wealth of his subjects for war purposes. For him direct taxation was a novelty that did not easily raise an adequate revenue. He fell back, therefore, on getting the most out of his regalian rights, and his rights of coinage proved by far the most profitable of these.

In 1295 Philip IV, under stress of war, embarked on a decade of debasements. Accounts for the year ending All Saints' Day 1296 show that he received 101,000 livres parisis from the mints, out of a total income of 550,974 livres parisis accounted for through the Trésor du Louvre. As the debasements became more dramatic, the profits became higher. In a period of just over eighteen months in 1298–9, the mints brought in 1,200,000 livres tournois, whilst the remainder of his income came to under 800,000 livres tournois.[3] Philip the Fair had worked his mint profits up to such a pitch that they formed the larger part of his income!

Philip IV's lawyers defended this action, quite clearly and explicitly: 'Abaisser la monnaie est privilege seul et special au roi, de son droit royal, et n'appartient a nul autre, mais a lui seul.' In the short run the profit was enormous and this is what was

---

[1] See below, pp. 316–18.
[2] See p. 95.
[3] A. Landry, *Essai économique sur les mutations des monnaies dans l'ancienne France de Philippe le Bel à Charles VII*, Bibliothèque de l'École des Hautes Études IV: Sciences Historiques et Philologiques CLXXXV (Paris, 1910; repr. 1969), 203–6.

necessary for the war. However prices always tended to rise in periods of debasement. This meant that in the longer term debasement reduced the purchasing power of every man whose income was traditional and fixed, and this principally meant the landlords.

It is not surprising that, towards the end of his first decade of debasement, political opinion about the right to change the coinage began to crystallise in reaction. Its first manifestation in France was in 1303–4, when the bishops, in their *declaratio prelatorum*, expressed the wish that the king should not take any action about the coinage without the approval of the bishops and greater barons.[1] It is significant whose approval they thought ought to be given. No further pressure was brought to bear on Philip IV by his subjects at this stage, for peace had already been made with England in 1303, and was shortly afterwards also made with Flanders. Philip IV's first period of debasement was therefore able to come to an end in 1305 and the occasion for complaint removed. It was in the interest of the king, as well as of the nobility and all those dependent on rents, to see a more substantial coinage once again. It was, however, much harder to impose an improvement of the coinage on those who held coin than a debasement. Nevertheless a staggering attempt was made to bring the coinage back to what it had been before the war with England. Barely had it been achieved, than the costs of the renewed war with Flanders compelled Philip IV in 1311 to resort once again to debasement. Once again it provided the money for the war. Once again it began to arouse animosities. Complaints about the debilitating effects of debasement loomed large amongst the grievances of the provincial nobility in the series of revolts that clouded the last months of Philip IV's reign. These nobles, of course, primarily lived on fixed money-rents. Promises of a return to sound money loomed equally large in the flood of parchment with which his son and successor smothered the revolts.[2] Again an attempt was made to restore the 'good money of St Louis'.

Meanwhile in England, although no debasement had taken place, speculation was rife that there might be one. The worry found expression in petitions presented in Parliament at Stamford in 1309, to which Edward II caused the reassuring reply to be made: 'Le Roy la voet maintenir aussi bone come elle soleit estre.'[3] The nobility were not to be reassured. Rumours persisted that Edward II was about to debase the coinage, with the assistance of his Italian bankers, the Frescobaldi. Consequently, when a group of the higher nobility compelled Edward II to assent to the ordinances of 1311, they contained the clause: 'Pur ceo qe a totes les foiz qe

[1] F. Lot and R. Fawtier, *Histoire des institutions françaises au Moyen Age*, vol. II, 'Institutions royales' (Paris, 1958), 215, quoting J. R. Strayer and C. H. Taylor, *Studies in Early French Taxation* (Cambridge, Mass., 1939), pp. 99–103.
[2] A. Artonne, *Le Mouvement de 1314 et les chartes provinciales de 1315* (Paris, 1912).
[3] *Rotuli Parliamentorum*, I, 444 (a).

eschange de mone se fet en Realme tut le people est grantement grevez en multz des maners; Nous ordenons qe quant mestre sera et quant le Roi voille eschange faire, qe il face par comun conseil de son Barnage et ceo en parlement.'[1] The Frescobaldi were expelled from the country by the ordainers and Edward II did not debase the coinage, despite the continued and extreme financial pressures of the Scottish wars, and despite the French example of the profitability of debasement as a source of war finance.

At about the same time in Brabant, the towns joined the nobility in compelling their duke, John III, to recognise in 1314 that: 'c'on ne fera ne forgera nul denier dedens Brabant, se ce n'est dedens frances villes et par le conseil desdites villes ou du pays; et ce denier on eswardera et tenra en bon point par le conseil desdites villes et du pays.'[2] In Aragon in 1307 James II was permitted to alter the coinage at a session of the *Cortes*, and bound himself by oath to maintain the coinage at the new standard, perpetually the same in type, weight and alloy.

Thus, within the space of ten years at the beginning of the fourteenth century the clergy of France had expressed the wish that the king should obtain magnate approval to changes in the coinage; the nobility of England had temporarily imposed the view that the king must obtain baronial advice for any such changes; the subjects of the Duke of Brabant had permanently obliged him to seek their counsel, although not yet their consent to monetary change; and the King of Aragon had in practice obtained consent in his *Cortes* to such a change.

Nevertheless no successful revolution in thought had yet occurred. The principle that the coinage belongs to the community had not yet been explicitly expressed. It was merely that the politically vocal elements in the community, the now newly institutionalised 'natural counsellors', having been hurt by debasement, or fearing that they would be, had begun to feel, pragmatically, that coinage was their concern. Coinage in their view had ceased merely to be the concern of the prince alone, and had become the concern of prince and magnates together.

In practice during the decades that separated the crisis of the opening years of the fourteenth century from that of the Hundred Years War the Kings of France did consult their subjects. General assemblies of the Langue d'Oil were held in 1320, 1321, 1329 and 1333 so that the king could obtain the advice of the three estates on the problem of coinage.[3] The Kings of France found it convenient to consult a national assembly over changes in the coinage but had not yet been convinced that this was obligatory. In a crisis they could dispense with the luxury of consultation.

The opening of the Hundred Years War placed the most severe strain on the royal

---

[1] Ordinance 30; 27 September 1311 (*Statutes of the Realm*, I, 285).
[2] Charte romane, *het Waals Charter*, article 2; quoted from E. Lousse, 'Les deux Chartes romanes brabançonnes du 12 juillet 1314', *Bulletin de la Commission Royale d'Histoire*, XCVI (Brussels, 1932), 24.
[3] G. Picot, *Histoire des États Généraux*, 1st ed., I (Paris, 1872), *passim*.

finances in both kingdoms that they had yet experienced. From the opening of hostilities Philip VI took very considerable profits from debasing the coinage, without any consideration of obtaining counsel or consent. The extent of the debasement may be measured by the amount of coin minted from a mark weight of silver. Up to the end of 1336 sixty gros tournois were struck from a mark of *argent-le-roi*, the standard French mixture for coining, consisting of 96% silver and 4% alloy. On 26 June 1342, by the seventh downward change in the quality of the coinage, Philip VI ordered his mints to produce 240 grossi turonenses novi from each mark of *argent-le-roi*. Each new gros was to be exactly half the weight and half the fineness of those being minted only 5½ years before.[1] Philip VI only temporarily returned to good money in 1343, in return for the grant by an assembly of estates in Paris of a sales-tax of 4 deniers in the livre.[2]

When in 1346 the process of debasement commenced again, the preamble to the royal ordinance that commanded it, included the significant assertion that: 'a nous seul et à nostre Majesté royale appartient seulement et pour le tout, en nostre royaume, le mestier, le fait, la provision et toute l'ordonnance de monnaye'.[3]

This was a return to the traditional royal point of view in France. It was just this point of view that Oresme was about to attack. Not only was the theory clear, but the results were impressively successful. In 1349, *recepta monetagii* provided 522,000 livres out of total receipts of 782,000 livres.[4] By the ordinance of 9 November 1355 no fewer than 480 gros were to be minted from the mark of *argent-le-roi*. The individual gros contained only 20% silver and 80% alloy.[5]

Men at the time were perfectly clear about what the consequences were of different ways of dealing with the coinage, and who gained and lost. In a remarkably objective piece of advice, Guillaume le Soterel, the treasurer general of Navarre, explained the various options to his king, Philippe of Evreux.

Everywhere there are three sorts of men, each of which wishes the currency to be to their advantage, and there are four sorts of coinage, and I am going to explain what are the sorts of men, and what the sorts of coinage.

The first sort of men are those who have rents . . . , especially those who have their rents in money of account. This sort of men clearly wish one sort of money, that is, money of strong alloy . . .

The second sort of men are those who engage in commerce, who wish for another sort of money. That is a middle sort of money . . . Trade is always poor except when money is in a middle state. To write all the reasons in this document would be too lengthy.

The third sort of men are those who live from the work of their bodies. These would wish

---

[1] J. Lafaurie, *Les Monnaies des rois de France*, I (Paris, 1951), nos. 265–7, pp. 42–3.

[2] R. Cazelles, *La Société politique et la crise de la royauté sous Philippe de Valois* (Paris, 1958), pp. 163–4.

[3] Ordinance of 16 January 1346 (*Ordonnances*, II, 254).

[4] R. Fawtier, *Comptes du trésor royal*, p. lxiv, quoted in Lot and Fawtier, *Institutions françaises au Moyen Age*, II (Paris, 1958), 236.

[5] Lafaurie, *Les Monnaies des rois de France*, no. 303d., p. 53.

to have weak money . . . When money is current which is not strong, everything always becomes cheap, and there is always enough currency, and all the feeble money draws the strong money to itself.

The fourth sort of money is desired by lords when they are at war, and he (*sic*) can thus strike coin as feeble as he likes to have the means to pay his troops to defend him and his people and his land. But at the end of the war, he ought to take this money in again.[1]

That was written in or about 1340, when the war was still young – in so many ways it is a much more honest document than Oresme's special pleading on the part of the landed interest.

Oresme had nothing good to say of what Le Soterel called money in a middle state, let alone weak money. Oresme's argument is purely one-sided; for him the only sort of good money was strong money. He attacked debasement with the emotive eloquence of the skilled rhetorician:

. . . because of these alterations, good merchandise or natural riches cease to be brought into a kingdom in which money is so changed, since merchants, other things being equal, prefer to pass over to those places in which they receive sound and good money. Furthermore, in such a kingdom internal trade is disturbed and hindered in many ways by such changes, and while they last, money-rents, yearly pensions, leases, cesses (*censure*) and the like, cannot be well and justly assessed, or valued, as is well known. Neither can money safely be lent or credit given. Indeed many refuse to give such charitable help on account of such alterations. And yet a sufficiency of bullion, of merchants, and of all these other things, are either necessary, or highly useful, to humanity and their lack is prejudicial and hurtful to the whole civil commonwealth.[2]

A closer look at Oresme's argument shows that as far as trade was concerned he was only interested in the import-trade, that is in the supply of luxury goods to the landowning classes. Even his arguments about trade are tinged with party interest.

At the same time as the violent debasements in France, Louis de Male, the Count of Flanders, was also debasing his coinage, but not in nearly so violent a fashion. Professor Hans van Werveke has shown that in 1354 and the immediately following years, in other words in the very years that Oresme was writing, Louis de Male was drawing 20,000 livres parisis and upwards each year from his mints, at a time when his receiver general was accounting for total revenues of around 130,000 livres parisis. In other words Louis de Male was adding an extra 20% or so to his regular income. Professor van Werveke has shown that this much milder debasement, although undertaken to provide money for war, had the unintentional effect of protecting the declining Flemish cloth industry. Debasement reduced the selling-price of Flemish cloth on foreign markets and made it more competitive. It did this largely by the direct means of cheapening exports, as a modern devaluation

---

[1] Béatrice Leroy, 'Théorie monétaire et extraction minière en Navarre vers 1340', *Revue Numismatique*, 6th series, XIV (1972), 110.
[2] *De Moneta*, chapter XX.

would do, but also by the indirect means of lowering the real wages of the craftsmen, whose labour made up a larger proportion of the cost of production than the raw materials which, being imported, naturally rose in price with successive debasements.[1]

The fourteenth-century attack on debasement was double-pronged. On the one hand there were the straightforward objections, as summarised by Oresme, to the ill effects of debasement. On the other were the objections to the profit being made by the prince. As Oresme himself recognised: 'I am of the opinion that the main and final cause why the prince pretends to the power of altering the coinage is the profit or gain which he can get from it.'[2]

In a major debasement the king was taking a percentage of the wealth of all who had coin in his realm. A debasement was in effect a tax, equitable and unavoidable, on the wealth of his subjects, fairly rapidly collectable, and easy to administer. It could be collected in the face of opposition, even rebellion, on the part of his subjects. Their individual self-interest dictated that, however much they might disapprove of the process, they preferred more new coins to fewer old ones.

But if the ability to change the coinage lay within the prince's prerogative, then he had access to a major source of extraordinary taxation that, unlike most other forms of extraordinary taxation, was outside the control of his leading subjects when gathered in the national political assembly. The leading subjects quite naturally objected to the degree of independence retained by the prince through his control of the coinage. The prince, equally, objected to any attempts to curtail his authority yet further. There was thus, in the mid fourteenth century, a struggle for the political control of the coinage, mixed up with the direct protests about the deleterious effects of debasement.

Magnates much preferred overt taxation, which they could control and which they could also escape. It was in these very years, whilst the new orthodoxy of 'strong', community-controlled, coinage was being worked out, that France at last acquired an effective taxation system. The ransom of John II was not paid out of the proceeds of fresh debasements, but from the *taille*, a hearth-tax imposed at the very heavy rate of 6 francs on every town hearth and 2 francs on every rural hearth, and from a sales-tax, at the rate of 12 deniers in the livre.[3] Although Charles V abolished the *taille* in 1380 on his deathbed, the precedent of an effective taxation system had been established.

Oresme's view, as I have already suggested, became the new orthodoxy in France in 1358 and France returned to a policy of strong money, combined with

---

[1] Hans van Werveke, 'Currency manipulation in the Middle Ages: the case of Louis de Male, Count of Flanders', *Transactions of the Royal Historical Society*, 4th series, xxxi (1949), 115–27, repr. in his *Miscellanea mediaevalia* (Ghent, 1968), pp. 255–67.

[2] *De Moneta*, chapter xv.

[3] 'L'Établissement de l'impôt' in Lot and Fawtier, *Institutions françaises au Moyen Age*, ii, 256ff.

direct taxation, from which the nobility were exempt, and of which the nobility took an increasing share.

Oresme's treatise obviously had a wide circulation. Not only were copies influentially placed in the libraries of rulers, but it became part of the common stock of academic discourse. At Paris Oresme's views were naturally taken up by other nominalists, and subscribed to by such writers as Henry of Langenstein, who, significantly, also wrote in favour of summoning a general council to cope with the Great Schism in the Church. Views favouring 'community', effectively 'magnate', control of the coinage fitted well with views favouring conciliar control of the Church. Not only at Paris was this line taken, but also at Padua and Bologna by Nicolo de Tudeschi, the canon lawyer who became Archbishop of Palermo, and hence 'Panormitanus', in 1435. He too favoured conciliar control of the Church at Basel, against Eugenius IV.

Later in the fifteenth century Gabriel Biel, one of the first professors at Tübingen in 1484, wrote a *Tractatus de potestate et utilitate monetarii* in which he quoted Oresme and Panormitanus with approval. For him, too, authority to regulate the coinage was vested in the community.[1]

Against this background of academic orthodoxy, it is interesting to see what actually happened in five countries, France, the Netherlands, Castille, Aragon and England.

In France the period of debasement had at last come to an end in 1360 with the issue of new gros tournois, which although somewhat lighter than before the war, were again made of 96% silver and only 4% alloy. For over half a century the strong money policy of the noble group led by the Meluns was continued in France. The gros remained completely unchanged in alloy for twenty-five years, until 1385, and hardly changed for another thirty.[2] The gros of 1413 were still 93% silver. It was only in a period of renewed civil war that this policy of stability was abandoned. By 1417 there were three different administrations in France, those of Henry V, of John the Fearless of Burgundy in the name of Charles VI, and of the dauphin. From October 1417 onwards they all engaged in violent debasements in desperation to pay for the costs of war. In May and June 1420 the gros of Paris, issued in the name of Charles VI, and that of Rouen, issued in the name of Henry V, only contained 20% silver. The accounts of Charles VI's receiver general, Pierre de Gorremont, show how effective the debasement was in raising money for the war. His second account shows that the mints provided him with 547,247 livres tournois out of a total of 678,596 livres tournois; in other words they provided more than four times as much revenue as all the other sources combined.[3] The next year the

[1] Gabriel Biel, *Treatise on the Power and Utility of Moneys*, trans. and ed. R. B. Burke (Philadelphia, 1930).
[2] I have continued to refer to the weight and fineness of the gros in this chapter for the sake of continuity, although after 1385 the blanc became the standard silver coin in France. See below, pp. 323–4.
[3] Maurice Rey, *Le Domaine du roi et les finances extraordinaires sous Charles VI 1388–1413* (Paris, 1965), p. 125.

contrast was even more dramatic. The mints produced about eleven times as much as all the other sources of revenue combined. The intention of producing war finance was abundantly fulfilled. The effect on landlords was to permit their tenants to pay them the same nominal rents with less than a fifth of the amount of silver. At the same time prices were rising, on this occasion not only as a natural byproduct of the debasement, but also as a consequence of war and poor harvests. The squeeze on the purchasing power of landlords was never precisely proportionate to the amount by which coinage was debased. Inflation was normally slower than debasement, and often milder, but on this occasion it appears to have been more severe. It is little wonder that there was a return to strong money at the earliest possible moment. In December 1420, when the two kings, Charles VI and Henry V, entered Paris together after the Treaty of Troyes, new money was ordained for the whole of northern France. The gros again contained 92% silver. On this occasion, as on many others, the return to strong money was accompanied by regulation of the existing coinage. When the new, good gros was issued it had $5\frac{1}{3}$ times as much silver in it as the most recent debased gros. Had they been called down in proportion to the improvement of the coinage, the last debased gros, which had been worth 16d. parisis, should have been revalued at 3d. Instead they were cried down to 2d. The intention of this was to make it attractive to bring base gros to the mint for reminting. The effect was to multiply eight-fold the amount of debased money needed to pay the same nominal rents. This more than redressed the effects of debasement on landlords' incomes, and effectively raised rents in silver 50% above their pre-war levels. It is hardly surprising that in 1421 the anonymous Parisian noted in his journal that the poor of Paris felt that the new level of rents was so crippling that many of them reacted first by rioting, when the proclamation was made, and later by abandoning their tenements and leaving the city.[1]

The war, however, was not over. The dauphin, later to be Charles VII, did not subscribe to his own disinheritance and continued the struggle. In the parts of the country controlled by him the debasement continued. The pieces struck for the dauphin grew progressively worse, until the issue of gros ordered by him in June 1422 contained only 3% silver and 97% alloy. The effects of such a debasement were, as before, good for the payers of fixed dues, particularly the peasants, and bad for the recipients, particularly the landlords. In 1422 Alain Chartier made the knight in his *Quadriloque invectif* say that the peasants' purse was 'like the cistern which has gathered and is gathering the waters and gutters of all the wealth in the kingdom'.[2] This is no more than a picturesque gloss to Oresme's statement, made

---

[1] *Journal d'un bourgeois de Paris*, trans. and ed. Janet Shirley as *A Parisian Journal 1405–1449* (Oxford, 1968).

[2] P. S. Lewis, *Later Medieval France* (London, 1968), p. 56, quoting Alain Chartier, *Le Quadriloque invectif*, ed. E. Droz, 2nd ed. (1950), p. 34.

under similar circumstances seventy years before, that 'the devalued state of the currency has effectively cut down for *them* the amount they have to pay *us* in dues and rents amongst other things'. It is little wonder that for the noble group of Angevin and Orleanist advisers who surrounded the dauphin, debasement was a policy to be used only in the dire straits in which they found themselves. The landed interests of southern and central France who were backing the dauphin desperately needed a return to strong currency at the earliest possible opportunity. When Henry V died, at an improbably early age, at the end of August 1422, the dauphin and his government took the opportunity of reverting to a strong currency within a few weeks, in the hope that the death of their principal opponent would so change the balance of military and political power that they could manage without the revenue from the coinage. Just as in the 1360s, a series of assemblies in the 1420s and 30s repeatedly voted for direct taxation instead of debasement. The *taille* was revived and became the mainstay of Charles VII's finances for the reconquest of northern France and Gascony. Whilst the war continued it was not entirely possible to keep to the strong coinage of September 1422. There was a series of debasements from August 1427 onwards to meet the costs of defending the Loire against Bedford's campaign. They were not so severe as those between 1417 and 1422, and were brought to an end as soon as possible, after the raising of the siege of Orléans, the battle of Patay, and the coronation of Charles VII at Rheims in the early summer of 1429.

In 1429 strong money became permanent, and in the 1430s the *taille* gradually became a regular tax. The formulations of Oresme were once again not only the stock-in-trade of monetary theorists, but also the practical guidelines for royal action.

The debasements of the years 1417 to 1422 and 1427 to 1429 were thus ephemeral aberrations from the stability achieved in 1360. Consecutive rulers of France, Charles V, his brother and nephew Philip and John of Burgundy, acting for Charles VI, the Marmosets, the Cabochiens, and then Charles VII and Louis XI all did their best to keep the money stable. It was not until after John Law became controller general of French finances in 1720 that there was another major perturbation in the coinage of France. That is not to say that the coinage was without change for over 350 years. The sheer wear and tear on the coin in circulation necessitated a gentle reduction in weight once every generation.[1] Such gentle and practical changes were perfectly consonant with stability. After 1360 the scourge of debasement was largely a thing of the past in France.

Conditions in the Netherlands were not the same as in France. Debasement had begun later in Flanders than in France, 1353/4 rather than 1337, and had been

---

[1] See below, pp. 312 and 316–18.

considerably less violent. It added only 20% to the count's regular income, rather than tripling it. As well as the fiscal advantages to the ruler, there were also large sections of Flemish society, like the woollen-cloth producers and exporters, who benefited from this relatively moderate debasement, just as Le Soterel had explained to the King of Navarre in 1340.[1]

The noble takeover in France in 1358 had no counterpart in Flanders, and Louis de Male was still engaging in moderate debasements of his coinage right up to his death in 1384. His son-in-law and successor, Philip the Bold of Burgundy, had, however, been strongly influenced by the ideals of the group of nobility and higher clergy who dominated the government of his brother, Charles V of France. In 1384 he at once tried to introduce 'strong money' in Flanders, and increased the silver content of the Flemish groot by over a fifth. He immediately found that it was not possible to regulate the coinage of any one principality in the Netherlands, unless coinage of the neighbouring principalities was similarly adjusted, since they all had a virtually common currency. Over the next four years, Philip himself debased or reduced the weight of the silver coinage of Flanders no less than four times, although never by any considerable amount. It was only after his victory in the *guerre monétaire* against the Duchess Jeanne of Brabant that he was able to introduce a 'strong money' that had any chance of survival. In 1389, he was able to restore nearly a third of the lost silver content of the Flemish groot, and to keep it stable for the rest of his reign, despite the violent reactions of rent-payers and wage-labourers.

His son and successor, John the Fearless, began by adhering to the same aristocratic tradition of strong money as his father and uncle. He had a French translation of Oresme's *De Moneta* made for his own use, and in 1407 even managed to increase the silver content of the Flemish groot further, with the support of the Four Members of Flanders. In 1409 he proposed a further increase of 7% in its silver content, combined with an increase in value of a quarter.[2] However, the strains of renewed war in France caused him to break with tradition and debase his coinage, both in his French territories of the two Burgundies, and also, briefly, in the Netherlands. In the two Burgundies, the mints provided the duke with over 90,000 livres tournois of revenue in 1416 and 1417, over 260,000 livres tournois in 1418, and over 210,000 livres tournois in 1419. This was at a time when the 'normal' revenue passing through the *recette-général* of the two Burgundies amounted to around 60,000 livres tournois.[3] In other words, John the Fearless, in need, more

[1] See above, pp. 305–7.
[2] Willem P. Blockmans, 'La Participation des sujets flamands à la politique monétaire des ducs de Bourgogne (1384–1500)', *Revue Belge de Numismatique*, CXIX (1973), 103–34.
[3] Michel Mollat (ed.), *Comptes généraux de l'état bourguignon entre 1416 et 1420* (Paris, 1965); and Françoise Dumas-Dubourg, 'A propos de l'atelier royal de Dijon. Aperçus sur la politique monétaire des ducs de Bourgogne, Jean sans Peur et Philippe le Bon', *Annales de Bourgogne*, XXXIV (1962), 5–48.

than quintupled his 'normal' revenue from the two Burgundies by debasing the coinage there. The debasement in Flanders was less violent, and much shorter-lived. It also began there in 1416, but in 1418 John was already sending his son and heir, Philip, to swear on his behalf that no further change would be made in the coinage for fifteen years. Fifteen years later, Philip, by then duke himself, made a fresh promise of an unchanging coinage for a further period of twenty years and extended it to the whole Burgundian Netherlands. Twenty years later still, Philip, although released from his promise, only altered the gold coinage, and retained the existing coinage of good silver and the divisionary coinage of billon unchanged.[1] Philip expressed his policy in the preambles to his monetary ordinances. In that of 1433, for example, he said: 'Nous considerans que ung des principaulx poins de toutes bonnes policies, surquoy le bien publique tant du prince comme du peuple est fonde es davoir *monnoye ferme et durable*, tant d'or comme d'argent.'[2]

However it was not possible to keep on striking silver and billon coins unchanged for ever. As the weight of 'silver' coins generally in circulation was gradually worn down, so the price of fine silver in terms of current coin crept upwards. After a time it naturally passed even the highest price that the mint could afford to pay for bullion in new coins, without reducing the weight or fineness of the coin offered. A reduction in the weight of newly minted coin was therefore necessary every generation or so, which slightly exceeded the wear and tear on the coin already in circulation.[3] If this was not done, money-changers and other suppliers ceased to bring any bullion to the mint. No fresh coin could then be minted, and the mint naturally had to close until the prince was able and willing for the silver content to be reduced enough. The lack of a continuous supply of new coins led to a variety of inconveniences. The 'foreign' coins that would otherwise have been reminted remained in circulation, particularly the most wretched. The best surviving coins, on the other hand, were culled out of circulation and frequently exported to a mint in whichever neighbouring state was offering the highest mint price for them as bullion. In return further miserable 'foreign' coins were brought back. Coinage thus rapidly deteriorated in quality when the mints were shut. There also seems to have been a surprisingly rapid fall in the quantity of currency circulating at such times. This is not altogether explicable, but hoarding no doubt played a part.

Such necessary reductions in the weight or fineness once in a generation must be carefully distinguished from the great debasements practised in wartime as a means of taxation.

---

[1] For a more detailed description of these events, and those which follow, see Peter Spufford, 'Coinage, taxation and the Estates General of the Burgundian Netherlands', *Standen en Landen*, XL (1966), 61–87, and Peter Spufford, *Monetary Problems and Policies in the Burgundian Netherlands 1433–96* (Leiden, 1970), chapter 5, 'The profit of the Duke', pp. 130–46.

[2] Archives du Nord, Lille, B. 639/15625.   [3] See above, p. 310, and below, pp. 316–18.

At the end of the reign of Philip the Good, there had been no reduction in the weight or fineness of the 'silver' coinage for over thirty years. In 1466, the duke attempted a slight weight reduction, but it was too small to bring in much bullion. His son Charles, on his accession, therefore made a rather larger reduction in weight, which was effective. The two changes together only reduced the metal content of the coins by about a sixth. In 1474, Charles made a further slight adjustment in the metal content of his 'silver' coins when he changed their types. He did not tamper with the coinage to pay for his wars. Even at the end of his reign, Charles kept up the tradition of 'monnoye ferme et durable' begun by his grandfather, although he was hard-pressed to replace the armies lost at Grandson and Morat. Charles was naturally supported in this policy by his close counsellors, since he surrounded himself with nobles, not with lawyers. The community, represented through assemblies of estates, could, according to Oresme, in time of war, have authorised the duke to take a large profit from a major debasement. However from the latter years of Philip the Good onwards, the assemblies of estates were themselves dominated by the nobility and the upper clergy. Even the representatives of the towns, hitherto the dominant element in assemblies in the Netherlands, were now frequently noblemen or lawyers whose interests were landed rather than commercial.[1] Even after the battle of Nancy, when the expense of defending the Netherlands was greater still, Mary, surrounded by her father's group of noble counsellors, resisted the temptation to debase the coinage. It was only after her death that Maximilian, acting as guardian for her infant son, Philip the Handsome, when faced with a major revolt of his subjects, broke with the traditional policy of strong money. He embarked on a series of major debasements, from which he drew enormous sums, which he used directly to pay the wages of the German and Swiss troops that he employed to fight his rebellious subjects.[2]

During the period of 'monnoye ferme et durable' the dukes had taken 2, 3, 4 and occasionally 5 gros as seigneuriage on each mark of silver minted. Philip the Good's total revenue from his mints had only been in the region of 240 li.gr. per year, whilst Charles had received around 500 li.gr. per year, from a much greater volume of coinage. These were negligible sums, of no use for military adventures. The entire profits of all his mints for the whole of his reign did not exceed Charles' expenditure on clothing for his entourage when he went to Trier to meet the Emperor!

Maximilian, on the other hand, took seigneuriage at a much greater rate. In 1485 he took no less than 24 gros from each mark of silver minted. In 1488 he took 62

---

[1] Willem Blockmans, 'De samenstelling van de Staten van de Bourgondische Landsherlijkheden omstreeks 1464', *Standen en Landen* (1968), 59–112.

[2] At the same time, in the bishopric of Liège, surrounded on all sides by Burgundian principalities, Jean de Hoorn embarked on a parallel series of debasements to pay for his own civil war against the Marck faction.

gros per mark, and in 1489, 120 gros per mark. In 1488, Maximilian received 14,000 li.gr. from the mints of Brabant, Guelders, Hainault and Holland. At that time the mint of Flanders was not in his hands. The mints thus provided nearly a quarter of all the revenues passing through the hands of Maximilian's receiver general.

The nobility insisted that this policy of debasement should last as short a time as possible, for the links between landed interests and a strong money policy naturally remained as close as ever. When Maximilian, just before Christmas in 1489, returned to 'monnoye ferme et durable' he was therefore assured of the support of the nobility. The chronicler Molinet expressed the connection in this way:

A cause de l'entretenement et nourreture des guerres dures et austères ès pays de monseigneur l'archiduc, les monnoyes estoyent tellement montées en valeur que une pièche d'or valloit trois, samblablement d'argent, qui estoit grant dhommage et desplaisir tant pour *ceulx qui avoyent rentes comme pour des gens d'eglises* . . . qui estoit chose exorbitant et hors de règle, dont pluseurs consaulz et assemblées se tindrent à Malines sur la reduction d'icelle. Jehan de Lannoy, abbé de Saint-Bertin, chancelier de la Thoison d'Or, principal directeur de ceste matière, fit convocquier de pluseurs quartiers gens experimentéz en ceste faculté, affin d'y remedier ou mieulx que possible seroit.[1]

Molinet makes it quite clear that the prime mover in this matter was a member of one of the greatest noble families of the Netherlands. He was a Lannoy, who was at the same time an abbot and chancellor of the aristocratic Order of the Golden Fleece, the Burgundian equivalent of the Garter. He was acting effectively on behalf of all those 'qui avoyent rentes'.

The very worst sequence of debasements in the whole of fourteenth- and fifteenth-century Europe can be seen in Castille. By 1480 the unchanging Florentine florin was exchanged for around 375 Castilian maravedis, whereas 130 years earlier it had been exchanged for around 20 maravedis. In other words, the Castilian money of account had lost around 95% of its value in the intervening years, a greater long-term fall in value than that of any other European money. This is just one measure of how spectacularly awful were the debasements practised on Castille by an impoverished crown. The debasements came in four waves, and each wave was very clearly intended to meet the costs of either foreign or civil war. The first wave of debasements began around 1354 to pay the royal troops of Pedro 'the Cruel' in his attempts to suppress the revolts amongst his nobility. Debasement was continued by both sides when these revolts evolved into a fully fledged civil war between Pedro, supported by English troops under the Black Prince and Henry of Lancaster, and his half-brother Henry, Count of Trastamara, supported by French troops under Du Guesclin. Both the English and the French naturally

---

[1] *Chroniques de Jean Molinet*, ed. G. Doutrepont and Omer Jodogne, III, Académie Royale de Belgique (Brussels, 1937), chapter CCXI, p. 173.

expected to be paid for their services, and debasement provided part of the means of payment.[1]

A second short, but exceedingly sharp, wave of debasements began in 1386 to pay for the costs of the defence of the kingdom, which was by then ruled by Henry's son John, against the threatened invasion by John of Lancaster on behalf of his wife, Pedro's daughter Constance. A third wave of debasements began in 1429 to pay for the war with Navarre and Aragon, and lasted through two decades, to finance the internal struggles of John II and Alvaro de Luna against the Aragonese party among the Castilian nobility.[2] A final wave of debasements began in 1463 to pay for another war with Navarre, and was continued to maintain Henry IV and his favourites, particularly Beltran de Cueva, in their struggles with the nobility.

As a result of these four waves of debasement, the Castilian crown experienced a catastrophic decline in its ordinary revenues. The nobility, however, suffered an even greater drop in their incomes. It is no wonder that the nobility, as elsewhere in Europe, stood out for a strong money policy and managed to impose temporary reforms of the currency on the crown whenever they had the chance, in 1371, in 1391, in 1441–2 and in 1471–3. Although such reforms may have pleased the nobility they severely damaged other groups in society, so much so that, in both 1391 and 1473, currency reform led to urban rioting.[3]

In 1371, at the *Cortes* of Toro, the noble faction who had supported Henry of Trastamara began to receive the reward for their support. The nominal value of the base coin issued by Henry and Pedro during the civil war was reduced at one stroke to a third of what it had been, and new 'strong' money issued in its place. Like his ally, Charles V of France, Oresme's patron, Henry ruled in close co-operation with his nobility. His reign was marked by his singular generosity to them in gifts of lands and privileges. It was at the same time an oasis of monetary stability for them between the two great fourteenth-century waves of debasement. The regime of Juan Pacheco, Marquis of Villena, in the middle of the fifteenth century, provided a similar oasis of monetary stability between the two fifteenth-century waves of

[1] 'King Henry, being in Burgos, took counsel because, since he had to make large payments to Mesen Beltrán (Du Guesclin) and to the other foreigners who had come with him as well as his own men, he could not fulfil (these obligations) however great the taxes which might be repartitioned throughout the kingdom . . . For all these reasons he decided to mint money . . . These coins were of low fineness . . . and then he took advantage (of these operations) and paid Mosen Betrán (*sic*) and the foreigners who had come to serve him . . . and also much of what he owed to many of his own men. But these coins caused a great deal of harm for a considerable time because things became so expensive' (Pedro López de Ayala, *Crónica de Enrique II de Castilla*, as trans. and cited by Angus MacKay, *Money, Prices and Politics in Fifteenth-Century Castile*, Royal Historical Society (London, 1981), p. 94).

[2] For the fifteenth-century debasements and their consequences see MacKay, *ibid.* I am not entirely convinced by his argument that Alvaro de Luna was deliberately trying to impoverish the nobility by his debasements of the coinage, although it is clear that the debasement had that effect in practice.

[3] MacKay, *ibid.* pp. 101–4, and 'Popular movements and pogroms in fifteenth century Castile', *Past and Present*, LV (May 1972), 33–67.

debasement, as a consequence of a conscious attempt once again to link the interests of the nobility with those of the crown. Even if Oresme's writings were not, to my knowledge, used by the rulers of Castille, as they were in France and the Netherlands, the ideas enshrined in them informed the policies of Henry II in the 1370s and of Villena in the 1450s.

By contrast England and Aragon were both exempt from the waves of debasement that intermittently afflicted the nobility of France and Castille so badly. Successive English and Aragonese kings kept to a strong money policy throughout both the fourteenth century and the fifteenth, and never succumbed to the temptation to debase the coinage to pay for their wars. The English, at least, had a far more sophisticated and efficient taxation system.[1]

Both the Aragonese and English kings had, however, like the fifteenth-century kings of France and the Burgundian rulers of the Netherlands, to reduce the weight of the coinage slightly at intervals, to keep their mints open.[2] In Aragon, this was a matter of some formality and involved the *Cortes*. The twelfth-century bargains between king and community, by which the king exchanged his profitable right to renew the coinage at intervals for direct taxation, lasted at most for a king's own lifetime. However in 1247, James I had sworn an oath, not only for himself, but for his successors, never to change the coinage in type, weight or alloy, and received from an assembly of his subjects a grant of *monedaje* in exchange, to be collected at intervals for ever. As the years passed, the promise of a perpetual, unchanging coinage naturally ceased to make economic sense. Sixty years later, the kingdom was suffering from an increasing dearth of currency as a consequence. At a session of the *Cortes* in 1307, James II was unbound from his grandfather's oath, and bound himself and his successors anew to keep the coinage perpetually the same in type, weight and alloy, but at a slightly lower standard. The whole process had to be repeated again, two generations later, by Pedro IV in 1350. Since the rare and infrequent changes of the previous century and a half had taken place in the context of political assemblies, it was hardly surprising that it came to be believed that no change in the coinage could be made without the consent of the *Cortes*. Pedro IV, 'the Ceremonious', seems to have kept his promise not to tamper with his Aragonese coinage, although he drew a considerable profit from the Zaragoza mint between 1367 and 1371, by striking imitations of base Castilian coins, during the Castilian civil war. At the *Cortes* of Zaragoza in 1372, his subjects protested that even minting these imitation Castilian coins infringed the rights of the *Cortes*. The king referred the constitutional point to that peculiar Aragonese figure, the *justicia*, for a decision, and in the meanwhile promised to stop minting imitation Castilian coins immediately.[3] This was not a very costly promise, since the recent 'strength-

---

[1] See below, p. 383.   [2] See above, pp. 310 and 312.
[3] *Feuros y Observancias del Reyno de Aragón*, 1 (Zaragoza, 1667), fo. 175v.

ening' of the coinage in Castille had already taken away any profit from imitating it.

Over the whole two centuries those occasional reductions in the silver content of the Aragonese coinage reduced the value of money of Jacca by less than a half. A stronger contrast with its neighbour Castille cannot be imagined.

The English experience was yet more enviable still. The weight of the penny remained unchanged for sixty-five years from 1279 to 1344. Three changes over the next seven years reduced its weight by less than a fifth. The standard established in 1351 remained unchanged for sixty-one years, when it was reduced by a sixth. The weight established in 1412 remained unchanged for fifty-two years, when it was reduced by a fifth, and that established in 1464 remained unchanged for a further sixty-two years. These reductions in weight by a fifth or a sixth every two generations could not correspond exactly to the average amount of wear that the coins had suffered in the interval,[1] for the coinage had to be reduced by a small extra amount to cover the actual costs of recoinage. The Kings of England did not expect to profit vastly from such recoinages, but had no intention of subsidising them. In 1345–6, for example, the gross receipts of the mints came to £1827 after Edward III's reduction in the weight of the coinage for the first time in sixty-five years. The costs of minting absorbed over 1000 pounds, leaving Edward with a modest, net revenue of around 800 pounds.[2] This contrasts vividly with Philip VI's inflated income from his mints at this very time, which only three years later reached the sum of 522,000 livres, almost exactly a hundred times as much as Edward's.[3] The Kings of England, who had a tradition of relatively frequent, direct taxation by parliamentary grant, and of a continued revenue from the customs, particularly the wool-customs, were in a favoured position compared with their French enemies. The English kings could mobilise a much greater proportion of the wealth of their smaller kingdom without recourse to debasements. It was the early growth of an efficient system of lay subsidies that saved the English nobility from the scourge of debasement.

If the English kings made very little profit from these minor reductions in weight

[1] The earliest exact calculations that we have for coin wear come from the nineteenth century, but are not altogether different from the amount of wear suggested by the scale of these reductions. The late-fourteenth-century half-groat, at 2.34 grams, was slightly lighter than the nineteenth-century sixpence, at 2.61 grams, although broader and thinner and therefore very slightly more liable to wear. In 1833, 900 sixpences, struck in equal numbers in 1817, 1821 and 1825, were weighed and found to have suffered from an average annual wear of 0.362% (Philip Grierson, 'Coin wear and the frequency table', presidential address to the Royal Numismatic Society 1963, *Numismatic Chronicle*, 7th series, III (1963), x–xi, quoting from *Tables of the Revenues, Population, Commerce etc. of the United Kingdom and its Dependencies*, Part III (Parl. Papers, vol. XIX (Accounts and papers, vol. 15), 1835), 16). Wear at this rate over a period of sixty-one years would greatly exceed the sixth by which the weight of coins was reduced in 1412, from which the unremarkable conclusion can be drawn that half-groats, although the most used denomination in the late fourteenth century, were used a great deal less than sixpences in the early nineteenth century.

[2] G. L. Harriss, *King, Parliament and Public Finance in Medieval England to 1369* (Oxford, 1975), p. 148.

[3] In 1369 the French livre tournois was worth about 2s. 8d. sterling. Calculated from Peter Spufford, *Handbook of Medieval Exchange* (Royal Historical Society, London, 1986).

once every two generations, neither did the public. Major profit-making debasements, like Philip VI's, only usefully provided urgently needed funds for a war actually in progress, if the public could be persuaded to bring their old coin to the mints very quickly indeed. In order to persuade them to act fast, the mint price for old coin had to be set far above its face value, so that it was not worth while to go on using it. The same sort of inducement could not be offered with these English minor reductions in weight. A consequent disadvantage was that large numbers of old coins were never reminted as they should have been. Anybody who happened to have old coins in good condition that were still appreciably heavier than the new coins was tempted to clip them instead, that is to cut small pieces of silver from the edge to bring them down to the weight of the new coins, and then to sell the clippings. Although the practice was illegal, it was much simpler to do this than to go to the trouble of taking them to a royal exchange. The profit to be made might even be marginally greater.

The scourge of debasement was no scourge for the English landlord in the late Middle Ages. He could expect to receive the same rents for the same lands as his father and grandfather had done. If his rents fell, it was not because he received them in debased coin, but because he deliberately lowered them himself in order to attract or retain tenants in the competitive situation brought about by the fourteenth- and fifteenth-century fall in population. Only once was there any disquiet amongst English landlords that they might suffer from debasement. That was in 1351, when Edward III had adjusted the coinage for the third time in seven years, and when Philip VI of France was in the midst of a series of major debasements. Edward III, however, was not about to follow his enemy's example. In 1352 Edward III dispelled anxieties by promising that the standards of the coinage would in future only be changed by Act of Parliament.[1]

In France, the Netherlands and Castille, the overwhelming expenses of war provoked the rulers to violent debasements for the sake of the revenue to be obtained. The economic effects of such debasements were in general favourable for the payers of fixed dues, particularly for those peasantry who paid fixed money-rents. They were commensurately bad for the recipients of these dues, particularly for those landowners who lived on money-rents. Similarly debasements made exports more competitive and were good for the producers of export goods, whilst imports became more expensive and so were bad for the consuming classes in general. It is little wonder that, in or out of assemblies of estates, the nobility and upper clergy reacted against debasements as strongly as they did. The Aragonese and English nobility were both fortunate and unusual, in a way they may not have fully appreciated.

---

[1] R. R. Ruding, *Annals of the Coinage*, 3rd ed. (3 vols., London, 1840; repr. 1974), I, quoting the Statute of Purveyors from *Statutes of the Realm*.

14

The Money of Europe around 1400

By the early fifteenth century three distinct levels of coin and credit had developed in western Europe, and each of these levels was characterised by a different sort of coin: gold, silver and billon. Each sort of coin had a different function.

At the highest level there were by the early fifteenth century 'national' gold coinages in most parts of Europe, as well as the great 'international' gold coinages of Florence and Venice that had been gradually replacing the currency of uncoined gold and of silver ingots since the mid thirteenth century.[1] Even in the early fifteenth century the florin and the ducat still preserved something of their original role for making large international commercial payments. The 'national' coinages served primarily for large internal payments, although these 'national' gold pieces were very frequently also used for international transactions. Moreover, the 'national' pieces very frequently had some close relationship to the 'international' pieces. When the minting of gold spread in the fourteenth century, the first gold coins in many countries had been direct imitations of Florentine florins.[2]

A hoard concealed in the Veneto around 1370 provides an astonishing example of the 'international' circulation of the florin–ducat denomination at that date. It contained 100 ducats minted in Venice itself, and a further 176 florins from other North Italian cities (Florence 90, Genoa 82, Savona 4), as well as 103 florins that had come from the general direction of the Kremnica goldfield (Hungary 92, Austria 8, Bohemia 3). It also contained, however, 52 derivatives of Florentine florins minted in the Rhône valley, 47 derivatives minted in the Rhine valley, 28 from the southern

---

[1] The ducat maintained its original weight and fineness throughout the Middle Ages. They were even maintained under the stress of the Genoese and Milanese wars from 1387 to 1405, when the silver content of the grossi was reduced; see below, p. 326. Modern assays suggest that the ducats of Doges Antonio Venier and Michele Steno were of at least 23½ carat gold (Philip Grierson, 'The Fineness of late Venetian ducats', paper read at Symposium on the use of Scientific Techniques for studying the coinage of Europe and the Mediterranean World A.D. 500–1500 (London, April 1984)). Professor Grierson's assays suggest that those carried out for Dr Bacharach, ostensibly on ducats of these two doges, were in fact on Levantine imitations of them. They were of 22- and 21-carat gold (Jere L. Bacharach, 'The dinar versus the ducat', *International Journal of Middle East Studies*, IV (1973), 93–6). The Florentine florin also retained its gold content, except for a few months in 1402 when its weight dropped from 3.52 grams to 3.33 grams.

[2] See above, pp. 183, 268, 278–80 and 288.

Netherlands, and 20 others from 8 different issuers in various parts of Europe, including one florin from as far away as Lübeck on the Baltic.[1]

In some cases the relationship had remained close. The florins or ducats of Hungary, the principal source of gold within Europe, had begun as straightforward imitations of the Florentine florin in type as well as in weight and fineness. Although their appearance had changed, their weight and fineness remained of the same standards as the Italian florins and ducats right through the fifteenth century.

In other cases the direct relationship had been broken little by little. The florins or gulden of Germany, whether struck for the emperors or for the great Rhineland electors, had also been the same as the Florentine florin when they were first introduced in the mid fourteenth century, but by the fifteenth century they had gradually lost a considerable degree of fineness, as well as a certain amount of weight. By the conventions between the Rhineland rulers from 1419 to 1488 they were only 19 carats fine instead of the nominal 24 carats of the Italian florins and ducats, so that they offered an alternative standard for a large area of Europe.[2]

Not all the new, gold coins of fourteenth-century Europe were of this 'international' denomination. When first issued in 1351, the English gold 'noble' had been a piece well over twice the weight of a florin or ducat. However, when it was reduced in weight in 1412, it essentially became a double florin. 'Half-nobles' were also struck which were essentially florins.

The French écu was, like the noble, not directly related to the florin when it was first struck in 1385. However, it too, after a number of reductions in weight, ended up in 1424 as the same weight as the florin.

The salut, struck for the Lancastrian 'King' of France, Henry VI of England, in the French mints under his control, was from 1423 to 1449 also a coin of this weight and fineness. The new, gold 'riders' introduced in Brittany in the 1420s by Duke John V were also of the same standard.[3] When a unified coinage was introduced in 1433 for the new 'kingdom' created in the Netherlands by Philip, Duke of Burgundy, he too struck gold 'riders' or 'cavaliers' which similarly contained almost exactly as much gold as the florin.[4]

In transactions between western Europe and the Levant the Venetian ducat was, from the mid fourteenth century, by far the most important means of payment.[5]

---

[1] *Coin Hoards*, I (1975), hoard no. 429.
[2] W. Diepenbach, 'Der rheinische Münzverein', in A. F. Napp-Zinn and M. Oppenheim (eds.), *Kultur und Wirtschaft im Rheinischen Raum. Festschrift zu Ehren Christian Eckert* (Mainz, 1949), pp. 89–120.
[3] Michael Dhénin, 'Florin et double florin de Bretagne', *Revue Numismatique*, 6th series, xv (1973), 190–215, suggests that they were consciously and directly imitating the florin. Since Charles VII's écu à la couronne, and both Henry VI's French salut and his English half-noble were of this weight, it is possible that the florin standard was being imitated at second hand.
[4] Peter Spufford, *Monetary Problems and Policies in the Burgundian Netherlands 1433–1496* (Leiden, 1970), pp. 30–2.
[5] See above, pp. 284–6, and below, pp. 353–6. In the Levant itself, the Mamluk rulers of Egypt struck 'ashrafi', derived from the ducat, from 1425 onwards.

However, inside western Europe the Florentine florin was clearly of more importance until the fifteenth century, when the ducat achieved such a position of dominance that 'ducat' came to replace 'florin' as the generic name for gold pieces of this size and fineness. Even in Florence itself the dominance of the ducat was recognised in May 1422, when the city increased the weight of its florin very slightly to make it more nearly equivalent to the ducat, so that it could be used in the Levant alongside the ducat, and thus assist Florentine merchants using the galleys newly established at Porto Pisano to break into the lucrative trade with Egypt.[1]

When the caravelles of Henry the Navigator began to bring back appreciable quantities of gold, shortly after the middle of the fifteenth century, the Kings of Portugal began also to mint a 'national' gold coinage, of gold cruzados, pieces of the same weight and fineness as the ducat. From this point onwards the ducat was more and more consciously a standard. At about this date the Kings of Naples also began to strike ducats, and in the 1470s the Kings of Aragon deliberately replaced their florins, which were only 18 carats fine (three-quarters gold), by fine gold ducados. Finally at the end of the century Ferdinand and Isabella abolished the traditional doblas of Castille and minted 'excelentes' instead, which they consciously modelled on the ducat: 'E porque se hallo que las monedas de ducados son mas comunes per todos los reynes e provincias de christianes e mas usadas en todos las contractaciones e essi les parescia que nos deviamos mandar labrar moneda de oro de la ley e talla e peso de ducados' (*Pragmatica* of Medina del Campo, 13 June 1497).

Despite the evolution of international banking, gold coins were essential in the fourteenth century for great political payments between princes. The ransom of John II of France, the dowry of Isabella of France, bride of Richard II of England, or the agreement by which John of Gaunt abandoned his claims to the kingdom of Castille had all been settled by payments of hundreds of thousands of gold francs or écus. They continued to be useful in just the same way in the fifteenth century. The ransom of James I of Cyprus was paid in 4 instalments of 50,000 Venetian ducats from 1429 onwards.[2]

However the value of these gold pieces was so great that the vast majority of men never used gold at all. Gold coins were for noblemen, government officials and merchants trading on a large scale. When they were first issued in 1433 the new, gold cavaliers of the Netherlands were worth 6 sous gros of Brabant, that is to say 72 gros. The following year, at Antwerp, the master masons working on the church of Notre-Dame were paid at 8 gros per day, and their journeymen at $4\frac{1}{2}$ gros per day. Craftsmen who were working outside the town received lower wages.

---

[1] P. Grierson, 'The weight of the gold florin in the fifteenth century', *Quaderni Ticinesi di Numismatica e Antichita Classiche*, x (Lugano, 1981), 421–31.
[2] See above, p. 255, and below, pp. 390–2.

Table 6. *The florin–ducat standard in the fifteenth century*

			weight in grams	fineness in carats
Florence,	florin	issue began 1252		
		1390–1402	3.52	24 nominally
		1402	3.33	24 nominally
		1402–1422	3.54	24 nominally
		1422–c. 1433	3.55	24 nominally
		c. 1433 onwards	3.54	24 nominally
		issue continued to 16th c.		
Genoa,	genovino	issue began 1252	3.56	24 nominally
Venice,	ducat	1284–c. 1840	3.56	24 nominally
Bologna,	bolognino d'oro	issue began 1380	3.55	24 nominally
Hungary,	florin or ducat	issue began 1328	3.54	24 nominally
England,	noble	1351–1412	7.78	24 nominally
		1412–1465	7.0	24 nominally
	half-noble	1412–1464	3.5	24 nominally (actually 23⅞)
France,	écu	1358–1388	4.08	24 nominally
	reduced by	1424 to	3.5	24 nominally
	debased by	1429 to	3.5	18
	restored	1435	3.5	24 nominally
	(écu à la couronne)			
	salut	1423–1449	3.5	24
Brittany,	rider	introduced 1420	3.05	24
Burgundian Netherlands,	philippus, rider or cavalier (Flanders, Brabant, Holland, Hainault)	1433–1447	3.63	23¹³⁄₁₆
Burgundy,	cavalier	1439–1443	3.63	23¹³⁄₁₆
		1443–1451	3.63	23
Egypt,	ashrafī	issued from 1425 onwards	3.41	24 nominally
Portugal,	cruzado	issued from 1457	3.74	23¾
Naples,	ducat	issued from Alfonso I (d. 1458)		
Sicily,	reali	issued from 1466	3.95	
Aragon,	florin	1369–1475/6	3.48	18
	ducado	issued from 1475/6	3.5	24 nominally
Castille,	excelente	issued from 1477	3.74	23¾

The carpenters working for the hospital of Saint Elizabeth received only 5 gros per day.[1] Yet these were all highly skilled men, and most men receiving day-wages were not skilled men. Nevertheless it was still necessary for such skilled men to work between 9 and 16 working days to earn 72 gros, the value of a single gold cavalier. Although wages were slightly higher in southern England at this time, it still took a similarly skilled master craftsman in the building industry 7 working

[1] Ch. Verlinden, *Dokumenten voor de Geschiedenis van Prijzen en Loonen in Vlaanderen en Brabant (XVᵉ–XVIIIᵉ eeuw)* (Ghent, 1959 and 1965).

days to earn the equivalent of a gold half-noble, or 10 days for a building labourer.[1] No sooner have these wages been expressed in terms of gold than it is clear that even highly skilled craftsmen, let alone the ordinary run of men, hardly ever used gold coins, and that most men in the fifteenth century never handled gold coins at all.

For most men, however, silver coins were much more important, and the key silver coins that had evolved by the early fifteenth century were of a value that was useful for the major payments of everyday life – wages, rents, taxes.

In the kingdom of France the key coin, from the second half of the fourteenth century right through to the sixteenth, was the blanc. This was a coin of approximately 3 grams in weight and made of slightly less than half silver.[2] It thus contained about a third of the silver of its pre-Hundred Years War predecessor, the gros tournois, which weighed about 4 grams and was made of silver as fine as was practicable, so-called *argent-le-roi*, which was pure silver with only one twenty-fourth part of alloy.

For most of its period of issue the blanc was of a fixed basic type, with the arms of France in a shield on the obverse and a square-headed cross on the reverse between lilies and crowns. Similar pieces were struck in their own mints by the great semi-independent princes in and around France like the Dukes of Brittany or Savoy.[3] The blanc was thus a familiar and unchanging object in the purses of Frenchmen for five generations and for the great part of its long period of issue it retained the same

---

[1] E. H. Phelps Brown and S. V. Hopkins, 'Seven centuries of building wages', *Economica*, XXII (1955), repr. in E. M. Carus-Wilson (ed.), *Essays in Economic History*, II (London, 1962), 168–78. They give craftsmen's daily wages as 5d. (1360–1402); 5d. to 6d. (1402–12); 6d. (1412–1532); and labourers' daily money-wages as 3d. (1371–1402); 3d. to 4d. (1402–12); 4d. (1412–1545). The half-noble remained at 3s. 4d. (40d.) from 1351 to 1464.

[2] The blanc which was to become a really permanent coin was the blanc first issued in 1385 and nicknamed the 'guénar'. It began to be made of half *argent-le-roi* and half alloy (48% pure silver), and 75 were struck from the mark of metal (it thus weighed 3.26 grams). It declined in weight and fineness very slowly and by the time that civil war broke out in 1413 it was still being made of $\frac{5}{12}$ *argent-le-roi*, and 80 were being struck from the mark of metal. During the next few years, under the stress of civil war and the English invasion, there was monetary chaos. A wide variety of blancs were issued during this short period, many of them at the same weight and fineness as the last guénars. When Charles VII re-stabilised the coinage, after he had reconquered Paris in 1436, he had a variant of the traditional guénar struck, called the 'blanc à la couronne' or 'parpaillole' which went on being minted until the reign of Louis XII (d. 1515). This too was initially of the same fineness and weight as the last guénars and only declined in fineness and weight very slowly. The 1507 issue was still being made of $\frac{9}{24}$ *argent-le-roi* and 86 were being struck from the mark of metal. The blancs issued before 1385 were really poor variants of the gros and had much the same appearance although of poorer metal and lower weight. The early wartime 'blancs à l'épi' of John II, which were struck from 1352, initially weighed almost exactly 3 grams and were 35% silver. By contrast the old pre-war gros tournois of Philip VI had weighed 4.08 grams and had been 96% silver. As the war continued, these blancs grew rapidly poorer and lighter. Charles V's standard silver coin from 1365 to 1380, the 'blanc au K', was a great improvement on the last wartime blancs. It was stable in weight and fineness, but only weighed 2.55 grams and was only 32% silver. For full details of all these blancs see Jean Lafaurie, *Les Monnaies des rois de France*, I (Paris, 1951), 52–131 *passim*, and plates.

[3] A hoard concealed in Normandy, in 1420, contained blancs guénars of Charles VI of France; John, Duke of Brittany; Philip and John, Dukes of Burgundy; and John, Lord of Rummen, indiscriminately mixed together (*Revue Numismatique*, 6th series, XX (1978), 131–56).

value – 10 deniers tournois or 8 deniers parisis. The anonymous Parisian who kept a vivid journal from 1405 to 1449 automatically used blancs when writing about wages by the day. According to him, the day-wages for an ordinary working man seem to have been around 3 blancs, after 1436 when the currency was finally restored. He also used blancs to express the prices of small quantities of semi-luxuries, butter or candles by the pound, oil or honey by the *pinte*, or of more ordinary commodities in larger amounts, eggs by the *quarteron* (=25 eggs?), whole cheeses, and vegetables and fruit, turnips, peas, beans, apples and walnuts by the bushel. From his description of the problems facing the poor in 1421 and 1422 during the initial attempt to restore the coinage after four years of extreme wartime debasement, it is quite apparent that, although house-rents in Paris were fixed in terms of money of account, so many francs a quarter, they were actually paid in *monnaie blanche*; since, as he said, 'most people had no other coin'. He expressed the prices of grain or of flour, which was sold by the Paris *setier*, a great tub holding something over 100 kilograms (220 pounds), in money of account, in francs and sous, but he noted down the cost of milling the grain into flour in blancs. He equally expressed the price of meat, of whole animals, oxen, pigs and sheep, in money of account, but the sales-taxes on them in blancs.[1] Parisian millers and tax-collectors in the 1430s and 1440s were thus paid in blancs, just as contemporary wage-earners were, and indeed had been already for two generations. The wages paid to master masons and master carpenters in Forez between 1378 and 1418 varied considerably, from 30 to 45 deniers tournois a day, as did those of their assistants, from 15 to 35 deniers, but they were always expressed in multiples of 5 deniers tournois, so that they could be paid conveniently in 10-denier blancs and 5-denier petits-blancs.[2] At Dijon during much of the fifteenth century a blanc was the normal fee that public prostitutes charged their clients for a standard half-hour session.[3]

The standard silver coin of the new Burgundian 'kingdom' in the Netherlands was a piece in the same range as the French blanc. When it was first issued in 1433 the patard or stuiver was made half of *argent-le-roi* and half of alloy, and weighed slightly more than the blanc at 3.44 grams (72 were struck from the mark troy of metal). It too declined very slowly in weight and fineness.[4] Because it was struck in four different principalities (Flanders, Brabant, Hainault and Holland) united by the Burgundians, it was also known as a 'vierlander', but it had a much wider

---

[1] *Journal d'un bourgeois de Paris*, trans. and ed. Janet Shirley as *A Parisian Journal 1405–1449* (Oxford, 1968).

[2] Étienne Fournial, *Les Villes et l'économie d'échange en Forez aux XIIIe et XIVe siècles* (Paris, 1967), pp. 643–6.

[3] J. Rossiaud, 'Prostitution, jeunesse et société dans les villes du sud-est au XVe siècle', *Annales E.S.C.*, XXI (1976), 304 and 322.

[4] In 1466, 82$\frac{1}{2}$ were struck from the mark and in 1467, 84$\frac{1}{2}$ from the mark. In 1474 its appearance was changed and its alloy was reduced to $\frac{5}{12}$ *argent-le-roi*, and its weight increased; 80 were made from the mark of metal until 1487. In 1492–6, 85 were still being made from the mark. For fuller details of these patards see H. Enno van Gelder and M. Hoc, *Les Monnaies des Pays-Bas bourguignons et espagnols* (Amsterdam, 1960), or Spufford, *Monetary Problems in the Burgundian Netherlands*, pp. 40–2.

currency than that, and became the common coin of the whole Netherlands, whether Burgundian or not. Philip the Good himself struck patards in the Duchy of Luxemburg when he began to rule it in the 1440s. The Bishops of Liège and Utrecht also struck patards, and the Dukes of Guelders did the same. The King of France also ordered his mintmaster at Tournai to strike patards instead of blancs, but Philip compelled the citizens of Tournai to stop the royal mint operating. Thus of the eleven principal mints of the Low Countries, only that of the King of England at Calais did not strike, or attempt to strike, patards.[1]

The patard, like the blanc, was a convenient denomination for wages. In Brabant it was valued at 3 gros in the 1430s. At Antwerp the daily wages of carpenters and masons then ranged between 4½ and 8 gros.[2] In Flanders, in the middle of the fifteenth century, the patard was worth 2 gros. A priest there could then hope to be paid 2 patards or 3 gros for singing a mass.[3]

The differing expectations of differing social groups are neatly revealed in the story told by Chastellain of what happened on one occasion when the Duke, Philip the Good, was hunting outside Brussels. He became detached from his hunting party and was lost in the forest. He was succoured by a woodcutter, who gave him bread and water at his fireside. Although it was after midnight, the Duke wished to get home, so he asked the woodcutter to take him to the main road. 'And', he said, 'I promise, I will give you four patards.' 'Four patards!' said the good man, 'Where are they?' And then the Duke put his hand in the little game-bag he was carrying and pulled out a (gold) florin of the Rhine, saying: 'My friend, I seem to be out of loose cash, but this will pay you them (the four patards). If you have any change, you can pay yourself and let me have the change.' 'Change!' said the good man, 'To change a florin! I am not well enough off to change a patard: it is rotten of you to ask me for change, I think you must be teasing me.'[4]

In northern Italy, the most commercially advanced area of medieval Europe, the dominant power from the middle of the fourteenth century was Milan, ruled by the Visconti. Unlike the Burgundian state in the Netherlands, which was mostly built up by successful marriages, the Visconti state was largely built up by military conquest. By the beginning of the fifteenth century the Duke of Milan rivalled the leading kings of Europe for wealth and military power. At his death in 1402 Gian Galeazzo was ruling over the former city-states of Bergamo, Brescia, Verona,

---

[1] Towards the end of the century a number of minor mints in the area, such as that of the town of Leeuwarden, also struck patards of the current Burgundian type.

[2] See above, p. 321.

[3] Revealed by a story, number 83, in the *Cent Nouvelles Nouvelles*, written between 1456 and 1467, which begins with a friar who 'se pourmenoit, attendant que quelque ung le feist chanter pour gaigner deux patars ou trois gros. [A widow] a qui print pitié du pouvre religieux, luy fist dire messe, et par son varlet bailler deux patars, et encores prier de disner . . .' and so the story takes off.

[4] G. Chastellain, *Oeuvres*, ed. Kervyn de Lettenhove, III (Brussels, 1863), 261–2. I am indebted to Prof. Pierre Cockshaw for this reference.

Vicenza, Cremona, Parma, Pavia and Piacenza in Lombardy, and those of Lucca, Pisa and Siena in Tuscany.

Just as the gros tournois was replaced in France by the blanc under the pressures of war in the mid fourteenth century, so the Milanese grosso of St Ambrose, a coin of the same size as the gros tournois, was replaced by the half-silver pegione at the same period. This naturally became the dominant silver coin of northern Italy just as the blanc did in France, or the patard in the Netherlands.

The only major city north of the Apennines to remain independent of Milan was Venice, the original home of the grosso. After a period when none were minted, the issue of grossi was revived there in 1379. They were still made of fine silver (95%) and their new weight was 1.99 grams.

By this time the Milanese were filling northern Italy with pegioni, of double the weight, but half the fineness. The revived Venetian grosso, although very different in appearance, was therefore a coin of approximately the same value as the pegione. Unlike the first Venetian grossi, which remained unchanged in weight and fineness for a century and a half, the new Venetian grossi were gradually lightened under the stress of war. They lost about a fifth of their weight during the war years from 1387 to 1405, and a further quarter during the next period of war, from 1426 to 1454. Since the pegioni of their Milanese adversaries equally declined, the values of the Venetian grossi and of the pegioni remained approximately the same.

Less important grossi of the same scale as the Venetian ones were those of Bologna and Ancona. Both these were widely imitated by the minor states to the east of the Apennines.[1] A Florentine coin list of about 1464 placed bolognini and anconitani in the same range of values as the grossi of Venice and the pegioni of Milan. All had approximately the same value as the blancs à la couronne of France, which appear as 'parpagliole di Francia'.[2]

Similar pieces to the blanc, the patard and the pegione were being struck in other parts of Europe. In Germany, for example, albus or weisspfennige were being minted in the Rhineland; schillings were being minted in the Hanseatic cities on the Baltic; and in south Germany Prague groschen, debased between 1360 and 1390 to this standard, were circulating widely along with Milanese pegioni.[3] In Bohemia

---

[1] Grossi bolognini were minted not only in Bologna by the commune and by the papacy, but also in Ferrara, Mantua, Modena, Ascoli, Macerata and even Ancona. Grossi agontani, or anconitani, were minted not only in Ancona, but also in Ravenna, Rimini, Ascoli, Camerino and even Bologna.

[2] U. Pasqui (ed.), 'Monete d'oro e d'argento correnti in Firenze nel secolo XV', *Rivista Italiana di Numismatica*, XXX (1917), 76–84.

[3] Hans Krusy, 'Der Fund von Aufhofen, Krs. Biberach Riss, vergraben 1435–40', *Hamburger Beiträge zur Numismatik*, VI (1964/5), 95–110. Both Prague groschen and Milanese pegioni were countermarked to give them currency in South Germany. Very few indigenous pieces were struck there at this time. However those that were, were of this standard. In Upper Bavaria in 1373 the co-dukes promised the assembled estates to keep the fineness of the silver coins unchanged in future at 9 lot, i.e. 9 sixteenths (0.563) (Wilhelm Jesse (ed.), *Quellenbuch zur Münz- und Geldgeschichte des Mittelalters* (Halle, 1924; repr. 1968), pp. 98–9).

itself, rural day-labourers and unskilled city-labourers were both being paid a debased Prague groschen a day around 1400, and skilled craftsmen 2 groschen a day.[1] Such half-silver *monnaie blanche* was generically known to Englishmen of the fifteenth century as 'whyght mony'.

England's own coinage, however, was itself still minted entirely of good silver. The key coin, even in the fifteenth century, was a heavy groat of good silver. Even after the weight reduction of 1411–12, it still weighed 3.89 grams and was 0.925 pure silver. Up to then, the original weight standard of 4.67 grams had still survived. These groats were worth rather more than double the French blancs or the patards of the Low Countries, but with half-groats, which were also minted, were still just suitable for the payment of day-wages. In southern England, in the first half of the fifteenth century, wages were fairly high and static; those of journeymen masons were generally a groat a day, whilst those of master masons were generally a groat and a half a day.[2]

In a few other places large grossi of good silver were still issued in the first half of the fifteenth century. The carlini of Sicily were still of 85% silver, and weighed just over 3 grams,[3] and the grossi of Florence were still of 96% silver, and weighed just under 3 grams.[4] In Florence in 1464 the range of value of such pieces was approximately double that of the pegioni and the Venetian grossi,[5] since they were the same weight and double the fineness of the former, and the same fineness and double the weight of the latter. Nevertheless even such large grossi were still usable for wages, when they were available, for they were only struck in very limited quantities. In the 1370s, building-labourers in Florence were normally paid 10 soldi or 2 grossi a day (for the grosso was then a piece of 5 soldi), and master masons and carpenters 3 grossi a day or more.[6]

Although these were the principal denominations of silver in circulation around 1400, they were not the only ones. As well as blancs in France, there were also half- or petits-blancs, of the same alloy, but half the weight. As well as patards or double gros in Flanders, there were also gros, again half the weight, and of the same alloy. As well as grossi in Venice, there were also half-grossi or mezzanini.

[1] John Martin Klassen, *The Nobility and the Making of the Hussite Revolution* (New York, 1978), pp. 15 and 17. Josef Janáček, 'L'Argent tchèque et la Méditerranée (xive et xve siècles)', in *Mélanges en l'honneur de Fernand Braudel*, I (Toulouse, 1973), 253–4, describes them as having become suitable for medium-scale urban uses ('catégories bourgeoises moyennes').

[2] Phelps Brown and Hopkins, 'Seven centuries of building wages'.

[3] Carmello Traselli, *Note per la storia dei banchi in Sicilia nel XV secolo*, vol. I, 'Zecche e monete' (Palermo, 1959), table VI.

[4] Mario Bernocchi, *Le monete della repubblica fiorentina*, III (Florence, 1976), 209, 212.

[5] Pasqui, 'Monete in Firenze'. The Florentine grossone was valued at 6s. 8d., and the carlino of Sicily at 5s. 6d., whilst the grossi of Venice, Bologna and Ancona, the pegioni and the French blancs were valued from 3s. 4d. down to 2s. 4d.

[6] Charles M. de la Roncière, 'Pauvres et pauvreté à Florence au xive siècle', in Michel Mollat (ed.), *Études sur l'histoire de la pauvreté*, II (Paris, 1974), 679–85.

There were even smaller denominations of 'white' silver. The minting of soldini began in Venice in 1328–9. As its name, 'little shilling', suggests, it was worth a soldo, or 12 Venetian denari piccoli. It was a tiny coin, half silver and half alloy. When grossi had ceased to be readily available, the Great Council in 1335 ordered that wages should no longer be paid in grossi as in the past, but in soldini instead. When grossi were again available in Venice in usable quantities in the early fifteenth century, soldini still went on being minted. Numerous other Italian city-states struck such soldini in the fourteenth and fifteenth centuries. They were introduced in Milan at about the same time as in Venice. They were still being issued in Florence in 1462, still half silver and half alloy, and weighed about three quarters of a gram. In Florence, Florentine soldini were, of course, worth a soldo, but the soldini of other cities varied in value according to the extent by which their currencies had depreciated. As listed in 1464 they all fell into the same general range, from 1 soldo and 5 denari, down to 8 denari.[1]

A certain number of Venetian soldini were carried to England on the galleys in the early fifteenth century, and had a certain currency there because of the lack of royal halfpence. They were nicknamed 'galyhalpens' and circulated from about 1400 to 1416 despite frequent prohibition.[2] The English currency contained no 'white' money of half-silver at all.

At the lowest level there ought to have been, in the cities at least, a plentiful supply of small change made of billon for daily purchases, for the small quantities of bread and meat, beer or wine that the ordinary city-dweller might need to buy for everyday living.[3]

The mites of Flanders and of Brabant performed this function in the early fifteenth century in the cities of the southern Netherlands, the second most urbanised area of Europe after northern Italy.

Above these mites were other pieces that might also be classified as small change. There were courtes, worth 2 Flemish mites or 3 Brabançon ones. There were gigots, worth 6 Flemish mites or 9 Brabançon ones, and so nicknamed 'little sixes' ('zeskins') or 'little-nine-men' ('negenmannekens') in the respective principalities. All these pieces came beneath the Flemish gros or groot, the basis of the monetary system of the Netherlands. This gros or groot, which, when it had first been issued, had been the great silver coin of Flanders, had by the debasements of the mid

---

[1] Pasqui, 'Monete in Firenze'.

[2] Peter Spufford, 'Continental coins in late medieval England', *British Numismatic Journal*, XXXII (1964), 132–7. Doge Mocenigo estimated that 100,000 ducats-worth of soldini, over 10 million of them, were sent to England every year. This is the same in both Marino Sanuto, *Vite de Duchi de Venezia*, ed. L. A. Muratori, Rerum Italicarum Scriptores, XXII (Milan, 1733), col. 960, and in Codice Marciana, *Italiani*, cl. VII, cod. 794, c. 24, published in *Bilanci generali della Repubblica di Venezia*, vol. I, part I, Documenti finanziari della Repubblica di Venezia, 2nd series (Venice, 1912), doc. 81, pp. 94–7 and 577.

[3] For further discussion of the function of small change see above, pp. 237–9, and below, pp. 360–2, 371–3, and 386.

fourteenth century itself become a piece of *monnaie blanche*.[1] The mite of Flanders was the twenty-fourth part of it, and the mite of Brabant the thirty-sixth part of it.

Although these tiny sub-multiples of the gros superficially look as if they are made entirely of copper, they were theoretically silver coins, although the quantity of silver in them is negligible. The mites of Brabant should legally have contained only one part of silver alloyed with ninety-five parts of copper. It is no wonder that they were called *monnaie noire*, 'black money'. If the masters of the mints struck such pieces honestly, following the mint ordinances to the letter, they would have made practically no profit on them, or sometimes even made a loss.[2] As a result they often did not make them at all. Consequently, in practice official *monnaie noire* was frequently lacking in fifteenth-century cities. In the first six years after the unification of the coinage of the Netherlands by the Burgundian Duke, Philip the Good, in 1433, his mints at Ghent for Flanders, at Brussels for Brabant, at Valenciennes for Hainault and at Dordrecht for Holland struck only just over 2 million pieces of *monnaie noire*. This was during a brief period of recoinage, when the mints of the Netherlands were very active and the mintmasters could afford the luxury of keeping to the rules. Nevertheless in the same space of time the same mints produced over 30 million 'white' silver patards, with nearly 150 times greater value as currency. In the place of official 'black money' men often used tokens, or 'black money' struck by petty noblemen in frontier zones, who had no compunction about not putting the ninety-sixth part of silver into their coins. Such *hagemunte* or 'hedge money', struck by minor noblemen in the Duchy of Limburg or the Bishopric of Liège, circulated freely to the west amongst the city-dwellers of the Burgundian Netherlands.

Similar sorts of official black money should have circulated wherever there were city-dwellers who needed small change for the sort of minor, day-to-day purchases that we take for granted in a post-industrial society, but in a pre-industrial society were peculiar to city life. Such 'black money' was therefore necessary in great capital cities, such as Paris or London and above all in northern Italy, where the greatest concentration of cities in Europe lay, even more than in the Netherlands.

In the cities of northern Italy the old denari or piccoli had already become black money in the thirteenth century and were exceedingly small. The mercers' statutes of Venice obliged them to make purses 'taliter quod *unus denarius parvus* non possit per eam exire'.[3] In some cities, like Florence or Pisa, the further decline in value of these denari in the fourteenth century meant that by 1400 they were no longer worth minting. Here the smallest coins were 'black' quattrini, 4-denari pieces, the

---

[1] See above, pp. 310–12.

[2] For examples from the Netherlands, see Spufford, *Monetary Problems in the Burgundian Netherlands*, p. 44.

[3] G. Monticoli, *I capitolari dello arte veneziane* (Rome, 1898–1904), Marzeri, XLII, 1279–83. I owe this reference to Dr Richard MacKenney.

price of a standard loaf of bread. As elsewhere the price of a loaf remained standard and its size increased or diminished with the price of grain. In the 1320s grain was normally around 16 soldi the *staio*. However, when in 1329 grain reached 1 florin a *staio* on the free market, and the florin was then around 66 soldi, the city stepped in and appointed commissioners to import grain from Sicily. This grain did not go onto the free market, instead it was baked and sold directly as quattrino loaves. Despite a hefty subsidy from the city, these loaves only weighed 170 grams or 6 ounces![1] Prices were still quoted in denari, but payments were primarily made in quattrini. For example in Pistoia, which used Florentine denari, a pound of mutton in 1407 cost 16 denari, i.e. 4 quattrini. A pound of pork cost 18 denari, and a pound of beef 26 denari.[2] When grossi were not available, wages too were paid in quattrini, and very inconvenient it must have been in the 1370s, when even gardeners at the great Florentine hospital of Santa Maria Nuova were often paid 10 soldi a day, 30 quattrini.[3] In a Florentine court in 1398 Antonio di Zanobi testified of a prostitute that 'he had copulated with Angela and that for that act she demanded 19 quattrini'.[4]

The anonymous citizen of Paris whose use of blancs has been noticed already, expressed the price of ordinary everyday purchases in *monnaie noire*, which in his case were deniers, half-deniers and double deniers tournois and deniers parisis. He shows us fruit and vegetables being sold by the pound, or in other small quantities, for *monnaie noire*. A denier could buy a small bundle of leeks, and even, during a glut, a double denier could buy as many as 100 large peaches! In normal years the most basic commodities of all, the loaf of bread, the joint of meat, and the *pinte* of wine, were naturally paid for in *monnaie noire*. In 1441 the diarist recorded that the sizes of the 2-denier loaves were so regulated that the loaf of white bread weighed 24 ounces, and the wholemeal loaf 32 ounces. In 1448, when food was cheap, he noted that a working man could buy a day's supply of bread for himself for a double tournois, and a *pinte* of wine for another 2 deniers. The next year prices were much the same. It was a measure of a bad year that he had to express the price of joints of meat or loaves of bread in blancs, rather than *monnaie noire*. In April 1438 he noted the alarming information that the standard loaf, which had shot up in price to 2 blancs, had shrunk in weight to no more than 11 ounces. As in the Netherlands, there was frequently a lack of small change, because there was no profit in it for the mintmaster. By November 1421 the Paris diarist recorded that without small change, no one could buy anything at all. 'There was now such a lack of coin in Paris that poor people got little or no alms.'[5] Black money had long been

[1] Giovanni Villani, *Cronica*, Book x, chapter cxviii. Villani was himself one of the commissioners.
[2] David Herlihy, *Medieval and Renaissance Pistoia* (Newhaven, Conn., 1967), p. 127.
[3] La Roncière, 'Pauvres à Florence'.
[4] G. Brucker (ed.), *The Society of Renaissance Florence. A Documentary Study* (New York, 1971), p. 192.
[5] *Parisian Journal*, trans. Shirley, pp. 152 and 164.

recognised as suitable for alms-giving. The denier parisis had consequently been nicknamed the 'denier de l'aumosnerie' from the middle of the fourteenth century.[1] As well as the lack of black money, the Parisian diarist also commented on the uncertainty caused by debasements. In June 1419, the new pieces 'provoked perpetual discussions when one bought bread, wine or anything else'.[2]

London, a rather smaller, but still considerable, capital city, had a problem over small change all of its own, for the English kings never had black money struck at all. The smallest coins were farthings, quarter-pennies, but these were minuscule coins of good silver (for two generations after 1411 they weighed just under a quarter of a gram), which were minted in such negligible quantities that they could not have been very freely available. They were still supplemented by cutting pennies into quarters at the end of the fourteenth century.[3] As elsewhere, the lack of small change was marked, and for the same reasons. A parliamentary petition of 1393 complained that 'the sustenance of poor beggars' was imperilled by the shortage of halfpence and farthings, for 'worthy persons' were unwilling to disburse as much as a whole penny in charity if there were no hope of receiving change.[4] It is no wonder that the Venetian soldini were welcome in London at this time.[5]

Prices, as fixed by city ordinances in times of dearth and scarcity, could, moreover, be expressed in divisions of half-farthings, the eighth part of a penny,[6] although no such pieces were ever officially issued in England. One of the characters in the play *Mankind*, probably datable to 1465–70, says:

> I haue a grett purse, ser, but I have no monay
> By e masse, I fayll to farthyngys of an halpeny[7]

This would seem to imply that halfpennies were cut in quarters, as well as pennies, although no such fractional pieces actually survive.

From the mid thirteenth century onwards the official coinage, so singularly lacking in either 'white' or 'black' money, may have been supplemented in London by lead 'tokens'. It is not yet clear whether the lead pieces that survive were

[1] Lafaurie, *Les Monnaies des rois de France*, I, 118.
[2] The diarist recorded that the gold mouton had been revalued from 16 sous to 24 sous parisis, implying a debasement of the parisis by one third. The particular pieces of which he complained were lubres, pieces of 8d. parisis. They were nominally blancs, but, as he pointed out, 'in practice they were as red as tokens'. By mid-August 1420 no one would accept these lubres, which by then had only half the silver content of the previous summer.
[3] Robert Seaman on the post-1377 Dunwich hoard(s?) in which there were an enormous number of cut halfpennies and farthings (*British Numismatic Journal*, XLI (1972), 27–33).
[4] *Rotuli Parliamentorum*, III, 319, as quoted by Philip Grierson, 'The monetary pattern of sixteenth century coinage', *Transactions of the Royal Historical Society*, 5th series, XXI (1971), 50.
[5] See above, p. 328.
[6] For example the price of veal in London was fixed at $\frac{5}{8}$d. per pound, as late as 1428 (Grierson, *ibid*. p. 51).
[7] Mark Eccles (ed.), *The Macro Plays*, Early English Text Society CCLXII (1969), lines 478–9. I am indebted to Dr Francis Celoria for this reference.

intended as reckoning counters or as tokens. If they were indeed tokens, we have as yet no idea of what value was placed on them. Sixteenth-century lead tokens were sometimes worth a farthing, sometimes a half, and sometimes a third of a farthing. The only medieval evidence that they may have been tokens is provided by a reference to tokens in a parliamentary petition of 1402 complaining about the lack of small change.[1] A century later, in an address to Henry VIII, a minter named Nicholas Tyery included among wrongs in need of reform: 'Suffraunce to lett tokyns to be curraunt within your citie of London in deression of your coyne.'[2]

When Erasmus stayed in England in 1508–13, he observed that the token coinage in England was of lead, whereas he was familiar with copper tokens in Flanders.[3]

As Erasmus noticed, London was not alone in possessing a token coinage in the later Middle Ages. Indeed it is possible that the idea of producing tokens was introduced into London from northern France. The earliest, thirteenth-century, English lead counters or tokens are derived from French prototypes. They also spread from northern France into the Low Countries, but barely into Germany until the sixteenth century. Outside England, the tokens and counters, although first made in lead, were later more frequently made of brass or copper, and it was with these that Erasmus was familiar. In many cases it is impossible to tell which of the surviving French and Low Country pieces are tokens and which are reckoning counters. Many of the tokens had a charitable origin and were intended to be exchanged only for specific quantities of bread, wine, meat, charcoal or peat, and were not intended to have a cash value.[4]

Perhaps the three levels of currency can be most clearly seen by looking at the immense distances that separated the three types of coinage, gold, good silver and black money. In Sicily in 1466 the gold reali were worth 20 good silver carlini, each of which was worth 60 black piccoli. Since very few carlini were struck, the currency in Sicily in the first half of the fifteenth century basically consisted of North Italian ducats and florins and black piccoli – the one worth 1000 times the other. In Florence in the early fifteenth century the range was not so wide. The gold florin was officially worth just over 14 good silver grossi, and the grosso $16\frac{1}{2}$ black quattrini, pieces of 4 denari.[5] The market relationship between the florin and the

[1] *Rotuli Parliamentorum*, III, 498, as quoted by David Sorenson, 'Lead tokens of London: a survey' (Thesis for the Diploma of Historical Studies, Cambridge, 1982). Mr Sorenson is now convinced that they are reckoning-counters and is preparing an article to demonstrate this.

[2] Quoted in notes to Thomas Smith, *A Discourse of the Common Weal of this Realm of England*, ed. Elizabeth Lamond (London, 1893), pp. 182–5.

[3] *Adagia* (1533 ed.), no. 5109, commented on in Philip Grierson, 'Notes on early Tudor coinage', *British Numismatic Journal*, XLI (1972), 85–7.

[4] William J. Courtenay, 'Token coinage and the administration of Poor Relief during the late Middle Ages', *Journal of Interdisciplinary History*, III (1972), 275–95. See also below, p. 361.

[5] Rates for 1415 (Nagl, 'Die Goldwährung und die handelsmässige Goldrechnung im Mittelalter', *Numismatische Zeitschrift*, XXVI (1894), 118–19).

grosso varied from year to year, even from month to month, and day to day. In the early fifteenth century the value of the florin in grossi was relatively stable, fluctuating only between 14 and 18 grossi. Unfortunately good silver grossi were rare after the middle of the fourteenth century and the Florentine currency, like the Sicilian, really consisted of two levels only, gold and black money. As early as 1336–8, in his justly famous description of the city, Giovanni Villani wrote of the mint striking 350,000 florins in a normal year, or even 400,000 in some years, and 20,000 pounds of black quattrini, just under 5 million a year, but he made no reference to grossi in his description.[1] In Villani's time the florin was worth 186 quattrini, but by the time of the Ciompi 'revolution' of 1378–80, it was worth 225 quattrini. In the 'revolution' the *popolo*'s concern was with florins and with the quattrini, in which their wages were paid, not with grossi. The cloth-workers, significantly, described the quattrini as 'lanaiuoli', the same word as they used for their employers.

Woollen-cloth manufacture was the dominant industry in Florence and cloth-manufacturers had, until then, played a considerable role in the government of the city. The cloth-workers felt that their employers had abused their position to manipulate the currency, so that the florin rose in terms of quattrini. They believed that this had been done so that the manufacturers could make excessive profits at the expense of their employees, for the cloth-manufacturers sold their rolls of cloth by the florin, but paid their workforce by the soldi, in quattrini. The representatives of the minor guilds, temporarily in power, legislated that 2000 florins-worth of quattrini should be withdrawn from circulation every year for the next 8 years. They hoped that this would bring down not only the price of the florin, but also that of other commodities. Veal, they pointed out, was selling in 1380 for 2s. 8d. the pound, although the official maximum price was 2 soldi the pound.

Their legislation had no significant effect. By the early fifteenth century the florin was worth 240 quattrini. This was not such a wide gap as in Sicily, but still a startlingly wide one. A currency consisting only of gold florins, on the one hand, worth half a month's pay for the humblest city employees, like the water-carriers of the *Stinche*, the commune's prison, and black quattrini on the other, 30 of which were needed for a single day's pay for a building-labourer, was not conveniently balanced for use.

In Venice it was not quite so bad. In the early fifteenth century Venice minted more grossi than any other city in Italy, because of its access to the Serbian silver-mines.[2] Furthermore the plentiful soldini were pieces of white money, even though small ones. However, a very high proportion of the grossi minted in early fifteenth-century Venice did not circulate there, but were exported to Egypt and

---

[1] Giovanni Villani, *Cronica*, Book XI, chapter xciv.
[2] See below, pp. 349–52.

Syria, so that the currency in Venice itself remained essentially one of ducats and soldini, and small pieces of black money. In 1413 the ducat was worth 124 soldini, a much narrower gap between denominations than in Sicily or even Florence.

Outside Italy the middle range of blancs, patards and weisspfennige was much more in evidence. When silver was available, and it was not always available,[1] the most frequently struck coins in the mints of fifteenth-century Europe were not the lowest denominations of black money used for small change, but this range of white money.[2] They are also the pieces most frequently met with today, not only in hoards, but more significantly as isolated finds, whether turned up in the rebuilding operations in city centres, or in deliberate archaeological excavations.

It is no wonder, with such wide gaps between the denominations in use, that the changing of money between denominations was constantly required. The function of professional money-changers was thus primarily to carry out exchanges between different levels of the same currency, rather than between different currencies. Money-changers claimed, and sometimes obtained, an official monopoly of internal exchanging. In November 1421 the Parisian diarist recorded that the president of the Parlement of Paris had 'decreed that no one but the money-changers – no goldsmith nor any other craftsman, however urgent the need, whether for a friend or anyone else – should exchange gold for currency or currency for gold'.[3] The *quid pro quo* of a monopoly was a maximum fee. The diarist went on: 'Nor was there any money-changer who would dare take more than two deniers tournois for changing a gold écu'. This was just over 1% of the value of the écu.[4]

In a famous article on the economic use of money in France in the sixteenth and seventeenth centuries, Jean Meuvret not only pointed out that only a small part of the population ever handled gold coin, but also suggested that people in general did not then even use silver money except for important purchases, and that the only really current money was 'fractional money' by then made of copper, and that many transactions were carried out without money.[5]

The situation in the fourteenth century was quite different from that described by Jean Meuvret. As far as silver is concerned, the evidence from the fourteenth century is quite clear. People in general were then accustomed to use silver money regularly and had been doing so since the thirteenth century and in some cases the

[1] See below, pp. 339–62.
[2] See above, p. 329, for the proportions struck in the Burgundian Netherlands.
[3] *Parisian Journal*, trans. Shirley, p. 164.   [4] See below, p. 393.
[5] 'Seule une petite partie de la population – négociants, fonctionnaires des finances – connaissait la monnaie d'or, que le peuple, dans son ensemble, n'utilisait la monnaie d'argent que pour des achats importants, que la seule monnaie courante était le billon, ou la monnaie divisionnaire, et qu'enfin beaucoup de besoins étaient satisfaits par l'autoconsommation, l'économie fermée ou le troc' (Jean Meuvret, 'Circulation monétaire et utilisation économique de la monnaie dans la France du XVI⁰ et du XVII⁰ siècle', in *Études d'histoire moderne et contemporaine*, I (Paris, 1947), 15–28, repr. in his *Études d'histoire économique*, Cahiers des Annales, XXXII (Paris, 1971), pp. 127–37).

twelfth. In cities it was in use for wages and rents, for example, and in the countryside the peasant was normally paid for his produce in silver. It is even apparent that quite ordinary people occasionally used gold. Occasionally, and exceptionally, Florentine building-craftsmen were paid by the job, rather than by the day, and were paid in gold.[1] More commonly peasantry, who after all sold a great deal at limited times of the year, handled gold at the time of their annual sales of farm produce.[2] Most late-medieval peasants handled a great deal of money, but only on a seasonal basis.[3] The richer ones amongst them were, however, able to save. From the 1330s the richest of the peasantry of Provence would provide their daughters with dowries of up to 50 florins in gold.[4] The fourteenth-century complaints were, in general, about the lack of small change. Far from the excessive, and perhaps inflationary, quantities of billon available in some countries in the seventeenth century,[5] the quantity of black money in fourteenth-century Europe seems to have been too small, even when eked out by *hagemunte* and by lead and copper tokens. Apart from the ill-founded complaint of the 'Ciompi', there is no evidence at all of any excess of billon. However, the effects of currency debasements in the fourteenth and fifteenth centuries, and even more the effects of the bullion famines of the fifteenth century did, in some places at any rate, reduce the reliance on coined money in the economy.[6] *If* Jean Meuvret's analysis of the economic use of money in seventeenth-century France is indeed correct, it implies that the retreat in the use of money that took place in the fifteenth century was paralleled by an even more major retreat from the use of money two centuries later.[7]

Although I have tried to characterise the three levels of currency, gold, white money and black money, by their different functions, it must not be thought that different use of different mediums of payment was by any means rigid or exclusive. On the one hand there are Florentine workmen occasionally paid in gold, and on the other international merchants paid in black money. On one occasion in the second half of the fifteenth century, when the Celys sold a parcel of English wool in Flanders for 100 Flemish pounds groot, they actually received £71 6s. 0d. in gold, £27 14s. 0d. in white money and £1 1s. 8d in black money.[8]

[1] C. M. de la Roncière, *Florence centre économique régional au XIVᵉ siècle*, II (5 vols., Aix en Provence, 1976), 310–13.
[2] *Ibid.* pp. 528ff, provides Tuscan examples from the fourteenth century.
[3] See below, pp. 382–5.
[4] Georges Duby, *Rural Economy and Country Life in the Medieval West* (Paris, 1962; Eng. trans. 1968), pp. 283–4.
[5] C. M. Cipolla, 'The big problem of the petty coins', *Money, Prices and Civilisation in the Mediterranean World* (Princeton, 1956), pp. 27–37. Professor Cipolla there attempts to generalise from the seventeenth-century evidence backwards to the fourteenth century, but I do not find this convincing.
[6] See below, pp. 348 and 376.
[5] My limited knowledge of the seventeenth century suggests that Meuvret's analysis, if true at all, should not be taken as a Europe-wide generalisation. It certainly did not apply to England, although it may well have applied to Sicily.
[8] Spufford, *Monetary Problems in the Burgundian Netherlands*, p. 39.

Alongside black money, white money and gold there were three parallel levels of credit.

Of the day-to-day credit on a petty scale, extended for example by small tradesmen to their customers, we know and can know next to nothing, because such transactions created no documents. Such credit was absolutely necessary when black money was scarce, or when the smallest denominations of official coin were larger than the payments involved in the purchase of ordinary daily requirements of bread or meat, beer or wine. If the lead pieces that survive were tokens, they evidently bore some relationship to such petty credit, even though we do not precisely understand their function or value.[1]

Medium-term credit for moderate sums was provided by Jews, Cahorsins, Lombards and, in Italy from the later fifteenth century, by public, civic pawnshops. We have more knowledge about this scale of credit. There were loans to peasant farmers, more often made in grain than in coin, but usually to be repaid in coin at the next harvest when 'all would be well' for the countryman, with money in his purse, for a short season of the year at any rate.[2] There were also loans to urban craftsmen, more often in coin, usually for several months, until an expected time of relative affluence was reached, like the completion of the weaving of a roll of cloth. It was extremely rare for this sort of loan to last for more than a year, as shown by a recent study of Jewish money-lending in Carpentras and its market area at the beginning of the fifteenth century. Such credit was very dear. The borrowers were charged 20% to 40% for each loan, and in the case of countrymen, plots of peasant land were taken as pledges in case the borrower could not repay his debts. We know of Rouen money-changers, who were also money-lenders to peasants, ending up with extensive lands, which they had gained tiny plot by tiny plot, by foreclosing on improvident or unfortunate peasant borrowers.[3] It was the same everywhere. A bad harvest, or worse still two together, or a family disaster, or even too much spent on dowries, was enough for peasants and craftsmen alike to find themselves in the hands of these loan sharks.

The way that these Rouen money-changers accumulated their property was that used by such lenders of money all over Europe from the time when a free market in peasant land began. It is rather acidly set out in an anonymous, early-sixteenth-century German dialogue on usury. In it a wealthy townsman explains:

You want to know who gave me my money? I shall tell you. A peasant comes knocking at my door and asks me to lend him ten or twenty gulden. I inquire of him whether he owns a plot of good pasture land or a nice field for plowing. He says: 'Yes, burgher, I have a good meadow and a fine field, worth a hundred gulden the two of them.' I reply: 'Excellent! Pledge your meadow and your field as collateral, and if you will undertake to pay one

---

[1] See above, pp. 331–2.   [2] See below, p. 383.
[3] Michel Mollat, *Le Commerce maritime normand à la fin du Moyen Age* (Paris, 1952), pp. 394–5.

gulden a year as interest, you can have your loan of twenty gulden.' Happy to hear the good news, the peasant replies: 'I gladly give you my pledge'. 'But I must tell you', I rejoin, 'that if ever you should fail to pay your interest on time, I will take possession of your land and make it my property.' As this does not worry the peasant, he proceeds to assign his pasture and field to me as his pledge. I lend him the money and he pays interest punctually for a year or two; then comes a bad harvest and soon he is behind in his payments. I confiscate his land, evict him, and meadow and field are mine. Thus I gain both money and property. And I do this not only with peasants but with artisans as well. If a craftsman owns a good house I lend him a sum of money on it, and before long the house belongs to me. In this way I acquire much property and wealth.[1]

It was because such loans were so frequently ruinous to artisans that charitable *montes pietati*, pawnshops, were set up in many Italian cities for the benefit of their citizens in distress. The Florentine civic *montes pietati* charged only 6% on loans after 1462, a completely different order of interest from that charged by professional money-lenders.[2] The Florentine *montes pietati* were financed by compulsory loans from the richer citizens, arranged by the city government. No such institutions existed for the benefit of the rural needers of loans.

Professional rural credit was not new in the fifteenth century, but stretched back for a couple of centuries.[3] It was supplemented, particularly in England, by the loans made by the richer peasants, or the rural clergy, to their co-villagers.[4] This sort of lending in rural society between neighbours was usually not at charitable rates of interest. It can be documented from the thirteenth century at least to the seventeenth in England, and helped to polarise village society – the few richer peasants, the creditors, became richer, by foreclosing on the many poorer, debtor, peasants, some of whom were eventually squeezed off the land into the class of rural labourers. Outside England this pattern of loans between villagers existed to a lesser extent, and credit was much more dominated by professional town-based money-lenders (*wuchers*, *usuriers*), whether Jews like those of Carpentras or Perpignan, or Italians like those at Rouen, or the 'Lombards' from Asti, who lent heavily in the market towns and villages of the Savoy Alps or the Rhône valley.[5]

But above and beyond this small and medium credit, of black money or of white, was really large-scale 'golden' credit extended to merchants, and noblemen,

[1] *Von der gült: Hie Kompt ein Beuerlein zu einem reichen Burger . . .* (*c.* 1521), trans. in G. Strauss (ed.), *Manifestations of Discontent in Germany on the Eve of the Reformation* (Indiana U.P., Bloomington, 1971), pp. 109–15.

[2] Professional money-lenders had been charging between 32½% and 43½% (Sidney Homer, *A History of Interest Rates* (Rutgers, U.P., 1963), pp. 69–143).

[3] Herlihy, *Pistoia*, pp. 141 and 145, suggests that the role of the usurer was less in the fifteenth century than it had been earlier, after the balance between town and country had shifted in favour of the latter in the second half of the fourteenth century. 'The usurer also entered on bad times at least in the countryside.'

[4] For the thirteenth century, M. M. Postan, 'Medieval agrarian society in its prime. England.' *Cambridge Economic History of Europe*, 2nd ed., 1 (1966), 627–8.

[5] For Perpignan Jews in the thirteenth century and 'Lombards' in Savoy in the fourteenth see Duby, *Rural Economy*, docs. 72 and 73, pp. 425–7.

princes and civic authorities. This had developed rapidly from the mid thirteenth century.[1] In the beginning it had been largely developed by the great Tuscan banking-houses, which had many branches spread through the great merchant and capital cities of Europe. Bankers on this scale naturally preferred to make straight-forward business loans to merchants who wanted to use the money in productive, commercial ventures. Such loans were much more secure and bore a much lower rate of interest than consumption loans. They were often involved with the bankers' other activity of transferring money from one place to another, from Barcelona to Bruges for example, or from Bruges to Barcelona. Another very common variant of this commercial loan was the credit sale (for the bankers were normally also merchants themselves), in which the purchaser did not need to pay for the goods for a fixed length of time, giving him a chance to trade with them or manufacture something for sale from them.

Loans to princes, or noblemen, were much less secure, for such men tended to resort to loans only under difficult circumstances, such as the sudden need to anticipate revenue brought on by war or the threat of war. Unlike peasants they could not be foreclosed on if they could not, or would not, repay, so the interest rates were even higher. A much safer form of public credit were the rent-charges sold by city governments, either by subscription or by compulsion. These bore a fixed interest rate and lasted for either one or more lifetimes or in perpetuity. Such city state-bonds could be resold by the initial lender and successive purchasers acquired the right to the interest, which was usually very low because of the high security of the loan. Occasionally such rent-charges were also sold by princes or even by private individuals, although not on such favourable terms.

Not only was Europe in 1400 a continent in which three levels of coin circulated and in which there were three parallel levels of credit, black, white and gold, but it had been so for some time. In some parts of Europe this had been so for over two centuries. By 1400 all groups in society were regularly involved in transactions using money and credit at one or more of these levels.

---

[1] See above, pp. 259–62.

15

The Bullion-Famines of the Later Middle Ages

As well as the enormous variety of particular changes in exchange rates in particular countries, which resulted from local circumstances, there were a number of long-run trends that can be seen right across Europe, which depended on the changing relationship in the supplies of gold and of silver available for coinage.

As silver became more and more available in the thirteenth century, its value in terms of gold dropped accordingly. When gold became more available after the 1320s, the value of gold in terms of silver dropped back. When for 20 years, from around 1390, and for a further 30 years, from around 1435, the availability of silver was greatly restricted, its price in terms of gold rose correspondingly, and when it began to become more freely available again in the 1460s, its price once more sank. The whole period from the 1320s to the 1460s was one of the predominance of gold, and the increased use of gold has already been touched on. The decreased use of silver, even to the point of its nearly total disappearance in some countries in the mid fifteenth century, is a separate, although closely related, phenomenon.

It was not the first time that the stock of silver had diminished in western Europe. In the sixth century silver had ebbed out of the west completely, and when silver-penny coinages began in the seventh century, they made a completely new beginning. No other break was as complete as that. In the ninth century the stock of silver had diminished greatly, to be renewed again in the late tenth century, particularly from the Goslar mines. In the eleventh century there was a much less extensive diminution. This was reversed in the late twelfth century, before it became very severe, by the opening-up of the Freiberg and Friesach mines. These sequences of ebb and flow took place in an economy that was entirely reliant on silver for its currency. The high point reached by each wave of silver was higher than the last, and when the tide was reversed the quantity remaining was still greater than at the last ebb. The quantity of silver in circulation in the mid eleventh century was much greater than it had been in the ninth on the eve of the Viking attacks, whilst the quantity available in the early fourteenth century was much greater than at the high points in the eleventh century.

The silver-famines of the late fourteenth and the fifteenth centuries therefore take their place in a series of fluctuations. These fluctuations, as in the past, depended on the opening of new mines, or the closing of old ones, on the wear and tear on coin in circulation, on hoarding and dishoarding, on loss in use and in recoinage, and on the balances of payments with parts of the world outside Europe.

Despite these familiar themes, however, in the light of our present knowledge, the silver-famines of the late fourteenth and the fifteenth centuries appear more severe than anything that had taken place since the seventh century. Moreover the late medieval silver-famines took place in an economy which had grown a great deal more complex than in the eleventh or earlier centuries, and in which men were a great deal more reliant on the use of money than their ancestors. The late medieval economy was also different in some other respects. The money supply no longer consisted exclusively of silver, but also included large and growing quantities of gold, and far from insignificant quantities of bank money and other forms of negotiable paper. Moreover a great deal more was committed to writing in fifteenth-century society so that we have a great deal more evidence about what was going on.

At the total recoinage of England's currency in 1278–80, Edward I caused some 100 tonnes of silver to be reminted. There was also an unknowable quantity of uncoined silver available for large payments, in ingots and other forms. Hoard evidence shows that practically none of the previous currency escaped the mints' melting-pots. Although a certain amount of foreign silver was drawn into the country by the recoinage itself, this 100 tonnes bears some relationship to the silver currency available in England at that time. At the similar recoinage of England's currency in 1412–14, Henry IV was only able to arrange for some 2 tonnes of silver to be reminted, together with a quantity of gold equivalent in value to another 70 tonnes of silver. Silver in ingot form was no longer in use. The amount of newly coined money available in England after the first two years of Henry IV's recoinage was thus under three quarters of the amount in circulation four generations earlier. This is not in itself startling, in view of the vast sums paid out and received back over the intervening period as the costs and profits of a long series of major wars, over and above the changes brought about through trade. What is startling is the reduction in the amount of money available in the form of silver coin for the whole range of ordinary transactions, from the very smallest purchases up to the level of the payment of wages and rents.

England was more fortunate than many countries in Europe in possessing even as much silver as this during the first silver-famine at the beginning of the fifteenth century. England was still better off in the second, and more severe, silver-famine of the middle of the century, when a high proportion of the mints elsewhere in Europe were closed for two decades on end for lack of bullion. How had this situation come about? Quite obviously, there had been a mammoth exchange of silver for gold. When there were recoinages in England itself, in the Low Countries, or in northern France, it sometimes became worthwhile to send coin made of one metal in one direction, and coin made of the other in the opposite direction. This was because the ratios between the mint purchase-price for silver and that for gold were made to differ between a group of countries by a recoinage in any one of them.

Even when a specific debasement had not made it profitable to exchange gold directly for silver, there was generally a slight difference in the ratios between the market values of gold and silver from place to place. This made it worthwhile to make payments in one direction in one metal and in the reverse direction in the other metal. This applied not only to commercial payments but also to political ones. For example, much of Edward III of England's war expenditures on the continent, or that part of it funded from his English resources, was in silver,[1] whilst the profits of war, and in particular the ransom of John II of France, were brought to England in gold.

'Political' or rather 'administrative' movements of coin might take place even within a 'state'. In the Burgundian 'state' around 1440 there was a difference in the ratio of gold to silver between Holland and Flanders. Gold was more valued in the north and silver in the south. The ducal receiver general's accounts therefore had a section on the profit to the duke made by taking taxes and dues in one part of his territories and spending them in another. The directions of these flows changed from time to time because of either market conditions or government action. For example, in the second quarter of the fifteenth century it was more sensible to make payments from the Low Countries to England in silver, and out of England to the Low Countries in gold, instead of the other way round.

After the agreement of 1327 by which Bohemian silver was no longer sent through Austria to Italy, the whole silver-production of the Bohemian mines flowed westwards and northwards across Germany.[2] Much of it was sent by way

---

[1] Edmund B. Fryde, 'Parliament and the French war 1336–40', in T. A. Sandquist and M. R. Powicke (eds.), *Essays in Medieval History presented to Bertie Wilkinson* (Toronto, 1969), pp. 250–69, repr. in E. B. Fryde and Edward Miller (eds.), *Historical Studies of the English Parliament*, 1 (Cambridge, 1970), 242–61, describes how heavily taxation bore on the peasantry. 'Now the fifteenth [the subsidy] runs in England year after year . . . the common people must sell their cows, their utensils and even clothing' (Anon., 1338–40). The country was emptied of the silver collected: 'There is a desperate shortage of cash among the people. At market the buyers are so few that a man can do no business, although he may have cloth or corn, pigs or sheep to sell, because so many are destitute' (Anon., in *Anglo-Norman Songs*, dated by Fryde to 1338–9). J. R. Maddicott, *The English Peasantry and the Demands of the Crown*, Past and Present Supplement 1 (1975), covers much the same ground, and N. Mayhew, 'Numismatic evidence and falling prices in the fourteenth century', *Economic History Review*, 2nd series, XXVII (1974), 1–15, attempts to measure the decline in the stock of silver in England.

[2] See above, pp. 269–70. The spread of Bohemian silver westwards and northwards across Germany in the fourteenth century can be illustrated by the countermarks with which the German cities stamped Bohemian Prague groats to give them local currency. This system began by 1382, as a reaction to the renewed debasement of the Prague groat from 1378. It had already been debased in the early 1360s. Countermarking continued until

of the Frankfurt Fairs to the Rhineland, in exchange for goods, particularly cloth from the Low Countries. From the middle of the fourteenth century English cloth was also available at Frankfurt.[1] So much silver was available that high-quality cloth and other luxuries were imported into Bohemia in such enormous quantities that they stifled the growth of native Bohemian manufacture.[2] From the Rhineland, silver flowed into the Low Countries and France, from which gold as well as goods were received in exchange. Between the Low Countries and France the general flow was of silver southwards and of gold northwards. In the same way between France and Italy, as well as goods, which were carried in both directions, there was a flow of gold from Italy into France and of silver from France to Italy. This long route round was, of course, short-circuited at various points. Men from the Rhône valley used gold to buy silver in Geneva from South German merchants.[3] South German merchants also carried Bohemian silver directly to Italy, and brought gold, as well as goods northwards from Italy.[4] The gold itself reached Italy from Hungary and, less importantly in the fifteenth century, from Africa via Spain, in return for goods. Italy, particularly Venice, exported either gold or silver to the Levant according to the relative ratios in Italy and the Levant, in Venice and Alexandria. There were additional sources of silver within the Mediterranean world itself, in Sardinia and in Serbia and Bosnia, but these did not supply Europe outside Italy. The main exceptions were the Aragonese receipt of silver from the Sardinian mines, which they controlled in the mines' declining years, and the English receipt of Serbian silver from Venice for the purchase of wool and woollens in the fifteenth century.

Whether or not gold- and silver-flows in opposite directions equalled each other depended on the balance of trade and the balance of 'political' and 'religious' payments. The general balance of these was in favour of southern Europe and against northern Europe. In general, more goods and services were sold by Italians

---

the middle of the fifteenth century. Countermarking took place in dozens of cities and towns, not only in Regensburg and Nuremberg, to which trade-routes ran directly from Prague, but also in places as far afield as Ulm and Constance in Swabia, Würzburg on the Main, and Göttingen, Hildesheim and Paderborn in Westphalia. In these places, old, sometimes very old, 'tekende groschen' or 'Gut bemesche, myt enen tekene', which had presumably travelled there before the 1380s, were to be accepted, and newer base ones, not so marked, refused (Hans Krusy, 'Gegenstempelte Prager Groschen', *Hamburger Beiträge zur Numismatik*, VI (1966), 525–30).

[1] English cloth first appeared alongside that of the Low Countries at the great cloth, and bullion, fairs at Frankfurt in 1341 (H. Ammam, 'Deutschland und die Tuchindustrie Nordwesteuropas im Mittelalter', *Hanisische Geschichtsblätter*, LXXII (1954), 39–42, 55–6).

[2] Josef Janáček, 'Der böhmische Aussenhandel in der Hälfte des 15 Jahrhunderts', *Historica*, IV (Prague, 1962), 39–58.

[3] Jean Furet, master of the Mâcon mint, bought silver, with gold, from Nuremberg merchants between 1416 and 1421 (Alain Guerreau, 'L'Atelier monétaire royal de Mâcon (1239–1421)', *Annales E.S.C.*, XXIX (1974), 384–5 and 388).

[4] The Runtinger carried gold, from Venice, onwards from Regensburg to Prague 1383–1401 (František Graus, 'La Crise monétaire du 14ᶜ siècle', *Revue Belge de Philologie et d'Histoire*, XXIX (1951), 445–54).

to those beyond the Alps than the other way round.[1] More was spent by outsiders, Germans, Provençals, Aragonese, Bohemians and Hungarians on military expeditions to Italy than they usually received in loot, ransoms and income from conquered territory. Payments to the papacy, although small in comparison with commercial or military expenditure, flowed to Avignon or Rome, and frequently onwards from Avignon to the papal states even when the papacy was in Avignon. Curial visitors and pilgrims brought more money to Avignon and Rome, over and above the dues paid to the papacy itself. From Italy the balance continued eastwards. The value of the imports of alum, silk, pepper and other spices, besides those of grain, oil and wine, greatly exceeded that of the linens and cheap woollens exported by the Italians. The difference had to be made up in gold or silver.[2] The revival of the slave-trade in the second half of the fourteenth century added to the imbalance, and so did pilgrimages to the Holy Land or Sinai.[3] The occasional crusades, to the Aegean in the 1350s or to Nicopolis in 1396, did the same. So did the ransoms following the latter.

All this had been built up on the assumption that a continuous flow of silver from central European mines was constantly being made available to pay for it. The problem of the later fourteenth century and of the fifteenth was that the supplies of precious metal, and in particular silver, were no longer adequate for the demands put on them. Through the thirteenth century great finds of silver at Freiberg, Iglau and Kutná Hora had succeeded each other, so that, when one group of mines began to be exhausted, another took over. After the Kutná Hora mines, however, there was no major new discovery of silver until the 1460s. The production of silver at Kutná Hora was in gradual decline throughout the second half of the fourteenth century and came to a standstill in the Hussite wars of the early fifteenth century.[4]

---

[1] Raymond de Roover, 'La Balance commerciale entre les Pays-Bas et l'Italie au quinzième siècle', *Revue Belge de Philologie et d'Histoire*, xxxvii (1959), 374–86; and H. A. Miskimin, *The Economy of Early Renaissance Europe 1300–1460* (Englewood Cliffs, 1969), pp. 138–58.

[2] Eliyahu Ashtor, *Les Métaux précieux et la balance des payements du Proche-Orient à la Basse Époque* (Paris, 1971), and E. Ashtor, 'Observations on Venetian trade in the Levant in the xivth century', *Journal of European Economic History*, v (1976), 533–86. The imbalance was so great that it was barely touched by the conquest of the Middle East by cheap European textiles, particularly linens and cheap Lombard woollens, at the end of the fourteenth century.

[3] The effects of the slave-trade on bullion flows have already been noted for earlier periods (above, pp. 49–50 and 65–9). In the late fourteenth century and the fifteenth, Asian slaves were sold in very considerable numbers through Caffa in the Crimea, principally girls to Europeans, and boys to Muslims. Ashtor, *Les Métaux précieux*, pp. 89–94, has commented on the extraordinary deleterious effect of the purchase of boy slaves on the supply of precious metals in the Muslim Near East. For European purchases of Asiatic slaves, see Charles Verlinden, *L'Esclavage dans l'Europe médiévale* (2 vols., 1955 and 1977).

[4] Unlike the Sardinia mines, which seem to have been worked out relatively suddenly, the decline at Kutná Hora seems to have been very slow indeed. Silver, which had been produced at the rate of over 20 tons a year in the first half of the fourteenth century (see above pp. 124–5), was probably still being produced at the rate of around 10 tons a year throughout the second half of the century. The mines did not close down until the sack of Kutná Hora by Sigismund's troops in 1422. Even then some were re-opened quite quickly, although most remained unworked until the 1450s and 60s. (Josef Janáček, 'L'Argent tchèque et la Méditerranée (xive et xve siècles)', in

Since silver continued to be sent onwards along the trade-routes without replenishment from the mines, the accumulated stocks of silver that had been built up in western Europe during the long thirteenth century were gradually eroded by the continuation of export without import or internal production of fresh silver.

In some respects the new supplies of gold coming from Hungary did a great deal to make up for the diminution in supplies of silver. For large-scale transactions, bank transfers, bills of exchange and gold coins were much more convenient than silver, but they were quite unsuitable to cope with the everyday needs of the bulk of the population.[1]

The damaging social effects of a dearth of silver coin can be more readily understood when it is realised how gold coins were no substitute. Even if they were available, they were no use for many purposes. The availability of gold was itself not always something that could be taken for granted in the fourteenth and fifteenth centuries. Although the production of gold in Hungary does not seem to have been much diminished until the 1440s, there were periods when its arrival in Italy was temporarily interrupted. The open war between Venice and Sigismund of Hungary in 1412 was followed by two decades of uneasy political relations, in which direct commercial contacts were very slight. Levantine goods did, however, reach Hungary from Venice by way of Milan and South Germany. Hungarian gold reached Venice by the same route, but not as regularly as hitherto.[2] The supply of gold from West Africa was, surprisingly, less vulnerable to change. The supply of West African gold to Seville never diminished significantly.[3] Much of this gold was sent on to Italy, not only because of the deficit in trade from Spain to Italy, but also because of the deficits in trade from Spain to Flanders, and from Flanders to Italy.[4] A general lack of gold was felt nevertheless in many parts of Europe from the late 1390s until the second decade of the fifteenth century, and in some places for another twenty years.[5] This was patently a byproduct of the silver-famine.

The imbalances of payments and the working-out of the mines were in themselves enough to create a critical lack of silver in Europe, but the dearth of

---

Mélanges en l'honneur de Fernand Braudel, I (Toulouse, 1973), 255). On the other hand, Graus, 'La Crise monétaire du 14ᵉ siècle', believed that the mines were not yet beginning to be worked out by 1400, and therefore that there was no decline in silver-production at all during the fourteenth century.

[1] See above, pp. 321–3.

[2] György Szekely, 'Les Facteurs économiques et politiques dans les rapports de la Hongrie et de Venise à l'époque de Sigismond', in V. Branca (ed.), *Venezia e Ungheria nel Rinascimento* (Florence, 1973), pp. 37–57.

[3] See above, pp. 287–8; Angus MacKay, *Money, Prices and Politics in Fifteenth-Century Castile*, Royal Historical Society (London, 1981), presents a convincing case for the continuity of supplies of gold to Spain, against J. Day, 'The great bullion famine of the fifteenth century', *Past and Present*, LXXIX (1978), 3–54.

[4] Raymond de Roover, *The Bruges Money Market around 1400* (Brussels, 1968), pp. 43–5, explains how this worked. Bills of exchange were used for purchases from Spain to Flanders, and further bills from Flanders to Italy, which meant that eventually Spanish merchants found themselves owing Italians for Flemish goods and had to send gold.

[5] Day, 'Great bullion famine', *passim*.

silver was exacerbated by two other factors of very different kinds, wear and fear.

We have no satisfactory estimates for wear from the Middle Ages beyond the scale of the necessary reductions in weight of silver coinage at intervals of half a century or so in countries that were maintaining stable currencies. These were of the order of a fifth or sixth of the previous weight, but this includes an element to induce the public to bring its old coin in for recoining and to cover the costs of reminting itself. Countries that indulged in no greater weight reductions than these still had silver coinages in 1500 with over half the silver content of 1300.[1] The loss by wear, therefore, over 200 years was thus very much less than a half. Nevertheless, wear, by itself, made a small, but continued, demand for fresh supplies of silver for the continual renewal of the coinage. There was also, of course, a certain amount of metal lost every time coin was reminted. Figures from two batches of Gascon coin being minted at the Tower mint in London for despatch to Bordeaux in 1325 give losses of $1\frac{3}{4}\%$ and of just under 2% on the metal brought to the mint.[2] These figures seem credible. However, it is harder to believe that nearly 9% of the metal sent to the Sicilian mint in 1471 for producing 'black' piccoli was lost in the minting processes.[3]

Besides loss by wear and loss by reminting, a certain amount of coin was also lost in use. The stray finds that we have from archaeological excavations are symptomatic of this sort of loss in use.[4]

The other exacerbating factor was fear. Fear of disorder made men conceal their coin. Fear of not being able to replace coin, made men the keener to keep their assets liquid. With a scarcity of coin went a reluctance to spend or invest what one had in hand, so that there was a sluggish circulation, which in itself was equivalent to a further reduction in the available quantity of coin. Fear of debasements and the instability of money made men happier to keep their silver in the form of plate, in addition to the desire for ostentation.

All these methods of hoarding, from the few petty coins put aside by poorer men in earthen vessels, to the vast sums locked up in chests by the greatest of the land, removed a great deal of coin from circulation. When he died in 1377, Richard, Earl

---

[1] See above, pp. 316–18. The only direct figures that I know for wear are provided by the Tower mint in London. In 1325, £280 of sterlings were counted out. At 243 to the pound, they had weighed $276\frac{1}{2}$ lb. when minted. They were found to weigh $267\frac{1}{6}$ lb. when received at the mint. They had therefore lost about $3\frac{1}{2}\%$ of their weight by wear, but the timespan over which this wear had taken place is not knowable (John D. Brand, 'A medieval mint account', *British Numismatic Journal*, XLVI (1976), 78–9). In 1381 the Warden and Master of the Tower mint said that the coin that had escaped export had lost a tenth of its weight, gold and silver alike. The previous recoinage had been thirty years earlier (John Craig, *The Mint* (Cambridge, 1953), p. 82).

[2] Brand, 'A medieval mint account'.

[3] Carmello Traselli, *Note per la storia dei banchi in Sicilia nel XV secolo*, vol. I, 'Zecche e monete' (Palermo, 1959), pp. 124–5.

[4] Despite attempts to do so, for example by C. C. Patterson, 'Silver stock and losses in ancient and medieval times', *Economic History Review*, XXV (May, 1972), 205–35, and by N. Mayhew, 'Falling prices', pp. 1–15, I remain unconvinced that any figure can be put on this sort of loss.

of Arundel, had nearly 44,000 marks of silver coin 'in the keep of the high tower of Arundel', together with a further 17,000 marks in coffers at St Pauls.[1] Gold was, of course, also hoarded. Oliver de Clisson, Constable of France, had a vast hoard of over 133,000 gold coins in his Breton chateau when he died in 1407.[2] However, even the great also hoarded black money! Margaret of Bavaria, the widow of John the Fearless, Duke of Burgundy, had more than 1850 marks of it on her death in 1424.[3]

As well as the amount that great men hoarded in coin, whether silver, gold or black money, they withdrew a great deal more from circulation in the form of plate. Not only was there a continued accretion of gifts of precious objects to churches and shrines, but also a spectacular increase in the amount of secular plate. This competed directly with the coinage for the available supplies of bullion. In February 1409 the Paris mint came to a standstill ostensibly because the money-changers refused to supply it with bullion as they ought to have done. When called upon to explain their action, one pointed out that Monseigneur de Berry needed gold to mount his collection of gems, others added that Monseigneur de Guyenne and the King of Sicily 'désiraient des calices' and jewellery, and so they could not respond to the wishes of the mint.[4] When Arnoul Braque had given up the mastership of the Paris mint a decade earlier, in February 1397, he said that he did so because there was no bullion to be had, and he too accounted for this lack of gold in Paris by alleging that it had all been turned into gold plate.[5] In each country only a handful of extremely rich families, particularly those of princes of the blood, had the surplus income required to build up such prestigious collections of plate.[6] These collections of plate were, however, normally very ephemeral. Their owners generally placed little value on the skill of the goldsmith's work involved. They treated their plate as a store of wealth and had no compunction about melting it down.[7] Very little of it has, therefore, survived to delight us, unlike the illuminated manuscripts commissioned at this time by members of these same princely groups, the Dukes of Berry, Orléans or Anjou, for example. Lesser men made lesser accumulations of plate. In the Toulouse region, silver cups, weighing precisely a

---

[1] L. F. Salzman (ed.), 'Property of Richard, Earl of Arundel 1377', *Sussex Archaeological Collections*, XCI (1953), 33ff.

[2] P. S. Lewis, *Later Medieval France* (London, 1968), p. 214.

[3] Henri Dubois, 'Commerce international, métaux précieux et flux monétaires aux confins orientaux du royaume de France XIIIᵉ–XVᵉ siècles', in *La Moneta nell'economia europea, secoli XIII–XVIII* (Prato, 1983).

[4] Maurice Rey, *Le Domaine du roi et les finances extraordinaires sous Charles VI 1388–1413* (Paris, 1965), p. 131.

[5] *Ibid*. p. 137.

[6] K. B. Macfarlane showed how in England some forty or so extraordinarily rich and powerful families of greater, titled, nobility emerged during the course of the fourteenth and fifteenth centuries out of an undifferentiated mass of some 2000 'noble' families at the beginning of the fourteenth century. If this pattern was repeated across the length and breadth of Europe, it would explain why there was such a concentration of hoardable wealth at this time.

[7] George Henderson, *Gothic* (London, 1967), pp. 135–9.

mark in weight, were a handy form in which to maintain a store of wealth.[1] To contemporaries it seemed that 'thesaurisation' was the main cause of the bullion famines. In retrospect it appears that it was itself in part a response to the famine. Nevertheless it made that shortage worse, although the export of precious metals from Europe now seems more important, combined with the failure of the mines to make good the losses. But whether or not contemporaries were right in the analysis of its causes, the fact of a bullion famine, not only of silver, but also of gold, was clear for all to see at the end of the fourteenth century. In the middle of the fifteenth century, it was yet worse.

Finally fear of the failure to repay, cut back on credit.[2] This too was partially a consequence of the shortage of money, and was also a cause of yet further shortage. As Spooner, writing of the sixteenth century, said, credit doubles money – when money is freely available, credit is also, when money is scarce, so is credit.[3]

In many parts of Europe the banking-system built up in the thirteenth century and the early fourteenth century began to be eroded. Fifteenth-century Venice, for example, frequently saw 'runs' on the local deposit banks, followed by their collapse. There was consequently a diminution of the possibilities of making payments by assignments on bank accounts, or in other terms a shrinkage in the amount of bank money available. Only in South Germany was there an extension of banking- and credit facilities at this time.[4] A clear symptom of the generally declining availability of credit is to be seen in rising interest rates at all levels. Even the most credit-worthy cities had to raise the interest rates they offered slightly. The general level in the first half of the fourteenth century in Italy was between $4\frac{7}{8}\%$ and $8\frac{3}{8}\%$. A hundred years later it was from 6% to over 10%.[5] For example, in Venice, the city in Europe in which coin and credit were most freely available, although the city government continued to pay 4% on its state bonds, the *monte*, in the first quarter of the fifteenth century, the market price stood at 66 ducats, per 100 ducats nominal, so that they bore a real interest rate of 6%.[6] Banks offered their depositors higher interest rates too. The Peruzzi from 1300 to 1325 gave a fixed 8% on deposits. In the first half of the fifteenth century the Medici often paid 10%.[7] The

---

[1] Ph. Wolff, *Commerce et marchands de Toulouse (vers 1350–vers 1450)* (Paris, 1954), p. 346.

[2] Fear of failure to repay could, for commercial loans, stem directly from the shortage of money. In political loans, a banker's assessment of the ability of a city or ruler to repay was usually based on expectations of whether or not foreseeable taxation would meet commitments (E. B. Fryde and M. M. Fryde, 'Public credit, with special reference to North-Western Europe', *Cambridge Economic History of Europe*, III (Cambridge, 1965), 430–553).

[3] Frank C. Spooner, *The International Economy and Monetary Movements in France 1493–1725* (Paris, 1956; English ed., Harvard U.P., 1972).

[4] W. von Strömer, *Oberdeutsche Hochfinanz 1350–1450*, Vierteljahrschrift für Sozial- und Wirtschaftsgeschichte, supplement LV–LVII (1970).

[5] Sidney Homer, *A History of Interest Rates* (Rutgers U.P., 1963), pp. 69–143.

[6] At 66 by 1402, and still at 66 in 1423 (Frederic C. Lane, *Venice, A Maritime Republic* (Baltimore, 1973), pp. 197 and 238).

[7] Homer, *Interest Rates*, pp. 69–143.

rates at which they could make commercial loans rose correspondingly. They were frequently some 2% higher than the banks paid their depositors. Consumption loans, whether to peasants and artisans, or to noblemen and princes, had always been at much higher rates of interest, because of the uncertainty involved.

Therefore when the fifteenth century opened there was in many parts of, although not throughout, western Europe, a dearth both of coin and of credit, and that at all levels. In Toulouse, for example, between 1400 and 1420 men were frequently reduced to using currency substitutes and to barter on a scale to which they had been unaccustomed for centuries.[1]

As stated above, when the silver-mines of central Europe had been productive, a river of silver had flowed across Germany towards the Rhineland and the Low Countries and had then watered England and France before finally reaching the Mediterranean world. However, by the end of the fourteenth century the streams that fed the river of silver were being reduced to mere trickles, and dried up entirely with the final closure of the Bohemian silver-mines during the Hussite wars of the early fifteenth century.[2] The flow of goods in the reverse direction diminished less rapidly than the production of silver. Silver thus drained out of South Germany, the Rhineland, the Low Countries, England and France towards the Mediterranean without any corresponding renewal from central Europe. The result was a progressive dearth of silver, which began to be felt in most countries of Europe in the fourteenth century.

The first signs of silver generally becoming rarer were experienced in the 1340s and 1360s. There were of course particular local shortages earlier, like the dearth of silver in Venice after 1327, caused by the prohibition on sending Bohemian silver on the trade-route through Austria,[3] or the dearth of silver in England in 1338–9 caused by the export of most of England's silver to pay for the French war.[4]

After an abnormally long lifespan the silver-mines of Argentiera in Sardinia suddenly began to be worked out in the 1340s.[5] This may perhaps lie behind the

---

[1] Wolff, *Commerce et marchands de Toulouse*, p. 346.

[2] The Runtinger of Regensburg stopped dealing with Prague in 1401, as the combination of political uncertainty and contracting market meant that it was no longer worth while trying to sell goods to Bohemia (John Martin Klassen, *The nobility and the making of the Hussite Revolution* (New York, 1978), p. 17).

[3] See above, pp. 283–4. This was soon alleviated by Regensburg merchants and other enterprising South Germans, who took the opportunity to open up the route across the Brenner and brought a certain amount of Bohemian silver to Italy in this way.

[4] See above, p. 341 n. 1.

[5] In the mid-1340s the minting of silver alfonsini at Iglesias dropped from over 600,000 a year to under 300,000 a year. At this date the Aragonese were managing to ensure that the larger part of the produce of the mines was being minted. I owe this information to Dr John Day. It is partially derived from his own research in the Archives of the Crown of Aragon, and partially from those of F. Ulina Martorell, 'Un aspecto de la evolución económica sarda en la siglo xiv: la acuñación de moneda', in *VI Congreso de la Historia de la Corona de Aragón 1957* (Madrid, 1959), pp. 647–61.

monetary difficulties experienced in Florence in 1345.[1] The Sardinian mines were finally exhausted around 1365. The Sardinian mint closed at this time, since there was no more newly mined silver to be had.[2] There was no silver minted in Genoa either and the whole Mediterranean was affected. A little later, supplies from Kutná Hora began to decline appreciably. The minting of silver groš at Kremnica came to an end as early as 1364 and was not resumed for over a century.[3]

Northern Europe also began to be affected by a shortage of silver in the 1370s. Flemish mint production, primarily silver coin, dropped significantly in the late 1370s, although it still remained quite considerable until the 1390s.[4] This was only the beginning of a chronic shortage of silver, which in many areas of Europe reached famine proportions in the 1390s.[5] In northern Italy a desperate lack of silver was felt. The minting of silver ceased in Florence in 1393, whilst serious concern was expressed about the lack of silver in Milan at the same time. By 1398 deposit bankers in Genoa were finding great difficulty in paying cash to their depositors. The city government therefore authorised bankers to make a 4% charge on withdrawals in cash. Only 50 florins of coin could be drawn out in any one day.[6] In France, too, the minting of silver declined greatly from 1392, and in Sweden minting stopped altogether at this time, for over 20 years.[7] The famine affected the southern Netherlands rather later, although the minting of silver ceased in Malines in 1392, and in Louvain in 1395 'for lack of bullion'. The bullion that should have gone to the Brabant mint went to that in Flanders instead. The latter was still able to mint considerable quantities of silver through the 1390s.[8]

Only the Venetians partially escaped the effects of this silver-famine, for they had access to the mines of Serbia and Bosnia, which had begun to make some contribution to the Venetian supply of silver from the late 1370s. Venice had been

[1] 'Multiplices querelas . . . de defectu monete argenti, que ad presens non cuditur et non est in usu in dicta civitate Florentie' (23 August 1345) (Mario Bernocchi, *Le monete della repubblica fiorentina*, vol. I, 'Il libro della Zecca' (Florence, 1974), p. 82). 'Nel detto anno 1345 . . . tutte le monete d'argente si fondeamo e portavansi oltremare' (Villani, *Cronica*, Book XII, chapter liii). Presumably the export of silver only afflicted the city in this way because it was not being replaced from Sardinia.

[2] John Day, 'The decline of a money economy: Sardinia in the late Middle Ages', in *Studi in memoria di Federigo Melis*, III (Naples, 1978), 155–76.

[3] Štefan Kazimír (ed.), *Kremnická mincovňa 1328–1978* (Kremnica, 1978), p. 233.

[4] John H. Munro, 'Mint policies, ratios and outputs in the Low Countries and England 1335–1420', *Numismatic Chronicle*, CXLI (1981), 106, translates mint production into modern weights. The mean annual striking of silver coin in the Flanders mint between 1365 and 1374 used over 9000 kilograms of pure silver, that between 1375 and 1384 used under 3000 kilograms of pure silver.

[5] Day, 'Great bullion famine', by far the most important description of the chronic, late-medieval shortage of silver, concentrates in great detail on the first of the bullion-famines, that between 1395 and 1415. Much of the general outline of what follows, pp. 349–50, is derived from Day's work.

[6] John Day, introduction to *Les Douanes de Gênes, 1376–1377* (Paris, 1963).

[7] Add to the very numerous references cited by Day, 'Great bullion famine', Brita Malmer, *Den senmedeltida penningen i Sverige (Late medieval coins in Sweden)* (Stockholm, 1980).

[8] Munro, 'Mint policies in the Low Countries and England', p. 106.

able to start minting silver grossi again in 1379. Even Venice was not immune to the silver-shortages of the 1390s, and restrictions were imposed on the export of silver in 1396. In 1400 fresh regulations to cope with the continuing shortage were framed in Genoa, and similar regulations followed the next year in Bruges. The Bruges mint, which had been able to mint considerable quantities of silver through the 1390s, suddenly found itself in difficulties in 1401 and closed in 1402.[1]

However in the next few years the greatly increased quantities of silver from Serbia dramatically changed the picture in Italy, temporarily at least.[2]

Apart from very small quantities that went overland to Constantinople, almost all of the Serbian and Bosnian silver was shipped out from Dubrovnik (Ragusa).[3] Most of this went to Venice, but some went to Florence, Pesaro and the towns of southern Italy and Sicily. Some of the silver that reached Venice filtered into the Venetian territories in Italy like Padua or Verona, some went in the galleys to England, and some remained in Venice itself. The Serbian gold went exclusively to Venice. (See Map 33.) In 1402 the minting of silver grossi began again in Florence, and some piccoli had even been minted the previous year. By 1404, minting of silver had been resumed in Genoa, and by 1407 there was sufficient silver in Venice for restrictions on its export to be waived. Over the next twenty years the imports from the east through Venice were largely paid for in Venetian silver grossi, which for a time were common coins in Syria and Egypt. In the Netherlands, the end of this famine, like its beginning, came rather later. It was not until 1410 that minting of silver was resumed in Flanders, but immediately on quite a large scale. The negligible amount of silver available in England for the recoinage of 1412–14 has already been discussed.

From Mediterranean Europe precious metals flooded eastwards to, and through, the Levant. In 1423 the dying doge, Tomaso Mocenigo, in a famous speech to senators gathered around his sickbed, attempting to persuade them against electing a war candidate as his successor, outlined the benefits that peace had given Venice whilst he had been doge. He said, in passing, that no less than 500,000 ducats worth of grossi were sent to Syria and Egypt each year and a further 100,000 ducats worth of grossi and soldini to the Venetian overseas territories in the Latin Orient.[4] Since

---

[1] The Flanders mint, at Bruges, had been able to use over 7000 kilograms of silver for minting in 1397 and 1398, but was unable to attract more than 2000 kilograms in 1401 (Munro, *ibid.*).

[2] Desanka Kovacevic, 'Dans la Serbie et la Bosnie médiévales: les mines d'or et d'argent', *Annales E.S.C.,* xv (1960), 248–58.

[3] B. Krekić, *Dubrovnik (Raguse) et le Levant au Moyen Âge* (Paris, 1961).

[4] Marino Sanuto, *Vite de Duchi de Venezia,* ed. L. A. Muratori, col. 960. The text in *Bilanci generali della Repubblica di Venezia,* vol. 1, part 1, Documenti finanziari della Repubblica di Venezia, 2nd series (Venice, 1912), doc. 81, p. 97, says 5000 marks a year exported to Syria and Egypt but is not clear if marks of ducats or of grosseti are meant. If this was 5000 marks of gold it would be 335,000 ducats, a probable figure; if 5000 marks of silver, it would be about three quarters of a million grossi, an improbably small amount. Also this text only gives 50,000 ducats of grossi and soldini exported to the overseas territories.

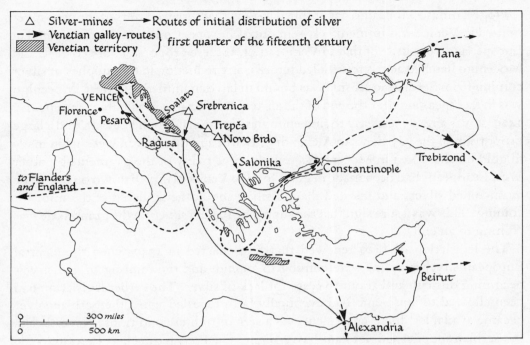

Map 33. Bosnian and Serbian silver

the ducat was then worth 22 grossi, this means an export of 13,200,000 grossi a year, or approximately 20 tonnes of silver. This is an exceedingly large sum.[1] It was only possible because of the production of the Serbian and Bosnian silver-mines. Venice was the only part of Europe still to possess silver in this sort of quantity. On the night of Christmas Eve in 1414 a fire swept through part of the city and threatened the Venetian mint with destruction. It did not go up in flames, which was very fortunate, as there was no less than 120,000 ducats-worth of coin within it.[2] Nowhere else in Europe could a mint be found at this period carrying this amount of money, unless it was in the exceptional circumstances of a recoinage.

In 1423 Venice not only had silver on this scale, but was regularly able to export it. However, the Serbian and Bosnian mines inevitably dried up in due course. Some were worked out as early as 1420, and the peak of their production was passed at some point in the 1420s.[3]

---

[1] Gino Luzzatto, 'Sull'attendibilità di alcune statistiche economiche medievali', *Giornale degli Economisti* (1929), repr. in *Studi di storia economica veneziana* (Padua, 1954), pp. 271–84, has shown that Mocenigo's figures, where checkable, do indeed bear some close relationship to official statistics. This figure for the balance of trade fits with other figures collected by Ashtor, *Les Métaux précieux*. Ashtor considers that in the fifteenth century in general 40% of the oriental goods imported to Europe were paid for by western goods and 60% by precious metals. He also estimated that two thirds of this trade was in Venetian hands.

[2] Sanuto, *Vite de Duchi di Venezia*, col. 892.   [3] Kovacevic, 'Dans la Serbie et la Bosnie'.

Doge Tomaso Mocenigo had implied in 1423 that three quarters of the new silver minted in Venice was immediately sent out of Europe. Only a quarter remained in Europe, and very little of that in Venice itself. If these proportions are correct, and Mocenigo had had access to detailed returns, any reduction in the supplies of silver coming from Serbia and Bosnia was bound to have an immediate effect. Mocenigo was in fact speaking near the end of the all-too-brief respite in the silver-famine. By 1429, it was already less easy to find enough silver to send to the Levant, and a large proportion of the payments to Alexandria, Beirut and the Aegean were again made in gold ducats. Even in Mocenigo's own lifetime many of the payments by other West Europeans had been made in gold. In 1429 Venice clamped down on free trade in uncoined silver, and insisted that all silver should be tendered at the mint for coining. This was a sure sign that the supply of Balkan silver on the grand scale was coming to an end.

The legislation of 1429 renewed that first enacted in 1347 when the Central European silver supplies were coming to an end, and the minting of grossi was becoming difficult and about to cease for lack of silver. The earlier legislation had been allowed to lapse, and had eventually been repealed when the Serbian silver became available.[1] Its re-enactment was a sign of tighter conditions. Nevertheless the Serbian supplies did not vanish overnight. The French traveller, Bertranden de la Broquière, noted in 1433 that Novo Brdo, the most important of these mines, still produced 200,000 ducats of revenue a year.[2] However, as the silver ran out, the Venetians returned to the export of gold, just as they had done in the fourteenth century before the Serbian mines were opened up. Mocenigo's speeches of 1423 indicate how gold was already flowing into Venice, if not through it. In his deathbed oration he estimated that the balance of trade between Florence and Venice was such that Florentines sent 392,000 ducats of gold a year to Venice,[3] despite the value of the wide variety of Florentine cloth that the Florentines sent to Venice. The Venetians exported it southwards to Apulia, the Regno, Sicily and Barbary; eastwards to Egypt, Syria, Cyprus, Rhodes, Crete, Constantinople and the Morea; and westwards to Catalonia, Castille and Portugal. In a speech two years earlier he had argued for keeping peace with Milan, despite a Florentine embassy urging war. He then pointed out that the Venetian *banchi di scritta* recorded the receipt of 1,600,000 ducats a year from the possessions of the Duke of Milan, over and above the enormous quantity of cloth and provisions received by the

---

[1] A. Nagl, 'Die Goldwährung und die handelsmäässige Goldrechnung im Mittelalter', *Numismatische Zeitschrift*, XXVI (1894), pp. 146–8.

[2] It is almost impossible to turn this into a quantity mined, even if revenue meant production not profit, since the mine produced a mixture of about $\frac{5}{6}$ silver and $\frac{1}{6}$ gold – so it could mean a production of something like $2\frac{1}{2}$ tonnes of silver and $\frac{1}{2}$ tonne of gold (Kovacevic, 'Dans la Serbie et la Bosnie', pp. 248–58).

[3] Sanuto, *Vite de Duchi di Venezia*, col. 960. The text in *Bilanci generali*, I, i, 97, gives an annual total of 150,000 ducats, but, inconsistently, the same weekly total of 7000 ducats as the Sanuto version.

Venetians. He valued these at some 1,200,000 ducats, so that Lombardy was 'a veritable garden to Venice, to be tilled in peace and not destroyed by war'. It was on this occasion that he declared 'tutto l'oro del mondo viena nella vestra Terra'.[1]

In other words, not only was silver draining out of western Europe to the Mediterranean, but gold was doing the same. Whether gold or silver was sent on to the Near East depended on the relative ratios between the two metals in Europe and in the Near East. This, of course, depended on the availability of the two metals, which was in turn a function of how much was being mined, and how much was already being transported away from either area. In this connection, it must be emphasised that although the Near East appeared to West Europeans or North Africans as the terminus for their trade, and for their precious metals, it was in reality only a staging-point on the way further eastwards. Professor Ashtor has shown very clearly how West African gold and European silver and gold, far from accumulating in the Mamluk dominions, passed through them, frequently leaving them denuded of precious metals.[2] It is a picture that reminds one of the fate of Spain in the latter sixteenth century and the seventeenth, becoming impoverished although the wealth of America flowed through it.

A brief glance at the somewhat simplified Table 7 will show the main lines of the evolution of the ratio of the values of gold and silver in Egypt and Venice.

At the end of the first quarter of the fourteenth century, silver was more highly valued in terms of gold in Egypt than in Venice, because Egypt had less of it than Venice, and in consequence the imbalance of trade was settled by sending shipments of silver from Venice to Egypt as had been done for the previous century or more.[3] During the next quarter-century gold became more plentiful in both Egypt and Venice, and supplies of silver diminished in Venice. By the middle of the fourteenth century the ratios were the same in both places and the imbalance of trade was settled by sending shipments of whichever metal was more available and more convenient. This usually turned out to be gold.[4]

As soon as silver was again available in Venice, grossi, minted once more from 1379, as well as gold ducats, were sent to Egypt. Lodovico Frescobaldi saw both ducats and grossi circulating in Egypt in 1384.[5] Two large hoards of coins concealed at Hamath before the end of the century confirm this observation. They contained large numbers of matapans of Antonio Venier (doge 1382–1400).[6] Since gold was still more highly valued in Egypt than in Venice, more gold than silver

---

[1] Sanuto, *Vite de Duchi di Venezia*, col. 957. Also in *Bilanci generali*, I, i, 94–7 and 577–9.

[2] Ashtor, *Les Métaux précieux*, final chapters: 'La balance des payements' and 'La disparition des métaux précieux et la faillite', pp. 65–108.

[3] See above, pp. 148–53.   [4] See above, pp. 283–5.

[5] J. Glenisson and J. Day, *Textes et documents d'histoire du Moyen Age XIVe–XVe siècles*, vol. I, 'Les "Crises" et leur cadre' (Paris, 1970), doc. 30.

[6] Eliyahu Ashtor, 'Observations on Venetian trade in the Levant in the XIVth century', *Journal of European Economic History*, V (1976), 565.

Table 7. *Gold–silver ratios in Egypt and Venice, in the fourteenth and fifteenth centuries*

Egypt		Venice		logical action to be taken
1324–36	1:10.3	1305–30	1:14.2	send silver
		1331–2	1:13.1	send silver
		1346	1:10.5	send silver
		1349	1:10.5	send silver
1338–59	1:9.4			
		1350	1:9.4	send metal available, i.e. gold
		1353–7	1:9.6	send metal available, i.e. gold
		1374	1:9.9	send gold
1375	1:11.3	1379	1:10.2	send gold
		1380	1:11.4	send either silver or gold
		1382	1:10.7	send either silver or gold
1384	1:14.7			send gold
		1398	1:11	send gold
1399	1:12.7	1399	1:11.3	send gold
1400–9	1:14	1408	1:11.2	send gold
1410	1:11			send either silver or gold
1415	1:8.1			send silver
1416–21	1:10.7	1417	1:12.5	send silver
1422–4	1:7			send silver
1425–38	1:11	1429	1:10.6	send metal available, increasingly gold

From: E. Ashtor, *Les Métaux précieux*, pp. 48–9; Carlo Cipolla, *Studi di storia della moneta*, vol. I, 'I movimenti dei cambi in Italia dal secolo XIII al XV' (Pavia, 1948), pp. 153–4; Jere L. Bacharach, 'Circassian monetary policy: silver', *Numismatic Chronicle*, 7th series, XI (1971), 267–81; Reinhold C. Mueller, 'La crisi economica–monetaria veneziana di meta quattrocento nel contesto generale', in *Aspetti della vita economica medievale* (Florence, 1985).

was therefore carried to Egypt. Maqrīzī commented that by A.H. 800 (A.D. 1397–8) the Venetian ducat, which he called 'ifranty', had become the current coin of 'all the principal cities of the world: Cairo, Fostât, Syria, the Hejaz and the Yemen', and was widely imitated in Cairo.[1] The continuous preference for sending gold for half a century meant that the supply of silver in Egypt was precariously small. When restrictions were imposed on the export of silver from Venice in 1396 a silver-famine immediately ensued in Egypt.[2] As a consequence, the value of silver rose in Egypt in terms of gold, whilst at the same time, with the opening-up of further Bosnian and Serbian silver-mines, the value of silver dropped in Venice. It made sense once more to export silver. In 1407, the Venetian senate lifted its interdict on exporting silver. By 1412 there were large quantities of Venetian grossi ('bunduqi') in Syria; so much so that the dirhams issued there by the Amir Navrūz during his revolt were imitations of Venetian grossi. The revolt was put down in 1414 and by then there were again adequate supplies of silver in Cairo as well.[3] Supplies of silver in Venice were still erratic and precarious. The Soranzo company did not buy any

[1] Glenisson and Day, *Textes et documents XIVᵉ–XVᵉ siècles*, I, doc. 31 (written A.D. 1415–16).
[2] Qualchaquandi observed that it was not only that Europeans ceased to bring silver but that Egyptians had wasted so much on ornamenting saddles and on vases! (*ibid.* doc. 29).
[3] Bacharach, 'Circassian monetary policy'.

silver, either in bars or in grossi for shipment to the Levant between January 1414 and July 1423. Instead they drew gold ducats from the bank 'per navegar'.[1] Indeed in mid-1417 the silver-mint of Venice was again almost at a standstill ('è andà in dissolution e reduta quasi a niente') since no silver was being imported.[2] In 1423 Tomaso Mocenigo was again able to speak of the export of silver to Egypt and Syria. In 1426 the Soranzo *fraterna* were purchasing quantities of *arzento di bolla* for export in the Levant galleys on the *viazo d'Aman*.[3] However, by 1429 it was once again less easy to find enough silver. This time the difficulty was of longer duration. The production of the Serbian and Bosnian mines had already passed its peak. Furthermore, less of that silver was coming to Venice, for it was exported direct from Ragusa to the Levant.[4] Silver was scarcer in Venice than it had been earlier and the ratio between gold and silver had consequently dropped. It was already on much the same level as in Egypt, so that it was again a matter of convenience and availability which metal was carried out of Venice. As a consequence, the stream of gold that was already flowing so strongly into Venice in Mocenigo's time began to flow onwards, alongside silver, and eventually, replacing it, to and through Egypt and Syria. No less than 460,000 ducats worth of gold and silver coin were on board the galleys leaving Venice for Beirut and Alexandria in July 1433.[5]

However, the ducat never again became what it had been in the latter fourteenth century, common coin in Syria, Egypt and Arabia.

In 1425, just at the time when the number of ducats sent to the Mamluk Empire was increasing again, the Sultan al-Ashraf Barsbây produced a new dinar, the ashrafî, of pure gold and very slightly lighter than the ducat.[6] Use of the ducat was banned in the Mamluk Empire. Those which were already circulating were called in and reminted into ashrafî.

The Mamluks already exercised considerable control over European traders. These were restricted to their own *funduqs*, or factories, where they could buy goods, primarily spices from further east, only under strict supervision. Control was now extended to require that all coin paid over to Islamic traders for goods, or to Mamluk officials by way of taxes, should be sent to be reminted, primarily into ashrafî. The success of Barsbây's new ashrafî was given a particular boost in 1426

---

[1] Reinhold C. Mueller, 'The role of bank money in Venice 1300–1500', *Studi Veneziani*, new series, III (1979), 88–9.

[2] *Ibid.* pp. 70–1, quoting N. Papadopoli, *Le monete di Venezia*, I (Venice, 1893), doc. 21.

[3] *Ibid.* p. 64. Note the brief revival of the use of ingots, with the temporary change back from gold to silver as the medium for large, long-distance payments.

[4] Krekić, *Dubrovnik et le Levant*, p. 75, suggests that Ragusan trade with the Levant increased after 1430.

[5] *Cronaca Morosini*, as quoted in P. Grierson, 'La moneta veneziana nell'economia mediterranea del Trecento e Quattrocento', in *La civiltà Veneziana del Quattrocento* (Fondazione Giorgio Cini, Florence, 1957), pp. 86 and 97. This information was explicitly said to be provided by officers of the customs. Prof. Grierson considered this abnormally large for a single shipment, but points out that it may be explained by the fact that it was the first fleet to sail after trade had been interrupted by war with Genoa.

[6] About 3.41 grams as opposed to 3.56 grams.

by the success of his Cypriot expedition, in which he captured the king, James I, and over 1000 other men worth ransoming. As the instalments of James I's ransom of 200,000 ducats arrived from 1429 onwards, they were at once reminted as ashrafî. After this, isolated references show that a few ducats still circulated, but their wide use had ended.[1] Instead, it was the ashrafî, into which the ducats were reminted, which not only became the standard coin for a century in the Mamluk Empire itself, but also influenced the later coinage of the Ottomans and of Persia.

In the Aegean, the ducat again became the common coin, since there was no central authority to stop its use. A second wave of ducat imitations began to be minted, as in the 1350s, at Rhodes, Mytylene, Chios and Phocaea and also at Pera, the Genoese port of Constantinople.[2]

This continued outflow of precious metals, first of silver and then of gold, then again of silver, and once more of gold, could not be sustained after the middle of the fourteenth century. The quantities of the two metals mined in western Europe, together with the gold that continued to come in from Africa, were too small. Neither the Hungarian nor the African gold, nor yet the Serbian and Bosnian silver, sufficed to meet this vast export of precious metals, in which the trade was dominated by Venice, but was shared to a lesser extent by other ports, above all Genoa and Barcelona. There may also have been an interruption in gold-mining at Kremnica at this time. Certainly no ducats were minted there between 1440 and 1453.[3] In consequence, there were erratic shortages in turn of silver and, less often, gold, until eventually, by the late 1430s and early 1440s both were lacking together.[4]

At this point many mints in western Europe were compelled to close down altogether, for lack of bullion, not merely for weeks or months on end, or even for years, as in the famine of the 1390s, but for decades.

Even in the commercially sophisticated Netherlands, the mints had to be closed, although under Philip the Good they were one of the few areas of Europe not scourged by war from the 1420s to the 1450s.

The mint of the Duchy of Brabant, at Brussels, was closed down in 1437, and minted no silver coins of any sort for the next twenty-nine years. It was shut up completely for seventeen of these years and neither gold nor silver was minted

---

[1] For the ducat and the ashrafî see Jere L. Bacharach, 'The dinar versus the ducat', *International Journal of Middle East Studies*, IV (1973), 77–96.

[2] See above, pp. 284–6 (for the 1350s); and H. E. Ives and Philip Grierson, *The Venetian Gold Ducat and its Imitations*, Numismatic Notes and Monographs CXXVIII (American Numismatic Society, New York, 1954); and Philip Grierson, 'La moneta veneziana'.

[3] Kazimír (ed.), *Kremnická mincovňa*, p. 233.

[4] I had already delivered the substance of what follows (pp. 356–62) on the second bullion-famine of the fifteenth century (*c.* 1440–64) as one of my lectures for the Chair of Burgundian Studies at the University of Louvain in 1972, before I became aware of John Day's notable work on the first bullion-famine (*c.* 1395–1415), which was later published as 'The great bullion famine'.

there. It was much the same in the other Burgundian principalities. Even in the county of Flanders, still the most developed of these principalities, where the mint at Ghent stayed open longest, it only struck the very smallest quantities of silver coin after 1439, and none at all from 1447 to 1454 and from 1456 to 1466. The mints of the counties of Holland and of Hainault, at Dordrecht and Valenciennes, were only open for one and two years respectively to strike either gold or silver for two whole decades after 1446 and 1444.[1]

In the neighbouring territories the same thing occurred. The English mint at Calais struck practically nothing after 1439 and closed down for ever in 1442. The mints at Amiens and St Quentin struck practically nothing after 1440 and nothing at all after 1447. The mint of the King of France at Tournai was closed down for political reasons in 1435, but when it was permitted to reopen after 1440, it was often impossible to find any bullion for minting. Only very minimal quantities were struck in seven of the following twenty-seven years, and in the rest nothing at all.[2]

The great Rhineland electors were forced to close down their mints one after another from 1440 to 1443. The only mint in north-western Europe that stayed open was the English royal mint in the Tower of London, but even here only derisory quantities were struck in the 1440s. The small amounts struck there did, incredibly, increase slightly in the 1450s, when other mints were closed. In the 1450s England appears to have had favourable balances of trade in all directions, from its own merchants trading in the Low Countries, from Hanseatic merchants trading with the Baltic, and from Genoese and Venetian merchants as well.[3] The latter continued to bring a minor quantity of Serbian and Bosnian silver into the country year by year in the galley fleet.

With this single exception the mints in all the countries of north-western Europe struck virtually nothing, and frequently nothing at all, from around 1440 for twenty-five years.

It was not only in north-western Europe that mints were compelled to close. In Austria there was no bullion at all, even though Vienna lay astride the former route for silver from Bohemia to Venice. In 1455 the Austrians, at a South German meeting about the lack of bullion, complained 'sy mochten neben unns nicht munssen'.[4] In 1448 men from the Flemish cities had failed to find silver where they apparently most expected it, in Breslau, Cracow, and Magdeburg.[5] In 1447 the

[1] Peter Spufford, *Monetary Problems and Policies in the Burgundian Netherlands 1433–1496* (Leiden, 1970), pp. 55–6, 85, 88, 94–5, 103–5, 116.
[2] M. Hoc, *Histoire Monétaire de Tournai* (Brussels, 1970), pp. 112ff.
[3] J. L. Bolton, *The Medieval English Economy 1150–1500* (London, 1980), pp. 287–319.
[4] T. Mayer, *Der auswärtige Handel des Herzogtums Österreich im Mittelalter*, Forschungen zur inneren Geschichte Österreichs, ed. A. Dopsch, VI (Innsbruck, 1909).
[5] Werner Hillebrand, 'Der Goslarer Metallhandel im Mittelalter', *Hansische Geschichtsblätter*, LXXXVII (1969), 35–6.

mints of Languedoc were recorded as having been already closed for several years. That of Toulouse was already shut by 1437.[1] Navarre had stopped minting as early as 1432.[2] Castille, like England, suffered less than other places from the dearth of silver, because it too was a major exporter of wool. This, combined with an unimpaired supply of gold from Africa, meant that Castille hardly shared at all in the general European experience of trade being curtailed for lack of the means of payment.[3] Other parts of Spain were, however, affected. The mint at Barcelona was reduced to striking minimal quantities after 1444. In 1447 the city council recognised that the lack of silver was not a problem peculiar to Barcelona. As they said 'a questes coses toquen lo univerç' ('the same things apply throughout the universe').[4]

Things went from bad to worse. Mints closed everywhere in the 1440s and generally remained shut throughout the 1450s, and well into the 1460s. Silver coins were no longer to be had. In such conditions, if one had any ready cash, one held on to it and did not spend it. The velocity of circulation was gravely reduced, to the great damage of both international trade and daily life. (See Map 34.)

In 1451 two galleys, one of Jacques Coeur, the *argentier* of Charles VII of France, the other from Florence, came into the port of Valencia. Neither sold anything of their cargoes, since there were no means available in the city for anyone to make any purchases from them.[5]

As well as the appalling direct effect that lack of money had on trade, it also caused the disappearance of business facilities. If there was not enough liquid money about, there was no longer any livelihood to be made for money-changers. At Dieppe, already one of the principal ports of northern France, there was not enough money to keep even a single money-changer in business after 1446, for thirty years.[6]

Attempts were made to remedy the lack of silver by mining, or attempting to mine, at various places in Europe.

It was only worthwhile to mine the small deposits of silver in the Lyonnais with silver so scarce. Nevertheless the astute Jacques Coeur thought it useful to incorporate them in his commercial empire.[7] In 1449 and again in 1453 Philip the

[1] Wolff, *Commerce et marchands de Toulouse*, pp. 342–3.
[2] Earl J. Hamilton, *Money, Prices and Wages in Valencia, Aragon and Navarre 1351–1500* (Cambridge, Mass., 1936), p. 211.
[3] MacKay, *Money in Fifteenth Century Castile*, pp. 23–41.
[4] Claude Carrère, *Barcelone, centre économique 1380–1462* (2 vols., Paris, 1967), II, 842.
[5] *Ibid.* pp. 743–6.
[6] Michel Mollat, *Le Commerce maritime normand à la fin du Moyen Age* (Paris, 1952), pp. 393–4. In the previous bullion-famine the number of money-changers in Marseilles had shrunk from sixteen in 1384 to three in 1411 (E. Baratier and F. Reynaud, *Histoire du commerce de Marseille*, vol. II, '1291–1480' (Paris, 1950), 844–6).
[7] Guerreau, 'L'Atelier monétaire royal de Mâcon', pp. 369–92, affirms that the mines of Beaujolais and Lyonnais were never of any importance for the Mâcon mint, despite royal optimism.

Map 34. Bullion-famine *c.* 1440–1464

Good vainly sponsored mining-experts to seek for deposits of silver in the two Burgundies.[1]

In England, in Parliament, the commons petitioned for the old silver-mines of the south-west to be reopened at any cost, in order to produce just a little silver to put into circulation.

Eventually even Venice was afflicted by the bullion-famine. The Turks overran Serbia and then Bosnia in the 1450s and 1460s. The production of silver and gold, which had been declining since the 1420s, came, as far as Venice was concerned, to an abrupt halt. The principal mines of Serbia, those at Novo Brdo, fell into Turkish hands in 1455, and the principal mines of Bosnia, those at Srebrenica, fell in 1460.[2]

The Venetian silver grosso, which had been drastically reduced in weight under the Doge Foscari during the long years of war with Milan from 1426 to 1454, had barely begun to recover after the Peace of Lodi, when the cutting-off of Serbian and Bosnian silver supplies brought its long life to a pitiful close in 1462. The last grossi of Cristoforo Moro weighed well under two thirds of the weight of the pre-war

[1] R. Vaughan, *Philip the Good* (London, 1970), p. 256.
[2] Kovacevic, 'Dans la Serbie et la Bosnie'.

grossi of forty years before, and much less than half of those original grossi of 1201, which had been the first in Europe, and had then been so assiduously maintained in weight and fineness by Venetian rulers for a century and a half.

There were never to be any more grossi after 1462. In 1464 Venice suffered the fate that other European cities had been suffering for twenty years. On 17 March the Marquis of Mantua's agent, Giovanni de Strigi, wrote to him that Venice had sent off all her liquid currency with the Syrian galleys. Her stocks of silver, her *arzenti*, were all at sea, 'sono navegati per questi navi di Siria', leaving the city bled white and temporarily paralysed.[1]

In November 1468 the heads of the workshops in the silver mint in Venice complained to the Senate that they were reduced to poverty 'cum in nostra cecha presentialiter non cudantur monete iuxta solitum'. In 1468 the mint of Milan was also totally inactive.[2] 1464 was probably the worst year of the bullion-famine. The Genoese city bonds sank to their lowest point ever, and in Florence there were a series of spectacular bank collapses, including that of the Strozzi bank, second only to the Medici. Even the Medici themselves were severely shaken.[3] As Angelo Acciaiuoli wrote in December, 'it is the greatest calamity that has happened in this city since 1339'.[4]

In the latter years of the bullion-famine even black money, which had never been as plentiful as it ought to have been, began to disappear, as well as white silver and gold. It was, perhaps, carried out of Europe. At first sight this seems improbable, but it may really have been the case. In 1424 officers of the King of France caught up with a convoy of 29 mules and horses travelling from Rodez to one of the Geneva Fairs. It was illegally carrying money out of the kingdom, not gold or white silver, But nearly 3 tonnes of black money![5] From Rodez to Geneva is 400 kilometres (250 miles) as the crow flies. If it was worthwhile to carry such vast quantities of petty currency for so long a distance by land in order to be able to make any purchases at all, it was much cheaper and easier to carry it even further by sea. The dearth of small change was accentuated by those who hoarded black money as their predecessors might have hoarded gold and silver. They did so, of course, in much

---

[1] F. Braudel, *The Mediterranean and the Mediterranean World in the Age of Philip II*, 2nd ed., I (Paris, 1966; English trans. London, 1972), 378.

[2] Reinhold C. Mueller, 'Guerra monetaria tra Venezia e Milano nel Quattrocento', in G. Gorini (ed.), *La Zecca di Milano* (Milan, 1984), p. 350.

[3] Raymond de Roover, *The Rise and Decline of the Medici Bank 1397–1494* (Cambridge, Mass., 1963), pp. 358–60 and 480–1.

[4] Glenisson and Day, *Textes et documents XIVᵉ–XVᵉ siècles*, I, doc. 33.

[5] R.H. Bautier, 'Trafics clandestins d'argent par le Dauphiné vers les foires de Genève (1424)', *Bulletin Philologique et Historique du Comité des Travaux Historiques* (1963), 669–88. Although the most striking, this was far from the only example of carrying black money to the Geneva Fairs. There are numerous cases involving men from the Duchy of Burgundy, including even Odot Molain himself, the most successful merchant in Burgundy (Dubois, 'Commerce international aux confins orientaux de France').

larger physical quantities to produce the same result in terms of value. The chronicler Molinet wrote of those who 'avoient de longtemps faict leur amas de petits gros et hallebardes par milliers en petits vaisseaulx'.[1] Enormous quantities of black money could, of course, be melted down to extract the small amounts of silver in it.[2]

One way or another, a general lack of black money began to develop throughout Europe, which particularly afflicted ordinary people and impeded the ordinary dealings of everyday life. A symptom of this growing lack was the petition of the town authorities of Maastricht in Limburg to their duke, Philip the Good of Burgundy, to be permitted to set up a town mint to strike black money, pieces of small change to be worth a fortieth part of a patard.[3] In 1463 Philip the Good authorised the chapter of Maubeuge to strike 32 pounds of 'deniers de plonc' for the townsmen to use in 'oeuvres de petite despense'.[4]

Another symptom was the attempt to profit from the lack of official black money by minor lords. Black money with extremely little silver content, or none at all, was struck by the Lords of Rummen and Kinrooi, and by other similar minor rulers of the eastern Netherlands. They were taking profitable advantage of the inability of the mints of the great principalities to cope legitimately with the growing lack of black money.[5] Similarly imitations with little or no silver content were widely made of the black Venetian quattrini struck for use on her mainland territories in 1453.[6]

This lack of black money throughout Europe reached crisis proportions during the seven worst years of the bullion-famine, from 1457 to 1464. Governments and city authorities took desperate measures to deal with the problem. In 1458 the King of France, Charles VII, authorised the master of his mint at Tournai to reopen it to strike black money, deniers parisis and little black deniers tournois, 'au soulagement du povre peuple', even if he made a loss in doing so.[7] He also gave subsidies on two occasions so as to have this sort of money struck in the Paris mint in 1458

---

[1] Spufford, *Monetary Problems in the Burgundian Netherlands*, p. 44.

[2] When copper coins were introduced by Venice in 1472, the impossibility of melting them down like black money for their silver content was regarded as one of their prime advantages (Reinhold C. Mueller, 'L'imperialismo monetario veneziano nel Quattrocento', *Società e Storia*, VIII (1980), 293).

[3] Spufford, *Monetary Problems in the Burgundian Netherlands*, p. 201.

[4] R. Chalon, *Recherches sur les monnaies des comtes de Hainault* (Brussels, 1848), pp. 230–3.

[5] Spufford, *Monetary Problems in the Burgundian Netherlands*, p. 200. They did not limit themselves to striking imitations of Burgundian black money, but were prepared to supply more distant markets as well. In 1456 two men from Dieppe were arrested when carrying home 3000 false French deniers, bought for 3 écus at Liège (Mollat, *Le Commerce maritime normand*, p. 73).

[6] Mueller, 'L'imperialismo monetario veneziano', p. 289.

[7] F. de Saulcy, *Recueil de documents relatifs à l'histoire des monnaies frappées par les rois de France, depuis Philippe II jusqu'à François Ier*, III (Paris, 1892), 225. He was to strike 45 marks of silver into black money, and to be paid 10s. tournois per mark for doing so. This would have produced 80,000 parisis or 100,000 tournois.

and 1461.[1] It is astonishing to find medieval rulers prepared to pay for the striking of money instead of expecting to make a profit from it.

In southern Europe conditions were the same. The city councillors of Barcelona responded in the same way as the King of France. They said that they would pay for the cost of minting the silver, if anybody would produce it. They sought for it everywhere, even offering a higher price than the normal mint price. In September 1460 they tried, unsuccessfully, to compel every money-changer to come to the mint each week bringing with him a single mark of silver. But the money-changers said that they could not even lay their hands on this quarter of a kilo (half a pound) of silver a week.[2]

In Holland in 1463 no master or warden survived from the old mint, since it had been shut down for so long, but a former die-engraver, Philip Pellegrineszoon van Waetselair, was still about. The Count of Holland, Duke Philip the Good of Burgundy, ordered him to reopen the disused mint buildings in Dordrecht specially to strike black money – 'oirtkins', 'doitkins' and 'pennyncxkins'.[3]

In Venice a novel idea was put forward to solve the problem of small change. In 1463 its rulers debated whether to authorise the striking of coins of pure copper, without trace of silver.[4] For the future it was the right solution, but for the next decade it was nothing more than an idea to discuss.

It is quite likely that pure copper coins actually existed in Europe in 1463, but not with the official blessing of a major government. The black money struck in the minor seigneuries of the eastern Netherlands at this time may well have had no silver content.[5] The pennies attributed to Bishop Kennedy of St Andrews in Scotland (1440–65) and the farthings and half-farthings struck in Ireland about 1460 may also have been entirely made of copper.[6]

And thus, with a lack even of black money, as well as of white silver and gold, the bullion-famine reached its worst point in the early 1460s. The economy of Europe ground to a halt at every level, from the humblest purchases of bundles of leeks, up to the great merchants, whose galleys had to row away with goods unsold.

---

[1] *Ibid.* pp. 225 and 234–5. He gave 55 marks of silver in 1458 and 20 marks in 1461, to produce 100,000 and 36,000 parisis, or 120,000 and 43,000 tournois.

[2] Carrère, *Barcelone, centre économique*, p. 895.

[3] Spufford, *Monetary Problems in the Burgundian Netherlands*, p. 201.

[4] See below, pp. 371–2.

[5] Spufford, *Monetary Problems in the Burgundian Netherlands*, pp. 200–2.

[6] Philip Grierson, 'The monetary pattern of sixteenth century coinage', *Transactions of the Royal Historical Society*, 5th series, XXI (1971), 50.

16

Money on the Eve
of the Price Revolution

The extreme difficulties of the dearth of coin and credit in the early 1460s disappeared very suddenly with the opening-up of new sources of silver.

A whole series of new discoveries of silver ore were made in the Alps and in the Erzgebirge, particularly at Schwaz in the Tirol and at Schneeberg in Saxony. At the same time a series of technical innovations, for example in the refining of silver, and in the development of pumps for draining the mines, made it profitable to reopen old mines. These revived mines included those at Kutná Hora in Bohemia, at Freiberg in Saxony and at Goslar in the Harz, each of which had already possessed the richest silver-mines in Europe in turn. The second period of exploitation of these revived mines produced relatively small amounts, however, compared with their first period of exploitation, or compared with the most important of the new mines being opened up in the second half of the fifteenth century.

The ore at Schwaz and at Schneeberg had been discovered before 1460, but it was not until well after 1460 that the mines at either place really began to produce silver in important quantities. The mines at Schneeberg in Saxony were developed the faster of the two. By the early 1470s over 30,000 marks of silver a year were being produced there, and a maximum annual production of nearly 45,000 marks was reached there between 1476 and 1485. The mines at Schwaz in the Tirol were slightly slower to develop. Nevertheless they were producing over 25,000 marks of silver each year in the late 1470s and reached their maximum annual production, of over 45,000 marks, a decade later.[1] That is to say, during the 1480s enough ore was being dug out of the mines at each place to produce between 10 and 11 tonnes of pure silver annually. These were only the two richest of the many groups of mines being opened up in Europe. Such quantities sound enormous to us. In the fifteenth century they gave the same impression, especially when placed against the background of a general dearth of silver throughout Europe. It is always impressive to dine off a table of solid silver, as the Elector of Saxony did in one of his mines,[2] but it is the more impressive when others were altogether lacking any silver at all.

[1] J. U. Nef, 'Silver production in Central Europe, 1450–1618', *Journal of Political Economy*, XLIX (1941), 578–86.
[2] Georgius Agricola, *De re metallica*, trans. and ed. H. C. and L. H. Hoover (London, 1912).

It is no wonder that, as in the thirteenth century, other rulers fostered a new wave of prospecting for precious metals. Successive popes called in a long sequence of mining experts such as 'Giovanni' Klug of Freiberg in 1479, and offered them lavish concessions if they should find silver in the papal states.[1] All was in vain. The popes were not enabled to emulate the Duke of Saxony, or Count Sigmund *der Münzreiche* of the Tirol in their mineral wealth.

The starving mints of Europe eagerly consumed this silver as fast as they could obtain it. The mints of the Burgundian Netherlands were reopened in 1466, and those in the Rhineland and in France at the same time. Those in Bohemia were reopened in 1469, the year after the Kutná Hora mines began to be exploited once again.[2] In northern Italy silver was again plentiful by 1471.

Frankfurt and Milan became the two focal points for the precious-metal trade. It was through Frankfurt that a very large proportion of this new silver passed to the mints of northern and western Europe. In 1472 a certain Frankfurt bullion-merchant, Martin Römer, of Zwickau in Saxony, wrote from Frankfurt to the city of Cologne, that he had already bought and sold more than 20,000 marks of this silver on his own account and offered his services as a purveyor of silver to the city of Cologne, which was then in the process of negotiating for the right to mint its own coinage.[3] In the same year the Count Palatine of the Rhine gave a safe conduct to merchants of Cologne who wished to cross his lands to purchase silver at Frankfurt.[4] In 1477 citizens of Cologne were to be found at Frankfurt purchasing not merely silver, but also shares in the Schneeberg silver-mines themselves.[5] The city of Cologne continued to buy silver regularly at Frankfurt to supply its new civic mint. For example in the year 1492–3, it bought silver to a value of 6000 florins of the Rhine.[6] The officers of the Burgundian and English mints similarly went to Frankfurt to buy silver.

In the Burgundian Netherlands it is possible to make a comparison with the major recoinage of a generation earlier. The initial quantities of fine silver coins struck after the 1466 recoinage hardly exceeded the fine silver coins struck after the recoinage of 1433, which suggests that, despite the difficulties of the previous two decades, enough silver had been hoarded in the Netherlands, or was attracted in for the recoinage itself, to bring the silver currency in the late 1460s back to the level of the mid-1430s.

[3] Gino Barbieri, *Industria e politica mineraria nello stato ponteficio dal '400 al '600* (Rome, 1940), pp. 31–48.
[1] Karel Castelin, *Grossus Pragensis. Der Prager Groschen und seine Teilstücke, 1300–1547*, 2nd ed. (Brunswick, 1973).
[2] B. Kuske (ed.), *Quellen zur Geschichte des Kölner Handels und Verkehrs im Mittelalter*, II (Bonn, 1917), 291–2.
[3] *Ibid.* p. 272.
[5] *Ibid.* pp. 381–5, 425, 436–7. From the 1460s the 'free' miners gave way as mine-owners to investors in central Europe. Absentee shareholders now provided the capital there, as they had earlier done in Tuscany and Sardinia; see above, pp. 129–30. It was this injection of capital, much of it from southern Germany, that enabled expensive new mining-equipment to be developed.
[6] *Ibid.* pp. 653, 659–60, 668.

This sort of comparison rests, of course, on the unprovable assumption that, in any major recoinage, a sufficiently high proportion of the circulating currency of a country was melted down and reminted, in the first two years, to give a fair impression of the total currency available.

In the 1430s the amount of silver struck in the Burgundian mints diminished very rapidly after the first two years of the new common coinage in the Netherlands, but in the 1460s and 1470s the amount struck in the Burgundian mints was maintained at a high level even after the first two years, thanks to the stream of newly mined silver that was flowing from Saxony to the Netherlands by way of Frankfurt and Cologne.

The Burgundian government estimated this import of raw silver from Germany at 60,000 marks (about 15 tonnes) a year.[1] It naturally flowed first into Brabant, and from 1475 onwards the minting of silver in Brabant exceeded that in Flanders. In Flanders, which had more immediate access to Portuguese gold, the minting of gold exceeded that in Brabant until the Portuguese moved their 'house' from Bruges to Antwerp in 1498.[2]

The concept of the 'purchase' *of* silver is an interesting one, and shows a radical change in attitudes since the thirteenth-century mining-boom. Then it was silver that took an active role. Goods were bought *with* silver, and mining directly promoted trade. In the late fifteenth-century mining-boom, silver took a passive role. It was bought, with gold, and mining promoted bi-metallic flows as well as, if not more than, trade. The gainers were financiers and bullion-brokers as much as merchants. In one sense the change had already reached northern and western Europe in the fourteenth century. The purchase of gold at Bruges for the Lübeck mint,[3] is an obvious early example of this sort of metal trade, and the exchange of a very large part of England's supply of silver for gold in the second half of the fourteenth century was partially the result of many similar transactions. Now the same process was taking place in reverse; silver was being purchased with gold, rather than gold with silver.

During the long century in which the stock of silver in Europe had almost shrunk away to nothing, the individual silver coins had also become progressively lighter and baser.[4] With the return of silver, larger and finer pieces began to be struck. Initially only the lost levels of the past were regained. In 1466 fine silver double patards began to be struck in the Burgundian Netherlands, containing about 3 grams of silver, double that in the half-silver patards, which had up to then been the

---

[1] Raymond van Uytven, 'What is new socially and economically in the sixteenth-century Netherlands', *Acta Historiae Neerlandicae*, VII (1974), 19–22.

[2] *Ibid.*; and Peter Spufford, *Monetary Problems and Policies in the Burgundian Netherlands 1433–1496* (Leiden, 1970), pp. 180–3, 194–7.

[3] See above, pp. 280–1.

[4] See above, pp. 323–8.

standard coins of the area. They had a great success and rapidly replaced the patards as the standard coins. In Milan the duke, Galeazzo-Maria Sforza, at about the same time, began to strike new, good, silver 'grossi da 5 soldi' in place of the half-silver pegioni, which had been the standard pieces for much of the previous 100 years. The new pieces contained nearly as much silver as the grossi ambrosini of the late thirteenth century.

It was in Italy too that the next step was taken, the production of silver coins of a greater weight than ever before, exceeding in silver content even the heaviest and best grossi of the late thirteenth and early fourteenth centuries.

In 1472 the Doge of Venice, Nicolo Tron, ordered the striking of a coin worth a whole Venetian lira, containing 6 grams of silver. It was probably not intended as more than a temporary measure, a stop-gap use of the plentiful Tirolean silver until more gold arrived from Hungary. However no more gold was to arrive from Hungary, and for a whole generation Venice had to put up with a currency almost without gold. Silver lire proved very useful under these circumstances as not-too-inconvenient substitutes for the more valuable gold ducats that were lacking. They came to be known as 'mocenighi', after Pietro Mocenigo, doge from 1474, who began to issue them in considerable quantities. Also in 1474, the Duke of Milan, Galeazzo-Maria Sforza, followed suit and ordered the striking of a Milanese lira that weighed more than 9 grams of silver. The obverse type, a magnificent portrait of the duke's head in profile, gave the pieces their nickname 'testoni' or 'head-pieces'. Successive Dukes of Milan were the most prolific issuers of these testoni, but the rulers of Ferrara, Mantua and Savoy and many of the Swiss Cantons soon followed the examples of Venice and Milan,[1] as quite naturally did Genoa while under Milanese rule.

Although the large-scale issue of testoni was for long limited to the Alps and the duchies between the Alps and the Apennines, the pieces themselves spread through Europe in an international way, in a pattern much more like that for gold coins than the normal pattern for silver coins, which, since the victory of gold in the fourteenth century, had tended to remain within the 'coinage province' in which they were issued. Soon placards printed in the Low Countries showed 'Milaensche penning metten hoofde' and 'Testones van Savoyen'. This was not merely the whimsy of a compiler trying to cram every outlandish coin he could think of into his list, for such pieces actually circulated in the Low Countries. A hoard from Courcelles in Hainault, probably buried about, or just after, 1493, contained 6 testoni of Galeazzo-Maria Sforza. The context in which they circulated is clearly illustrated by the fact that the remaining 31 pieces in the hoard were all of gold.[2]

---

[1] Philip Grierson, 'The monetary pattern of sixteenth-century coinage', *Transactions of the Royal Historical Society*, 5th series, XXI (1971), 53–5.
[2] Spufford, *Monetary Problems in the Burgundian Netherlands*, p. 71.

One of the first pieces of this new, large format to be struck outside Italy was the 7-gram, silver réal struck in 1487 in the name of Philip the Handsome in the Netherlands. But the numbers of réals, and their successors the grand doubles, struck were insignificant. A mere 76,000 were minted over 10 years, at the same time as over 5 million double patards and over 8 million patards. The testoon size and type of coin came to England and France even later. Henry VII of England began a limited issue of 9-gram testoons in 1504, and Louis XII of 9½-gram testoons in France in 1514, but such large pieces did not find a regular place in the currency of north-western Europe for another generation, because there was no lack of gold in this area of Europe. Even under Francis I (1515–47), testoons were largely struck for the payment of Swiss mercenaries and did not remain in France.[1]

During the last decades of the fifteenth century the absolute dearth of silver had disappeared, but there was still not enough to satisfy all the rapidly growing needs of commerce, as it began to develop once again.

The imbalance in trade between Europe and the Levant still continued, and so did the export of silver to pay for the excess of oriental goods imported, over the western goods exported. Arnold van Haeff, who was in Egypt in 1496, estimated that the annual balance paid in coin then amounted to the equivalent in silver of 300,000 ducats.[2] However the export of silver from Europe to the Levant on this scale no longer caused the same difficulties as it had done in the middle of the century.[3] The necessity of exporting gold to the east to supplement the inadequate supplies of silver came to an end, and one of the paradoxical effects of the increased mining of silver was therefore to make gold more readily available in Europe. The decline of the Magyar gold-mines, after a final high peak of production during the reign of Matthias Corvinus, nevertheless made gold a great deal less available in certain parts of Europe, notably in Venice, where the first silver lire have already been seen to have been struck to provide larger silver coins to recompense for the lack of gold ones. Venetians like Nicolo and Alvise Barbarigo found it profitable to take silver from Venice in the late 1460s and the 1470s to Tunis,[4] which by now was firmly in the Venetian trading-orbit, to purchase West African gold that had followed the traditional camel-caravan route, across the Sahara. (See Map 35.)

A certain proportion of West African gold was by now being brought back directly from the West African coast by merchants and adventurers, and reached Europe through Lisbon, where it was minted from 1457 onwards by the Kings of

[1] Grierson, 'Sixteenth century coinage', p. 59.
[2] Eliyahu Ashtor, *Les Métaux précieux et la balance des payements du Proche-Orient à la Basse Époque* (Paris, 1971), pp. 66–7, 70ff.
[3] See above, pp. 359–60.
[4] Frederic C. Lane, *Andrea Barbarigo, Merchant of Venice 1418–49* (Baltimore, 1944), pp. 140–81 and 'Venture accounting in medieval business management' (1945), repr. in *Venice and History: Collected Papers* (Baltimore, 1966), p. 105.

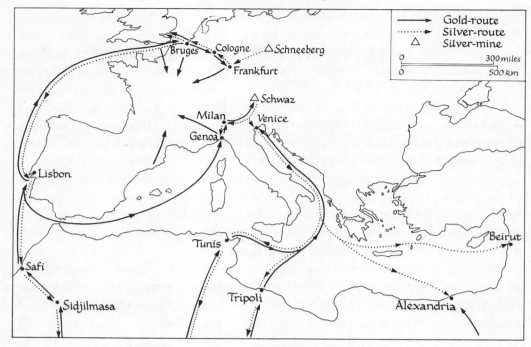

Map 35. Flows of gold and silver 1465 – *c.* 1500

Portugal into ducat-sized cruzados. This gold found its way into wide areas of western Europe, overland into Castille, for instance, or by sea to Genoa, or, from the 1460s, to Bruges, and thence to England and Frankfurt.

The Genoese used some of this West African gold to purchase Tirolean silver in Milan.[1] A little of this gold even ended up in the Tirol itself, where gold gulden were struck for Count Sigmund from 1478 onwards, although he was only able to issue a quarter of a million of them over a period of eight years.[2] It is not clear whether this Portuguese gold represented any increase at all in the amount of gold reaching Europe from West Africa, or merely a diversion of the means by which it came, away from the traditional camel-caravan routes across the Sahara.

There were still very large profits to be made in the trans-Saharan trade. The western 'Sudan' was persistently lacking in salt and since its inhabitants desperately needed it, they were always prepared to pay sufficiently highly for it in gold or slaves to make trans-Saharan trade, despite its risks, very attractive to the inhabitants of the Maghreb and Egypt. Not only rich men, but men of comparatively modest fortune were prepared to invest their capital in the trade. As well as salt, it was also highly profitable to carry copper and silver across the Sahara. The

[1] Carlo M. Cipolla, 'Argento tedesco e monete genovesi alla fine del quattrocento', *Rivista Italiana di Numismatica*, LVIII (1956), 100–7.
[2] Grierson, 'Sixteenth century coinage', p. 55.

weight–value ratio between silver and gold in the western 'Sudan' was as low as 3:1, whilst in the Mediterranean world it was everywhere above 9:1, and in some times and places much higher. It was the continual arrival of fresh supplies of gold and slaves in the Maghreb that attracted the interest of western Europeans in their place of origin.[1]

In 1450 it was estimated that the West African gold passing through Sidjilmasa to the ports of Morocco amounted to 400,000 dinars a year (some 1500–1800 kilograms or 30–35 cwts.), whilst further quantities travelled along more easterly caravan routes to Tunis, Tripoli and Egypt. At the end of the fifteenth century the Portuguese alone were still acquiring over 40,000 doblas of gold (over 600 kilograms or 12 cwts.) annually at Safi in Morocco, besides purchasing lesser quantities, with silver, at other Moroccan ports. In addition they were acquiring much smaller amounts by trading up the Gambia river and at Sierra Leone, but their prime source of African gold was San Jorge 'da Mina' and the other lesser trading-posts along the coast of what is now Ghana. For many years a monthly caravel service ran between Lisbon and 'El Mina'. In one direction it carried European cloth and clothing, copper and latten goods, glassware and a variety of other European goods, including even white wine. In the other it mainly carried gold. In 1505 it was estimated that 170,000 doblas of gold (some 750 kilograms or 15 cwts.) came back from El Mina, and lesser quantities from the other ports on this coast. Added together, the total quantity of gold coming into Portugal each year at the end of the fifteenth century cannot have been very different from that passing through Sidjilmasa half a century before.[2]

Nevertheless the diversion of even part of the gold-trade from the trans-Saharan routes did have a very marked adverse effect on the commerce of the whole of North Africa from Morocco eastwards to Tunis and Tripoli, and even as far as Egypt.[3]

It seems to me probable that the overall quantity of gold in Europe did increase, despite the decline in Hungarian gold-mining, and despite wear and tear, partially because of the cessation of exports of it to the Levant. Certainly the weight–value ratio of gold and silver did not go on increasing, despite the enormously enlarged quantities of silver available, and in many places it even dropped. This might be because there were greater quantities of gold available, or because the continued and rapidly increasing demand for silver still outstripped the fast-growing amounts being mined. The use of larger, silver coins as gold-substitutes or supplements further complicated the pattern of demand for the two metals.

[1] Marian Malowist, 'Quelques observations sur le commerce de l'or dans le Soudan occidental au moyen âge', *Annales E.S.C.*, xxv (1970), 1630–6.
[2] P. Vilar, *A History of Gold and Money, 1450–1920* (Barcelona, 1969; English trans., London, 1976).
[3] Ashtor, *Les Métaux précieux*, pp. 106–7.

In Venice the ratio between silver and gold, which had been up to 12.1:1, was down to 10.7:1 in 1472, when gold ran short. In Milan where it had been up to 12.7:1, it was down to 11.0:1 in 1474.[1] In the Netherlands, where the ratio between the prices offered for gold and silver by the Burgundian mints in 1456 had been 12.9:1, the ratio had fallen to 10.9:1 in 1467.

In England on the other hand the ratio between the mint prices rose from 10.9:1 in the 1450s, when England was one of the few places in Europe still minting any silver at all, to 12.1:1 in 1466.[2] One of the consequences of this relatively high, official value put on gold in England was that after 1465 and 1466, the first two years of the recoinage, the value of gold minted in London exceeded the value of silver by quite considerable amounts. Nevertheless the quantity of silver minted, although small by the standards of the 1470s, was rather greater than the quantity minted in the decade before 1464 which had in fact been very large by the standards of that decade. The Saxon silver had changed men's notions of what was a small mint-output and what was a large one. In 1469 an agreement was drawn up, but never ratified, permitting Burgundian coin to circulate freely in England, and a certain number of silver double patards actually did so. These were pieces of approximately the same size and silver content as the English groat. There was thus more Saxon silver flowing into England than might appear from the mint records. Double patards made up at least 10%, and possibly getting on for a quarter, of the English silver currency when their use was at its most extensive in the 1480s and 1490s.[3] Nevertheless, in England at any rate, Portuguese gold was more important than Saxon silver.

In France, too, the value placed on gold went on rising, and there is some evidence to suggest that in some parts of France the market price of gold was even ahead of the official values. In 1478–9 gold was being accepted in Normandy for a higher value of silver than the official value, which itself gave a silver:gold ratio of 11.3:1. The same was still true in 1480–1, when the official ratio was up to 11.8:1; and in 1488–9, when it was up again to 12.2:1.[4] But there were local differences in the values placed on the precious metals. Gold was priced higher in Rouen than in Paris, and higher still in Dieppe than Rouen.

As a consequence of the high values set on gold in France, it came in from all sides, from the Rhineland, from Savoy, from Aragon and from England, as well as

[1] Carlo M. Cipolla, *Studi di storia della moneta*, vol. I, 'I movimenti del cambi in Italia dal secolo XIII al XV' (Pavia, 1948), p. 154.
[2] See above, p. 357. The ratios are worked out from the mint prices printed by John H. Munro, *Wool, Cloth and Gold. The Struggle for Bullion in Anglo-Burgundian Trade 1340–1478* (Brussels–Toronto, 1973), pp. 199–200.
[3] Peter Spufford, 'Burgundian double patards in late medieval England', *British Numismatic Journal*, XXXIII (1964), 110–17.
[4] Michel Mollat, *Le Commerce maritime normand à la fin du Moyen Age* (Paris, 1952), pp. 382–3.

from the Burgundian Netherlands.[1] It is not clear whether this was balanced by an outflow of silver, or goods or both.

We have already seen how the general dearth of black money caused great difficulties around 1460 in the ordinary, small, everyday transactions of urban life. We have also seen the desperate attempts of princes and cities to resolve this problem by having even the smallest quantities of black money minted, whatever the cost, and how the complete lack of silver defeated these attempts.[2]

When, in 1463, the Venetians discussed the possibility of striking coins of pure copper, containing no silver at all, instead of 1% or 2% of silver, it was 'ut pauperes persone et alii, qui minutim lucrantur [earn very little], vitam ducere possint'.[3]

Nine years later, in 1472, the members of the Venetian Council of Ten again discussed the need for small change in everyday life 'ut habeatur moneta, qua necessitati quotidiani victus suppleatur'. In the meantime the great medieval silver-famine had come to an end, so that it was natural for them to think once again of the traditional solution. They ordered that out of the silver that happened to be in the mint whilst their discussions were taking place, 30,000 ducats-worth should be coined into soldini, small coins of poor silver, which had already been struck on and off for well over a century.[4] It is a remarkable sidelight on the change that had taken place that the council could take it for granted that there would be at least 30,000 ducats-worth of silver in the mint waiting to be coined, instead of having to make arrangements to try to squeeze the odd mark or two of silver out of individual money-changers with great difficulty.

However, the really extraordinary thing was that in the following year they decided that the mint of Venice should actually strike coins of a new type, 'bagattini', which were made entirely of copper. Paradoxically, this innovation did not take place under the pressure of the silver-famine, but a decade later, when there was adequate silver to mint the traditional, base-silver coinage.[5] The change from black money to a true copper coinage was not a revolutionary change, at least not at the beginning, for the Venetians insisted that their new copper coins should contain their value in copper, less the actual cost of minting them. This was precisely the

[1] Georges Lesage, 'La Circulation monétaire en France dans la seconde moitié du xvᵉ siècle', *Annales E.S.C.*, III (1948), 315–16. He would like to see this influx of gold as evidence of a favourable balance of trade.

[2] See above, pp. 361–2.

[3] Wilhelm Jesse (ed.), *Quellenbuch zur Münz- und Geldgeschichte des Mittelalters* (Halle, 1924; repr. 1968), no. 292, pp. 158–9.

[4] Jesse (ed.), *Quellenbuch*, no. 293, p. 159.

[5] The Council of Ten decided to mint pure copper coins for quite different reasons. Pure copper coins could not be melted down, as billon coins were, to extract the silver. Those who had profited by making false billon coins without any silver content, could make nothing out of imitating pure copper coins: 'ita quod volentes illam adulterare pro lucrando, non possint' (Reinhold C. Mueller, 'L'imperialismo monetario veneziano nel Quattrocento', *Società e Storia*, VIII (1980), 293).

same principle that had been applied to the traditional black money, which was almost entirely of copper.

It is not surprising that it was at Venice, the greatest commercial city in Europe, that the striking of copper coins should have first been discussed, for throughout the second half of the fifteenth century Venice was the major European centre for the growing trade in the copper of the Alps and Carpathians, until it was supplanted by Antwerp in the first decade of the sixteenth century.[1] It is, however, rather surprising that it was in Naples that the idea actually became a reality. It was in Naples, possibly already the largest capital city in Europe, that the first copper coins, cavalli, were struck in 1472. Once again it was clearly a matter of free choice and not of necessity, for quite enough silver existed in southern Italy at this time to mint traditional black money. Across the water in Sicily the mint at Palermo was able to strike more than 25 million piccoli, containing $2\frac{1}{2}$% silver, in the years 1471 to 1475.

The changeover from small change of base silver to small change of copper spread through the cities of Europe extremely slowly. In the Burgundian Netherlands pure copper was first used for coins in 1502, but this was for a limited issue of mailles, to circulate only in and around Namur, one of the centres of the copper-industry along the Meuse. It was not until 1543 that pure copper was used for minting courtes, to circulate throughout the cities of the Low Countries. This was over seventy years after copper had first been introduced into the city of Naples, but pure copper was not used for coinage in France and England until even later. In France it was first used in 1578, but did not become of importance until after 1654; whilst in England it was first used as late as 1613, but did not become of importance until after 1660.

Throughout the period with which this book is concerned, it is not necessary to draw any distinction between black money and copper coinage. It was the sum total of the two that supplied, or failed to supply, the small change necessary for urban daily life.

The problem of the inflationary excess of petty coins of copper was a problem of a later epoch. In the seventeenth century it became necessary to limit the quantities of copper coins that should be struck, but in the late fifteenth century the problem was still what it had been since the major growth of cities in the thirteenth century, to find enough small change to go round.[2]

Thus on the eve of the price revolution, the stock of gold in Europe was static or perhaps either growing or diminishing slightly; the stock of good silver coin was

[1] Herman van der Wee, *The Growth of the Antwerp Market and the European Economy*, 1 (The Hague, 1963), 523.

[2] Carlo M. Cipolla, 'The big problem of the petty coins', in his *Money, Prices and Civilization in the Mediterranean World* (Princeton, 1956), pp. 27–37, provides much useful and interesting evidence of seventeenth-century fears of the inflationary excess of copper coin, but also attributes the same fears to men in the fourteenth and fifteenth centuries without any supporting evidence.

growing rapidly, but by the end of the fifteenth century it was still far from reaching the level of the early fourteenth century; and the stock of small change, whether old, black money or new copper, was beginning to be enough to satisfy the needs of ordinary people.

The return of adequate coinage brought its own problems. When Louis XI came to the throne in 1461, such little currency as was available for use in France was either French or Burgundian in origin. Even in the next five years, as the situation began to ease, foreign coins began to creep back into use. In 1466 nine different types of foreign coin were permitted to circulate in France. Five years later the situation was much more complex. In 1471 no less than twenty-one sorts of non-French coin were allowed to be current in France, apart from those which circulated without such official authorisation. Even the officers of the king's own household used foreign coin.[1] This renewed complexity in the currency circulating in any one country reflected not only the increased supply of coin, but the increased velocity of its circulation, not merely at a local level, but at an international level. Under such circumstances it is not surprising that an official money-changer was appointed again at the port of Dieppe in 1475, after a period of thirty years during which the supply of money and the sluggishness of its circulation had been too slight to support one.[2] From 1481 onwards there was enough business to support more than a single money-changer.[3]

The first generation of the sixteenth century saw an acceleration of the same processes that had marked the end of the fifteenth century. Prospectors continued to discover and exploit new sources of silver. The mines of Annaberg in Saxony and those of the Joachimsthal in Bohemia were the most important for this new generation, as those at Schneeberg and at Schwaz had been for the previous generation. The total production of silver in Europe went on growing until it reached a peak around the 1530s and then began to diminish.[4]

Just as the striking of large silver testoons had symbolised growing availability of silver in late-fifteenth-century Europe, so the yet larger supplies of silver available in the early sixteenth century were symbolised by the striking of yet larger silver coins, silver guldiner, gulden groschen or talers, of the general size later adopted for English silver crowns and American silver dollars. The earliest such pieces were struck at Hall, near Schwaz, in the Tirol in 1486, but the first large-scale issues were minted at Annaberg in Saxony after 1500, and at Joachimsthal in Bohemia after 1519.[5] As their name suggests, they were designed to be the equivalent, in silver, of gold gulden and interchangeable with them.

It is interesting to notice how the process of restoration, followed by increasing

[1] Lesage, 'La Circulation monétaire', pp. 310–14.   [2] See above, p. 358.
[3] Mollat, *Le Commerce maritime*, pp. 393–4.   [4] Nef, 'Silver production in Central Europe'.
[5] Grierson, 'Sixteenth Century Coinage', pp. 52–7.

the size of the denominations minted, in two stages, followed a parallel course in the fifteenth and early sixteenth centuries to that in the twelfth and early thirteenth centuries, although moving rather more boldly and rapidly through the transition process.

It is necessary not merely to describe the situation brought about by the end of the silver-famine and the increasing quantities of European silver available throughout the two generations from the 1460s to the 1520s, but to ask what effect this had on the European economy, and on the life of ordinary Europeans.

As stated earlier, during the silver-famine it had been natural for anyone who had any silver at all to keep it and not to use it unless absolutely necessary. In this way the stock of coined money that was actually current had been much reduced by hoarding and the velocity of circulation had become very slow. When the quantity of silver available began to increase, even slightly, individuals began to relax and feel more able to use the silver that they had. In this way the influx of silver from outside the economy also brought about the release of hoarded silver within it, and so the effects both of the silver-famine and of its end, were doubled by the hopes and fears of individuals.

The quantity of silver and the velocity of its circulation were thus at this time not two distinct, independent variables, but two variables very tightly bound together. The impact on the volume of transactions was thus not only the stimulus to exports provided by the demand generated by the newly mined silver, but also the stimulus stimulus to internal trade provided by the newly dis-hoarded silver. The impact on the price level was similarly greater than that merely derived from the additional demand created by the newly mined silver.

But over and above the doubling of the newly mined silver by dis-hoarded silver there was yet a further doubling of the money supply by the remarkable increase in credit. A simple example of how this happened is provided by the giro banks of Venice, which, by 1500, were operating on a liquidity of around 8%. The remainder of the deposits were represented by loans to other customers, trade ventures overseas, holdings of city bonds, and investments in shipping and property. The bank had already invested elsewhere almost all the money actually deposited, but the depositor could equally use his deposit for purchases, investment and other payments, provided he was dealing with another customer, or potential customer, of the same or another Venetian giro bank. When a German merchant brought Tirolean silver to a bank (and by 1500 it was usual to sell to a bank) he was immediately credited with its value in the books of the bank. As a result he could at once begin to make purchases of goods from Venetians by book-transfer. The bank meanwhile sent the silver to the mint, and when minted silver coin came back, the bank could either add it to its reserves or extend its own operations. This double use of the silver continued until some depositor actually demanded cash from the bank.

If more than about 8% of its deposits were demanded at the same time, a bank found itself in difficulties and might be forced to close down, even if its overall assets, when eventually realised, could more than satisfy its creditors.

Our evidence of how the system worked is in fact derived from the documentation provided when banks did close down, either because of an inability to satisfy their depositors, or because of the death of the principal banker, Alvise Pisani for example, and the dissolution of the partnership that ran it.[1]

Bills of exchange to a certain extent acted in the same way at an international level as transfers in the books of a bank did within the city, and were often met in a city such as Venice or Genoa by book-transfer rather than the payment of cash. But the acceptance both of payment by a bill of exchange on an international level, and of payment by a transfer in the books of a bank, depend in the last resort on the trust and expectation that coined money will be forthcoming if asked for. If there is no such expectation, there can be no credit.

The extreme example of this situation was provided by the situation in Valencia in 1451, when the stock of money was so low that no one was prepared to part with what he had. The velocity of circulation was zero and no one was prepared to extend credit. Demand was so inhibited that goods from the galley of Jacques Coeur could not find purchasers at any price.

If merchants did not believe that they could sell in a particular market, they would not bother to adventure their goods in it. If enough markets were blocked in this way, merchants would cease to trade and invest their capital in other ways. It seems to me that the low level of trade, and the low level of prices, outside the Low Countries, was in this way tightly bound up with the silver-famine – and the revival of trade, and a new buoyancy in prices, with the end of the famine.[2]

It is essential to point out that the levels of trade and of prices were equally bound up with a range of other factors, above all the demographic factor. If one believes that population, or rather its growth, acted as the motor of the economy, it is equally necessary to believe that money, or rather its lack, acted as the brake. It was necessary to release the brake before the economy could move forward.

When money was lacking, ordinary people kept what they had and merchants refrained from investing in commerce, but invested their money in land, life-rents, perpetual rents, city bonds or even in objects of culture, such as books, paintings, sculpture and buildings. It is just this that Lopez and Miskimin observed in Florence during the bullion-famine.[3] One evident consequence of this reluctance to invest in

---

[1] Frederic C. Lane, 'Venetian bankers 1496–1533', *Journal of Political Economy*, XLV (1937), 187–206, repr. in *Venice and History*, pp. 69–86.

[2] F. Braudel and Frank C. Spooner, 'Prices in Europe from 1450 to 1750', *Cambridge Economic History of Europe*, IV (1967), 401.

[3] R. S. Lopez and H. A. Miskimin, 'The economic depression of the Renaissance', *Economic History Review*, 2nd series, XIV (1962), 408–26.

trade was the rise in interest rates for commercial loans at that period – and the corollary, after 1465, was the fall in interest rates. A high liquidity preference and high rate of interest were themselves brakes upon commerce, and their reduction made trade much easier.

The overall demand for luxury objects in Europe by those classes who lived off rents was greatly reduced by the universal fall in rents, except in the Low Countries – but it was further reduced by the transformation of rents paid in money to rents paid partially or wholly in kind. This coincided with the greatest extension of the system of *métayage* or *mezzadria*. But with the end of the bullion-famine there was a swing back from rents in kind to money-rents. A further consequence of the disappearance and reappearance of money was the growth and decline of barter in trade, in parallel with the growth and decline of rents in kind.

Barter had never entirely disappeared, but its revival in place of payment in money was very natural in circumstances like the arrival of the galley of Jacques Coeur in Valencia. Mme Thielemans has observed it in the commerce between England and Burgundy.[1] After nearly twenty years of increase in the money supply, barter still remained important, even in quite large-scale commerce. In 1480–1, a merchant from Bristol in England, in the course of a trading-journey to Portugal, during the reign of Afonso V, 'the African', had exchanged 22 whole cloths directly against 32 tuns, 1 pipe and 1 hogshead of wine and 5 cwt. of oranges, and only sold 19 whole cloths for money, with part of which he proceeded to purchase more wine.[2] As late as 1498, a merchant from Paris trading at Rouen in Normandy had accepted leather and two sorts of cloth from England in part exchange for 53 puncheons of Auxerre wine, and only the balance was paid him in silver.[3]

The governments of western Europe had a great many problems in the fifteenth century, but very many of these problems were made much heavier by their financial difficulties. The landed revenues of princes were reduced in part by imprudent alienations to over-mighty subjects, but they were equally reduced by the general fall in rents. Those extraordinary revenues which were taken directly from trade fell and rose with it, so that the state of trade made a considerable difference to the well-being of princes. With the return of silver such revenues rose. For example the *alcabala* in Castille, where it had not been commuted for lump sums, was a tax on all sales in the interior of the country. It rose in the last quarter of the fifteenth century, at the same time as the customs revenue of England, which by now came primarily from the increased export of cloth, particularly to the lands of

---

[1] Marie-Rose Thielemans, *Bourgogne et Angleterre* (Brussels, 1966), p. 359.
[2] T. F. Reddaway and Alwyn A. Ruddock (eds.), 'Accounts of John Balsall, Purser of *Trinity of Bristol* 1480–1', Camden 4th series, VII, Royal Historical Society (London, 1969), pp. 21–3.
[3] Mollat, *Le Commerce maritime*, p. 387.

the Burgundian state. One of the distinctive marks of the renewal of monarchy from the 1470s was that the collection of taxes became much more efficient. This new efficiency was greatly assisted by the increased availability of coin, just as the previous inability to collect was in part due to the lack of ready cash with which to pay on the part of tax-payers.

It seems to me that the monetary differences between the two generations on either side of the year 1465 tie up very closely indeed with a great number of other changes taking place in Europe at the same time.

The importance for daily living of the disappearance and reappearance of black money was immediately recognised at the time. It is much easier for us in retrospect to look back to this time as the turning-point between gradually dropping prices and rents and gradually rising prices and rents; between stable or even rising real wages, and falling real wages; between rising interest rates and falling interest rates; between a tendency to pay rents increasingly in kind, or through *métayage*, and a tendency to pay rents once again in cash; between an increasing resort to barter and a decreasing use of direct exchange of goods; between an erratic diminution in the scale of commerce and banking, and a steady increase in their scale; between decreasing princely revenues collected with difficulty, and increasing princely revenues collected with ease. All these mark out the 1460s as a turning-point in the economy of Europe and strongly suggest that the noticeable change in the money supply at just that point in time played a key role in those changes.

Conclusion

Looking back over the history of money in the Middle Ages, it becomes apparent that it falls into two distinct periods. The first, which ran from the seventh century to the twelfth, was an era of silver coins variously called pennies, deniers, denari, pfennigs, or pennings, depending on the language used. The second period, which began in the thirteenth century, was a much more complex era of large silver coins, which since they were 'great' in comparison with the pennies, were variously called groats, groschen, gros or grossi. There was no gold in circulation in the first period in western Europe, but in the second period gold was again used for currency for the first time since its disappearance in the Dark Ages. First of all there were the gold coins of the Italian trading-cities for international use in the Mediterranean world, and later, with the fourteenth-century conquest of western Europe by gold coin, a variety of 'national' coinages like French écus or English nobles. In the later fifteenth century larger and yet larger silver coins began to be introduced, first testoni, testons or testoons, and then gulden groschen and, in the sixteenth century, thalers and silver écus and crowns.

Alongside the silver pennies of the first period a large amount of silver also circulated in the form of ingots, or bars, of fixed fineness, whilst some payments were fixed in terms of commodities other than silver, such as pepper. Alongside the silver groats and gold florins of the second period many large-scale payments between the more advanced commercial centres of western Europe were made by bills of exchange, and, within the most advanced of these, by credit transfers in the books of certain banks, the *banchi di scritta* or *del giro*.

The first period was characterised by fairly limited payments in coin, the second by very extensive use of money. This applied at all levels of society from the bottom to the top. In the first period the bulk of peasant rent took the form of payments in service and in kind, with only relatively unimportant annual payments of dues in coin. In the second period the bulk of peasant rent took the form of payments in coin, with only residual services, except in those areas where *métayage* or *mezzadria* predominated, and here too a large part of the shared produce was destined for sale for money.

378

In the first period rulers lived primarily on the products of their demesnes and the services of their vassals, although this was supplemented by some revenues in money, for example from the renewal of the coinage itself at regular intervals. In the second period rulers lived primarily from taxes in money paid by their subjects, and the older sources of revenue were also turned into money; the demesnes were leased out for money-rents or their products sold on the market, and the services commuted for cash payments. Therefore, in the first period rulers paid the embryonic civil services in their households, and their warriors, by allowances of food, clothing and other goods, and by grants, often hereditary, of land (fiefs) for their maintenance. In the second period rulers paid their civil servants and their professional indentured soldiery with money.

Even if the use of money was relatively inconsiderable in the first period, and even slighter in the preceding 'Dark' Ages, it never actually fell out of use, in any area of western Europe in which it had been used in antiquity, except in England from the fifth century to the seventh. Indeed the use of coin spread across the Roman frontier to areas where it had never been used before, culminating in the issue of indigenous coins in Bavaria and Bohemia, in Saxony and Denmark in the tenth century, in Hungary in the eleventh, and in Poland, Sweden and Scotland in the twelfth century.

Although the thirteenth century looks like a clear turning-point, changes were very gradual and often took a very long time to spread outwards from Italy. The first grossi were struck in Venice in 1201, but a successful groat coinage did not get under way in England until 1351. The first gold fiorini were issued in Genoa and Florence, in 1252, but even Flanders and Brabant, which were economically advanced, did not strike gold coins until the 1330s. In many parts of Europe the currency of silver ingots was only replaced by that of gold coins a great deal later. On the other hand, the changes of the thirteenth century were prepared for at the end of the twelfth century by a greatly increased issue of silver-penny coinages, nourished by prolific new silver-mines. The most important were those at Freiberg in Meissen, Friesach in Carinthia, and Montieri in Tuscany. The older penny coinages did not disappear in the thirteenth century with the introduction of grossi and fiorini, but continued to be struck, not always in adequate quantities, for 'small' change. They therefore became known as piccioli, denari minuti, menuts or parvi, in distinction to grossi or 'great' coins. These petty coins had already been debased before the introduction of the 'great' coins and continued to be debased afterwards, until their alloy was so poor that they were commonly known as 'black money' or *monnaie noire*. They were eventually replaced by pure copper coins, from the late fifteenth century onwards. Again there was a very considerable time-lag between different parts of Europe. Naples and Venice began to use copper coins in 1472 and 1473. London did not do so until 1613.

This extraordinarily long time-lag in the adoption of innovations between the different parts of Europe meant that at any one time there were very distinct regional differences in the type and amount of money available and in the way it was used. It also makes it difficult to break down the period into shorter spans of time with distinctive characteristics. In so far as this can be done it is on the basis of the varying quantities of new silver, or gold, being pumped into circulation from the mines of Europe. Against the variables of mining production, which sometimes altered suddenly, must be set the variables of loss by wear, by hoarding and by export to the east, which changed much less fast. These factors formed a constant group, but the relative importance of each varied from time to time. The larger the number of coins in circulation the greater the wear; the more disorderly the times the more likely that temporary hoarding would become a permanent loss from circulation; and the higher the standard of living of the élites, and the more numerous they were, the greater the drain to the east.

The false dawn of the medieval economy in the Carolingian period seemed to rely on the silver mined at Melle. The mines declined, and so did the supply of money. When the silver from distant Tashkent and from Goslar brought about a tenth-century revival in coinage, the monetary pattern of the Carolingian period was renewed. There seems to have been a fresh decline in the late eleventh century and the early twelfth and so a retreat in the use of money, immediately before the late-twelfth-century surge of silver from the mines at Freiberg, Friesach and Montieri. This time the quantitative changes seem to have been sufficiently great to promote qualitative changes that were not to be reversed. When the mines at Freiberg and Friesach expired, their place was taken by other silver-mines, like those at Jihlava, Brskovo and Kutná Hora in turn. For over a century and a half silver, therefore, continued to enter into circulation in quantities much larger than those in the eighth or the tenth centuries. Although silver-mining declined rapidly in the fourteenth century, the gold-mines around Kremnica opened up to provide the means for large-scale payments, although the increasing dearth of silver caused very great problems for payments on a smaller scale. But even in the midst of dearth, the Bosnian and Serbian silver-mines alleviated the lack of silver for a generation at the beginning of the fifteenth century, before the bullion-famine really became acute in the middle years of the fifteenth century. The last generation of the fifteenth century saw the opening of new silver-mines in the Erzgebirge and the Tirol, and the arrival of African gold by sea just at the time that the Hungarian gold began to peter out.

The maximum amount of silver mined at Kutná Hora in the early fourteenth century seems to have been not very different from the maximum of 21 tonnes mined in the Joachimsthal in 1533, two centuries later. However, it seems that, although the maxima of the two most important mines may not have been very different, the total amount of silver available in Europe in the early fourteenth century may easily have exceeded that available two centuries later, and possibly even that available at the end of the sixteenth century, after American silver had taken over from the Central European mines.

It is difficult to make any reasonable comparisons over a long stretch of time because of the changing relative importance of different areas. In 1300, England was important for the general European economy only as a key supplier of raw materials, particularly wool and tin. By the end of the sixteenth century England was becoming one of the more important countries of Europe in economic terms. Nevertheless its currency in 1600, taking coined gold and silver together, was only of the same magnitude as the coined silver currency had been three centuries earlier.[1] In 1300 there had been an unknowable amount of silver in the form of bars and ingots in addition to the coined silver. This serves to stress the importance of the thirteenth-century growth in money and its use. In the late thirteenth century the amount of silver in Italy must very greatly have exceeded that in England, whilst in the late sixteenth century the amount of coin in England was probably only exceeded by the amount in the United Provinces.

The regional differences may be illustrated from the scale of minting. In the late 1330s, when the Kremnica gold was first surging through Europe, the quantity of gold minted in Florence, the principal banking-city in all Europe at that time, as well as the principal industrial city of Italy, was around 350,000 florins a year. At the same date the Count of Flanders was able to mint 100,000 florins a year at Ghent, at that time the leading industrial city north of the Alps; whilst the city of Lübeck, the headquarters of the Hanseatic League and the most important commercial city on the Baltic, or, indeed, anywhere north of London, only struck 35,000 florins a year at the same period. The ranking order of the most advanced areas of Europe, northern Italy, the southern Netherlands and the Hanseatic cities, could not be more clearly illustrated. The difference in scale was maintained. Ninety years later, when gold was perhaps at its most plentiful, the mint at Venice, then by far the most important port in the Mediterranean, was striking 1,200,000 ducats a year, whilst the combined mints of the Burgundian Netherlands were striking gold coins equivalent to about 300,000 ducats a year. In view of the difference in scale of the monetary base, it is hardly surprising that the qualitative differences in credit arrangements should have been very different in different areas of Europe. Much Hanseatic trade involved no credit at all; a great deal was straightforwardly bought and sold for money or silver bars. At the other extreme, Heers quotes the Genoese merchant who did 160,000 lire of business in 4 years with under 12,000 lire of coin.[2] This difference in the credit superstructure meant that

---

[1] See above, p. 205, for detailed estimates.
[2] Jacques Heers, *Gênes au XVᵉ siècle* (Paris, 1971), p. 90.

the real difference in the scale of operations between northern and southern Europe was even greater than the supply of coined money would suggest.

As well as the great difference in the scale of operations between different areas of Europe, there was also the radical difference within every region of Europe in the use of coin between town and country.

One of the striking features of the changes in the long thirteenth century was the 'monetisation' of the rural economy. Yet, when that has been said, it still remains true that, even after this fundamental change, the use of money in the city and the country was quite different. The new pattern for the use of money in the countryside was essentially seasonal, for the thirteenth century witnessed the creation of a great seasonal flow and ebb of coined money, into and out of the countryside. In rural society the procession of the seasons was of primary importance. In urban society it was also important, but only of secondary importance. In rural society things can only be done at the appropriate time of the year. In urban society much can be done at any time of year. Rural society is geared to an annual 'harvesting'. The timing of the seasonal flow, or flows, of money depended on the nature of the principal product, or products, of any particular region. Peasant producers had a great deal to offer for sale, but their sales were generally made all at once.[1] This frequently happened at only one time of year, when the grain had been threshed, the grapes, olives or cheeses pressed, the sheep sheared, the cattle fattened or the woad balled. As the concentration on production for the market increased during the long thirteenth century, so specialisation increased, so that the most suitable products for a region tended also to become the only products. Vineyards took the place of fields of grain in parts of France, at the same time as vineyards disappeared in England. Specialised products were increasingly sold at regular fairs, which brought enormous sums of money into the countryside very suddenly. In the grain-growing areas of eastern England annual sales of grain took place round Michaelmas (29 September), at, for example, the Stourbridge Fair near Cambridge. In Apulia, where cheese and oil were the principal products, there were two sets of fairs, one in late April and early May, the other late in the autumn. The dating of the establishment of such fairs is illuminating. In England royal charters permitting the establishment of new fairs began to be granted in the 1180s and were common by the 1220s.[2]

At these times, large amounts of current coin, usually good silver, suddenly reached the purses of the peasantry. At these times of year, the richer peasant paid such labour as he employed. Those who hired full-time labour paid their perma-

---

[1] All except the richest peasants had to sell immediately after 'harvest', because of the concentration of financial demands on them at this season. This was, however, the cheapest time of year to sell produce. The richest, and only the richest, peasants could afford to wait until prices rose later in the year, and so became richer still.

[2] Adolphus Ballard and James Tait, _British Borough Charters, 1042–1216 and 1216–1307_ (Cambridge, 1913 and 1923).

nent employees, like full-time shepherds and ploughmen, their annual wages now. Those who only employed casual labour by the day did so for specific jobs. The most numerous of these were related to 'harvesting', and so were paid for at 'harvest' times. The additional hands for grain-harvesting, sheep-shearing and grape-picking, the great labour-intensive operations of the farming year, thus earned their wages now.

The major peasant purchases of manufactured goods, such as ploughshares and other iron tools, also took place at these times of year when the purchasers could afford them. They were frequently bought at the same fairs at which the produce of the countryside was sold to the city. The existence of an extensive network of small, weekly markets from the thirteenth century onwards, implies the use of money in a minor key throughout the year, when the minor products of the countryside, such as eggs, could be sold and the money spent on urban products, or at least on products, such as salt, that were distributed through towns. At 'harvest' times the poorer peasants also paid off such debts as they had contracted, whether to richer neighbours, or to specialised lenders, who multiplied as the thirteenth century progressed. The new wave of urban money-lenders to be found in thirteenth-century France, Jews, Cahorsins or Lombards from Asti and thereabouts, expected repayment by peasants at fixed times of year. In the Île de France loans by Jews to peasants had to be repaid at All Saints (1 November) by a royal ordinance of 1230. At Carpentras, Jewish loans of grain to peasants were repaid in money in the autumn, and at Perpignan in August and September.[1]

Payment of tithe, sometimes also commuted for money, naturally took place at this time of year. Payment of taxes in money, another of the new impositions of the long thirteenth century made possible by the availability of money,[2] also took place at this time of year. The imposition of direct taxation in money became possible on a much larger scale than anything attempted since antiquity. In England, for example, direct taxation began at the end of the twelfth century, and the thirteenth-century subsidies exacted by Henry III and Edward I were based on a proportionate levy, frequently a fifteenth part, of the 'goods' of the peasantry, i.e. of their produce as available for sale at Michaelmas.[3] The tradition of assessing rural taxation at Michaelmas continued in England at least until the hearth-taxes of the late seventeenth century. Seasonal direct taxation of production thus came to be the typical form of rural taxation throughout the later Middle Ages and the early modern period. By contrast, the dominant form of urban taxation much more frequently took the form of all-the-year-round, indirect taxation of consumption,

---

[1] Gerard Nahon, 'Le Crédit et les juifs dans la France du XIIIᵉ siècle', *Annales E.S.C.*, XXIV (1969), 1121–48; R. W. Emery, *The Jews of Perpignan in the XIII Century* (New York, 1959).
[2] See above, pp. 246–7.
[3] J. R. Maddicott, *The English Peasantry and the Demands of the Crown*, Past and Present Supplement, 1 (1975).

for example by gate-taxes on goods passing into the city. This difference in taxation reflects the essentially different use of money in town and countryside.

Such money as remained in peasant purses was saved against the great expenses of peasant life, most notably the accumulation of dowries for daughters or the purchase of additional land. But saving did not necessarily mean the hoarding of coin, although it frequently did so. Peasants very frequently also lent money one to another, against the security of their tenements. Nevertheless the majority of hoards of coins that have been discovered from the Middle Ages were secreted in the countryside rather than the town. Equally the labourer tried to save, and hoard, against the great expense of setting up as a peasant tenant, and of the marriage that went with it. Despite these aspirations, little of the coin that reached the purses of the peasantry at these seasons of harvest had any chance of remaining there. Most of it returned to the city as quickly as it had come out, and left the countryside within a few weeks. Some returned at once from sales at the fairs themselves, some almost at once as loans, tithes and taxes were collected in, but the larger part was concentrated into the hands of the landlords and their stewards.[1] Rent-day was named to coincide with the sale of the harvest. In southern England, for example, most cash-rents were paid at Michaelmas, 29 September, immediately after the grain-harvest was sold, although, in some cases, minor payments were also due at Easter, presumably after the spring sale of lambs. In Bohemia, whose harvest is slightly later, rent-day was normally 16 October. In Lorraine the cycle was differently timed again. Major payments of money-rents were made at Martinmas, 11 November, and minor payments on St John's day, 24 June. When, and where, direct cultivation of the demesnes was still practised, the seasonal pattern was very little different. In such cases it was the landlords' stewards who received the proceeds from the sales of produce, who paid out the wages, the tithes and in some cases the taxes, and purchased the ploughshares and so forth, before remitting the balance to the landlords.

Sometimes the system was partially short-circuited by landlords, and much less money entered the countryside. This happened when certain landlords arranged for collection of local produce, grain or wool or cattle, and themselves transported it to a distant major city, where it could command a higher price than at a local fair or market. The seller or his agents then frequently spent the bulk of the money on the spot and returned with luxury goods for himself, and with only a relatively small amount of coin to distribute in the countryside from the balance of sales, less rent and charges for transport. This sort of practice can be found in various parts of Europe from the thirteenth century onwards. It still went on, even as late as the eighteenth century, in some parts of Europe. In seventeenth- and eighteenth-century Poland, for example, the great landlords of the interior arranged for the

---

[1] See above, pp. 241–5, for the change to money-rents.

transport of rye, not only for themselves, but also for their tenants and for smaller landlords, down the rivers to Danzig and Königsberg. This was very profitable, since the price of rye at the ports was up to double that in the interior. The larger part of the money involved in these transactions never left Danzig or Königsberg at all.

Within weeks of being filled with good silver the purses of all but the richest peasants were almost empty of money and remained so for the rest of the year. Some of the money had already returned to the city, in the purses of urban casual labourers, who had come out for the harvest, in the purses of urban money-lenders, in the purses of those who sold urban products at the fairs, or in the coffers of tax-collectors. Some was in the hands of the clergy, some remained with the richest peasants, but most had been paid to the nobility or their stewards. This, too, returned to the city in due course, since so many noblemen came to be resident in the city for all or part of the year and had their revenues remitted to them there by their stewards. Some of the *hôtels*, *alberghi* and inns in the capitals built from the thirteenth century on, like the palace of the Bishops of Winchester and the *hôtel* of the abbots of Cluny, still survive. It was in the capital cities that these absentees spent the money, received in the country, on urban goods and services. It was in the capitals that they bought their luxury requirements not only for consumption in their city houses, but equally for their consumption in the country. Lesser landlords similarly spent their money on a narrower range of luxuries in the principal town of their region.[1]

The net effect of this rapid, seasonal cycle of money payments was the temporary wide diffusion of coin followed by its sudden re-concentration as the city sucked the countryside dry again of the cash that it had sent out. By and large the countryside was denuded of all but the smallest of small change from one 'harvest' to the next. David Herlihy, working on Pistoia and its *contado*, observed, however, that in the fifteenth-century 'depression', the relationship between town and country changed. The city was no longer able each year to suck back all the cash that it had sent out. Over a period of several years the countryside thus began to fill up with coin in a way that it had not done before, and was not to do again once the 'depression' was over.

It has been suggested that this seasonal pattern of ebb and flow between city and country, established in the long thirteenth century, continued throughout the pre-industrial period, and, in rare cases, even up to the present. As late as the sixteenth century most of the money in England was to be found concentrated in London and the seaports, and in seventeenth-century Sicily it was found in Palermo and Messina. A study of the Sarakatsan shepherds of Zagori in Greece in the 1950s revealed a rural community that then still only used money seasonally.[2]

---

[1] See above, pp. 249–51. [2] J. K. Campbell, *Honour, Family and Patronage* (Oxford, 1964), pp. 247–53.

Only in the hinterland of the great cities of the southern Netherlands or northern Italy did a semi-urban pattern of using money all the year round develop, since there was scope there for market gardening, or for town-dependent occupations such as spinning at piece-rates for money.

The urban pattern was quite different. Money was used in cities all the year round. The seasonal nature of the use of money in the countryside obviously had an effect on urban life, as did the seasonal nature of certain long-distance travel. The closing of the Alpine passes in the winter brought its own annual rhythm to trade by land outward from Italy, and trade by sea equally had its own rhythm. The galleys to Flanders and England travelled in convoy at specific times of year, as did those to Syria and Egypt. But these were rhythms within a continued use of money as a day-by-day urban phenomenon.

Urban wages were more generally day-wages or piece-work wages, paid all the year round, rather than annual wages. Urban rents might be annual, but they might also be paid monthly. Townsmen bought bread by the loaf, whereas countrymen bought, or sold, grain by the bushel. Loaves need repeated purchase, grain can be bought once a year. Townsmen bought meat by the pound, whereas countrymen bought, or sold, whole animals. The countryman therefore needed his money less often, in fewer, larger sums than the townsman, who used his money all the year round for a myriad of minor transactions, just as we are accustomed to do in our industrialised society. Black money and, later, copper coins were therefore really only suitable for town use. White money and good silver could, however, be appropriately used in either town or country.

At the other end of the scale of money, gold coin was also more useful in urban conditions. Transactions of a size for which gold was useful rarely took place in the countryside. The produce of the individual peasant holding would normally most suitably be sold for silver. The produce of a demesne farm, or the collected produce from a range of holdings might, by contrast, reach a scale suitable for sale against gold. As has already been seen, such a vendor could afford to transport this produce further than the nearest small, local, market centre, to a large city, where it might be sold at a higher price. In such cases, gold was paid out for rural produce, whether it was foodstuffs or raw materials. This gold often never left the city. This dichotomy, which characterised the whole of the *ancien régime*, still continued in eighteenth-century Lombardy. The great landlords sold for gold in the great cities, on an international market; whilst the small, independent peasantry sold for silver in small market towns on the local, internal market.

It is possible to devise a scheme, which is a rough approximation to the truth, that would suggest that at the end of the Middle Ages, the *monnaie noire* of a city circulated frequently and continuously throughout the year within that city, but hardly anywhere else. The silver coin of a city circulated within that city, and between it and other cities in the same 'coinage province' continuously throughout the year. It was also used seasonally, very rapidly, in large quantities for a very short time in the small towns and villages of the countryside served by those cities. The gold coin of a city circulated internationally in that city or in any other city in Christendom, but very rarely in the countryside. Until the enormous increase in the quantity of gold coin in the fourteenth century this international role in large-scale transactions between, and within, cities was filled by silver currency bars. Even after the great expansion of gold coinage, silver coin was of course carried outside its own 'coinage province', but usually as part of a bi-metallic flow, in which case it was normally immediately carried to the mint on arrival in the new country.

The various maps in this volume represent the principal international flows of silver and, where appropriate, gold. These are, of course, the major trade-routes of Europe seen in reverse, for a balance of payments in one direction, normally represented a balance of goods in the opposite direction.

It is quite clear that newly mined silver or gold very soon left the area in which it was mined. The long-term benefits of mineral wealth did not accrue to the mining communities. The Czech historian Janáček has even suggested that the silver-mines had an adverse effect on the Bohemian economy in the Middle Ages, because the ease with which manufactured goods could be purchased abroad, particularly cloth from the Netherlands, meant that there was a positive disincentive to build up a manufacturing-base to the Bohemian economy.[1] Even inside the mining communities, the evidence from similar communities later was to suggest that the miners themselves were not the principal beneficiaries, and that they were either unsuccessful and hopeful, or successful and then rapidly fleeced of their sudden wealth by an army of gamblers, prostitutes, lodging-house proprietors and sellers of food and clothing at inflated prices. It was as much these people as the miners themselves who generated the demand for luxuries, in return for which the newly mined silver, or gold in the Hungarian case, was sent out of the country. The prince, the landowner, and the Church all took minor portions of the proceeds of mining. Their portions were generally transmitted to the country's capital city at once, from Kutná Hora to Prague for example, or from Kremnica to Buda. This silver and gold was responsible for building up those cities quite remarkably, and underpinning the political importance of their rulers. The power of the house of Luxemburg was transformed by the acquisition of Bohemia and its mineral wealth. In some cases too, absentee capitalist backers had shareholdings in the mines, so that a portion of the profits was remitted directly to them, from the mines of Iglesias in Sardinia to investors at Pisa, for example, late in the thirteenth century, or nearly two centuries later from the mines on the Schneeberg in Saxony to

---

[1] See above, pp. 341–2.

investors in Cologne. In the sixteenth century Agricola took shareholding in mines by absentee investors for granted.

All this set the new silver and gold moving away from its source, and stimulated the economy, and the political and cultural life, of Europe at a variety of points more or less distant from the actual sources of the metal. Some intermediate cities on the trade-routes benefited, such as Vienna or, later, Frankfurt. The major benefits, however, accumulated in the two most commercially developed areas of Europe, the southern Netherlands and northern Italy. All the evidence, from the period of the silver of Goslar, to that of the silver of the Schneeberg and of Schwaz, suggests that the new silver and gold gravitated to these two areas of Europe. It was in these two areas that capital accumulation took place, and commercial and industrial transformations were possible. Between the two leading areas the commercial dominance of northern Italy was reflected in a continual balance of payments in its favour and a consequent flow of specie from north-west to south-east.

It was North Italian businessmen, not Flemings or Brabançons, who penetrated all parts of Europe, exploiting the opportunities of inter-regional trade, and managing the flow of money from place to place. They did this by bills of exchange, or by straightforward, physical transport of it by the cartload. They, too, provided the skilled, entrepreneurial management for the mint factories of Europe, whether in Kutná Hora or in London, in Lübeck or in Paris, or even in Ghent. It is no accident that my maps show that so much of the precious metal of Europe ended up in northern Italy. The business was managed and organised with just that intention. Europe north of the Alps was economically exploited in the later Middle Ages by Italians in much the same way that the British exploited India in the eighteenth century. The hope that inspired so many young Italians when they set out to go to far-flung corners of Europe as factors of great business houses was that they would return to Italy in their middle years as rich 'nabobs' to play an important role in the economic, social and political life of their home cities.

England provided the only significant exception to this continuous drain of precious metals to northern Italy, either directly or by way of the Netherlands, for England's wool put it in much the same position as a modern oil-producing country, able to use threats of economic embargoes to raise the price of English wool on the Flemish or Florentine markets and to twist the arms of the international banking-houses.[1] England was a rich 'colonial' territory for Tuscans to exploit, but it could equally be dangerous; potential 'nabobs' could return from it bankrupted and broken men, as well as immensely enriched. In the tenth century, and again

---

[1] In the fifteenth century northern Castille, increasingly important as an alternative source of high-quality wool, found itself in the same exceptional position as England (Angus MacKay, *Money, Prices and Politics in Fifteenth-Century Castile*, Royal Historical Society (London 1981)).

continuously from the twelfth century onwards, England remained an island well supplied with money, because of its wool, even when the rest of Europe was suffering from a bullion shortage. In the 1420s Mocenigo reported that the Venetians were carrying Bosnian and Serbian silver to England, but to nowhere else in Europe, and in the 1450s the London mint still went on striking new coins from imported silver when most of the mints in the rest of Europe were closed because of the acuteness of the silver-famine. It was the exceedingly high share in the revenues of the wool-trade taken by the crown, like the state share in modern oil-revenues, that gave the kings of England a political importance out of all proportion to the size and population of the kingdom that they ruled.

In the seventeenth century Thomas Mun defended the vast sums of silver that the English East India Company were sending out to the east, against the attacks of narrow-minded mercantilists. He did so on the grounds that the oriental products imported into England were re-exported to other parts of Europe at such a profit that the stock of money in England was in no way diminished by this outflow of silver, but rather increased by it. The same argument applied, on a larger scale, to the activities of the Dutch East India Company at the same time. The Dutch and the English East India Companies were merely, for the time being, the agents of a flow of silver, and sometimes gold, from Europe to Asia that had continued on a varying scale from the Dark Ages through the time of Mun's apologia for it. It went on until the flow was reversed, for the first time ever, by European industrialisation and European conquest in Asia, in the late eighteenth century. Professor Ashtor has estimated that in the fourteenth and fifteenth centuries, taking good times and bad ones together, European exports of goods to the Levant were exceeded by European imports of goods to a value approaching 400,000 ducats a year, which had to be settled in coin.[1]

In the early fifteenth century it was the Venetians who held the role later occupied by the Dutch and the English. Like Mun, Doge Mocenigo had no objection to the vast quantities of silver being exported to the Levant, indeed he gloried in them and in the profit gained by Venetian merchants from the re-sale of oriental goods, so much so that he saw all the gold of Christendom being drawn into Venice as a

[1] Eliyahu Ashtor, *Les Métaux précieux et la balance des payements du Proche-Orient à la Basse Époque* (Paris, 1971), p. 96, where he proposes the following balance for the fifteenth century:

The Venetians sent out	*The Venetians brought back*
300,000 ducats in coin	400,000 ducats of spices from further east
200,000 ducats in goods	80,000 ducats of goods from the Near East
	20,000 ducats in coin

Other Europeans sent out	*Other Europeans brought back*
100,000 ducats in coin	130,000 ducats of spices
60,000 ducats in goods	20,000 ducats of goods from the Near East
	10,000 ducats in coin

giving a net imbalance of 370,000 ducats in coin on a total trade worth 660,000 ducats a year.

result. This continuous outflow of silver or gold from Europe needs to be borne in mind as a background to the flow of precious metals into Italy.

Nevertheless, as Mocenigo and Mun pointed out, it was in the countries that were the agents of the import of oriental goods to Europe that the greatest concentration of money accumulated, rather than in the countries, like Meissen in the twelfth century, or Spain in the seventeenth century, through which the precious metals were first introduced into Europe. The maximum amount of money remained in the country reached last by the flow of specie rather than in that reached first.

For the economic historian it is these commercial flows that are most important. For the political historian the occasional, but dramatic, movements of money from one place to another are more interesting. The ransom of Richard I of England provides a good example. Richard was captured by Leopold of Austria on his way back from the Third Crusade in 1192 and handed over to the Emperor Henry VI. Two years later he was released against the payment of no less than 100,000 Cologne marks of silver, just over 23 tonnes of it, which was collected in London and shipped up the Rhine to Henry, in precisely the opposite direction to the normal commercial balance of payments. An additional 50,000 marks was due to be paid later, but only just over a fifth was actually sent, mostly from Normandy.[1] Much of this vast quantity of silver was presumably in the form of ingots, although some was certainly in coin. It provided Henry VI with the means to invade Italy successfully and make good his claims to his wife Constance's kingdom of Sicily. Twenty years later, in 1214, Richard I's brother and successor, John, shipped another 40,000 marks of silver to Germany from England. This time it was not a ransom, but a subsidy to support his nephew, the Saxon Emperor Otto IV, in their common fight against Philip II of France. Much of this subsidy was certainly in the form of English silver pennies, which suddenly came to circulate extensively in Westphalia and were vigorously imitated there. Just over forty years later still, in 1257, John's younger son, Richard of Cornwall, carried a rather smaller sum of silver from England to the Rhineland in his own attempt to establish himself as King of the Romans. A generation later still, Richard's nephew, Edward I of England, shipped a much greater quantity of silver, to pay his troops and subsidise his allies in the Low Countries, between 1294 and 1298. This was the greatest of these political payments to date. It weighed over 120 tonnes, and was worth around £350,000 sterling. It was largely sent in the form of pennies sterling. Indeed sterlings suddenly came to form much of the currency in the Low Countries, where they were heavily imitated, and remained so for the next two decades.

The scale and expense of these vast political shipments of coin is best illustrated by the fact that, for the initial subsidies of 1294, the silver was sent across the North

[1] Heinz Quirin, *Einführung in das Studium der mittelalterlichen Geschichte*, 2nd ed. (Brunswick, 1961), pp. 151–2.

Sea by Edward I to his paymaster Robert de Segre in no less than 17 ships, manned by 756 sailors, who were, of course, paid by the king.[1]

Impressive though these sums seem, it was possible four times in a century to ship such quantities of silver out of an England that had only derisorily small silver-mines of its own, simply because the cumulative effects of the balance of trade were even more considerable. The quantity of coin in the country not only recovered its previous level between these political exports of silver, but considerably increased in each generation up to the 1290s. After the political shipments of coin in the 1290s, which carried away a very large proportion of the circulating medium of the country, it took much less than a generation for the money supply of England to be restored to its high point. Many of these very sterlings, exported for political reasons, returned to England by way of trade, unfortunately accompanied by large numbers of their continental imitations.

It is obviously easier to judge the impact of such political movements of coin when they run clean contrary to the balance of trade, than when they run with it, and merely accelerate the existing trends. It is easier to see Richard's ransom draining silver out of England and the rest of the Angevin 'empire', than it is to see it pouring silver into Italy, into which so much new silver was already flowing commercially at the same time. The payment of Richard's ransom was made only seven years before the Venetians reached the stage of striking the first grossi. It might perhaps be agreeable to think that Henry VI's radical transformation of the Norman copper coinage of Sicily into a northern type of silver-penny coinage owed something to the silver sent from England, but such a hypothesis is not yet proven. Nor is it possible to pick up the monetary traces of some of the later military expeditions into Italy, although the quantities of Kutná Hora silver brought by John the Blind of Luxemburg, and later by his son the Emperor Charles IV, were very considerable. So were the quantities of Kremnica gold brought by Elizabeth of Hungary in 1343–4, when she secured the succession to the throne of Naples, which was still one of the richest kingdoms in Europe, for her younger son Andrew and his wife Joanna I. Her elder son Louis (the Great), who had only recently become King of Hungary, provided her with 21,000 marks of gold, and 27,000 marks of silver. These were both apparently uncoined, since the chronicler adds that she also took with her almost half a bushel of florins ('de florenis fere cum media garleta'), and 'de denariis vero parvis usque ad exitum regni multum'.[2] Andrew's resources for taking over the throne weighed, in modern terms, over 5 tonnes of gold and nearly 7 tonnes of silver. Italy had recently become accustomed

---

[1] Michael Prestwich, *War, Politics and Finance under Edward I* (London, 1972), pp. 171–5.

[2] Chronicle of John, Archdeacon of Küküllö quoted by Balint Homan, 'La circolazione delle monete d'oro in Ungheria dal x al xiv secolo e la crisi europea dell' oro nel secolo xiv', *Rivista Italiana di Numismatica*, 2nd series, v (1922), 152–3.

to receiving Hungarian gold by way of trade. Andrew's resources therefore had much less impact than the very similar quantities of gold paid out on behalf of Edward III and Philip VI seven years earlier. This was carried to the Low Countries and the Rhineland to subsidise their respective allies there. The latter payments had so much more impact because they were carried to areas hitherto totally unused to gold as currency. Edward's and Philip's subsidies were therefore movements of coin entirely against the general pattern dictated by the balance of trade. These enormous sums paid as ransoms and dowries, and to purchase allies and secure thrones, were frequently very much greater than the sums transmitted in the course of commerce in any one year. Commerce, however, went on year after year, decade after decade, and in the longer term even these vast amounts of coin paled into insignificance against the tide of commerce: 370,000 ducats-worth of coin a year leaving the ports of Europe for the Levant by way of trade, amounting very roughly to 1¼ tonnes of gold or 13 tonnes of silver, according to which metal was sent, adding up year after year, very rapidly surpasses even the largest of these political payments, and, seen in the perspective of decades or even centuries, makes them seem small and ephemeral.

Nevertheless it was these sudden political payments that seemed more likely to lead to the production of imitative coins, rather than the continuous payments by way of trade. In the period when silver was still used for political payments, the silver pence of John of England were imitated in Westphalia, those of his grandson Edward I in the southern Netherlands, and the gigliati of Naples in the Aegean during the Crusade of the Archipelago. In the period when gold took over this role, it was the écus of Philip VI and the florins of Florence, sent on Edward III's behalf, that were imitated in the Low Countries. The ducats of Venice were imitated in the Aegean during the Venetian–Genoese war there.

The flow of money to the papacy was one that raised a great deal of emotion in the Middle Ages. The average income available to John XXII, pope from 1316 to 1334, amounted to under 230,000 florins a year. This was less than half the income enjoyed by the contemporary Kings of France, Naples or even England,[1] and no more than that handled by the chamberlains of the city of Florence. Royal and city revenues, however, were usually spent again in the same countries in which they had been raised, so that taxation and government expenditure merely circulated the money within one principality. If it moved from one place to another it was as part of the general reflux of money from the country to the city. Papal revenues were quite different. They came from all parts of Europe and were spent in one part of Europe. This was generally Italy, for even when the papacy was at Avignon, the

---

[1] These can only ever be very rough estimates, for the popes, like medieval kings, spent a great deal of their revenues by assigning payment on local collectors, so that only a portion of their income ever passed through the central treasury.

larger part of the revenues were spent in Italy on the maintenance of papal armies. Papal payments in this direction ran along the general currents of trade. Indeed the cameral merchants to whom prelates and papal collectors frequently entrusted the transport of the money due to the *camera apostolica* were most commonly the leading banking-houses of the day. They already had a multitude of branches in many parts of Christendom, and were already managing the commercial flow of money around Europe. They were naturally accustomed to moving sums of money in the same direction with great regularity. Firms such as the Buonsignori of Siena, the Bardi, the Peruzzi and the Acciaiuoli of Florence, the Malabayla of Asti, and the Alberti and Medici of Florence handled this business in turn. Prelates sent the 'common services' and other sums that they owed at their own expense. However papal collectors did so at the expense of the *camera*. The cameral accounts therefore give a clear picture of how the system worked in practice. The papal collectors gathered a great deal of the money involved in small sums, in silver and even in black money. They had to take what they had collected to a local money-changer and exchange it for gold, since, at this point, they were moving from the circuit of silver to the circuit of gold. For example in March 1386, Pons de Cros, the papal collector at Le Puy in France, paid 8 livres to change 400 livres tournois of silver into gold. This represented the exchange of nearly 10,000 blancs, or of even more coins if it was in smaller denominations, presumably from a great iron-bound chest in which it had been accumulated, into 400 gold francs, which one may equally presume were in a small leather bag. Other evidence suggests that the usual charge for such a service was between 4d. and 6d. in the pound. This was, of course, the opposite operation from the service performed by money-changers for manufacturers who sold their goods, cloth for example, on the international market for gold, but needed to pay their employees in silver. The papal collector then had the choice of carrying the gold to the *camera* himself, sending someone whom he trusted with it, or else purchasing a bill of exchange. Inside Italy these could be acquired very easily, for practically every city of importance was a banking-place, but outside Italy fully fledged banking-places were much more spread out. Montpellier and Paris in France, Barcelona and Seville in the Iberian Peninsula, London in England and Bruges in the Netherlands were the only places at which bills of exchange could certainly be purchased over long periods of time. At the greater international fair towns, initially those of Champagne, and later Geneva, and then Lyons, or Medina del Campo, bills of exchange could also usually be purchased during a fair. At a great many other cities they could sometimes be found, for example in those cities of south Germany that were to become of such importance from the late fifteenth century. Because 'banking-places' were so widely disposed outside Italy, papal collectors had frequently to travel some distance to purchase bills of exchange. The papal collector at Toledo, for example, had to go to Seville, over 480 kilometres (300 miles) away. For some it was even worse. The papal collector in Poland had usually to choose between Bruges and Venice, and Pope Benedict XII was unable to persuade the Bardi to set up a branch in Cracow.[1] In March 1386 Pons de Cros was very fortunate in finding someone in Le Puy itself from whom he could purchase a bill of exchange with the 400 gold francs that he had obtained from the money-changer. He usually had to take the risks of carrying the gold himself, but on this occasion he was able to carry a bill of exchange to Avignon instead. He was also fortunate in that this service only cost him 5 francs, just over 1% of the sum involved. Bills of exchange rarely cost as little as this. Up to 5% of the sum transferred was commonly charged. Over long distances it could be much higher. For example, at Seville in June 1393 the papal sub-collector Miguel Rodriguez purchased a bill of exchange from the Genoese Francesco di Gentile with 400 gold doblas, payable at Avignon by Frederigo Imperiale within 15 days of being presented to him. On this occasion the sub-collector was not going to Avignon himself, nor had he a messenger to send, so that di Gentile himself transmitted the bill of exchange to Imperiale, who, just under 6 weeks later, paid the sum of 480 cameral florins into the papal treasury in gold. But in Seville, 400 doblas were worth 533 cameral florins. Rodriguez had in effect paid 53 florins, 10% of the sum remitted, for the service provided.[2] All these were straightforward bills of exchange. They were used quite simply to remit sums of money from one place to another. A service was provided and charged for. How di Gentile and Imperiale carried out the business between them was no concern of Rodriguez. Patently they were in regular correspondence with each other, had accounts with each other, and could draw bills on each other as well as send goods to each other. From time to time they would naturally have to settle up, but if possible they would do so by buying a bill from a third party, drawn on a fourth party, who wanted money transmitted in the opposite direction. However, there were basic imbalances between certain places. In the last resort gold had actually to be carried from place to place. Gold, for example, was commonly carried from Seville to Genoa. Before this stage was reached, a very great deal of business had passed in each direction, so that the gold actually carried represented a much greater volume of transactions. The combination of a great body of bills of exchange with occasional remittances in gold, represented an enormous commercial advance on the older pattern of carrying a vast bulk of silver in bars on practically every occasion. The overall contribution of the papacy to this business was slight, although for the limited number of firms who acted as papal bankers it was of

---

[1] Armando Sapori, 'Gli Italiani in Polonia fino a tutto il quattrocento', *Studi di storia economica – secoli XIII, XIV, XV*, III (Florence, 1967), 149–76.

[2] Jean Favier, *Les Finances pontificales à l'époque du grand Schisme d'Occident 1378–1419*, Bibliothèque des Écoles Françaises d'Athènes et de Rome CCXI (Paris, 1966), pp. 451–79.

considerable importance. However, owing to the preservation of papal records it is the papal business that is most clearly visible to us. The papacy were only using a system set up for commercial purposes, for which the records, of course, generally do not survive.

Bills of exchange were also used, and, it was sometimes suggested, abused by those who did not wish to transmit money from one place to another at all. Such persons would sell a bill of exchange to a banker, drawn on a third party in another place, who, when the bill was presented to him, would meet it by another bill, drawn on the original seller of the first bill, who would have to meet it by repaying the banker, together with the accrued charges. These might be the genuine charges for the double exchange, based on the difference in exchange rates between the two places, in which case there was a risk element for the banker, or they might be specified in advance, in which case the banker was certain of his profit. The profit could then be considered a disguised form of interest, and the original sum paid for the bill of exchange a disguised loan. The disguise became rather thinner if the third party in either city was either fictitious or another branch of the same bank. However such a use, or misuse, of the system of bills of exchange as an instrument of credit, depended on the existence of the system itself for genuine commercial transactions.

It must be emphasised that all this superstructure of international payments was only a superstructure, and that the great body of commercial transactions, and in consequence of monetary payments, was intensely local in character. The majority of men were fed and clothed by the products of their own vicinities. Even the town-dwelling minority were largely dependent on the surrounding countryside for their needs. Only the very largest cities, like Venice and Florence, drew their basic necessities from great distances. The interplay between town and country was far more important than the interplay between one town and another.

Inside the town, as in the country, most transactions were met by payment in coin. Only in an extraordinarily limited number of cities, such as Genoa and Venice, was there a sufficiently developed system of *banchi del giro* or *banchi di scritta* for payment to be made frequently and easily by transfer in the books of the bank. The earliest surviving Florentine cheque so far discovered was drawn on the Castellani bank by two patrician Tornaquinci in November 1368 to pay a draper, Sengnia Ciapi, for black cloth for a family funeral. Within a hundred years cheques were in use there by very modest men for modest purposes. In 1477, a Florentine haberdasher wrote a cheque to pay for the emptying of a cesspit.[1] Where they were available, primarily in the great commercial cities of North Italy, such banking facilities were used by a surprisingly large number of people. Around 1500, perhaps

[1] Marco Spallanzani, 'A note on Florentine banking in the Renaissance: orders of payment and cheques', *Journal of European Economic History*, VII (1978), 145–65; and see above, p. 257.

as many as 4000 out of a total adult male population of 30,000 in Venice had current bank accounts, and a high proportion, precisely half, of these were not patricians.[1] If the wealth and tax structure of Venice in 1500 had been anything like that of Florence in 1457, these 4000 account-holders would have enjoyed around three quarters of the taxable income of the city. Nevertheless, even in Venice, by far the most commercially sophisticated city in Europe in 1500, a vast number of small transactions had still to be carried out with actual metallic coin. In less advanced cities the use of coin remained dominant. It was not until the seventeenth century, and then only in England and Holland, which were by then the most advanced countries, that anything except coined money made a really significant contribution to the internal money supply outside the few favoured cities. Even in the nineteenth century the role of coined money was in many places dominant, and everywhere important. It is virtually only in the twentieth century that coin has been relegated to the role of small change in the money supply. These later developments took place in societies that were increasingly urban and industrialised. Medieval Europe was predominantly rural and overwhelmingly agricultural. In such a society the money supply was the supply of metallic coin although with significant exceptions.

[1] Frederic C. Lane, 'Venetian bankers 1496–1533', *Journal of Political Economy*, XLV (1937), 187–206, repr. in *Venice and History: Collected Papers* (Baltimore, 1966); Robert S. Lopez, 'Une Histoire à trois niveaux: la circulation monétaire', in *Mélanges en l'honneur de Fernand Braudel*, II (1973), 335–41, extrapolating from de Roover's work, suggested that in Bruges around 1400, only one in forty of the total population, perhaps one in ten of the adult males, had bank accounts.

Appendix I

The Coins Most Commonly in Use in the Middle Ages, Together With Details of their Country and Period of Origin, their Weight and Fineness, their Initial Values and the Names under which They Were Current

Weight in medieval documents was normally expressed in terms of the number of coins that were struck from a standard weight, usually a pound or a mark, but sometimes from a smaller unit, such as an ounce or lot. These weights naturally varied from time to time and from place to place, although there were some, such as the marks of Cologne or Troyes, that had a long and widespread use. Alternatively weights were expressed in terms of carats or grains. The carat or siliqua (the seed of the carob, *Ceratonia siliqua*) was the standard basic weight in antiquity in the Mediterranean world, and continued in use in the Byzantine Empire in the Middle Ages. In the Germanic west, however, it fell out of use in the sixth and seventh centuries in favour of systems in which cereal grains were the basic units. Both barley grains, later called Troy grains, and wheat grains, later called Paris grains, were used. The former weighed 0.065 grams and the latter 0.053 grams. The last Merovingian gold trientes and the first Merovingian silver deniers could therefore be described either as weighing 20 grains of barley or as weighing 24 grains of wheat. In this table all weights are reduced to grams.

Fineness in medieval documents was normally expressed in terms derived from systems of weight used at an earlier time. For silver, the system used right through the Middle Ages was derived from weighing in grains, as it had been used in the first centuries of the circulation of the denier. At that point a solidus, or shilling, had meant 12 silver deniers, and at the critical period each denier had weighed 24 grains (a pennyweight – dwt.). This was fossilised, so that pure silver, or, more often *argent-le-roi* (standard, nearly pure, silver) was described as having a fineness of 12 d(eniers). Similarly half-silver and half-alloy was described as having a fineness of 6d. (out of 12 being understood), and so forth. Thus silver coins described as having a fineness of 4d. 18gr., consisted of $4\frac{3}{4}$-twelfths silver and $7\frac{1}{4}$-twelfths alloy. An alternative system, used around the Baltic, described fineness in terms of lots. A mark weight was divided into 16 lots. Pure silver was therefore described as having a fineness of 16 lots; half-silver and half-alloy as having a fineness of 8 lots and so forth. When gold was used again in western Europe, the Byzantine system was taken over. Here the solidus was still a gold piece, which weighed 24 carats. Pure gold was accordingly described as 24 carats fine and so forth. Gold coins described as 19½ ct. fine, therefore, consisted of 19½ twenty-fourths of gold, and 4½ twenty-fourths of alloy. The finenesses of medieval gold coins were much higher than those of modern jewellery: 18 ct. fine was poor for a gold coin, but is rather good for jewellery. In this table I have given some finenesses in their original terms, but have also added a modern fineness expressed as a decimal. Unity here represents pure metal.

IMPERIAL GOLD

solidus or solidus aureus (in Latin) or nomisma (in Greek)	Byzantine Empire, from Constantine *c.* 309, to 963. Nominally fine gold. Initially at least 0.98 fine. Wt. 24 siliquae/carats; 72 to pound (4.5 grams). Principal mint: Constantinople. Half=semissis; third=tremissis or triens (1.5 grams).
histamenon (=standard)	Standard nomisma, from Nicephoras Phocas, 963, to *c.* 1085. Retained original weight and fineness until abrupt decline in eleventh century.
tertarteron	Light-weight nomisma, struck at Constantinople 963–*c.* 1085.
hyperpyron (='pure') or iperpero or perper	Restored nomisma, from Alexius I, *c.* 1085 to *c.* 1341. Initially 20½ ct., 0.85 fine. Deteriorated in thirteenth century; issued in very small numbers after Andronicus II (d. 1328). The hyperpyron continued as an accounting unit until the end of the Byzantine Empire.

BARBARIAN GOLD
Visigoths

solidus and triens (= third)	In names of Emperors Anastasius, Justin and Justinian; issued by Alaric II (484–507) to Leovigild (568–86).
triens	In names of kings from Leovigild (from *c.* 580) to Achila II (*c.* 710–14). Debased by comparison with Byzantine triens, badly debased by the middle of the seventh century.

Merovingians

solidus and triens	In names of Emperors Anastasius, Justin and Justinian; issued until, in northern Gaul, Theodebert I of Austrasia (534–48) and, in Provence, Heraclius (610–41). In names of kings from Theodebert I to Dagobert II (674–9). Weight in sixth century on two standards: solidus at 24 and 21 siliquae (4.5 and 3.9 grams) and triens at 1.5 and 1.3 grams; surviving trientes of the seventh century

weigh mostly 1.15–1.3 grams. Most solidi from Provence.

Lombards

triens
: In names of emperors from *c.* 571 onwards. In names of kings from Cunincpert (680–700) to Charlemagne (until 781). Fineness and weight initially near Byzantine triens, but by Charlemagne 0.39 fine, wt. 0.97 gram.

Anglo-Saxons

triens or thrymsa
: Mainly issued in last quarter of seventh century. Mints: Canterbury and London. Wt. of surviving examples 1.25–1.35 grams. Value thought to be 1 shilling.

ISLAMIC

dinar
: Standard gold coin issued by Ummayad and Abbasid caliphs from Damascus mint, from Abd al-Malik, A.H. 77 (=A.D. 696/7). Nominally fine gold, wt. 4.25 grams. Dinar *manqûsh*=engraved dinar.

copies
: Dinar of Offa of Mercia (after 774). Wt. 4.28 grams.

dinar or mancus
: Issued by later Ummayads in Spain, Abd-al-Rahman III to Sulaijman (928–1013). Fineness and weight of surviving dinars vary greatly: fineness 0.79–0.98; wt. 3.43–4.71 grams.

copies
: Mancusos de oro of Berengar Raymond I and Raymond Berengar I, Counts of Barcelona (1018–76).

dinar or morabetino
: Issued by Almoravids in North Africa and Spain (*c.* 1085–*c.* 1170). Wt. 3.88 grams.

copies
: Morabetinos or maravedis issued by Kings of Castille, of Leon and of Portugal (1172–*c.* 1221).

dobla
: Double of dinar or mazmudina issued by Mazmuda or Almohads in North Africa and Spain, Abdelmumin (1129–62) to fall of Granada (1492). Wt. 4.60 grams.

copies
: Doblas of kings of Castille from Ferdinand III (1217–52) onwards.

rubā'i
: Quarter-dinar issued in Ummayad Spain, North Africa and Muslim Sicily.

copies
: Taris of Salerno (*c.* 1050–1194), Amalfi (*c.* 1050–1220+) and Christian Sicily (1072–1278).

dirhams
: Derived from Sassanian direm. Standard silver coin of Ummayad caliphate from Abd al-Malik, A.H. 79 (=A.D.

698/9). Initial wt. 2.97 grams. Issued by successor king-
doms from central Asia to Spain. Irregular weight in
Samanid emirate: early tenth century, 2.6–3.2 grams.
Extremely irregular to *c.* 930: 2.7–4.5 grams.

In Spain, slow decline in weight and fineness:

> Early eighth century: fineness 0.95–0.99; wt. 2.81
> grams.
> Late tenth and early eleventh centuries: fineness
> 0.73–0.78; wt. 3.11–3.13 grams.
> Almoravids (*c.* 1085–*c.* 1170): wt. 2 grams.
> Almohads: wt. 1.5 grams.

millares	Christian name in the thirteenth century for square dirhams of North Africa.
copies	Spain, southern France, Italy. See pp. 171–5.

PENNY COINAGE

Penny=penning=pfennig=denarius=denaro=denier=dinero=dinhero
Halfpenny=obolus=obole=medaglia=maille
Farthing=ferling=pougeoise=pogesa
12 pennies=shilling=schilling=skilling=solidus=sou=soldo=sueldo (except in Bavaria
and Austria where 30 pfennigs=schilling)
240 pennies=pound=pfund=pond=libra=livre=lira

Merovingian Gaul

denier or denarius

c. 673–5, in name of Childeric II of Austrasia and of many
ecclesiastics and some laymen during the remainder of
the seventh and first half of the eighth century. Majority
of surviving examples weigh 1.2–1.3 grams. Probable
standard *c.* 1.3 grams.

Frisian and Anglo-Saxon coasts

penning or penny

From the end of the seventh to the third quarter of the
eighth century. Miscalled sceat or sceatta.

Carolingian Empire

denier

Replaced Merovingian denier, from 755, and Frisian
penning. 755: wt. 1.3 grams (?); 794: wt. 1.7 grams. After
end of Carolingians, issue continued in some places with
immobilised types, into eleventh century.

France

Feudal deniers issued throughout West Frankia after
break-up of Carolingian Empire.

denier provinois	Minted at Provins in the name of the Count of Troyes and then of the Count of Champagne (end tenth century– after 1265). Basis of money of account for Champagne, Barrois and Lorraine. From 1210 of same standard as denier tournois.
copies	Denaro provisino issued by Senate of Rome.
denier melgorien	Issued by Count of Melgueil or Mauguio, then Bishop of Maguelonne (tenth century – after 1282). 1125: fineness 0.42; wt. 1.10 grams. 1215: fineness 0.33; wt. 1.09 grams.
denier parisis	Issued by Kings of France, Louis VII–Charles V.

Louis VII (1137–80): wt. of surviving examples 0.85–1.28 grams.

Charles V (last issued 1365): fineness 0.16; wt. 1.28 grams.

Other local deniers issued by Capetians from end tenth century.

denier tournois	Issued by Abbey of St Martin of Tours, from tenth century to 1204. Wt. declining: 1.2–0.95 grams. Issued by Kings of France (1204–1649).

Philip Augustus (d. 1223): wt. of surviving examples 0.78–1.01 grams.

Charles VIII (1483 issue): fineness 0.08; wt. 1.02 grams.

Empire
Italy

denari	Issued by or in name of Carolingians, of native Kings of Italy and of German Emperors from Otto I (962). Initially of Charlemagne's standard (794: wt. 1.7 grams), but declining. Principal mint for Lombardy: Pavia; for Tuscany: Lucca.

Lombardy

denari imperiali	Reformed denari, issued from about 1155/61 by emperors and later rulers of Milan and Pavia. Initially, Frederick I, double preceding denari: fineness 0.5; wt. 1 gram.

Venice

denari	Issued by city from ninth century. In name of ruling doge, instead of long-dead emperor, from around 1170.

Tuscany

denari	Issued by imperial mint at Lucca, taken over by city, and by new civic mints, at Pisa about 1151, Volterra about

1165, and Siena about 1191. Denari of Tuscan cities kept at identical fineness and weight by monetary conventions. Second half of twelfth century: wt. 0.6 gram. First half of thirteenth century: wt. 0.25 gram.

Rome

denari

Issued jointly in names of pope and emperor from Leo III and Charlemagne to late tenth century.

denari provisini

Issued by Senate from *c.* 1180. Of same type as denier provinois of Champagne.

Germany

pfennig

Imperial pfennigs theoretically on Charlemagne's standard, 240 to pound, wt. 1.7 grams; or from twelfth century, 160 to mark of Cologne, wt. 1.46 grams. In practice:
Pfennig at Trier, 1160: wt. 0.97 gram.
Pfennig of Luxemburg, early thirteenth century: wt. 0.73 gram.
Bracteate pfennig at Minden, 1265: fineness 0.8; wt. 0.67 gram.

Hungary

denar

From Stefan I (1008–38) onwards. Bracteate denars, Béla IV (1235–70) to Otto (1305–7).

England

penny (called 'sterling' from the eleventh century)

Struck on broader flan, to replace 'sceatta' type of penny, from about 775/80 by Heaberht and Ecgberht, Kings of Kent, and from about 783/4 by Offa, King of Mercia. Thereafter issued by all Anglo-Saxon kingdoms, by Viking kingdom in York, and by Norman kings.
Until 1156/7 fineness and weight fluctuated considerably from issue to issue. Wt. within limits 1–1.8 grams.
1156/7–1279: fineness 0.925; wt. 1.46 gram:
'Tealby' coinage, 1156/7–80.
short-cross pennies, 1180–1247.
long-cross pennies, 1247–78.
1279 onwards: fineness 0.925; wt. declining. 1279: 1.44 grams; 1412–64: 0.97 grams; 1464–1526: 0.78 gram.

copies

See Scotland and Ireland. Also:
Of Anglo-Saxon pennies in Scandinavia, in large numbers, particularly of Aethelred II.

Of short-cross pennies in Westphalia.
Of long-cross pennies in the Rhineland.
Of pennies of Edward I in Low Countries, in large numbers.

Scotland

penny

Derived from English penny, issued from David I, *c.* 1140, onwards. Fineness and weight as English penny to *c.* 1367:
> short-cross pennies, *c.* 1195–1250
> long-cross pennies, *c.* 1250–80
> As Edward I of England from 1280.

Ireland

penny

Derived from English penny, issued from John, 1190s, onwards. Issue very intermittent. Fineness and weight as English penny to 1460:
> short-cross pennies, *c.* 1204–11
> long-cross pennies, *c.* 1251–3
> Edward I, as in England, *c.* 1280–5, 1294–1302
> Until 1460 no further issues except 1339, 1425.

Spain

Barcelona
dinero

From early eleventh century by Counts of Barcelona (later also Kings of Aragon). Declining fineness and weight:
> 1067: fineness 0.33; wt. 1.14 grams.
> Mid twelfth century: fineness 0.2; wt. 0.66 gram.
> *c.* 1174–7, reformed dinero of Alfonso II: fineness 0.33; wt. 1.08 grams.
> 1256: fineness 3d. (0.25), hence called 'ternales'; wt. 1.08 grams.

Aragon
dinero iaccensis or dinero jaquesa

Issued by kings from Sancho Ramirez (1063–94) at Jacca and other mints. Under Alfonso II (of Barcelona), 1175: fineness 0.33; wt. 1.08 grams.

Castille
dinero

Issued by kings from Fernando I (1035–65) onwards.

LARGER SILVER

Grossus denarius=great coin=grosso=gros=groschen=groot=croat=groat. Thenceforth older penny coinages became petty coins, piccoli, parvi, petits, minutii, menuts etc.

Italy

Venice
Grosso or ducato d'argento or matapan

First issued by Doge Enrico Dandolo. 1201–1355: fineness 0.965; wt. 2.18 grams. 1379, new issue: fineness 0.95; wt. 1.99 grams; declined in fifteenth century. Initial value probably 24d.=2 soldi.

Genoa
grosso

Probably issued in first decade of thirteenth century: wt. 1.4 grams. Initial value probably 4d.

grosso

Probably issued from second decade of thirteenth century: wt. 1.7 grams. Initial value probably 6d.

Verona
grosso or aquilino

First issued in 1220s: wt. 1.7 grams. Value 20d., hence sometimes called vigintiarius.

  copies

By Bishop of Trento, from 1230s.
By Count of Tirol, from 1271. Known as kreuzer, zwanziger or tirolino.

Siena
grosso

First issued in 1220s: wt. 1.7 grams. Initial value 12d.=Sienese soldo.

Pisa
grosso

First issued in 1220s: wt. 1.7 grams. Initial value 12d.=Pisan soldo. Later thirteenth century Pisan grossi, known as aquilini, circulated widely in Tuscany, not to be confused with grossi aquilini of Verona (and the Tirol) which circulated widely in north-eastern Italy.

Florence
grosso or fiorino d'argento

First issued in 1230s: wt. 1.7 grams. Initial value 12d.= Florentine soldo.

Milan
grosso or ambrosino

First issued by second quarter of thirteenth century, possibly from 1190s. Initial value probably 12d. imperiali=Milanese soldo.

Rome
grosso or romanino

First issued 1253 by Brancaleone d'Andolo (Senator 1253–5): wt. 3.5 grams. Initial value 12d. provisini=Roman soldo.

Naples
grosso or carlino

First issued 1278 by Charles I of Anjou. Fineness 0.93; wt. 3.34 grams.

grosso or gigliato

Charles II (from 1302) to Louis XII of France (King of Naples 1501–4). Initially fineness 0.93; wt. 4 grams. Weight fairly constant, surviving examples of Louis XII still 3.4–3.6 grams.

  copies

Provence, from Robert of Naples (1309–43) onwards. These gros appear in papal accounts at Avignon as 'iulhati'.
Cyprus from Henry II (1288–1324) onwards. Hungary from 1329 (Charles Robert of Naples) onwards. Emirates of Mentesche and Aidin in Asia Minor.

Sicily
reale or pierreale

From Pedro of Aragon (1282–5) onwards. Original fineness 0.93; wt. 3.34 grams.

Spain

Barcelona/Aragon
grosso de plata or croat

First issued 1284 by Pedro III. Fineness 0.96; wt. 3.24 grams. Initial value 12d. ternales=sueldo of Barcelona. Croats of same weight and fineness to sixteenth century.

Castille
maravedi de plata

Alfonso X, isolated issue 1258; wt. surviving examples 5.4–6.0 grams.

real

First issued by Pedro I (1350–69). Standard unchanged to late fifteenth century; fineness 11d. 4 gr. (0.93); wt. 3.48 grams. Initial value 3 maravedis.

France

gros tournois

St Louis to Charles VI. Fineness 0.96. 1266–1322: wt. 4.22 grams. 1329–64: wt. declining to 2.55 grams. 1266–90 valued at sou tournois.

  copies

Provence 1267. Otherwise almost entirely fourteenth century, principalities within France, in Low Countries, and in Rhineland.

Low Countries

Hainault and Flanders
cavalier

From 1269, issue by Margaret of Constantinople of double sterlings, with type of mounted knight ('cavalier') at Valenciennes, lion-shield at Ghent, eagle at Alost. Wt. about 2.6 grams.

  copies

Many principalities in Low Countries to about 1320.

Flanders
gros

Derivatives from gros tournois, from Jean de Namur (1302–3), for twenty years.

groot

Distinctive indigenous type from Louis de Nevers (1322–46). Initial wt. 3.6 grams. Valued at 3 Flemish sterlings. 1433: fineness 0.48; wt. 1.7 grams. 1492: fineness 0.32; wt. 1.78 grams.

Bohemia

grossus pragensis or prager-groschen or prague groat

From 1300 to 1547. Initially fineness 0.93; wt. 3.97 grams; value 12d. Standard declined, at first slowly: 1378, fineness 0.89, wt. 3.62 grams, thereafter rapidly: 1405, fineness 0.67; wt. 2.7 grams.

England

groat

Edward I, isolated issue 1279: fineness 0.925; wt. 5.77 grams. Edward III onwards, from 1351, 0.925 fine; declining in weight: 1351, wt. 4.67 grams; under Henry VII, wt. 3.11 grams. Valued throughout at 4 English sterlings.

  copies

Scotland from 1357.

GOLD
Italy

Sicily
augustale

Frederick II, 1231, struck at Messina and Brindisi mints. Fineness 0.854; wt. 5.3 grams=double dinar.

Florence
florin or fiorino d'oro

Issued 1252–1533. Nominally pure gold. Initial value 1 lira, wt. 3.54 grams. Wt. varied: 3.33–3.55 grams.
  1252–1422: fiorino d'oro stretto.
  1422–1533: fiorino d'oro largo.

  copies

Rhône valley, Low Countries, Rhineland, Austria, Hungary, Aragon.

Genoa

genovino or genoin — From 1252. Nominally pure gold. Wt. 3.53 grams. Initial value 8s. Also quartarolo or quarter-florin (cf. tari or quarter-dinar), and eighth-florin or soldo d'oro.

Venice

ducato d'oro or ducat or zecchino or sequin — 1284–*c.* 1840. Nominally pure (0.997 by assay); wt. 3.56 grams.

 copies — Rome, Latin Orient, Muslim Levant, India.

Gold florins also issued by Perugia (*c.* 1259), Lucca (by 1275), Milan (Ambrosino d'oro, before end of thirteenth century), and Bologna (bolognino d'oro, 1379; wt. 3.55 grams).

Papacy

cameral florins — Struck at Avignon from 1322, later at Rome.

Spain

Castille

dobla — From Fernando III (1217–52) to 1497. Nominally pure gold. Wt. 4.6 grams. Also multiple doblas, double, tenfold, twenty-fold and even fifty-fold! Alongside good doblas, also poor doblas de la banda under John II and Enrique IV (1406–74): fineness only 0.79; wt. still 4.6 grams. First excelente of Catholic kings was double dobla, wt. 9.2 grams.

 copies — Dobra in Portugal from Pedro I (1357–67) onwards.

Aragon/Barcelona

florin — From 1369 (Pedro IV) to 1475/6 (John II). Fineness 0.75; wt. 3.48 grams.

ducado d'oro — From 1475/6 to 1535. Fineness 0.99; wt. 3.54 grams.

 copies — Ducado adopted as unit in Castille in 1497, nominally pure gold, wt. 3.5 grams. New excelente was double ducado, wt. 7 grams.

Portugal

cruzado — From 1457. Fineness 0.99; wt. 3.78 grams.

France

écu — St Louis, 1266, nominally fine; wt. 4.2 grams, initial value 10s. tournois.

petit royal or florin — Philip IV from 1290; nominally fine; wt. 3.55 grams.

chaise or clinkaert | Philip IV from 1303: double of royal or florin.

agnel or mouton | Philip IV from 1311, continued by his successors.

écu d'or or écu à la chaise or chaise | Philip VI and John II, from 1337 to 1351. Wt. 4.53 grams; fineness declines: 1337, nominally pure gold; 1351, 0.75.

franc à cheval or cavalier | John II, from 1360; nominally fine; wt. 3.89 grams; i.e. half English noble.

écu or scutum or schilt | Charles VI–Louis XIV:
1385: nominally fine; wt. 4.08 grams.
1388–1475, écu à la couronne or crown: nominally fine; wt. in 1388, 3.99 grams declining.
From 1475, écu au soleil: fineness 0.96; wt. in 1475, 3.5 grams declining.

salut | Charles VI–Henry VI; nominally fine:
1421–3; wt. 3.89 grams
1423–49; wt. 3.5 grams.

Hungary

florins of St Ladislaus or ducats | From Charles Robert (1308–42) onwards; nominally fine; wt. 3.54 grams.

Empire

Emperors

Imperial gulden or florins from Louis of Bavaria (from 1339). Wt. and fineness declined with Rhinegulden (below).

Bohemia

Florins, ducats or gulden from 1325.

Lübeck

gulden or ducats | 1340–1801. Nominally fine gold; wt. 3.59 grams. Not controlled by the Wendish monetary agreements.

Rhineland

rhinegulden, florins of the Rhine, electoral florins, electoral gulden | Struck by electors and other Rhineland princes under a series of agreements from 1354–1626, declining in weight and fineness:
1354: fineness 0.98; wt. 3.54 grams
1419: fineness 0.79; wt. 3.51 grams
1626: fineness 0.77; wt. 3.24 grams.

Hamburg and Lüneburg

Issued gulden of the same fineness and weight as the imperial gulden and rhinegulden after 1435 and 1440 respectively.

England

gold penny   Henry III, isolated issue, 1257. Nominally pure gold; wt. 2.92 grams=that of 2 silver pennies; valued at 20d. sterling.

noble   Edward III–James I. Nominally pure gold. 1344–1464, valued at 6s. 8d. sterling. 1344–6: wt. 8.97 grams. 1346–51: wt. 8.33 grams. 1351–1412: wt. 7.78 grams. 1412–64: wt. 7 grams.
              From 1464, rose-noble or ryal, valued at 10s. sterling. In 1464, wt. 7.78 grams.

angel   From 1464, valued at 6s. 8d. sterling; nominally fine; wt. 5.18 grams.

Burgundy or Burgundian Netherlands

philippus or cavalier or rider   Philip the Good (1433–51); valued in 1433 at 4s. groot of Flanders; fineness 0.99; wt. 3.63 grams.

lion or leeuw   Philip the Good (1454–60); valued in 1454 at 5s. groot of Flanders; fineness 0.96; wt. 4.25 grams.

florin of St Andrew or St Andriesgulden   Philip the Good to Philip the Handsome (1466–96); valued in 1466 at 3s. 5d. groot of Flanders; fineness 0.79; wt. 3.4 grams, as rhinegulden.

BLANCS

White money=blancs, albus, weisspfennige, blancas.

France

blanc au K   1365–80. Fineness 0.32; wt. 2.55 grams.

blanc or guénar   1385–1413. Initially fineness 0.48; wt. 3.26 grams; declined very slowly. 1413: fineness 0.4; wt. 3.06 grams. Value 10d. tournois.

blanc à la couronne or parpaillole   1436–1515. Initially fineness 0.4; wt. 3.06 grams; declined slowly. 1507–15: fineness 0.36; wt. 2.85 grams. 1436–88, value 10d. tournois; after 1488, value 12d. tournois.

copies   Dukes of Brittany, Burgundy, Savoy.

Appendix I

Burgundian Netherlands

patard or stuiver or vierlander — From 1433 to sixteenth century. Initially fineness 0.48; wt. 3.44 grams.

Rhineland

weisspfennig or albus — Struck by electors and other Rhineland princes under a series of agreements commencing in 1354.

Hanseatic cities

Coinage (pfennigs, witten (4pf.), sechslinge (6pf.) and schillinge) minted by six 'Wendish' towns – Lübeck, Hamburg, Lüneburg, Rostock, Stralsund and Wismar – under a series of monetary conventions commencing in 1379.

schillinge — Minted from 1432 to sixteenth century. Initially fineness 0.625; wt. 2.54 grams.

Appendix II
Money of Account

In most parts of late medieval Europe, and in many places up to the eighteenth or even the nineteenth century, a dichotomy existed in the functions of money. On the one hand money of account was the *measure of value*, whilst on the other, the actual coin was the *medium of exchange*, and the *store of wealth*.

Money of account derived its name from its function. As a measure of value it was used almost exclusively for accounting purposes. Most financial transactions were first determined and expressed in money of account, although payments were naturally made subsequently in coin, or surprisingly often in other goods. Coin itself was valued as a commodity in terms of money of account, and, as with any other commodity, its value frequently varied. This variation of the value of coin in terms of money of account has been the cause of much confusion of thought about the nature of money of account. This confusion of thought has resulted in the expression of a differing concept of money of account by practically every writer on medieval money.

With the decline of the denier at different rates in different places in the eleventh and twelfth centuries, a standard of reference was needed for the wide variety of deniers that might be circulating in any region in addition to the indigenous coinage. Such a need was particularly felt in such regions as Champagne because of the fairs. With the introduction in the thirteenth century of the fine silver grosso and the gold florin in addition to the often base denaro, a common denominator became necessary to express the varying values of gold, silver and billon coins. Money of account supplied both these needs.

Although the necessity for money of account did not arise until the eleventh and, more seriously, the twelfth and thirteenth centuries, the form taken by money of account dated from a much earlier period. As early as the eighth century and probably the seventh, the system of pounds and shillings had been in use. With regional modifications the relationship of 12 deniers or pennies to the sou or shilling, and of 20 shillings to the livre or pound, had gradually become established throughout western Europe. As has been seen, this was basically a system of counting coins, rather than a system of money. A shilling meant a dozen coins, and a pound meant a score of dozens. Marc Bloch maintained that before the thirteenth century the sou and the livre were no more than 'unités numériques'. The principal variants on the system were in Bavaria, and places, like Austria, which were settled from Bavaria, where the schilling meant 30 coins and the pfund or talent meant 8 sets of 30 coins. In England the mark, which was there a weight two-thirds of the size of the pound, had been transformed into a unit of account, two-thirds of the pound sterling, and was freely used alongside it. At Cologne and Lübeck marks were also transformed into units of account of 12 and 16 schillings respectively.

In some cases the development of money of account was facilitated by a transitional stage in which the new coins neatly represented the old multiples of deniers. The grossi of Florence and Rome, the earliest gros tournois and the earliest Prague groschen were all originally intended to be soldi, sous or schillings, containing 12 times as much silver as their respective deniers, but they soon ceased to fulfil this function. Similarly the Florentine florin and the French chaise à l'écu were originally intended to represent the Florentine lira and the French livre tournois, but both were soon elevated in value. The English noble was only kept at a fixed value, half of the mark sterling or one third of the pound sterling, by reducing the weight of gold that it contained from time to time.

The habit of counting coins in dozens and scores of dozens was so ingrained that when a new coin did not coincide neatly with a multiple of the pre-existing coins, a new system of pounds, shillings and pence was automatically constructed on the basis of the new coin. In Venice, after the creation of the matapan, two concurrent systems of money of account came into use, the one based on the old little (*piccolo*) denier, the other on the new great (*grosso*) denier. There was no firm relationship between the two systems of accounting, for whereas the base denaro of the lira, soldo and denaro *piccolo* system sank further and further in quality, eventually becoming undisguised copper in the late fifteenth century, the denaro of the £.s.d. *grosso* system very largely conserved its fineness and weight.

Two concurrent, and divergent, systems of money of account similarly came into existence in Florence, with the creation of the silver florin or grosso, and in France, with the creation of the gros tournois. In Venice and France alike, the system of account based on the larger coin expired when the relevant grosso or gros ceased to circulate, several decades after it ceased to be issued.

In Castille although the maravedi had only an ephemeral life as a large silver coin, it survived for over two centuries as a unit of account, with the meaning of 10 small Castilian dineros.

In other places the newer gros ousted the older deniers so completely that methods of accounting based on the denier either ceased, or continued to be used only on the basis of a notional relationship between the defunct denier and the surviving gros.

This occurred in Flanders early in the fourteenth century, when the new groot penning supplanted both the Flemish version of the French denier parisis and the Flemish version of the English sterling. The new groot was held to be worth 3 of the old Flemish sterlings and 12 of the old Flemish deniers parisis. The Flemish systems of account based on their groot, their sterling and their parisis were thereafter fossilised in this relationship. All three moneys of account were thus in reality tied to the groot. A similar transition to reckoning in the new great coins took place not only in neighbouring Brabant, which also had its gros, but in other places as far away as Naples and Bohemia, where accounting came to be carried out in terms of gigliati and Prague groschen respectively. Initially the Prague (and Meissen) groschen were struck at 60 to the local mark weight of silver, so that the mark was a convenient multiple of these groats. Even when they ceased to be minted at 60 to the mark they continued to be reckoned for convenience in multiples of 60, each called a 'sexagena' or 'schock'. Reckoning in schocks or sixties occasionally spread to other denominations, and was reinforced in the mid fifteenth century, when a schock of the Meissen groschen was temporarily worth an imperial gold gulden.

Not only were new systems of money of account constructed using the larger silver pieces as denari or soldi, but others were built up using the new gold pieces as lire. The Florentine gold florin, the French franc and the Electoral rhinegulden all became pounds of account. Unfortunately for simplicity of comprehension, the value of all three coins became in time detached from the pounds of account with the same names.

In Florence the gold florin began as the lira in the system of money based on the denaro piccolo, whilst the grosso, or silver florin, was still the soldo. The gold florin thus began as equal to 20 silver florins or 20 soldi affiorino. As the denaro piccolo and the fiorino grosso evolved differently, the gold florin came to have different values in grossi and in piccoli. This evolution came to an end in 1279, when the silver fiorino ceased to be struck. By that time the gold florin had become worth 29 silver florins (29 soldi affiorino). Silver florins remained in circulation until they were withdrawn in 1296. Accounting in lire, soldi and denari affiorini did not vanish with the fiorino grosso, like most other systems based on large silver coins, but continued into the fourteenth century, because it had effectively become based on the gold florin, rather than the silver florin, at the fossilised rate of 29 soldi to the gold florin.

The French case was much simpler. The gold franc was first issued at the value of a livre tournois; it then increased in value in tournois money as the silver coinage was debased, but the word 'franc' remained as an alternative term for the livre tournois, not only when gold francs of a different, higher, value were actually in circulation, but for long after gold francs had ceased to circulate.

In the Netherlands the electoral florins from the Rhineland were commercially current in the 1440s at 40 Flemish groten and in the 1450s officially current at that rate, and so became equated in men's minds with the pound of 40 groten. The principal silver coin in circulation in the Netherlands, the Burgundian stuiver or patard, formed a natural shilling for this pound, being valued at 2 groten. Although by 1467 the gold rhinegulden had officially become worth 42 Flemish groten and, by 1488, 90 Flemish groten, gulden still remained, into the sixteenth century, as the name of the pound of 40 groats. This was indeed a strange fossilised system, yet it continued to attach itself to monetary reality by its fixed relationship to the Flemish groot.

Similar fossilised systems existed elsewhere. In France the system of livre, sou and denier parisis, based, until its disappearance in 1365, on the denier parisis, continued in use for at least another century and a half, keeping contact with reality by the fossilisation of the mid-fourteenth-century relationship of 5:4 with the denier tournois. In Flanders their system of livre, sou and denier parisis was kept in contact with reality, as has already been seen, through the perpetuated equivalence of the Flemish sou parisis to the Flemish groot. After 1433 there was no distinct Brabançon coinage, yet the Brabançon money of account continued to be used; it was also kept in contact with reality by the fossilisation of its relationship with the Flemish money of account, as it had been in 1433, when 3 Brabançon livres had equalled 2 Flemish livres. Thereafter Brabançon money of account was based on the Flemish groot.

The misnomer 'imaginary money' has often been applied to late-medieval money of account, perhaps because the real coin on which the money of account was resting was not always evident on first inspection, as in the cases above. To untangle the maze of moneys of account that were created in the last centuries of the Middle Ages is beyond the scope of this Appendix, but it may be taken as axiomatic that on closer inspection an historical explanation may be found for the existence of each money of account, and that such an historical explanation will indicate to which real coin the system continued to be attached.

For transactions inside any one 'country', accounting naturally took place in local money of account, and payment, unless made by assignment on a bank, was made in coins available on the spot, in gold, silver or billon, according to the scale of the transaction. For transactions across 'national' boundaries, however, this was not adequate. The different moneys had to be reduced to a common denominator. Since the people most frequently concerned in such inter-'national' transactions were papal officials and Italian merchants, it was natural that it should be Italian money that was used as the common denominator, and it was most frequently the Florentine florin that was so used, for the Florentine florin was the gold coin *par excellence* of Tuscany and it was Tuscan merchants above all others who provided the multi-branched commercial and banking network within which so many of these transactions took place. It was only rarely that papal treasurers and even papal collectors used cameral merchants from outside a charmed circle of Florentines, Lucchese and Sienese for the transmission of funds across Europe, whether from collectors in fourteenth-century England to the papal curia at Avignon, or onwards from Avignon to paymasters in Perugia for papal troops in central Italy. The amount due from a new Archbishop of York was thus fixed in florins, although, of course, paid over to the transmitting bankers in sterling. In noting the cost of sending English wool to Porto Pisano for cloth-manufacture in Tuscany, Pegolotti expressed the various sums actually to be paid out along the way in relevant local moneys of account, but then summarised the costs by conversion into Florentine florins. For the purpose of making comparisons between sums in the money of different countries, for example the prices of iron in various parts of Europe, we can do no better than systematise one of the principal threads in the actual accounting procedures of the Middle Ages. The table on pp. 291–3 gives the value of florins, usually Florentine, in the principal moneys of account of western Europe at fifty-year intervals.

Appendix III

Production at Some Later Medieval Mints

Table 1. *Estimated levels of mint production in kilograms of gold and silver*

years	gold	silver	gold	silver
Italy	*Florence*		*Genoa*	
1301–1310	— [1]	—	—	—
1311–1320	—	—	—	—
1321–1330	—	—	—	—
1331–1340	1,315 (GV)[2]	1,125 (GV)	—	—
1341–1350	828 (5)[3]	2,772 (5)	595 (1)	1,819 (1)
1351–1360	276 (7)	1,355 (2)	—	—
1361–1370	120 (8)	489 (8)	800 (2)	1,959 (1)
1371–1380	72 (4)	1,299 (5)	178 (2)	101 (2)
1381–1390	127 (9)	261 (2)	—	—
1391–1400	322 (1)	*187*[4] (10)	—	—
1401–1410	—	—	98 (2)	743 (2)
1411–1420	—	—	153 (2)	*1,682* (2)
1421–1430	191 (4)	1,022 (4)	275 (2)	*1,779* (2)
1431–1440	128 (6)	122 (6)	108 (3)	2,123 (3)
1441–1450	79 (7)	190 (7)	168 (5)	548 (5)
1451–1460	204 (1)	773 (1)	308 (1)	263 (1)
1461–1470	297 (1)	0 (1)	121 (1)	—
1471–1480	99 (3)	*1,752* (6)	202 (5)	—
1481–1490	66 (10)	1,479 (10)	132 (1)	—
1491–1500	82 (7)	142 (7)	83 (3)	—

Lacking: Venice, Milan, Naples, Palermo, Rome and a multitude of minor mints.

[1] Dashes indicate lack of evidence, not lack of minting.
[2] GV=Giovanni Villani's estimate.
[3] The figures in parentheses indicate the number of years per decade covered by the data, except where otherwise indicated.
[4] Figures in italics denote major recoinages.

Table 1. *cont.*

years	gold	silver	gold	silver
Iberia	*Barcelona*		*Valencia*	
1301–1310	—	—	—	—
1311–1320	0 (10)	6,208 (4)	—	—
1321–1330	0 (10)	2,796 (8)	—	—
1331–1340	0 (10)	3,734 (6)	—	—
1341–1350	0 (10)	1,378 (6)	—	—
1351–1360	0 (10)	1,378 (10)	—	—
1361–1370	0 (8)	1,378 (2)	—	—
1371–1380	—	—	—	—
1381–1390	—	0 (4)	106 (9)	0 (10)
1391–1400	—	0 (6)	0 (10)	—
1401–1410	—	—	0 (10)	—
1411–1420	36 (3)	485 (6)	32 (10)	0 (10)
1421–1430	18 (2)	—	3 (10)	0 (10)
1431–1440	11 (10)	164 (1)	0 (10)	0 (10)
1441–1450	30 (2)	—	27 (10)	4 (10)
1451–1460	8 (2)	246 (2)	24 (10)	0 (10)
1461–1470	—	—	34 (10)	508 (10)
1471–1480	—	—	62 (10)	0 (10)
1481–1490	—	—	63 (10)	0 (10)
1491–1500	—	—	94 (10)	0 (10)
	Navarre		*Sardinia*	
1301–1310	—	—	—	—
1311–1320	—	—	—	—
1321–1330	—	—	0 (10)	789 (7)
1331–1340	—	—	9 (10)	1,919 (10)
1341–1350	—	—	0 (10)	713 (10)
1351–1360	—	—	0 (10)	913 (10)
1361–1370	—	—	0 (10)	158 (9)
1371–1380	6 (2)	3,059 (4)	0 (10)	0 (10)
1381–1390	1 (10)	230 (10)	0 (10)	0 (10)
1391–1400	0 (10)	0 (10)	0 (10)	9 (10)
1401–1410	0 (10)	0 (10)	0 (10)	0 (10)
1411–1420	0 (10)	0 (10)	0 (10)	0 (10)
1421–1430	0 (10)	128 (10)	0 (10)	55 (10)
1431–1440	0 (10)	86 (10)	—	—
1441–1450	0 (10)	0 (10)	0 (10)	102 (8)
1451–1460	0 (10)	0 (10)	0 (10)	29 (10)
1461–1470	0 (10)	0 (10)	—	—
1471–1480	0 (10)	0 (10)	—	—
1481–1490	20 (10)	4 (10)	—	—
1491–1500	45 (3)	0 (3)	—	—

Lacking: Castilian, Aragonese and Portuguese mints.

—

Table 1. *cont.*

years	gold	silver	gold	silver
Netherlands	*Brabant*		*Holland*	
1301–1310	—	—	—	—
1311–1320	—	—	—	—
1321–1330	—	—	—	—
1331–1340	—	—	—	—
1341–1350	—	—	—	—
1351–1360	—	—	—	—
1361–1370	—	—	—	—
1371–1380	567 (6)	435 (6)	—	—
1381–1390	37 (10)	497 (10)	—	—
1391–1400	51 (5)	1,154 (5)	—	—
1401–1410	27 (6)	802 (6)	—	—
1411–1420	15 (10)	570 (10)	—	—
1421–1430	81 (10)	475 (10)	251 (5)	190 (5)
1431–1440	312 (10)	664 (10)	231 (10)	791 (10)
1441–1450	0 (10)	0 (10)	0 (6)	0 (6)
1451–1460	161 (10)	29 (10)	29 (10)	4 (10)
1461–1470	28 (10)	735 (10)	2 (7)	62 (7)
1471–1480	156 (10)	4,069 (10)	0 (8)	0 (8)
1481–1490	111 (10)	2,506 (10)	23 (9)	1,801 (10)
1491–1500	39 (9)	1,849 (9)	21 (2)	387 (2)
	Hainaut-Namur		*Flanders*	
1301–1310	—	—	—	—
1311–1320	—	—	—	—
1321–1330	—	—	—	—
1331–1340	—	—	412 (3)	6,644 (5)
1341–1350	—	—	1,211 (3)	5,931 (5)
1351–1360	—	—	2,433 (8)	8,075 (8)
1361–1370	—	—	2,030 (10)	7,444 (9)
1371–1380	—	—	1,145 (6)	3,233 (6)
1381–1390	—	—	819 (5)	3,613 (5)
1391–1400	—	—	321 (10)	4,831 (10)
1401–1410	—	—	22 (10)	931 (10)
1411–1420	—	—	5 (10)	2,678 (10)
1421–1430	179 (9)	761 (9)	212 (10)	8,452 (10)
1431–1440	502 (8)	398 (8)	280 (10)	3,813 (10)
1441–1450	0 (6)	0 (6)	57 (10)	53 (10)
1451–1460	113 (10)	27 (10)	241 (10)	47 (10)
1461–1470	3 (10)	51 (10)	94 (10)	1,490 (10)
1471–1480	0 (10)	0 (10)	164 (10)	4,345 (10)
1481–1490	—	—	16 (8)	1,762 (8)
1491–1500	—	—	39 (9)	1,177 (10)

Table 1. cont.

France[1] years	gold		silver	
1301–1310	—		3,488	(8)
1311–1320	1,207	(2)	3,908	(8)
1321–1330	—		—	
1331–1340	986	(11)	5,567	(11)
1341–1350	—		—	
1351–1360	277	(6)	1,780	(10)
1361–1370	455	(7)	692	(6)
1371–1380	127	(5)	147	(6)
1381–1390	208	(6)	360	(5)
1391–1400	171	(3)	966	(4)
1401–1410	93	(15)	418	(17)
1411–1420	82	(10)	1,346	(13)
1421–1430	113	(10)	945	(18)
1431–1440	84	(12)	418	(13)
1441–1450	42	(8)	88	(8)
1451–1460	47	(14)	252	(15)
1461–1470	32	(13)	143	(11)
1471–1480	25	(13)	247	(13)
1481–1490	22	(13)	223	(13)
1491–1500	49	(24)	346	(24)
England				
1301–1310	0	(10)	25,845	(9)
1311–1320	0	(10)	8,737	(9)
1321–1330	0	(10)	671	(10)
1331–1340	0	(10)	406	(10)
1341–1350	461	(10)	3,597	(10)
1351–1360	1,738	(10)	10,798	(10)
1361–1370	2,078	(10)	1,009	(10)
1371–1380	521	(10)	336	(10)
1381–1390	421	(9)	313	(9)
1391–1400	511	(10)	184	(10)
1401–1410	134	(8)	47	(8)
1411–1420	1,617	(9)	1,005	(9)
1421–1430	1,497	(10)	5,013	(10)
1431–1440	175	(10)	4,489	(10)
1441–1450	79	(10)	354	(10)
1451–1460	44	(10)	1,437	(10)
1461–1470	1,005	(6)	4,637	(6)
1471–1480	487	(9)	1,625	(9)
1481–1490	178	(9)	961	(9)
1491–1500	294	(6)	2,340	(6)

[1] In this section of the table (France) the figures in parentheses indicate the number of mints in each ten-year period. The amount given is the average output per mint.

Table I. *cont.*

years	gold	silver

Germany: almost entirely lacking.

Bohemia: lacking.

Hungary: lacking.

General Averages[1]

years	gold	silver
1301–1310	—	14,666 (2)
1311–1320	402 (3)	6,284 (3)
1321–1330	—	1,419 (3)
1331–1340	454 (6)	3,232 (6)
1341–1350	452 (7)	2,702 (6)
1351–1360	678 (7)	4,050 (6)
1361–1370	699 (8)	1,876 (7)
1371–1380	327 (8)	1,076 (8)
1381–1390	215 (8)	586 (9)
1391–1400	172 (8)	916 (8)
1401–1410	47 (8)	420 (7)
1411–1420	242 (8)	971 (8)
1421–1430	235 (12)	1,711 (11)
1431–1440	166 (11)	1,188 (11)
1441–1450	40 (12)	122 (11)
1451–1460	98 (12)	259 (12)
1461–1470	162 (10)	847 (9)
1471–1480	120 (10)	1,338 (9)
1481–1490	70 (9)	1,092 (8)
1491–1500	83 (9)	780 (8)

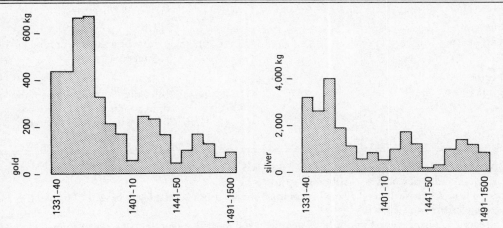

Graph IV. Minting activity in the late Middle Ages (general averages)

[1] In this section of the table (General Averages) the figures in parentheses indicate the number of 'countries' in each ten-year sample.

Appendix III

Table 2. *Estimates of European monetary stocks in the late Middle Ages (in tons)*

years	gold	silver	gold×10 +silver	notes
England				
1278–1290	(0)	285	(285)	Mayhew's estimate.[1]
1311–1324	(0)	352–66	(352–66)	Mayhew's estimate.
1348–1353	—	—	125–46	Mayhew's estimate.
1351–1356	10.2	95.8	198.6	6 years of recoinage.
1412–1417	12.6	7.9	133.9	6 years of recoinage.
1465–1469	8.4	34.2	118.2	5 years of recoinage. Extrapolated for 1467–8.
France				
1307–1312	—	184.0	—	6 years of recoinage in 8 mints. Extrapolated for 1307–8.[2]
1311–1318	12.4	—	—	8 years recoinage of gold at Paris mint.[2]
1340	21.8	122.4	340.4	6 months of recoinage×4 in 11 mints.
1418–1436	10.8	96.8	204.8	Recoinages during 2 cycles of mutations÷4. 20 mints. Numerous extrapolations.
Flanders				
1347–1361	13.9	54.3	193.3	15-year cascade of recoinages÷2. Extrapolated for 1347 (gold) and 1354–5.
Burgundian Netherlands				
1434–1439	5.7	46.5	103.5	6 years of recoinage.
Florence				
1347–1351	(3.6)	15.6	(51.6)	5 years of gold coinage and silver recoinage.
Venice				
c. 1423	(4.2)	30.4	(72.4)	Mocenigo's estimate of annual mint production during recoinage of silver money and normal coinage of gold.[3]

[1] Mayhew, 'Numismatic evidence and falling prices in the fourteenth century', *The Economic History Review*, 2nd series, XXVII, 1 (February 1974), 1–15.

[2] John Day, ' "Crise du féodalisme" et conjoncture des prix à la fin du Moyen Âge', *Annales E.S.C.*, XXXIV (1979), 305–18.

[3] Frederic C. Lane, 'Les Exportations vénitiennes d'or et d'argent 1200–1400', in John Day (ed.), *Études d'histoire monétaire XIIᵉ–XIXᵉ siècles* (Lille, 1984), 29–48.

Source: John Day, 'The question of monetary contraction in late medieval Europe', *Nordisk Numismatisk Årsskrift* (1981), 20–9, by kind permission of the author. The statistics that formed the basis of Dr Day's calculations in 'The great bullion famine', *Past and Present*, LXXIX (1978), 3–54, have been completed and in some cases rectified.

Italy

Florence: Based on Giovanni Villani's estimate for *c.* 1338 and surviving annual or semi-annual mint reports, 1345–1497. Sources: Giovanni Villani, *Cronica* (*Rerum Italicarum Scriptores*, ed. L. A. Muratori, vol. XIII col. 827); Mario Bernocchi, *Le monete della repubblica fiorentina*, vol. I, 'Il libro della zecca' (Florence, 1974), *passim.*

Genoa: Sources: *Archivio di Stato*, Genoa, Diversorum negotiorum comperarum capituli 1342, Compere e mutui 1096, fol. 40r–41r; Cechae introytus et exitus 1365, Zecca antica I, fol. 4v–11r; Comperae capituli introitus et exitus 1371, Compere e mutui 1003, fol. 3v; Magistrorum rationalium communis Ianuae sententiae 1374, Antico Comune 73, fol. 15r–15v; Cechae introytus et exitus 1380, Zecca antica 2; Cechae introytus et exitus, Zecca antica 4–6 (1404–6 and 1412–14); G. Felloni, *Profilo economico delle monete genovesi dal 1139 al 1814* (Genoa, 1975), pp. 309–24; G. Felloni, 'Ricavi e costi della zecca di Genova dal 1341 al 1450'; in *Studi in memoria di Federigo Melis*, III (Naples, 1978), 141–53.

Iberia

Barcelona: Effective or projected mint output. Sources: J. Botet y Siso, *Les monedes catalanes* (3 vols., Barcelona, 1908–11), vol. III, docs. XXII, XXXII, LI, LII; J. Salat, *Tratado de las monedas labradas en el Principado de Cataluña* (2 vols., Barcelona, 1818), vol. II, docs. XXII–XXIII; F. Udina Martorell, 'La ceca de Barcelona en tiempos de Fernando de Antequera y de Alfonso el Magnánimo . . .', *Numisma*, VIII (1958), 37–47; Claude Carrère, *Barcelone, centre économique à l'époque des difficultés, 1380–1462* (2 vols., Paris, 1967), p. 840 (1440).

Valencia: The record, according to Hamilton, is 'very nearly complete' for gold, 1382–1500, and for silver, 1410–1500. Source: Earl J. Hamilton, *Money, Prices and Wages in Valencia, Aragon and Navarre, 1351–1500* (Cambridge (Mass.), 1936), pp. 207–10.

Navarre: The record is reasonably complete, 1377–1493; Mint: Pamplona. Source: Hamilton, *Money in Valencia, Aragon and Navarre*, pp. 210–12.

Sardinia: Effective output, 1324–91; projected output thereafter. Mints: Iglesias, Cagliari (1324–5, 1338). Sources: F. Udina Martorell, 'Un aspecto de la evolución económica sarda en el siglo XIV: la acuñación de moneda', in *VI Congreso de Historia de la Corona de Aragón* (Madrid, 1959), pp. 647–61; John Day, 'The decline of a money economy: Sardinia in the late Middle Ages', in *Studi in memoria di Melis*, III, 155–76.

Netherlands

Brabant: Mints: Antwerp, Brussels, Louvain, Maastrict, Vilvoorde. Sources: John H. Munro, 'Monnayage, monnaies de compte et mutations monétaires au Brabant à la fin du Moyen Age', in John Day (ed.), *Études d'histoire monétaire XIIᵉ–XIXᵉ siècles* (Lille, 1984); Munro, *Wool, Cloth and Gold*, pp. 187–97; Spufford, *Monetary Problems in the Burgundian Netherlands*, pp. 172–99.

Holland: Mints: Dordrecht, The Hague. Source: Munro, *Wool, Cloth and Gold*, pp. 187–97.

Hainaut and Namur: Mints: Valenciennes, Namur. Source: Munro, *Wool, Cloth and Gold*, pp. 187–97.

Flanders: Mints: Bruges, Ghent, Malines (1357–93), Fauquemont (1397–9). Sources: Victor Gaillard, *Recherches sur les monnaies des Comtes de Flandre jusqu'à l'avènement de la maison de Bourgogne*, 2nd ed. (Ghent, 1857), pp. 31–61, 158–69; John H. Munro, *Wool, Cloth and Gold. The Struggle for Bullion in Anglo-Burgundian Trade, 1340–1478* (Brussels–Toronto, 1973), pp. 187–97; Peter Spufford, *Monetary Problems and Policies in the Burgundian Netherlands, 1433–1496* (Leiden, 1970), pp. 172–99; H. Enno van Gelder and M. Hoc, *Les Monnaies des Pays-Bas bourguignons et espagnols* (Amsterdam, 1960), p. 35.

France

Based for the most part on the number of coins from each issue sent to Paris for essay, but also on the projected minimum coinage stipulated in mint-farm contracts. Mints: Tournai, St Quentin-Amiens, Paris, Troyes, Chaumont, St Menehould/Châlons, Rouen, Saint Lô, Rennes, Nantes, Angers, Tours, Bourges, Montreuil-Bonnin/Poitiers, La Rochelle, Limoges, Dijon/Lyons, St Pourçain, Cremieu, Romans, Côte-St-André, Grenoble, Embrun-Briançon/Mirabel/Montélimar, Beaucaire, Sommières/Montpellier/Villeneuve-St-André, Toulouse, Villefranche de Rouergue, Mont-de-Dôme, Bordeaux, Perpignan, Bayonne. Sources: F. de Saulcy (ed.), *Recueil de documents relatifs à l'histoire des monnaies frappées par les rois de France depuis Philippe II jusqu'à François 1er* (4 vols., Paris, 1879–92); F. de Saulcy, 'Recherches sur les monnaies du système flamand frappées à Tournai au nom de Charles VII', *Mémoires de la Société Nationale des Antiquaires de France*, XXXVII (1877), 17–36; M. Rey, 'Les Émissions d'écus à la couronne à l'Hôtel de Monnaies de Paris vers la fin du XIVᵉ siècle et dans les premières années du XVᵉ siècle, 1385–1413', in *Mélanges d'histoire de Moyen Age dédiés à la memoire de Louis Halphen* (Paris, 1951), pp. 595–603; M. Rey, 'Le ZIB 305 (deuxième partie). Etude d'histoire monétaire en France au début du XVᵉ siècle', *Annales littéraires, Université de Besançon*, 1 (1954), 28–35; F. Dumas-Dubourg, 'À propos de l'atelier royal de Dijon. Aperçus sur la politique monétaire des ducs de Bourgogne Jean sans Peur et Philippe le Bon', *Annales de Bourgogne*, XXXIV (1962), 5–45; Alain Guerreau, 'L'Atelier monétaire royal de Mâcon (1239–1421)', *Annales E.S.C.*, XXIX (1974), 369–92; Frank C. Spooner, *L'Économie mondiale et les frappes monétaires en France, 1493–1680* (Paris, 1956), appendices; Jean Lafaurie, *Les Monnaies des rois de France* (Paris and Basel, 1951).

England

Mints: London, Canterbury (1301–46), York (1353–5, 1470–5), Bristol (1470–2), Calais (1363–84, 1387–1403, 1422–46). Sources: John Craig, *The Mint* (Cambridge, 1953), pp. 408–13; C. G. Crump and C. Johnson, 'Tables of bullion coined under Edward I, II and III', *Numismatic Chronicle*, 4th series, XIII (1913), 200–45; G. C. Brooke and E. Stokes, 'Tables of bullion coined from 1377 to 1550', *Numismatic Chronicle*, 5th series, IX (1929), 27–69; Peter Spufford, 'Calais and its mint: Part One', in N. J. Mayhew (ed.), *Coinage in the Low Countries (880–1500)*, British Archaeological Reports, International Series LIV (Oxford, 1979).

Bibliography

GENERAL

The standard bibliography is

    Grierson, Philip. *Bibliographie numismatique.* 2nd ed., Brussels, 1979.

From the point of view of the economic historian the best attempt at a general history of money available up to now is the incomplete and posthumously published

    Bloch, Marc. *Esquisse d'une histoire monétaire de l'Europe.* Cahiers des Annales IX. Paris, 1954.

and the intriguing but brief series of lectures published as

    Cipolla, Carlo M. *Money, Prices and Civilization in the Mediterranean World.* Princeton, 1956. Italian version: *Moneta e civiltà mediterranea.* Venice, 1957.

and by myself:

    Spufford, Peter. 'Coinage and currency', in *Cambridge Economic History of Europe,* II. 2nd ed. Cambridge, 1987.

From the numismatist's point of view the best introductory work is

    Porteous, John. *Coins in History.* London, 1969.

The standard work of reference for the coinage of medieval Europe is

    Engel, A., and Serrure, R. *Traité de numismatique du moyen âge.* 3 vols. Paris, 1891–1905. Repr. 1964.

This, however, is outdated in many particulars, and it is in many ways now preferable to refer first to the magnificently illustrated volume

    Grierson, Philip. *Monnaies du moyen âge.* Fribourg, 1976.

and to follow up the references given there. Other useful reference works are the volume of documents

    Jesse, Wilhelm (ed.). *Quellenbuch zur Münz- und Geldgeschichte des Mittelalters.* Halle, 1924. Repr. 1968.

and the dictionary

    Schrötter, F. von (ed.). *Wörterbuch der Münzkunde.* Berlin–Leipzig, 1930. Repr. 1970.

An interesting introductory essay on numismatics as an ancillary discipline of history is

    Grierson, Philip. 'Numismatics', in J. M. Powell (ed.), *Medieval Studies. An Introduction,* Syracuse, N.Y., 1976, pp. 103–50.

The standard work of numismatics is now

    Grierson, Philip. *Numismatics.* Oxford, 1975.

which does not entirely replace

    Luschin von Ebengreuth, A. *Allgemeine Münzkunde und Geldgeschichte.* 2nd ed. Berlin and Munich, 1926. Repr., 1969.

Economic historians and numismatists joined together at a remarkable conference in 1975, the proceedings of which are being published as

    La moneta nell'economia europea secoli XIII–XVIII. Settima Settimana di Studio 1975. Istituto Internazionale di Storia Economica 'Francesco Datini', Prato, 1983.

Economic historians and numismatists have also joined together in a volume of essays

    Day, John (ed.). *Études d'histoire monétaire XIIe–XIXe siècles.* Lille, 1984.

A particular range of new numismatic techniques is covered by the proceedings of a specialist conference

    Hall, E. T., and Metcalf, D.M. (eds.). *Methods of Chemical and Metallurgical Investigation of Ancient Coinage.* Royal Numismatic Society. London, 1972.

Particularly useful is

Metcalf, D. M. 'Analyses of the metal contents of medieval coins'. *Ibid.* pp. 385–434.

ROMAN–BARBARIAN DISCONTINUITY

An extremely useful series of papers is printed in

Moneta e scambi nell'alto medioevo. Settimane di Studi del Centro Italiano di Studi sull'alto medioevo VIII. Spoleto, 1961.

Barral y Altet, Xavier. *La Circulation des monnaies suèves et visigothiques. Contribution à l'histoire économique du royaume visigot. Francia,* supplement 4. Munich, 1976.

Bernareggi, Ernesto. *Il sistema economico della monetazione dei Langobardi nell'Italia superiore.* Milan, 1960.

Doehaerd, Renée. *Le Haut Moyen Age occidental: économies et sociétés.* Paris, 1971.

The Early Middle Ages in the West: Economy and Society. English trans., Amsterdam, 1978.

Grierson, Philip. 'Commerce in the Dark Ages; a critique of the evidence'. *Transactions of the Royal Historical Society,* 5th series, IX (1959), 123–40. Repr. in a collection of twenty-nine articles: *Dark Age Numismatics.* London, 1979.

'La Fonction sociale de la monnaie en Angleterre aux VIIe et VIIIe siècles', in *Moneta e scambi nell'alto medioevo* (as above). Reprinted as above.

Grierson, Philip, and Blackburn, Mark. *Medieval European Coins with a Catalogue of the Coins in the Fitzwilliam Museum, Cambridge.* I: 'The Early Middle Ages (5th–10th centuries)'. Cambridge, 1986.

Lafaurie, Jean. 'Essai sur le monnayage d'argent franc des Ve et VIe siècles'. *Annales de Normandie,* XIV (1964), 173–222.

Latouche, Robert. *Les Origines de l'économie occidentale.* Paris, 1956; 2nd ed., 1967. English trans.: *The Birth of Western Economy.* London, 1961.

Le Gentilhomme, Pierre. 'Le Monnayage et la circulation monétaire dans les royaumes barbares en Occident V^e–VIIIe siècles'. *Revue Numismatique,* 5th series, VII (1943), 46–112, and VIII (1948), 13–59. A general survey, now replaced in many particulars.

Miles, G. C. *The Coinage of the Visigoths in Spain: Leovigild to Achila II.* American Numismatic Society, New York, 1952.

Tomasini, W. H. *The Barbaric Tremissis in Spain and Southern France: Anastasius to Leovigild.* Numismatic Notes and Monographs CLII. American Numismatic Society, New York, 1964.

BYZANTINE EMPIRE

Bertele, Tommaso. 'L'iperpero bizantino dal 1261 al 1453'. *Rivista Italiana di Numismatica,* LIX (1957), 70–89.

'Lineamenti principali della numismatica bizantina'. *Rivista Italiana di Numismatica,* LXVI (1964), 33–118. Trans. into French by Cecile Morrisson in T. Bertele, *Numismatique byzantine.* Wetteren, 1978.

Grierson, Philip. *Byzantine Coins.* London, 1982.

Hendy, Michael F. 'Byzantium 1081–1204: an economic reappraisal'. *Transactions of the Royal Historical Society,* 5th series, XX (1970), 31–52.

Coinage and Money in the Byzantine Empire 1081–1261. Dumbarton Oak Studies XII. Washington, 1969.

Studies in the Byzantine Monetary Economy c. 300–1450. Cambridge, 1985.

Lopez, R. S. 'The dollar of the middle ages'. *Journal of Economic History*, XI (1951), 209–34.

FROM THE ORIGINS OF THE DENIER TO THE CAROLINGIANS

Dhondt, Jean. 'L'Essor urbain entre Meuse et Mer du Nord a l'époque mérovingienne', in *Studi in onore di Armando Sapori*, I. Milan, 1975, 55–78.

Frère, Hubert. 'Le Denier carolingien, spécialement en Belgique', in *Numismatica Lovaniensa*, I. Louvain-la-Neuve, 1977. Includes useful documents.

Grierson, Philip. 'Money and coinage under Charlemagne', in W. Braunfels (ed.), *Karl der Grosse: Lebenswerk und Nachleben*, I, Dusseldorf, 1965, 501–36.

Hill, David, and Metcalf, D. M. *Sceattas in England and on the Continent.* British Archaeological Reports CXXVIII. Oxford, 1984.

Lafaurie, Jean. 'Monnaies d'argent mérovingiennes des VIIᵉ et VIIIᵉ siècles', *Revue Numismatique*, 6th series, XI (1969), 98–219.

Morrison, Karl F. 'Numismatics and Carolingian trade: a critique of the evidence', *Speculum*, XXXVIII (1963), 403–32.

Morrison, Karl F., and Grunthal, Henry. *Carolingian Coinage.* Numismatic Notes and Monographs CLVIII. American Numismatic Society, New York, 1967.

THE AGE OF THE VIKINGS

Blackburn, M. A. S., and Metcalf, D. M. (eds.). *Viking-Age Coinage in the Northern Lands.* British Archaeological Reports. International Series CXXII. 2 vols., Oxford, 1981.

Blunt, Christopher E. 'The coinage of Athelstan 924–939; a survey'. *British Numismatic Journal*, XLII (1974), 35–160.

Dolley, R. H. M. (ed.). *Anglo-Saxon Coins: Studies Presented to F. M. Stenton.* London, 1961.

Anglo-Saxon Pennies. British Museum, London, 1964.

Viking Coins of the Danelaw and of Dublin. British Museum, London, 1965.

Dumas-Dubourg, Françoise. 'Le Début de l'époque féodale en France d'après les monnaies'. *Bulletin du Cercle d'Études Numismatiques*, X (1973), 65–77.

Le Trésor de Fécamp et le monnayage en Francia occidentale pendant la seconde moitié du Xᵉ siècle. Bibliothèque Nationale, Paris, 1971.

Grierson, Philip. 'Mint output in the tenth century'. *Economic History Review*, 2nd series, IX (1957), 462–6.

'The volume of Anglo-Saxon currency'. *Economic History Review*, 2nd series, XX (1967), 153–60.

Hatz, Gert. *Handel und Verkehr zwischen dem Deutschen Reich und Schweden in der späten Wikingerzeit.* Lund, 1974.

Kiersnowski, Ryszard. *Pieniadz Kruscowy w Polsce wczesnosredniowieczney.* Warsaw, 1960 (with French résumé).

Kraume, Emil, and Hatz, Vera. 'Die Otto–Adelheid-Pfennige und ihre Nachprägungen'. *Hamburger Beiträge zur Numismatik*, new series, XV (1961–3), 13–23, and appendices.

Lewicki, Tadeusz. 'Le Commerce des Sāmānides avec l'Europe orientale et centrale à la lumière des trésors de monnaies coufiques', in D. K. Kouymjian (ed.), *Near Eastern Numismatics, Iconography, Epigraphy and History. Studies in Honor of George C. Miles*, Beirut, 1974, pp. 219–33

Metcalf, D. M. 'How large was the Anglo-Saxon currency?' *Economic History Review*, 2nd series, XVIII (1965), 475–82.

'The prosperity of North-Western Europe in the eighth and ninth centuries'. *Economic History Review*, 2nd series, XX (1967), 344–57.

'Continuity and change in English monetary history c. 973–1086'. *British Numismatic Journal*, L (1980), 20–49; LI (1981), 52–90.

Metcalf, D. M., and Northover, J. P. 'Debasement of the coinage in southern England in the age of Alfred'. *Numismatic Chronicle*, CXLV (1985), 150–76.

Petersson, H. Bertil A. *Anglo-Saxon Currency; King Edgar's Reform to the Norman Conquest*. Lund, 1969.

Rasmusson, N. L., and Lagerqvist, L. O. (eds.). *Commentationes de Nummis Saeculorum IX–XI in Suecia Repertis*. 2 vols. Stockholm, 1961–8.

Sawyer, Peter H. *The Age of the Vikings*. 2nd ed. London, 1971.

'The wealth of England in the eleventh century'. *Transactions of the Royal Historical Society*, 5th series, XV (1965), 145–64.

Suchodolski S. 'Études sur la monnaie polonaise de la fin du Xe et au début du XIe siècle', *Archaeologia Polona*, XI (1969), 91–192.

Yanin, V. L. 'Les Problèmes généraux de l'échange monétaire russe aux IXe–XIIe siècles', in *Moneta e scambi nell'alto medioevo*. Spoleto, 1961, pp. 485–505.

RURAL USE OF MONEY

Bloch, Marc. 'Économie-nature et économie-argent; un pseudo-problème'. *Annales d'Histoire Économique et Sociale*, VI (1933), 7–16. Repr. in *Mélanges historiques*, II, Paris, 1963, 869–77. Trans. as 'Natural economy and money economy; a pseudo-dilemma', in *Land and Work in Medieval Europe*, London, 1967, pp. 230–43.

Dollinger, Philippe. *L'Évolution des classes rurales en Bavière*. Paris, 1949.

Duby, Georges. *The Early Growth of the European Economy*. London, 1974. Originally published as *Guerriers et paysans aux VIIe–XIIe siècles*. Paris, 1973.

Rural Economy and Country Life in the Medieval West. Paris, 1962. English trans., 1968.

Fossier, Robert. *La Terre et les hommes en Picardie jusqu'à la fin du XIIIe siècle*. Paris–Louvain, 1968.

Herlihy, David. 'The agrarian revolution in southern France and Italy 801–1150'. *Speculum*, XXXIII (1958), 23–41.

'Treasure hoards in the Italian economy, 960–1139', *Economic History Review*, 2nd series, X (1957–8), 1–14.

Meuvret, J. 'Circulation monétaire et utilisation économique de la monnaie dans la France du XVIe et du XVIIe siècle', in *Études d'histoire moderne et contemporaine*, I, Paris, 1947, 15–28. Repr. in *Études d'histoire économique*, Cahiers des Annales XXXII, Paris, 1971, pp. 127–37.

Postan, M. M. 'The chronology of labour services'. *Transactions of the Royal Historical Society*, 4th series, XX (1937), 169–93.

'The rise of a money economy'. *Economic History Review*, XIV (1944), 123–34

Both repr. in *Essays on Medieval Agriculture and General Problems of the Medieval Economy*, Cambridge, 1973, pp. 89–106 and 28–40.

Toubert, Pierre. *Les Structures du Latium médiéval . . . du IXᵉ à la fin du XIIᵉ siècle*. Bibliothèque des Écoles Françaises d'Athènes et de Rome CCXXI. Rome, 1973.

MINING AND TRADE IN PRECIOUS METALS

See also the chapter and bibliography in the *Cambridge Economic History of Europe*, II, Cambridge, 1952, 430–92 and 561–7.

Agricola, Georgius. *De veteribus et novis metallis*. Basle, 1546. English trans. in *Georgius Agricola De re metallica*, Trans. and ed. H. C. and L. H. Hoover. London, 1912.

Albertus Magnus. *Book of Minerals*. Trans. and ed. Dorothy Wyckoff. Oxford, 1967.

Cipolla, Carlo. M. 'Argento tedesco e monete genovesi alla fine del quattrocento'. *Rivista Italiana di Numismatica*, LVIII (1956), 100–7.

Herrmann, Walther. 'Bergbau und Kultur'. *Freiberger Forschungshefte*, series D, II (1953), 7–22.

Hillebrand, Werner. 'Der Goslarer Metallhandel im Mittelalter'. *Hansische Geschichtsblätter*, LXXXVII (1969), 31–57.

Kovacevic, Desanka. 'Dans la Serbie et la Bosnie médiévales: les mines d'or et d'argent. *Annales E.S.C.*, XV (1960), 248–58.

Nef, J. U. 'Silver production in Central Europe 1450–1618'. *Journal of Political Economy*, XLIX (1941), 575–91.

Spufford, Peter. *The Routes of Trade in Medieval Europe* (London, forthcoming).

MONEY IN THE COMMERCIAL REVOLUTION

For the 'Commercial Revolution' in general see the *Cambridge Economic History of Europe*, II, 2nd ed. (1987) and III (1963), particularly the chapters by R. S. Lopez and Raymond de Roover.

Barnard, F. P. *The Casting-Counter and the Counting-Board*. Oxford, 1916.

Berghaus, *see under* Nohejlova-Pratova.

Castelin, K. *Grossus Pragensis. Der Prager Groschen und seine Teilstücke 1300–1547*. 2nd ed. Brunswick, 1973.

Cipolla, C. 'Currency depreciation in medieval Europe'. *Economic History Review*, 2nd series, XV (1963), 413–22. Repr. in Sylvia Thrupp (ed.). *Change in Medieval Society*, New York, 1964, pp. 227–36.

Courtenay, William J. 'Token coinage and the administration of Poor Relief during the late Middle Ages'. *Journal of Interdisciplinary History*, III (1972), 275–95.

De Roover, Raymond. *Business, Banking and Economic Thought in Late Medieval and Early Modern Europe. Selected Studies of R. de Roover*. Ed. Julius Kirshner. Chicago, 1974.

Grierson, *see under* Nohejlova-Pratova.

Grunzweig, Armand. 'Les Incidences internationales des mutations monétaires de Philippe le Bel'. *Moyen Age*, LIX (1953), 117–72.

Homan, Balint. 'La circolazione delle monete d'oro in Ungheria dal X al XIV secolo e la crisi europea dell'oro nel secolo XIV'. *Rivista Italiana di Numismatica*, 2nd series, V (1922), 109–56.

Homer, Sidney. *A History of Interest Rates*. Rutgers, New Brunswick, 1963.

Koch, Bernhard. 'Goldgeld und Groschenmünzen im österreichischen Geldverkehr des Mittelalters'. *Numismatische Zeitschrift*, LXXXI (1965), 3–13.

Lafaurie, *see under* Nohejlova-Pratova.

Lane, Frederic C. 'Le vecchie monete di conte Veneziane ed il ritorno all'oro'. *Atti del Istituto Veneto di Scienze, Lettere ed Arti*, CXVII (1959), 51–78.

'La mobilità e l'utilità delle monete di conto'. *Rivista di storia economica*, new series I (1984).

Lopez, R. S. 'Prima del ritorno all'oro nell'occidente duecentesco: i primi denari grossi d'argento'. *Rivista Storica Italiana*, LXXIX (1967), 174–81.

'Settecento anni fa: il ritorno all'oro nell'occidente duecentesco'. *Rivista Storica Italiana*, LXV (1953), 19–55, 161–98. A shorter version appeared in English as 'Back to gold, 1252', *Economic History Review*, 2nd series, IX (1956), 219–40.

Murray, Alexander. 'Piety and impiety in thirteenth-century Italy', in G. J. Cuming and Derek Baker (eds.), *Popular Belief and Practice*. Studies in Church History VIII. Cambridge, 1972.

Nagl, Alfred. 'Die Goldwährung und die handelmässige Goldrechnung im Mittelalter'. *Numismatische Zeitschrift*, XXVI (1894), 41–258.

Nohejlova-Pratova, E. (ed.). 'Les Commencements de la grosse monnaie et de la monnaie d'or en Europe Centrale (1250–1350)', special number of *Numismatický Sborník*, XII (Prague, 1971–2).

As well as Central European papers this also includes

Berghaus, P. 'Die Ausbreitung der Goldmünze und des Groschens in Deutschen Landen zu Beginn des 14. Jahrhunderts', pp. 211–43.

Grierson, Philip. 'The origins of the Grosso and of gold coinage in Italy', pp. 33–48.

Lafaurie, Jean. 'Le gros tournois en France', pp. 49–64.

Spufford, Peter. 'Le Rôle de la monnaie dans la révolution commerciale du XIIIᵉ siècle', in John Day (ed.), *Études d'histoire monétaire*, Lille, 1984, pp. 355–95.

Van Werveke, Hans. 'Monnaie de compte et monnaie reelle'. *Revue Belge de Philologie et d'Histoire*, XII (1934), 123–52. Repr. in *Miscellanea mediaevalia*, Ghent, 1968, pp. 133–58.

'Monnaie, lingots ou marchandises? Les instruments d'échange aux XIᵉ et XIIᵉ siècles'. *Annales d'Histoire Économique et Sociale*, IV (1932), 452–68. Repr. in *Miscellanea mediaevalia*, Ghent, 1968, pp. 191–208.

A great deal of information about money is to be found in merchants' notebooks. The following are arranged in the order of their compilation.

Tarifa zoè Noticia dy pexi e mexure di Luogi e tere che s'adovra mercadantia per el mondo. Reale Istituto Superiore di Scienze Economiche e Commerciali di Venezia. (Ed. V. Orlandi. Introduction by R. Cessi.) Venice, 1925. (1290?)

Stussi, Alfredo (ed.). *Zibaldone da Canal, manoscritto mercantile del secolo XIV*. Fonti per la Storia di Venezia. V. Venice, 1967. (*c.* 1311.)

Pegolotti, Francesco Balducci. *La pratica della mercatura*. Ed. Allan Evans. Medieval Academy of America XXIV. Cambridge, Mass., 1936. (Completed Florence, *c.* 1340.)

To be consulted together with

Evans, Allan. 'Some coinage systems of the fourteenth century'. *Journal of Economic and Business History*, III (1931), 481–96.

and

Grierson, Philip. 'The coin list of Pegolotti', in *Studi in onore di Armando Sapori*, I, Milan, 1957, 483–92.

Ciane, Cesare (ed.). *La 'pratica di mercatura' datiniana*. Milan, 1964. (Compiled Pisa/Prato, *c.* 1385/6.)

Borlandi, Antonia (ed.). *Il manuale di mercatura da Saminiato de' Ricci*. Genoa, 1963. (Genoa, 1396, and Florence, 1416–18.)

Borlandi, Franco (ed.). *El libro di mercatantie et usanze de' Paesi*. Turin, 1936. (Florence, pre-1425.)

Pagnini della Ventura, G. F. (ed.). '*La pratica della mercatura scritta de Giovanni di Antonio da Uzzano*', *della decima e delle altre gravezze*. IV. Lisbon–Lucca, 1766. (Florence, *c.* 1442.)

THE INTERNATIONAL MONEY-MARKET

Cipolla, Carlo M. *Studi di storia della moneta*. I: 'I movimenti dei cambi in Italia dal secolo XIII at XV'. Pavia, 1948.

The Dawn of Modern Banking. Center for Medieval and Renaissance Studies, University of California, Los Angeles. New Haven, Conn. 1979.

De Roover, Raymond. 'Le Marché monétaire au Moyen Âge et au début des temps modernes. Problèmes et méthodes'. *Revue Historique*, CCXLIV (1970), 5–40.

Favier, Jean. *Les Finances pontificales à l'époque du grand Schisme d'Occident 1378–1419*. Bibliothèque des Écoles Françaises d'Athènes et de Rome CCXI. 1966.

Lunt, W. E. *Papal Revenues in the Middle Ages*. 2 vols. New York, 1934.

Piquet, J. *Des banquiers au moyen âge. Les Templiers. Étude de leurs opérations financières*. Paris, 1935.

Renouard, Yves. *Les Relations des papes d'Avignon et des compagnies commerciales et bancaires de 1316 à 1378*. Bibliothèque des Écoles Françaises d'Athènes et de Rome CLI. Paris, 1941.

Schafer, H. *Die Ausgaben der apostolischen Kammer unter Johann XXII. Vatikanische Quellen zur Geschichte der päpstlichen Hof- und Finanzverwaltung, 1316–1375*. II. Paderborn, 1911.

Sprandel, Rolf. 'Excurs uber Geld', in *Das Eisengewerbe im Mittelalter*. Stuttgart, 1968.

Spufford, Peter, *Handbook of Medieval Exchange*. Royal Historical Society, London, 1986.

Usher, A. P. *The Early History of Deposit Banking in Mediterranean Europe*. Cambridge, Mass., 1943.

THE FLOW OF MONEY AND BULLION IN AND OUT OF WESTERN EUROPE

Ashtor, Eliyahu. *Les Métaux précieux et la balance des payements du Proche-Orient à la Basse Époque*. Paris, 1971.

Attman, A. *The Bullion Flow Between Europe and the East 1000–1750*. Acta Regiae Societatis Scientiarum et Litterarum Gothoburgensis. Humaniora XX. Göteborg, 1981.

Bacharach, Jere L. 'The dinar versus the ducat'. *International Journal of Middle East Studies*, IV (1973), 77–96.

Balog, Paul. *The Coinage of the Mamluk Sultans of Egypt and Syria*. Numismatic Studies XII. American Numismatic Society, New York, 1964.

Bautier, Robert H. 'L'Or et l'argent en Occident de la fin du XIIIe siècle au début du XIVe siècle'. *Académie des Inscriptions et Belles Lettres, Comptes Rendus des Séances* (1951), 169–74.

Bloch, Marc. 'Le Problème de l'or au moyen âge'. *Annales d'Histoire Economique et Sociale,* v (1933), 1–34. Repr. in *Mélanges Historiques,* II, Paris, 1963, 839–67. English trans. as 'The problem of gold in the Middle Ages', in *Land and Work in Medieval Europe,* London, 1967, pp. 186–229.

Bolin, Sture. 'Mohammed, Charlemagne and Ruric'. *Scandinavian Economic History Review,* I (1953), 5–39, and

Cipolla, C. 'Sans Mahomet, Charlemagne est inconcevable'. *Annales E.S.C.,* XVII (1962), 130–6, and

Perroy, E. 'Encore Mohamet et Charlemagne'. *Revue Historique,* CCXII (1954), 232–8.

Braudel, F. 'Economies: precious metals, money and prices', in *The Mediterranean and the Mediterranean World in the Age of Philip II,* 2nd ed., I. Paris, 1966. English trans. London, 1972, pp. 462–542.

Cahen, Claude. 'Quelques problèmes concernant l'expansion économique musulmane au haut moyen âge'. *L'Occidente e l'Islam nell' alto medioevo.* Settimane di Studi del Centro Italiano di Studi sull'Alto Medioevo XII, Spoleto, 1965, pp. 391–432.

Cipolla, *see under* Bolin.

Duplessy, Jean. 'La Circulation des monnaies arabes en Europe occidentale du VIIIe au XIIIe siècles'. *Revue Numismatique,* 5th series, XVIII (1956), 101–63.

Goitein, S. D. *A Mediterranean Society. The Jewish Communities of the Arab World as portrayed in the Documents of the Cairo Geniza.* 1: 'Economic foundations'. Berkeley, 1967.

Grierson, Philip. 'Muslim coins in thirteenth century England', in D. K. Kouymjian (ed.), *Near Eastern Numismatics, Iconography, Epigraphy and History. Studies in Honor of George C. Miles,* Beirut, 1974, pp. 387–91.

Hazard, Harry W. *The Numismatic History of Late Medieval North Africa.* Numismatic Studies VIII. American Numismatic Society: New York, 1952.

Heyd, Wilhelm von. *Histoire du Commerce du Levant au Moyen Age.* 2nd French ed. 2 vols. Leipzig, 1885–6. 1st German ed., *Geschichte des Levantehandels im Mittelalter.* 2 vols. Stuttgart, 1879.

Lombard, Maurice. 'Les Bases monétaires d'une suprématie économique. L'or musulman du VIIe au XIe siècle'. *Annales E.S.C.,* II (1947), 143–60. Repr. in *Espaces et réseaux du haut moyen âge,* Paris, 1972, pp. 7–29.

Études d'économie médiévale. 1: 'Monnaie et histoire d'Alexandre à Mahomet', Paris, 1971, 133–222.

Lopez, R.S., Miskimin, H., and Udovitch, A. 'England to Egypt 1350–1500: long term trends and long distance trade', in M. A. Cook (ed.), *Studies in the Economic History of the Middle East,* London, 1970.

Malowist, Marian. 'Quelques observations sur le commerce de l'or dans le Soudan occidental au moyen âge'. *Annales E.S.C.,* XXV (1970), 1630–6.

Perroy, *see under* Bolin.

Richards, J. F. (ed.). *Precious Metals in the Later Medieval and Early Modern Worlds.* Carolina Academic Press, 1983.

Schlumberger, G. *Numismatique de l'Orient Latin.* Paris, 1878. *Supplément,* 1882. Repr. Graz, 1954.

Van der Wee, Herman, and Peeters, Theo. 'Un modèle dynamique de croissance interséculaire, du commerce mondial xiiᵉ–xviiiᵉ siècles'. *Annales E.S.C.*, xxv (1970), 100–26.

Watson, Andrew. 'Back to gold – and silver'. *Economic History Review*, 2nd series, xx (1967), 1–34.

MINT ORGANISATION

Bailhache, J. 'Chambre et Cour des Monnaies xivᵉ, xvᵉ, xviᵉ siècles. Aperçu historique'. *Revue Numismatique,* 4th series, xxxvii (1934), 63–99, 175–97; xxxviii (1935), 67–99; xxxix (1936), 157–79, 327–45.

Beardwood, Alice. 'The royal mints and exchanges', in J. F. Willard and W. A. Morris (eds.), *The English Government at Work 1327–1336.* iii, Cambridge, Mass., 1950, 35–66.

Carson, R. A. G. (ed.). *Mints, Dies, and Currency.* London, 1971.

Craig, John. *The Mint.* Cambridge, 1953. Being replaced by a volume edited by C. Challis.

Lopez, R. S. 'Continuità e adattamento nel medio evo: un milennio di storia delle associazioni di monetieri nell' Europa meridionale', in *Studi in onore di Gino Luzzatto,* Milan, 1949, pp. 74–117.

Mate, Mavis. 'A mint of trouble 1279–1307'. *Speculum,* xliv (1969), 201–12.

Reddaway, T. F. 'The king's mint and exchange in London 1343–1543'. *English Historical Review,* lxxxii (1967), 1–23.

Spufford, Peter. 'Mint organisation in the Burgundian Netherlands in the fifteenth century', in C. N. L. Brooke, B. H. I. H. Stewart, J. G. Pollard and T. R. Volk (eds.), *Studies in Numismatic Method Presented to Philip Grierson.* Cambridge, 1983.

Spufford, Peter, and Mayhew, N. J. (eds.). *Mint Organisation in Medieval Europe.* British Archaeological Reports, International Series, Oxford, 1987.

MONEY AND GOVERNMENT

Bisson, T. 'Coinages and royal monetary policy in Languedoc during the reign of Saint Louis'. *Speculum,* xxxii (1957), 443–69.

Conservation of Coinage, Monetary Exploitation and its Restraint in France, Catalonia and Aragon c. 1000–1225 A.D. Oxford, 1979.

Blockmans, Willem P. 'La Participation des sujets flamands à la politique monétaire des ducs de Bourgogne (1384–1500)'. *Revue Belge de Numismatique,* cxix (1973), 103–34.

Bolin, Sture. 'Tax money and plough money'. *Scandinavian Economic History Review,* ii (1954), 3–21.

Campbell, James. 'Observations on English government from the tenth to the twelfth century'. *Transactions of the Royal Historical Society,* 5th series, xxv (1975), 39–54.

Miskimin, H. A. *Money and Power in Fifteenth Century France.* New Haven, Conn., 1984.

Spufford, Peter. 'Assemblies of estates, taxation and control of coinage in medieval Europe', in *Studies presented to the International Commission for the History of Representative and Parliamentary Institutions,* xxxi. Louvain–Paris, 1966, 115–30.

'Coinage, taxation and the Estates General of the Burgundian Netherlands', *Standen en Landen,* xl (1966), 61–87.

THE SILVER-FAMINES OF THE LATER MIDDLE AGES

Day, John. 'The decline of a money economy: Sardinia in the late Middle Ages', in *Studi in memoria di Federigo Melis*, III, Naples, 1978, 155–76.

'The great bullion famine of the fifteenth century'. *Past and Present*, LXXIX (1978), 3–54.

Girard, A. 'Un phénomène économique: la guerre monétaire (XIVᵉ–XVᵉ siècles)'. *Annales d'Histoire Sociale*, II (1940), 207–18.

Graus, Franisek. 'La Crise monétaire du 14ᵉ siècle'. *Revue Belge de Philologie et d'Histoire*, XXIX (1951), 445–54.

Heers, Jacques. 'Il commercio nel Mediterraneo alla fine del sec. XIV e nei primi anni del XV'. *Archivio Storico Italiano*, CXIII (1955).

L'Occident aux XIVᵉ et XVᵉ siècles. Aspects économiques et sociaux. 2nd ed. Paris, 1966.

Miskimin, H. A. 'Monetary movements and market structure: forces for contraction in fourteenth and fifteenth century England'. *Journal of Economic History*, XXIV (1964), 470–95.

Money, Prices and Foreign Exchange in Fourteenth Century France. New Haven, Conn., 1963.

Mollat, Michel. *Le Commerce maritime normand à la fin du Moyen Âge*. Paris, 1952.

Munro, John H. *Wool, Cloth and Gold. The Struggle for Bullion in Anglo-Burgundian Trade*, 1340–1478. Brussels–Toronto, 1973.

Perroy, E. 'A l'origine d'une économie contractée: les crises du XIVᵉ siècle'. *Annales E.S.C.*, IV (1949), 167–82.

'Wage labour in France in the later Middle Ages'. *Economic History Review*, 2nd series, VIII (1955), 232–9. Reprinted in Sylvia Thrupp (ed.), *Change in Medieval Society*, New York, 1964, pp. 237–46.

THEORY OF MONEY

Babelon, Ernest. 'La Théorie féodale de la monnaie'. *Mémoires de l'Académie des Inscriptions et Belles-Lettres*, XXXVIII (first part), Paris, 1908, 179–347.

Biel, Gabriel. *Treatise on the Power and Utility of Moneys*. Trans. and ed. R. B. Burke. Philadelphia, 1930.

Bridrey, E. *La Théorie de la monnaie au XIVᵉ siècle, Nicole Oresme*. Caen, 1906.

De Roover, R. 'Les Doctrines économiques des scolastiques: à propos du traité sur l'usure d'Alexandre Lombard'. *Revue d'Histoire Ecclésiastique*, LIX (1964), 854f.

Gordon, Barry. *Economic Analysis before Adam Smith*. London, 1957.

Ibanes, J. *La Doctrine de l'Église et les réalités économiques du XIIIᵉ siècle. L'intérêt, les prix et la monnaie*. Paris, 1967.

Monroe, A. E. *Monetary Theory before Adam Smith*. Harvard, 1923.

Noonan, J. T. *The Early Scholastic Analysis of Usury*. Cambridge, Mass., 1957.

Oresme, Nicholas. *De Moneta*. Latin text, ed. with English trans. by Charles Johnson. Edinburgh and London, 1956.

MONEY ON THE EVE OF THE PRICE REVOLUTION

Ehrenberg, R. *Das Zeitalter der Fugger, Geldkapital und Kreditverkehr im 16. Jahrhundert.* 3rd ed. Jena, 1922. Shorter English version: *Capital and Finance in the Age of the Renaissance.* London, 1928.

Grierson, Philip. 'The monetary pattern of sixteenth century coinage'. *Transactions of the Royal Historical Society,* 5th series, XXI (1971), 45–60. Collected in a volume of reprints of 22 articles: Philip Grierson. *Late Medieval Numismatics (11th–16th Centuries).* London, 1979.

Lesage, Georges. 'La Circulation monétaire en France dans la seconde moitié du XVe siècle'. *Annales E.S.C.,* III (1948), 304–16.

Spooner, F. C. *L'Économie mondiale et les frappes monétaires en France, 1493–1780.* Paris, 1956. English ed., *The International Economy and Monetary Movements in France 1493–1725.* Harvard, U.P., 1972.

Vilar, P. *A History of Gold and Money 1450–1920.* Barcelona, 1969. English trans. London, 1976.

MONEY AND COMMERCE

General bibliography, arranged by countries.

The States of Italy

Cipolla, Carlo M. *Le avventure della lira.* Milan, 1958.
    Storia dell'economia italiana. Saggi di storia economica. I: 'Secoli VII–XVII'. Turin, 1959.
Corpus Nummorum Italicorum. 20 out of 21 vols. published. Rome, 1910–61.
Grierson, Philip. 'The origins of the Grosso and of gold coinage in Italy'. *Numismatický Sborník,* XII (1971–2), 33–48.
Herlihy, David, Lopez, R. S., and Slessarev, Vsevolod (eds.). *Economy, Society and Government in Medieval Italy. Essays in Memory of Robert L. Reynolds.* Kent, Ohio, 1969. Also appeared as *Explorations in Economic History,* VII (1969).
Romano, R. and Tucci, U. (eds.). *Economia naturale, economia monetaria.* Storia d'Italia. Annali VI. Turin, 1983.
Sambon, G. *Repertorio generale delle monete coniate in Italia,* I. Paris, 1912.
Schulte, Aloys. *Geschichte des mittelalterlichen Handels und Verkehrs zwischen Westdeutschland und Italien mit Ausschluss von Venedig.* Leipzig, 1900.

Venice

Cessi, Roberto (ed.). *Problemi monetari Veneziani.* Documenti finanziari della Repubblica di Venezia, 4th series, I. Padua, 1937.
Grierson, Philip. 'La moneta veneziana nell'economia mediterranea del Trecento e Quattrocento', in *La civiltà veneziana del Quattrocento.* Fondazione Giorgio Cini, Florence, 1957, pp. 77–97.
Ives, H. E., and Grierson, Philip. *The Venetian Gold Ducat and its Imitations.* Numismatic Notes and Monographs CXXVIII. American Numismatic Society, New York, 1954.
Lane, Frederic C. *Venice, A Maritime Republic.* Baltimore, 1973.
    Venice and History: Collected Papers. Baltimore, 1966. Including 'Investment and usury',

repr. from *Explorations in Entrepreneurial History*, 2nd series, II (1964), 3–15, and 'Venetian bankers 1496–1533', repr. from *Journal of Political Economy*, XLV (1937), 187–206.

Lane, Frederic C., and Mueller, Reinhold C. *Money and Banking in Medieval and Renaissance Venice*, I. Baltimore, 1985; II, forthcoming.

Luzzatto, Gino. 'Il costo della vita a Venezia nel Trecento', *Ateneo Veneto*, CXXV (1934). Repr. in *Studi di storia economica veneziana*, Padua, 1954, pp. 285–97.

'L'oro e l'argento nella politica monetaria veneziana dei secoli XIII–XIV'. *Rivista Storica Italiana* (1937). Repr. in *Studi di storia economica veneziana*, Padua, 1954, pp. 259–70.

Mueller, Reinhold C. 'L'imperialismo monetario veneziano nel Quattrocento'. *Società e Storia*, VIII (1980), 277–97.

'The role of bank money in Venice 1300–1500'. *Studi Veneziani*, new series, III (1979), 47–96.

Papadopoli, N. *Le Monete di Venezia*. 4 vols. Venice, 1893–1919.

Stahl, Alan M. *The Venetian Tornesello. A Medieval Colonial Coinage*. Numismatic Notes and Monographs CLXIII. American Numismatic Society, New York, 1985.

Genoa

Chiaudano, Mario. 'La moneta di Genova nel secolo XII', in *Studi in onore di Armando Sapori*, I, Milan, 1957, 189–214.

Day, John. *Les Douanes de Gênes, 1376–1377*. Paris, 1963.

Heers, Jacques. *Gênes au XVe siècle: activité économique et problèmes sociaux*. Paris, 1961. Abridged ed. Paris, 1971.

Pesce, G., and Felloni, G. *Le monete genovesi*. Genoa, 1975.

Florence

Bernocchi, Mario. *Le monete della repubblica fiorentina*. I: 'Il libro della Zecca'. Florence, 1974. II: '*Corpus Nummorum Florentinum*'. Florence, 1975. III: 'Documentazione'. Florence, 1976. IV: 'Valute del fiorino d'oro 1389–1432'. Florence, 1978.

Cipolla, Carlo M. *The Monetary Policy of Fourteenth Century Florence*. Berkeley–Los Angeles, 1983.

De Roover, Raymond. *The Rise and Decline of the Medici Bank 1397–1494*. Cambridge, Mass., 1963.

La Roncière, Charles M. De. *Un changeur florentin du Trecento, Lippo di Fede del Sega 1285 env. – 1363 env.* Paris, 1973.

Florence, centre économique régional au XIVe siècle. 5 vols. Aix-en-Provence, 1976.

Pasqui, U. (ed.). 'Monete d'oro e d'argento correnti in Firenze nel secolo XV'. *Rivista Italiana di Numismatica*, XXX (1917), 76–84.

Sapori, Armando. *Una compagnia di Calimala ai primi del Trecento*. Biblioteca Storica Toscana VII. Florence, 1932.

Studi di storia economica medievale – secoli XIII, XIV, XV. I and II 3rd ed., Florence, 1955; III, Florence, 1967.

Tuscany

Day, John. 'La Circulation monétaire en Toscane en 1296'. *Annales E.S.C.*, XXIII (1968), 1054–66.

Milan

Gnecchi, F. and E. *Le monete di Milano*. Milan, 1884.

Gorini, G. (ed.). *La Zecca di Milano*. Milan, 1984.

Rome

Grierson, Philip. 'I Grossi "senatoriali" di Roma, parte I, del 1253 al 1282'. *Rivista Italiana di Numismatica*, LVIII (1956), 36–69.

Sicily

Traselli, Carmello. *Note per la storia dei banchi in Sicilia nel XV secolo*. I: 'Zecche e monete'. Palermo, 1959. II: 'I banchieri ed i loro affari'. Palermo, 1968.

The Kingdoms of the Iberian Peninsula

Bonnassié, Pierre. *La Catalogne du milieu du Xe à la fin du XIe siècle. Croissance et mutations d'une société*. 2 vols. Toulouse, 1975–6.

Carrère, Claude. *Barcelone, centre économique à l'époque des difficultés, 1380–1462*. 2 vols. Paris, 1967.

Dufourcq, C. E., and Gautier-Dalché, J. *Histoire économique et sociale de l'Espagne chrétienne au moyen âge*. Paris, 1976.

Gil Farres, Octavio. *Historia de la moneda española*. 2nd ed. Madrid, 1976.

Hamilton, Earl J. *Money, Prices and Wages in Valencia, Aragon and Navarre, 1351–1500*. Cambridge, Mass., 1936.

MacKay, Angus. *Money, Prices and Politics in fifteenth-century Castille*. Royal Historical Society, London, 1981.

Magalhaes Godhino, Vitorino. *L'Économie de l'empire portugais aux XVe et XVIe siècles*. Paris, 1969.

Miles, George C. *The Coinage of the Umayyads of Spain*. American Numismatic Society, New York, 1950.

   The Coins of the Spanish Mulūk al-Tawā'if. American Numismatic Society, New York, 1954.

Teixeira de Aragao, A. G. *Descripção geral e historica das moedas cunhadas em nome dos reis, regentes e governadores de Portugal*. 3 vols. Lisbon, 1874–80.

France

Blanchet, A., and Dieudonné, A. *Manuel de numismatique française*. 4 vols. Paris, 1912–36. II: 'Monnaies royales françaises depuis Hugues Capet jusqu'à la Révolution'. Paris, 1916. IV: 'Monnaies féodales françaises'. Paris, 1936.

Guilhermoz, P., and Dieudonné, A. 'Chronologie des documents monétaires de la numismatique royale des origines à 1330 et 1337'. *Revue Numismatique*, XXXII (1929), 209–26, and XXXIII (1930), 85–118, 233–54.

Lafaurie, Jean. *Les Monnaies des rois de France*, I. Paris and Basel, 1951.

Saulcy, F. de (ed.). *Recueil de documents relatifs à l'histoire des monnaies frappées par les rois de France depuis Philippe II jusqu'à François Ier*. 4 vols. Paris, 1879–92.

Royal coins

Cazelles, Raymond L. 'La Stabilisation de la Monnaie par la création du franc (decembre 1360): blocage d'une société'. *Traditio*, XXXII (1976), 293–311.

'Quelques réflexions à propos des mutations de la monnaie royale française, 1295–1360'. *Le Moyen Age*, LXXII (1966), 83–105, 251–78.

Gandilhon, René. *Politique économique de Louis XI*. Rennes, 1940.

Guerreau, Alain. 'L'Atelier monétaire royal de Mâcon (1239–1421)', *Annales E.S.C.*, XXIX (1974), 369–92.

Landry, A. *Essai économique sur les mutations des monnaies dans l'ancienne France de Philippe le Bel à Charles VII*. Bibliothèque de l'École des Hautes Études. IV. Sciences Historiques et Philologiques CLXXXV. Paris, 1910. Repr. 1969.

Rey, Maurice. *Le Domaine du roi et les finances extraordinaires sous Charles VI 1388–1413*. Paris, 1965.

Les Finances royales sous Charles VI. Les causes du déficit 1388–1413. Paris, 1965.

Feudal coins

Blancard, Louis, *Essai sur les monnaies de Charles Ier comte de Provence*. Paris, 1868-79.

Capra, P. 'Les Espèces, les ateliers, les frappes et les émissions monétaires en Guyenne anglo-gasconne aux XIVe et XVe siècles'. *Numismatic Chronicle*, 7th series, XIX (1979), 139–54, and XX (1980), 132–64.

Caron, E. *Monnaies féodales françaises*. Paris, 1882.

Castaing-Sicard, Mireille. *Monnaies féodales et circulation monétaire en Languedoc (X^e–XIIIe siècles)*. Cahiers de l'Association Marc Bloch de Toulouse, Études d'Histoire Méridionale IV. Toulouse, 1961.

Dumas, Françoise, and Barrandon, Jean-Noel. 'Le Titre et le poids de fin des monnaies sous le règne de Philippe Auguste'. *Cahiers Ernest Babelon*, I (1982).

Giard, Jean-Baptiste. 'Le Florin d'or au Baptiste et ses imitations en France au XIVe siècle'. *Bibliothèque de l'École des Chartes*, CXXV (1967), 94–141.

Poey d'Avant, Faustin. *Les Monnaies féodales de la France*. 3 vols. Paris, 1858–62.

Rey, Maurice. 'La Monnaie estevenante des origines à la fin du XIVe siècle'. *Mémoires de la Société d'Émulation du Doubs*, new series (1958), 35–66.

Richebé, Claude. *Les Monnaies féodales d'Artois du Xe au début du XIVe siècle*. Paris, 1963.

Rolland, Henri. *Monnaies des Comtes de Provence, XIIe–XVe siècles*. Histoire Monétaire, Économique et Corporative. Paris, 1956.

Commerce

Baratier, E., and Reynaud, F. *Histoire du commerce de Marseille*. II: '1291–1480'. Paris, 1950.

Bautier, R.-H. 'Marchands, voituriers et contrebandiers du Rouergue et de l'Auvergne. Trafics clandestins d'argent par le Dauphiné vers les foires de Genève (1424)'. *Bulletin Philologique et Historique du Comité des Travaux Historiques* (1966 for 1963), 669–88.

Combes, Jean. 'Les Commerçants et les capitalistes de Montpellier aux XIIIe et XIVe siècles'. *Revue Historique*, CLXXXIX (1940), 341–77.

De Roover, R. 'Le Marché monétaire à Paris du règne de Philippe le Bel au début du XVe siècle'. *Comptes rendus de l'Académie des Inscriptions et Belles Lettres* (1968), 548–58.

Dubois, Henri. *Les Foires de Chalon-sur-Saône et le commerce dans la vallée de la Saône à la fin du moyen âge*. Paris, 1975.

Emery, R. W. *The Jews of Perpignan in the XIII Century.* New York, 1959.

Favreau, Robert. 'Les Changeurs du Royaume sous le règne de Louis XI'. *Bibliothèque de l'École des Chartes,* CXXII (1964), 216–51.

Fournial, Étienne. *Les Villes et l'économie d'échange en Forez aux XIIIᵉ et XIVᵉ siècles.* Paris, 1967.

Nahon, Gerard. 'Le Crédit et les juifs dans la France du XIIIᵉ siècle'. *Annales E.S.C.,* XXIV (1969), 1121–48.

Wolff, Philippe. *Commerces et marchands de Toulouse (vers 1350–vers 1450).* Paris, 1954.

Principalities of the Low Countries

Bigwood, Georges. *Le Régime juridique et économique du commerce de l'argent dans la Belgique du moyen âge.* Mémoires de l'Académie Royale de Belgique, Classe des Lettres et des Sciences Morales et Politiques, Collection in 8°, 2nd series, XIV (Brussels, 1921–2).

Chautard, J. *Les Imitations des monnaies au type esterlin.* Nancy, 1871. Now complemented by N. J. Mayhew, *Sterling Imitations of Edwardian Type.* London, 1983.

De Roover, Raymond. *The Bruges Money Market around 1400.* Brussels, 1968.

Money, Banking and Credit in Medieval Bruges. Cambridge, Mass., 1948.

Enno van Gelder, H. 'De munten van Vlaanderen onder Lodewijk van Nevers en Lodewijk van Male'. *Jaarboek voor Munt- en Penningkunde,* XXXIII–XXXIV (1946–7), 122–31.

'De Muntpolitik van Philips de Schone 1482–1496'. *Jaarboek voor Munt- un Penningkunde,* XXXVIII (1951), 42–54.

Enno van Gelder, H., and Hoc, M. *Les Monnaies des Pays-Bas bourguignons et espagnols.* Amsterdam, 1960. Supplement, 1964.

Grierson, Philip. 'Coinage in the Cely Papers'. *Miscellanea mediaevalia in memoriam Jan Frederik Niermeyer,* Groningen, 1967, pp. 379–404.

Laurent, H. *La Loi de Gresham au moyen âge. Essai sur la circulation monétaire entre la Flandre et le Brabant à la fin du XIVᵉ siècle.* Brussels, 1933.

Mayhew, N. J. (ed.). *Coinage in the Low Countries (880–1500).* British Archaeological Reports, International Series LIV. Oxford, 1979.

Spufford, Peter. 'Dans l'espace bourguignon: 1477 – un tournant monétaire?' *Cinq-centième anniversaire de la Bataille de Nancy (1477).* Actes du Colloque Organisé par l'Institut de Recherche Régionale en Sciences Sociales, Humaines et Économiques de l'Université de Nancy II. Nancy, 1977.

Monetary Problems and Policies in the Burgundian Netherlands 1433–1496. Leiden, 1970.

Van der Wee, Herman. 'L'Échec de la réforme monétaire de 1407 en Flandre, vu par les marchands italiens de Bruges', in *Studi in onore di Amintore Fanfani,* III, Milan, 1962, 579–589.

The Growth of the Antwerp Market and the European Economy. 3 vols. The Hague, 1963.

Van Uytven, Raymond. 'La Flandre et le Brabant, "Terres de Promission" sous les dus de Bourgogne'. *Revue du Nord,* XLIII (1961), 281–317.

'Social-economische evoluties in de Nederlanden voor de Revoluties (viertiende-zestiende eeuw)'. *Bijdragen en Mededelingen betreffende de Geschiedenis der Nederlanden,* LXXXVII (1972), 60–93. English trans.: 'What is new socially and economically in the sixteenth-century Netherlands'. *Acta Historiae Neerlandicae,* VII (1974), 18–53.

Van Werveke, Hans. 'Currency manipulation in the Middle Ages: the case of Louis de

Male, Count of Flanders'. *Transactions of the Royal Historical Society*, 4th series, XXXI (1949), 115–27. Repr. in *Miscellanea mediaevalia*, Ghent, 1968, pp. 255–67.

'De economische en sociale gevolgen van de muntpolitik der graven an Vlaanderen 1337–1433', *Annales de la Société d'Émulation de Bruges*, LXXIV (1931), 1–15. Repr. in *Miscellanea mediaevalia*, Ghent, 1968, pp. 243–54.

Southern Low Countries

Chalon, R. *Recherches sur les monnaies des comtes de Hainault*. Brussels, 1848. Supplements, 1852, 1854, 1857 and by A. E. Witte, 1891.

Chestret de Haneffe, J. de. *Numismatique de la Principauté de Liège*. Brussels, 1890. Supplement, Liège, 1900.

Deschamps de Pas, L. 'Essai sur l'histoire monétaire des comtes de Flandre de la maison de Bourgogne'. *Revue Numismatique*, new series, VI (1861), VII (1862), XI (1866), XIV (1869), XV (1874), and *Revue Belge de Numismatique*, XXXII (1876).

De Witte, A. *Histoire monétaire des comtes de Louvain, ducs de Brabant*. 3 vols. Antwerp, 1894–9.

Gaillard, Victor. *Recherches sur les monnaies des Comtes de Flandre . . . jusqu'à l'avènement de la maison de Bourgogne*. 2nd ed. Ghent, 1857.

Ghyssens, J. *Les Petits Deniers de Flandre du XIIe et XIIIe siècles*. Brussels, 1971.

Northern Low Countries

Chijs, P. O. van der. *De munten der Nederlanden van de vroogste tijden tot aan de Pacificatie van Gend (1576)*. 9 vols. Haarlem, 1851–66.

Enno van Gelder, H. *De Nederlandse Munten*. Utrecht–Antwerp, 1966.

Ketner, F. 'The Utrecht monetary system', in N. W. Posthumus. *Inquiry into the History of Prices in Holland*. II, Leiden, 1966, 12–30.

British Isles

Blunt, C. E., and Brand, J. D. 'Mint output of Henry III'. *British Numismatic Journal*, XXXIX (1970), 61–6.

Challis, C. E. *The Tudor Coinage*. Manchester, 1978.

Crump, C. G., and Johnson, C. 'Tables of bullion coined under Edward I, II, and III', *Numismatic Chronicle*, 4th series, XIII (1913), 200–45.

Dolley, Michael. 'Anglo-Irish monetary policies, 1172–1637', in *Historical Studies*, VII, London, 1969, 45–64.

Feaveryear, A. E. *The Pound Sterling*. 2nd ed. Oxford, 1962.

Fryde, Edmund B. 'Financial resources of Edward I in the Netherlands, 1294–1298'. *Revue Belge de Philologie et d'Histoire*, XL (1962), 1168–87.

'Financial resources of Edward III in the Netherlands, 1337–40'. *Revue Belge de Philologie et d'Histoire*, XLV (1967), 1142–216.

'Parliament and the French War 1336–40', in T. A. Sandquist and M. R. Powicke (eds.), *Essays in Medieval History Presented to Bertie Wilkinson*, Toronto, 1969, pp. 250–69. Repr. in E. B. Fryde, and Edward Miller (eds.), *Historical Studies of the English Parliament*, I, Cambridge, 1970, 242–61.

Harvey, P. D. A. 'The English inflation of 1180–1220'. *Past and Present*, LXI (1973), 3–30.

Ives, Herbert E. *Foreign Imitations of the English Noble*. Numismatic Notes and Monographs XCIII. American Numismatic Society, New York, 1941.

Mate, Mavis, 'High prices in early fourteenth century England: causes and consequences', *Economic History Review*, 2nd series, XXVIII (1975), 1–16.

'Monetary policies in England 1272–1307'. *British Numismatic Journal*, XLI (1972), 34–79.

Mayhew, N. J. (ed.). *Edwardian Monetary Affairs (1279–1344)*. British Archaeological Reports XXXVI. Oxford, 1977.

'Numismatic evidence and Falling prices in the fourteenth century'. *Economic History Review*, 2nd series, XXVII, 1 (1974), 1–15.

Metcalf, D. M. (ed.). *Coinage in Medieval Scotland (1100–1600)*. The Second Oxford Symposium on Coinage and Monetary History. British Archaeological Reports XLV. Oxford, 1977.

North, J. J. *English Hammered Coinage*. 2nd ed. 2 vols. London, 1975–80.

Oman, Charles. *The Coinage of England*. Oxford, 1931.

Prestwich, Michael. 'Edward I's monetary policies and their consequences'. *Economic History Review*, 2nd series, XXXII (1969), 406–16.

War, Politics and Finance under Edward I. London, 1972.

Ruding, R. R. *Annals of the Coinage*. 3rd ed. 3 vols. London, 1840. Repr. 1974.

Spufford, Peter. 'Burgundian double patards in late medieval England'. *British Numismatic Journal*, XXXIII (1964), 110–17.

'Continental coins in late medieval England'. *British Numismatic Journal*, XXXII (1964), 127–39.

Stewart, I. H. *The Scottish Coinage*. 3rd ed. London, 1967.

Stokes, Ethel. 'Tables of bullion coined from 1377 to 1550'. *Numismatic Chronicle*, 4th series, XIII (1913), 200–45.

Sutherland, C. H. V. *English Coinage 600–1900*. London, 1973.

Sylloge of Coins of the British Isles. British Academy, London, 1958–.

Thompson, J. D. A. *Inventory of British Coin Hoards AD 600–1500*. British Numismatic Society, London, 1956.

German States

Bastian, F. (ed.). *Das Runtingerbuch 1383–1407 und verwandtes Material zum Regensburger-südostdeutschen Handel and Münzwesen*. 3 vols. Regensburg, 1935–44.

Berghaus, Peter. 'Die Münzpolitick der deutschen Städte im Mittelalter', in *Pro Civitate, Collection Historie in 8°*, VII, Brussels, 1964, 75–85.

'Die Perioden des Sterlings in Westfalen, dem Rheinland und in den Niederlanden'. *Hamburger Beiträge zur Numismatik* I (1947), 34–53.

'Umlauf und Nachprägung des Florentinen Guldens Nordlich der Alpen', in *Congresso Internazionale di Numismatica*, II: 'Atti', Rome, 1965, 595–607.

Berghaus, Peter, and Hatz, G. (eds.), *Dona Numismatica – Walter Hävernick zum 23. Januar 1965 dargebracht*. Hamburg, 1965.

Cahn, Julius, *Der Rappenmünzbund*. Heidelberg, 1901.

Diepenbach, W. 'Der Rheinische Münzverein', in A. F. Napp-Zinn and M. Oppenheim (eds.), *Kultur und Wirtschaft im Rheinischen Raum. Festschrift zu Christian Eckert*, Mainz, 1949, pp. 89–120.

Hävernick, Walter. *Der Kölner Pfennig im 12. und 13. Jahrhundert.* Vierteljahrschrift für Sozial- und Wirtschaftsgeschichte, supplement XVIII. Stuttgart, 1931.

Hess, W. 'Das rheinisches Munzwesen im 14 Jahrhundert'. *Der deutsche Territorialstaat im 14 Jahrhundert.* Vorträge und Forschungen XIII. Sigmaringen, 1970.

Jesse, Wilhelm, *Der Wendische Münzverein.* Lübeck, 1928. Repr. Brunswick, 1966–71, with 32 extra pages, 2nd ed.

Krusy, H. *Gegenstempel auf Münzen des Spätmittelalters.* Frankfurt, 1974.

Metcalf, D. M. *The Coinage of South Germany in the Thirteenth Century.* London, 1961.

Schulte, A. *Geschichte der Grossen Ravensberger Handelsgesellschaft 1380–1530.* Stuttgart–Berlin, 1923.

Stromer, W. von. *Oberdeutsche Hochfinanz 1350–1450.* Vierteljahrschrift fur Sozial- und Wirtschaftsgeschichte, supplements LV–LVII. Wiesbaden, 1970.

Suhle, Arthur. *Deutsche Münz- und Geldgeschichte von den Anfängen bis zum 15. Jahrhundert.* 2nd ed. Berlin, 1964.

Northern Europe

See also above under 'The Age of the Vikings'.

Bendixen, Kirsten. *Denmark's Money.* Copenhagen, 1967.

Jensen, J.S. (ed.). *Coinage and monetary circulation in the Baltic area c. 1350–c. 1500.* Special number of *Nordisk Numismatisk Årsskrift,* 1981.

'Danish money in the fourteenth century'. *Mediaevalia Scandinavia,* VI (1973), 161–71.

Jesse, Wilhelm. *Der Wendische Münzverein.* Lübeck, 1928. Repr. Brunswick, 1966–71, with 32 extra pages. 2nd ed.

Lagerqvist, L. O. *Svenska mynt under Vikingtid och Medeltid ca. 995–1521 samt Gotlandska mynt ca. 1140–1565.* Stockholm, 1969.

Malowist, Marian. *Croissance et régression en Europe XIVe–XVIIe siècles: recueil d'articles.* Cahiers des Annales XXXIV. Paris, 1972.

Sprandel, Rolf. *Das mittelalterliche Zahlungssystem nach Hansisch-Nordischen Quellen des 13.–15. Jahrhunderts.* Stuttgart, 1975.

Central and Eastern Europe

Baumgartner, Egon. 'Die Blütezeit der Friesacher Pfennige'. *Numismatische Zeitschrift,* LXXIII (1949), 75–106, LXXVIII (1959), 14–57, and LXXIX (1961), 28–63.

Castelin, K. *Ceska drobna mince doby predhusitcke a husitske 1300–1471.* Prague, 1953. (With résumé in French.)

Grossus Pragensis. Der Prager Groschen und seine Teilstücke, 1300–1547. 2nd ed. Brunswick, 1973.

Graus, F. 'Die Handelsbeziehungen Böhmens zu Deutschland und Österreich im 14. und zu Beginn des 15. Jahrhunderts'. *Historica,* II (1960), 77–110.

Kazimír, Štefan (ed.). *Kremnická mincovňa 1328–1978.* Kremnica, 1978.

Kiersnowski, R. *Wstep de numizmatyki polskiej wiekow srednich.* Warsaw, 1964.

Lohr, A. *Österreichische Geldgeschichte.* Vienna, 1946.

Metcalf, D. M. *Coinage in South-Eastern Europe 820–1396,* 2nd ed. Royal Numismatic Society, London, 1979.

Probszt, Gunther. *Quellenkunde der Münz- und Geldgeschichte der ehemaligen Osterreichisch-Ungarischen Monarchie.* Graz, 1953. Supplements, 1960 and 1963.

Rethy, L. (ed.). *Corpus Nummorum Hungarie.* 1899–1907. German trans., Graz, 1958.

Spasskij, I. G. *The Russian Monetary System.* Amsterdam, 1967; English trans. from *Russkaya monetnaya sistema.* 3rd ed. Leningrad, 1962.

Suchodolski. Stanisław. 'Renovatio Monetae in Poland in the 12th century'. *Wiadomosci Numizmatyczne,* v (1961), 57–75.

Coin Index

This index should be used in conjunction with Appendix I. It is arranged alphabetically, whilst the appendix is arranged by groups of coins. There are many coins which appear here which do not appear in the appendix. Penny coinages appear under particular names and issuers, not under denar, denaro, denier, dinero, penny, pfennig.

General Index

Cross-references to individual denominations in the General Index refer to entries in the Coin Index

447